T0215686

Lecture Notes in Artificial Intelligence 9161

Subseries of Lecture Notes in Computer Science

LNAI Series Editors

Randy Goebel
   University of Alberta, Edmonton, Canada
Yuzuru Tanaka
   Hokkaido University, Sapporo, Japan
Wolfgang Wahlster
   DFKI and Saarland University, Saarbrücken, Germany

LNAI Founding Series Editor

Joerg Siekmann
   DFKI and Saarland University, Saarbrücken, Germany

More information about this series at http://www.springer.com/series/1244

Sébastien Destercke · Thierry Denoeux (Eds.)

Symbolic and Quantitative Approaches to Reasoning with Uncertainty

13th European Conference, ECSQARU 2015
Compiègne, France, July 15–17, 2015
Proceedings

 Springer

Editors
Sébastien Destercke
Université de Technologie de Compiègne
Compiègne
France

Thierry Denoeux
Centre de Recherches de Royallieu
Université de Technologie de Compiègne
Compiègne
France

ISSN 0302-9743   ISSN 1611-3349 (electronic)
Lecture Notes in Artificial Intelligence
ISBN 978-3-319-20806-0   ISBN 978-3-319-20807-7 (eBook)
DOI 10.1007/978-3-319-20807-7

Library of Congress Control Number: 2015942629

LNCS Sublibrary: SL7 – Artificial Intelligence

Springer Cham Heidelberg New York Dordrecht London

Printed on acid-free paper

Springer International Publishing AG Switzerland is part of Springer Science+Business Media
(www.springer.com)

Preface

The biennial ECSQARU conferences constitute a forum for advances in the theory and practice of reasoning under uncertainty. Contributions typically come from researchers who are interested in advancing technology and from practitioners using uncertainty techniques in real-world applications. The scope of the conference series encompasses fundamental issues, representation, inference, learning, and decision making in qualitative and numeric uncertainty paradigms.

Previous ECSQARU events were held in Marseille (1991), Granada (1993), Fribourg (1995), Bonn (1997), London (1999), Toulouse (2001), Aalborg (2003), Barcelona (2005), Hammamet (2007), Verona (2009), Belfast (2011), and Utrecht (2013). The 13th European Conference on Symbolic and Quantitative Approaches to Reasoning with Uncertainty was held in Compiègne, France, during July 15–17, 2015. The 49 papers presented at the conference and included in this volume were selected from 69 submitted manuscripts. Each submission underwent rigorous reviewing by at least two members of the ECSQARU Program Committee.

ECSQARU 2015 further included keynote talks by three outstanding researchers in the field: Edith Elkind (University of Oxford), Teddy Seidenfeld (Carnegie Mellon University) and Marco Zaffalon (Istituto "Dalle Molle" di Studi sull'Intelligenza Artificiale, IDSIA).

We would like to thank all those who have contributed with their papers to this volume, the Program Committee members and the additional referees for their efforts, as well as our sponsors for their financial support.

May 2015

Sébastien Destercke
Thierry Denoeux

Organization

Program Committee

Leila Amgoud	IRIT-CNRS, France
Alessandro Antonucci	IDSIA, Switzerland
Nahla Ben Amor	Institut Supérieur de Gestion de Tunis, Tunisia
Boutheina Ben Yaghlane	LARODEC-ISG, IHEC Carthage, Tunisia
Salem Benferhat	Cril, CNRS UMR8188, Université d'Artois, France
Philippe Besnard	IRIT-CNRS, France
Martin Caminada	University of Aberdeen, UK
Giulianella Coletti	University of Perugia, Italy
Fabio Cozman	Universidade de Sao Paulo, Brazil
Fabio Cuzzolin	Oxford Brookes University, UK
Cassio De Campos	Queen's University Belfast, UK
Luis M. De Campos	University of Granada, Spain
Thierry Denoeux	Université de Technologie de Compiegne, France
Sébastien Destercke	CNRS, UMR Heudiasyc, France
Didier Dubois	IRIT/RPDMP, France
Zied Elouedi	Institut Supérieur de Gestion de Tunis, Tunisia
Helene Fargier	IRIT-CNRS, France
Lluis Godo	Artificial Intelligence Research Institute, IIIA-CSIC
Andreas Herzig	IRIT-CNRS, France
Anthony Hunter	University College London, UK
Gabriele Kern-Isberner	Technische Universität Dortmund, Germany
Sébastien Konieczny	CRIL-CNRS, France
Rudolf Kruse	University of Magdeburg, Germany
Christophe Labreuche	Thales R&T, France
Jérôme Lang	LAMSADE, France
Pedro Larranaga	University of Madrid, Spain
Jonathan Lawry	University of Bristol, UK
Jan Lemeire	Vrije Universiteit Brussel, Belgium
Philippe Leray	LINA/DUKe - Nantes University, France
Churn-Jung Liau	Academia Sinica, Taipei, Taiwan
Weiru Liu	Queen's University Belfast, UK
Peter Lucas	Radboud University Nijmegen, The Netherlands
Thomas Lukasiewicz	University of Oxford, UK
Pierre Marquis	CRIL-CNRS and Université d'Artois, France
Vincenzo Marra	University of Milan, Italy
Andres R. Masegosa	University of Granada, Spain
David Mercier	Université d'Artois, France

Thomas Meyer	Centre for Artificial Intelligence Research, UKZN and CSIR Meraka, South Africa
Enrique Miranda	University of Oviedo, Spain
Serafin Moral	University of Granada, Spain
Vincent Mousseau	LGI, Ecole Centrale Paris, France
Kristian Olesen	Aalborg Universtet, Denmark
Ewa Orlowska	National Institute of Telecommunications
Odile Papini	LSIS UMR CNRS 6168, France
Simon Parsons	University of Liverpool, UK
Jose M. Peña	Linköping University, Sweden
Henri Prade	IRIT-CNRS, France
Erik Quaeghebeur	Centrum Wiskunde & Informatica, The Netherlands
Steven Schockaert	Cardiff University, UK
Roman Slowinski	Poznan University of Technology, Poland
Matthias Troffaes	Durham University, UK
Linda C. van der Gaag	Utrecht University, The Netherlands
Leon van der Torre	University of Luxembourg, Luxembourg
Barbara Vantaggi	Università La Sapienza, Italy
Paolo Viappiani	CNRS and LIP6, Université Pierre et Marie Curie, France
Jirka Vomlel	Academy of Sciences, Czech Republic

Additional Reviewers

Braune, Christian
Doell, Christoph
Halland, Ken
Held, Pascal
Kratochvíl, Václav
Liao, Beishui

Manfredotti, Cristina
Pichon, Frédéric
Pouyllau, Hélia
Quost, Benjamin
Rens, Gavin
Varando, Gherardo

Contents

Graphical Models

Bayesian Networks

Belief Functions

Logic

Probabilistic Graphical Models for Scalable Data Analytics

Decision Theory and Preferences

Minimizing Regret in Dynamic Decision Problems

Joseph Y. Halpern and Samantha Leung[(✉)]

Cornell University, Ithaca, NY 14853, USA
{halpern,samlyy}@cs.cornell.edu

Abstract. The menu-dependent nature of regret-minimization creates subtleties when it is applied to dynamic decision problems. It is not clear whether forgone opportunities should be included in the menu. We explain commonly observed behavioral patterns as minimizing regret when forgone opportunities are present. If forgone opportunities are included, we can characterize when a form of dynamic consistency is guaranteed.

1 Introduction

Savage [12] and Anscombe and Aumann [3] showed that a decision maker maximizing expected utility with respect to a probability measure over the possible states of the world is characterized by a set of arguably desirable principles. However, as Allais [2] and Ellsberg [4] point out using compelling examples, sometimes intuitive choices are incompatible with maximizing expected utility. One reason for this incompatibility is that there is often *ambiguity* in the problems we face; we often lack sufficient information to capture all uncertainty using a single probability measure.

To this end, there is a rich literature offering alternative means of making decisions (see, e.g., [1] for a survey). For example, we might choose to represent uncertainty using a set of possible states of the world, but using no probabilistic information at all to represent how likely each state is. With this type of representation, two well-studied rules for decision-making are *maximin utility* and *minimax regret*. Maximin says that you should choose the option that maximizes the worst-case payoff, while minimax regret says that you should choose the option that minimizes the *regret* you'll feel at the end, where, roughly speaking, regret is the difference between the payoff you achieved, and the payoff that you could have achieved had you known what the true state of the world was. Both maximin and minimax regret can be extended naturally to deal with other representations of uncertainty. For example, with a set of probability measures over the possible states, minimax regret becomes minimax expected regret (MER) [10,15]. In this paper, we consider a generalization of minimax expected regret

---

Work supported in part by NSF grants IIS-0812045, IIS-0911036, and CCF-1214844, by AFOSR grants FA9550-08-1-0438, FA9550-09-1-0266, and FA9550-12-1-0040, and by ARO grant W911NF-09-1-0281.

S. Destercke and T. Denoeux (Eds.): ECSQARU 2015, LNAI 9161, pp. 3–13, 2015.
DOI: 10.1007/978-3-319-20807-7_1

called minimax *weighted* expected regret (MWER) that we introduced in an earlier paper [7]. For MWER, uncertainty is represented by a set of *weighted* probability measures. Intuitively, the weight represents how likely the probability measure is to be the true distribution over the states, according to the decision maker (henceforth DM).

Real-life problems are often dynamic, with many stages where actions can be taken; information can be learned over time. Before applying regret minimization to dynamic decision problems, there is a subtle issue that we must consider. In static decision problems, the regret for each act is computed with respect to a *menu*. That is, each act is judged against the other acts in the menu. Typically, we think of the menu as consisting of the *feasible acts*, that is, the ones that the DM can perform. The analogue in a dynamic setting would be the feasible *plans*, where a plan is just a sequence of actions leading to a final outcome. In a dynamic decision problem, as more actions are taken, some plans become *forgone opportunities*. These are plans that were initially available to the DM, but are no longer available due to earlier actions of the DM. Since regret intuitively captures comparison of a choice against its alternatives, it seems reasonable for the menu to include all the feasible plans at the point of decision-making. But should the menu include forgone opportunities?

Consequentialists would argue that it is irrational to care about forgone opportunities [8,11]; we should simply focus on the opportunities that are still available to us, and thus not include forgone opportunities in the menu. And, indeed, when regret has been considered in dynamic settings thus far (e.g., by Hayashi [10]), the menu has not included forgone opportunities. However, introspection tells us that we sometimes do take forgone opportunities into account. For example, when considering a new job, one might compare the available options to what might have been available if one had chosen a different career path years ago. As we show, including forgone opportunities in the menu can make a big difference in behavior. Consider procrastination: we tell ourselves that we will start studying for an exam (or start exercising, or quit smoking) tomorrow; and then tomorrow comes, and we again tell ourselves that we will do it, starting tomorrow. This behavior is hard to explain with standard decision-theoretic approaches, especially when we assume that no new information about the world is gained over time. However, we give an example where, if forgone opportunities are not included in the menu, then we get procrastination; if they are, then we do not get procrastination.

This example can be generalized. Procrastination is an example of *preference reversal*: the DM's preference at time t for what he should do at time $t + 1$ reverses when she actually gets to time $t + 1$. We prove in Sect. 3 that if the menu includes forgone opportunities and the DM acquires no new information over time (as is the case in the procrastination problem), then a DM who uses regret to make her decisions will not suffer preference reversals. Thus, we arguably get more rational behavior when we include forgone opportunities in the menu.

What happens if the DM does get information over time? It is well known that, in this setting, expected utility maximizers are guaranteed to have no preference reversals. Epstein and Le Breton [5] have shown that, under minimal assumptions, to avoid preference reversals, the DM must be an expected utility maximizer. On the other hand, Epstein and Schneider [6] show that a DM using MMEU never has preference reversals if her beliefs satisfy a condition they call *rectangularity*. Hayashi [10] shows that rectangularity also prevents preference reversals for MER under certain assumptions. Unfortunately, the rectangularity condition is often not satisfied in practice. Other conditions have been provided that guarantee dynamic consistency for ambiguity-averse decision rules (see, e.g., [1] for an overview).

We consider the question of preference reversal in the context of regret. Hayashi [10] has observed that, in dynamic decision problems, both changes in menu over time and updates to the DM's beliefs can result in preference reversals. In Sect. 4, we show that keeping forgone opportunities in the menu is necessary in order to prevent preference reversals. But, as we show by example, it is not sufficient if the DM acquires new information over time. We then provide a condition on the beliefs that is necessary and sufficient to guarantee that a DM making decisions using MWER whose beliefs satisfy the condition will not have preference reversals. However, because this necessary and sufficient condition may not be easy to check, we also give simpler sufficient condition, similar in spirit to Epstein and Schneider's [6] rectangularity condition.

2   Preliminaries

2.1   Static Decision Setting and Regret

Given a set S of states and a set X of outcomes, an *act* f (over S and X) is a function mapping S to X. We use $\mathcal{F}$ to denote the set of all acts. For simplicity in this paper, we take S to be finite. Associated with each outcome $x \in X$ is a utility: $u(x)$ is the utility of outcome x. We call a tuple (S, X, u) a *(non-probabilistic) decision problem*. To define regret, we need to assume that we are also given a set $M \subseteq \mathcal{F}$ of acts, called the *menu*. The reason for the menu is that, as is well known, regret can depend on the menu. We assume that every menu M has utilities bounded from above. That is, we assume that for all menus M, $\sup_{g \in M} u(g(s))$ is finite. This ensures that the regret of each act is well defined. For a menu M and act $f \in M$, the regret of f with respect to M and decision problem (S, X, u) in state s is $reg_M(f, s) = \left(\sup_{g \in M} u(g(s))\right) - u(f(s))$. That is, the regret of f in state s (relative to menu M) is the difference between $u(f(s))$ and the highest utility possible in state s among all the acts in M. The regret of f with respect to M and decision problem (S, X, u), denoted $reg_M^{(S,X,u)}(f)$, is the worst-case regret over all states: $\max_{s \in S} reg_M(f, s)$. We typically omit superscript (S, X, u) in $reg_M^{(S,X,u)}(f)$ if it is clear from context. The minimax regret decision rule chooses an act that minimizes $\max_{s \in S} reg_M(f, s)$. In other words, the minimax regret choice function is $C_M^{reg,u}(M') = \operatorname{argmin}_{f \in M'} \max_{s \in S} reg_M(f, s)$; the choice function returns the set of all acts in M' that minimize regret with respect to M.

Note that we allow the menu M', the set of acts over which we are minimizing regret, to be different from the menu M of acts with respect to which regret is computed. For example, if the DM considers forgone opportunities, they would be included in M, although not in M'.

If there is a probability measure Pr over the states, then we can consider the *probabilistic decision problem* (S, X, u, Pr). The *expected regret* of f with respect to M is $reg_M^{\text{Pr}}(f) = \sum_{s \in S} \text{Pr}(s) reg_M(f, s)$. If there is a set $\mathcal{P}$ of probability measures over the states, then we consider the $\mathcal{P}$-decision problem $\mathcal{D} = (S, X, u, \mathcal{P})$. The maximum expected regret of $f \in M$ with respect to M and $\mathcal{D}$ is $reg_M^{\mathcal{P}}(f) = \sup_{\text{Pr} \in \mathcal{P}} \left(\sum_{s \in S} \text{Pr}(s) reg_M(f, s) \right)$. The minimax expected regret (MER) decision rule minimizes $reg_M^{\mathcal{P}}(f)$.

In an earlier paper, we introduced another representation of uncertainty, *weighted set of probability measures* [7]. A weighted set of probability measures generalizes a set of probability measures by associating each measure in the set with a weight, intuitively corresponding to the reliability or significance of the measure in capturing the true uncertainty of the world. Minimizing weighted expected regret with respect to a weighted set of probability measures gives a variant of minimax regret, called Minimax Weighted Expected Regret (MWER). A set $\mathcal{P}^+$ of *weighted probability measures* on a set S consists of pairs $(\text{Pr}, \alpha_{\text{Pr}})$, where $\alpha_{\text{Pr}} \in [0, 1]$ and Pr is a probability measure on S. Let $\mathcal{P} = \{\text{Pr} : \exists \alpha (\text{Pr}, \alpha) \in \mathcal{P}^+\}$. We assume that, for each $\text{Pr} \in \mathcal{P}$, there is exactly one α such that $(\text{Pr}, \alpha) \in \mathcal{P}^+$. We denote this number by α_{Pr}, and view it as the *weight of* Pr. We further assume for convenience that weights have been normalized so that there is at least one measure $\text{Pr} \in \mathcal{P}$ such that $\alpha_{\text{Pr}} = 1$.

If beliefs are modeled by a set $\mathcal{P}^+$ of weighted probabilities, then we consider the $\mathcal{P}^+$-decision problem $\mathcal{D}^+ = (S, X, u, \mathcal{P}^+)$. The maximum weighted expected regret of $f \in M$ with respect to M and $\mathcal{D}^+ = (S, X, u, \mathcal{P}^+)$ is

$$reg_M^{\mathcal{P}^+}(f) = \sup_{\text{Pr} \in \mathcal{P}} \left(\alpha_{\text{Pr}} \sum_{s \in S} \text{Pr}(s) reg_M(f, s) \right).$$

If $\mathcal{P}^+$ is empty, then $reg_M^{\mathcal{P}^+}$ is identically zero. Of course, we can define the choice functions $C_M^{reg, \text{Pr}}$, $C_M^{reg, \mathcal{P}}$, and $C_M^{reg, \mathcal{P}^+}$ using reg_M^{Pr}, $reg_M^{\mathcal{P}}$, and $reg_M^{\mathcal{P}^+}$, by analogy with C_M^{reg}.

2.2   Dynamic Decision Problems

A *dynamic decision problem* is a single-player extensive-form game where there is some set S of states, nature chooses $s \in S$ at the first step, and does not make any more moves. The DM then performs a finite sequence of actions until some outcome is reached. Utility is assigned to these outcomes. A *history* is a sequence recording the actions taken by nature and the DM. At every history h, the DM considers possible some other histories. The DM's *information set* at h, denoted $I(h)$, is the set of histories that the DM considers possible at h. Let $s(h)$ denote the initial state of h (i.e., nature's first move); let $R(h)$ denote all the moves the DM made in h after nature's first move; finally, let $E(h)$ denote the set of states that the DM considers possible at h; that is, $E(h) = \{s(h') : h' \in I(h)\}$. We assume that the DM has *perfect recall*: this means that $R(h') = R(h)$ for all $h' \in I(h)$, and that if h' is a prefix of h, then $E(h') \supseteq E(h)$.

A *plan* is a (pure) strategy: a mapping from histories to histories that result from taking the action specified by the plan. We require that a plan specify the same action for all histories in an information set; that is, if f is a plan, then for all histories h and $h' \in I(h)$, we must have the last action in $f(h)$ and $f(h')$ must be the same (so that $R(f(h)) = R(f(h'))$). Given an initial state s, a plan determines a complete path to an outcome. Hence, we can also view plans as acts: functions mapping states to outcomes. We take the acts in a dynamic decision problem to be the set of possible plans, and evaluate them using the decision rules discussed above.

A major difference between our model and that used Epstein and Schneider [6] and Hayashi [9] is that the latter assume a *filtration* information structure. With a filtration information structure, the DM's knowledge is represented by a fixed, finite sequence of partitions. More specifically, at time t, the DM uses a partition $F(t)$ of the state space, and if the true state is s, then all that the DM knows is that the true state is in the cell of $F(t)$ containing s. Since the sequence of partitions is fixed, the DM's knowledge is independent of the choices that she makes, and her options and preferences cannot depend on past choices. This assumption significantly restricts the types of problems that can be naturally modeled. For example, if the DM prefers to have one apple over two oranges at time t, then this must be her time t preference, regardless of whether she has already consumed five apples at time $t - 1$. Moreover, consuming an apple at time t cannot preclude consuming an apple at time $t + 1$. Since we effectively represent a decision problem as a single-player extensive-form game, we can capture all of these situations in a straightforward way. The models of Epstein, Schneider, and Hayashi can be viewed as a special case of our model.

In a dynamic decision problem, as we shall see, two different menus are relevant for making a decision using regret-minimization: the menu with respect to which regrets are computed, and the menu of feasible choices. We formalize this dependence by considering *choice functions* of the form $C_{M,E}$, where $E, M \neq \emptyset$. $C_{M,E}$ is a function mapping a nonempty menu M' to a nonempty subset of M'. Intuitively, $C_{M,E}(M')$ consists of the DM's most preferred choices from the menu M' when she considers the states in E possible and her decision are made relative to menu M. (So, for example, if the DM is making her choices choices using regret minimization, the regret is taken with respect to M.) Note that there may be more than one plan in $C_{M,E}(M')$; intuitively, this means that the DM does not view any of the plans in $C_{M,E}(M')$ as strictly worse than some other plan.

What should M and E be when the DM makes a decision at a history h? We always take $E = E(h)$. Intuitively, this says that all that matters about a history as far as making a decision is the set of states that the DM considers possible; the previous moves made to get to that history are irrelevant. As we shall see, this seems reasonable in many examples. Moreover, it is consistent with our choice of taking probability distributions only on the states space.

The choice of M is somewhat more subtle. The most obvious choice (and the one that has typically been made in the literature, without comment) is that M consists of the plans that are still feasible at h, where a plan f is *feasible* at a history h if, for all strict prefixes h' of h, $f(h')$ is also a prefix of h. So f is feasible at h if h is compatible with all of f's moves. Let M_h be the set of plans feasible at h. While taking $M = M_h$ is certainly a reasonable choice, as we shall see, there are other reasonable alternatives.

Before addressing the choice of menu in more detail, we consider how to apply regret in a dynamic setting. If we want to apply MER or MWER, we must update the probability distributions. Epstein and Schneider [6] and Hayashi [9] consider *prior-by-prior updating*, the most common way to update a set of probability measures, defined as follows: $\mathcal{P}|^p E = \{\Pr|E : \Pr \in \mathcal{P}, \Pr(E) > 0\}$.

Prior-by-prior updating can produce some rather counter-intuitive outcomes. For example, suppose we have a coin of unknown bias in $[0.25, 0.75]$, and flip it 100 times. We can represent our prior beliefs using a set of probability measures. However, if we use prior-by-prior updating, then after each flip of the coin the set $\mathcal{P}^+$ representing the DM's beliefs does not change, because the beliefs are independent. Thus, in this example, prior-by-prior updating is not capturing the information provided by the flips.

We consider another way of updating weighted sets of probabilities, called *likelihood updating* [7]. The intuition is that the weights are updated as if they were a second-order probability distribution over the probability measures. Given an event $E \subseteq S$, define $\overline{\mathcal{P}}^+(E) = \sup\{\alpha_{\Pr}\Pr(E) : \Pr \in \mathcal{P}\}$; if $\overline{\mathcal{P}}^+(E) > 0$, let $\alpha_{\Pr,E} = \sup_{\{\Pr' \in \mathcal{P}:\Pr'|E=\Pr|E\}} \frac{\alpha_{\Pr'}\Pr'(E)}{\overline{\mathcal{P}}^+(E)}$. Given a measure $\Pr \in \mathcal{P}$, there may be several distinct measures $\Pr'$ in $\mathcal{P}$ such that $\Pr'|E = \Pr|E$. Thus, we take the weight of $\Pr|E$ to be the sup of the possible candidate values of $\alpha_{\Pr,E}$. By dividing by $\overline{\mathcal{P}}^+(E)$, we guarantee that $\alpha_{\Pr,E} \in [0,1]$, and that there is some measure $\Pr$ such that $\alpha_{\Pr,E} = 1$, as long as there is some pair $(\alpha_{\Pr}, \Pr) \in \mathcal{P}$ such that $\alpha_{\Pr}\Pr(E) = \overline{\mathcal{P}}^+(E)$. If $\overline{\mathcal{P}}^+(E) > 0$, we take $\mathcal{P}^+|^l E$, the result of applying likelihood updating by E to $\mathcal{P}^+$, to be $\{(\Pr|E, \alpha_{\Pr,E}) : \Pr \in \mathcal{P}, \Pr(E) > 0\}$.

In computing $\mathcal{P}^+|^l E$, we update not just the probability measures in $\mathcal{P}$, but also their weights. Intuitively, probability measures that are supported by the new information will get larger weights than those not supported by the new information. Clearly, if all measures in $\mathcal{P}$ start off with the same weight and assign the same probability to the event E, then likelihood updating will give the same weight to each probability measure, resulting in measure-by-measure updating. This is not surprising, since such an observation E does not give us information about the relative likelihood of measures.

Let $C_M^{reg,\mathcal{P}^+|^l E}(M')$ be the set of acts in M' that minimize weighted expected regret when the regret is computed with respect to menu M and beliefs $\mathcal{P}^+|^l E$. If $\mathcal{P}^+|^l E$ is empty then $C_M^{reg,\mathcal{P}^+|^l E}(M') = M'$. We can similarly define $C_M^{reg,\mathcal{P}|E}$ and $C_M^{reg,\Pr|E}$.

3   Forgone Opportunities

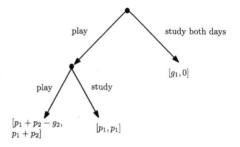

As we have seen, when making a decision at a history h in a dynamic decision problem, the DM must decide what menu to use. In this section we focus on one choice. Take a *forgone opportunity* to be a plan that was initially available to the DM, but is no longer available due to earlier actions.

Fig. 1. An explanation for procrastination.

As we observed in the introduction, while it may seem irrational to consider forgone opportunities, people often do. Moreover, when combined with regret, behavior that results by considering forgone opportunities may be arguably *more* rational than if forgone opportunities are not considered. Consider the following example.

Example 1. Suppose that a student has an exam in two days. She can either start studying today, play today and then study tomorrow, or just play on both days and never study. There are two states of nature: one where the exam is difficult, and one where the exam is easy. The utilities reflect a combination of the amount of pleasure that the student derives in the next two days, and her score on the exam relative to her classmates. Suppose that the first day of play gives the student $p_1 > 0$ utils, and the second day of play gives her $p_2 > 0$ utils. Her exam score affects her utility only in the case where the exam is hard and she studies both days, in which case she gets an additional g_1 utils for doing much better than everyone else, and in the case where the exam is hard and she never studies, in which case she loses $g_2 > 0$ utils for doing much worse than everyone else. Figure 1 provides a graphical representation of the decision problem. Since, in this example, the available actions for the DM are independent of nature's move, for compactness, we omit nature's initial move (whether the exam is easy or hard). Instead, we describe the payoffs of the DM as a pair $[a_1, a_2]$, where a_1 is the payoff if the exam is hard, and a_2 is the payoff if the exam is easy.

Assume that $2p_1 + p_2 > g_1 > p_1 + p_2$ and $2p_2 > g_2 > p_2$. That is, if the test were hard, the student would be happier studying and doing well on the test than she would be if she played for two days, but not too much happier; similarly, the penalty for doing badly in the exam if the exam is hard and she does not study is greater than the utility of playing the second day, but not too much greater. Suppose that the student uses minimax regret to make her decision. On the first day, she observes that playing one day and then studying the next day has a worst-case regret of $g_1 - p_1$, while studying on both days has a worst-case regret of $p_1 + p_2$. Therefore, she plays on the first day. On the next day, suppose that she does not consider forgone opportunities and just compares her two available options, studying and playing. Studying has a worst-case regret of p_2, while playing has a worst-case regret of $g_2 - p_2$, so, since $g_2 < 2p_2$, she plays again on the second day. On the other hand, if the student had included the forgone opportunity in the menu on the second day, then studying would have regret $g_1 - p_1$, while playing would have regret $g_1 + g_2 - p_1 - p_2$. Since $g_2 > p_2$, studying minimizes regret.   □

Example 1 emphasizes the roles of the menus M and M' in $C_{M,E}(M')$. Here we took M, the menu relative to which choices were evaluated, to consist of all plans, even the ones that were no longer feasible, while M' consisted of only feasible plans. In general, to determine the menu component M of the choice function $C_{M,E(h)}$ used at a history h, we use a *menu-selection function* μ. The menu $\mu(h)$ is the menu relative to which choice are computed at h. We sometimes write $C_{\mu,h}$ rather than $C_{\mu(h),E(h)}$.

We can now formalize the notion of *no preference reversal*.

Definition 1 (No Preference Reversal). *A family of choice functions $C_{\mu,h}$ has no preference reversals if, for all histories h and all histories h' extending h, if $f \in C_{\mu,h}(M_h)$ and $f \in M_{h'}$, then $f \in C_{\mu,h'}(M_{h'})$.*

The fact that we do not get a preference reversal in Example 1 if we take forgone opportunities into account here is not just an artifact of this example. As we now show, as long as we do not get new information and also use a constant menu (i.e., by keeping all forgone opportunities in the menu), then there will be no preference reversals if we minimize (weighted) expected regret in a dynamic setting.

Proposition 1. *If, for all histories h, h', we have $E(h) = S$ and $\mu(h) = \mu(h')$, and decisions are made according to MWER (i.e., the agent has a set $\mathcal{P}^+$ of weighted probability distributions and a utility function u, and $f \in C_{\mu,h}(M_h)$ if f minimizes weighted expected regret with respect to $\mathcal{P}^+|^l E(h)$), then no preference reversals occur.*

Table 1. $\alpha_{Pr_1} = 1, \alpha_{Pr_2} = 0.6.$

	Hard		Easy	
	Short	Long	Short	Long
Pr_1	1	0	0	0
Pr_2	0	0.2	0.2	0.2
Play-study	1	0	5	0
Play-play	0	3	0	3

Proposition 1 shows that we cannot have preference reversals if the DM does not learn about the world. However, if the DM learns about the world, then we can have preference reversals. Suppose, as is depicted in Table 1, that in addition to being hard and easy, the exam can also be short or long. The student's beliefs are described by the set of weighted probabilities Pr_1 and Pr_2, with weights 1 and 0.6, respectively.

We take the option of studying on both days out of the picture by assuming that its utility is low enough for it to never be preferred, and for it to never affect the regret computations. After the first day, the student learns whether the exam will be hard or easy. One can verify that the ex ante regret of playing then studying is lower than that of playing on both days, while after the first day, the student prefers to play on the second day, regardless of whether she learns that the exam is hard or easy.

4   Characterizing No Preference Reversal

We now consider conditions under which there is no preference reversal in a more general setting, where the DM can acquire new information. While including all forgone opportunities is no longer a sufficient condition to prevent preference reversals, it is necessary, as the following example shows: Consider

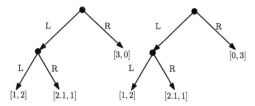

Fig. 2. Two decision trees.

the two similar decision problems depicted in Fig. 2. Note that at the node after first playing L, the utilities and available choices are identical in the two problems. If we ignore forgone opportunities, the DM necessarily makes the same decision in both cases if his beliefs are the same. However, in the tree to the left, the ex ante optimal plan is LR, while in the tree to the right, the ex ante optimal plan is LL. If the DM ignores forgone opportunities, then after the first step, she cannot tell whether she is in the decision tree on the left side, or the one on the right side. Therefore, if she follows the ex ante optimal plan in one of the trees, she necessarily is not following the ex ante optimal plan in the other tree.

In light of this example, we now consider what happens if the DM learns information over time. Our no preference reversal condition is implied by a well-studied notion called *dynamic consistency*. One way of describing dynamic consistency is that a plan considered optimal at a given point in the decision process is also optimal at any preceding point in the process, as well as any future point that is reached with positive probability [14]. For menu-independent preferences, dynamic consistency is usually captured axiomatically by variations of an axiom called *Dynamic Consistency* (DC) or the *Sure Thing Principle* [13]. We define a *menu-dependent* version of DC relative to events E and F using the following axiom. The second part of the axiom implies that if f is strictly preferred conditional on $E \cap F$ and at least weakly preferred on $E^c \cap F$, then f is also strictly preferred on F. An event E is *relevant to a dynamic decision problem D* if it is one of the events that the DM can potentially learn in D, that is, if there exists a history h such that $E(h) = E$. Given a decision problem D, we take the *measurable sets* to be the σ-algebra generated by the events relevant to D. The following axioms hold for all measurable sets E and F, menus M and M', and acts f and g.

Axiom 1 (DC-M). *If $f \in C_{M,E \cap F}(M') \cap C_{M,E^c \cap F}(M')$, then $f \in C_{M,F}(M')$. If, furthermore, $g \notin C_{M,E \cap F}(M')$, then $g \notin C_{M,F}(M')$.*

Axiom 2 (Conditional Preference). *If f and g, when viewed as acts, give the same outcome on all states in E, then $f \in C_{M,E}(M')$ iff $g \in C_{M,E}(M')$.*

Axiom 3. $C_{M,E}(M') \subseteq M'$ *and* $C_{M,E}(M') \neq \emptyset$ *if* $M' \neq \emptyset$.

Axiom 4 (Sen's α). *If $f \in C_{M,E}(M')$ and $M'' \subseteq M'$, then $f \in C_{M,E}(M'')$.*

Theorem 1. *Given a dynamic decision problem D, if Axioms 1–4 hold, and $\mu(h) = M$ for some fixed menu M, then there will be no preference reversals in D.*

We next provide a representation theorem that characterizes when Axioms 1–4 hold for a MWER decision maker. The following condition says that the unconditional regret can be computed by separately computing the regrets conditional on $E \cap F$ and on $E^c \cap F$.

Definition 2 (SEP). *The weighted regret of f with respect to M and $\mathcal{P}^+$ is separable with respect to $|^l$ if for all measurable sets E and F,*

$$reg_M^{\mathcal{P}^+|^l F}(f) = \sup_{\text{Pr} \in \mathcal{P}^+} \alpha_{\text{Pr}} \left(\text{Pr}(E \cap F) reg_M^{\mathcal{P}^+|^l (E \cap F)}(f) + \text{Pr}(E^c \cap F) reg_M^{\mathcal{P}^+|^l (E^c \cap F)}(f) \right),$$

and if $reg_M^{\mathcal{P}^+|^l (E \cap F)}(f) \neq 0$, then

$$reg_M^{\mathcal{P}^+|^l F}(f) > \sup_{\text{Pr} \in \mathcal{P}^+} \alpha_{\text{Pr}} \, \text{Pr}(E^c \cap F) reg_M^{\mathcal{P}^+|^l (E^c \cap F)}(f). \tag{1}$$

While (1) may seem complicated, note that a a sufficient condition for satisfying it for all plans f is that $\inf_{(\text{Pr}, \alpha_{\text{Pr}}) \in \mathcal{P}^+} \alpha_{\text{Pr}} \, \text{Pr}(E \cap F) > 0$.

We now show that Axioms 1–4 characterize SEP. Say that a decision problem D is *based on* a σ-algebra Σ if Σ is the σ-algebra generated by the set of events relevant to D. In the following results, we will also make use of an alternative interpretation of weighted probability measures. Define a *subprobability measure p* on S to be like a probability measure, in that it is a function mapping measurable subsets of S to $[0, 1]$ such that $p(T \cup T') = p(T) + p(T')$ for disjoint sets T and T', except that it may not satisfy the requirement that $p(S) = 1$. We can identify a weighted probability distribution (Pr, α) with the subprobability measure $\alpha \, \text{Pr}$. (Note that given a subprobability measure p, there is a unique pair (α, Pr) such that $p = \alpha \, \text{Pr}$: we simply take $\alpha = p(S)$ and $\text{Pr} = p/\alpha$.) Given a set $\mathcal{P}^+$ of weighted probability measures, we let $C(\mathcal{P}^+) = \{p \geq \mathbf{0} : \exists c, \exists \text{Pr}, (c, \text{Pr}) \in \mathcal{P}^+ \text{ and } p \leq c \, \text{Pr}\}$.

Theorem 2. *If $\mathcal{P}^+$ is a set of weighted distributions on S such that $C(\mathcal{P}^+)$ is closed, then the following are equivalent:*

(a) *For all decision problems D based on Σ and all menus M in D, Axioms 1–4 hold for the family $C_M^{reg, \mathcal{P}^+|^l E}$ of choice functions.*

(b) *For all decision problems D based on Σ, states $s \in S$, and acts $f \in M_{\langle s \rangle}$, the weighted regret of f with respect to $M_{\langle s \rangle}$ and $\mathcal{P}^+$ is separable with respect to $|^l$.*

It is not hard to show that SEP holds if the set $\mathcal{P}$ is a singleton. But, in general, it seems difficult to determine whether a set of weighted probabilities satisfies SEP. We thus provide a condition on $\mathcal{P}^+$ sufficient for SEP to hold that should be easier to check.

Definition 3 (Richness). *A set $\mathcal{P}^+$ of weighted probability measures is rich if for all measurable sets E and F,*

(a) if $(\mathrm{Pr}_1, \alpha_1), (\mathrm{Pr}_2, \alpha_2), (\mathrm{Pr}_3, \alpha_3) \in \mathcal{P}^+$, then

$$\alpha_{\mathrm{Pr}_3} \mathrm{Pr}_3(E \cap F) \frac{\alpha_1 \mathrm{Pr}_1(E \cap F)}{\overline{\mathcal{P}}^+(E \cap F)} \mathrm{Pr}_1|^l(E \cap F)$$
$$+ \alpha_{\mathrm{Pr}_3} \mathrm{Pr}_3(E^c \cap F) \frac{\alpha_2 \mathrm{Pr}_2(E^c \cap F)}{\overline{\mathcal{P}}^+(E^c \cap F)} \mathrm{Pr}_2|^l(E^c \cap F) \in C(\mathcal{P}^+),$$

(b) for all $(\mathrm{Pr}, \alpha) \in \mathcal{P}^+$, $\alpha \mathrm{Pr}(E \cap F) > 0$, and

(c) for some $(\mathrm{Pr}, \alpha) \in \mathcal{P}^+|^l F$, $\alpha \mathrm{Pr}(E \cap F) = \overline{\mathcal{P}}^+(E \cap F)$ and $\alpha \mathrm{Pr}(E^c \cap F) = \overline{\mathcal{P}}^+(E^c \cap F)$.

As the following result shows, richness is indeed sufficient to give us Axioms 1–4 under likelihood updating.

Theorem 3. *If $\mathcal{P}^+$ is rich and $C(\mathcal{P}^+)$ is closed, then Axiom 1 holds for the family of choices $C_M^{reg,\mathcal{P}^+|^l E}$.*

References

1. Al-Najjar, N., Weinstein, J.: The ambiguity aversion literature: a critical assessment. Econ. Philos. **25**, 249–284 (2009)
2. Allais, M.: Le comportement de l'homme rationnel devant le risque: Critique des postulats et axiomes de l'ecole americaine. Econometrica **21**(4), 503–546 (1953)
3. Anscombe, F., Aumann, R.: A definition of subjective probability. Ann. Math. Stat. **34**, 199–205 (1963)
4. Ellsberg, D.: Risk, ambiguity, and the savage axioms. Q. J. Econ. **75**(4), 643–669 (1961)
5. Epstein, L.G., Le Breton, M.: Dynamically consistent beliefs must be Bayesian. J. Econ. Theor. **61**(1), 1–22 (1993)
6. Epstein, L.G., Schneider, M.: Recursive multiple-priors. J. Econ. Theor. **113**(1), 1–31 (2003)
7. Halpern, J.Y., Leung, S.: Weighted sets of probabilities and minimax weighted expected regret: new approaches for representing uncertainty and making decisions. In: Proceedings of Twenty-Ninth Conference on Uncertainty in Artificial Intelligence (UAI 2012), pp. 336–345 (2012)
8. Hammond, P.J.: Changing tastes and coherent dynamic choice. Rev. Econ. Stud. **43**(1), 159–173 (1976)
9. Hayashi, T.: Stopping with anticipated regret. J. Math. Econ. **45**(7–8), 479–490 (2009)
10. Hayashi, T.: Context dependence and consistency in dynamic choice under uncertainty: the case of anticipated regret. Theor. Decis. **70**, 399–430 (2011)
11. Machina, M.J.: Dynamic consistency and non-expected utility models of choice under uncertainty. J. Econ. Lit. **27**(4), 1622–1668 (1989)
12. Savage, L.J.: The theory of statistical decision. J. Am. Stat. Assoc. **46**, 55–67 (1951)
13. Savage, L.J.: The Foundations of Statistics. Wiley, New York (1954)
14. Siniscalchi, M.: Dynamic choice under ambiguity. Theor. Econ. **6**(3), 379–421 (2011)
15. Stoye, J.: Axioms for minimax regret choice correspondences. J. Econ. Theor. **146**(6), 2226–2251 (2011)

Extracting Decision Rules from Qualitative Data Using Sugeno Integral: A Case-Study

Didier Dubois[1], Claude Durrieu[2], Henri Prade[1], Agnès Rico[3](✉), and Yannis Ferro[2]

[1] IRIT, Université Paul Sabatier, 118 route de Narbonne,
31062 Toulouse cedex 9, France
{dubois,prade}@irit.fr
[2] LEHNA-ENTPE, UMR 5023, rue Maurice Audin,
69518 Vaulx-en-velin cédex, France
{claude.durrieu,yannis.ferro}@entpe.fr
[3] ERIC, Université Claude Bernard Lyon 1, 43 bld du 11 novembre,
69100 Villeurbanne, France
agnes.rico@univ-lyon1.fr

Abstract. This paper deals with knowledge extraction from experimental data in multifactorial evaluation using Sugeno integrals. They are qualitative criteria aggregations where it is possible to assign weights to groups of criteria. A method for deriving such weights from data is recalled. We also present results in the logical representation of Sugeno integrals. Then we show how to extract if-then rules expressing the selection of good situations on the basis of local evaluations, and rules to detect bad situations. We illustrate such methods on a case-study in the area of water ecosystem health.

1 Introduction

Sugeno integrals are aggregation functions that make sense on any completely ordered scale, and can then be called qualitative aggregation operations. Like many aggregation operations in multifactorial evaluation, they return a global evaluation lying between the minimum and the maximum of the partial ratings. In a Sugeno integral each group of criteria receives an importance weight, whereby interactions between criteria can be modeled.

Sugeno integrals are used both in multiple criteria decision making and in decision under uncertainty [2,6,8]. While many results exist proposing formal characterizations of Sugeno integral [10,11], fewer papers address the identification of Sugeno integrals from data, and the interpretation of this aggregation method in terms of decision rules. The former problem is addressed by Prade *et al.* [12,13]: they calculate a family of capacities, if any, that determine Sugeno integrals that account for a set of empirically rated objects both locally with respect to criteria, and globally, each object receiving an overall evaluation. The second issue was first addressed by Greco *et al.* [9]. Representing a Sugeno integral by a set of rules make it more palatable in practical applications.

© Springer International Publishing Switzerland 2015
S. Destercke and T. Denoeux (Eds.): ECSQARU 2015, LNAI 9161, pp. 14–24, 2015.
DOI: 10.1007/978-3-319-20807-7_2

More recently, a possibilistic logic rendering of Sugeno integral has been proposed, in the form of weighted formulas the satisfaction of which is sufficient to ensure a minimal global evaluation [5].

Such a possibilistic logic base can be used to obtain some rules associated to the given data modeled by a Sugeno integral. This paper combines both a technique for identifying a family of capacities at work in a Sugeno integral applied to subjective multifactorial evaluation data, and a technique for extracting decision rules from the obtained family of Sugeno integrals. At the theoretical level it completes the results obtained in [5] by considering the extraction of decision rules that give conditions for an object to have a global evaluation less than a given threshold. Overall, we then get rules that can accept good objects and rules that can discard bad ones. As an illustration the paper presents an application of these results on a case-study on the effects of rainwater pollution on the development of algae. In a nutshell, this application focuses on the following question: what do we learn about the given data on algae when representing the global evaluation by an aggregation of local ones via a discrete Sugeno integral? Papers using fuzzy set methods in ecology are not so numerous; let us however mention the use in classification of another family of aggregation functions, named symmetric sums [15].

The paper is structured as follows: Sect. 2 begins with a brief reminder about some theoretical results concerning Sugeno integral. Next it presents results on the identification of Sugeno integral and its expression in the form of rules. Section 3 presents the data of the case-study. Section 4 deals with the application of the theoretical results to the given dataset.

2   Interpreting Evaluation Data Using Sugeno Integrals

We use the terminology of multiple criteria decision-making where some objects are evaluated according to criteria. We denote by $C = \{1, \cdots, n\}$ the set of criteria, 2^C the power set and L a totally ordered scale with top 1, bottom 0, and the order-reversing operation denoted by ν (ν is involutive and such that $\nu(1) = 0$ and $\nu(0) = 1$). An object is represented by a vector $x = (x_1, \cdots x_n)$ where x_i is the evaluation of x according to the criterion i.

In the definition of Sugeno integral the relative weights of the set of criteria are represented by a capacity (or fuzzy measure) which is a set function $\mu :$ $2^C \rightarrow L$ that satisfies $\mu(\emptyset) = 0$, $\mu(C) = 1$ and $A \subseteq B$ implies $\mu(A) \leq \mu(B)$. In order to translate a Sugeno integral into rules we shall also need the notion of conjugate capacity. More precisely, the conjugate capacity of μ is defined by $\mu^c(A) = \nu(\mu(A^c))$ where A^c is the complementary of A. The Sugeno integral of function x with respect to a capacity μ is originally defined by [16,17]: $S_\mu(x) = \max_{\alpha \in L} \min(\alpha, \mu(x \geq \alpha))$, where $\mu(x \geq \alpha) = \mu(\{i \in C | x_i \geq \alpha\})$. It can be equivalently written under various forms [3,10,11], especially:

$$S_\mu(x) = \max_{A \subseteq C} \min(\mu(A), \min_{i \in A} x_i) = \min_{A \subseteq C} \max(\mu(A^c), \max_{i \in A} x_i) \qquad (1)$$

2.1 Eliciting Sugeno Integrals

In this paper, our first aim is to elicit a family of Sugeno integrals that are compatible with a given dataset. Let us recall how to calculate the bounds of this family.

The set of data is a collection of $(x^k, \alpha_k)_k$ where x^k are tuples of local evaluations of objects $k = 1, \ldots, N$ and α_k is the global evaluation of object k. This data set is supposed to be provided by some expert, or the result of a data collection. We want to know if there exists a capacity μ such that $S_\mu(x^k) = \alpha_k$ for all k, and if so, we want to calculate at least one solution. In [14], the following result is proved:

Proposition 1. *For a given data item (x, α), $\{\mu | S_\mu(x) = \alpha\} = \{\mu | \check{\mu}_{x,\alpha} \leq \mu \leq \hat{\mu}_{x,\alpha}\}$ where $\check{\mu}_{x,\alpha}$ and $\hat{\mu}_{x,\alpha}$ are capacities defined by*

$$\check{\mu}_{x,\alpha}(A) = \begin{cases} \alpha \ if \ \{i | x_i \geq \alpha\} \subseteq A \\ 0 \ otherwise \end{cases} \quad and \quad \hat{\mu}_{x,\alpha}(A) = \begin{cases} \alpha \ if \ A \subseteq \{i | x_i > \alpha\} \\ 1 \ otherwise. \end{cases}$$

Remark: It is easy to see that $\check{\mu}_{x,\alpha}$ is a necessity measure with respect to the possibility distribution $\check{\pi}_{x,\alpha}(i) = \begin{cases} 1 \ if \ x_i \geq \alpha \\ \nu(\alpha) \ otherwise \end{cases}$, and $\hat{\mu}_{x,\alpha}(A)$ is a possibility measure with respect to the possibility distribution $\hat{\pi}_{x,\alpha}(i) = \begin{cases} 1 \ if \ x_i \leq \alpha \\ \alpha \ otherwise \end{cases}$.

Hence we can calculate the bounds of the compatible Sugeno integrals:

Proposition 2. *The set of compatible capacities with the given data $(x^k, \alpha_k)_k$ is $\{\mu | \max_k \check{\mu}_{x^k, \alpha_k} \leq \mu \leq \min_k \hat{\mu}_{x^k, \alpha_k}\}$.*

As a consequence, $\max_k \check{\mu}_{x^k, \alpha_k}$ and $\min_k \hat{\mu}_{x^k, \alpha_k}$ can be any kind of capacity, since any capacity is the eventwise minimum of necessity measures and the eventwise maximum of possibility measures [4]. Moreover, it is not always the case that $\{\mu | \max_k \check{\mu}_{x^k, \alpha_k} \leq \mu \leq \min_k \hat{\mu}_{x^k, \alpha_k}\} \neq \emptyset$, that is, the set of solutions can be empty.[1]

2.2 Extracting If-Then Rules Using Possibilistic Logic

Based on the above results and procedures described in [12], suppose we have a family of Sugeno integrals compatible with the evaluation data. Now, we try to express if-then rules associated to these integrals, thus facilitating the interpretation of the data.

Selection Rules. First let us recall how Sugeno integral can be encoded by means of a possibilistic logic base with positive clauses (see [5] for more details).

---

[1] In order to compare $\max_k \check{\mu}_{x^k, \alpha_k}$ and $\min_k \hat{\mu}_{x^k, \alpha_k}$ it is not necessary to calculate their values and to compare them on each subset of criteria. It is proved in [14] that the set of compatible capacities is not empty if and only if for all $\alpha_k < \alpha_l$ we have $\{i | x_i^l \geq \alpha_l\} \not\subseteq \{i | x_i^k > \alpha_k\}$.

We need to use the inner qualitative Moebius transform of a capacity μ which is a mapping $\mu_\# : 2^C \to L$ defined by

$$\mu_\#(E) = \mu(E) \text{ if } \mu(E) > \max_{B \subset E} \mu(B) \text{ and } 0 \text{ otherwise.}$$

A set E such that $\mu_\#(E) > 0$ is called a focal set. The set of the focal sets of μ is denoted by $\mathcal{F}(\mu)$. Moreover we denote by $\mathcal{F}(\mu)^\alpha$ the set of the focal sets E such that $\mu(E) = \alpha$. Note that Sugeno integral can be expressed in terms of $\mu_\#$ using Equation (1) as follows: $S_\mu(x) = \max\limits_{E \in \mathcal{F}(\mu)} \min(\mu_\#(E), \min\limits_{i \in E} x_i)$.

Using the definition of the Sugeno integral it is easy to get the following result [5]:

Proposition 3. *The inequality $S_\mu(x) \geq \gamma$ is equivalent to $\exists T \in \mathcal{F}(\mu)^\gamma$ such that $\forall i \in T, x_i \geq \gamma$.*

So each focal T of μ with level $\mu_\#(T)$ corresponds to the selection rule:

$$R_T^s: \text{ If } x_i \geq \mu_\#(T) \text{ for all i } \in T \text{ then } S_\mu(x) \geq \mu_\#(T).$$

This set of rules can be encoded in possibilistic logic as a set of weighted cubes. Define for each criterion i a family of Boolean predicates $x_i(\alpha), \alpha > 0 \in L$ such that $x_i(\alpha) = 1$ if $x_i \geq \alpha$ and 0 otherwise. Then we consider weighted Boolean formulas of the form $[\phi, \alpha]$ which are interpreted as lower possibility distribu-

tions on the set of objects: $\pi_{[\phi,\alpha]}^-(x) = \begin{cases} \alpha \text{ if } x \models \phi; \\ 0 \text{ otherwise} \end{cases}$. Then the lower possibil-

ity distribution associated to a weighted cube is $[\wedge_{j \in T} x_j(\alpha), \alpha]$ interpreted as

$\pi_{[T,\alpha]}^-(x) = \begin{cases} \alpha \text{ if } x_i \geq \alpha, \forall i \in T; \\ 0 \text{ otherwise} \end{cases}$. Each weighted cube $[\wedge_{j \in T} x_j(\mu(T)), \mu_\#(T)]$

for a focal set T corresponds to a rule R_T^s as stated above.

The lower possibility distributions associated to a set of such weighted formulas is interpreted as the maximum of the lower possibility distributions associated to each weighted formula. Now consider the possibilistic base

$$B_\mu^- = \{[\wedge_{j \in T} x_j(\alpha), \alpha] : \mu(T) \geq \alpha > 0, T \in \mathcal{F}(\mu)\}$$

with lower possibility distribution $\pi_\mu^-(x) = \max_{\mu(T) \geq \alpha > 0, T \in \mathcal{F}(\mu)} \pi_{[\phi,\alpha]}^-(x)$.

Proposition 4 *(Proposition 4 in [5]).* $S_\mu(x) = \pi_\mu^-(x)$.

The proof takes advantage of the max-min form of Sugeno integral in Eq. (1).

Elimination Rules. The above rules and their logical encoding are tailored for the selection of good objects. Symmetrically, we can obtain rules for the rejection of bad objects associated to the Sugeno integral. In the following we prove results similar to those in [5] for the inequality $S_\mu(x) \leq \gamma$.

The idea is to use the min-max form of Sugeno integral in Eq. (1), which is the form of possibility distributions in standard possibilistic logic [1]. The focal sets of the conjugate of μ are sufficient to calculate the Sugeno integral:

Proposition 5. $S_\mu(x) = \min_{T \in \mathcal{F}(\mu^c)} \max(\nu(\mu_\#^c(T)), \max_{i \in T} x_i)$.

Proof. Note that we can write $S_\mu(x) = \min_{T \subseteq \mathcal{C}} \max(\nu(\mu^c(T)), \max_{i \in T} x_i)$. Hence, $S_\mu(x)$ is the minimum between $\min_{T \notin \mathcal{F}(\mu^c)} \max(\nu(\mu^c(T)), \max_{i \in T} x_i)$ and $\min_{T \in \mathcal{F}(\mu^c)} \max(\nu(\mu_\#^c(T)), \max_{i \in T} x_i))$.

If we consider $T \notin \mathcal{F}(\mu^c)$ then there exists $F \in \mathcal{F}(\mu^c)$ such that $F \subseteq T$ and $\mu^c(F) = \mu^c(T) = \mu_\#^c(F^c)$. Moreover $\max_{i \in F} x_i \leq \max_{i \in T} x_i$ which implies that $\max(\mu_\#^c(F), \max_{i \in F} x_i) \leq \max(\mu_\#^c(T), \max_{i \in T} x_i)$. □

Note that $S_\mu(x)$ takes the form "min →" using Kleene implication, like weighted minimum.

Proposition 6. $S_\mu(x) \leq \alpha$ if and only if $\exists F \in \mathcal{F}(\mu^c)$ with $\mu^c(F) \geq \nu(\alpha)$ s.t. $\forall x_i \in F \ x_i \leq \alpha$.

Proof. $S_\mu(x) \leq \alpha$ implies $\exists F \in \mathcal{F}(\mu^c)$ such that $\mu^\#(F^c) \leq \alpha$ and $\max_{i \in F} x_i \leq \alpha$. So we have $\nu(\mu_\#^c(F)) \leq \alpha$, i.e., $\mu_\#^c(F) \geq \nu(\alpha)$ and $\forall x_i \in F \ x_i \geq \alpha$. □

This proposition shows that for each focal set of the conjugate μ^c we have the following elimination rule:

R_F^e: If $x_i \leq \nu(\mu_\#^c(F))$ for all $i \in F$ then $S_\mu(x) \leq \nu(\mu_\#^c(F))$.

Let us give a possibilistic logic view of elimination rules associated to Sugeno integral, now as set of weighted clauses. Define for each criterion i a family of Boolean predicates $x_i(\alpha), \alpha > 0 \in L$ such that $x_i(\alpha) = 1$ if $x_i > \alpha$ and 0 otherwise. It is slightly different from the previous case. It is easy to check that $x_i = \min_{\alpha < 1} \max(x_i(\alpha), \alpha)$.

Here we consider weighted Boolean formulas of the form (ϕ, β) which are interpreted as upper possibility distributions on the set of objects:

$$\pi_{(\phi,\beta)}^+(x) = \begin{cases} 1 & \text{if } x \models \phi; \\ \nu(\beta) & \text{otherwise} \end{cases}.$$

The upper possibility distributions associated to a set of such weighted formulas is interpreted as the minimum of the upper possibility distributions associated to each weighted formula. Then the set of weighted clauses $\{(\bigvee_{j \in F} x_j(\alpha), \nu(\alpha)) : \alpha < 1\}$ induces an upper possibility distribution:

$$\pi_F(x) = \min_{\alpha < 1} \max(\alpha, \max_{j \in F} x_j(\alpha)) = \max_{j \in F} x_j.$$

Each weighted clause $(\bigvee_{j \in F} x_j(\mu^c(F)), \nu(\mu^c(F)))$ for a focal set F of μ^c corresponds to the elimination rule R_T^e stated above.

A logical rendering of the Sugeno integral in the min-max form is obtained as follows. First consider the following base of clauses $B_\mu^F = \{(\bigvee_{j \in F} x_j(\alpha), \nu(\alpha)) : \nu(\mu_\#^c(F)) \leq \alpha < 1\}$. We claim it encodes the term $\max(\nu(\mu_\#^c(F)), \max_{i \in F} x_i)$.

Proposition 7. $\pi^+_{B^F_\mu}(x) = \max(\nu(\mu^c_\#(F)), \max_{i\in F} x_i)$.

Proof. $\pi^+_{B^F_\mu}(x) = \min_{1>\alpha\geq\nu(\mu^c_\#(F))} \max(\alpha, \max_{j\in F} x_j(\alpha)) = \min_{1>\alpha} \max(\nu(\mu^c_\#(F)), \max(\alpha, \max_{j\in F} x_j(\alpha))) = \max(\nu(\mu^c_\#(F)), \max_{i\in F} x_i)$. $\square$

Now consider the possibilistic base

$$B^+_\mu = \{(\bigvee_{j\in F} x_j(\alpha), \nu(\alpha)) : \nu(\mu^c(F)) \leq \alpha < 1, F \in \mathcal{F}(\mu^c)\}$$

with upper possibility distribution $\pi^+_\mu(x) = \min_{F\in\mathcal{F}(\mu^c)} \pi^+_{B^F_\mu}(x)$.

Proposition 8. $S_\mu(x) = \pi^+_\mu(x)$.

3 Data for the Case Study

Samples were collected on retention basins in the Eastern suburbs of Lyon before groundwater seepage (see [7] for more details). Some samples are obtained by rainy weather and others are obtained by dry weather. We then speak about "rain waters" and "dry waters" respectively. The waters contain many pollutants (like heavy metals, pesticides, hydrocarbons, PCB, ...) and our aim is to assess their impact on the water ecosystem health. This is why the unicellular algal compartment is considered hereafter. Algae are chosen for their high ecological representativeness at the first level of the food chain.

First, algal growth (C) was measured as a global indicator of algal health with standardized bioassay (NF EN ISO 8692), then bioassays more specific of different metabolic pathways were carried out: chlorophyll fluorescence (F) as phosynthesis indicator and two enzymatic activities, Alkaline phosphatase Activity (APA) and Esterase Activity (EA) as nutrients metabolism indicators. Assays were performed after 24 h exposure to samples collected during 7 different rainfall events and for different periods of the year for dry weather. Results, presented in Table 1 in which each row represents a sample, are expressed as

Table 1. Original data

data under rainy weather

data under dry weather

AE	APA	F	C	AE	APA	F	C	AE	APA	F	C
								509	55, 02	111, 64	110, 69
83	36, 46	185, 45	45, 39	24, 65	104, 93	153, 51	67, 58	209, 28	109, 1	73, 18	102, 30
131, 64	25, 88	10, 69	0	17, 6	466, 4	123, 62	15, 76	1964, 58	95, 93	6, 96	0
35, 6		167, 06	0	33, 22	47, 6	163, 58	55, 17	122, 62	98, 61	137, 09	69, 30
16, 36	81, 25	194, 97	7, 17	96, 78	35, 17	21, 51	9, 71	5, 6		143, 12	38, 81
107, 82	72, 64	167, 04	0	74, 06	92, 3	123, 43	26, 59	45, 35	78, 27	129, 45	56, 82
58, 18		116, 57	63, 39	64, 55	73, 32	163, 08	0	64, 88	331, 37		0
698, 37	42, 15	90, 18	92, 70	5, 12	206, 87	111, 56	92, 17	143, 63			65, 52
									31, 92	44, 23	75, 78

percent of activity of control (control being algae before exposure to rain waters). The effects are considered significant when the values are far from 100. The values obtained are less than 100 in the case of inhibition and greater than 100 in the case of activation. The expert translates the results to the totally ordered scale $L = \{15, 25, 50, 85, 100\}$. Level 100, interpreted as a complete lack of effect of the rainwater, is the best evaluation; and the farther an evaluation is from 100, the worse it is. More precisely we have the following interpretation:

15	25	50	85	100
very strong effect	strong effect	effect	weak effect	no effect

With these rescaled data the expert can give a global evaluation (global eval.) in the scale L. The results are presented in Table 2.

Table 2. Rescaled data

data under rainy weather

AE	APA	F	C	global eval.	AE	APA	F	C	global eval.
85	25	50	50	50	15	100	50	50	50
85	25	15	15	25	15	15	85	25	25
25		50	15	25	25	50	50	50	50
25	85	25	15	25	100	25	25	15	25
100	85	50	15	50	85	100	85	25	85
50		85	50	50	50	85	50	15	50
15	50	100	85	50	15	15	100	100	50

data under dry weather

AE	APA	F	C	global eval.
15	50	100	100	85
15	100	85	100	85
15	100	15	15	25
100	100	85	50	85
15		85	25	50
50	85	85	50	50
50	15		15	25
85			50	50
	25	50	85	50

The evaluation scale is equipped with the reversing order map ν defined by: $\nu(15) = 100$, $\nu(25) = 85$, $\nu(50) = 50$.

These experiment results can be modeled by an aggregation operation: the four criteria will be APA, AE, F and C, and we try to elicit Sugeno integrals which represent the given global evaluation. Next the obtained Sugeno integrals are translated into rules whose conditions use the criteria.

4   Experimental Results

In this section, we try to interpret the above data in terms of selection and elimination rules built via a Sugeno integral.

Data Under Rainy Weather. We consider the data under rainy weather and we compute the bounds of the set of compatible capacities $\check{\mu}$, $\hat{\mu}$ and their conjugate capacities (Table 3).

We have $\check{\mu} \leq \hat{\mu}$ so it is possible to represent the data with a Sugeno integral. Let us denote by μ a capacity with $\check{\mu} \leq \mu \leq \hat{\mu}$.

Table 3. Weights for criteria groups for rainy weather

criteria	$\check{\mu}$	$\hat{\mu}$	$\check{\mu}^c$	$\hat{\mu}^c$	criteria	$\check{\mu}$	$\hat{\mu}$	$\check{\mu}^c$	$\hat{\mu}^c$	criteria	$\check{\mu}$	$\hat{\mu}$	$\check{\mu}^c$	$\hat{\mu}^c$
$\{AE\}$	15	25	50	15	$\{APA\}$	15	25	50	15	$\{F\}$	15	25	85	15
$\{C\}$	15	50	25	15	$\{AE,APA\}$	25	50	50	50	$\{AE,F\}$	15	100	100	15
$\{AE,C\}$	15	100	100	15	$\{APA,F\}$	15	100	100	15	$\{APA,C\}$	15	100	100	15
$\{F,C\}$	50	50	85	50	$\{AE,APA,F\}$	85	100	100	50	$\{AE,APA,C\}$	25	100	100	85
$\{AE,F,C\}$	50	100	100	85	$\{APA,F,C\}$	50	100	100	85	$\{AE,APA,F,C\}$	100	100	100	100

Remark 1. As $\check{\mu} \leq \mu \leq \hat{\mu}$, $\mu(\{F,C\}) = 50$. Since $\mu(F) \leq 25$, either C is a focal element with level 50 or $\{F,C\}$ is a focal element with level 50.

Remark 2. Since $S_{\check{\mu}} \leq S_{\mu} \leq S_{\hat{\mu}}$, then we are going to consider $\check{\mu}$ (resp. $\hat{\mu}^c$) to obtain selection (resp. elimination) rules. Indeed, testing $\check{\mu}$ is larger than a threshold and $\hat{\mu}^c$ less than this threshold give sure decisions despite the limited knowledge about μ.

- Let us consider $\check{\mu}$. The focal sets are $\mathcal{F}(\check{\mu})^{100} = \{\{AE, APA, F, C\}\}$, $\mathcal{F}(\check{\mu})^{85} = \{\{AE, APA, F\}\}$, $\mathcal{F}(\check{\mu})^{50} = \{\{F,C\}\}$, $\mathcal{F}(\check{\mu})^{25} = \{\{AE, APA\}\}$, and we obtain the following selection rules
  - If $x_{AE} \geq 85$, $x_{APA} \geq 85$ and $x_F \geq 85$ then $S_{\check{\mu}}(x) \geq 85$.
  - If $x_F \geq 50$ and $x_C \geq 50$ then $S_{\check{\mu}}(x) \geq 50$.
  - If $x_{AE} \geq 25$ and $x_{APA} \geq 25$ then $S_{\check{\mu}}(x) \geq 25$.
- Let us consider $\hat{\mu}^c$. We have $\mathcal{F}(\hat{\mu}^c)^{50} = \{\{APA, AE\}, \{F,C\}\}$, $\mathcal{F}(\hat{\mu}^c)^{85} = \{\{AE, APA, C\}, \{AE, F, C\}, \{APA, F, C\}\}$, $\mathcal{F}(\hat{\mu}^c)^{100} = \{\{AE, APA, F, C\}\}$ which produces the following elimination rules:
  - if $x_{APA} \leq 50$ and $x_{AE} \leq 50$ then $S_{\hat{\mu}}(x) \leq 50$.
  - if $x_F \leq 50$ and $x_C \leq 50$ then $S_{\hat{\mu}}(x) \leq 50$.
  - if $x_{APA} \leq 25$ and $x_{AE} \leq 25$ and $x_C \leq 25$ then $S_{\hat{\mu}}(x) \leq 25$.
  - if $x_{AE} \leq 25$ and $x_F \leq 25$ and $x_C \leq 25$ then $S_{\hat{\mu}}(x) \leq 25$.
  - if $x_{APA} \leq 25$ and $x_F \leq 25$ and $x_C \leq 25$ then $S_{\hat{\mu}}(x) \leq 25$.

Sugeno integral $S_{\mu}(x)$ complies with all rules, hence the following comments:

- If criteria AE, APA and F are satisfied enough then the global evaluation is good;
- When criterion C has a bad rating, two other criteria also need to have a bad rating in order to obtain a bad global evaluation.
- However if criteria other than C get bad ratings it is not enough to get a bad global evaluation.

Let us consider fictitious examples of data and predict the global evaluation given with $S_{\check{\mu}}$ and $S_{\hat{\mu}}$ obtained above. We get an interval-valued evaluation given by the range of compatible capacities $S_{\check{\mu}} \leq S_{\mu} \leq S_{\hat{\mu}}$. In the left-hand table we consider that only one criterion is perfect and the others get the worst value. In the right-hand table we consider that only one criterion has the worst value and the other are satisfied.

AE	APA	F	C	$S_{\check{\mu}}$	$S_{\hat{\mu}}$
15	15	15	100	15	50
100	15	15	15	15	25
15	15	100	15	15	25
15	100	15	15	15	25

AE	APA	F	C	$S_{\check{\mu}}$	$S_{\hat{\mu}}$
100	100	100	15	85	100
100	100	15	100	25	100
100	15	100	100	50	100
15	100	100	100	50	100

Some comments concerning the global evaluation: Criterion C is not sufficient to downgrade it under 85, and it is not sufficient to bring it above 50. No other criterion is sufficient to alone bring it above 25. Criterion F is not sufficient to downgrade it under 25, and criteria AE and APA are not sufficient to downgrade it alone under 50. These remarks give a good idea of the relative importance of criteria.

Data Under Dry Weather. This section is similar to the previous one. First we compute the bounds of the capacities as per Table 4. Since $\check{\mu} \leq \hat{\mu}$, it is possible to represent the data with a Sugeno integral. We remark that the set of solutions $\check{\mu} \leq \mu \leq \hat{\mu}$ is not compatible with the previous one since they have an empty intersection.

Remark 3. We have $\mu(\{F, C\}) = 85$ and since $\mu(F) \leq 50$, either C is a focal element with level 85 or $\{F, C\}$ is a focal element with level 85.

- Let us consider $\check{\mu}$. The focal sets form $\mathcal{F}(\check{\mu})^{100} = \{\{AE, APA, F, C\}\}$, $\mathcal{F}(\check{\mu})^{85} = \{\{F, C\}, \{AE, APA, F\}\}$, $\mathcal{F}(\check{\mu})^{25} = \{\{APA\}\}$. It produces the following rules:
  - If $x_{AE} \geq 85$, $x_{APA} \geq 85$ and $x_F \geq 85$ then $S_{\check{\mu}}(x) \geq 85$;
  - If $x_F \geq 85$ and $x_C \geq 85$ then $S_{\check{\mu}}(x) \geq 85$;
  - If $x_{APA} \geq 25$ then $S_{\check{\mu}}(x) \geq 25$.
- Let us consider $\hat{\mu}^c$. We have $\mathcal{F}(\hat{\mu}^c)^{25} = \{\{AE, APA\}, \{AE, F\}, \{F, C\}\}$, $\mathcal{F}(\hat{\mu}^c)^{50} = \{\{AE, C\}\}$, $\mathcal{F}(\hat{\mu}^c)^{85} = \{\{AE, F, C\}\}$, $\mathcal{F}(\hat{\mu}^c)^{100} = \{\{AE, APA, F, C\}\}$, which produces the following rules:
  - if $x_{AE} < 100$ and $x_{APA} < 100$ then $S_{\hat{\mu}}(x) < 100$;
  - if $x_{AE} < 100$ and $x_F < 100$ then $S_{\hat{\mu}}(x) < 100$;
  - if $x_F < 100$ and $x_C < 100$ then $S_{\hat{\mu}}(x) < 100$;
  - if $x_{AE} \leq 50$ and $x_C \leq 50$ then $S_{\hat{\mu}}(x) \leq 50$;
  - if $x_{AE} \leq 25$ and $x_F \leq 25$ and $x_C \leq 25$ then $S_{\hat{\mu}}(x) \leq 25$.

Table 4. Weights for criteria groups for dry weather

Criteria	$\check{\mu}$	$\hat{\mu}$	$\check{\mu}^c$	$\hat{\mu}^c$	Criteria	$\check{\mu}$	$\hat{\mu}$	$\check{\mu}^c$	$\hat{\mu}^c$	Criteria	$\check{\mu}$	$\hat{\mu}$	$\check{\mu}^c$	$\hat{\mu}^c$
$\{AE\}$	15	85	25	15	$\{APA\}$	25	25	25	15	$\{F\}$	15	50	85	15
$\{C\}$	15	85	25	15	$\{AE,APA\}$	25	85	25	25	$\{AE,F\}$	15	100	85	25
$\{AE,C\}$	15	100	85	50	$\{APA,F\}$	25	50	100	15	$\{APA,C\}$	25	85	100	15
$\{F,C\}$	85	85	85	25	$\{AE,APA,F\}$	85	100	100	25	$\{AE,APA,C\}$	25	100	100	50
$\{AE,F,C\}$	85	100	85	85	$\{APA,F,C\}$	85	100	100	25	$\{AE,APA,F,C\}$	100	100	100	100

A Sugeno integral $S_\mu(x)$, where $\breve{\mu} \leq \mu \leq \hat{\mu}$, complies with all rules, hence, if C, F and AE have a bad evaluation then the global evaluation is bad. As previously, we consider fictitious examples and derive the bounds of the global evaluation given by S_μ.

AE	APA	F	C	$S_{\breve{\mu}}$	$S_{\hat{\mu}}$	AE	APA	F	C	$S_{\breve{\mu}}$	$S_{\hat{\mu}}$
15	15	15	100	15	85	100	100	100	15	85	100
100	15	15	15	15	85	100	100	15	100	25	100
15	15	100	15	15	50	100	15	100	100	15	100
15	100	15	15	25	25	15	100	100	100	85	100

Some comments concerning the global evaluation: Each of C and AE is not sufficient to alone bring it above 85 or to downgrade it under 85. F is not sufficient to alone bring it above 50 or to downgrade it under 25. APA is not sufficient to bring it above 25 but it can downgrade it to 15. If C and NF have a good evaluation the global evaluation will be good. It is the same if C is replaced by AE and APA.

Discussion. The rules presented in this section include pieces of knowledge familiar to experts in the application area. For example, parameters C and F are used to evaluate the global health of algae, unlike APA and AE which refer to specific pathways metabolism. So, when C and F show no effect or weak effect, the global evaluation is good, while a significant effect on the APA and EA only, is known not to allow degradation of the overall score. Moreover, rules extracted from the obtained Sugeno integrals show stronger effects with rain samples than those obtained after dry weather samples exposure. These results are in perfect agreement with those obtained directly with bioassays.

5   Conclusion

This paper shows the usefulness of qualitative aggregation operations such as Sugeno integrals to extract knowledge from data. The key asset of the approach is the capability of Sugeno integral to lend itself to a complete logical rendering of its informative content, which is typical of qualitative approaches, while a direct handling of the numerical data would make this step more difficult to process. A comparison between the results obtained by this approach and results obtained by standard machine learning methods would be worthwhile in a future work. Of course one objection is that only special kinds of rules can be expressed by Sugeno integral: a single threshold is used in all conditions of each rule [9]. This limited expressive power may be a cause of failure of the approach if no capacity can be identified from the data. Extracting more expressive rules would need qualitative aggregation operations beyond Sugeno integrals.

References

1. Dubois, D., Lang, J., Prade, H.: Possibilistic logic. In: Gabbay, D.M., Hogger, C.J., Robinson, J.A., Nute, D. (eds.) Handbook of Logic in Artificial Intelligence and Logic Programming, pp. 439–513. Oxford University Press, Oxford (1994)

2. Dubois, D., Marichal, J.-L., Prade, H., Roubens, M., Sabbadin, R.: The use of the discrete Sugeno integral in decision making: a survey. Int. J. Uncertainty Fuzziness Knowl. Based Syst. **9**, 539–561 (2001)

3. Dubois, D., Prade, H.: Qualitative possibility functions and integrals. In: Pap, E. (ed.) Handbook of Measure Theory, pp. 1469–1521. Elsevier, Amsterdam (2002)

4. Dubois, D., Prade, H., Rico, A.: Representing qualitative capacities as families of possibility measures. Int. J. Approximate Reasoning **58**, 3–24 (2015)

5. Dubois, D., Prade, H., Rico, A.: The logical encoding of Sugeno integrals. Fuzzy Sets Syst. **241**, 61–75 (2014)

6. Dubois, D., Prade, H., Sabbadin, R.: Decision-theoretic foundations of qualitative possibility theory. Eur. J. Oper. Res. **128**, 459–478 (2001)

7. Ferro, Y.: Evaluation de l'impact de rejets urbains par temps de pluie sur le compartiment algal et mise au point d'outils pour la surveillance des milieux récepteurs. Ph. D. Thesis INSA, Lyon (2013)

8. Grabisch, M., Murofushi, T., Sugeno, M.: Fuzzy Measures and Integrals. Theory and Applications. Physica-Verlag, Heidelberg (2000)

9. Greco, S., Matarazzo, B., Slowinski, R.: Axiomatic characterization of a general utility function and its particular cases in terms of conjoint measurement and rough-set decision rules. Eur. J. Oper. Res. **158**, 271–292 (2004)

10. Marichal, J.-L.: Aggregation Operations for Multicriteria Decision Aid. Ph.D. Thesis, University of Liège, Belgium (1998)

11. Marichal, J.-L.: On Sugeno integrals as an aggregation function. Fuzzy Sets Syst. **114**(3), 347–365 (2000)

12. Prade, H., Rico, A., Serrurier, M.: Elicitation of Sugeno integrals: a version space learning perspective. In: Rauch, J., Raś, Z.W., Berka, P., Elomaa, T. (eds.) ISMIS 2009. LNCS, vol. 5722, pp. 392–401. Springer, Heidelberg (2009)

13. Prade, H., Rico, A., Serrurier, M., Raufaste, E.: Eliciting Sugeno integrals: methodology and a case study. In: Sossai, C., Chemello, G. (eds.) ECSQARU 2009. LNCS, vol. 5590, pp. 712–723. Springer, Heidelberg (2009)

14. Rico, A., Labreuche, C., Grabisch, M., Chateauneuf, A.: Preference modeling on totally ordered sets by the Sugeno integral. Discrete Appl. Math. **147**, 113–124 (2005)

15. Silvert, W.: Ecological impact classification with fuzzy sets. Ecolog. Modell. **96**, 1–10 (1997)

16. Sugeno, M.: Theory of Fuzzy Integrals and its Applications, Ph.D. Thesis, Tokyo Institute of Technology, Tokyo (1974)

17. Sugeno, M.: Fuzzy measures and fuzzy integrals: a survey. In: Gupta, M.M., Saridis, G.N., Gaines, B.R. (eds.) Fuzzy Automata and Decision Processes, pp. 89–102. North-Holland, Amsterdam (1977)

Elicitation of a Utility from Uncertainty Equivalent Without Standard Gambles

Christophe Labreuche[1]([⊠]), Sébastien Destercke[2], and Brice Mayag[3]

[1] Thales Research and Technology, Palaiseau, France
`christophe.labreuche@thalesgroup.com`
[2] Heudiasyc, Université de Technologie de Compiègne, Compiègne, France
`sebastien.destercke@hds.utc.fr`
[3] LAMSADE, University of Paris Dauphine, Paris, France
`brice.mayag@dauphine.fr`

Abstract. In the context of decision under uncertainty, standard gambles are classically used to elicit a utility function on a set X of consequences. The utility of an element x in X is derived from the probability p for which a gamble giving the best outcome in X with probability p and the worst outcome in X otherwise, is indifferent to getting x for sure. In many situations, uncertainty that can be observed on the true value of X concerns only neighbour values. Uncertainty is then represented by a probability distribution whose support is an interval. In this case, standard gambles are unrealistic for the decision maker. We consider uncertainty represented by an equi-probability over an interval of X. This paper addresses the elicitation of a utility function on X by obtaining the certainty equivalent of an equi-probability over an interval of X. We show that not all utility models are suitable to accomplish this task.

1 Introduction

The elicitation of a utility function u over a set X is an important aspect of decision theory. It can be performed in decision under uncertainty by observing the attitude of the decision maker towards risk over gambles defined on X [18]. The most classical way to elicit u is based on standard gambles. A *standard gamble* (or *standard lottery*) denotes a vector $\langle p, x^\top; 1 - p, x^\perp \rangle$ where the best outcome $x^\top$ (resp. the worst outcome $x^\perp$) in X is realized with probability p (resp. $1 - p$). For some $x \in X$, one gets from the decision maker the probability p for which the standard gamble $\langle p, x^\top; 1 - p, x^\perp \rangle$ is indifferent to the sure outcome x. Under the expected utility (EU) model, one obtains $u(x) = p$, after fixing $u(x^\top) = 1$ and $u(x^\perp) = 0$ [18,19]. This elicitation approach has been used for instance to construct the utility of the remaining years to live, for medical decisions. Such a gamble can be a $50 - 50$ gamble resulting in either 20 years of good health or immediate death [20].

The idea of the previous approach is to elicit $u(x)$ by identifying an uncertain situation (a probability distribution over the set X of consequences) that has x as certainty equivalent. The uncertain situation is then a standard gamble based

S. Destercke and T. Denoeux (Eds.): ECSQARU 2015, LNAI 9161, pp. 25–35, 2015.
DOI: 10.1007/978-3-319-20807-7_3

on the extreme consequences $x^\top$ and $x^\perp$. There are many applications where standard gambles do not make sense to the decision maker. Let us consider the following example.

Example 1. In crisis management, if heavy rain is expected, the local authority would like to forecast the peak flood level in a city. Before the flood arises, the decision maker only has an uncertain estimate of the peak flood level X. The problem is then to define a utility function on this variable, to be combined with other criteria to make a decision on the evacuation of a residential area. The flood propagation models typically return an extreme value distribution.

In the previous example, it might not be easy to elicit the utility function on X on the basis of the distribution on the peak flood level provided by the models as it is relatively complex. We note that this distribution has a support which is a closed interval of X. Hence it would not be realistic to use standard gambles, like $\langle p, 15m; 1 - p, 0m \rangle$, as the decision maker will not face such a situation in a real crisis management. We propose in this paper to use uniform distribution law on a close interval like $[10m, 14m]$. The uniform law can be seen as an approximation of the extreme value distribution, which is simple to grasp for a decision maker. We restrict ourselves to uniform probability laws over intervals of X, such as a uniform probability on $[10m, 14m]$ in Example 1.

We are interested in constructing a utility function on X from the certainty equivalent $\hat{x}$ of a uniform probability law on an interval $[a, b]$ of X. Utility functions are parameterized for elicitation purposes. The certainty equivalent $\hat{x}$ can potentially be any element in interval $[a, b]$. Then a family of parameterized utility functions is admissible if, for any $\hat{x} \in [a, b]$, there exists a value of the parameters for which the expected value of the utility function over $[a, b]$ is equal to $\hat{x}$. We show that the most commonly used models do not fulfilled this requirement. We propose some models that satisfy it.

In practice, one cannot expect to identify accurately the certainty equivalent of a probability law over X. Hence we do not obtain a unique utility function but rather a family of compatible utility functions, from which decisions are to be taken. We adopt a cautious approach to recommend decisions [8,16].

Section 2 presents the general elicitation approach. We address in Sect. 3 piecewise affine utility functions, which is a commonly used representation in multi-criteria decision making. We then consider in Sect. 4 an analytical formula, as it is done in decision under uncertainty. Section 5 presents the related works. Finally some conclusions are drawn.

2   General Approach for the Elicitation of a Utility Function

Let X be an interval of $\mathbb{R}$. Without loss of generality, we will consider in the whole paper only strictly increasing utility functions over X. In an elicitation phase, one cannot expect to uniquely identify the utility function. Hence we assume a family U of compatible utility functions, where U is to be determined.

2.1   Decision Model Under Uncertainty

We define a *gamble* on X as a probability density function on X. We wish to represent a preference relation over these gambles, given the set U. Here two gambles describe two different uncertainties on X, and we are interested in the attitude of the decision maker toward such uncertainty. Note that this definition of a gamble is different from that used in subjective probability [6,22], where a gamble is a reward associated to each state of nature.

The basic decision rule in decision under uncertainty is based on expected utility:

$$\mathrm{EU}_u(g) = \int_X u(x)\, p(x)\, dx,$$

where p is the probability density function associated to gamble g. There are many different decision rules to compare gambles when the parameters of the model are imprecise: [21] for imprecise probabilities, [8] for imprecise utilities, and [16] for both imprecise probabilities and utilities. Lower and upper expectations are often used. We use a cautious way to make a decision on the gambles, facing U (imprecise utilities), where the relation holds if the preference is true for **all** utility functions in U:

$$g \succsim_U g' \text{ (resp. } g \succ_U g' \text{ or } g \sim_U g') \quad \Longleftrightarrow \quad \qquad (1)$$
$$\forall u \in U, \ \mathrm{EU}_u(g) \geq \mathrm{EU}_u(g') \text{ (resp. } \mathrm{EU}_u(g) > \mathrm{EU}_u(g') \text{ or } \mathrm{EU}_u(g) = \mathrm{EU}_u(g'))$$

Relation induced by $\succsim_U$ is usually incomplete.

2.2   Elicitation Process

Once the utility is known, the decision model $\succsim_U$ can be applied to probability laws p that are very complex (as for the flood peak level in Example 1). However, during the elicitation process, we restrict ourselves to uniform probability laws over intervals of X in order to reduce the cognitive load. We denote by $\langle 1, [a, b]\rangle$ (with $[a, b] \subseteq X$ and $b > a$) the gamble described by the uniform probability density function p given by $p(x) = \frac{1}{b-a}$ if $x \in [a, b]$ and $p(x) = 0$ else. The sure outcome $x \in X$ is also noted $\langle 1, [x, x]\rangle$. We set $\mathcal{G}_X = \{\langle 1, [a, b]\rangle, \ [a, b] \subseteq X\}$ including both cases. We have $\mathrm{EU}_u(\langle 1, [a, b]\rangle) = \frac{1}{b-a}\int_a^b u(x)\, dx$ if $b > a$, and $\mathrm{EU}_u(\langle 1, [a, b]\rangle) = u(a)$ if $a = b$.

In order to ease the elicitation process, we are interested in families of parameterized utility functions. This is classically done in decision under uncertainty, with for instance family $u_\lambda(x) = x^\lambda$ [13,17]. We denote by γ the vector of parameters, by Γ its range, and by u_γ the associated utility function. Let $\mathcal{U} = \{u_\gamma, \gamma \in \Gamma\}$. The set of admissible utility functions corresponds to a subset Γ_A of Γ, where $U = \{u_\gamma, \gamma \in \Gamma_A\}$.

Generalizing the elicitation process based on standard gambles, Γ_A may be derived by asking to the decision maker the certainty equivalent $\hat{x}$ of a gamble $\langle 1, [a, b]\rangle$, given interval $[a, b]$. The *certainty equivalent* of gamble $\langle 1, [a, b]\rangle$ is an element $\widehat{x} \in [a, b]$ such that $\langle 1, [a, b] \rangle$ is indifferent to $\langle 1, [\widehat{x}, \widehat{x}] \rangle$. Then Γ_A is the set of values γ satisfying relation $\frac{1}{b-a} \int_a^b u_\gamma(x) \, dx = u_\gamma(\widehat{x})$.

In practice, a decision maker is not expected to provide a value $\widehat{x}$ that is close to the extreme values a and b. Hence one might often have

$$\langle 1, [a + \varepsilon, a + \varepsilon] \rangle \prec_U \langle 1, [a, b] \rangle \prec_U \langle 1, [b - \varepsilon, b - \varepsilon] \rangle \tag{2}$$

for some $\varepsilon > 0$ which depends on the attitude of the decision maker. Note that ε can be very small if the decision maker is extremely risk averse or risk seeking. We will show in Sect. 3.1, that a classical family of utility functions satisfies (2) with $\varepsilon = \frac{b-a}{4}$. This value is relatively large (only half of interval $[a, b]$ is reachable), and we guess that this family is not versatile enough.

As it is not easy to set some value for ε and we do not want to rule out some extreme attitudes of decision makers, we would ideally like to represent the case where the certainty equivalent of gamble $\langle 1, [a, b] \rangle$ can be any element in the open interval (a, b).

Condition Comp(a, b) – Completeness (with $b > a$): For every $\overline{x} \in (a, b)$,

$$\exists \gamma \in \Gamma \qquad \frac{1}{b-a} \int_a^b u_\gamma(x) \, dx = u_\gamma(\overline{x}). \tag{3}$$

Conversely, from the intermediate value theorem, we know that if function u_γ is continuous, then for every $\gamma \in \Gamma$, there exists a point $\overline{x} \in [a, b]$ such that (3) holds.

One can readily see that if function u_γ is constant, then condition **Comp**(a, b) is trivially satisfied for every interval $[a, b]$. Hence we consider only strictly increasing utility functions.

In practice, it is unrealistic to ask directly to the decision maker to provide the value of the certainty equivalent of a gamble. The certainty equivalent $\widehat{x}$ can be approximated, by asking questions of the following form (with $\langle 1, [a, b] \rangle \in \mathcal{G}_X$ and $\overline{x} \in (a, b)$)

"Is$\langle 1, [a, b] \rangle$ less preferred / preferred / indifferent / incomparable to $\langle 1, [\overline{x}, \overline{x}] \rangle$?" (4)

for different values of $\overline{x}$, proceeding by dichotomy on $\overline{x}$. The so-obtained dichotomy process for approximating $\widehat{x}$ given gamble $\langle 1, [a, b] \rangle$ is called **Certainty Equivalent Estimate (CEE)**. If the answer is *"less preferred"* (resp. *"preferred"* or *"indifferent"*), then for all $\gamma \in \Gamma_A$, $\mathrm{EU}_{u_\gamma}(\langle 1, [a, b] \rangle) - u_\gamma(\overline{x}) < 0$ (resp. > 0 or $= 0$). At the end, Γ_A is the set of all values γ satisfying these constraints. *"Incomparability"* answers are not explicitly represented as constraints.

The remaining of this paper is devoted to finding models of utility that fulfil **Comp**. We will see that condition **Comp** is not fulfilled with the most commonly used classes of utility functions. This condition will be used to select suitable families $\mathcal{U}$.

3   Case of Piecewise Affine Utility Functions

Piecewise affine utility functions are classically used in multi-criteria decision making [1]. The decision maker provides a finite set of elements in X: $x_1 < x_2 < \cdots < x_m$. We set

$$u_\gamma(x_1) = 0 \quad \text{and} \quad u_\gamma(x_m) = 1. \tag{5}$$

The unknowns are the utility at the points $x_2, \ldots, x_{m-1}$: $\gamma = (u_2, \ldots, u_{m-1})$, where $u_k = u_\gamma(x_k)$, $u_1 = 0$ and $u_m = 1$. As u_γ is strictly increasing, we assume that $u_1 < u_2 < \cdots < u_{m-1} < u_m$. The utility function which interpolates between the points $(x_1, u_1), \ldots, (x_m, u_m)$, is denoted u_γ^{PA} (where PA stands for *Piecewise Affine*):

$$u_\gamma^{\mathrm{PA}}(x) = \begin{cases} 0 & \text{if } x \leq x_1 \\ u_k + \dfrac{x - x_k}{x_{k+1} - x_k}\left(u_{k+1} - u_k\right) & \text{if } x \in [x_k, x_{k+1}] \\ 1 & \text{if } x \geq x_m \end{cases} \tag{6}$$

We first show that form (6) does not fulfill condition **Comp**. Then we propose another form of piecewise affine utility function.

3.1   Verification of Condition Comp with u_γ^{PA}

As the elements $x_1, \ldots, x_m$ have a special meaning to the decision maker, we can ask questions of the form (4) with the value of a and b being elements in $x_1, \ldots, x_m$.

Lemma 1. *Condition* **Comp** *is not fulfilled with* u_γ^{PA}. *More precisely, for every* $p, q \in \{1, \ldots, m\}$ *with* $q > p$, *there exists* γ *such that* (3) *holds with* $a = x_p$ *and* $b = x_q$ *iff*

$$\overline{x} \in \left[x_p + (x_{p+1} - x_p)\, \frac{x_q - \frac{1}{2}x_{p+1} - \frac{1}{2}x_p}{x_q - x_p}, x_{q-1} + (x_q - x_{q-1})\, \frac{x_q - x_{q-1}}{2(x_q - x_p)} \right] \tag{7}$$

Proofs are omitted due to space limitation. The idea is that, in order to allow having $\overline{x}$ close to the lower bound $a = x_p$ (resp. upper bound $b = x_q$), the utility function should be close to the Heaviside function at x_p (resp. x_q) – see function u^1 (resp. u^2) in the right part of Fig. 1. Lemma 1 shows that this is not the case with u_γ^{PA}. Interval in (7) is strictly included in $[x_p, x_q]$. For instance for $X = [0, 1]$, $p = 1$, $q = m = 3$ and $x_1 = 0$, $x_2 = \frac{1}{2}$, $x_3 = 1$, interval in (7) is $[\frac{1}{4}, \frac{3}{4}]$, to be compared with interval $[0, 1]$. It follows that the expected utility $\mathrm{EU}_{u_\gamma^{\mathrm{PA}}}(\langle 1, [x_p, x_q] \rangle)$ cannot take any value in $[x_p, x_q]$. This comes from the fact that the points $x_1, \ldots, x_m$ are fixed. Hence we need to find another representation.

3.2   Piecewise Affine Function Around a Diagonal

Instead of fixing the value of x and letting the associated utility be a variable, the idea is to allow both the value of x and its utility to be variable (but not independently).

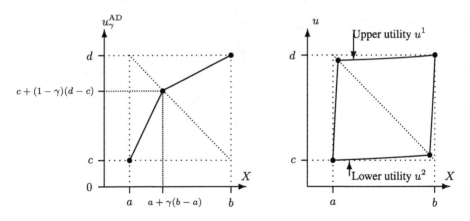

Fig. 1. Piecewise affine utility function around the diagonal $(a, d) - (b, c)$.

We start by defining a utility function, depending on only one parameter γ, in an interval $[a, b]$ and with fixed values of the utility at the boundary: $u_\gamma(a) = c$ and $u_\gamma(b) = d$. The values of $a, b \in X$ and $c, d \in \mathbb{R}$ are fixed. We consider a piecewise affine function with an intermediate point in the diagonal line between (a, d) and (b, c) (see the left part of Fig. 1). Let $\gamma \in [0, 1]$; the intermediate point has coordinates $(a + \gamma(b - a), c + (1 - \gamma)(d - c))$. On the whole, u_γ performs an affine interpolation between the points (a, c), $(a + \gamma(b - a), c + (1 - \gamma)(d - c))$ and (b, d). We denote this utility function u_γ^{AD} (where AD stands for *Affine around a Diagonal*).

In order to elicit γ, we use the Dichotomy method **CEE** based on Question (4) with interval $[a, b]$. The next result shows that it completely makes sense.

Lemma 2. *Condition* **Comp**(a, b) *is fulfilled with* u_γ^{AD}. *Moreover, if* $\langle 1, [a, b] \rangle$ *is less preferred (resp. preferred or indifferent) to* $\overline{x} \in (a, b)$, *then* $\gamma < \frac{\overline{x} - a}{b - a}$ *(resp.* $\gamma > \frac{\overline{x} - a}{b - a}$ *or* $\gamma = \frac{\overline{x} - a}{b - a}$ *).*

The main advantage of this approach is that whatever the answer $\overline{x}$ of the decision maker in the interval $[a, b]$, one can find the value of parameter $\gamma \in [0, 1]$. Moreover the correspondence between $\overline{x}$ and γ is very simple, as the mean value of u_γ^{AD} is attained precisely at the breaking point $(a + \gamma(b - a), c + (1 - \gamma)(d - c))$ on the diagonal. In particular, the value of γ is independent of the values of c and d. We will use this property in the next section, where c and d may be unknown.

The previous pattern can be applied only once to $a = x_1$, $b = x_2$, $c = 0$ and $d = 1$.

3.3   Proposal with More Parameters

If we want more intermediate points, we can apply the previous patterns several times. In Fig. 2, we apply the pattern two times, where the three values x_1, x_2, x_3 are fixed. More precisely, we use the pattern a first time on the input interval

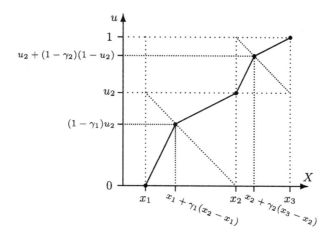

Fig. 2. Parametric piecewise affine utility function using two patterns.

$[x_1, x_2]$ and output interval $[0, u_2]$, and a second time on the input interval $[x_2, x_3]$ and output interval $[u_2, 1]$.

We have three unknowns: $\gamma = (\gamma_1, \gamma_2, u_2)$. We use three times the process Dichotomy method **CEE**.

The first use of Dichotomy method **CEE** is on interval $[x_1, x_2]$. If $\langle 1, [x_1, x_2] \rangle$ is less preferred (resp. preferred or indifferent) to $\overline{x}_{1,2} \in [x_1, x_2]$, then, by Lemma 2

$$\gamma_1 < \frac{\overline{x}_{1,2} - x_1}{x_2 - x_1} \left(\text{resp. } \gamma_1 > \frac{\overline{x}_{1,2} - x_1}{x_2 - x_1} \text{ or } \gamma_1 = \frac{\overline{x}_{1,2} - x_1}{x_2 - x_1} \right). \tag{8}$$

The identification of γ_1 is independent of unknown u_2.

The second use of Dichotomy method **CEE** is on interval $[x_2, x_3]$. If $\langle 1, [x_2, x_3] \rangle$ is less preferred (resp. preferred or indifferent) to $\overline{x}_{2,3} \in [x_2, x_3]$, then

$$\gamma_2 < \frac{\overline{x}_{2,3} - x_2}{x_3 - x_2} \left(\text{resp. } \gamma_2 > \frac{\overline{x}_{2,3} - x_2}{x_3 - x_2} \text{ or } \gamma_2 = \frac{\overline{x}_{2,3} - x_2}{x_3 - x_2} \right). \tag{9}$$

The identification of γ_2 is independent of unknown u_2.

Finally, the last use of Dichotomy method **CEE** is on the interval $[x_1, x_3]$. The decision maker is asked to compare $\langle 1, [x_1, x_3] \rangle$ with the sure outcome $\overline{x}_{1,3} \in [x_1, x_3]$. As

$$\text{EU}_{u_\gamma}(\langle 1, [x_1, x_3] \rangle) = \frac{x_2 - x_1}{x_3 - x_1}(1 - \gamma_1)u_2 + \frac{x_3 - x_2}{x_3 - x_1}(u_2 + (1 - \gamma_2)(1 - u_2)), \tag{10}$$

One can derive from (10) constraints on u_2, given the answer of the comparison of $\langle 1, [x_1, x_3] \rangle$ with the sure outcome $\overline{x}_{1,3}$, and upper and lower bounds on γ_1 and γ_2.

4 Parametric Utility Functions

We consider in this section parametric utility functions. We restrict ourselves to $X = [0, 1]$. We start with family $u_\gamma^{\mathrm{pow}}(x) = x^\gamma$, with $\gamma > 0$, already mentioned previously [13,17] (see also [7] for a quadratic model). Another family will then be considered.

4.1 Power Function

Lemma 3. *Condition* **Comp**$(0, 1)$ *is not fulfilled with* u_γ^{pow}. *More precisely, there exists γ such that (3) holds with $a = 0$ and $b = 1$ iff $\overline{x} \in \left(\frac{1}{e}, 1\right)$.*

With model u_γ^{pow}, the decision maker is not allowed to provide a value of $\overline{x}$ outside interval $\left(\frac{1}{e}, 1\right)$. Utility function u_γ^{pow} tends to the Heaviside function at 0 when γ tends to 0. However it does not imply that condition **Comp**$(0, 1)$ is not necessarily satisfied with $\overline{x}$ arbitrarily close to 0. The shape of u_γ^{pow} is such that its mean value v_γ tends to 1 when $\gamma \to 1$, but $(u_\gamma^{\mathrm{pow}})^{-1}(v_\gamma)$ does not tend to 0.

4.2 MinMaxVar Parametric Function

As Lemma 3 shows that the power utility function u_γ^{pow} is not suitable, we consider another parametric function called *MinMaxVar* [5] taking the following expression:

$$u_\gamma^{\mathrm{MMV}}(x) = 1 - \left(1 - x^{\frac{1}{\gamma}}\right)^\gamma \tag{11}$$

where $u_\gamma^{\mathrm{MMV}}(0) = 0$ and $u_\gamma^{\mathrm{MMV}}(1) = 1$ (see conditions (5)). Parameter γ belongs to $\Gamma = (0, \infty)$, where function u_γ^{MMV} is convex for $\gamma < 1$ and is concave for $\gamma > 1$.

Function u_γ^{MMV} has an useful symmetry property. Indeed one can readily check that

$$y = u_\gamma^{\mathrm{MMV}}(x) \qquad \Longleftrightarrow \qquad 1 - x = u_\gamma^{\mathrm{MMV}}(1 - y). \tag{12}$$

Hence points (x, y) and $(1-y, 1-x)$ are symmetric w.r.t. the diagonal connecting points $(1, 0)$ and $(0, 1)$ (see Fig. 3). As a result, curve u_γ^{MMV} is symmetric w.r.t. this diagonal. Note that u_γ^{AD} (Sect. 3.2) satisfies a similar property as it is also symmetric w.r.t. diagonal $(a, d) - (b, c)$.

Moreover, curve u_γ^{MMV} intersects the diagonal $(1, 0) - (0, 1)$ at a point with coordinates $(\beta, 1 - \beta)$, with $1 - \beta = u_\gamma^{\mathrm{MMV}}(\beta)$. Hence $\left(1 - \beta^{\frac{1}{\gamma}}\right)^\gamma = \beta$, i.e. $\beta = \left(\frac{1}{2}\right)^\gamma$.

The next result shows that Dichotomy method **CEE** can be used on interval $[0, 1]$.

Lemma 4. *Condition* **Comp**$(0, 1)$ *is fulfilled with* u_γ^{MMV}.

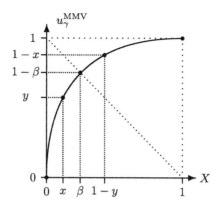

Fig. 3. Parametric function u_γ^{MMV}.

Given any $\overline{x} \in (0,1)$, one can easily find by dichotomy or a Gradient method the value $\overline{\gamma}$ such that $\int_0^1 u_{\overline{\gamma}}^{\mathrm{MMV}}(x)\, dx = u_{\overline{\gamma}}^{\mathrm{MMV}}(\overline{x})$. Moreover, the next lemma provides bounds on γ given the comparison of the decision maker.

Lemma 5. *For any $\overline{x} \in (0,1)$, there exists a unique $\overline{\gamma} > 0$ such that $\int_0^1 u_{\overline{\gamma}}^{\mathrm{MMV}}(x)\, dx = u_{\overline{\gamma}}^{\mathrm{MMV}}(\overline{x})$. Moreover, $\langle 1, [0,1] \rangle$ is less preferred (resp. preferred or indifferent) to $\overline{x} \in [0,1]$, iff $\gamma > \overline{\gamma}$ (resp. $\gamma < \overline{\gamma}$ or $\gamma = \overline{\gamma}$).*

5   Related Works

The elicitation process based on standard gambles has been enriched in different ways. It has been used in AI as a baseline technique to elicit elaborate models such as the Generalized Additive Independence (GAI) model [3,9]. If the set of possible utilities is U, the decision rule can be the *expected* expected utility where the expectation is taken over the set of outcomes but also over the space U of possible utility functions [2]. The probability over utilities is updated during elicitation using Bayes' rule in [4]. Standard gambles are used to elicit an imprecise utility in the framework of multi-attribute utility theory in [7].

   It has been noticed in the litterature that the elicitation of the utility using standard gambles may result in wrong assessments of u or in inconsistencies. Experiments indeed indicate that human beings as subject to a number of biases that distort their judgment about the perception of uncertainty. A canonical list of biases can be found in [12]. For further references, see also [11,14]. The most commonly encountered biases are: (1) probability weighting (individuals do not treat probabilities linearly, and tend to overestimate small objective probabilities, and under-estimate large ones [20]); (2) loss aversion (individuals are more sensible to losses than to gains) [13,17].

   Under the Expected Utility model, risk averse individuals (they prefer for instance a sure outcome x to the gamble $\langle \frac{1}{2}, 0; \frac{1}{2}, 2x \rangle$) are represented by concave utility functions. However, it has been noticed that the standard gamble method tends to exaggerate the concavity of the utility function to capture risk aversion [10]. Rank dependent expected utility treats the probability weighting bias by transforming the probability with a distortion function [15]. This model is generalized in the prospect theory, where gains and losses (demarcating a neutral level) are handled differently [13,17]. Prospect theory models the two biases.

6 Conclusion

We have proposed in this paper the elicitation of a utility function over a set X by comparing a gamble proposing x in an interval $[a, b] \subseteq X$ with equiprobability, to a sure outcome $\overline{x} \in X$. This is a generalization of the elicitation process based on standard gambles. A consistency condition called *Comp* has been defined: it tells that for any $\overline{x} \in [a, b]$, there shall exist a value γ of the parameters such that $\langle 1, [a, b] \rangle$ is indifferent to sure outcome $\overline{x}$. The piecewise affine model u_γ^{PA} and power model u_λ^{pow} do not fulfill this condition. We propose the use of two models that fulfill this condition. The first one u_γ^{AD} is piecewise affine with an intermediate point where both the abscissa and ordinate numbers varies at the same time on a diagonal. This pattern can be repeated several times in adjacent intervals (for instance, in $[x_1, x_2]$, $[x_2, x_3]$, etc.). The second one is the MinMaxVar function u_γ^{MMV}, which shares a symmetry property with u_γ^{AD}. In both cases, we can derive constraints on the parameters of the utility model from any comparison of gamble $\langle 1, [a, b] \rangle$ to the sure outcome $\overline{x}$. Risk aversion occurs when $\langle 1, [a, b] \rangle$ is strictly less preferred to sure outcome $\frac{a+b}{2}$. Under our models, this implies concavity of utility functions. Similar results are obtained with standard gambles.

We can extend this work in several directions. We can extend the expected utility model that we used to represent some cognitive bias. One can think of rank dependent expected utility which is based on the Choquet integral. One can also think of other types of uncertainties, such as the reliability of sources. One would then compare making a decision from a source with low reliability providing a value $x \in X$ to another source with high reliability providing another value $x' \in X$. We can also think of other models for information $[a, b]$, such as the set of probabilities having this support.

Acknowledgments. This work has been partly supported by the European project FP7-SEC-2013-607697, PREDICT "PREparing the Domino effect In crisis siTuations". The authors would like to thank an anonymous review for helpful comments.

References

1. Bana e Costa, C.A., De Corte, J., Vansnick, J.-C.: MACBETH. Int. J. Inform. Techno. Decis. Making **11**, 359–387 (2012)
2. Boutilier, C.: On the foundations of expected expected utility. In: Proceedings of the Eighteenth International Joint Conference on Artificial Intelligence (IJCAI-03), pp. 285–290, Acapulco (2003)

3. Braziunas, D., Boutilier, C.: Minimax regret based elicitation of generalized additive utilities. In: Proceedings of the Twenty-third Conference on Uncertainty in Artificial Intelligence (UAI-07), pp. 25–32, Vancouver (2007)
4. Chajewska, U., Koller, D., Parr, R.: Making rational decisions using adaptive utility elicitation. In: Proceedings of the Seventeenth National Conference on Artificial Intelligence (AAAI-00), pp. 363–369, Austin (2000)
5. Cherny, A., Madan, D.: New measures for performance evaluation. Rev. Financ. Stud. **22**, 2571–2606 (2009)
6. de Finetti, B.: Theory of Probability: A Critical Introductory Treatment. Wiley, Chichester (1974)
7. Farrow, M.: Sample size determination with imprecise risk aversion. In: 8th International Symposium on Imprecise Probability: Theories and Applications (ISIPTA'2013), Compiègne, July 2013
8. Farrow, M., Goldstein, M.: Almost-pareto decision sets in imprecise utility hierarchies. J. Stat. Theory Pract. **3**, 137–155 (2009)
9. Gonzales, C., Perny, P.: GAI networks for utility elicitation. In: Proceedings of the 9th International Conference on the Principles of Knowledge Representation and Reasoning (KR), pp. 224–234, (2004)
10. Hershey, J.C., Schoemake, P.J.H.: Probability versus certainty equivalence methods in utility measurement: Are they equivalent? Manage. Sci. **31**, 1213–1231 (1985)
11. Hogarth, R.: Cognitive processes and the assessment of subjective probability distributions. J. Am. Stat. Assoc. **70**, 271–294 (1989)
12. Kahneman, D., Slovic, P., Tversky, A.: Judgment Under Uncertainty: Heuristics and Biases. Cambridge University Press, Cambridge (2001)
13. Kahneman, D., Tversky, A.: Prospect theory: an analysis of decision under risk. Econometrica **47**, 263–291 (1979)
14. Morgan, M., Henrion, M.: Uncertainty: A Guide to Dealing with Uncertainty in Quantitative Risk and Policy Analysis. Cambridge University Press, New York (1990)
15. Quiggin, J.: Generalized Expected Utility Theory: The Rank-Dependent Model. Kluwer Academic, Boston (1993)
16. Seidenfeld, T., Schervish, M., Kadane, J.: A representation of partially ordered preferences. Ann. Stat. **23**, 2168–2174 (1995)
17. Tversky, A., Kahneman, D.: Advances in prospect theory: cumulative representation of uncertainty. J. Risk Uncertainty **5**, 297–323 (1992)
18. von Neumann, J., Morgenstern, O.: Game Theory and Economic Behavior. Princeton University Press, Princeton (1953)
19. von Winterfeldt, D., Edwards, W.: Decison Analysis and Behavioral Research. Cambridge University Press, Cambridge (1986)
20. Wakker, P., Stiggelbout, A.: Explaining distortions in utility elicitation through the rank-dependent model for risky choices. Med. Decis. Making **15**(2), 180–186 (1995)
21. Walley, P.: Statistical Reasoning with Imprecise Probabilities. Chapman and Hall, London (1991)
22. Walley, P.: Towards a unified theory of imprecise probability. Int. J. Approximate Reasoning **24**, 125–148 (2000)

Possibilistic Conditional Preference Networks

Nahla Ben Amor[1], Didier Dubois[2], Héla Gouider[1]([✉]), and Henri Prade[2]

[1] LARODEC, Institut Supérieur de Gestion Tunis, 2000 Le Bardo, Tunisie
`nahla.benamor@gmx.fr, gouider.hela@gmail.com`
[2] IRIT – CNRS, 118, Route de Narbonne, Toulouse, France
{`dubois,prade`}`@irit.fr`

Abstract. The paper discusses the use of product-based possibilistic networks for representing conditional preference statements on discrete variables. The approach uses non-instantiated possibility weights to define conditional preference tables. Moreover, additional information about the relative strengths of symbolic weights can be taken into account. It yields a partial preference order among possible choices corresponding to a symmetric form of Pareto ordering. In the case of Boolean variables, this partial ordering coincides with the inclusion between the sets of preference statements that are violated. Furthermore, this graphical model has two logical counterparts in terms of possibilistic logic and penalty logic. The flexibility and the representational power of the approach are stressed. Besides, algorithms for handling optimization and dominance queries are provided.

1 Introduction

Since the direct assessment of a preference relation between elements of Cartesian products is usually not feasible, current work in preference modeling aims at proposing compact preference models achieving a good compromise between elicitation easiness and computational efficiency. Conditional preference networks (CP-nets) [4] are a popular example of such setting. However, in spite of their appealing graphical nature, CP-nets may induce debatable priorities between decision variables and lack a logical counterpart. Symbolic possibilistic logic bases stand as another approach to represent preferences [9]. This setting overcomes the above mentioned CP-nets limitations. Moreover, it leaves complete freedom for stating relative priorities between variables. But, it is not a graphical model.

This paper explores the representation of preferences by possibilistic networks, outlined in [1] and establishes formal results about them. This approach preserves a possibilistic logic representation, while offering a graphical compact format convenient for elicitation.

The paper is organized as follows. Section 2 provides a formal definition of product-based possibilistic network with symbolic weights, and shows the nature of its preference ordering. Section 3 deals with the case of Boolean decision variables and provides two logical counterparts of this model, in possibilistic logic and in penalty logic. Section 4 discusses optimization and dominance queries.

© Springer International Publishing Switzerland 2015
S. Destercke and T. Denoeux (Eds.): ECSQARU 2015, LNAI 9161, pp. 36–46, 2015.
DOI: 10.1007/978-3-319-20807-7_4

2   Possibilistic Preference Networks

This section provides a short refresher on possibilistic networks, and then describes how conditional preferences can be encoded by a possibilistic network. Moreover, we show that the use of product-based conditioning leads us to define a preference ordering that amounts to compare vectors by a symmetric extension of the Pareto ordering.

2.1   Background on Possibilistic Networks

Possibility theory can be used for representing preferences. It relies on the idea of a possibility distribution π, which is a mapping from a universe of discourse Ω to the unit interval $[0, 1]$. Possibility degrees $\pi(\omega)$ estimate how satisfactory the solutions ω is. Since alternative choices are usually described by means of several decision variables, we need to manipulate possibility distributions on a Cartesian product $\Omega = D_{A_1} \times \cdots \times D_{A_N}$. Namely, each composite decision $\omega = (a_1, \ldots, a_N)$ (denoted for short by $a_1 \ldots a_N$), corresponds to an instantiation of the N variables $V = \{A_1, \ldots, A_N\}$, where A_i ranges on domain $D_{A_i} = \{a_{i1}, \ldots, a_{in}\}$. If $U \subseteq V$, then $\omega[U]$ denotes the restriction of solution ω to variables in U. Conditioning is defined from the Bayesian-like equation $\pi(A_i, A_j) = \pi(A_i|A_j) \otimes \pi(A_j)$ [3], where $\otimes$ stands for the product in a quantitative (numerical) setting or for min in a qualitative (ordinal) setting. Thus, the joint possibility distribution on Ω can be decomposed using conditional possibility distributions by means of the *chain rule* $\pi(A_1, \ldots, A_N) = \bigotimes_{i=1..N} \pi(A_i \mid Pa(A_i))$ where the set $Pa(A_i) \subseteq \{A_{i+1}, \ldots, A_N\}$ forms the parents of A_i. A_i is conditionally dependent on its parent variables only. This decomposition has a graphical counterpart, called possibilistic network, where each node encodes a variable related to each its parents by a directed arc. In the following, we use possibilistic networks for representing preferences (rather than uncertainty as it has been the case until now).

2.2   Preference Specification

The user is supposed to express his preferences under the form of comparison statements between variable instantiations, conditional on some other instantiated variables. Therefore, in the particular case of Boolean variables, we deal with preferences of the form: "I prefer a to $\neg a$" if the preference is not conditioned, and of the form "in the context where c is true, I prefer a to $\neg a$" if conditioned. More formally,

Definition 1. *A preference statement s is a preference relation between values $a_{ik} \in D_{A_i}$ of a variable A_i, in the form of a complete preorder, i.e., we have only 2 different cases:*

(i) $u_i: a_{ik} \succ a_{im}$: in the context u_i, a_{ik} is preferred to a_{im};
(ii) $u_i : a_{ik} \sim a_{im}$: in the context u_i, the user is indifferent between a_{im} and a_{ik}, where u_i is an instantiation of all variables that affect the user preferences concerning the values of A_i. If $u_i = \emptyset$, then A_i is an independent variable.

Table 1. Conditional preference specification

$(s_1)\ j_b \succ j_r$
$(s_2)\ p_b \succ p_w$
$(s_3)\ j_b p_b:\ s_b \succ s_r \succ s_w$
$(s_4)\ j_b p_w:\ s_w \succ s_b \succ s_r$
$(s_5)\ j_r p_b:\ s_r \succ s_b \succ s_w$
$(s_6)\ j_r p_w:\ s_b \sim s_r \sim s_w$

$\pi(j_b)$	$\pi(j_r)$
1	α

$\pi(p_b)$	$\pi(p_w)$
1	β

$\pi(.|.)$	$j_b p_b$	$j_b p_w$	$j_r p_b$	$j_r p_w$
s_b	1	δ_3	δ_5	1
s_r	δ_1	δ_4	1	1
s_w	δ_2	1	δ_6	1

Fig. 1. A possibilistic preference network

The running Example 1, inspired from [4], illustrates such preference statements.

Example 1. *Consider a preference specification about an evening dress over 3 decision variables $V = \{J, P, S\}$ standing for jacket, pants and shirt respectively, with values in $D_J = \{Red\ (j_r),\ Black\ (j_b)\}$, $D_P = \{White\ (p_w),\ Black\ (p_b)\}$ and $D_S = \{Black\ (s_b),\ Red\ (s_r),\ White\ (s_w)\}$. The conditional preferences are given in Table 1. Preference statements (s_1) and (s_1) are unconditioned. Note that the user is indifferent between the values of variable S in context $u_j = j_b p_w$.*

2.3 Graphical Possibilistic Encoding of Preferences

As already said, conditional preference statements can be associated to a graphical structure. In this paper, this graphical structure is understood as a possibilistic network where each node is associated with a conditional possibility table used for representing the preferences. For each particular instantiation u_i of $Pa(A_i)$, the preference order between the values of A_i stated by the user will be encoded by a local conditional possibility distribution. So, each node A_i is associated with a conditional preference table. We call this model possibilistic conditional preference network (π-*Pref net* for short).

Definition 2. *A possibilistic preference network (π-Pref net) ΠG over a set $V = \{A_1, \ldots, A_N\}$ of variables is a preference network where we associate to each node $A_i \in V$ a possibilistic preference table (π_i-table for short), such that to each instantiation u_i of $Pa(A_i)$ is associated a symbolic conditional possibility distribution defining an ordering between the values of A_i:*

- *If $a_{ik} \prec a_{im}$ then $\pi(a_{ik}|u_i) = \alpha, \pi(a_{im}|u_i) = \beta$ where α and β are non-instantiated variables on (0, 1] we call symbolic weights, and $\alpha < \beta \leq 1$;*
- *If $a_{ik} \sim a_{im}$ then $\pi(a_{ik}|u_i) = \pi(a_{im}|u_i) = \alpha$ where α is a symbolic weight such that $\alpha \leq 1$;*
- *For each instantiation u_i of $Pa(A_i)$, $\exists\ a_i \in D_{A_i}$ such that $\pi(a_i|u_i) = 1$.*

Let $\mathcal{C}$ be the set storing the constraints existing between the symbolic weights introduced as above. This set can be completed by additional constraints, directly provided by the user.

By a symbolic weight, we mean a symbol representing a real number whose value is unspecified. However, inequalities or equalities between such unspecified values may be enforced, as in Definition 2, between conditional possibilities, or independently stated in $\mathcal{C}$. Since the symbolic weights stand for real numbers, relations $\leq$ and $<$ are transitive.

As usual in possibilistic networks, the normalization condition (expressed by the third item in Definition 2) is crucial for conditional possibility distributions. For example, consider a variable A such that $D_A = \{a_1, a_2, a_3\}$ and its context instantiation u, and assume that the user is indifferent between the values of A in that context. Then, $\pi(a_1|u) = \pi(a_2|u) = \pi(a_3|u) = \alpha$. Then, in order to satisfy normalization, α should be equal to 1 (see Example 1). In addition to the preferences encoded by a π-Pref net, additional constraints in $\mathcal{C}$ can be taken into account. Such constraints may, in particular, reflect the relative importance of variables by making all preferences associated to a variable more imperative than the ones associated to another variable, or express the relative importance of preferences associated to different instantiations of parent variables of the same variable. In the case one can not infer any relation between two weights by transitivity (distinct from 1), we consider them as incomparable.

Example 2. *Given the preference statements of Example 1, we can associate the possibilistic preference network ΠG in Fig. 1 encoding the user preference over V. The preference statements corresponds to the set of constraints $\mathcal{C} = \{\delta_2 < \delta_1,\ \delta_4 < \delta_3,\ \delta_6 < \delta_5\}$. Consider, for instance, the preference statement s_6. Due to the normalization condition, $\pi(s_b|j_r p_w) = \pi(s_r|j_r p_w) = \pi(s_w|j_r p_w) = 1$.*

In this work, we explore the properties of possibilistic networks where conditioning is based on product. It has sometimes a greater discriminating power than the minimum operator, in the sense that $\alpha \cdot \beta < \alpha$, while we only have $\min(\alpha, \beta) \leq \alpha$. For instance, if $\alpha = \gamma < \delta < \beta$ then min considers (α, β) and (γ, δ) as equal, while we have $(\alpha, \beta) > (\gamma, \delta)$ with the product. However, if $\alpha < \gamma < \delta < \beta$ then $(\alpha, \beta) < (\gamma, \delta)$ with the min while the product operator fails to order them.

Example 3. *Let us consider the possibilistic preference network of Example 2. Using the chain rule, we obtain the following symbolic joint possibility distribution: $\pi(j_b p_b s_b) = 1$, $\pi(j_b p_b s_r) = \delta_1$, $\pi(j_b p_b s_w) = \delta_2$, $\pi(j_b p_w s_b) = \beta \cdot \delta_3$, $\pi(j_b p_w s_r) = \beta \cdot \delta_4$, $\pi(j_b p_w s_w) = \beta$, $\pi(j_r p_b s_b) = \alpha \cdot \delta_5$, $\pi(j_r p_b s_r) = \alpha$, $\pi(j_r p_b s_w) = \alpha \cdot \delta_6$, $\pi(j_r p_w s_b) = \pi(j_r p_w s_r) = \pi(j_r p_w s_w) = \alpha \cdot \beta$.*
Indeed, for instance, $\pi(j_r p_b s_b) = \pi(j_r) \cdot \pi(p_b) \cdot \pi(s_b|j_r p_b) = \alpha \cdot \delta_5$. Now, assume that the user considers the choice of the color of his pants as more important than the color of his shirt, then $\mathcal{C}$ is augmented with the additional constraint $\beta < \{\delta_1, \delta_2, \delta_3, \delta_4, \delta_5, \delta_6\}$. In this case, we can compare for instance $j_r p_b s_b \succ j_r p_w s_b$.

The preference specification is partial when the preference statements do not cover all the domains values of all the parent instantiations. A default principle, in case of missing information, may be to assume indifference, which amounts to assigning equal possibility degree to all corresponding options. From now on, we assume the complete specification of conditional preferences, i.e., in each possible context, the user provides a complete preordering of the values of the considered variable in terms of strict preference or indifference. As can be seen in the running example, our representation setting shares the same graphical structure as CP-nets [4]. But we are not adopting the worsening flips semantics of the latter, rather we use the chain rule and compare products of symbolic weights attached to solutions for defining the partial order between them.

2.4   Partial Ordering Induced by π-Pref Nets

The purpose of preference modeling is to compare all possible solutions in Ω. Each possibility degree of a solution, computed from the product-based chain rule, expresses the satisfaction level of the solution. This leads to the following definition of the induced ordering.

Definition 3. *Preference ordering: Given a set of solutions Ω, a joint possibility distribution $\pi_{\Pi G}$ computed from a possibilistic preference network ΠG and a set C of constraints between the symbolic weights. Let ω_i and ω_j be two solutions of Ω. We have: (i) $\omega_i \succ \omega_j$ iff $\pi_{\Pi G}(\omega_i) > \pi_{\Pi G}(\omega_j)$; (ii) $\omega_i \sim \omega_j$ iff $\pi_{\Pi G}(\omega_i) = \pi_{\Pi G}(\omega_j)$; (iii) $\omega_i \pm \omega_j$ iff $\pi_{\Pi G}(\omega_i) \pm \pi_{\Pi G}(\omega_j)$, ($\pm$ denotes non comparability).*

Each solution $\omega = a_1 \ldots a_N$ is associated with a vector $\vec{\omega} = (\alpha_1, \ldots, \alpha_N)$, where $\alpha_i = \pi(a_i|u_i)$ and $u_i = \omega[Pa(A_i)]$. A natural ordering of such vectors is the Symmetric Pareto ordering $\succ_{SP}$, such that $\vec{\omega} \succ_{SP} \vec{\omega}'$ iff there exists a permutation σ of the components of $\vec{\omega}' = (\beta_1, \ldots, \beta_N)$, yielding a vector $\vec{\omega}'_\sigma = (\beta'_1, \ldots, \beta'_N)$, s.t. $\vec{\omega} \succ_{Pareto} \vec{\omega}'_\sigma$ (where $\vec{\omega} \succ_{Pareto} \vec{\omega}'_\sigma$ iff $\forall k$, $\alpha_k \geq \beta'_k$ and $\exists s$ s.t. $\alpha_s > \beta'_s$). The next proposition checks that the Symmetric Pareto ordering $\succ_{SP}$ on solutions is the same as the one induced by a product-based π-Pref net.

Proposition 1. $\omega \succ_{SP} \omega'$ iff $\pi_{\Pi G}(\omega) > \pi_{\Pi G}(\omega')$.

Proof (Informal). ($\Rightarrow$) This direction is obvious. ($\Leftarrow$) Assume that $\omega \succ_{SP} \omega'$ does not hold. If $\omega' \succeq_{SP} \omega$, then, clearly $\pi_{\Pi G}(\omega') \geq \pi_{\Pi G}(\omega)$. If $\omega \pm_{SP} \omega'$, then one possibility is that for each permutation, two pairs of components from each vector are ordered in opposite ways, another is that for each permutation, some components are incomparable. In each case, it is possible to find instantiations of the weights in such a way that their products leads to the domination of one vector over the other, and of the latter over the former. Hence the product ordering also yields incomparability.

3   Boolean π-Pref Nets and Their Logical Encodings

Boolean π-Pref nets are a particular case of interest. In this case, π-Pref nets can be equivalently expressed in terms of possibilistic logic, or penalty logic.

3.1   Agreement with the Inclusion Ordering in the Boolean Case

If variables are *binary*, it is easy to define the violation of the preference statement associated to variable A_i by a solution. A solution ω violates the preference statement $u_i : a_{i1} > a_{i2}$ associated to variable A_i if and only if $\omega[Pa(A_i)] = u_i$ and $\omega[A_i] = a_{i2}$. A solution can violate only one preference statement per variable. Then an intuitive ranking of solutions is the inclusion ordering in the sense that if a solution ω violates all the preference statements violated by another solution ω' plus some other(s), then ω' is strictly preferred to ω. When no additional preference constraint is available, the ordering induced from the product-based π-Pref net boils down to this order.

Proposition 2. *Let ΠG be a possibilistic preference network with binary decision variables. Let ω, ω' be two solutions and $\pi_{\Pi G}$ be the joint possibility distribution induced from ΠG. Then ω falsifies all the preference statements falsified by ω' plus some other(s) if and only if $\pi_{\Pi G}(\omega) < \pi_{\Pi G}(\omega')$.*

Proof. It is enough to notice that the Symmetric Pareto ordering then reduces to the inclusion ordering between subsets of violated preference statements.

Example 4. *Let V and W be two Boolean variables standing respectively for "vacations" and "weather" and these preference statements $w \succ \neg w$, $\neg w : v \sim \neg v$ and $w : v \succ \neg v$ (with $w = $ 'good weather', $v = $ 'having vacations'), giving birth to a π-Pref net ΠG: $\pi_{\Pi G}(w) = 1$, $\pi_{\Pi G}(\neg w) = \alpha$, $\pi_{\Pi G}(v|\neg w) = \pi_{\Pi G}(\neg v|\neg w) = 1$, $\pi_{\Pi G}(\neg v|w) = \beta$, $\pi_{\Pi G}(v|w) = 1$. We have $\pi_{\Pi G}(wv) = 1 > \pi_{\Pi G}(\neg wv) = \pi_{\Pi G}(\neg w \neg v) = \alpha$ and $\pi_{\Pi G}(wv) = 1 > \pi_{\Pi G}(w \neg v) = \beta$. Note that wv satisfies the two preference statements, while the other solutions only satisfy one. Moreover, $\neg w \neg v$ and $\neg wv$ satisfy the same preference statement. Thus, the ordering deduced from π-Pref net is indeed the same as the inclusion ordering.*

We should mention that although it is conjectured [9] that CP-nets are consistent with the inclusion order in the above sense, it was never formally proved.

3.2   Logical Possibilistic Encoding

Since the possibilistic setting offers different representation formats, π-Pref nets also have a logical counterpart offering another reading of the preferences, which may be of interest for reasoning purposes. Such a logical counterpart is a symbolic possibilistic base of the form $\Sigma = \{(f_1, c_1), \ldots, (f_m, c_m)\}$ which is a finite set of weighted formulas f_i where $c_i > 0$ is understood as a lower bound of a necessity degree $N(f_i)$ [8]. Its semantics is a possibility distribution $\pi_\Sigma(\omega) = min_{i=1,n} \pi_{\{(f_i,c_i)\}}(\omega) = 1$ if $\omega \vDash f_i$ and $1 - c_i$ if $\omega \vDash \neg f_i$. Each complete preorder on Ω can be represented by a possibility distribution. Moreover, any distribution can be associated with a possibilistic logic base, and also equivalently represented by a possibilistic network [3]. We now consider the possibilistic base associated to complete preference preorder at each node of the π-Pref net:

Definition 4. *The symbolic possibilistic base Σ_i associated to a Boolean variable A_i in a possibilistic network ΠG is defined as follows:*

– *For each preference statement $u_i : a_{i1} \succ a_{i2}$ between the two possible values of a variable A_i, $(\neg u_i \vee a_{i1}, \beta) \in \Sigma_i$ where $\pi(a_{i2}|u_i) = 1 - \beta < 1$ in ΠG.*
– *There is no formula induced by preference statements $u_i : a_{i1} \sim a_{i2}$.*

For Example 4, we get $\Sigma_W = \{(w, 1 - \alpha)\}$ and $\Sigma_V = \{(\neg w \vee v, 1 - \beta)\}$.

Proposition 3. *If π_i is the possibility distribution induced by Σ_i associated with node A_i, then $\pi_i(\omega[\{A_i\} \cup Pa(A_i)]) = \pi(a_i|u_i)$ where $a_i = \omega[A_i]$, $u_i = \omega[Pa(A_i)]$.*

Thus, $\pi_{\Pi G}(A_1, \ldots, A_N) = \times_{i=1,\ldots,N} \pi_i(\omega[\{A_i\} \cup Pa(A_i)])$.

The possibilistic base associated with a π-Pref net ΠG can be obtained by fusing the elementary bases Σ_i ($i = 1, \ldots, N$) associated to its nodes. Since we are in the product-based setting, the combination of these possibilistic bases is defined iteratively as $Comb(\Sigma_1, \Sigma_2) = \Sigma_1 \cup \Sigma_2 \cup \{(p_i \vee q_j, \alpha_i + \beta_j - \alpha_i \times \beta_j) : i \in I, j \in J, p_i \vee q_j \neq \top\}$, where $\Sigma_1 = \{(p_i, \alpha_i) : i \in I\}$ and $\Sigma_2 = \{(q_j, \beta_j) : j \in J\}$. The base resulting from this product-based combination is a (possibly large) possibilistic base that encodes the same possibility distribution as $\pi_{\Pi G}$, see [8]. For Example 4 it reduces to $\Sigma_W \cup \Sigma_V$, as the third formula is a tautology.

3.3   Links with Penalty Logic

This subsection points out another logical counterpart of a π-Pref net ΠG (with distribution $\pi_{\Pi G}$), in terms of a penalty logic base PK [7], where weights are additive. More precisely, this logic associates to each formula the cost (in $[0, +\infty)$) to pay if this formula is violated. The penalty $k_{PK}(\omega)$ relative to a solution ω is the sum of the elementary penalties of the violated formulas. This contrasts with possibilistic logic, where weights are combined by an idempotent operation. The best solution has a cost equal to 0. This logic with a cost interpretation has a close relationship with product-based π-Pref nets. Indeed, the cost of a solution induced by a penalty logic base corresponds actually to the possibility degree computed from a π-Pref net. Namely, in each possibilistic base Σ_i associated to a node A_i we can at most violate one formula. Thus, for each possibilistic base $\Sigma_i = \{(f_{i1}, \alpha_{i1}), \ldots, (f_{ik}, \alpha_{ik})\}$ there exists a penalty logic base $PK_i = \{(f_{i1}, -\ln(\alpha_{i1})), \ldots, (f_{ik}, -\ln(\alpha_{ik}))\}$ such that the ordering induced by π_i is the same as the order induced by the cost function of the penalty logic. This mirrors the fact that $\pi_{\Pi G}(\omega) = \alpha_1 \cdot \cdots \cdot \alpha_N \Leftrightarrow k_{PK}(\omega) = -(\ln(\alpha_1) + \cdots + \ln(\alpha_N))$. Contrarily to possibilistic bases, the combination between penalty bases is the union of all PK_i ($i = 1, \ldots, N$). This yields the same ordering as π-Pref nets. But there is no proof system for penalty logic yet.

4   Optimization and Dominance Queries

In π-Pref nets, conditional preferences correspond to nodes associated with conditional possibility tables. We restrict ourselves to π-Pref nets that are Directed Acyclic Graphs (DAG). On this basis and using the chain rule, one can compute the symbolic possibilities of completely instantiated alternatives, which can then be compared. Two types of queries are usually considered: Optimization queries (for finding the optimal solution), and dominance queries (for comparing solutions). We now study the two types of queries are presented.

4.1   Optimization

For acyclic CP-nets, the optimization query is linear in the size of the network (using a forward sweep algorithm), and there is always a unique optimal solution [4]. In our case, this query may return several solutions since, contrarily to CP-nets, we allow the user to express indifference. Clearly, the best solutions are those having a joint possibility degree equal to 1. Indeed, such a solution exists since the joint possibility distribution associated to the possibilistic network is normalized, thanks to the normalization of each conditional possibility table (i.e. for each variable A_i, each instantiation u_i of $Pa(A_i)$: $\max(\pi(a_i \mid u_i), \pi(\neg a_i \mid u_i)) = 1$ where $\{\neg a_i\} = D_{A_i}/\{a_i\}$ with $a_i \in D_{A_i}$). Thus, we can always find an optimal solution, starting from the root nodes where we choose each time the most or one of the most preferred value(s) (i.e. with possibility equal to 1). Then, depending on the parents instantiation, each time we again choose an alternative with a conditional possibility equal to 1. At the end of the procedure, we get one or several completely instantiated solutions having a possibility equal to 1. Consequently, partial preference orders with incomparable maximal elements can not be represented by a π-Pref net.

Example 5. *Let us reconsider Example 2 and its joint possibility degree in Example 3. Then, $j_b p_b s_b$ is the preferred solution since its joint possibility is equal to 1, and this is the only one.*

The complexity of optimization queries in possibilistic networks is the same as the CP-nets forward sweep procedure if the network omits indifference. In a more general case where indifference is allowed, we can use the same principle as when searching for the best explanations in Bayesian networks [6]. In fact the Most Probable Explanations (MPE) can be obtained by adapting the propagation algorithm in junction trees [12] by replacing summation by maximum. This algorithm has the same complexity as probability propagation (i.e. NP-hard) except in the particular case when the DAG is a polytree since the MPE task can be accomplished efficiently using Pearl's polytree algorithm [14]. The adaptation of this algorithm for the possibilistic framework can be easily performed on the product-based Junction tree algorithm [2] with the same complexity as the standard MPE. A possible variant of the optimization problem is to compute the M most possible configurations using a variant of the MPE [13]. This query is not proposed in CP-nets and can be interesting in π-Pref nets even if the answer is not always obvious to obtain in presence of incomparable solutions.

4.2   Dominance

The comparison between the symbolic possibility degrees can be found using Algorithm 1.1 that takes as input the set of constraints $\mathcal{C}$ between the symbolic weights and two vectors. Let us consider two solutions ω_i and ω_j with simplified respective vectors $\overrightarrow{\omega_i^*} = (\alpha_1, \dots, \alpha_k)$ and $\overrightarrow{\omega_j^*} = (\beta_1, \dots, \beta_m)$ where the components equal to 1 have been deleted, with $k \leq m \leq N$. Then, the algorithm proceeds by first deleting all pairs of equal components between the vectors so to get

1.1. Comparison between two joint possibility degrees

Data: $\vec{\omega}_i$, $\vec{\omega}_j$, $\mathcal{C}$

Result: R

begin

    $equality(\vec{\omega}_i, \vec{\omega}_j, \mathcal{C})$;

    if $(empty(\vec{\omega}_i)$ *and* $empty(\vec{\omega}_i))$ **then** $R \leftarrow \omega_i = \omega_j$; **else** $s \leftarrow true$;

    $s \leftarrow sort(\vec{\omega}_i, \vec{\omega}_j, \mathcal{C})$;

    if $s = true$ **then** $R \leftarrow \omega_i \succ \omega_j$;

    else $R \leftarrow \omega_i \pm \omega_j$;

    return R

end

totally different components. Second, if there exists a permutation where each component α_i is higher than β_s such that $s \in [1, ..., k]$ then $\omega_i \succ \omega_j$, otherwise they remain non comparable. Thus the algorithm is based on the sequential application of:

(1) The function *equality* that deletes the common values between $\vec{\omega}_i$ and $\vec{\omega}_j$.
(2) The function *sort* that returns *true* if given $\alpha_c \in \vec{\omega}_i$, there exists a constraint $\alpha_c > \delta$ in $\mathcal{C}$ such that $\delta \in \vec{\omega}_j$. Each component of $\vec{\omega}_j$ can be used only one time in the comparison process.

Example 6. *Let us consider the π-Pref net ΠG of Example 2. Using Algorithm 1.1, the ordering between the solutions is defined in Fig. 2 such that a link from ω_i to ω_j means that ω_i is preferred to ω_j. For instance, consider $\overrightarrow{j_b p_w s_r} = (\beta, \delta_4)$ and $\overrightarrow{j_r p_w s_r} = (\alpha, \beta)$. First, we should delete common values, namely the symbolic weight β. Then, we should check if $\mathcal{C}$ entails $\alpha < \delta_4$ or the inverse. Here, α and δ_4 are not comparable. Thus, we have $j_b p_w s_r \pm j_r p_w s_r$.*

The complexity of dominance in CP-nets depends on the network structure. For singly connected binary-valued CP-nets it has been proved that the problem is NP-complete (using a reduction to 3SAT). In the general case [10] shows that it is a PSPACE-complete. Clearly, for π-Pref nets, the complexity is due to the comparison step in Algorithm 1.1 (since the computation of the possibility

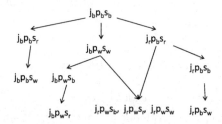

Fig. 2. Possibilistic order relative to Example 2

degrees is a simple matter using the chain rule) and in particular to the *sort* function where the matching between the two vectors needs the definition of different possible arrangements i.e. the algorithm is of time complexity O(n!).

5   Conclusion

This paper has established the main properties of possibilistic conditional preference networks. This modeling is appropriate to represent conditional preferences without having the CP-nets limitations, namely the enforced priority in favor of parent nodes. Moreover, we have shown that π-Pref nets produce a symmetric Pareto ordering of solutions, and in the Boolean case are endowed with logical counterparts allowing an equivalent modeling suitable for inference.

This work calls for several developments. In fact, we might think of partially specified preferences as well as the handling of impossible situations. Also, it would be interesting to conduct a deep comparison with other preference models such as GAI networks [11] and UCP-net [5] since they both use additive utilities.

References

1. Ben Amor, N., Dubois, D., Gouider, H., Prade, H.: Possibilistic networks: a new setting for modeling preferences. In: Straccia, U., Calì, A. (eds.) SUM 2014. LNCS, vol. 8720, pp. 1–7. Springer, Heidelberg (2014)
2. Ben Amor, N., Benferhat, S., Mellouli, K.: Anytime possibilistic propagation algorithm. In: Proceedings of the 1st International Conference Computing in an Imperfect World, pp. 263–279 (2002)
3. Benferhat, S., Dubois, D., Garcia, L., Prade, H.: On the transformation between possibilistic logic bases and possibilistic causal networks. Int. J. Approx. Reasoning **29**(2), 135–173 (2002)
4. Boutilier, C., Brafman, R.I.: A tool for representing and reasoning with conditional ceteris paribus preference statements. J. Artif. Intell. Res. **21**, 135–191 (2004)
5. Brafman, R.I., Domshlak, C.: Introducing Variable Importance Tradeoffs Into CP-nets. CoRR, New York (2013)
6. Dawid, A.P.: Applications of a general propagation algorithm for probabilistic expert systems. Stat. Comput. **2**(1), 25–36 (1992)
7. Dupin de Saint-Cyr, F., Lang, J., Schiex, T.: Penalty logic and its link with Dempster-Shafer theory. In: Proceedings of the 10th Conference UAI, pp. 204–211, Morgan Kaufmann (1994)
8. Dubois, D., Prade, H.: Possibilistic logic: a retrospective and prospective view. Fuzzy Sets Syst. **144**(1), 3–23 (2004)
9. Dubois, D., Prade, H., Touazi, F.: Conditional Preference-nets, possibilistic logic, and the transitivity of priorities. In: Proceedings of the 33rd SGAI Intenational Conference, pp. 175–184. Springer, Heidelberg (2013)
10. Goldsmith, J., Lang, J., Truszczynski, M., Wilson, N.: The computational complexity of dominance and consistency in CP-nets. J. Artif. Intell. Res. **33**, 403–432 (2008)
11. Gonzales, C., Perny, N.: GAI networks for utility elicitation. In: Proceedings of the 9th International Conference Principles of Knowledge Representation and Reasoning, pp. 224–234 (2004)

12. Jensen, F.V., Lauritzen, S.L., Olesen, K.G.: Bayesian updating in causal proba-
    bilistic networks by local computations. Comput. Stat. Q. **4**, 269–282 (1990)
13. Nilsson, D.: An efficient algorithm for finding the m most probable configurations
    in probabilistic expert systems. Stat. Comput. **8**(2), 159–173 (1998)
14. Pearl, J.: Probabilistic Reasoning in Intelligent Systems: Networks of Plausible
    Inference. Morgan Kaufmman, San Francisco (1988)

Argumentation

On Supported Inference and Extension Selection in Abstract Argumentation Frameworks

Sébastien Konieczny, Pierre Marquis[(⊠)], and Srdjan Vesic

CRIL, CNRS and Université d'Artois, Lens, France
{konieczny,marquis,vesic}@cril.fr

Abstract. We present two approaches for deriving more arguments from an abstract argumentation framework than the ones obtained using sceptical inference, that is often too cautious. The first approach consists in selecting only some of the extensions. We point out several choice criteria to achieve such a selection process. Choices are based either on the attack relation between extensions or on the support of the arguments in each extension. The second approach consists of the definition of a new inference policy, between sceptical and credulous inference, and based as well on the support of the arguments. We illustrate the two approaches on examples, study their properties, and formally compare their inferential powers.

1 Introduction

An abstract argumentation system is often represented as an *oriented graph*, where nodes correspond to *arguments* and arcs correspond to *attacks* between them [15]. Different *semantics* are used to calculate *extensions* (sets of arguments that can be accepted together). From the extensions, a *status*, accepted or rejected, is assigned to each argument, using some *acceptance policy*. They are two main acceptance policies. In the first one, the *sceptical* policy, an argument is accepted if (there are extensions and) it appears in each extension. For the second one, the *credulous* policy, an argument is accepted if it belongs to (at least) one extension.

When the number of extensions is large, using a sceptical / credulous approach can be sub-optimal. Namely, if there is a lot of extensions, only few (if any) arguments are in all of them. Thus, using sceptical inference gives almost no information. Conversely, the credulous approach may result in too many arguments.

There exist settings for abstract argumentation where preferences, weighted attacks or similar extra information are considered [2,8,11,16,20,21]. Those additional data can be exploited to reduce the number of extensions. Contrastingly, the problem addressed in this paper is to increase the number of accepted arguments when there is no further data, i.e., other data except the arguments and the attacks between them.

We investigate this problem and present two approaches for dealing with it. The first one consists in selecting only some of the extensions (the "best"

© Springer International Publishing Switzerland 2015
S. Destercke and T. Denoeux (Eds.): ECSQARU 2015, LNAI 9161, pp. 49–59, 2015.
DOI: 10.1007/978-3-319-20807-7_5

ones, for a given semantics). The idea is to discriminate the extensions by taking advantage of the attack relation. The selection achieved in this way leads to increase the number of sceptically accepted arguments. Two methods for selecting extensions are pointed out. The first one is based on a pairwise comparison of extensions. The second method is based on a global evaluation of each extension, followed by a selection of the best evaluated ones. The second approach we developed goes through the definition of a new policy for accepting arguments. We introduce a third acceptance policy, which can be viewed as a trade-off between the credulous and the sceptical policy. The very idea is to consider the number of times an argument appears in the extensions. For the sceptical policy a "good" argument is one that appears in all extensions. If no such argument exists, then it makes sense to consider that arguments that appears in every extension but one are "quite good", and better than the ones that appear in less extensions.

A technical report [19] containing all the proofs, more explanations, more examples and more figures is available online at http://www.cril.fr/~vesic.

2   Formal Setting

This section introduces basic definitions and notations we use throughout the paper. An *argumentation system* (AS) is a pair $\mathscr{F} = (\mathscr{A}, \mathscr{R})$ where $\mathscr{R} \subseteq \mathscr{A} \times \mathscr{A}$. $\mathscr{A}$ is called the set of *arguments* and $\mathscr{R}$ is called the *attack relation*. We restrict ourselves to the case when $\mathscr{A}$ is finite.

Let $\mathscr{F} = (\mathscr{A}, \mathscr{R})$ be an AS, and let $\mathscr{E}, \mathscr{E}', \mathscr{E}'' \subseteq \mathscr{A}$ and $a \in \mathscr{A}$. $\mathscr{E}$ is *conflict-free* if and only if there exist no arguments $a, b \in \mathscr{E}$ such that $a \mathscr{R} b$. $\mathscr{E}$ defends a if and only if for every $b \in \mathscr{A}$ we have that if $b \mathscr{R} a$ then there exists $c \in \mathscr{E}$ such that $c \mathscr{R} b$. Argument a is strongly defended from $\mathscr{E}'$ by $\mathscr{E}''$ (written $sd(a, \mathscr{E}', \mathscr{E}'')$) if and only if $(\forall b \in \mathscr{E}')$ if $(b\mathscr{R}a)$ then $(\exists c \in \mathscr{E}'' \setminus \{a\})((c\mathscr{R}b) \wedge sd(c, \mathscr{E}', \mathscr{E}'' \setminus \{a\}))$.

Usual semantics for Dung's AS are considered, especially the complete, preferred, grounded [15], semi-stable [7] and ideal semantics [14]. A semantics σ is said to return conflict-free sets iff for every AS $\mathscr{F}$, every extension of $\mathscr{F}$ is conflict-free. For an argumentation system $\mathscr{F} = (\mathscr{A}, \mathscr{R})$ we denote $\text{Ext}_\sigma(\mathscr{F})$; or, by a slight abuse of notation, $\text{Ext}_\sigma(\mathscr{A}, \mathscr{R})$ the set of its extensions with respect to semantics σ. We use abbreviations c, p, s, ss, g and i for respectively complete, preferred, stable, semi-stable, grounded and ideal semantics. For example, $\text{Ext}_p(\mathscr{F})$ denotes the set of preferred extensions of $\mathscr{F}$.

An *acceptance policy* is a function $\text{Inf}_\sigma : \text{Ext}_\sigma(\mathscr{F}) \to 2^{\mathscr{A}}$. The two main acceptance policies are sceptical and credulous policies. We say that x is *sceptically accepted* under semantics σ (or in short *s-sceptically accepted*) iff $\text{Ext}_\sigma(\mathscr{F}) \neq \emptyset$ and $x \in \bigcap_{\mathscr{E} \in \text{Ext}_\sigma(\mathscr{F})} \mathscr{E}$. x is *credulously accepted* under semantics σ iff $x \in \bigcup_{\mathscr{E} \in \text{Ext}_\sigma(\mathscr{F})} \mathscr{E}$. We denote the set of sceptically accepted arguments by $\text{Sc}_\sigma(\mathscr{F})$ and the set of credulously accepted arguments by $\text{Cr}_\sigma(\mathscr{F})$. We denote by $\mathscr{R}_{\downarrow \mathscr{E}}$ the restriction of attack relation $\mathscr{R}$ on set $\mathscr{E}$.

3   Comparing Extensions by Pairwise Comparison

This section studies the way to select the "best" extensions based on the following process:

1. Compare all pairs of extensions based on a given criterion (e.g. the number of arguments in one extension not attacked by the other extension)
2. Choose the "best" extension(s) given the winners of pairwise comparisons

Definition 1 (Pairwise Comparison Criteria). *Let $\mathscr{F} = (\mathscr{A}, \mathscr{R})$ be an AS, σ a semantics and $\text{Ext}_\sigma(\mathscr{F})$ the set of extensions of $\mathscr{F}$. Let $\mathscr{E}, \mathscr{E}' \in \text{Ext}_\sigma(\mathscr{F})$. Then:*

1. *$\mathscr{E} \succeq_{nonatt} \mathscr{E}'$ if the number of arguments in $\mathscr{E}$ non attacked by $\mathscr{E}'$ is greater than or equal to the number of arguments in $\mathscr{E}'$ non attacked by arguments of $\mathscr{E}$*
2. *$\mathscr{E} \succeq_{strdef} \mathscr{E}'$ if the number of arguments in $\mathscr{E}$ strongly defended from $\mathscr{E}'$ by $\mathscr{E}$ is greater than or equal to the number of arguments in $\mathscr{E}'$ strongly defended from $\mathscr{E}$ by $\mathscr{E}'$*
3. *$\mathscr{E} \succeq_{delarg} \mathscr{E}'$ if the cardinality of any largest subset S of $\mathscr{E}$ such that if all the attacks from S to $\mathscr{E}'$ are deleted then $\mathscr{E}$ is an extension of $(\mathscr{E} \cup \mathscr{E}', \mathscr{R}_{\downarrow \mathscr{E} \cup \mathscr{E}'})$ is greater than or equal to the cardinality of any largest subset S' of $\mathscr{E}'$ such that if all the attacks from S' to $\mathscr{E}$ are deleted then $\mathscr{E}$ is an extension of $(\mathscr{E} \cup \mathscr{E}', \mathscr{R}_{\downarrow \mathscr{E} \cup \mathscr{E}'})$*
4. *$\mathscr{E}' \succeq_{delatt} \mathscr{E}'$ if the maximal number of attacks from $\mathscr{E}$ to $\mathscr{E}'$ that can be deleted such that $\mathscr{E}$ is still an extension of $(\mathscr{E} \cup \mathscr{E}', \mathscr{R}_{\downarrow \mathscr{E} \cup \mathscr{E}'})$ is greater than or equal to the maximal number of attacks from $\mathscr{E}'$ to $\mathscr{E}$ that can be deleted such that $\mathscr{E}'$ is still an extension of $(\mathscr{E} \cup \mathscr{E}', \mathscr{R}_{\downarrow \mathscr{E} \cup \mathscr{E}'})$*

The two first criteria are based on the number of non attacked or (strongly) defended arguments. The last two ones are based on a notion of robustness from attacks stemming from the other extension. One could also consider other criteria, for example by comparing the total number of attacks from $\mathscr{E}$ to $\mathscr{E}'$ and the total number of attacks from $\mathscr{E}'$ to $\mathscr{E}$. For a criterion γ, we write $\mathscr{E} \succ_\gamma \mathscr{E}'$ iff $\mathscr{E} \succeq_\gamma \mathscr{E}'$ and it is not the case that $\mathscr{E}' \succeq_\gamma \mathscr{E}$. We also write $\mathscr{E} \sim_\gamma \mathscr{E}'$ iff $\mathscr{E} \succeq_\gamma \mathscr{E}'$ and $\mathscr{E}' \succeq_\gamma \mathscr{E}$.

Example 1. Consider the AS $\mathscr{F}_1 = (\mathscr{A}_1, \mathscr{R}_1)$ with $\mathscr{A}_1 = \{a, b, c, d\}$ and $\mathscr{R}_1 = \{(a, c), (a, d), (b, c), (c, a), (d, b)\}$. $\text{Ext}_p(\mathscr{F}_1) = \{\mathscr{E}, \mathscr{E}'\}$ with $\mathscr{E} = \{a, b\}$, $\mathscr{E}' = \{c, d\}$. All the arguments are attacked, so $\mathscr{E} \sim_{nonatt} \mathscr{E}'$. No argument is strongly defended, so $\mathscr{E} \sim_{strdef} \mathscr{E}'$. We also have $\mathscr{E} \succ_{delarg} \mathscr{E}'$ since for $S = \{b\}$ $\mathscr{E}$ is still an extension even if all the attacks from S are deleted; whereas there are no $S' \subseteq \mathscr{E}'$ with $S' \neq \emptyset$ such that $\mathscr{E}'$ is still a preferred extension even after deleting all the attacks from S'. Finally, $\mathscr{E} \succ_{delatt} \mathscr{E}'$ since even if the attack from a to c is deleted, $\mathscr{E}$ is still a preferred extension, whereas as soon as one attack from $\mathscr{E}'$ is deleted, $\mathscr{E}'$ is no longer a preferred extension.

Definition 2 (Copeland-Based Extensions). *Let $\gamma \in \{nonatt, strdef, delarg, delatt\}$ be one of the criteria from Definition 1. Let $\mathscr{F} = (\mathscr{A}, \mathscr{R})$ be* an argumentation system, σ a semantics and $\text{Ext}_\sigma(\mathscr{F})$ the set of extensions of $\mathscr{F}$ with respect to σ. We define the set of Copeland-based extensions (CBE) as follows

$$\text{CBE}_{\sigma,\gamma}(\mathscr{F}) = \underset{\mathscr{E} \in \text{Ext}_\sigma(\mathscr{F})}{\arg\max} \; |\{\mathscr{E}' \in \text{Ext}_\sigma(\mathscr{F}) \mid \mathscr{E} \succeq_\gamma \mathscr{E}'\}| - |\{\mathscr{E}'' \in \text{Ext}_\sigma(\mathscr{F}) \mid \mathscr{E}'' \succeq_\gamma \mathscr{E}\}|$$

We call this selection "Copeland-based" since it is inspired by the Copeland's rule from voting theory [22]. Of course, one can envisage other ways to select the extensions given criterion γ, for instance all voting methods based on the majority graph (such as Miller, Fishburn, Schwartz, Banks or Slater's methods [6]). Clearly, selecting some extensions is a way to increase the number of sceptically accepted arguments (and to decrease the number of credulously accepted arguments):

Fact 1. For every $\gamma \in \{nonatt, strdef, delarg, delatt\}$, for every semantics σ, for every AS $\mathscr{F} = (\mathscr{A}, \mathscr{R})$, for every $x \in \mathscr{A}$:

- $\text{CBE}_{\sigma,\gamma}(\mathscr{F}) \subseteq \text{Ext}_\sigma(\mathscr{F})$
- if x is σ-sceptically accepted then x is $\text{CBE}_{\sigma,\gamma}$-sceptically accepted
- if x is $\text{CBE}_{\sigma,\gamma}$-credulously accepted then it is σ-credulously accepted.

Example 2. Consider the argumentation system from Example 1. For example, we have that $\text{CBE}_{\sigma,delarg}(\mathscr{F}_1) = \text{CBE}_{\sigma,delatt}(\mathscr{F}_1) = \{\mathscr{E}\}$.

Baroni and Giacomin [4] pointed out a set of extension evaluation criteria that can be seen as properties for characterizing good semantics. We now show that the semantics defined in this section satisfy the same properties as the underlying semantics they are built from, with the exception of directionality.

Proposition 1. *Let x be any property among I-maximality, Admissibility, Strong Admissibility, Reinstatement, Weak Reinstatement, CF-Reinstatement [4].*

If the semantics σ satisfies property x, then the semantics $\text{CBE}_{\sigma,\gamma}$ satisfies property x.

Note that the relations among different semantics do not carry over in case of CBE approach. For instance, it is not guaranteed that each CBE-stable extension is also a CBE-preferred extension.

4   Comparing Extensions by Global Evaluation

In Sect. 3 we considered different criteria for *pairwise comparison* of extensions. In this section we define the score of an argument as the number of extensions it appears in. One may justify this choice of score as some kind of generalization of the principles behind sceptical acceptance. For sceptical acceptance a "good" argument is an argument that appears in all extensions. But, if no such argument exists, it could make sense to consider that arguments that appears in every extension but one are "good", and typically better than the ones that appears in less extensions. Note that one can use other scores in the construction and obtain similar results.

Definition 3 (Scores and Support Vectors). *Let $\mathscr{F} = (\mathscr{A}, \mathscr{R})$ be an argumentation system, σ a semantics, x be an argument, and $\mathrm{Ext}_\sigma(\mathscr{F})$ the set of extensions of $\mathscr{F}$ with respect to σ. We define* ne *as the number of extensions x appears in. Formally,* $\mathrm{ne}_\sigma(x, \mathscr{F}) = |\{\mathscr{E} \in \mathrm{Ext}_\sigma(\mathscr{F}) \mid x \in \mathscr{E}\}|$. *For an extension $\mathscr{E} \in \mathrm{Ext}_\sigma(\mathscr{F})$, with $\mathscr{E} = \{a_1, \ldots, a_n\}$ we define its support as* $\mathrm{vsupp}_\sigma(\mathscr{E}, \mathscr{F}) = (\mathrm{ne}_\sigma(a_1, \mathscr{F}), \ldots, \mathrm{ne}_\sigma(a_n, \mathscr{F}))$.

When $\mathscr{F}$ and σ are clear from the context, we write $\mathrm{ne}(x)$ *and* $\mathrm{vsupp}(\mathscr{E})$ *instead of* $\mathrm{ne}_\sigma(x, \mathscr{F})$ *and* $\mathrm{vsupp}_\sigma(\mathscr{E}, \mathscr{F})$.

Definition 4 (Aggregation Functions). *Let $v = (v_1, \ldots, v_n)$ be a vector of natural numbers. We denote by $sum(v)$ the sum of all elements of v, by $max(v)$ the maximal element of v, by $min(v)$ the minimal element of v, by $leximax(v)$ the re-arranged version of v where $v_1, \ldots, v_n$ are put in decreasing order, by $leximin(v)$ the re-arranged version of v where $v_1, \ldots, v_n$ are put in increasing order.*

For example, if $v = (2, 1, 4, 2, 5)$, then we have $sum(v) = 14$ and $leximin(v) = (1, 2, 2, 4, 5)$. Note that there exist other ways to aggregate vectors [13].

For the next definition we need the notion of lexicographic order $<_{lex}$ (for *leximin* and *leximax*). Let $v = (v_1, \ldots, v_n)$ and $v' = (v'_1, \ldots, v'_n)$ be two vectors of natural numbers. We have $v <_{lex} v'$ iff $\exists j \in 1, \ldots, n (\forall i \in 1, \ldots, j-1, v_i = v'_i)$ and $v_j < v'_j$. We also have $v <_{leximin} v'$ iff $leximin(v) <_{lex} leximin(v')$ and $v <_{leximax} v'$ iff $leximax(v) <_{lex} leximax(v')$.

Definition 5 (Order-Based Extensions). *Let $\mathscr{F} = (\mathscr{A}, \mathscr{R})$ be an argumentation system, σ a semantics, $\mathrm{Ext}_\sigma(\mathscr{F})$ be the set of extensions of $\mathscr{F}$ with respect to σ, and γ be an aggregation function. We have* $\mathrm{OBE}_{\sigma,\gamma}(\mathscr{F}) = arg\,max_{\mathscr{E} \in \mathrm{Ext}_\sigma(\mathscr{F})} \gamma(\mathrm{vsupp}_\sigma(\mathscr{E}, \mathscr{F}))$.

The idea of the previous definition is to calculate the popularity of an extension by taking into account the popularity of the arguments it contains.

Example 3. Let $\mathscr{F}_3 = (\mathscr{A}_3, \mathscr{R}_3)$ be AS $\mathscr{F}_3 = (\mathscr{A}_3, \mathscr{R}_3)$ with $\mathscr{A}_3 = \{a, b, c, d, e, f, g, h\}$ and $\mathscr{R}_3 = \{(a, b), (b, a), (e, f), (f, e), (b, g), (f, g), (g, h), (h, d), (d, c), (c, d)\}$. There are five preferred extensions: $\{a, e, g, c\}$, $\{a, e, g, d\}$, $\{a, f, h, c\}$, $\{b, h, c, e\}$, $\{b, h, c, f\}$. So $\mathrm{ne}_p(a, \mathscr{F}_3) = 3$, $\mathrm{ne}_p(b, \mathscr{F}_3) = 2$, $\mathrm{ne}_p(c, \mathscr{F}_3) = 4$, $\mathrm{ne}_p(d, \mathscr{F}_3) = 1$, $\mathrm{ne}_p(e, \mathscr{F}_3) = 3$, $\mathrm{ne}_p(f, \mathscr{F}_3) = 2$, $\mathrm{ne}_p(g, \mathscr{F}_3) = 2$, $\mathrm{ne}_p(h, \mathscr{F}_3) = 3$.

We obtain $\mathrm{OBE}_{\sigma,max}(\mathscr{F}_3) = \mathrm{OBE}_{\sigma,min}(\mathscr{F}_3) = \{\{a, e, g, c\}, \{a, f, h, c\}, \{b, h, c, e\}, \{b, h, c, f\}\}$. So, whereas $\mathrm{Sc}_p(\mathscr{F}_3) = \emptyset$, we have $\mathrm{Sc}_{\mathrm{OBE}_{p,min}}(\mathscr{F}_3) = \{c\}$. Similarly, we have $\mathrm{OBE}_{\sigma,sum}(\mathscr{F}_3) = \mathrm{OBE}_{\sigma,leximin}(\mathscr{F}_3) = \mathrm{OBE}_{\sigma,leximax}(\mathscr{F}_3) = \{\{a, e, g, c\}, \{a, f, h, c\}, \{b, h, c, e\}\}$.

Fact 2. For every $\gamma \in \{sum, max, min, leximin, leximax\}$, for every semantics σ, for every AS $\mathscr{F} = (\mathscr{A}, \mathscr{R})$, for every $x \in \mathscr{A}$:

- $\mathrm{OBE}_{\sigma,\gamma}(\mathscr{F}) \subseteq \mathrm{Ext}_\sigma(\mathscr{F})$
- if x is σ-sceptically accepted then x is $\mathrm{OBE}_{\sigma,\gamma}$-sceptically accepted
- if x is $\mathrm{OBE}_{\sigma,\gamma}$-credulously accepted then it is σ-credulously accepted.

Proposition 2. *Let x be any property among I-maximality, Admissibility, Strong Admissibility, Reinstatement, Weak Reinstatement, CF-Reinstatement [4].*

If the semantics σ satisfies property x, then the semantics $\mathsf{OBE}_{\sigma,\gamma}$ satisfies property x.

Like in Sect. 3, directionality is not always satisfied by the OBE approach.

A natural issue is to determine how the proposed criteria are connected. Do some of the rules coincide? Are some of them refinements of others? In the rest of this section we provide the answer to this question. Essentially, all the criteria give different results; the exceptions come from the obvious fact that *leximin* (resp. *leximax*) refines min (resp. max). We used the preferred semantics to construct the counter-examples; a similar study can be conducted for the other semantics.

Definition 6. *Let Γ and Γ' be two functions. We write $\Gamma \sqsubseteq \Gamma'$ iff for every $\mathcal{F}$, $\Gamma(\mathcal{F}) \subseteq \Gamma'(\mathcal{F})$. The relation $\sqsubseteq$ is a pre-order. Let us denote its strict part by $\sqsubset$, its symmetric part by $\doteq$ and its negation by $\not\sqsubseteq$. We write Γ ind Γ' iff $\Gamma \not\sqsubseteq \Gamma'$ and $\Gamma' \not\sqsubseteq \Gamma'$.*

Proposition 3. *For every acceptability semantics σ,*

$$\mathsf{OBE}_{\sigma,leximin} \sqsubseteq \mathsf{OBE}_{\sigma,\min} \ and \ \mathsf{OBE}_{\sigma,leximax} \sqsubseteq \mathsf{OBE}_{\sigma,\max}$$

We now provide a complete comparison between pairs of criteria under preferred semantics.

Proposition 4. *It holds that $\mathsf{OBE}_{p,leximin} \sqsubset \mathsf{OBE}_{p,\min}$ and $\mathsf{OBE}_{p,leximax} \sqsubset \mathsf{OBE}_{p,\max}$. The other pairs of rules (x,y) with $x,y \in \{\mathsf{OBE}_{sum}, \mathsf{OBE}_{\min}, \mathsf{OBE}_{\max}, \mathsf{OBE}_{leximin}, \mathsf{OBE}_{leximax}\}$, $x \neq y$ are incomparable, i.e., x ind y.*

5   Support-Based Acceptance Policy

This section presents a completely different approach for selecting arguments. We focus on arguments that have the greatest supports among extensions to construct what we call "candidate sets". Then, an argument is called *supportedly accepted* if it is in all the candidate sets.

Definition 7 (Candidate Sets). *Let $\mathcal{F} = (\mathcal{A}, \mathcal{R})$ be an AS and let σ be a semantics. Let $\succeq$ be any pre-order defined on $\mathcal{A}$. Let $|\mathcal{A}| = m$. For a permutation θ of $\{1,\ldots,m\}$, let $>_\theta$ be the linear order on $\mathcal{A}$ defined by $a_{\theta(1)} >_\theta \ldots >_\theta a_{\theta(m)}$. $>_\theta$ is said to be compatible with $\succeq$ iff $a_{\theta(1)} \succeq \ldots \succeq a_{\theta(m)}$. A set $\mathcal{E} \subseteq \mathcal{A}$ is a candidate set of $\mathcal{F}$ under semantics σ w.r.t. $\succeq$ iff there exists a permutation θ of $\{1,\ldots,m\}$ such that $>_\theta$ is compatible with $\succeq$ and $\mathcal{E}$ is obtained by the following greedy procedure:*

$$S := \emptyset;$$
$$for \ j = 1,\ldots,m \ do$$
$$\quad if \ (\mathsf{ne}_\sigma(a_{\theta(j)}, \mathcal{F}) \geq 1) \ and \ (S \cup \{a_{\theta(j)}\} \ is \ conflict\text{-}free)$$
$$\quad then \ S := S \cup \{a_{\theta(j)}\}$$
$$end \ for;$$
$$\mathcal{E} := S.$$

In the following, we consider the pre-order $\succeq$ on $\mathscr{A}$ defined by for all $x, y \in \mathscr{A}$, $x \succeq y$ iff $\mathsf{ne}_\sigma(x, \mathscr{F}) \geq \mathsf{ne}_\sigma(y, \mathscr{F})$. We denote the set of candidate sets of $\mathscr{F}$ under σ w.r.t. this pre-order by $\mathsf{CS}_\sigma(\mathscr{F})$.

Note that, in general, neither each candidate set is an extension nor each extension is a candidate set. Observe also that the construction of candidate sets is reminiscent to the one of preferred subbases from a stratified belief base with respect to the inclusion-based ordering [5]; here the belief base consists of all the arguments and the stratification is based on the $\mathsf{ne}_\sigma(., \mathscr{F})$ score.

Definition 8 (Supported Acceptance). *Let $\mathscr{F} = (\mathscr{A}, \mathscr{R})$ be an AS, σ be a semantics and let $x \in \mathscr{A}$. We say that x is supportedly accepted under semantics σ iff $x \in \bigcap_{\mathscr{E} \in \mathsf{CS}_\sigma(\mathscr{F})}$. We denote the set of supportedly accepted arguments $\mathsf{Sp}_\sigma(\mathscr{F})$.*

We can show that supported inference is "between" sceptical and credulous inference.

Proposition 5. *For every AS $\mathscr{F} = (\mathscr{A}, \mathscr{R})$, for every semantics σ returning conflict-free extensions:*

$$\mathsf{Sc}_\sigma(\mathscr{F}) \subseteq \mathsf{Sp}_\sigma(\mathscr{F}) \subseteq \mathsf{Cr}_\sigma(\mathscr{F}).$$

Note that the condition telling that σ returns conflict-free extensions is necessary to ensure the link between sceptical and supported acceptance. However, this is not an issue, since all the well-known semantics return conflict-free sets.

Example 4. Let $\mathscr{F}_4 = (\mathscr{A}_4, \mathscr{R}_4)$ be an AS with $\mathscr{A}_4 = \{a, b, c, d, e, f, g, h\}$ and $\mathscr{R}_4 = \{(a, b), (b, a), (b, g), (c, d), (d, c), (d, g), (e, f), (f, e), (f, g), (g, h)\}$. There are eight preferred extensions: $\{a, c, e, g\}$, $\{a, d, e, h\}$, $\{a, c, f, h\}$, $\{a, d, f, h\}$, $\{b, c, e, h\}$, $\{b, d, e, h\}$, $\{b, c, f, h\}$, $\{b, d, f, h\}$. There are no sceptically accepted arguments, i.e. $\mathsf{Sc}_p(\mathscr{F}_4) = \emptyset$. But h is accepted by seven out of the eight extensions, and it is supportedly accepted, i.e., $\mathsf{Sp}_p(\mathscr{F}_4) = \{h\}$.

In the above example the set of candidates is a subset of the set of extensions, but this is not always the case. Consider for instance the AS from Example 3, where there is only one candidate set $\{c, a, e, h\}$, that is *not* an extension. So it is interesting to note that on this example there are four supportedly inferred arguments, whereas with the OBE methods only c is inferred.

A major drawback of credulous inference is that the set of inferred arguments is not always conflict-free. This is problematic since all these arguments cannot be accepted together in such a case. Sceptical inference does not suffer from this problem since the set of inferred arguments is ensured to be conflict-free. Interestingly, supported inference offers the same important property:

Fact 3. *For any $\mathscr{F}$, the set of supportedly accepted arguments is conflict-free.*

Note that this set is not necessarily admissible. This should not be shocking since the same observation can be made for the set of sceptically accepted arguments.

Finally, an interesting issue is to determine whether some connections exist between supported inference and the approaches presented in the previous sections. We provide a systematic study of the links between the two approaches under preferred semantics.

Proposition 6. *For every* $\gamma \in \{sum, min, max, leximin, leximax\}$, *$OBE_\gamma$ and CS are incomparable under preferred semantics, i.e., OBE_γ ind CS.*

Let us first show that every $OBE_{\sigma,\max}$-sceptically accepted argument is also supportedly accepted, for every semantics that returns conflict-free extensions.

Proposition 7. *Let σ be a semantics returning conflict-free extensions. We have*

$$Sc_{OBE_{\sigma,\max}} \sqsubseteq Sp_\sigma.$$

Let us now illustrate the indifference between γ-sceptical acceptance and supported acceptance for $\gamma \neq max$, again on the case of preferred semantics.

Proposition 8. *The links between Sc_γ and Sp under preferred semantics are as follows:*

1. $Sc_{OBE_{p,\max}} \sqsubset Sp_p$.
2. *for every* $\gamma \in \{sum, min, leximin, leximax\}$, $Sc_{OBE_{p,\gamma}}$ ind Sp_p.

The two previous propositions show that OBE and supported inference, although both using the scores of arguments defined as the number of extensions they belong to, induce intrinsically different reasoning mechanisms.

6   Conclusion and Related Work

This paper aimed at defining approaches for a better inference from abstract argumentation framework. Indeed, a large number of extensions results in a low number of sceptically accepted arguments. Several approaches have been described for dealing with this problem. First, different criteria for pairwise comparison of extensions and a method for selecting only the best extensions given the winners of pairwise duels have been pointed out. Second, several criteria for ordering the extensions have been presented. Both approaches result in a decrease of the number of extensions; consequently, the number of sceptical arguments increases (and the number of credulous arguments diminishes). The third approach we have put forward does not choose between existing extensions. Instead, it uses extensions to assign a score to every argument (the score of an argument is the number of extensions it belongs to). Then, starting from the arguments having the maximal score, candidate sets can be generated and on this ground supportedly accepted arguments have been defined.

Several papers in the literature are relevant to our work in the sense that their objectives are somehow similar. Thus, some previous work aimed at defining different levels of acceptability for arguments [3,9,18,23]. Such levels can be obtained by attaching numerical scores between 0 and 1 to each argument, or by ranking arguments over an ordinal scale. Contrastingly, the goal of the present paper is not to tackle the problem of gradual acceptance. In this work our objective is not to question the classical binary framework for inference, where an argument is inferred or not, but to define inference relations allowing to infer more arguments than sceptical inference; to make a parallel with logical inference, a similar distinction exists between paraconsistent logics and some weighted logics (such as possibilistic or fuzzy logics).

Settings where argumentation systems are based on preferences or attack weights can also be exploited for reducing the number of extensions. However, those approaches suppose the availability of some extra information such as weights or preferences, whereas our approach is based solely on the argumentation system $\mathscr{F} = (\mathscr{A}, \mathscr{R})$.

Other approaches calculate arguments' scores / statuses without relying on the notion of extension [1,12]. Unlike our approach, semantics (e.g., stable, preferred) are not used at all. Here, we suppose the use of an (arbitrary) semantics to calculate extensions and then point out a way to augment the number of arguments which are accepted. Our criteria are orthogonal to the notion of semantics, so that each criterion can be combined with each semantics.

Another related work is [10] which addresses the problem of defining more prudent inference relations for Dung's argumentation frameworks (i.e., the objective is to derive less arguments). Contrariwise to the present paper, instead of selecting some extensions or defining a new inference policy, the approach consists in strengthening the usual (direct) conflict-freeness property to indirect conflict-freenesss. Thus a prudent extension cannot contain two arguments when there exists an indirect attack among the first one and the second one. When the credulous policy and the preferred semantics (or the stable semantics) are considered, the set of derivable arguments from prudent extensions is included in the set of arguments derivable from the standard extensions.

Baroni et al. [3] show how to define some fine-grained argument justification statuses for abstract argumentation frameworks. For extension-based semantics, the justification status of an argument basically depends on the existence of extensions containing it and the existence of extensions attacking it. Clearly enough, the problem of selecting extensions is orthogonal to the problem of defining argument justification statuses; thus, Baroni's et al. results can be exploited as soon as some extensions exist, even if they come from a selection process. Our notion of supported inference is closer to their proposal since it induces an intermediate argument status, supported acceptance, between sceptical acceptance and credulous acceptance. However, the mechanisms at work for defining this intermediate status and its rationale are quite different from those considered in Baroni's et al. paper: in our work, the support of an argument is based on the number of extensions containing it.

Our approach also departs from the work by Dunne et el. [17] which focusses on ideal semantics. Indeed, ideal acceptance is more demanding than sceptical acceptance. As such, it proves useful when sceptical acceptance is not prudent enough, i.e. when unexpected arguments are sceptically accepted. Contrastingly, our work is motivated by the remaining cases, when sceptical inference is too cautious and discards some expected arguments.

Caminada and Wu [23] defined different labelling-based justification statuses of arguments. Indeed, they propose to attach to each argument the set of its possible labels (i.e. the collection of all labels it obtains in all complete labellings). Whereas Dung-based approach allows to split the arguments into three classes (sceptically accepted, credulously accepted, rejected), their contribution provides a way for fine-graded classification, by defining six different justification statuses: $\{\mathtt{in}\}$, $\{\mathtt{in},\mathtt{undec}\}$, $\{\mathtt{undec}\}$, $\{\mathtt{in},\mathtt{out},\mathtt{undec}\}$, $\{\mathtt{out},\mathtt{undec}\}$ and $\{\mathtt{out}\}$. The work of Caminada and Wu is related to our work since it could also be used to reason in cases when there are no (or when there are not enough) accepted arguments. However, the actual way to do it is drastically different from our approach.

References

1. Amgoud, L., Ben-Naim, J.: Ranking-based semantics for argumentation frameworks. In: Liu, W., Subrahmanian, V.S., Wijsen, J. (eds.) SUM 2013. LNCS, vol. 8078, pp. 134–147. Springer, Heidelberg (2013)
2. Amgoud, L., Vesic, S.: Rich preference-based argumentation frameworks. Int. J. Approximate Reasoning **55**, 585–606 (2014)
3. Baroni, P., Caminada, M., Giacomin, M.: An introduction to argumentation semantics. Knowl. Eng. Rev. **26**(4), 365–410 (2011)
4. Baroni, P., Giacomin, M.: On principle-based evaluation of extension-based argumentation semantics. Artif. Intell. J. **171**, 675–700 (2007)
5. Benferhat, S., Cayrol, C., Dubois, D., Lang, J., Prade, H.: Inconsistency management and prioritized syntax-based entailment. In: Proceedings of the International Joint Conference on Artificial Intelligence (IJCAI 1993), pp. 640–647 (1993)
6. Brams, S.J., Fishburn, P.C.: Voting procedures. In: Kenneth, A.K.S., Arrow, J., Suzumura, K. (eds.) Handbook of Social Choice and Welfare. Handbook of Social Choice and Welfare, vol. 1, pp. 173–236. Elsevier, Amsterdam (2002)
7. Caminada, M.: Semi-stable semantics. In: Proceedings of the 1st International Conference on Computational Models of Argument (COMMA 2006), pp. 121–130 (2006)
8. Cayrol, C., Devred, C., Lagasquie-Schiex, M.-C.: Acceptability semantics accounting for strength of attacks in argumentation. In: Proceedings of the European Conference on Artificial Intelligence (ECAI 2010), pp. 995–996 (2010)
9. Cayrol, C., Lagasquie-Schiex, M.-C.: Graduality in argumentation. J. Artif. Intell. Res. **23**, 245–297 (2005)
10. Coste-Marquis, S., Devred, C., Marquis, P.: Prudent semantics for argumentation frameworks. In: 17th IEEE International Conference on Tools with Artificial Intelligence (ICTAI 2005), pp. 568–572 (2005)
11. Coste-Marquis, S., Konieczny, S., Marquis, P., Ouali, M.A.: Selecting extensions in weighted argumentation frameworks. In: Proceedings of the 4th International Conference on Computational Models of Argument (COMMA 2012), pp. 342–349 (2012)
12. da Costa Pereira, C., Tettamanzi, A., Villata, S.: Changing one's mind: erase or rewind? In: Proceedings of the International Joint Conference on Artificial Intelligence (IJCAI 2011), pp. 164–171 (2011)

13. Dubois, D., Fargier, H., Prade, H.: Refinements of the maximin approach to decision-making in fuzzy environment. Fuzzy Sets Syst. **81**, 103–122 (1996)
14. Dung, P., Mancarella, P., Toni, F.: Computing ideal skeptical argumentation. Artif. Intell. J. **171**, 642–674 (2007)
15. Dung, P.M.: On the acceptability of arguments and its fundamental role in non-monotonic reasoning, logic programming and n-person games. Artif. Intell. J. **77**, 321–357 (1995)
16. Dunne, P., Hunter, A., McBurney, P., Parsons, S., Wooldridge, M.: Weighted argument systems: basic definitions, algorithms, and complexity results. Artif. Intell. J. **175**(2), 457–486 (2011)
17. Dunne, P.E., Dvořák, W., Woltran, S.: Parametric properties of ideal semantics. Artif. Intell. J. **202**, 1–28 (2013)
18. Dvořák, W.: On the complexity of computing the justification status of an argument. In: Modgil, S., Oren, N., Toni, F. (eds.) TAFA 2011. LNCS, vol. 7132, pp. 32–49. Springer, Heidelberg (2012)
19. Konieczny, S., Marquis, P., Vesic, S.: On supported inference and extension selection in abstract argumentation frameworks. Technical report, CRIL, CNRS - Univ. Artois (2015)
20. Martínez, D., García, A., Simari, G.: Strong and weak forms of abstract argument defense. In: Proceedings of the 2nd International Conference on Computational Models of Argument (COMMA 2008), pp. 216–227. IOS Press (2008)
21. Martínez, D.C., García, A., Simari, G.: An abstract argumentation framework with varied-strength attacks. In: Proceedings of the 11th International Conference on Principles of Knowledge Representation and Reasoning (KR 2008), pp. 135–144 (2008)
22. Moulin, H.: Axioms of Cooperative Decision Making. Cambridge University Press, New York (1988)
23. Wu, Y., Caminada, M.: A labelling-based justification status of arguments. Stud. Logic **3**(4), 12–29 (2010)

Representing and Reasoning About Arguments Mined from Texts and Dialogues

Leila Amgoud[1]([✉]), Philippe Besnard[1], and Anthony Hunter[2]

[1] CNRS, IRIT, Université de Toulouse, Toulouse, France
amgoud@irit.fr
[2] University College London, London, U.K.

Abstract. This paper presents a target language for representing arguments mined from natural language. The key features are the connection between possible reasons and possible claims and recursive embedding of such connections. Given a base of these arguments and counterarguments mined from texts or dialogues, we want be able combine them, deconstruct them, and to analyse them (for instance to check whether the set is inconsistent). To address these needs, we propose a formal language for representing reasons and claims, and a framework for inferencing with the arguments and counterarguments in this formal language.

1 Introduction

There is growing interest in the computational linguistics community in identifying arguments and relations between them in natural language (see for example [1–3]). Consider also the First ACL Workshop on Argument Mining held in 2014 [4], and the IBM Debating Technologies being developed by IBM Research for extracting arguments from sources such as Wikipedia [5,6].

An interesting challenge that is arising from attempts to mine arguments (seen as *reasons* about *claims*) is the choice of target formalism for representing the extracted arguments. In computational models of argument, abstract argumentation (as proposed by Dung [7]) and logical or structured argumentation (as proposed in [8–11]) are the two key options. Neither is ideal as a target formalism as we outline below.

Abstract Argumentation: Each argument is atomic. Thus, as a target language, it is quite weak since there is no formal differentiation of reason and claim. A ramification of this is that there can be no recursive embedding (e.g. reasons for the claim *"x is a reason for claim y"* cannot be represented in abstract argumentation). Also, it does not allow for Boolean combinations of reasons like *"x or y is a reason for z"*. In addition, it does not differentiate between i) *"x being a reason for not claiming y"* and ii) *"x not being a reason for claiming y"*. Introducing a support relation partly addresses some shortcomings of abstract argumentation, but not the ones mentioned above. Note that the notion of a supporting argument is not necessarily the same as the notion of a reason.

© Springer International Publishing Switzerland 2015
S. Destercke and T. Denoeux (Eds.): ECSQARU 2015, LNAI 9161, pp. 60–71, 2015.
DOI: 10.1007/978-3-319-20807-7_6

Logical Argumentation: Each argument is a set of formulae entailing a claim. As a target language, its expressiveness does not fit with the above needs. Firstly, all the logical formulae for the premises and claims need to be identified. It is currently not feasible to aim for translating argumentation in text and dialogues into logical formulae such that all the premises are represented explicitly and the claim follows logically from the premises. One great challenge for this is that most arguments in text and dialogues are *enthymemes*. That is, some or all of the premises are *implicit*, and even the claim may be implicit. For more on computational modelling of enthymemes, see [12]. Logical argumentation is also insufficient because it does not capture embedded relationships (like *"(x is not a reason for y) is a reason for z"*) nor does it explicitly capture *"x is not a reason for claim y"* or *"x is a reason for not claiming y"*. So, as a target language, logical argumentation captures details that cannot be extracted in the short term by argument mining and it lacks some features potentially valuable for argument mining.

Our proposal here is partly motivated by the need for a better formalism for representing argumentation coming from natural language. There is a second motivation. Given a set of arguments and counterarguments represented in our target language, we can infer further arguments and counterarguments. This is not possible with abstract argument since it has no inference machinery over argument graphs. This is also not possible directly with logical argumentation. Given logical arguments A_1 and A_2, we cannot infer a new logical argument A_3 (other than by extracting the support in each argument and using that as a knowledge base for generating further logical arguments).

To address these, we propose a formal language for representing reasons and claims, as well as a framework for inferring with arguments and counterarguments in this language. The implied arguments will be deconstructions, e.g. obtained by flattening the recursive structure in an argument, and constructions obtained by combining arguments. This framework is flexible in that different choices for inference rules can be made.

2   Formal Syntax

We now present our formalism for representing arguments, inspired by Apothéloz [13]. The formalism is built upon a propositional language $\mathbb{L}$ with the connectives $\neg$, $\vee$, $\wedge$, $\rightarrow$, $\leftrightarrow$. There are also two operators $\mathcal{R}(.)$ and $\mathcal{C}(.)$ and an additional negation $-$. Thus, two negation operators are needed: $\neg$ for denying propositional formulas ($\neg x$ denotes that x is false), and $-$ for denying $\mathcal{R}(.)$ and $\mathcal{C}(.)$. Please note that $\neg\neg x$ is identified with x and $--\mathcal{R}(.)$ is identified with $\mathcal{R}(.)$ (similarly, $--\mathcal{C}(.)$ is identified with $\mathcal{C}(.)$).

Definition 1 (Formula). The set of formulas L_A is the smallest set such that a *formula* is of the form $(-)\mathcal{R}(y) : (-)\mathcal{C}(x)$ where each of x and y is *either* a formula of $\mathbb{L}$ *or* is itself a formula.

Each formula is either an argument or a rejection of an argument, to be defined next.

Definition 2 (Argument). An *argument* is a formula of L_A of the form $\mathcal{R}(y) : (-)\mathcal{C}(x)$.

An *argument* is a reason for concluding a claim. It has two main parts: *premises* (the reason) and a *conclusion*. The functions $\mathcal{R}$ and $\mathcal{C}$ respectively play the roles of *giving reason* and *concluding*. Indeed, an argument is interpreted as follows: its conclusion holds *because* it follows, according to a given notion, from the premises. The notion refers to the nature of the link between them (e.g., the premises imply the conclusion), formally identified by the colon in the definition. However, the contents may be true while the functions do not hold and vice versa. The intuitive reading is as follows:

$$\mathcal{R}(y) : \mathcal{C}(x) \text{ means that "} y \text{ is a reason for concluding } x \text{"}$$
$$\mathcal{R}(y) : -\mathcal{C}(x) \text{ means that "} y \text{ is a reason for not concluding } x \text{"}$$

The first kind of expression captures two forms of argument about a proposition x: One in which x is supported ($\mathcal{R}(y) : \mathcal{C}(x)$) and one in which its negation is supported ($\mathcal{R}(y) : \mathcal{C}(\neg x)$). As to the expression $\mathcal{R}(y) : -\mathcal{C}(x)$, it encompasses two cases:

- the case where y is a reason for concluding $\neg x$;
- the case that y does not support $\neg x$ but still does not support x either.

Example 1. *In the dialogue next, Mary's argument supports $\neg fe$, a claim opposing Paul's but John's argument is only meant to* stop concluding fe *without committing to $\neg fe$.*

Paul: Carl will fail his exams (fe). He did not work hard ($\neg wh$). $\mathcal{R}(\neg wh) : \mathcal{C}(fe)$
Mary: No, he will not fail. The exams will be easy (ee). $\mathcal{R}(ee) : \mathcal{C}(\neg fe)$
John: Carl is very smart! (sm). $\mathcal{R}(sm) : -\mathcal{C}(fe)$

Unlike existing definitions of argument where a conclusion x follows from premises y using a notion of *derivation* [8], Definition 2 does not make the link explicit. We aim at a general definition that allows us to represent any argument in text or dialogue, e.g. enthymemes [12], without judging whether it is a good argument. Also, reasons can be hypothetical (assumed for the purpose of the argument). And our approach is meant to capture links of whatever nature including non-deductive links as in the causal argument

Ice on its wings (iw) could cause a plane to crash (pc). $\mathcal{R}(iw) : \mathcal{C}(pc)$

or abductive links as in the following argument:

Tim and Jack have recently had a row that ended their friendship (x). Clara just saw them jogging together (y). Thus, they are friends again (z). $\mathcal{R}(x \wedge y) : \mathcal{C}(z)$

So far, the negation operator "$-$" has been used to deny the concluding function. Now, the function of *giving reason* can be denied as well by placing "$-$" in front of $\mathcal{R}$. What is denied in this case is not the premises but rather the idea that the premises justify the conclusion of the argument. Such a form is called *rejection* of argument.

Definition 3 (Rejection). A *rejection of an argument* is a formula of L_A of the form $-\mathcal{R}(y) : (-)\mathcal{C}(x)$.

The intuitive meaning for these formal expressions is as follows:

$-\mathcal{R}(y) : \mathcal{C}(x)$ means that "y is not a reason for concluding x"
$-\mathcal{R}(y) : -\mathcal{C}(x)$ means that "y is not a reason for not concluding x"

Example 2. *Consider the following dialogue.*

Eric: *The fact that Carl is smart is not a reason to stop concluding that he will fail his exams.* $\qquad -\mathcal{R}(sm) : -\mathcal{C}(fe)$

John: *Anyway, the fact that Carl did not work hard is not a reason to conclude that he will fail his exams.* $\qquad -\mathcal{R}(\neg wh) : \mathcal{C}(fe)$

Ann: *Being stressed is the reason that Carl will fail his exams, hence it is not the fact that he did not work hard (st).* $\mathcal{R}(\mathcal{R}(st) : \mathcal{C}(fe)) : \mathcal{C}(-\mathcal{R}(\neg wh) : \mathcal{C}(fe))$

Sara: *He is not stressed at all.* $\qquad \mathcal{R}(\neg st) : \mathcal{C}(-\mathcal{R}(st) : \mathcal{C}(fe))$

There can be many reasons for rejecting an argument $\mathcal{R}(y) : \mathcal{C}(x)$ as illustrated next:

1. y is true but is *irrelevant* to x.
   The fact that the weather is cloudy *(wcl)* is no reason to conclude that Carl will fail his exams. $\qquad -\mathcal{R}(wcl) : \mathcal{C}(fe)$
2. y is true, relevant to x but *not sufficient* to explain x.
   Paul: You should buy the same car as mine *(bc)*. It's fast *(f)*. $\mathcal{R}(f) : \mathcal{C}(bc)$
   John: If it's affordable! *(a)*. $\qquad \mathcal{R}(\mathcal{R}(f \wedge a) : \mathcal{C}(bc)) : \mathcal{C}(-\mathcal{R}(f) : \mathcal{C}(bc))$
3. y is false, thus y cannot be a reason for x.
   Sara's argument is an example.
4. y and x are both true but y is not the reason for x (there is a better reason for x).
   Ann's argument is an example.

Forms 1-3 of rejection amount to blocking the conclusion of the targeted argument. They give rise to arguments whose reason justifies rejecting the targeted argument and whose conclusion inhibits the conclusion of the targeted argument: Eric's rejection leads to $\mathcal{R}(-\mathcal{R}(sm) : -\mathcal{C}(fe)) : \mathcal{C}(fe)$ and John's to $\mathcal{R}(-\mathcal{R}(\neg wh) : \mathcal{C}(fe)) : -\mathcal{C}(fe)$. As to form 4, the reason and conclusion of the targeted argument are acknowledged. Such a rejection is less of a counterargument than a better argument for the conclusion.

No other logic-based approach to modelling argumentation provides a language for expressing rejection of arguments in the object language. This gives a more appropriate encoding of situations and allows us to differentiate between say $-\mathcal{R}(cr) : \mathcal{C}(bc)$ and $\mathcal{R}(cr) : -\mathcal{C}(bc)$ (let cr denote "*The car is red*" and bc denote "*We should buy the car*").

■ $-\mathcal{R}(cr) : \mathcal{C}(bc)$ could represent a rejection of the argument $\mathcal{R}(cr) : \mathcal{C}(bc)$ as we need to consider more than the colour of the car when choosing whether to buy it.

■ $\mathcal{R}(cr) : -\mathcal{C}(bc)$ could represent a rejection of $\mathcal{R}(cr) : \mathcal{C}(bc)$ because we do not like the colour red for a car.

Even if we identify the rejection $-\mathcal{R}(cr) : \mathcal{C}(bc)$, it is possible that we could identify another argument for buying the car using other criteria such as $\mathcal{R}(ec \wedge sp) : \mathcal{C}(bc)$ where ec denotes *"The car is economical"* and sp denotes *"The car is spacious"*.

3   Representing Mined Arguments

Our approach first aims at representing mined arguments. We want to use our language to represent arguments as they arise in natural language texts and dialogues. We believe that central to handling texts and dialogues is the need to provide support for nested arguments and rejections. To illustrate some of the richness of our approach, we give in Table 1 various forms (F_1-F_{12}) of arguments and rejections allowed by our definitions (x, y, z, t are propositional formulas to simplify matters). The table is not exhaustive.

In our approach, we are not identifying what constitutes a good argument (or a good rejection of an argument). Rather, we are providing a representation of arguments (and rejections thereof). If an argument or rejection occurs in a text or dialogue, then we want it to be mined, and we want to be able to represent it in our language.

A list of arguments below shows that all the forms F_i can be used as a target for natural language. It indicates how to use our language, rather than suggesting that there is a canonical translation of text in to the formal target language. As with translating a natural language sentence in to any logic, there is some subjectivity in how a sentence is exactly translated, depending on various factors.

F_1: Tweety can fly (f). It is a bird (b). $\mathcal{R}(b) : \mathcal{C}(f)$

Table 1. Forms of argument

Basic arguments	F_1	$\mathcal{R}(y) : \mathcal{C}(x)$
	F_2	$\mathcal{R}(y) : \mathcal{C}(\neg x)$
	F_3	$\mathcal{R}(y) : -\mathcal{C}(x)$
Single-embedding meta-arguments (in reason)	F_4	$\mathcal{R}(\mathcal{R}(z) : \mathcal{C}(y)) : \mathcal{C}(x)$
	F_5	$\mathcal{R}(\mathcal{R}(z) : \mathcal{C}(y)) : \mathcal{C}(\neg x)$
	F_6	$\mathcal{R}(\mathcal{R}(z) : \mathcal{C}(y)) : -\mathcal{C}(x)$
Single-embedding meta-arguments (in conclusion)	F_7	$\mathcal{R}(y) : \mathcal{C}(\mathcal{R}(z) : \mathcal{C}(x))$
	F_8	$\mathcal{R}(y) : \mathcal{C}(-\mathcal{R}(z) : \mathcal{C}(x))$
	F_9	$\mathcal{R}(y) : -\mathcal{C}(\mathcal{R}(z) : \mathcal{C}(x))$
Double-embedding meta-arguments	F_{10}	$\mathcal{R}(\mathcal{R}(z) : \mathcal{C}(y)) : \mathcal{C}(\mathcal{R}(t) : \mathcal{C}(x))$
	F_{11}	$\mathcal{R}(\mathcal{R}(z) : \mathcal{C}(y)) : \mathcal{C}(-\mathcal{R}(t) : \mathcal{C}(x))$
	F_{12}	$\mathcal{R}(\mathcal{R}(z) : \mathcal{C}(y)) : -\mathcal{C}(\mathcal{R}(t) : \mathcal{C}(x))$

F_2: Tweety cannot fly. It is a penguin (p). $\qquad$ $\mathcal{R}(p) : \mathcal{C}(\neg f)$

F_3: Carl is smart. Thus, it is not possible to conclude that he will fail his exams.
$$\mathcal{R}(sm) : -\mathcal{C}(fe)$$

F_4: That Tweety can fly because it is a bird, is a reason to conclude that Tweety has wings (w). $\qquad$ $\mathcal{R}(\mathcal{R}(b) : \mathcal{C}(f)) : \mathcal{C}(w)$

F_5: That Carl will fail his exams because he did not work hard is a reason to conclude that he is not so smart. $\qquad$ $\mathcal{R}(\mathcal{R}(\neg wh) : \mathcal{C}(fe)) : \mathcal{C}(\neg sm)$

F_6: Paul's car is in his job parking lot (pr) because it is broken (br), hence we cannot conclude that Paul is in his office (of). $\quad \mathcal{R}(\mathcal{R}(br) : \mathcal{C}(pr)) : -\mathcal{C}(of)$

F_7: The weather is sunny (su). Thus, rain (ra) will lead to rainbow (rb).
$$\mathcal{R}(su) : \mathcal{C}(\mathcal{R}(ra) : \mathcal{C}(rb))$$

F_8: The fact that Tweety is a penguin is a reason to conclude that being a bird is not a sufficient reason for Tweety being able to fly. $\mathcal{R}(p) : \mathcal{C}(-\mathcal{R}(b) : \mathcal{C}(f))$

F_9: The fact that all European countries have a strong economy (se) is a reason for not concluding that an economic crisis (ec) in Germany is a reason for a declining value of the euro (de). $\qquad$ $\mathcal{R}(se) : -\mathcal{C}(\mathcal{R}(ec) : \mathcal{C}(de))$

F_{10}: CFCs (cfc) cause damage to the ozone layer of the atmosphere (do). Man-made pollution (mp) causes global warming (gw).
$$\mathcal{R}(\mathcal{R}(cfc) : \mathcal{C}(do)) : \mathcal{C}(\mathcal{R}(mp) : \mathcal{C}(gw))$$

F_{11}: Stress is the reason that Carl will fail his exams, hence it is not the fact that he did not work hard (st). $\quad \mathcal{R}(\mathcal{R}(st) : \mathcal{C}(fe)) : \mathcal{C}(-\mathcal{R}(\neg wh) : \mathcal{C}(fe))$

F_{12}: The object looks red (lr). It is illuminated by red light (il). Thus, we cannot conclude that looking red implies the object being indeed red (re).
$$\mathcal{R}(\mathcal{R}(il) : \mathcal{C}(lr)) : -\mathcal{C}(\mathcal{R}(lr) : \mathcal{C}(re))$$

Examples in F_1-F_{12} illustrate that the outer reason and claim can be potentially identified using argument mining techniques, such as based on sentiment analysis techniques (e.g. [14]), text entailment techniques (e.g. [1]), or directly via machine learning techniques (e.g. [6]), and then by recursion, the inner reasons and claims can be identified by argument mining techniques. Thus, the nested structure appears better suited as a target language for arguments as they arise in natural language dialogues and texts.

4 Reasoning Systems

Our approach also aims at reasoning with mined arguments and rejections. We want to find what arguments and rejections follow from them. Note that deriving an argument α does *not* mean that α is accepted. Instead, inferring α means that the argument(s) used while deriving α cannot be held without α also being held. Inference captures *commitment* between arguments. Hence, if a foolish argument is used as a premise then a foolish α may result: If an agent holds a foolish argument, he henceforth commits to some other foolish arguments.

Our approach is to treat a set of arguments and rejections as a set of formulae from which we apply a reasoning system. A consequence operator ⊩ is the least closure of a set of *inference rules* extended with one *meta-rule*. Different reasoning systems can be defined by adopting different choices for the set of inference rules. In this paper, we only have space to introduce one reasoning system (in Sect. 5), but we will also indicate how alternative reasoning systems can be identified.

For the sake of simplicity, the rules are introduced using propositional formulas. However, they *all* hold in the general case. So, the variables x, y, z can be instantiated with propositional formulae, arguments, and rejections of arguments.

Let us introduce the meta-rule. In keeping with the meaning of $-\mathcal{R}(y) : \mathcal{C}(x)$, i.e., y is not a reason for x, which is the negation of the meaning of $\mathcal{R}(y) : \mathcal{C}(x)$, i.e., y is a reason for x, the *meta-rule* expresses that we can reverse any inference rule of the form

$$\frac{\mathcal{R}(y) : \Phi}{-\mathcal{R}(y) : \Psi} \qquad \text{into} \qquad \frac{\mathcal{R}(y) : \Psi}{-\mathcal{R}(y) : \Phi}$$

Of course, the same reversing process takes place whenever "$-$" occurs in front of a leftmost "$\mathcal{R}$" so that, in the general case, an inference rule[1] where $i, j \in \{0, 1\}$

$$\frac{-^{(i)}\mathcal{R}(y) : \Phi}{-^{(j)}\mathcal{R}(y) : \Psi} \qquad \text{can be reversed into} \qquad \frac{-^{(1-j)}\mathcal{R}(y) : \Psi}{-^{(1-i)}\mathcal{R}(y) : \Phi}$$

Now we turn to introducing the inference rules. As a start, consistency of arguments' reasons is a source of inferences (where x is a formula in $\mathbb{L}$).

$$\frac{\mathcal{R}(y) : \mathcal{C}(x)}{-\mathcal{R}(y) : -\mathcal{C}(x)} \qquad \frac{\mathcal{R}(y) : \mathcal{C}(x)}{\mathcal{R}(y) : -\mathcal{C}(\neg x)} \qquad \textbf{(Consistency)}$$

The leftmost rule means that if y is a reason for x then y is not a reason to doubt x. The rightmost rule means that if y is a reason for x then it is also a reason to doubt $\neg x$.

Proposition 1. *The inference rules below are derived from (Consistency) and the meta-rule (where x is a formula in $\mathbb{L}$ in the first, third and fourth inference rules).*

$$\frac{\mathcal{R}(y) : \mathcal{C}(x)}{-\mathcal{R}(y) : \mathcal{C}(\neg x)} \quad \frac{\mathcal{R}(y) : -\mathcal{C}(x)}{-\mathcal{R}(y) : \mathcal{C}(x)} \quad \frac{\mathcal{R}(y) : \mathcal{C}(\neg x)}{\mathcal{R}(y) : -\mathcal{C}(x)} \quad \frac{\mathcal{R}(y) : \mathcal{C}(\neg x)}{-\mathcal{R}(y) : \mathcal{C}(x)}$$

Any reasoning system for our language is to include the meta-rule and the derived rules. In Sect. 5, we consider specific inference rules for an example of a reasoning system.

5 Indicative Reasoning

Indicative reasoning is an example of a reasoning system for our language. We give for this system some simple inference rules that can be used with the meta-rule presented in Sect. 4. We discuss some inference rules that are not part of the set of rules for this example of a reasoning system and give some properties of the consequence relation.

---

[1] $-^{(1)}$ denotes a single occurrence of the hyphen and $-^{(0)}$ the absence of it.

5.1   Inference Rules

The first inference rule for indicative reasoning captures when reasons are interchangeable. This is when x is the reason for y and vice-versa. Hence the next inference rule.

$$\frac{\mathcal{R}(y):\mathcal{C}(x) \quad \mathcal{R}(x):\mathcal{C}(y) \quad \mathcal{R}(y):\mathcal{C}(z)}{\mathcal{R}(x):\mathcal{C}(z)} \qquad \textbf{(Mutual Support)}$$

As an illustration, let x stand for "Paul and Mary are married to each other" and y for "Paul and Mary are in love with each other".

The next rule gathers different reasons for the same conclusion within a single argument where y and z are formulas in $\mathbb{L}$.

$$\frac{\mathcal{R}(y):\mathcal{C}(x) \quad \mathcal{R}(z):\mathcal{C}(x)}{\mathcal{R}(y \vee z):\mathcal{C}(x)} \qquad \textbf{(Or)}$$

Cautious monotonicity means that the reason of an argument can be expanded with any premise it justifies. *Cut* expresses a form of minimality of the reason of an argument.

<table>
<tr><td style="text-align:center">(Cautious Monotonicity)</td><td style="text-align:center">(Cut)</td></tr>
<tr><td style="text-align:center">$\dfrac{\mathcal{R}(y):\mathcal{C}(z) \quad \mathcal{R}(y):\mathcal{C}(x)}{\mathcal{R}(y \wedge z):\mathcal{C}(x)}$</td><td style="text-align:center">$\dfrac{\mathcal{R}(y \wedge z):\mathcal{C}(x) \quad \mathcal{R}(y):\mathcal{C}(z)}{\mathcal{R}(y):\mathcal{C}(x)}$</td></tr>
</table>

The two next rules concern nesting of $\mathcal{R}(.)$ and $\mathcal{C}(.)$. *Exportation* shows how to simplify meta-arguments (where y and z are formulas in $\mathbb{L}$) and *Permutation* shows that for some forms of meta-arguments, permutations of reasons are possible.

<table>
<tr><td style="text-align:center">(Exportation)</td><td style="text-align:center">(Permutation)</td></tr>
<tr><td style="text-align:center">$\dfrac{\mathcal{R}(y):\mathcal{C}(\mathcal{R}(z):\mathcal{C}(x))}{\mathcal{R}(y \wedge z):\mathcal{C}(x)}$</td><td style="text-align:center">$\dfrac{\mathcal{R}(y):\mathcal{C}(\mathcal{R}(z):\mathcal{C}(x))}{\mathcal{R}(z):\mathcal{C}(\mathcal{R}(y):\mathcal{C}(x))}$</td></tr>
</table>

We show that the consequence operator $\Vdash$ defined upon the introduced inference rules is consistent. Indeed, $-\mathcal{R}(y):\mathcal{C}(x)$ cannot be schematically derived from $\mathcal{R}(y):\mathcal{C}(x)$ and that $-\mathcal{R}(y):-\mathcal{C}(x)$ cannot be schematically derived from $\mathcal{R}(y):-\mathcal{C}(x)$. By the inference rules in Property 1, Property 2 actually expresses that neither $\mathcal{R}(y):\mathcal{C}(\neg x)$ nor $\mathcal{R}(y):-\mathcal{C}(x)$ can be schematically derived from $\mathcal{R}(y):\mathcal{C}(x)$.

Proposition 2. *There is no $i,j \in \{0,1\}$ s.t. the following is a derived inference rule.*

$$\frac{-^{(i)}\mathcal{R}(y):-^{(j)}\mathcal{C}(x)}{-^{(1-i)}\mathcal{R}(y):-^{(j)}\mathcal{C}(x)}$$

5.2   Non-Inference

We turn to inference rules that are excluded from our example of a reasoning system. We explain why they are excluded but some of these could be in an alternative system.

Proposition 3. *Neither the (Reflexivity) axiom, i.e., $\mathcal{R}(x) : \mathcal{C}(x)$ for all $x \in \mathbb{L}$, nor the following rules hold in indicative reasoning.*

(Logical Consequence)

$$\frac{y \models x}{\mathcal{R}(y) : \mathcal{C}(x)}$$

(Left Logical Equivalence)

$$\frac{\mathcal{R}(y) : \mathcal{C}(x) \qquad \models y \leftrightarrow z}{\mathcal{R}(z) : \mathcal{C}(x)}$$

(Left Logical Consequence)

$$\frac{\mathcal{R}(y) : \mathcal{C}(x) \qquad z \models y}{\mathcal{R}(z) : \mathcal{C}(x)}$$

(Right Logical Consequence)

$$\frac{\mathcal{R}(y) : \mathcal{C}(x) \qquad x \models z}{\mathcal{R}(y) : \mathcal{C}(z)}$$

(Transitivity)

$$\frac{\mathcal{R}(z) : \mathcal{C}(y) \qquad \mathcal{R}(y) : \mathcal{C}(x)}{\mathcal{R}(z) : \mathcal{C}(x)}$$

(And)

$$\frac{\mathcal{R}(y) : \mathcal{C}(x) \qquad \mathcal{R}(y) : \mathcal{C}(z)}{\mathcal{R}(y) : \mathcal{C}(x \wedge z)}$$

Reflexivity is omitted because it seems unlikely that in full generality x be a reason for x, e.g., not when the link is causality. Hence *Logical Consequence* is inhibited as well. Indeed, being a reason for x is far *more restrictive* than having x as logical consequence. Here is an illustration. By classical logic, taking x to stand for "if I am in London then I am in England" while taking y to be $\neg z$ where z stands for "if I am in England then I am in Paris" yields $\neg z \models x$. However, $\neg z$ falls short of being a reason for x.

We refrain from adopting *Right Logical Consequence* in indicative reasoning again on the grounds that being a reason for x is in general far more restrictive than having x as a logical consequence. Indeed, the *nature* of the link plays an important role. E.g., consider the causal argument: flu is a reason for your body temperature to be in the range $39°\,\mathrm{C}-41°\,\mathrm{C}$. The fact that being in the range $36°\,\mathrm{C}-41°\,\mathrm{C}$ is a logical consequence of being in the range $39°\,\mathrm{C}-41°\,\mathrm{C}$ does not make flu a reason for your body temperature to be in the range $36°\,\mathrm{C}-41°\,\mathrm{C}$ (it is the only possible range unless you are dead!).

And cannot be adopted either for indicative reasoning. Consider the case where y, x and z stand respectively for "Paul is standing in the middle of the road while a car is approaching", "Paul should move forward", and "Paul should move back".

Transitivity does not hold either for indicative reasoning. Back to the F_6 example, the fact that Paul's car is broken does not support the conclusion "Paul is in his office".

In indicative reasoning, blocking a reason is different from blocking a conclusion:

(a) $\mathcal{R}(y) : -\mathcal{C}(\mathcal{R}(z) : \mathcal{C}(x))$ does not imply $\mathcal{R}(y) : -\mathcal{C}(x)$
(b) $\mathcal{R}(y) : -\mathcal{C}(x)$ does not imply $\mathcal{R}(y) : -\mathcal{C}(\mathcal{R}(z) : \mathcal{C}(x))$

Argument 1: *The fact that several European countries have a good economy (ge) is a reason for not concluding that an economic crisis (ec) in Spain is a reason for a declining value of the euro (de).*

Argument 1 has the form $\mathcal{R}(ge) : -\mathcal{C}(\mathcal{R}(ec) : \mathcal{C}(de))$ and illustrates case (a) because $\mathcal{R}(ge) : -\mathcal{C}(de)$ needs not hold since an economic crisis in Germany may lead to a declining value of the euro.

Argument 2: *The fact that Carl did not attend at all the course (ac) is a reason for him failing his exams.*

That Argument 2, formally captured as $\mathcal{R}(\neg ac) : \mathcal{C}(fe)$, is doubted on the grounds that Carl is smart can be written $\mathcal{R}(sm) : -\mathcal{C}(\mathcal{R}(\neg ac) : \mathcal{C}(fe))$. However, the latter argument needs not hold even in the presence of $\mathcal{R}(sm) : -\mathcal{C}(fe)$ (Carl being smart is a reason not to conclude him failing his exams) because $\neg ac$ is *more specific* than sm.

We insist that the indicative reasoning system we present here is only one option for a reasoning system with our approach. By giving this system, we also want to question the appropriateness of some simple inference rules that most notions of logic would adhere to. In particular, we suggest that reasoning with arguments needs not use the same inference rules as non-monotonic reasoning (cf e.g. Kraus *et al.* [15]). For instance, we may choose to set up a system such as the indicative reasoning system, that fails reflexivity (i.e. we do not accept that statement x is automatically a reason for claim x).

5.3   Consequence Relation

When $\Vdash$ is the smallest inference relation obeying the rules from Sect. 5.1, reflexivity, monotonicity and cut hold, meaning that with the $\Vdash$ consequence relation, manipulation of arguments by the inference rules is *well-founded*, in the logic tradition [16]. Indeed:

Proposition 4. *Let Δ be a set of (rejections of) arguments. Let α, and β be arguments.*

$$\Delta \Vdash \alpha \text{ if } \alpha \in \Delta \qquad\qquad \textbf{(Reflexivity)}$$
$$\Delta \cup \{\alpha\} \Vdash \beta \text{ if } \Delta \Vdash \beta \qquad\qquad \textbf{(Monotonicity)}$$
$$\Delta \Vdash \beta \text{ if } \Delta \cup \{\alpha\} \Vdash \beta \text{ and } \Delta \Vdash \alpha \qquad \textbf{(Cut)}$$

Also, the $\Vdash$ consequence relation is *paraconsistent* in the sense that it is not trivialized by contradiction (i.e., not all formulae of the language L_A follow from contradiction).

Proposition 5. $\{-^{(i)}\mathcal{R}(y) : -^{(j)}\mathcal{C}(x), -^{(1-i)}\mathcal{R}(y) : -^{(j)}\mathcal{C}(x)\} \nVdash L_A$.

$\Vdash$ is monotonic but involves a non-monotonic operator in its object language: $\mathcal{R}$. "being a reason" is a non-monotonic relation $\vDash$ as witnessed by transitivity failing (it can be that y is generally a reason for x although there are special cases where this fails). As an aside, please note that Mutual Support is a special instance of Transitivity. Anyway, the fact that $\mid\sim$ is formalized as an operator in our formalism makes the non-monotonicity confined to failure of inferring $\mathcal{R}(y \wedge z) : \mathcal{C}(x)$ from $\mathcal{R}(y) : \mathcal{C}(x)$. There is no effect on the logic. The case is similar to conditional logics (they *are* monotonic) because an operator capturing a counterfactual conditional must be *non*-monotonic: e.g., "were I to scratch this match, it would ignite" denoted $y \rightarrowtail x$ may hold while "were I to scratch this match, that is wet, it would ignite" denoted $y \wedge z \rightarrowtail x$ fails to hold.

6   Conclusion

We propose a logic for representing and reasoning about arguments in a way that is just not possible with existing formalisms. We think that the formalism is a promising target language for argument mining and that if we obtain arguments (and rejections of arguments) by argument mining, we can use our inference machinery to analyse them.

Our formalism captures arguments and rejections thereof, with definitions encompassing different roles of reasons (concluding and blocking statements), various forms of reasons (factual and hypothetical) and different kinds of links (deductive, abductive, inductive, . . .). Unlike existing computational models of argumentation where attack (support) between arguments is expressed by external relations on the set of arguments, any attack (support) can be expressed as an argument in our formalism.

Many well-known logics were first proposed as proof systems. For these logics, semantics were only obtained later. We have identified an alternative reasoning system (that preserves more of the classical inference rules such as reflexivity) with a three valued semantics. An exciting challenge is to identify a semantics for indicative reasoning. Future research includes exploring the space of reasoning systems, semantics for them, and investigating Boolean combinations of arguments (and rejections thereof).

References

1. Cabrio, E., Villata, S.: Generating abstract arguments: a natural language approach. In: Proceedings of the 4th Conference on Computational Models of Argument (COMMA'12), pp. 454–461. IOS Press (2012)
2. Florou, E., Konstantopoulos, S., Koukourikos, A., Karampiperis, P.: Argument extraction for supporting public policy formulation. In: Proceedings of the 7th Workshop on Language Technology for Cultural Heritage, Social Sciences, and Humanities, pp. 49–54. ACL (2013)
3. Peldszus, A., Stede, M.: From argument diagrams to argumentation mining in texts: a survey. Int. J. Cogn. Inf. Nat. Intell. **7**(1), 1–31 (2013)
4. Green, N., Ashley, K., Litman, D., Reed, C., Walker, V. (eds.).: Proceedings of the First ACL Workshop on Argumentation Mining (2014)
5. Aharoni, E., Polnarov, A., Lavee, T., Hershcovich, D., Levy, R., Rinott, R., Gutfreund, D., Slonim, N.: A benchmark dataset for automatic detection of claims and evidence in the context of controversial topics. In: Proceedings of the ACL Workshop on Argumentation Mining (2014)

6. Levy, R., Bilu, Y., Hershcovich, D., Aharoni, E., Slonim, N.: Context dependent claim detection. In: Proceedings of the 25th International Conference Computational Linguistics (COLING) (2014)
7. Dung, P.M.: On the acceptability of arguments and its fundamental role in nonmonotonic reasoning, logic programming and n-person games. Artific. Intelligence **77**, 321–357 (1995)
8. Besnard, P., Hunter, A.: Elements of Argumentation. MIT Press, Cambridge (2008)
9. Bondarenko, A., Dung, P., Kowalski, R., Toni, F.: An abstract, argumentation-theoretic approach to default reasoning. Artif. Intell. **93**, 63–101 (1997)
10. García, A., Simari, G.: Defeasible logic programming: an argumentative approach. Theory Pract. Logic Program. **4**(1–2), 95–138 (2004)
11. Prakken, H.: An abstract framework for argumentation with structured arguments. Argument Comput. **5**(1), 1–31 (2010)
12. Black, E., Hunter, A.: A relevance-theoretic framework for constructing and deconstructing enthymemes. J. Logic Comput. **22**(1), 55–78 (2012)
13. Apothéloz, D.: The function of negation in argumentation. J. Pragmatics **19**, 23–38 (1993)
14. Wang, L., Cardie, C.: Improving agreement and disagreement identification in online discussions with a socially-tuned sentiment lexicon. In: Proceedings of the ACL Workshop on Computational Approaches to Subjectivity, Sentiment and Social Media Analysis (2014)
15. Kraus, S., Lehmann, S., Magidor, D.: Nonmonotonic reasoning, preferential models and cumulative logics. Artif. Intell. **44**, 167–207 (1990)
16. Tarski, A.: Logic, Semantics, Metamathematics. Oxford University Press, Oxford (1956). Traslated by (Woodger., J. H)

Dialogue Games for Argumentation Frameworks with Necessities

Farid Nouioua[1]([⊠]) and Sara Boutouhami[2]

[1] LSIS - UMR CNRS 6168, Aix-Marseille University, Marseille, France
farid.nouioua@lsis.org
[2] RIIMA Lab, USTHB, Bab Ezzouar, Algeria
s_boutouhami@yahoo.fr

Abstract. In this paper, we present a generalization of dialectical proof procedures to argumentation frameworks with necessities, a bipolar generalization of Dung argumentation framework where the support relation has the meaning of necessity (an argument is necessary for another one). We show how to extend the existing approach by accommodating the new support relation. We consider in this paper dialectical proof procedures for acceptability under grounded semantics and credulous acceptability under preferred semantics.

Keywords: Dialogue games · Abstract argumentation · Argumentation frameworks with necessities · Preferred semantics · Grounded semantics

1 Introduction

Argumentation has become a central issue in artificial intelligence (AI) (see e.g. [1,19]). One of the very influential models of argumentation in AI is that of Dung abstract argumentation frameworks (AFs) [12]. This approach has been extensively studied and extended in different directions. One of the reasons of this popularity is undoubtedly its simplicity: an argumentation system consists on a set of abstract arguments and a binary attack relation between arguments. Indeed, this model does not assume any particular structure of arguments and focuses rather on their interaction. Hence, its use as a reasoning tool on concrete knowledge bases (KBs), requires first an instanciation step that constructs arguments from the KB. A number of works have been done in this direction and have pointed out the advantages and the limits of this model in dealing with logical KBs (see e.g. [2,13]) and with KBs expressed as logic programs [7].

In this paper, we stay at the abstract level, i.e., at the granularity level where the available model gives an abstraction of knowledge by means of arguments and their interactions. In this context, a main question is to find methods to compute extensions (sets of arguments that are collectively accepted) under a given semantics. Labeling algorithms (see e.g. [14]) brings answers to this question for Dung AFs. Another question is to decide whether a particular argument is accepted (skeptically or credulously) under a given semantics. Dialogue games give answers

© Springer International Publishing Switzerland 2015
S. Destercke and T. Denoeux (Eds.): ECSQARU 2015, LNAI 9161, pp. 72–82, 2015.
DOI: 10.1007/978-3-319-20807-7_7

to this question. A dialogue game takes place between two protagonists: *PRO* who is in favor of the considered argument and *OPP* who is against it. The rules of the game imposed to each protagonist depends on the used acceptability semantics. Dialogue games have been proposed for Dung AFs (see e.g. [6,14]) but also for other approaches extending Dung AFs (see e.g. [8,11]).

One of the numerous directions in extending Dung AFs is to represent positive interactions (supports) between arguments in addition to negative interactions (attacks) (see [3,5,9,10,18]). In a previous work [15], we have presented a proposal in this context that extends Dung AFs by incorporating a support relation having the specific meaning of necessity (an argument is necessary for another one). Thanks to the specific meaning given to the support relation, it was possible to generalize various results developed for Dung AFs to the case of AFs with necessities (AFNs), including: preferences handling [4,16], labeling algorithms [17] and relationships with logic programs [15].

In the continuation of this research line, we propose in this paper dialogue games for AFNs. Our objective is to extend the existing approach so that to accommodate the necessity relation. The key idea in this accommodation is to let a protagonist of a dialogue game able to take into account the necessity relation in challenging his adversary: in addition to answering to an argument by putting one of its attackers (this is the only possible way in the case of Dung AFs), a protagonist can also challenge his adversary by asking him to prove the acceptability of its necessary arguments. Besides, extensions of AFNs under any acceptability semantics are constrained to not contain any cycle of necessities (for more details, see [17]). The proposed dialogue games incorporate this constraint by restricting the dispute lines to those that do not involve necessity cycles.

The structure of the paper is as follows. In Sect. 2, we recall AFNs and their acceptability semantics. Section 3 presents general notions of dialogue games adapted to AFNs. In Sects. 4 and 5 we present dialogue games in AFNs for acceptability under grounded semantics and credulous acceptability under preferred semantics. In Sect. 6 we conclude the paper and give some perspectives for future work.

2 Preliminaries

2.1 Dung AFs

An AF [12] is a pair $\mathcal{H} = \langle \mathcal{A}, \mathcal{R} \rangle$ where $\mathcal{A}$ is a set of arguments and $\mathcal{R}$ is a binary attack relation on $\mathcal{A}$. A subset $\mathcal{E} \subseteq \mathcal{A}$ is conflict-free if there are no $a, b \in \mathcal{E}$ such that $a\mathcal{R}b$, $\mathcal{E}$ defends a if for each $b \in \mathcal{A}$, if $b\mathcal{R}a$ then $\exists c \in \mathcal{E}$ s.t. $c\mathcal{R}b$ and $\mathcal{E}$ is an admissible set if it is conflict-free and defends all its elements. We denote by $\mathcal{E}^+$ the set of arguments attacked by $\mathcal{E}$: $\mathcal{E}^+ = \{a \mid \exists b \in \mathcal{E} \text{ s.t. } b\mathcal{R}a\}$.

Several acceptability semantics have been defined for an AF. Let $\mathcal{H} = \langle \mathcal{A}, \mathcal{R} \rangle$ be an AF and $\mathcal{E} \subseteq \mathcal{A}$. $\mathcal{E}$ is a complete extension of $\mathcal{H}$ iff it is admissible and contains any argument it defends. $\mathcal{E}$ is a grounded extension of $\mathcal{H}$ iff it is the $\subseteq$-minimal complete extension. $\mathcal{E}$ is a preferred extension of $\mathcal{H}$ iff it is a $\subseteq$-maximal complete extension. $\mathcal{E}$ is a stable extension of $\mathcal{E}$ iff $\mathcal{E}$ is a compete extension that attacks any argument outside it (i.e., $\mathcal{E}^+ = \mathcal{A} \setminus \mathcal{E}$). Finally, $\mathcal{E}$ is a semi-stable extension iff $\mathcal{E}$ is a complete extension that maximizes $\mathcal{E} \cup \mathcal{E}^+$ (wrt. set inclusion).

2.2   AFs with Necessities

AFNs [15] are a kind of bipolar AFs that extend Dung AFs by considering, in addition to the attack relation, a support relation to represent positive interactions between arguments. In AFNs the support relation has the particular meaning of necessity.

Definition 1. *An AFN is defined by $\mathcal{G} = \langle \mathcal{A}, \mathcal{R}, \mathcal{N} \rangle$ where $\mathcal{A}$ is a set of arguments, $\mathcal{R} \subseteq \mathcal{A} \times \mathcal{A}$ is an attack relation and $\mathcal{N} \subseteq 2^{\mathcal{A}} \times \mathcal{A}$ is a necessity relation. $\mathcal{R}$ is interpreted exactly as in Dung AFs: $a\mathcal{R}b$ means that if a is accepted then b is not accepted. The new relation $\mathcal{N}$ is interpreted in a dual way as follows: For $E \subseteq \mathcal{A}$ and $b \in \mathcal{A}$, $E\mathcal{N}b$ means that if no argument of E is accepted then b is not accepted (the acceptance of at least one argument of E is necessary for the acceptance of b).*

Now, let us recall the concept of coherence of a subset of arguments. Intuitively, in a coherent subset $\mathcal{E}$, every argument is provided by enough arguments that satisfy its necessities and no deadlock due to necessity cycles is present. This is satisfied if for every argument $a \in \mathcal{E}$, we can construct a sequence of arguments of $\mathcal{E}$ such that: the first one does not require any subset of arguments, the last one is a and if an argument b of a sequence requires a subset of arguments, then at least one of the arguments of this subset precedes b in the sequence.

Definition 2. *Let $\mathcal{G} = \langle \mathcal{A}, \mathcal{R}, \mathcal{N} \rangle$ be an AFN and $\mathcal{E} \subseteq \mathcal{A}$. An argument a is powerful in $\mathcal{E}$ iff $a \in \mathcal{E}$ and there is a sequence $a_0, \ldots, a_k$ of arguments in $\mathcal{E}$ such that $a_k = a$, there is no $E \subseteq \mathcal{A}$ s.t. $E\mathcal{N}a_0$ and for $1 \leq i \leq k$: for each $E \subseteq \mathcal{A}$ s.t. $E\mathcal{N}a_i$, $E \cap \{a_0, \ldots, a_{i-1}\} \neq \emptyset$. $\mathcal{E}$ is coherent iff every $a \in \mathcal{E}$ is powerful in $\mathcal{E}$. Finally, $\mathcal{E}$ is strongly coherent iff $\mathcal{E}$ is coherent and conflict-free.*

Strong coherence plays in AFNs the same role of conflict-freeness in Dung AFs as a minimal requirement for any extension under any acceptability semantics.

The acceptability semantics defined on Dung AFs have been generalized to AFNs (see [15]). Besides, The labeling characterization of these semantics proposed for Dung AFs (see e.g. [14]) has been generalized in [17] to AFNs. In this paper, we are interested in two acceptability semantics: the grounded and the preferred semantics. We use the labeling approach to define them.

Let $\mathcal{G} = \langle \mathcal{A}, \mathcal{R}, \mathcal{N} \rangle$ be an AFN. A labelling is a function $\mathcal{L} : \mathcal{A} \longrightarrow \{in, out, undec\}$. We put $in(\mathcal{L}) = \{a \in \mathcal{A} | \mathcal{L}(a) = in\}$, $out(\mathcal{L}) = \{a \in \mathcal{A} | \mathcal{L}(a) = out\}$ and $undec(\mathcal{L}) = \{a \in \mathcal{A} | \mathcal{L}(a) = undec\}$. We write a labelling $\mathcal{L}$ as a triplet $(in(\mathcal{L}), out(\mathcal{L}), undec(\mathcal{L}))$. The notion of legal label is generalized in AFNs as follows [17].

Definition 3. *Let a be an argument and $\mathcal{L}$ be a labelling.*

– *a is legally in iff a is labelled in and the two following conditions hold: (1)
$\forall b \in \mathcal{A}$, if $b\mathcal{R}a$ then $b \in out(\mathcal{L})$ (all attackers of a are labelled out) and
(2) $\forall E \subseteq \mathcal{A}$, if $E\mathcal{N}a$ then $E \cap in(\mathcal{L}) \neq \emptyset$ (at least one argument from each
necessary set for a is labelled in).*
– *a is legally out iff a is labelled out and at least one of the two following
conditions holds: either (1) $\exists b \in \mathcal{A}$ s.t. $b\mathcal{R}a$ and $b \in in(\mathcal{L})$ (at least one
attacker of a is labelled in) or (2) $\exists E \subseteq \mathcal{A}$, s.t. $E\mathcal{N}a$ and $E \subseteq out(\mathcal{L})$ (all the
arguments of at least one necessary set for a are labelled out).*
– *a is legally undec iff a is labelled undec and the three following conditions hold:
(1) $\forall b \in \mathcal{A}$, if $b\mathcal{R}a$ then $b \notin in(\mathcal{L})$ (no attacker of a is labelled in), (2) $\forall E \subseteq \mathcal{A}$,
if $E\mathcal{N}a$ then $E \not\subseteq out(\mathcal{L})$ (not all the arguments of any necessary set for a
are labelled out) and (3) either $\exists b \in \mathcal{A}$ s.t. $b\mathcal{R}a$ and $b \notin out(\mathcal{L})$ or $\exists E \subseteq \mathcal{A}$
s.t. $E\mathcal{N}a$ and $E \cap in(\mathcal{L}) = \emptyset$ (either at least one attacker of a is not labelled
out or at least one necessary set for a does not contain any argument that is
labelled in).*

Notice that for $\mathcal{N} = \emptyset$, we find exactly the original definitions of legal labels
given in [14]. In addition to legality of labels, the presence of $\mathcal{N}$ imposes two
further constraints. Any argument which is not powerful in $\mathcal{A}$ does not belong
to any extension and must be labelled *out* and since each extension $\mathcal{E}$ under any
semantics must be coherent, the set of *in* arguments of any labelling characterizing any extension of an AFN must be coherent. Labellings that satisfy these
constraints are called *safe* labellings.

Definition 4. *We say that a labelling $\mathcal{L}$ is safe iff the set $in(\mathcal{L})$ is coherent and
for each $a \in \mathcal{A}$, if a is not powerful in $\mathcal{A}$ then $a \in out(\mathcal{L})$.*

Definition 5. *A labelling $\mathcal{L}$ is: complete iff $\mathcal{L}$ is safe and without any illegally
in, illegally out or illegally undec arguments; grounded iff $\mathcal{L}$ is complete and
$in(\mathcal{L})$ is $\subseteq$-minimal and preferred iff $\mathcal{L}$ is complete and $in(\mathcal{L})$ is $\subseteq$-maximal.*

In Dung AFs (i.e. AFNs where $\mathcal{N} = \emptyset$), any set of arguments is coherent and thus
any labeling is safe. In this case, we obtain exactly the classical definitions for
legally *in, out* and *undec* arguments and for the different kinds of labellings. The
relationship between labellings and acceptability semantics for AFNs is given as
follows.

Proposition 1. *$\mathcal{E}$ is a complete (resp. grounded, preferred) extension iff there
is a complete (resp. grounded, preferred) labelling $\mathcal{L}$ such that $\mathcal{E} = in(\mathcal{L})$.*

Example 1. *Let us consider the three AFNs $\mathcal{G}_i = \langle \mathcal{A}_i, \mathcal{R}_i, \mathcal{N}_i \rangle$ $(1 \leq i \leq 3)$
such that: $\mathcal{A}_1 = \mathcal{A}_2 = \mathcal{A}_3 = \{a, b, c, d\}$, $\mathcal{R}_1 = \mathcal{R}_2 = \{(c, d)\}$, $\mathcal{R}_3 =
\{(c, a), (b, d)\}$, $\mathcal{N}_1 = \{(\{a, b\}, c), (c, a), (c, b)\}$, $\mathcal{N}_2 = \{(\{a, b\}, c), (c, a)\}$ and
$\mathcal{N}_3 = \{(\{a\}, b), (\{d\}, c)\}$. Figure 1 depicts the three AFNs where attacks (resp.
necessities) are represented by continuous (resp. dashed) arcs.*
  *The only complete labelling of $\mathcal{G}_1$ is $\mathcal{L} = (\{d\}, \{a, b, c\}, \emptyset)$. It is also its
grounded and preferred labelling. The only complete labelling of $\mathcal{G}_2$ is $\mathcal{L}' =
(\{a, b, c\}, \{d\}, \emptyset)$. It is also its grounded and preferred labelling. $\mathcal{G}_3$ has three*

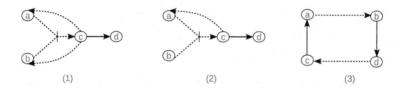

Fig. 1. Three examples of AFNs

complete labellings : $\mathcal{L}_1 = (\emptyset, \emptyset, \{a, b, c, d\})$, $\mathcal{L}_2 = (\{a, b\}, \{c, d\}, \emptyset)$ *and* $\mathcal{L}_3 = (\{c, d\}, \{a, b\}, \emptyset)$. $\mathcal{L}_1$ *is the grounded labelling of* $\mathcal{G}_3$ *and both* $\mathcal{L}_2$ *and* $\mathcal{L}_3$ *are its preferred labellings.*

3   Dialogue Games for AFNs

A dialogue game for an argument takes place between a protagonist *PRO* who defends the argument and a protagonist *OPP* who is against it. The legal moves that each protagonist is allowed to play depends on the considered acceptability semantics and acceptability criteria (skeptical, i.e., membership in all extensions; or credulous, i.e. membership in at least one extension). In AFNs, when a protagonist puts an argument a, the other protagonist may have two ways to challenge him. The first way (which is the only way used for Dung AFs) is to put an attacker of a. The second way is to put a subset E which is necessary for a. The idea of this move is to ask the other protagonist to prove the acceptability of at least one element of E. To answer this last challenge, any element of E may be put. This leads to the following definition of a dispute tree:

Definition 6. *Let* $\mathcal{G} = \langle \mathcal{A}, \mathcal{R}, \mathcal{N} \rangle$ *be an AFN, and let* $a \in \mathcal{A}$. *The dispute tree induced by* a *in* $\mathcal{G}$ *is a tree* $\mathcal{T}$ *having* a *as a root node, a node of* $\mathcal{T}$ *is either an argument or a subset of arguments* $E \subseteq \mathcal{A}$. *Let* x *be a node of* $\mathcal{T}$ *then:*

- *If* $x \in \mathcal{A}$, y *is a child of* x *iff:* $(y \in \mathcal{A} \text{ and } y\mathcal{R}x)$ *or* $(y = E, E \subseteq \mathcal{A} \text{ and } E\mathcal{N}x)$.
- *If* x *is a subset* E, y *is a child of* x *iff* $y \in E$.

Every branch in the tree is called a *dispute*. As extensions must not contain cycles of necessities, we are interested only in disputes that do not include such cycles.

Definition 7. *Let* $\mathcal{G} = \langle \mathcal{A}, \mathcal{R}, \mathcal{N} \rangle$ *be an AFN, let* $a \in \mathcal{A}$, $\mathcal{T}$ *the dispute tree induced by* a *in* $\mathcal{G}$ *and* d *a dispute of* $\mathcal{T}$. *The dispute* d *is said to be acyclic iff it does not involve a cycle constituted only from necessity links, i.e., d does not contain any sub-sequence of the form:* $a_1, E_1, \ldots, a_n, E_n, a_{n+1}$ *where* $a_i \in \mathcal{A}$ *for* $1 \le i \le n+1$, $E_j \subseteq \mathcal{A}$ *for* $1 \le j \le n$ *and* $a_1 = a_{n+1}$. *The acyclic dispute tree induced by* a *is the dispute tree induced by* a *and restricted to acyclic disputes.*

Now, we are ready to introduce the key notion of *winning strategy* in the case of AFNs. Intuitively, a winning strategy tells to *PRO* the move that he has to play against any move of *OPP* in order to guarantee that it will eventually win.

Definition 8. *Let* $\mathcal{G} = \langle \mathcal{A}, \mathcal{R}, \mathcal{N} \rangle$, $\mathcal{T}$ *the dispute tree induced by a in* $\mathcal{G}$, *and* $\mathcal{T}'$ *a sub-tree of* $\mathcal{T}$. $\mathcal{T}'$ *is a winning strategy for a iff:*

1. *The set* $D_{\mathcal{T}'}$ *of disputes in* $\mathcal{T}'$ *is a non-empty finite set such that each dispute* $d \in D_{\mathcal{T}'}$ *is finite and is won by PRO (terminates in a move played by PRO).*
2. $\forall d \in D_{\mathcal{T}'}, \forall d'$ *such that* d' *is some sub-dispute[1] of d whose last move is played by PRO, if this last move is:*
   - *an argument* x *then, for any* y *such that* $y\mathcal{R}x$ *(resp. E such that* $E\mathcal{N}x$*), there is* $d'' \in D_{\mathcal{T}'}$ *s.t.* $d' - y$ *(resp.* $d' - E$*)[2] is a sub-dispute of* d''*;*
   - *a subset of arguments E then, for any* y *such that* $y \in E$*, there is a* $d'' \in D_{\mathcal{T}'}$ *such that* $d' - y$ *is a sub-dispute of* d''*.*

The last notion we need is that of legal move function. It expresses the rules that a protagonist have to respect in playing any move.

Definition 9. *Let* $\mathcal{G} = \langle \mathcal{A}, \mathcal{R}, \mathcal{N} \rangle$, $\mathcal{T}$ *the dispute tree induced by a in* $\mathcal{G}$. *Let* $D_{\mathcal{T}}$ *be the set of all disputes in* $\mathcal{T}$. *Then a legal move function is a function* ϕ *such that* $\phi : D_{\mathcal{T}} \to 2^{\mathcal{A}} \cup 2^{\Gamma}$ *where* $\Gamma = \{E \mid E \subseteq \mathcal{A}\}$.

For a legal move function ϕ, we call ϕ-*winning strategy*, any winning strategy in the tree restricted to disputes where all moves are those given by the function ϕ.

Example 1 (Cont). Figure 2 depicts the dispute trees induced by the three AFNs of Example 1. The barred arcs in Fig. 2-(1) and (2) are those that introduce cycles of necessities. Such arcs are absent in Fig. 2-(3) since the system $\mathcal{G}_3$ has no cycle of necessities.

4 Dialogue Game for Grounded Semantics

We consider in this section a dialogue game for acceptability under grounded semantics. Since any AFN has a unique grounded extension, it does not makes sense to distinguish between skeptical and credulous criteria. In words, the only restriction made by the legal move function on *OPP* is to prevent him to put an argument that creates a cyclic dispute. Whereas, In addition to this same limitation, *PRO* is also constrained to not repeat any argument that is previously put in the current dispute.

Definition 10. *Given,* $\mathcal{G} = \langle \mathcal{A}, \mathcal{R}, \mathcal{N} \rangle$*, let d be a dispute s.t. x is the last move in d and PRO(d) be the arguments moved by PRO in d. Then,* ϕ_{G_1} *is a legal move function s.t.:*

- *If d is of odd length (next move is by OPP) then,*

---

[1] A sub-dispute of d is any subsequence of d starting with the same initial argument as d.

[2] If d is a dispute and x is an argument or a subset of arguments, then $d - x$ denotes the dispute which results from the continuation of d by x.

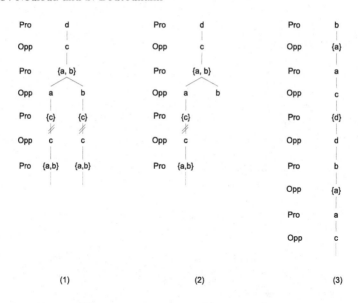

Fig. 2. Dispute trees of our examples

- if $x \in \mathcal{A}$, $\phi_{G_1}(d) = \{E \mid E \subseteq \mathcal{A} \text{ and } E\mathcal{N}x\} \cup \{y \mid y\mathcal{R}x \text{ and } d-y \text{ is acyclic}\}$;
- if $x = E$, $\phi_{G_1}(d) = \{y \mid y \in E \text{ and } d-y \text{ is acyclic}\}$.
- If d is of even length (next move is by PRO) then,
  - if $x \in \mathcal{A}$, $\phi_{G_1}(d) = \{E \mid E \subseteq \mathcal{A} \text{ and } E\mathcal{N}x\} \cup \{y \mid y\mathcal{R}x, d-y \text{ is acyclic and } y \notin PRO(d)\}$;
  - if $x = E$, $\phi_{G_1}(d) = \{y \mid y \in E, \ d-y \text{ is acyclic and } y \notin PRO(d)\}$.

ϕ_{G_1} captures the arguments accepted under grounded semantics in an AFN.

Theorem 1. *Let* $\mathcal{G} = \langle \mathcal{A}, \mathcal{R}, \mathcal{N} \rangle$ *be a finite AFN. Then, there exists a* ϕ_{G_1}*-winning strategy* T' *for* x *such that the set* $PRO(T')$ *of arguments moved by PRO in* T' *is conflict-free, iff* x *is in the grounded extension of* $\mathcal{G}$.

As in the case of Dung AFs, the proof procedure may be shortened by introducing two additional constraints in *PRO*'s moves.

- If the last move of *OPP* is an argument x, then it is useless that *PRO* moves against it an argument y such that $x\mathcal{R}y$. Indeed, in this case, it suffices to *OPP* to move x again and *PRO* can no more repeat the move of y.
- Since the *PRO*'s arguments must be conflict-free in the winning strategy, one can forbid *PRO* to move any argument which is in conflict with its precedent arguments. For a sub-dispute d, the set of forbidden arguments for *PRO* is defined by $Forb(d) = \{y \mid (y\mathcal{R}y) \text{ or } \exists z \in PRO(d) \text{ s.t. } (z\mathcal{R}y) \text{ or } (y\mathcal{R}z)\}$

Let ϕ_{G_2} be the winning strategy obtained by adding these two restrictions to ϕ_{G_1}. Then we have the following result:

Theorem 2. *Let* $\mathcal{G} = \langle \mathcal{A}, \mathcal{R}, \mathcal{N} \rangle$ *be a finite AFN. Then, there exists a* ϕ_{G_2}*-winning strategy* T' *for* x *iff* x *is in the grounded extension of* $\mathcal{G}$.

Example 1 (Cont). Figure 3-(1) (resp. 3-(2), 3-(3)) depicts the dispute tree of $\mathcal{G}_1$ (resp. $\mathcal{G}_2$, $\mathcal{G}_3$) induced by d (resp. d, b) and using ϕ_{G_2} (or ϕ_{G_1}) as legal move function.

In the dispute tree for $\mathcal{G}_1$ (Fig. 3-(1)), the two disputes are won by *PRO*. Indeed, in both disputes, the only possible next move of *OPP* which is c is forbidden since it leads to a cyclic dispute. The dispute tree itself is a ϕ_{G_2}-winning strategy for d. Thus, d belongs to the grounded extension of $\mathcal{G}_1$.

This same situation holds for $\mathcal{G}_2$ (Fig. 3-(2)) for the dispute $d - c - \{a, b\} - a - \{c\}$ won by *PRO*. However, the second dispute $d - c - \{a, b\} - b$ is won by *OPP*. Indeed, *PRO* cannot challenge b because b has neither attackers nor necessary subsets of arguments. There is no ϕ_{G_2}-winning strategy for d. Thus, d does not belong to the grounded extension of $\mathcal{G}_2$.

The dispute tree for $\mathcal{G}_3$ (Fig. 3-(3)) has one dispute which is won by *OPP*. In this dispute, the only possible next move of *PRO* which is b is forbidden since *PRO* has already moved it. There is no ϕ_{G_2}-winning strategy for b. Thus b does not belong to the grounded extension of $\mathcal{G}_3$.

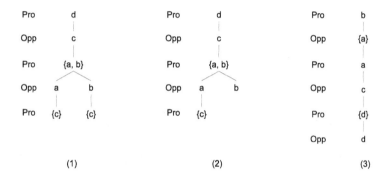

Fig. 3. ϕ_{G_2} dispute trees of our examples

5 Dialogue Games for Preferred Semantics

Now, let us turn to credulous acceptability under preferred semantics. Recall that an argument is credulously accepted under preferred semantics if it belongs to at least one preferred extension. It turns out that the credulous acceptability under preferred semantics corresponds roughly to inverting the roles of *PRO* and *OPP* in the dialogue game of grounded semantics. More precisely, *PRO* can repeat his arguments but he is restricted to arguments that do not create conflicts or cyclic disputes. Whereas, *OPP* is prohibited from repeating any argument he previously put in the current dispute or playing moves that create cyclic disputes. This is the corresponding legal move function.

Definition 11. *Given $\mathcal{G} = \langle \mathcal{A}, \mathcal{R}, \mathcal{N} \rangle$, let d be a dispute s.t. x is the last move in d and $OPP(d)$ be the arguments moved by OPP in d. Then, ϕ_{PC} is a legal move function s.t.:*

- If d is of odd length (next move is by OPP) then,
  - if $x \in \mathcal{A}$ then $\phi_{PC}(d) = \{E \mid E \subseteq \mathcal{A} \text{ and } E\mathcal{N}x\} \cup \{y \mid y\mathcal{R}x,\ d-y \text{ is acyclic and } y \notin OPP(d)\}$;
  - if $x = E$ then $\phi_{PC}(d) = \{y \mid y \in E,\ d-y \text{ is acyclic and } y \notin OPP(d)\}$.
- If d is of even length (next move is by PRO) then,
  - if $x \in \mathcal{A}$ then $\phi_{PC}(d) = \{E \mid E \subseteq \mathcal{A} \text{ and } E\mathcal{N}x\} \cup \{y \mid y\mathcal{R}x,\ d-y \text{ is acyclic and } y \notin Forb(d)\}$;
  - if $x = E$ then $\phi_{PC}(d) = \{y \mid y \in E,\ d-y \text{ is acyclic and } y \notin Forb(d)\}$.

This legal move function captures exactly the arguments credulously accepted under preferred semantics in an AFN.

Theorem 3. *Let $\mathcal{G} = \langle \mathcal{A}, \mathcal{R}, \mathcal{N} \rangle$ be a finite AFN. Then, there exists a ϕ_{PC}-winning strategy T' for x iff x is in an admissible (and hence preferred) extension of $\mathcal{G}$.*

Example 1 (Cont). Figure 4-(1) (resp. 4-(2), 4-(3)) depicts the dispute tree of $\mathcal{G}_1$ (resp. $\mathcal{G}_2$, $\mathcal{G}_3$) induced by d (resp. d, b) and using ϕ_{PC} as legal move function.

In the dispute tree for $\mathcal{G}_1$ (Fig. 4-(1)), the two disputes are won by PRO. Indeed, in both disputes, the only possible next move of OPP which is c is forbidden since it leads to a cyclic dispute. The dispute tree itself is a ϕ_{PC}-winning strategy for d. Thus d belongs to a preferred extension of $\mathcal{G}_1$. This same situation holds for $\mathcal{G}_2$ (Fig. 4-(2)) for the dispute $d - c - \{a, b\} - a - \{c\}$ won by PRO. However, the second dispute $d - c - \{a, b\} - b$ is won by OPP. Indeed, PRO cannot challenge b because b has neither attackers nor necessary subsets of arguments. There is no ϕ_{PC}-winning strategy for d. Thus d does not belong to any preferred extension of $\mathcal{G}_2$. The dispute tree for $\mathcal{G}_3$ (Fig. 4-(3)) has one dispute won by PRO. In this dispute, the only possible next move of OPP which is c is forbidden since OPP has already moved it. There is a ϕ_{PC}-winning strategy for b (the dispute tree itself). Thus, b is in a preferred extension of $\mathcal{G}_3$.

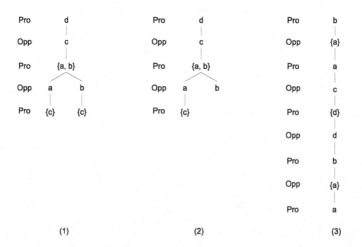

(1)   (2)   (3)

Fig. 4. ϕ_{PC} dispute trees of our examples

6 Conclusion

In this paper we presented dialogue games for argumentation frameworks with necessities. We have shown how to take into account the support relation in this dialogues by letting a protagonist (*PRO* or *OPP*) able to use both the attack and the support relations in challenging his adversary. The proposed dialogues for AFNs take into account also the constraint that cycles of necessities are prohibited in any extension.

We have considered in this paper dialogue games for acceptability under grounded semantics and credulous acceptability under preferred semantics. A natural future work is to extend our approach to other acceptability semantics (stable, semi-stable and ideal) for the skeptical and credulous criteria for multi-extensions semantics. Another important perspective is to exploit the link between AFNs and logic programs in order to obtain a complete querying system for abstract argumentation systems and logic programs which is parametrized by the acceptability semantics and the acceptability criteria.

Acknowledgments. This work has received support from the french Agence Nationale de la Recherche, ASPIQ project reference ANR-12-BS02-0003.

References

1. Bench-Capon, T., Dunne, P.: Argumentation in artificial intelligence. Artif. Intell. J. **171**(10–15) (2007)
2. Amgoud, L., Besnard, P.: Logical limits of abstract argumentation frameworks. J. Appl. Non-Class. Logics **23**(3), 229–267 (2013)
3. Boella, G., Gabbay, D.M., Van Der Torre, L., Villata, S.: Support in abstract argumentation. In: COMMA 2010, pp. 40–51. IOS Press (2010)
4. Boudhar, I., Nouioua, F., Risch, V.: Handling preferences in argumentation frameworks with necessities. In: ICAART 2012, pp. 340–345 (2012)
5. Brewka, G., Woltran, S.: Abstract dialectical frameworks. In: KR 2010, pp. 102–111 (2010)
6. Caminada, M.W.A., Wu, Y.: Towards an argument game for stable semantics. In: 8th CMNA Workshop (2008)
7. Caminada, M., Sá, S., Alcântara, J.: On the equivalence between logic programming semantics and argumentation semantics. In: van der Gaag, L.C. (ed.) ECSQARU 2013. LNCS, vol. 7958, pp. 97–108. Springer, Heidelberg (2013)
8. Cayrol, C., Devred, C., Lagasquie-Schiex, M.C.: Dialectical proofs accounting for strength of attacks in argumentation systems. In: ICTAI 2010, pp. 207–214 (2010)
9. Cayrol, C., Lagasquie-Schiex, M.C.: On the acceptability of arguments in bipolar argumentation frameworks. In: Godo, L. (ed.) ECSQARU 2005. LNCS (LNAI), vol. 3571, pp. 378–389. Springer, Heidelberg (2005)
10. Cayrol, C., Lagasquie-Schiex, M.-C.: Coalitions of arguments: a tool for handling bipolar argumentation frameworks. Int. J. Intell. Syst. **25**(1), 83–109 (2010)
11. Devred, C., Doutre, S., Lefèvre, C., Nicolas, P.: Dialectical proofs for constrained argumentation. In: COMMA 2010, pp. 159–170 (2010)

12. Dung, P.M.: On the acceptability of arguments and its fundamental role in non-monotonic reasoning, logic programming and n-person games. Artif. Intell. **77**(2), 321–357 (1995)
13. Gorogiannis, N., Hunter, A.: Instantiating abstract argumentation with classical logic arguments: postulates and properties. Artif. Intell. **175**(9–10), 1479–1497 (2011)
14. Modgil, S., Caminada, M.: Proof theories and algorithms for abstract argumentation frameworks. In: Rahwan, I., Simari, G. (eds.) Argumentation in Artificial Intelligence, pp. 105–129. Springer, Heidelberg (2009)
15. Nouioua, F., Risch, V.: Argumentation frameworks with necessities. In: Benferhat, S., Grant, J. (eds.) SUM 2011. LNCS, vol. 6929, pp. 163–176. Springer, Heidelberg (2011)
16. Nouioua, F.: Generalizing naive and stable semantics in argumentation frameworks with necessities and preferences. In: Hüllermeier, E., Link, S., Fober, T., Seeger, B. (eds.) SUM 2012. LNCS, vol. 7520, pp. 44–57. Springer, Heidelberg (2012)
17. Nouioua, F.: AFs with necessities: further semantics and labelling characterization. In: Liu, W., Subrahmanian, V.S., Wijsen, J. (eds.) SUM 2013. LNCS, vol. 8078, pp. 120–133. Springer, Heidelberg (2013)
18. Oren, N., Norman, T.J.: Semantics for evidence-based argumentation. In: COMMA 2008, pp. 276–284 (2008)
19. Rahwan, I., Simari, G. (eds.): Argumentation in Artificial Intelligence, pp. 105–129. Springer, Heidelberg (2009)

Explaining Bayesian Networks Using Argumentation

Sjoerd T. Timmer[1]([⊠]), John-Jules Ch. Meyer[1], Henry Prakken[1,2],
Silja Renooij[1], and Bart Verheij[3]

[1] Department of Information and Computing Sciences, Utrecht University,
Utrecht, The Netherlands
s.t.timmer@uu.nl
[2] Faculty of Law, University of Groningen, Groningen, The Netherlands
[3] Artificial Intelligence Institute, University of Groningen,
Groningen, The Netherlands

Abstract. Qualitative and quantitative systems to deal with uncertainty coexist. Bayesian networks are a well known tool in probabilistic reasoning. For non-statistical experts, however, Bayesian networks may be hard to interpret. Especially since the inner workings of Bayesian networks are complicated they may appear as black box models. Argumentation models, on the contrary, emphasise the derivation of results. However, they have notorious difficulty dealing with probabilities. In this paper we formalise a two-phase method to extract probabilistically supported arguments from a Bayesian network. First, from a BN we construct a *support graph*, and, second, given a set of observations we build arguments from that support graph. Such arguments can facilitate the correct interpretation and explanation of the evidence modelled in the Bayesian network.

Keywords: Bayesian networks · Argumentation · Reasoning · Explanation · Inference · Uncertainty

1 Introduction

Reasoning about probabilities and statistics, and independence in particular, is a difficult task that easily leads to reasoning errors and miscommunication. For instance in the legal or medical domain the consequences of reasoning errors can be severe. Bayesian networks, which model probability distributions, have found a number of applications in these domains (see [9] for an overview). However, the interpretation of BNs is a difficult task, especially for domain experts who are not trained in probabilistic reasoning. Argumentation is a well studied topic

This work is part of the research programme "Designing and Understanding Forensic Bayesian Networks with Arguments and Scenarios", which is financed by the Netherlands Organisation for Scientific Research (NWO). See http://www.ai.rug.nl/~verheij/nwofs/.

S. Destercke and T. Denoeux (Eds.): ECSQARU 2015, LNAI 9161, pp. 83–92, 2015.
DOI: 10.1007/978-3-319-20807-7_8

in the field of artificial intelligence (see Chap. 11 of [12] for an overview). Argumentation theory provides models that describe how conclusions can be justified. These models closely follow the same reasoning patters present in human reasoning. This makes argumentation an intuitive and versatile model for common sense reasoning tasks. This justifies a scientific interest in models of argumentation that incorporate probabilities. In this paper we formalise a new method to extract arguments from a BN, in which we first extract an intermediate support structure that guides the argument construction process. This results in numerically backed arguments based on probabilistic information modelled in a BN. We apply our method to a legal example but the approach does not depend on this domain and can also be applied to other fields where BNs are used.

In previous work [10] we introduced the notions of probabilistic rules and arguments and an algorithm to extract those from a BN. However, exhaustively enumerating every possible probabilistic rule and argument is computationally infeasible and also not necessary because many of the enumerated antecedents will never be met, and many arguments constructed in this way are superfluous because they argue for irrelevant conclusions. Improving on this work we proposed [11] a new method that solves these issues. We split the process of argument generation into two phases: from the BN we construct a *support graph* at first, from which argument can be generated in a second phase. We introduced an algorithm for the first phase but the second phase has only been described informally. In the current paper we show a number of properties of the support graph formalisms and we fully formalise the argument generation phase.

In Sect. 2 we will present backgrounds on argumentation and BNs. In Sect. 3 we formally define and discuss support graphs. Using the notion of a support graph we present a translation to arguments in Sect. 4. One of the advantages of this method is that the support graph presents a dynamic model of evidence because when observations are added to the BN it does not need to be recomputed. Only the resulting argumentation changes.

2 Preliminaries

2.1 Argumentation

In argumentation theory, one possibility to deal with uncertainty is the use of defeasible inferences. A defeasible (as opposed to strict) rule can have exceptions. In a defeasible rule the antecedents do not conclusively imply the consequence but rather create a presumptive belief in it. Using (possibly defeasible) rules, arguments can be constructed. Figure 1, for instance, shows (on the left) an argument graph with a number of arguments connected by two rules. From a psychological report it is derived that the suspect had a motive and together with a DNA match this is reason to believe that the suspect committed the crime. Different formalisation of such systems exist [5,7,8,14]. In this paper we will construct an argumentation system where the rules follow from the BN. Since a BN captures probabilistic dependencies the inferences will be defeasible. Figure 1 also shows a possible counter-argument. Undercutting and rebutting attacks between arguments with defeasible rules have been distinguished [7]. A rebuttal attacks the conclusion of an argument, whereas an undercutter directly attacks the inference (as in this example). An undercutter exploits the fact that a rule is not strict by posing one of the exceptional circumstances under which it does not apply. Using rebuttals and undercutters, counter-arguments can be formulated. Arguments can be compared on their strengths to see which attacks succeed as defeats. Then Dung's theory of abstract argumentation [1] can be used to evaluate the acceptability status of arguments.

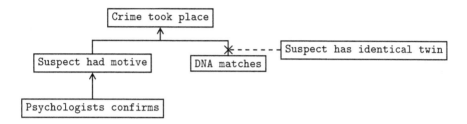

Fig. 1. An example of complex arguments and an undercutting counter-argument.

2.2 Bayesian Networks

A Bayesian network (BN) contains a directed acyclic graph (DAG) in which nodes correspond to stochastic variables. Variables have a number of mutually exclusive and collectively exhaustive outcomes: upon observing the variable, exactly one of the outcomes will become true. Throughout this paper we will consider variables to be binary for simplicity.

Definition 1 (Bayesian Network). *A Bayesian network is a pair $\langle G, P \rangle$ where G is a directed acyclic graph $(\mathbf{V}, \mathbf{E})$, with variables $\mathbf{V}$ as the set of nodes and edges $\mathbf{E}$, and P is a probability function which specifies for every variable V_i the probability of its outcomes conditioned on its parents $Par(V_i)$ in the graph.*

We will use $Cld(V_i)$ and $Par(V_i)$ to denote the sets of children and parents respectively of a variable V_i in a graph. $Cld(\mathbf{V'})$ (and $Par(\mathbf{V'})$) will likewise denote the union of the children (and parents respectively) of variables in a set $\mathbf{V'} \subseteq \mathbf{V}$.

Given a BN, observations can be entered by instantiating variables; this update is then propagated through the network, which yields a posterior probability distribution on all other variables, conditioned on those observations. A BN models a joint probability distribution with independences among its variables implied by d-separation in the DAG [6].

Definition 2 (d-Separation). *A trail in a DAG is a simple path in the underlying undirected graph. A variable is a head-to-head node with respect to a particular trail iff it has two incoming edges on that trail. A variable on a trail blocks that trail iff either (1) it is an unobserved head-to-head node without observed* *descendants, or (2) it is not a head-to-head on that trail and it is observed. A trail is* active *iff none of its variables are blocking it. Subsets of variables* $\mathbf{V}_A$ *and* $\mathbf{V}_B$ *are d-separated by a subset of variables* $\mathbf{V}_C$ *iff there are no active trails from any variable in* $\mathbf{V}_A$ *to any variable in* $\mathbf{V}_B$ *given observations for* $\mathbf{V}_C$.

If, in a given BN model, $\mathbf{V}_A$ and $\mathbf{V}_B$ are d-separated by $\mathbf{V}_C$, then $\mathbf{V}_A$ and $\mathbf{V}_B$ are probabilistically independent given $\mathbf{V}_C$. An example of a BN is shown in Fig. 2. This example concerns a criminal case with five variables describing how the occurrence of the crime correlates with a psychological report and a DNA matching report. The variables `Motive` and `Twin` model the presence of a criminal motive and the existence of an identical twin. The latter can result in a false positive in a DNA matching test. In the following we will also require the notions of a Markov blanket and Markov equivalence [13].

Definition 3 (Markov Blanket). *Given a BN graph, the* Markov blanket $MB(V_i)$ *of a variable* V_i *is the set* $Cld(V_i) \cup Par(V_i) \cup Par(Cld(V_i))$. *I.e., the parents, children and parents of children of* V_i.

Definition 4 (Markov Equivalence). *Given a BN graph, an* immorality *is a tuple* $\langle V_a, V_c, V_b \rangle$ *of variables such that there are directed edges* $V_a V_a \!\!-\!\!\triangleright V_c\, V_c$ *and* $V_b V_b \!\!-\!\!\triangleright V_c\, V_c$ *in the BN graph but no edges* $V_a\, V_a \!\!-\!\!\triangleright V_b\, V_b$ *or* $V_b\, V_b \!\!-\!\!\triangleright V_a\, V_a$. *Given two BN graphs, they are* Markov equivalent *if and only if they have the same underlying undirected graph, and they have the same set of immoralities.*

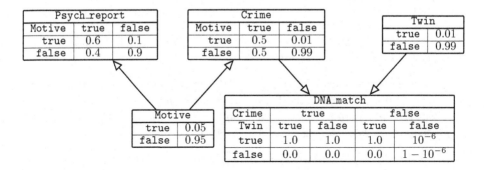

Fig. 2. A small BN concerning a criminal case. The conditional probability distributions are shown as tables inside the nodes of the graph.

3 Support Graphs

We will split the construction of arguments for explaining a BN in two steps. We first construct a support graph from a BN, and subsequently establish arguments from the support graph. In this section we define the support graph and its construction.

Given a BN and a variable of interest $V^\star$, the support graph is a template for generating explanatory arguments. As such, it does not depend on observations of variables but rather models the possible structure of arguments for a particular variable of interest. This means that it can be used to construct an argument for any variable of our choice given any set of evidence, as we will show in the next section. When new evidence becomes available the same support graph can be reused. This means that the support graph should be able to capture the dynamics in d-separation caused by different observations. To enable this, each node in the support graph (which we will refer to as *support nodes* from here on) will be labelled with a *forbidden set* of variables $\mathcal{F}$. Moreover, since one BN variable can be represented more than once in a support graph, a function $\mathcal{V}$ is used to assign a variable to every support node. The support graph can now be constructed recursively. Initially a single support node $N^\star$ is created for which $\mathcal{V}(N^\star) = V^\star$ and $\mathcal{F}(N^\star) = \{V^\star\}$.

Definition 5 (Support Graph). *Given a BN with graph $G = (\mathbf{V}, \mathbf{E})$ and a variable of interest $V^\star$, a support graph is a tuple $\langle \mathcal{G}, \mathcal{V}, \mathcal{F} \rangle$ where $\mathcal{G}$ is a directed graph $(\mathbf{N}, \mathbf{L})$, consisting of nodes $\mathbf{N}$ and edges $\mathbf{L}$, $\mathcal{V} : \mathbf{N} \mapsto \mathbf{V}$ assigns variables to nodes, and $\mathcal{F} : \mathbf{N} \mapsto \mathcal{P}(\mathbf{V})$ assigns sets of variables to each node, such that $\mathcal{G}$ is the smallest graph containing the node $N^\star$ (for which $\mathcal{V}(N^\star) = V^\star$ and $\mathcal{F}(N^\star) = \{V^\star\}$) closed under the following expansion operation:*

Whenever possible, a supporter N_j with variable $\mathcal{V}(N_j) = V_j$ is added as a parent to a node N_i (with $V_i = \mathcal{V}(N_i)$) iff $V_j \in MB(V_i) \setminus \mathcal{F}(N_i)$. The forbidden set $\mathcal{F}(N_j)$ of the new support node is

- $\mathcal{F}(N_i) \cup \{V_j\}$ *if V_j is a parent of V_i*
- $\mathcal{F}(N_i) \cup \{V_j\} \cup \{V_k \in Par(V_j) | \langle V_i, V_j, V_k \rangle \text{ is an immorality}\}$
                                                  if V_j is a child of V_i
- $\mathcal{F}(N_j) \cup \{V_j\} \cup (Cld(V_i) \cap Cld(V_j))$ *otherwise*

If a support node with this forbidden set and the same $\mathcal{V}(N_j)$ already exists, that node is added as the parent of N_i, otherwise a supporting node N_j is created.

To be able to represent d-separation correctly the *forbidden set* of variables assigns to every support node a set of variables that cannot be used in further support for that node. This forbidden set is inherited by supporters such that ancestors in the support graph cannot use variables from $\mathcal{F}$ either. Figure 3 shows the three cases of the forbidden set definition. The forbidden set of a new supporter N_i for variable V_i always includes the variable V_i itself which prevents circular reasoning. In a BN, parents of a common child often exhibit intercausal-interactions (such as explaining away) which means that the effect of one parent on the other is not the same as the combined effect from the parent to the child and then to the other parent. To support a variable V_i with one of its children and then support this child by a parent would incorrectly chain the inferences through a head-to-head node even though an intercausal-interaction is possible. Therefore we forbid the latter step by including any other parents that constitute immoralities in the second case. A reasoning step that uses the inference according to the intercausal-interaction is allowed by the third case.

Now let us consider the example BN from Fig. 2 and take `Crime` as the variable of interest. The initial support graph contains just one node with this

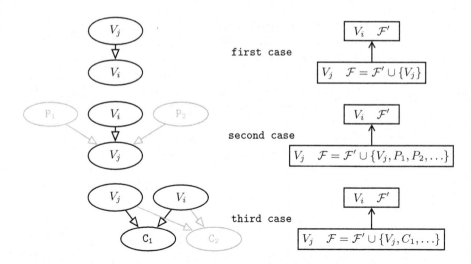

Fig. 3. Visual representation of the three cases in Definition 5. A support node for variable V_i can obtain support in three different ways from a variable V_j, depending on its graphical relation to V_i.

variable and the forbidden set {Crime}. As can be seen in Fig. 4, all of the three cases for $\mathcal{F}$ apply exactly once in this example. The Crime node can be supported by one parent (Motive), one child (DNA_match) and one parent of a child (Twin). In the first case the forbidden set leaves room to support the Motive node even further by adding a node for the Psych_report variable. This graph represents all possible dependencies in the BN model, where the actual dependencies will depend on the instantiation of evidence.

Property 1. Given a BN with $G = (\mathbf{V}, \mathbf{E})$, the constructed support graph contains $\mathcal{O}(|\mathbf{V}| * 2^{|\mathbf{V}|})$ nodes.

Proof (Sketch). Variables can occur multiple times in the support graph but never with the same $\mathcal{F}$ sets (see the definition). This set contains subsets of other variables and therefore $2^{|\mathbf{V}|}$ is a strict upper bound on the number of times any variable can occur in the support graph. The total number of support nodes is therefore limited to $|\mathbf{V}| * 2^{|\mathbf{V}|}$.   □

Property 2. In a given BN with a singly connected graph $G = (\mathbf{V}, \mathbf{E})$, every variable occurs exactly once in the support graph and the size of the support graph is $|\mathbf{V}|$.

Proof (Sketch). A variable can in theory occur multiple times in the support graph, but this only happens when the graph is loopy (multiply connected).   □

Theorem 1. *Given two Markov equivalent BN graphs G and G', and a variable of interest $V^{\star}$, the two resulting support graphs are identical.*

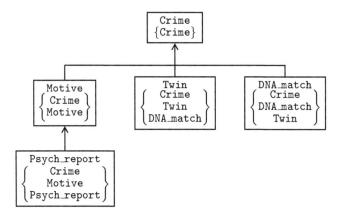

Fig. 4. The support graph corresponding to the example in Fig. 2 with $V^* = $ Crime. For every node N_i we have shown the variable name $\mathcal{V}(N_i)$ togehter with the forbidden set $\mathcal{F}(N_i)$.

Proof (Sketch). Consider the BN graph G and the corresponding support graph. In a Markov equivalent graph G' an arbitrary number of edges may be reversed but not if this would create or remove immoralities. Following the three possible support steps we see that every supporter follows an edge from the skeleton (which stays the same) or an immorality (which also stays the same). What remains to be shown is that the forbidden sets will also be equal. Let us consider the three cases of the $\mathcal{F}$ update from Definition 5 (see also Fig. 3). Suppose that in the support graph of G, N_i for variable V_i is supporting N_j for variable V_j:

- In the first case, reversal of the edge between V_i and V_j would change this to the second case in which variables V_k with an immorality $\langle V_i, V_j, V_k \rangle$ would be added to $\mathcal{F}$. However, since no immoralities are created those variables either do not exist, or the reversal is not allowed by the Markov equivalence.
- In the second case, reversal of any of the incoming edges of V_j is not allowed if V_j is involved in an immorality $\langle V_i, V_j, \_ \rangle$. If that is the case, reversal is allowed and we end up in the first case but the forbidden set will be exactly the same.
- In the third case, there is no immorality between V_i and V_j through any of the shared children because if there were, a direct edge exists and either of the former cases would have taken precedence. None of these edges may therefore be reversed in G'. □

What this theorem shows is that Markov equivalent models are mapped to the same support graph, which means that they will receive the same argumentative explanation. This takes one of the confusing aspects of BNs away, which is that the directions of edges do not have a clear intuitive interpretation.

4   Argument Construction

In previous work we have already shown a method to identify arguments in a BN setting and how they can be enumerated exhaustively [10]. A disadvantage of the exhaustive enumeration of probabilistic rules and rule combinations is the combinatorial explosion of possibilities, even for realistically sized models. Using a support graph can reduce the number of arguments that need to be enumerated because only rules relevant to the conclusion of the argument are considered.

Definition 6 (Bayesian Argument). *An argument A on the basis of a BN, a set of observations $\mathbf{O}$, and the corresponding support graph $\langle \mathcal{G} = (\mathbf{N}, \mathbf{L}), \mathcal{V}, \mathcal{F} \rangle$, is one of the following:*

- *$\langle N, o \rangle$ such that $(\mathcal{V}(N) = o) \in \mathbf{O}$, for which $Obs(A) = \{N = o\}$ or*
- *$\langle N_1, o_1 \rangle, \ldots, \langle N_n, o_n \rangle \Rightarrow \langle N, o \rangle$ such that $N_1, \ldots, N_n$ are parents of N in the support graph, $\langle N_1, o_1 \rangle$ through $\langle N_n, o_n \rangle$ are arguments, and o is the most probable outcome of $\mathcal{V}(N)$ given the observations $Obs(A)$, in which $Obs(A)$ is the union of $Obs(B)$ over subarguments B.*

In this definition $\langle N_1, o_1 \rangle$ through $\langle N_n, o_n \rangle$ are the immediate subarguments of $\langle N_1, o_1 \rangle, \ldots, \langle N_n, o_n \rangle \Rightarrow \langle N, o \rangle$.

Argument attack arises when two arguments assign outcomes to the same variable. We might be tempted to prefer the argument with the highest probability but that could lead to mistakes. For instance, when A, B and C collectively support a conclusion, situations can exist where the highest probability of that conclusion occurs when B is left out. It is, however, usually not acceptable to ignore evidence. The following definition meets this criterion:

Definition 7 (Superseding). *An argument A supersedes another argument B iff $Obs(A) \supseteq Obs(B)$.*

Indeed, we prefer one argument over another iff it includes a superset of evidence. This resembles Pollock's concept of *subproperty defeat of the statistical syllogism* [7]. Superseding can be seen as a special case of undercutting, so attack and defeat follow naturally:

Definition 8 (Undercutting Attack and Defeat). *An argument A undercuts another argument B iff it supersedes B or one of the sub-arguments of B. An undercutting attack always succeeds and therefore A also defeats B.*

It can be shown that this instantiates a special case of the ASPIC+ [5] model of argumentation but a proof of that is omitted for brevity. In this special case rebuttal and undermining are redundant due to the fact that for every rebuttal there is also an undercutter resolving the issue.

An interesting property of this approach is that conflicts between observations are resolved in the probabilistic setting within the argument and that the resolution is mirrored by the defeat relation of the extracted arguments, rather than decided by it. This means that the resulting argumentation system is rather simple which is ideal for a BN explanation method.

If we apply this system to the support graph from our example BN with the observations that `Psych_report=true` and `DNA_match=true`, we obtain (among others) the arguments shown in Fig. 5. The argument on the right is in fact the formal version of the argument that we already showed in Fig. 1. The undercutter from that figure was not extracted because no evidence for a twin was present in the set of observations.

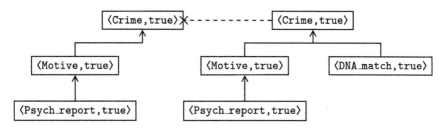

Fig. 5. Arguments resulting from our running example. The argument on the left is superseded by the one on the right. For readability we have only shown conclusions inside the nodes.

Property 3. Given a BN, a variable of interest, the resulting support graph and a set of observations, for every node in the support graph either no argument for this node exists at all, or exactly one of the arguments that exists supersedes all other arguments for the same node without itself being superseded.

Proof (Sketch). Suppose no such un-superseded argument exists, then there must be two arguments A and B that supersede each other, i.e. $\mathrm{Obs}(A) \setminus \mathrm{Obs}(B) \neq \emptyset$ and $\mathrm{Obs}(B) \setminus \mathrm{Obs}(A) \neq \emptyset$. However, in that case an argument C combining the immediate subarguments of A and B also exists that strictly supersedes both A and B.   □

Informally, the argument that includes all possible supporters that have ancestors in **O** will supersede any argument that includes fewer supporters. Since this holds for every node, there is in this argumentation system one unique tree in which every argument is supported by the maximal number of immediate subarguments given what is derivable from the evidence. Together with the fact that the outcome of the argument is based on the probability given the used observations, and that no d-separated paths are used in the argument this exactly mirrors the probabilistic reasoning.

5 Discussion

In this paper we formalised a two-phase argument extraction method. We have shown how support graphs help in the construction of arguments because they capture the argumentative structure that is present in a BN.

Many explanation methods for BNs (see e.g. [3,4]) focus on textual or visual systems. Other work on argument extraction includes that of Keppens [2], who focuses on Argument Diagrams. One advantage of structured argumentation is that counter-arguments can easily be modelled as well. Future research includes how arguments constructed from a BN can be combined with arguments from other sources, since often the available evidence is only partially probabilistic.

References

1. Dung, P.M.: On the acceptability of arguments and its fundamental role in non-monotonic reasoning, logic programming and n-person games. Artif. Intell. **77**, 321–357 (2005)
2. Keppens, J.: Argument diagram extraction from evidential Bayesian networks. Artif. Intell. Law **20**(2), 109–143 (2012)
3. Koiter, J.R.: Visualizing inference in Bayesian networks. Master's thesis, Delft University of Technology (2006)
4. Lacave, C., Díez, F.J.: A review of explanation methods for Bayesian networks. Know. Eng. Rev. **17**(2), 107–127 (2002)
5. Modgil, S., Prakken, H.: A general account of argumentation with preferences. Artif. Intell. **195**, 361–397 (2013)
6. Pearl, J.: Probabilistic Reasoning in Intelligent Systems: Networks of Plausible Inference. Morgan Kaufmann, San Francisco (1988)
7. Pollock, J.L.: Justification and defeat. Artif. Intell. **67**, 377–407 (1994)
8. Simari, G.R., Loui, R.P.: A mathematical treatment of defeasible reasoning and its implementation. Artif. Intell. **53**(2), 125–157 (1992)
9. Taroni, F., Aitken, C., Garbolino, P., Biedermann, A.: Bayesian Networks and Probabilistic Inference in Forensic Science. Wiley, Chichester (2006)
10. Timmer, S.T., Meyer, J.-J.C., Prakken, H., Renooij, S., Verheij, B.: Extracting legal arguments from forensic Bayesian networks. In: Hoekstra, R. (ed.) Legal Knowledge and Information Systems. JURIX 2014: The Twenty-Seventh Annual Conference, vol. 217, pp. 71–80 (2014)
11. Timmer, S.T., Meyer, J.-J.C., Prakken, H., Renooij, S., Verheij, B.: A structure-guided approach to capturing Bayesian reasoning about legal evidence in argumentation. In: Proceedings of the 15th International Conference on AI and Law (2015)
12. van Eemeren, F.H., Garssen, B., Krabbe, E.C.W., Henkemans, A.F.S., Verheij, B., Wagemans, J.H.M.: Handbook of Argumentation Theory. Springer, Dordrecht (2014)
13. Verma, T., Pearl, J.: Equivalence and synthesis of causal models. In: Proceedings of the Sixth Annual Conference on Uncertainty in Artificial Intelligence, UAI 1990, pp. 255–270. Elsevier Science Inc., New York (1991)
14. Vreeswijk, G.A.W.: Abstract argumentation systems. Artif. Intell. **90**(1), 225–279 (1997)

Conditionals

Transitive Reasoning with Imprecise Probabilities

Angelo Gilio[1], Niki Pfeifer[2], and Giuseppe Sanfilippo[3]([✉])

[1] Department SBAI, University of Rome "La Sapienza", Rome, Italy
angelo.gilio@sbai.uniroma1.it
[2] Munich Center for Mathematical Philosophy,
LMU Munich, München, Germany
niki.pfeifer@lmu.de
[3] Department of Mathematics and Computer Science,
University of Palermo, Palermo, Italy
giuseppesanfilippo@gmail.com

Abstract. We study probabilistically informative (weak) versions of transitivity by using suitable definitions of defaults and negated defaults in the setting of coherence and imprecise probabilities. We represent p-consistent sequences of defaults and/or negated defaults by g-coherent imprecise probability assessments on the respective sequences of conditional events. Finally, we present the coherent probability propagation rules for Weak Transitivity and the validity of selected inference patterns by proving p-entailment of the associated knowledge bases.

Keywords: Coherence · Default · Imprecise probability · Knowledge base · P-consistency · P-entailment · Reasoning · Syllogism · Weak transitivity

1 Motivation and Outline

While Transitivity is basic for reasoning, it does not hold in nonmonotonic reasoning systems. Therefore, various patterns of Weak Transitivity were studied in the literature (e.g., [17]). In probabilistic approaches, Transitivity is probabilistically non-informative, i.e., the premise probabilities, $p(C|B), p(B|A)$, do not constrain the probability of the conclusion $p(C|A)$ (for instance, the extension $p(C|A) = z$ of the assessment $p(C|B) = 1, p(B|A) = 1$ is coherent for any $z \in [0, 1]$; see [30,31]). In this paper, we study probabilistically informative versions of Transitivity in the setting of coherence ([4,13,22]). Transitivity has also

N. Pfeifer—Supported by the DFG grants PF 740/2-1 and PF 740/2-2 (both within the DFG Priority Programme SPP1516) and the Alexander von Humboldt-Foundation.

G. Sanfilippo—Supported by the INdAM–GNAMPA Project 2015 and by the FFR 2012-ATE-0585 Project of University of Palermo.

S. Destercke and T. Denoeux (Eds.): ECSQARU 2015, LNAI 9161, pp. 95–105, 2015.
DOI: 10.1007/978-3-319-20807-7_9

been studied in [7, 16]; among other differences, in our approach we use imprecise probabilities in the setting of coherence, where conditioning events may have zero probability.

After introducing some notions of coherence for set-valued probability assessments (Sect. 2), we present probabilistic interpretations of defaults and negated defaults (Sect. 3). We represent a knowledge base by sequence of defaults and/or negated defaults, which we interpret by an imprecise probability assessment on the associated sequence of conditional events. Moreover, we generalize definitions of p-consistency and p-entailment. In Sect. 4 we present the coherent probability propagation rules for Weak Transitivity (Theorems 3 and 4). We then exploit Theorem 3 to demonstrate the validity of selected patterns of (weak) transitive inferences involving defaults and negated defaults by proving p-entailment of the corresponding knowledge bases (Sect. 5).

2   Imprecise Probability Assessments

Given two events E and H, with $H \neq \bot$, the *conditional event* $E|H$ is defined as a three-valued logical entity which is *true* if EH (i.e., $E \wedge H$) is true, *false* if $\neg EH$ is true, and *void* if H is false. Given a finite sequence of $n \geq 1$ conditional events $\mathcal{F} = (E_1|H_1, \ldots, E_n|H_n)$, we denote by $\mathcal{P}$ *any precise* probability assessment $\mathcal{P} = (p_1, \ldots, p_n)$ on $\mathcal{F}$, where $p_j = p(E_j|H_j) \in [0, 1]$, $j = 1, \ldots, n$. Moreover, we denote by Π the set of *all coherent precise* assessments on $\mathcal{F}$. The coherence-based approach to probability has been adopted by many authors (see e.g., [4, 13, 18, 23, 24, 28, 30]); we therefore recall only selected key features of coherence in this paper. We recall that when there are no logical relations among the events $E_1, H_1, \ldots, E_n, H_n$ involved in $\mathcal{F}$, that is $E_1, H_1, \ldots, E_n, H_n$ are logically independent, then the set Π associated with $\mathcal{F}$ is the whole unit hypercube $[0, 1]^n$. If there are logical relations, then the set Π *could be* a strict subset of $[0, 1]^n$. As it is well known, $\Pi \neq \emptyset$; therefore, $\emptyset \neq \Pi \subseteq [0, 1]^n$.

Definition 1. *An* imprecise, *or* set-valued, *assessment $\mathcal{I}$ on a family of conditional events $\mathcal{F}$ is a (possibly empty) set of precise assessments $\mathcal{P}$ on $\mathcal{F}$.*

Definition 1, introduced in [19], states that an *imprecise (probability) assessment* $\mathcal{I}$ on a given family $\mathcal{F}$ of n conditional events is just a (possibly empty) subset of $[0, 1]^n$. Given an imprecise assessment $\mathcal{I}$ we denote by $\mathcal{I}^c$ the *complementary imprecise assessement* of $\mathcal{I}$, i.e. $\mathcal{I}^c = [0, 1]^n \setminus \mathcal{I}$. In what follows, we generalize the notions of g-coherence, coherence, and total-coherence for interval-valued probability assessments (see e.g., [21, Definitions 7a, 7b, 7c, respectively]) to the case of imprecise (in the sense of set-valued) probability assessments.

Definition 2. *Let a sequence of n conditional events $\mathcal{F}$ be given. An imprecise assessment $\mathcal{I} \subseteq [0, 1]^n$ on $\mathcal{F}$ is g-coherent if and only if there exists a coherent precise assessment $\mathcal{P}$ on $\mathcal{F}$ such that $\mathcal{P} \in \mathcal{I}$.*

Definition 3. *Let $\mathcal{I}$ be a subset of $[0, 1]^n$. For each $j \in \{1, 2, \ldots, n\}$, the projection $\rho_j(\mathcal{I})$ of $\mathcal{I}$ onto the j-th coordinate, is defined as*

$$\rho_j(\mathcal{I}) = \{x_j \in [0, 1] : p_j = x_j, \text{ for some } (p_1, \ldots, p_n) \in \mathcal{I}\}.$$

Definition 4. *An imprecise assessment $\mathcal{I}$ on a sequence of n conditionals events $\mathcal{F}$ is* coherent *if and only if, for every $j \in \{1, \ldots, n\}$ and for every $x_j \in \rho_j(\mathcal{I})$, there exists a coherent precise assessment $\mathcal{P} = (p_1, \ldots, p_n)$ on $\mathcal{F}$, such that $\mathcal{P} \in \mathcal{I}$ and $p_j = x_j$.*

Definition 5. *An imprecise assessment $\mathcal{I}$ on $\mathcal{F}$ is* totally coherent *if and only if the following two conditions are satisfied: (i) $\mathcal{I}$ is non-empty; (ii) if $\mathcal{P} \in \mathcal{I}$, then $\mathcal{P}$ is a coherent precise assessment on $\mathcal{F}$ (see [19, Definition 2]).*

Remark 1. We observe that:

$$\mathcal{I} \text{ is g-coherent} \iff \Pi \cap \mathcal{I} \neq \emptyset \iff \forall j \in \{1, \ldots, n\}, \rho_j(\Pi \cap \mathcal{I}) \neq \emptyset;$$
$$\mathcal{I} \text{ is coherent} \iff \forall j \in \{1, \ldots, n\}, \emptyset \neq \rho_j(\Pi \cap \mathcal{I}) = \rho_j(\mathcal{I});$$
$$\mathcal{I} \text{ is totally coherent} \iff \emptyset \neq \Pi \cap \mathcal{I} = \mathcal{I}.$$

Then, the following relations among the different notions of *coherence* hold:
$\mathcal{I}$ totally coherent $\Rightarrow \mathcal{I}$ coherent $\Rightarrow \mathcal{I}$ g-coherent .

Definition 6. *Let $\mathcal{I}$ be a non-empty subset of $[0,1]^n$. For each sub-vector $(j_1, \ldots, j_m)$ of $(1, \ldots, n)$, the projection $\rho_{(j_1, \ldots, j_m)}(\mathcal{I})$ of $\mathcal{I}$ onto the coordinates $(j_1, \ldots, j_m)$, with $1 \leq m \leq n$, is defined as the set $\rho_{(j_1, \ldots, j_m)}(\mathcal{I}) \subseteq [0,1]^m$ such that each vector $(x_{j_1}, \ldots, x_{j_m}) \in \rho_{(j_1, \ldots, j_m)}(\mathcal{I})$ is the sub-vector $(p_{j_1}, \ldots, p_{j_m})$ of some $\mathcal{P} = (p_1, \ldots, p_n) \in \mathcal{I}$.*

Let $\mathcal{I}$ be an imprecise assessment on the sequence $\mathcal{F} = (E_1|H_1, \ldots, E_n|H_n)$; moreover, let $E_{n+1}|H_{n+1}$ be a further conditional event and let $\mathcal{J} \subseteq [0,1]^{n+1}$ be an imprecise assessment on $(\mathcal{F}, E_{n+1}|H_{n+1})$. We say that $\mathcal{J}$ is an *extension* of $\mathcal{I}$ to $(\mathcal{F}, E_{n+1}|H_{n+1})$ if and only if $\rho_{(1, \ldots, n)}(\mathcal{J}) = \mathcal{I}$, that is: (i) for every $(p_1, \ldots, p_n, p_{n+1}) \in \mathcal{J}$, it holds that $(p_1, \ldots, p_n) \in \mathcal{I}$; (ii) for every $(p_1, \ldots, p_n) \in \mathcal{I}$, there exists $p_{n+1} \in [0,1]$ such that $(p_1, \ldots, p_n, p_{n+1}) \in \mathcal{J}$.

Definition 7. *Let $\mathcal{I}$ be a g-coherent assessment on $\mathcal{F} = (E_1|H_1, \ldots, E_n|H_n)$; moreover, let $E_{n+1}|H_{n+1}$ be a further conditional event and let $\mathcal{J}$ be an extension of $\mathcal{I}$ to $(\mathcal{F}, E_{n+1}|H_{n+1})$. We say that $\mathcal{J}$ is a* g-coherent extension *of $\mathcal{I}$ if and only if $\mathcal{J}$ is g-coherent.*

Theorem 1. *Given a g-coherent assessment $\mathcal{I} \subseteq [0,1]^n$ on $\mathcal{F}$, let $E_{n+1}|H_{n+1}$ be a further conditional event. Then, there exists a g-coherent extension $\mathcal{J} \subseteq [0,1]^{n+1}$ of $\mathcal{I}$ to the family $(\mathcal{F}, E_{n+1}|H_{n+1})$.*

Proof. As $\mathcal{I}$ is g-coherent, there exists a coherent precise assessment $\mathcal{P}$ on $\mathcal{F}$, with $\mathcal{P} \in \mathcal{I}$. Then, as it is well known, there exists (a non-empty interval) $[p', p''] \subseteq [0,1]$ such that $(\mathcal{P}, p_{n+1})$ is a coherent precise assessment on $(\mathcal{F}, E_{n+1}|H_{n+1})$, for every $p_{n+1} \in [p', p'']$ (Fundamental Theorem of Probability; see e.g., [4,10,12,15,25]). Now, let any $\Gamma \subseteq [0,1]$ be given such that $\Gamma \cap [p', p''] \neq \emptyset$; moreover, consider the extension $\mathcal{J} = \mathcal{I} \times \Gamma$ on $(\mathcal{F}, E_{n+1}|H_{n+1})$. Clearly, $(\mathcal{P}, p_{n+1}) \in \mathcal{J}$ for every $p_{n+1} \in \Gamma \cap [p', p'']$; moreover the assessment $(\mathcal{P}, p_{n+1})$ on $(\mathcal{F}, E_{n+1}|H_{n+1})$ is coherent for every $p_{n+1} \in \Gamma \cap [p', p'']$. So by Definition 2, $\mathcal{J}$ is a g-coherent extension of $\mathcal{I}$ to $(\mathcal{F}, E_{n+1}|H_{n+1})$. $\square$

Given a g-coherent assessment $\mathcal{I}$ on a sequence of n conditional events $\mathcal{F}$, for each coherent precise assessment $\mathcal{P}$ on $\mathcal{F}$, with $\mathcal{P} \in \mathcal{I}$, we denote by $[\alpha_{\mathcal{P}}, \beta_{\mathcal{P}}]$ the interval of coherent extensions of $\mathcal{P}$ to $E_{n+1}|H_{n+1}$; that is, the assessment $(\mathcal{P}, p_{n+1})$ on $(\mathcal{F}, E_{n+1}|H_{n+1})$ is coherent if and only if $p_{n+1} \in [\alpha_{\mathcal{P}}, \beta_{\mathcal{P}}]$. Then, defining the set

$$\Sigma = \bigcup_{\mathcal{P} \in \Pi \cap \mathcal{I}} [\alpha_{\mathcal{P}}, \beta_{\mathcal{P}}], \tag{1}$$

for every $p_{n+1} \in \Sigma$, the assessment $\mathcal{I} \times \{p_{n+1}\}$ is a g-coherent extension of $\mathcal{I}$ to $(\mathcal{F}, E_{n+1}|H_{n+1})$; moreover, for every $p_{n+1} \in [0,1] \setminus \Sigma$, the extension $\mathcal{I} \times \{p_{n+1}\}$ of $\mathcal{I}$ to $(\mathcal{F}, E_{n+1}|H_{n+1})$ is not g-coherent. Thus, denoting by Π' the set of coherent precise assessments on $(\mathcal{F}, E_{n+1}|H_{n+1})$, it holds that Σ is the projection onto the $(n+1)$-th coordinate of the set $(\mathcal{I} \times [0,1]) \cap \Pi'$, that is $\rho_{n+1}((\mathcal{I} \times [0,1]) \cap \Pi') = \Sigma$. We say that Σ is the *set of coherent extensions* of the imprecise assessment $\mathcal{I}$ on $\mathcal{F}$ to the conditional event $E_{n+1}|H_{n+1}$.

3   Probabilistic Knowledge Bases and Entailment

Let E and H denote events, where H is a not self-contradictory event. The sentence "E *is a plausible consequence of* H" is a *default*, which we denote by $H \mathrel{|\!\sim} E$. Moreover, we denote a *negated default*, $\neg(H \mathrel{|\!\sim} E)$, by $H \mathrel{|\!\!\not\sim} E$ (it is not the case, that: E is a plausible consequence of H). We interpret the negation of a default by classical negation ($\neg$). Thus, we require that $\neg(H \mathrel{|\!\!\not\sim} E) = \neg(\neg(H \mathrel{|\!\sim} E)) = (H \mathrel{|\!\sim} E)$. We define defaults and negated defaults in terms of probabilistic assessments as follows:

Definition 8. *Given two events E, H we say that $H \mathrel{|\!\sim} E$ (resp., $H \mathrel{|\!\!\not\sim} E$) holds iff our imprecise probability assessment $\mathcal{I}$ on $E|H$ is $\mathcal{I} = \{1\}$ (resp., $\mathcal{I} = [0,1[$).*

We observe that a default is negated by classical negation: the default $H \mathrel{|\!\sim} E$ is represented by the assessment $\{1\}$ on $E|H$ and the negated default $H \mathrel{|\!\!\not\sim} E$ is represented by the assessment $[0,1[$, which is the complementary set of $\{1\}$. Given two events E and H, with $H \neq \bot$, by coherence $p(E|H) + p(\neg E|H) = 1$ (which holds in general). Thus, the probabilistic interpretation of the following types of sentences $H \mathrel{|\!\sim} E$ (I), $H \mathrel{|\!\sim} \neg E$ (II), $H \mathrel{|\!\!\not\sim} E$ (III), and $H \mathrel{|\!\!\not\sim} \neg E$ (IV), can be represented in terms of imprecise assessments on $E|H$ (Table 1). We recall that the notion of p-consistency for a knowledge base, given by Adams in [1], has been also studied in the framework of coherence (see, e.g., [18]). In [18, Definition 4] Adams' p-consistency of a knowledge base is interpreted by the g-coherence of an imprecise assessment, where $p(H|E) \geq 1 - \varepsilon$ for every $\varepsilon > 0$, i.e. $p(H|E)$ is close to 1, for each default $H \mathrel{|\!\sim} E$ in the given knowledge base. Therefore, the notion of p-consistency is related to the notion of g-coherence. Moreover, as shown in [22, Definition 2, Remark 1, Theorem 4], p-consistency can be defined equivalently by requiring $p(H|E) = 1$ for each default $H \mathrel{|\!\sim} E$. Of course, for what concerns practical aspects, instead of the latter approach it is more useful to use imprecise assessments (see e.g., [5,6,18,22,23,29–31]). In this paper a knowledge base $\mathcal{K}$ is defined as a (non-empty) finite sequence of defaults and negated defaults. Let $\mathcal{K} = (H_1 \mathrel{|\!\sim} E_1, \ldots, H_n \mathrel{|\!\sim} E_n, D_1 \mathrel{|\!\!\not\sim} C_1, \ldots, D_m \mathrel{|\!\!\not\sim} C_m)$ be a knowledge base, with $n+m \geq 1$. We now define our probabilistic representation of the knowledge base $\mathcal{K}$ by a corresponding pair $(\mathcal{F}_\mathcal{K}, \mathcal{I}_\mathcal{K})$, where $\mathcal{F}_\mathcal{K}$ is the ordered family of conditional events $(E_1|H_1, \ldots, E_n|H_n, C_1|D_1, \ldots, C_m|D_m)$ and $\mathcal{I}_\mathcal{K}$ is the imprecise assessment $\underset{i=1}{\overset{n}{\times}}\{1\} \times \underset{j=1}{\overset{m}{\times}}[0,1[$ on $\mathcal{F}_\mathcal{K}$. We now define the notion of p-consistency of a given knowledge base in terms of g-coherence.

Table 1. Probabilistic interpretations of defaults (Types I and II) and negated defaults (Types III and IV), and their respective (imprecise) assessments $\mathcal{I}$ on a conditional event $E|H$.

Type	Sentence	Probabilistic constraint	Assessment $\mathcal{I}$ on $E\mid H$
I	$H \mathrel{\vdash\!\sim} E$	$p(E\vert H) = 1$	$\{1\}$
II	$H \mathrel{\vdash\!\sim} \neg E$	$p(\neg E\vert H) = 1$	$\{0\}$
III	$H \mathrel{\not\vdash\!\sim} E$	$p(E\vert H) < 1$	$[0,1[$
IV	$H \mathrel{\not\vdash\!\sim} \neg E$	$p(\neg E\vert H) < 1$	$]0,1]$

Definition 9. *A knowledge base $\mathcal{K}$ is p-consistent if and only if the imprecise assessment $\mathcal{I}_\mathcal{K}$ on $\mathcal{F}_\mathcal{K}$ is g-coherent.*

In other words, $\mathcal{K} = (H_1 \mathrel{\vdash\!\sim} E_1, \ldots, H_n \mathrel{\vdash\!\sim} E_n, D_1 \mathrel{\not\vdash\!\sim} C_1, \ldots, D_m \mathrel{\not\vdash\!\sim} C_m)$ is p-consistent if and only if there exists a coherent precise probability assessment $\mathcal{P} = (p_1, \ldots, p_n, q_1, \ldots, q_m)$ on $\mathcal{F}_\mathcal{K} = (E_1|H_1, \ldots, E_n|H_n, C_1|D_1, \ldots, C_m|D_m)$ such that $p_i = 1$, $i = 1, \ldots, n$, and $q_i < 1$, $i = 1, \ldots, m$.

Example 1. Let $H \neq \bot$ and Π be the set of all the coherent assessments $x = p(E|H)$. We distinguish three cases. (i) $H \wedge E = \bot$: $\Pi = \{0\}$, $(H \mathrel{\vdash\!\sim} E)$ is not p-consistent because the assessment $p(E|H) = 1$ is not coherent; $(H \mathrel{\not\vdash\!\sim} E)$ is p-consistent because the assessment $p(E|H) = 0$ is coherent, hence there exists a coherent assessment $p(E|H)$ such that $p(E|H) < 1$; (ii) $H \wedge \neg E = \bot$: $\Pi = \{1\}$, therefore by the same reasoning, $(H \mathrel{\vdash\!\sim} E)$ is p-consistent, while $(H \mathrel{\not\vdash\!\sim} E)$ is not p-consistent; (iii) $H \wedge E \neq \bot$ and $H \wedge \neg E \neq \bot$: $\Pi = [0,1]$, $(H \mathrel{\vdash\!\sim} E)$ and $(H \mathrel{\not\vdash\!\sim} E)$ are separately p-consistent.

We define the notion of p-entailment of a (negated) default from a p-consistent knowledge base in terms of coherent extension of a g-coherent assessment.

Definition 10. *Let $\mathcal{K}$ be p-consistent. $\mathcal{K}$ p-entails $A \mathrel{\vdash\!\sim} B$ (resp., $A \mathrel{\not\vdash\!\sim} B$), denoted by $\mathcal{K} \models_p A \mathrel{\vdash\!\sim} B$ (resp., $\mathcal{K} \models_p A \mathrel{\not\vdash\!\sim} B$), iff the (non-empty) set of coherent extensions to $B|A$ of $\mathcal{I}_\mathcal{K}$ on $\mathcal{F}_\mathcal{K}$ is $\{1\}$ (resp., a subset of $[0,1[$).*

Theorem 2. *Let $\mathcal{K}$ be p-consistent. $\mathcal{K} \models_p A \mathrel{\vdash\!\sim} B$ (resp., $\mathcal{K} \models_p A \mathrel{\not\vdash\!\sim} B$), iff there exists a (non-empty) sub-sequence $\mathcal{S}$ of $\mathcal{K}$: $\mathcal{S} \models_p A \mathrel{\vdash\!\sim} B$ (resp., $\mathcal{S} \models_p A \mathrel{\not\vdash\!\sim} B$).*

Proof. ($\Rightarrow$) Trivially, by setting $\mathcal{S} = \mathcal{K}$.

($\Leftarrow$) Assume that $\mathcal{S} \models_p A \mathrel{\vdash\mkern-9mu\sim} B$ (resp., $A \mathrel{\not\vdash\mkern-9mu\sim} B$). Then, for every precise coherent assessment $\mathcal{P} \in \mathcal{I}_{\mathcal{S}}$ on $\mathcal{F}_{\mathcal{S}}$, if the extension $(\mathcal{P}, z)$ on $(\mathcal{F}_{\mathcal{S}}, B|A)$ is coherent, then $z = 1$ (resp., $z \neq 1$). Let $\mathcal{P}' \in \mathcal{I}_{\mathcal{K}}$ be a coherent precise assessment on $\mathcal{F}_{\mathcal{K}}$. For *reductio ad absurdum* we assume that the extension $(\mathcal{P}', z)$ on $(\mathcal{F}_{\mathcal{K}}, B|A)$ is coherent with $z \in [0, 1[$ (resp., $z = 1$). Then, the sub-assessment $(\mathcal{P}, z)$ of $(\mathcal{P}', z)$ on $(\mathcal{F}_{\mathcal{S}}, B|A)$ is coherent with $z \in [0, 1[$ (resp., $z = 1$): this contradicts $\mathcal{S} \models_p A \mathrel{\vdash\mkern-9mu\sim} B$ (resp., $\mathcal{S} \models_p A \mathrel{\not\vdash\mkern-9mu\sim} B$). Therefore, $\mathcal{K} \models_p A \mathrel{\vdash\mkern-9mu\sim} B$ (resp., $\mathcal{K} \models_p A \mathrel{\not\vdash\mkern-9mu\sim} B$). $\square$

A similar approach has been developed in [13, Definition 26]. We observe that if the knowledge base $\mathcal{K}$ consists of defaults only, then Definitions 9 and 10 coincide with the notion of p-consistency and p-entailment, respectively, investigated from a coherence perspective in [22] (see also [5,23]). Moreover, p-entailment of the inference rules of the well known nonmonotonic System P has been studied in this context (e.g., [13,18], see also [3,14]).

Remark 2. By Table 1 the probabilistic interpretation of $\mathcal{K} = (H_1 \mathrel{\vdash\mkern-9mu\sim} E_1, \ldots, H_n \mathrel{\vdash\mkern-9mu\sim} E_n, D_1 \mathrel{\not\vdash\mkern-9mu\sim} C_1, \ldots, D_m \mathrel{\not\vdash\mkern-9mu\sim} C_m)$ can equivalently be represented by the assessment $\mathcal{I}_{\mathcal{K}} = \bigtimes_{i=1}^{n} \{1\} \times \bigtimes_{j=1}^{m}]0, 1]$ on $\mathcal{F}_{\mathcal{K}} = (E_1|H_1, \ldots, E_n|H_n, \neg C_1|D_1, \ldots, \neg C_m|D_m)$. Definitions 9 and 10 can be rewritten accordingly.

Example 2. Given three logically independent events A, B, C, with $A \neq \bot$ and $B \neq \bot$, in [18] (see also [23]) it has been proved that any assessment $(x, y) \in [0, 1]^2$ on $(C|A, C|B)$ is coherent. Furthermore, the extension $z = P(C|(A \vee B))$ of (x, y) on $(C|A, C|B)$ is coherent if and only if $z \in [z', z'']$, where

$$z' = \begin{cases} \frac{xy}{x+y-xy} > 0, & \text{if } x > 0 \wedge y > 0, \\ 0, & \text{if } x = 0 \vee y = 0, \end{cases} \quad z'' = \begin{cases} \frac{x+y-2xy}{1-xy} < 1, & \text{if } x < 1 \wedge y < 1, \\ 1, & \text{if } x = 1 \vee y = 1. \end{cases}$$

Then, in our framework we have (see also [13]): $(A \mathrel{\vdash\mkern-9mu\sim} C, B \mathrel{\vdash\mkern-9mu\sim} C) \models_p A \vee B \mathrel{\vdash\mkern-9mu\sim} C$ (Or); $(A \mathrel{\not\vdash\mkern-9mu\sim} C, B \mathrel{\not\vdash\mkern-9mu\sim} C) \models_p A \vee B \mathrel{\not\vdash\mkern-9mu\sim} C$ (Disjunctive Rationality).

Example 3. Given three logically independent events A, B, C, with $A \neq \bot$, any assessment $(x, y) \in [0, 1]^2$ on $(C|A, B|A)$ is of course coherent. Furthermore, the extension $z = P(C|AB)$ of (x, y) on $(C|A, B|A)$ is coherent if and only if $z \in [z', z'']$, where ([18])

$$z' = \begin{cases} \frac{x+y-1}{y} > 0, & \text{if } x + y > 1, \\ 0, & \text{if } x + y \leq 1, \end{cases} \quad z'' = \begin{cases} \frac{x}{y} < 1, & \text{if } x < y, \\ 1, & \text{if } x \geq y. \end{cases}$$

Then, we have (see also [13,17]): $(A \mathrel{\vdash\mkern-9mu\sim} C, A \mathrel{\vdash\mkern-9mu\sim} B) \models_p AB \mathrel{\vdash\mkern-9mu\sim} C$ (Cautious Monotonicity); $(A \mathrel{\not\vdash\mkern-9mu\sim} C, A \mathrel{\not\vdash\mkern-9mu\sim} \neg B) \models_p AB \mathrel{\not\vdash\mkern-9mu\sim} C$ (Rational Monotonicity).

4   Weak Transitivity: Propagation of Probability Bounds

In this section, we presents two results on the propagation of a precise, or interval-valued, probability assessment on $(C|B, B|A, A|A \vee B)$ to $C|A$.

Remark 3. Let A, B, C be logically independent events. It can be proved that the assessment (x, y, t) on $\mathcal{F} = (C|B, B|A, A|A \vee B)$ is coherent for every $(x, y, t) \in [0,1]^3$, that is the imprecise assessment $\mathcal{I} = [0,1]^3$ on $\mathcal{F}$ is totally coherent. Also $\mathcal{I} = [0,1]^3$ on $\mathcal{F}' = (C|B, B|A, C|A)$ is totally coherent.[1]

Theorem 3. *Let A, B, C be three logically independent events and $(x, y, t) \in [0,1]^3$ be a (coherent) assessment on the family $\big(C|B, B|A, A|(A \vee B)\big)$. Then, the extension $z = P(C|A)$ is coherent if and only if $z \in [z', z'']$, where*

$$[z', z''] = \begin{cases} [0,1], & t = 0; \\ [\max\{0, xy - (1-t)(1-x)/t\}, \min\{1, (1-x)(1-y) + x/t\}], & t > 0. \end{cases}$$

Due to the lack of space we omit the proof of Theorem 3. A detailed proof of the theorem is available in [20] and is obtained by applying the Algorithm 2 given in [4] in a symbolic way. Alternative proofs of Theorem 3 can be obtained by applying other equivalent methods ([8,9,13,32]).

Theorem 4. *Let A, B, C be three logically independent events and $\mathcal{I} = ([x_1, x_2] \times [y_1, y_2] \times [t_1, t_2]) \subseteq [0,1]^3$ be an imprecise (totally-coherent) assessment on $\big(C|B, B|A, A|(A \vee B)\big)$. Then, the set Σ of the coherent extension of $\mathcal{I}$ is the interval $[z^*, z^{**}]$, where $[z^*, z^{**}] =$*

$$\begin{cases} [0,1], & t = 0; \\ \Big[\max\Big\{0, x_1 y_1 - \frac{(1-t_1)(1-x_1)}{t_1}\Big\}, \min\Big\{1, (1-x_2)(1-y_1) + \frac{x_2}{t_1}\Big\}\Big], & t > 0. \end{cases}$$

Proof. We observe that $\Sigma = \bigcup_{\mathcal{P} \in \mathcal{I}}[z'_{\mathcal{P}}, z''_{\mathcal{P}}] = [z^*, z^{**}]$. If $t_1 = 0$, we obtain $[z^*, z^{**}] = [0,1]$ by Theorem 3. If $t_1 > 0$, the proof is straightforward by observing that the lower bound z' in Theorem 3 is non-decreasing in the arguments x, y, t; moreover, the upper bound z'' is non-decreasing in the argument x, while it is non-increasing in the argument y and t. □

Remark 4. By applying Theorem 4 with $x_1 = y_1 = 1 - \varepsilon$, $t_1 > 0$, and $x_2 = y_2 = t_2 = 1$ we obtain $z^* = \max\Big\{0, (1 - \varepsilon)^2 - \frac{(1-\varepsilon)\varepsilon}{t_1}\Big\}$ and $z^{**} = 1$, with $z^* = 0$ if and only if $\varepsilon = 1$ or $(\varepsilon < 1) \wedge (t_1 \leq \varepsilon/(1 - \varepsilon))$.

5 Weak Transitivity Involving (Negated) Defaults

Let A, B, C be logically independent. By Remark 3, the p-consistent knowledge base $(B \mathrel{\vdash\!\!\!\sim} C, A \mathrel{\vdash\!\!\!\sim} B)$ neither p-entails $A \mathrel{\vdash\!\!\!\sim} C$ nor p-entails $A \mathrel{\not\vdash\!\!\!\sim} C$. This will be denoted by $(B \mathrel{\vdash\!\!\!\sim} C, A \mathrel{\vdash\!\!\!\sim} B) \not\models_p A \mathrel{\vdash\!\!\!\sim} C$ and $(B \mathrel{\vdash\!\!\!\sim} C, A \mathrel{\vdash\!\!\!\sim} B) \not\models_p A \mathrel{\not\vdash\!\!\!\sim} C$, respectively.

---

[1] For proving total coherence of $\mathcal{I}$ on $\mathcal{F}$ (resp., $\mathcal{F}'$) it is sufficient to check that the assessment $\{0,1\}^3$ on $\mathcal{F}$ (resp., $\mathcal{F}'$) is totally coherent ([19, Theorem 7]), i.e., each of the eight vertices of the unit cube is coherent. Coherence can be checked, for example, by applying Algorithm 1 of [19] or by the CkC-package [2].

Theorem 5. $(B \mathrel{\vdash\!\!\!\sim} C, A \mathrel{\vdash\!\!\!\sim} B, A \vee B \mathrel{\not\vdash\!\!\!\sim} \neg A) \models_p A \mathrel{\vdash\!\!\!\sim} C.$

Proof. By Remark 3, the knowledge base $\mathcal{K} = (B \mathrel{\vdash\!\!\!\sim} C, A \mathrel{\vdash\!\!\!\sim} B, A \vee B \mathrel{\not\vdash\!\!\!\sim} \neg A)$ is p-consistent. Based on Remark 2, we set $\mathcal{I}_\mathcal{K} = \{1\} \times \{1\} \times \,]0,1]$ and $\mathcal{F}_\mathcal{K} = (C|B, B|A, A|(A \vee B))$. Let $\mathcal{P}$ be any precise coherent assessment on $\mathcal{F}_\mathcal{K}$ such that $\mathcal{P} \in \mathcal{I}_\mathcal{K}$, i.e., $\mathcal{P} = (1, 1, t)$, with $t \in \,]0,1]$. From Theorem 3, the interval of coherent extensions from $\mathcal{P}$ on $\mathcal{F}_\mathcal{K}$ to $C|A$ is $[z'_\mathcal{P}, z''_\mathcal{P}] = [1, 1]$. Then, by Eq. (1), the set of coherent extensions to $C|A$ from $\mathcal{I}_\mathcal{K}$ on $\mathcal{F}_\mathcal{K}$ is $\bigcup_{\mathcal{P} \in \mathcal{I}_\mathcal{K}}[z'_\mathcal{P}, z''_\mathcal{P}] = [1, 1]$. $\square$

Theorem 6. $(B \mathrel{\vdash\!\!\!\sim} C, A \mathrel{\not\vdash\!\!\!\sim} \neg B, A \vee B \mathrel{\not\vdash\!\!\!\sim} \neg A) \models_p A \mathrel{\not\vdash\!\!\!\sim} \neg C.$

Proof. By Remark 3, the knowledge base $\mathcal{K} = (B \mathrel{\vdash\!\!\!\sim} C, A \mathrel{\not\vdash\!\!\!\sim} \neg B, A \vee B \mathrel{\not\vdash\!\!\!\sim} \neg A)$ is p-consistent. Based on Remark 2, we set $\mathcal{I}_\mathcal{K} = \{1\} \times \,]0,1] \times \,]0,1]$ and $\mathcal{F}_\mathcal{K} = (C|B, B|A, A|(A \vee B))$. Let $\mathcal{P}$ be any precise coherent assessment on $\mathcal{F}_\mathcal{K}$ such that $\mathcal{P} \in \mathcal{I}_\mathcal{K}$, i.e., $\mathcal{P} = (1, y, t)$, with $y \in \,]0,1]$ and $t \in \,]0,1]$. From Theorem 3, the interval of coherent extensions from $\mathcal{P}$ on $\mathcal{F}_\mathcal{K}$ to $C|A$ is $[z'_\mathcal{P}, z''_\mathcal{P}] = [y, 1]$. Then, by Eq. (1), the set of coherent extensions to $C|A$ from $\mathcal{I}_\mathcal{K}$ on $\mathcal{F}_\mathcal{K}$ is $\bigcup_{(y,t) \in \,]0,1] \times \,]0,1]}[y, 1] = \,]0, 1]$. Therefore, the set of coherent extensions on $\neg C|A$ is $[0, 1[$. $\square$

Theorem 7. $(B \mathrel{\vdash\!\!\!\sim} C, A \mathrel{\vdash\!\!\!\sim} B, B \mathrel{\not\vdash\!\!\!\sim} \neg A) \models_p A \mathrel{\vdash\!\!\!\sim} C.$

Proof. It can be shown that the assessment $[0, 1]^3$ on $(C|B, B|A, A|B)$ is totally coherent. Then, $\mathcal{K} = (B \mathrel{\vdash\!\!\!\sim} C, A \mathrel{\vdash\!\!\!\sim} B, B \mathrel{\not\vdash\!\!\!\sim} \neg A)$ is p-consistent. We set $\mathcal{I}_\mathcal{K} = \{1\} \times \{1\} \times \,]0,1]$ and $\mathcal{F}_\mathcal{K} = (C|B, B|A, A|B)$. We observe that $A|B \subseteq A|(A \vee B)$, where the binary relation $\subseteq$ denotes the well-known Goodman and Nguyen inclusion relation between conditional events (e.g., [22]). Coherence requires that $p(A|B) \leq p(A|(A \vee B))$. Let $\mathcal{P}$ be any precise coherent assessment on $\mathcal{F}_\mathcal{K}$ such that $\mathcal{P} \in \mathcal{I}_\mathcal{K}$, i.e., $\mathcal{P} = (1, 1, w)$, with $w \in \,]0, 1]$. Thus, for any coherent extension $\mathcal{P}' = (1, 1, w, t)$ of $\mathcal{P}$ on $(\mathcal{F}_\mathcal{K}, A|(A \vee B))$, it holds that $0 < w \leq t$. Then, $\mathcal{K}' = (B \mathrel{\vdash\!\!\!\sim} C, A \mathrel{\vdash\!\!\!\sim} B, B \mathrel{\not\vdash\!\!\!\sim} \neg A, A \vee B \mathrel{\not\vdash\!\!\!\sim} \neg A)$ is p-consistent. Thus, by Theorem 5, $\mathcal{K}' \models_p A \mathrel{\vdash\!\!\!\sim} C$. Then, for every coherent extension $\mathcal{P}'' = (1, 1, w, t, z)$ of $\mathcal{P}'$ on $(\mathcal{F}_{\mathcal{K}'}, C|A)$ it holds that $z = 1$. By *reductio ad absurdum*, if for some $z < 1$ the extension $(1, 1, w, z)$ on $(\mathcal{F}_\mathcal{K}, C|A)$ of $\mathcal{P} \in \mathcal{I}_\mathcal{K}$ on $\mathcal{F}_\mathcal{K}$ were coherent, then—with $0 < w \leq t$ and $z < 1$—the assessment $(1, 1, w, t, z)$ on $(\mathcal{F}_{\mathcal{K}'}, C|A)$ would be coherent, which contradicts the conclusion $z = 1$ above. Thus, for every coherent extension $(1, 1, w, z)$ of $\mathcal{P} \in \mathcal{I}_\mathcal{K}$ on $(\mathcal{F}_\mathcal{K}, C|A)$ it holds that $z = 1$. $\square$

Theorem 8. $(B \mathrel{\vdash\!\!\!\sim} C, A \mathrel{\not\vdash\!\!\!\sim} \neg B, B \mathrel{\not\vdash\!\!\!\sim} \neg A) \models_p A \mathrel{\not\vdash\!\!\!\sim} \neg C.$

Proof. The proof exploits Theorem 6 and is similar to the proof of Theorem 7.

Remark 5. Of course by Definition 8, Theorem 5 to Theorem 8 can be rewritten in terms of probability constraints. Theorem 5, for example, would then read as follows: $p(C|B) = 1$, $p(B|A) = 1$, and $p(A|A \vee B) > 0$ implies $p(C|A) = 1$. We note that the corresponding results would also hold within standard approaches to probability where conditional probability $p(E|H)$ is defined by the ratio $p(E \wedge H)/p(H)$ (requiring positive probability of the conditioning event, $p(H) > 0$). However, in our coherence-based approach, our results *even* hold when conditioning events have zero probability. Furthermore, we observe that, by Theorem 3, $p(C|B) = 1$, $p(B|A) = 1$, and $p(A|A \vee B) = 0$ implies $0 \leq p(C|A) \leq 1$. This observation cannot be made in standard approaches to probability, as $p(A|A \vee B) = 0$ implies that the probability of the conditioning event A equals to zero, i.e., $P(A) = 0$.

6   Concluding Remarks

Our definition of negated defaults, based on imprecise probabilities (Sect. 3), can be seen as an instance of the *wide-scope* reading of the negation of a conditional. It offers an interesting alternative to the *narrow-scope* reading, where a conditional is negated by negating its consequent [27]. Moreover, we note that Theorem 5 can also be seen as a modern probabilistic formalization of classical (Aristotelian) syllogisms, specifically those of syllogistic Fig. 1. Figure 1 syllogisms are valid transitive argument forms which are composed of universally/existentially quantified statements and their respective negated versions (see, e.g., [26]). Examples of valid syllogisms are Modus Barbara (*All M are P, All S are M, therefore All S are P*) and Modus Darii (*All M are P, At least one S is M, therefore At least one S is P*). As suggested in [11], *All S are P* (resp., *At least one S is P*) can be interpreted probabilistically by the assessment $\mathcal{I} = \{1\}$ on $P|S$ (resp., $\mathcal{I} = [0,1[$). The probabilistic constraint $p(S|(S \vee M)) > 0$ can serve as an *existential import* assumption for Fig. 1 syllogisms, as the assessment $(p(P|M), p(M|S))$ on the (major and minor) premises alone do not constrain the probability of the conclusion ($p(P|S)$; see Remark 3). We observe that the probabilistic versions of these syllogisms can equivalently be expressed in terms of (negated) defaults with $S \vee M \not\hspace{-0.4em}\sim \neg S$, i.e. the probabilistic constraint $p(S|(S \vee M)) > 0$, as our existential import assumption: Theorem 5 is our default version of Modus Barbara and Theorem 6 is our default version of Modus Darii. Both syllogisms can also be expressed with the stronger notion of existential import $M \not\hspace{-0.4em}\sim \neg S$ (its probabilistic counterpart $p(S|M) > 0$ has been proposed in [16]): they are presented in Theorems 7 and 8. In all versions of the syllogisms we do not presuppose any positive antecedent probabilities in our framework. Assuming the positive antecedent probabilities $p(S) > 0$ would be yet another (stronger!) existential import assumption. Our preferred existential import assumption, i.e. the probabilistic constraint $p(S|(S \vee M)) > 0$, is weaker as it neither implies $p(S) > 0$ nor $p(S|M) > 0$. We are currently working on a coherence-based probability semantics for classical categorical syllogisms, where we exploit the ideas presented above.

Acknowledgments. We thank two anonymous referees for their very useful comments and suggestions.

References

1. Adams, E.W.: The Logic of Conditionals. Reidel, Dordrecht (1975)
2. Baioletti, M., Capotorti, A., Galli, L., Tognoloni, S., Rossi, F., Vantaggi, B.: CkC-package; version e5 (2009). www.dmi.unipg.it/~upkd/paid/software.html
3. Benferhat, S., Dubois, D., Prade, H.: Nonmonotonic reasoning, conditional objects and possibility theory. Artif. Intell. **92**, 259–276 (1997)
4. Biazzo, V., Gilio, A.: A generalization of the fundamental theorem of de Finetti for imprecise conditional probability assessments. Int. J. Approximate Reasoning **24**(2–3), 251–272 (2000)
5. Biazzo, V., Gilio, A., Lukasiewicz, T., Sanfilippo, G.: Probabilistic logic under coherence, model-theoretic probabilistic logic, and default reasoning in System P. J. Appl. Non-Class. Logics **12**(2), 189–213 (2002)
6. Biazzo, V., Gilio, A., Lukasiewicz, T., Sanfilippo, G.: Probabilistic logic under coherence: complexity and algorithms. Ann. Math. Artif. Intell. **45**(1–2), 35–81 (2005)
7. Bonnefon, J.F., Da Silva Neves, R., Dubois, D., Prade, H.: Qualitative and quantitative conditions for the transitivity of perceived causation. Ann. Math. Artif. Intell. **64**(2–3), 311–333 (2012)
8. Capotorti, A., Galli, L., Vantaggi, B.: Locally strong coherence and inference with lower-upper probabilities. Soft. Comput. **7**(5), 280–287 (2003)
9. Capotorti, A., Vantaggi, B.: Locally strong coherence in inference processes. Ann. Math. Artif. Intell. **35**(1–4), 125–149 (2002)
10. Capotorti, A., Lad, F., Sanfilippo, G.: Reassessing accuracy rates of median decisions. Am. Stat. **61**(2), 132–138 (2007)
11. Chater, N., Oaksford, M.: The probability heuristics model of syllogistic reasoning. Cogn. Psychol. **38**, 191–258 (1999)
12. Coletti, G., Scozzafava, R.: Characterization of coherent conditional probabilities as a tool for their assessment and extension. Int. J. Uncertainty Fuzziness Knowl. Based Syst. **04**(02), 103–127 (1996)
13. Coletti, G., Scozzafava, R.: Probabilistic Logic in a Coherent Setting. Kluwer, Dordrecht (2002)
14. Coletti, G., Petturiti, D., Vantaggi, B.: Coherent T-conditional possibility envelopes and nonmonotonic reasoning. In: Laurent, A., Strauss, O., Bouchon-Meunier, B., Yager, R.R. (eds.) IPMU 2014, Part III. CCIS, vol. 444, pp. 446–455. Springer, Heidelberg (2014)
15. de Finetti, B.: Foresight: Its logical laws, its subjective sources. In: Kyburg, H.J., Smokler, H.E. (eds.) Studies in Subjective Probability, pp. 55–118. Robert E. Krieger Publishing Company, Huntington, New York (1937/1980)
16. Dubois, D., Godo, L., Lóez De Màntaras, R., Prade, H.: Qualitative reasoning with imprecise probabilities. J. Intel. Inf. Syst. **2**(4), 319–363 (1993)
17. Freund, M., Lehmann, D., Morris, P.: Rationality, transitivity, and contraposition. Artif. Intell. **52**(2), 191–203 (1991)
18. Gilio, A.: Probabilistic reasoning under coherence in System P. Ann. Math. Artif. Intell. **34**, 5–34 (2002)
19. Gilio, A., Ingrassia, S.: Totally coherent set-valued probability assessments. Kybernetika **34**(1), 3–15 (1998)
20. Gilio, A., Pfeifer, N., Sanfilippo, G.: Transitive reasoning with imprecise probabilities (2015). http://arxiv.org/abs/1503.04135

21. Gilio, A., Sanfilippo, G.: Coherent conditional probabilities and proper scoring rules. In: Proceedings of the Seventh International Symposium on Imprecise Probability: Theories and Applications, pp. 189–198. SIPTA, Innsbruck (2011)
22. Gilio, A., Sanfilippo, G.: Probabilistic entailment in the setting of coherence: the role of quasi conjunction and inclusion relation. Int. J. Approximate Reasoning **54**(4), 513–525 (2013)
23. Gilio, A., Sanfilippo, G.: Quasi conjunction, quasi disjunction, t-norms and t-conorms: probabilistic aspects. Inf. Sci. **245**, 146–167 (2013)
24. Gilio, A., Sanfilippo, G.: Conditional random quantities and compounds of conditionals. Stud. Logica. **102**(4), 709–729 (2014)
25. Lad, F.: Operational Subjective Statistical Methods: A Mathematical, Philosophical, and Historical Introduction. Wiley, New York (1996)
26. Pfeifer, N.: Contemporary syllogistics: comparative and quantitative syllogisms. In: Kreuzbauer, G., Dorn, G.J.W. (eds.) Argumentation in Theorie und Praxis: Philosophie und Didaktik des Argumentierens, pp. 57–71. Lit Verlag, Wien (2006)
27. Pfeifer, N.: Experiments on Aristotle's thesis: towards an experimental philosophy of conditionals. The Monist **95**(2), 223–240 (2012)
28. Pfeifer, N.: Reasoning about uncertain conditionals. Stud. Logica. **102**(4), 849–866 (2014)
29. Pfeifer, N., Kleiter, G.D.: Coherence and nonmonotonicity in human reasoning. Synthese **146**(1–2), 93–109 (2005)
30. Pfeifer, N., Kleiter, G.D.: Framing human inference by coherence based probability logic. J. Appl. Logic **7**(2), 206–217 (2009)
31. Pfeifer, N., Kleiter, G.D.: The conditional in mental probability logic. In: Oaksford, M., Chater, N. (eds.) Cognition and Conditionals, pp. 153–173. Oxford Press, Oxford (2010)
32. Walley, P., Pelessoni, R., Vicig, P.: Direct algorithms for checking consistency and making inferences from conditional probability assessments. J. Stat. Plan. Infer. **126**(1), 119–151 (2004)

On the Algebraic Structure
of Conditional Events

Tommaso Flaminio[1], Lluis Godo[2]([✉]), and Hykel Hosni[3]([✉])

[1] Dipartimento di Scienze Teoriche e Applicate, Università dell'Insubria,
Via Mazzini 5, 21100 Varese, Italy
tommaso.flaminio@uninsubria.it
[2] Artificial Intelligence Research Institute (IIIA - CSIC),
Campus de la Univ. Autònoma de Barcelona s/n, 08193 Bellaterra, Spain
godo@iiia.csic.es
[3] London School of Economics, Houghton Street,
London WC2A 2AE, UK
h.hosni@lse.ac.uk

Abstract. This paper initiates an investigation of conditional measures as simple measures on conditional events. As a first step towards this end we investigate the construction of *conditional algebras* which allow us to distinguish between the logical properties of conditional events and those of the conditional measures which we can be attached to them. This distinction, we argue, helps us clarifying both concepts.

Keywords: Conditionals events · Uncertain reasoning · Conditional algebra

1 Introduction and Motivation

This paper offers a logico-algebraic perspective on conditionals which is motivated by a number of pressing problems in field of logic-based uncertain reasoning. Indeed, conditionals play a fundamental role both in qualitative and in quantitative uncertain reasoning. The former is a consequence of the very fruitful interaction between philosophical logic and artificial intelligence, which linked the semantic approaches to conditionals of the 1970s, mainly Stalnaker's and D. Lewis's to the proof-theoretic and model-theoretic development of non monotonic consequence relations in the 1990s (see [14]). But it is in quantitative uncertain reasoning that conditionals play their most delicate role leading to the key concept of conditional probability. Despite the apparent simplicity of the "ratio definition", on which more below, the notion of conditional probability is far from being uncontroversial. Makinson, for instance, points out in [15] how some rather undesirable behaviour can arise when conditioning on what he refers to as the "critical zone". Things get inevitably more complicated if we move to non-classical probability logic, i.e. probability defined on non-classical logics, a rapidly expanding research field. Yet the problem with conditional probability arises in much simpler contexts that those just mentioned.

© Springer International Publishing Switzerland 2015
S. Destercke and T. Denoeux (Eds.): ECSQARU 2015, LNAI 9161, pp. 106–116, 2015.
DOI: 10.1007/978-3-319-20807-7_10

Logician Ernest Adams is well-known for putting forward

Adam's Thesis: Conditional probability is the probability that the conditional is true.

The thesis is quite plausible if one reasons as follows. Let θ be a sentence in some propositional language, and let its probability be denoted by $\mu(\theta)$. Then it is very natural to interpret $\mu(\theta)$ as the *probability that θ is true*. This is certainly compatible with the Bayesian operational definition of subjective probability as the price a rational agent would be willing to bet on event θ [7]. Now, if θ is of the form $p \to q$, then $\mu(\theta)$ appears to be naturally intepreted as the probability that *q is true given that p is also true*, i.e. $\mu(p \mid q)$. But this gives rise to the

Lewis's Triviality: Adams' thesis implies that $\mu(\theta \mid \phi) = \mu(\theta)$.

So, either $\to$ is not truth-functional or Adams' thesis is wrong, and the two alternatives are exclusive.[1]

This paper initiates a research project which aims at tackling the foundational difficulties related to conditional probability by radically changing the perspective. In a nutshell our overall goal is to investigate conditional algebras in such a way as to see *conditional measures as simple measures (possibly with further properties) on conditional events*, i.e. the elements inhabiting conditional algebras. Hence we adopt a two-fold perspective on conditionals. First, we characterize conditional events as elements of an algebra which we term *conditional algebra*. Within such structures conditionals are *simple* objects, a terminology whose meaning will be apparent in a short while. Second, since we are interested in modelling various epistemic attitudes that agents may exhibit in connection to conditional events – and in particular rational belief under uncertainty – we are ultimately interested investigating appropriate *measures* to be attached to conditionals. This paper prepares the stage by focusing on the first objective.

Whilst we are unaware of other proposals which separate the logico-algebraic properties of conditionals from those of conditional measures, the notion of conditional algebra has been investigated in the context of the so-called *Goodman-Nguyen-van Fraassen algebras*. Since we will be in an ideal position to compare this approach with ours after having introduced some formal details, suffice it to mention now that the notion of Conditional Event Algebra (CEA) introduced in [10] differs quite substantially from our notion of conditional algebra.

Let θ, ϕ be sentences in a classical logic propositional language. We denote the conditional assertion "ϕ given θ" by $\phi \mid \theta$. It will sometimes be convenient to refer to ϕ as the *consequent* of the conditional and to θ as its *antecedent*. When presented with a conditional of this form, there are three *distinct* questions that we may ask:

---

[1] Among many other references, the reader may get an idea of the arguments in support of Adam's thesis which sees the probability of a conditional as conditional probability from [2,10,11,19], and from the arguments which reject it as ill-founded from [13,16].

(1) what are the syntactic properties of $\phi \mid \theta$?
(2) what are the semantic properties of $\phi \mid \theta$?
(3) what properties should be satisfied by a (rational) measure of belief on $\phi \mid \theta$?

This paper focusses on (1) and provides an algebraic interpretation for (2), leaving the investigation of question (3) as future research. The answers put forward in this paper can be informally illustrated as follows:

1. Though it makes perfectly good sense to distinguish, in the conditional $\phi \mid \theta$, the antecedent from the consequent, we will assume that conditional events are *simple* objects which live in a conditional structure. The fundamental consequence of this approach is that the "global" properties, so to speak, of conditionals are defined for the underlying algebraic structure and not at the object level of the conditional formula.

2. The semantic properties of conditionals are also given at the level of the conditional algebra. For instance, by suitably constraining the ideals of a particular freely generated Boolean algebra we will be in a position to characterize the semantic properties we want conditional events to satisfy. As will become apparent, all the results of this paper fail for *counterfactuals*. The reason for this lies in the adoption of a principle which we refer to as the *rejection constraint* according to which a conditional $\phi \mid \theta$ is (semanticaly) meaningless if the antecedent fails to be true (under a suitably defined valuation). This property, as we shall shortly see, is motivated by reflections on conditional events.

2   The Logic of Conditionals

The most general feature on conditionals is that they express some form of hypothetical assertion: the assertion of the consequent based *on the supposition* that the antecedent is satisfied (with respect, of course, to a suitably defined semantics). As Quine put it some four decades ago:

> [An] affirmation of the form 'if p then q' is commonly felt less as an affirmation of a conditional than as a conditional affirmation of the consequent. If, after we have made such an affirmation, the antecedent turns out true, then we consider ourselves committed to the consequent, and are ready to acknowledge error if it proves false. *If, on the other hand, the antecedent turns out to have been false, our conditional affirmation is as if it had never been made* ([20] Added emphasis)

The idea here is that the semantic evaluation of a conditional (in this interpretation) amounts to a two-step procedure. We first check the antecedent. If this is rejected, the conditional ceases to mean anything at all. Otherwise we move on to evaluating the consequent. Note that is in full consonance with de Finetti's semantics for conditional events, an interpretation which lies at the foundation of his *betting interpretation* of subjective probability [7] and which can be extended to more general measures of belief [8]. In particular, with respect to a fixed possible world v,

$$\text{a bet on } \theta \mid \phi \text{ is } \begin{cases} \text{won if} & v(\phi) = v(\theta) = 1; \\ \text{lost if} & v(\phi) = 1 \text{ and } v(\theta) = 0; \\ \text{called off if} & v(\phi) = 0. \end{cases}$$

The final clause is of course the most interesing one, for it states that under the valuation which assigns 0 to the conditioning event, a conditional bet must be called off (all paid monies are returned). This property is what we will henceforth name *Rejection Constraint* stating that in the process of realization of a conditional bet into a fixed world v, we must agree to invalidate bets made on conditionals whose antecedents are evaluated to 0.[2] An immediate consequence of this is that any expression of the form $\theta \mid \bot$ cannot be considered a conditional event. Indeed, in this interpretation, it does not make sense to bet on a conditional whose antecedent is false independently on the possible world v in which the conditional is realized, because it would be always rejected.

The latter observation, leads us to impose a second constraint to our analysis, namely we will require the algebra of conditional events to be Boolean. This property of conditionals is what we will call *Boolean Constraint* and it is essentially motivated to provide conditional events with an algebraic structure which is a suitable domain of uncertainty measures. Indeed, as recalled in Sect. 1, in our future work we will investigate simple (i.e. unconditional) uncertainty measures on conditional algebras. Moreover, Sect. 4 presents an algebraic construction that defines conditional Boolean algebras in a modular way.

3   Algebraic Preliminaries

For every Boolean algebra A we denote by $\delta : A \times A \to A$ the well known *symmetric difference* operator. In other words δ stands for the following abbreviation: for every $x, y \in A$,

$$\delta(x, y) = (x \vee y) \wedge \neg(x \wedge y) = \neg(x \leftrightarrow y). \tag{1}$$

In any Boolean algebra A, the following equations hold:

(i) $\delta(x, y) = \delta(y, x)$ (iv) $\delta(x, \bot) = x$

(ii) $\delta(x, \delta(y, z)) = \delta(\delta(x, y), z)$ (v) $\delta(x, x) = \bot$

(iii) $\delta(\delta(x, y), \delta(y, z)) = \delta(x, z)$

Therefore, in particular δ is (i) commutative; (ii) associative; and (iv) has $\bot$ as neutral element.

The following proposition collects further properties of δ. Owing to space limitations we are forced omit proofs.

Proposition 1. *The following hold in any Boolean algebra A:*

(a) $\delta(x, y) = \bot$ *iff* $x = y$ (c) $\delta(x, y) = \delta(\neg x, \neg y)$

(b) $\delta(x, z) \le \delta(x, y) \vee \delta(y, z)$ (d) $\delta(x \vee y, z \vee k) = \delta(x, z) \vee \delta(y, k)$.

---

[2] Note that the Rejection Constraint forces us to exclude counterfactual conditionals from our analysis.

A non-empty subset i of a Boolean algebra A is said to be an *ideal* of A if: (1) $\bot \in i$; (2) for any $x, y \in i$, $x \vee y \in i$; (3) if $x \in i$, and $y \leq x$, then $y \in i$. If $X \subseteq A$, denote by $\mathfrak{J}(X)$, the ideal generated by X, i.e. the least ideal (w.r.t. inclusion) containing X. For every $x \in A$, we denote by $\downarrow x$ the *principal ideal* of A generated by x, i.e. $\downarrow x = \{y \in A : y \leq x\} = \mathfrak{J}(\{x\})$.

Proposition 2. *Let A be a Boolean algebra, and let i be an ideal of A. Then for every $x, y \in A$, the equation $x = y$ is valid in the quotient algebra A/i iff $\delta(x, y) \in i$.*

Remark 1. The above Proposition 2 immediately implies that, whenever i is a proper ideal, and $\neg\delta(x, y) \in i$, then the quotient algebra A/i makes valid $\neg(x = y)$. In fact if $\neg\delta(x, y) \in i$, then $\delta(x, y) \notin i$ (otherwise $\delta(x, y) \vee \neg\delta(x, y) = \top \in i$, and hence i would not be proper) iff in A/i, $\neg(x = y)$ holds true i.e. $x \neq y$.

3.1   On the Conjunction of Conditionals

Let A be a Boolean algebra, and denote by $A \mid A$ the set $\{a \mid b : a, b \in A\}$. The problem of defining operations between the objects in $A \mid A$ has been discussed extensively in the context of measure-free conditionals [6].

Whilst widespread consensus exists about defining the negation of a conditional as $\neg(a \mid b) = \neg a \mid b$, there are at least three major proposals competing for the definition of conjunction:

(Schay, Calabrese) $(a \mid b) \&_1 (c \mid d) = [(b \rightarrow a) \wedge (d \rightarrow c) \mid (b \vee d)]$ (cf. [5, 21] and see also [1] where this conjunction between conditionals is called *quasi-conjunction*).

(Goodman and Nguyen) $(a \mid b) \&_2 (c \mid d) = (a \wedge c) \mid [(\neg a \wedge b) \vee (\neg c \wedge d) \vee (b \vee d)]$ (cf. [11])

(Schay) $(a \mid b) \&_3 (c \mid d) = (a \wedge c) \mid (b \wedge d)$ (cf. [21])

Disjunctions $\oplus_1, \oplus_2$ and $\oplus_3$ among conditionals, are defined by De Morgan's laws from $\&_1, \&_2$ and $\&_3$ above. Schay [21], and Calabrese [5] show that $\&_1$, and $\oplus_1$ are not distributive with respect to each other, and hence the class $A \mid A$ of conditionals, endowed with $\&_1$ and $\oplus_1$ is no longer a Boolean algebra. Therefore $\&_1$ does not satisfy the Boolean constraint mentioned in the introductory Section. For this reason we reject $\&_1$ as a suitable definition of conjunction.

Similarly, the Boolean constraint leads us to reject also $\&_3$, and $\oplus_3$ as candidates for defining conjunction and disjunction betwen conditionals. Indeed, if we defined the usual order relations by

1. $(a_1 \mid b_1) \leq_1 (a_2 \mid b_2)$ iff $(a_1 \mid b_1) \&_3 (a_2 \mid b_2) = (a_1 \wedge a_2 \mid b_1 \wedge b_2) = (a_1 \mid b_1)$,
2. $(a_1 \mid b_1) \leq_2 (a_2 \mid b_2)$ iff $(a_1 \mid b_1) \oplus_3 (a_2 \mid b_2) = (a_1 \vee a_2 \mid b_1 \wedge b_2) = (a_2 \mid b_2)$,

then $\leq_1 \neq \leq_2$. To see this, let a be a fixed element in A. Then $(a \mid \top) \&_3 (a \mid a) = (a \mid a)$ and hence $(a \mid a) \leq_1 (a \mid \top)$. On the other hand $(a \mid \top) \oplus_3 (a \mid a) = (a \mid a)$ as well, and therefore $(a \mid \top) \leq_2 (a \mid a)$ for every $a \in A$, and in particular for a such that $a \mid a \neq a \mid \top$. Conversely, it is easy to see that, if we restrict to the class of those conditionals $a_i \mid b$ with a fixed antecedent b, then $\leq_1 = \leq_2$. Therefore $\&_3$ is suitable as a definition of conjunction only for those conditionals $a_1 \mid b_1$ and $a_2 \mid b_2$, such that $b_1 = b_2$. Interestingly enough, when restricted to this class of conditionals, $\&_2$ and $\&_3$ do coincide.

It is worth noticing that the above conjunctions are defined in order to make the class $A \mid A$ of conditional objects closed under $\&_i$, and hence an algebra. Therefore for every $a_1, b_1, a_2, b_2 \in A$, and for every $i = 1, 2, 3$, there exists $c, d \in A$ such that, $(a_1 \mid b_1) \&_i (a_2 \mid b_2) = (c \mid d)$. This leads us to introduce a further constraint:

Context Constraint (CC): Let $a_1 \mid b_1$, $a_2 \mid b_2$ be conditionals in $A \mid A$. If $b_1 = b_2$, then the conjunction $(a_1 \mid b_1)$ AND $(a_2 \mid b_2)$ is a conditional in the form $c \mid d$, and in that case $d = b_1 = b_2$.

The Context constraint is better understood by pointing out that, whenever the object $(a_1 \mid b_1)$ AND $(a_2 \mid b_2)$ cannot be reduced to a conditional $c \mid d$, then necessarily $b_1 \neq b_2$.

Note that each of the $\&_i$'s above satisfy the stronger requirement, denoted by (CC)', that for every $a_1 \mid b_1$, and $a_2 \mid b_2$, $(a_1 \mid b_1)$ AND $(a_2 \mid b_2)$ is a conditional in the form $c \mid d$ (but in general $d \neq b_1$, and $d \neq b_2$). This stronger condition ensures in fact that $A \mid A$ is closed under $\&_i$, and hence makes $\&_i$ a total operator on $A \mid A$. On the other hand, as we are going to show in the next section, our construction of conditional algebra, defines a structure whose domain strictly contains all the elements $a \mid b$ for a in A, and b belonging to a particular subset of A guaranteeing the satisfaction of our Rejection constraint. This allows us to relax this condition of closure as stated above. Indeed, for every pair of conditionals of the form $a_1 \mid b_1$ and $a_2 \mid b_2$ belonging to the conditional algebra, their conjunction will always be an element of the algebra (i.e. the conjunction is a total, and not a partial, operation), but in general it will be not in the form $c \mid d$. Therefore we will provide a definition for conjunction between conditionals that satisfies (CC), but not, in general, (CC)'. Moreover our definition of conjunction behaves as $\&_2$, and $\&_3$ whenever restricted to those conditionals $(a_1 \mid b_1), (a_2 \mid b_2)$ with $b_1 = b_2$.

4   Conditional Boolean Algebras

We now show how a conditional Boolean algebra can be built up from any Boolean algebra A and a non-empty $\{\perp\}$-free subset of A, which we will call a *bunch* of A, and denote by A'.

Let A be any Boolean algebra and let $A \times A'$ be the cartesian product of A and A' (as sets). We denote by

$$\mathcal{F}(A \times A') = (\mathcal{F}(A \times A'), \wedge^{\mathcal{F}}, \vee^{\mathcal{F}}, \neg^{\mathcal{F}}, \perp^{\mathcal{F}}, \top^{\mathcal{F}})$$

the Boolean algebra freely generated by the pairs $(a, b) \in A \times A'$ (cf. [4][II §10]). Consider the following elements in $\mathcal{F}(A \times A')$: for every $x, z \in A$, $y, k \in A'$,

$x_1 \in A$ and $z_1 \in A'$ with $x_1 \ngeq z_1$, and $x_2 \in A$ and $y_2, z_2 \in A'$ such that $x_2 \to y_2 = y_2 \to z_2 = \top$.

(t1) $\delta((y,y), \top^{\mathcal{F}})$

(t2) $\delta((x,y) \wedge^{\mathcal{F}} (z,y), (x \wedge z, y))$

(t3) $\delta(\neg^{\mathcal{F}}(x,y), (\neg x, y))$

(t4) $\delta((x \wedge y, y), (x, y))$

(t5) $\neg\delta((x_1, z_1), (z_1, z_1))$

(t6) $\delta((x_2, z_2), (x_2, y_2) \wedge^{\mathcal{F}} (y_2, z_2))$.

Consider the proper ideal $\mathfrak{C}$ of $\mathcal{F}(A \times A')$ that is generated by the set of all the instances of the above introduced terms (t1)-(t6).

Definition 1. *For every Boolean algebra A and every bunch A' of A, we say that the quotient algebra $\mathcal{C}(A, A') = \mathcal{F}(A \times A')/\mathfrak{C}$ is the conditional algebra of A and A'.*

Thus, every conditional algebra $\mathcal{C}(A, A')$ is a quotient of a free Boolean algebra, whence is Boolean. So our Boolean constraint is satisfied.

We will denote atomic elements of $A \times A'$ by $a \mid b$ instead of (a, b). In a conditional algebra $\mathcal{C}(A, A')$ we therefore have *atomic conditionals* in the form $a \mid b$ for $a \in A$, and $b \in A'$, and also *compound conditionals* being those elements in $\mathcal{C}(A, A')$ that are the algebraic terms definable in the language of Boolean algebras, modulo the identification induced by $\mathfrak{C}$. The operations on $\mathcal{C}(A, A')$ are denoted using the following notation, which is to be interpreted in the obvious way:

$$\mathcal{C}(A, A') = (\mathcal{C}(A, A'), \cap_{\mathfrak{C}}, \cup_{\mathfrak{C}}, \neg_{\mathfrak{C}}, \bot_{\mathfrak{C}}, \top_{\mathfrak{C}}).$$

The construction of $\mathcal{C}(A, A')$, and in particular the role of the ideal $\mathfrak{C}$, is best illustrated by means of an example.

Example 1. Let A be the four elements Boolean algebra $\{\top, a, \neg a, \bot\}$, and consider the bunch $A' = A \setminus \{\bot\}$. Then $A \times A' = \{(\top, \top), (\top, a), (\top, \neg a), (a, \top), (a, a), (a, \neg a), (\neg a, \top), (\neg a, a), (\neg a, \neg a), (\bot, \top), (\bot, a), (\bot, \neg a)\}$. The cartesian product $A \times A'$ has cardinality 12, whence $\mathcal{F}(A \times A')$ is the free Boolean algebra of cardinality $2^{2^{12}}$, i.e. the finite Boolean algebra of 2^{12} atoms. The conditional algebra $\mathcal{C}(A, A')$ is then obtained as the quotient of $\mathcal{F}(A \times A')$ by the ideal $\mathfrak{C}$ generated by (t1)-(t6). Having in mind Proposition 2, we can easily see that the ideal $\mathfrak{C}$ of $\mathcal{F}(A \times A')$ specifically *forces* the free algebra $\mathcal{F}(A \times A')$ about which elements are equal as conditionals. For instance, following Proposition 3 (see below), in $\mathcal{C}(A, A')$ the following equations hold: $\top \mid \top = a \mid a = (\neg a) \mid (\neg a)$; $(\top \mid \top) \cap_{\mathfrak{C}} (a \mid \top) = (\top \wedge a) \mid \top = (a \mid \top)$; $\neg_{\mathfrak{C}}(\top \mid \top) = \bot \mid \top$, $\neg_{\mathfrak{C}}(a \mid \neg a) = (\neg a) \mid (\neg a) = \top \mid \top$.

Notice that the conditional algebra $\mathcal{C}(A, A')$ can be defined as a quotient of the free Boolean algebra $\mathcal{F}(X)$ by $\mathfrak{C}$, where X is the subset of $A \times A'$ whose pairs are not redundant under $\mathfrak{C}$, i.e. $X = \{(x_i, y_i) \in A \times A' : \forall i \neq j, \delta((x_i, y_i), (x_j, y_j)) \notin \mathfrak{C}\} = \{(\top, \top), (a, \top), (\neg a, \top), (\bot, \top)\}$. Therefore $\mathcal{F}(X)$ is the free Boolean algebra with 2^4 atoms.

Proposition 3. *Every conditional algebra* $\mathcal{C}(A, A')$ *satisfies the following equations:*

(e1) *For all* $y \in A'$, $y \mid y = \top_{\mathfrak{C}}$
(e2) *For all* $x, z \in A$ *and* $y \in A'$, $(x \mid y) \cap_{\mathfrak{C}} (z \mid y) = (x \wedge z) \mid y$
(e3) *For all* $x \in A$ *and* $y \in A'$, $\neg_{\mathfrak{C}}(x \mid y) = (\neg x \mid y)$
(e4) *For all* $x \in A$, *for all* $y \in A'$, $(x \wedge y \mid y) = (x \mid y)$
(e5) *For all* $x, y \in A$, *if* $(x \mid \top) = (y \mid \top)$, *then* $x = y$
(e6) *For all* $y \in A'$, $\neg y \mid y = \bot_{\mathfrak{C}}$
(e7) *For all* $x, z \in A$, *and* $y \in A'$, $(x \mid y) \cup_{\mathfrak{C}} (z \mid y) = (x \vee z \mid y)$
(e8) *For all* $x \in A$ *and* $y, z \in A'$ *such that* $x \rightarrow y = y \rightarrow z = \top$, $(x \mid z) = (x \mid y) \cap_{\mathfrak{C}} (y \mid z)$

Remark 2. (1) As we have already stated, for all $a_1 \mid b_1, a_2 \mid b_2 \in A \times A'$, their conjunction is the element $(a_1 \mid b_1) \cap_{\mathfrak{C}} (a_2 \mid b_2)$ that belongs to the conditional algebra by definition. Notice that $(a_1 \mid b_1) \cap_{\mathfrak{C}} (a_2 \mid b_2) = (c \mid d)$ iff, from Proposition 2, $\delta((a_1 \mid b_1) \cap_{\mathfrak{C}} (a_2 \mid b_2), (c \mid d)) \in \mathfrak{C}$. Therefore (**t2**) ensures that, if $b_1 = b_2 = d$, then $(a_1 \mid d) \cap_{\mathfrak{C}} (a_2 \mid d) = (c \mid d)$ (see Proposition 3 (**e2**)). Therefore our Context constraint (CC) is satisfied. Also notice that (CC)' is not satisfied in general by the conjunction we have defined in $\mathcal{C}(A, A')$. In fact, when $b_1 \neq b_2$, we cannot ensure in general $(a_1 \mid b_1) \cap_{\mathfrak{C}} (a_2 \mid b_2)$ to be atomic, and hence in the form $(c \mid d)$. In any case $\mathcal{C}(A, A')$ is closed under $\cap_{\mathfrak{C}}$.

(2) The Rejection constraint introduced in Sect. 2, forces our construction to drop $\bot$ from the algebra intended to contain the antecedents of conditionals. For this reason we defined the *bunch* as a bottom-free subset of A. Notice that if we allowed the conditional algebra to represent counterfactual conditionals (i.e. had we not imposed the Rejection constraint), the resulting algebraic structure would have not be Boolean as shown in [19, 22]. In this sense, the Rejection constraint can be seen as being closely connected to the Boolean one.

In a conditional algebra $\mathcal{C}(A, A')$, as in any Boolean algebra, one can define the order relation $\leq$ by the letting

$$(x \mid y) \leq (z \mid k) \text{ iff } (x \mid y) \cap_{\mathfrak{C}} (z \mid k) = (x \mid y). \tag{2}$$

Proposition 4. *In every conditional algebra* $\mathcal{C}(A, A')$ *the following hold:*

(o1) *For every* $x, y \in A$, *and for every* $z \in A'$, $(x \mid y) \leq (z \mid z)$; *moreover* $(x \mid z) \geq (z \mid z)$, *implies* $x \geq z$
(o2) *For every* $x, y \in A$ *and* $z \in A'$, *if* $x \leq y$, *then* $(x \mid z) \leq (y \mid z)$ *(where clearly* $x \leq y$ *means with respect to* A*).* In particular $x \leq y$ iff $(x \mid \top) \leq (y \mid \top)$
(o3) *For every* $x \in A$ *and* $y \in A'$, *if* $x \not\geq y$, *then* $(x \mid y) \neq (y \mid y)$, *and in particular* $(x \mid y) < (y \mid y)$
(o4) *For every* $x, y \in A$ *and* $z \in A'$, *if* $(x \mid z) \neq (y \mid z)$, *then* $x \neq y$. *In particular* $x \neq y$ iff $(x \mid \top) \neq (y \mid \top)$
(o5) *For every* $x \in A'$, $(\top \mid x) = (x \mid x) = \top_{\mathfrak{C}}$, *and* $(\bot \mid x) = (\neg x \mid x) = \bot_{\mathfrak{C}}$
(o6) *For every* $x, y \in A$ *and* $z, k \in A'$, $(x \mid k) \cap_{\mathfrak{C}} (y \mid z) = (x \mid k)$ iff $(x \mid k) \cup_{\mathfrak{C}} (y \mid z) = (y \mid z)$

Remark 3. As we have already observed, every conditional algebra $\mathcal{C}(A, A')$ is finite whenever A is finite. So, if A is finite, $\mathcal{C}(A, A')$ is atomic. Moreover, since the canonical homomorphism $h_{\mathcal{C}} : \mathcal{F}(A \times A') \to \mathcal{C}(A, A')$ is onto, we have:

$$2^{2^{|A \times A'|}} = |\mathcal{F}(A \times A')| \geq |\mathcal{C}(A, A')|.$$

Finally, recall that a conditional probability on a Boolean algebra A is a map $\mu : A \times A' \to [0,1]$, where A' is a bunch of A, such that:

(μ1) For all $x \in A'$, $\mu(x \mid x) = 1$,
(μ2) If $x_1, x_2 \in A$, $x_1 \wedge x_2 = 0$ and $y \in A'$, $\mu(x_1 \vee x_2 \mid y) = \mu(x_1 \mid y) + \mu(x_2 \mid y)$,
(μ3) If $x \in A$ and $y \in A'$, $\mu(x \mid y) = \mu(x \wedge y \mid y)$,
(μ4) If $x \in A$ and $y, z \in A'$ such that $x \to y = y \to z = \top$, then $\mu(x \mid z) = \mu(x \mid y) \cdot \mu(y \mid z)$.

Theorem 1. *Let A be a Boolean algebra, A' a bunch of A and let $\mu : \mathcal{C}(A, A') \to [0,1]$ be a simple (i.e. unconditional) probability further satisfying: for all $x \in A$ and $y, z \in A'$ such that $x \to y = y \to z = \top$*

$$\mu((x \mid y) \cap_{\mathcal{C}} (y \mid z)) = \mu(x \mid y) \cdot \mu(y \mid z). \tag{3}$$

Then, μ satisfies all the axioms of a conditional probability on A.

Proof. The properties (μ1) and (μ3) respectively follow from Proposition 3 (e1), (e4) together, with the normalization property for probability measures: $\mu(\top) = 1$. In order to show (μ2), notice that whenever $x_1 \wedge x_2 = \bot$, then from Proposition 3 (e2), for every $y \in A'$, $(x_1 \mid y) \cap_{\mathcal{C}} (x_2 \mid y) = (x_1 \wedge x_2 \mid y) = (\bot \mid y) = \bot_{\mathcal{C}}$. Therefore, since μ is additive, $\mu((x_1 \mid y) \cup_{\mathcal{C}} (x_2 \mid y)) = \mu(x_1 \mid y) + \mu(x_2 \mid y)$. Therefore ($\mu$2) also holds because by Proposition 3 (e7), $(x_1 \mid y) \cup_{\mathcal{C}} (x_2 \mid y) = (x_1 \vee x_2) \mid y$. Finally, by Proposition 3 (e8) together with (3), if $x \in A$ and $y, z \in A'$ are such that $x \to y = y \to z = \top$, $\mu(x \mid z) = \mu((x \mid y) \wedge_{\mathcal{C}} (y \mid z)) = \mu(x \mid y) \cdot \mu(y \mid z)$. $\qquad \square$

5   Conclusions and Further Work

The results reported in this paper constitute a first step towards providing a rather flexible framework for conditionals which builds on the distinction between the properties of a conditional event and those of a conditional measure. Our next step will involve relaxing the Boolean constraint, a relaxation which implies a substantial generalization of the Rejection constraint as well and that may have a significant impact on our understanding of conditional *many-valued* probability, a topic to which considerable research effort has been devoted in the past decade, see e.g. [9,12,17,18]). Another interesting prospective (pointed out by one of the referees) is to look at the conditional as a partial operation on a Boolean algebra and apply techniques of theory of partial algebras [3].

Acknowledgments The authors are very grateful for the interesting comments by two anonymous reviewers. Flaminio was supported by the Italian project FIRB 2010 (RBFR10DGUA_002). Godo acknowledges partial support of the Spanish MINECO project TIN2012-39348-C02-01. Hosni acknowledges the support of the EU Marie Curie IEF-GA-2012-327630 project *Rethinking Uncertainty: A Choice-based approach.*

References

1. Adams, E.W.: The Logic of Conditionals. D. Reidel, Dordrecht (1975)
2. Adams, Ernest W.: What is at stake in the controversy over conditionals. In: Kern-Isberner, Gabriele, Rödder, Wilhelm, Kulmann, Friedhelm (eds.) WCII 2002. LNCS (LNAI), vol. 3301, pp. 1–11. Springer, Heidelberg (2005)
3. Burmeister, P.: Partial algebras - an introductory survey. In: Rosenberg, I.G., Sabidussi, G. (eds.) Algebras and Orders. NATO ASI Series C, vol. 389, pp. 1–70. Kluwer Academic Publishers, Dordrecht (1993)
4. Burris, S., Sankappanavar, H.P.: A Course in Universal Algebra. Springer-Verlag, New York (1981)
5. Calabrese, P.: An algebraic synthesis of the foundations of logic and probability. Inf. Sci. **42**, 187–237 (1987)
6. Dubois, D., Prade, H.: Measure-free conditioning, probability and non-monotonic reasoning. In: Proceedings of IJCAI 1989, vol. 2, pp. 1110–1114 (1989)
7. Flaminio, T., Godo, L., Hosni, H.: On the logical structure of de Finettis notion of event. J. Appl. Logic **12**(3), 279–301 (2014)
8. Flaminio, T., Godo, L., Hosni, H.: Coherence in the aggregate: a betting method for belief functions on many-valued events. Int. J. Approximate Reasoning **58**, 71–86 (2015)
9. Gerla, B.: Conditioning a state by a Lukasiewicz event: a probabilistic approach to Ulam games. Theoret. Comput. Sci. **230**, 149–166 (2000)
10. Goodman, I.R., Mahler, R.P.S., Nguyen, H.T.: What is conditional event algebra and why should you care? In: Proceedings of the SPIE, vol. 3720 (1999)
11. Goodman, I.R., Nguyen, H.T.: Conditional objects and the modeling of uncertainty. In: Gupta, M.M., Yamakawa, T. (eds.) Fuzzy Computing: Theory, Hardware and Applications, pp. 119–138. North-Holland, Amsterdam (1998)
12. Kroupa, T.: Conditional probability on MV-algebras. Fuzzy Sets and Systems **149**(2), 369–381 (2005)
13. Lewis, D.: Probabilities of conditionals and conditional probabilities I-II. Philos. Rev. **85**(3), 297 (1976). And 54(4):581–589 (1986)
14. Makinson, D.: Bridges from Classical to Non-monotonic Logic. College Publications, London (2005)
15. Makinson, D.: Conditional probability in the light of qualitative belief change. In: Hosni, H., Montagna, F. (eds.) Probability, Uncertainty and Rationality. Edizioni della Normale, Pisa (2010)
16. Milne, P.: The simplest Lewis-style triviality proof yet? Analysis **63**(4), 300–303 (2003)
17. Montagna, F.: A notion of coherence for books on conditional events in many-valued logic. J. Logic Comput. **21**(5), 829–850 (2011)
18. Mundici, D.: Faithful and invariant conditional probability in łukasiewicz logic. In: Makinson, D., Malinowski, J., Wansing, H. (eds.) Towards Mathematical Philosophy. Trends in Logic, vol. 28, pp. 213–232. Springer, Netherlands (2009)

19. Nguyen, H.T., Walker, E.A.: A history and introduction to the algebra of conditional events and probability logic. IEEE Trans. Syst. Man Cybern. B Cybern. **24**(12), 1671–1675 (1994)
20. Quine, W.V.: Methods of Logic. Harvard University Press, Cambridge (1959)
21. Schay, G.: An algebra of conditional events. J. Math. Anal. Appl. **24**, 334–344 (1968)
22. Walker, E.A.: Stone algebras, conditional events and three valued logics. IEEE Trans. Syst. Man Cybern. B Cybern. **24**(12), 1699–1707 (1994)

In All, but Finitely Many, Possible Worlds: Model-Theoretic Investigations on 'Overwhelming Majority' Default Conditionals

Costas D. Koutras[1]([✉]) and Christos Rantsoudis[2]

[1] Department of Informatics and Telecommunications, University of Peloponnese,
End of Karaiskaki Street, 221 00 Tripolis, Greece
ckoutras@uop.gr
[2] Graduate Programme in Logic, Algorithms and Computation (MPLA),
Department of Mathematics, University of Athens,
Panepistimioupolis, 157 84 Ilissia, Greece
rants212@yahoo.gr

Abstract. Defeasible conditionals of the form '*if A then normally B*' are usually interpreted with the aid of a '*normality*' ordering between possible states of affairs: $A \Rightarrow B$ is true if it happens that in the most '*normal*' (least *exceptional*) A-worlds, B is also true. Another plausible interpretation of '*normality*' introduced in nonmonotonic reasoning dictates that $A \Rightarrow B$ is true iff B is true in '*most*' A-worlds. A formal account of '*most*' in this *majority*-based approach to default reasoning has been given through the usage of (weak) filters and (weak) ultrafilters, capturing at least, a basic core of a size-oriented approach to defeasible reasoning. In this paper, we investigate *defeasible conditionals* constructed upon a notion of '*overwhelming majority*', defined as '*truth in a cofinite subset of ω*', the first infinite ordinal. One approach employs the modal logic of the frame $(\omega, <)$, used in the temporal logic of discrete linear time. We introduce and investigate conditionals, defined modally over $(\omega, <)$; several modal definitions of the conditional connective are examined, with an emphasis on the nonmonotonic ones. An alternative interpretation of '*majority*' as sets *cofinal* (in ω) rather than cofinite (subsets of ω) is examined. For all these modal approaches over $(\omega, <)$, a decision procedure readily emerges, as the modal logic **KD4LZ** of this frame is well-known and a translation of the conditional sentences can be mechanically checked for validity. A second approach employs the conditional version of Scott-Montague semantics, in the form of ω, endowed with neighborhoods populated by its cofinite subsets. Again, different conditionals are introduced and examined. Although it is not feasible to obtain a completeness theorem, since it is not easy to capture 'cofiniteness-in-ω' syntactically, this research reveals the possible structure of '*overwhelming majority*' conditionals, whose relative strength is compared to (the conditional logic 'equivalent' of) KLM logics and other conditional logics in the literature.

Keywords: Defeasible conditionals · Default reasoning · Conditional logics of normality

© Springer International Publishing Switzerland 2015
S. Destercke and T. Denoeux (Eds.): ECSQARU 2015, LNAI 9161, pp. 117–126, 2015.
DOI: 10.1007/978-3-319-20807-7_11

1 Introduction

Artificial Intelligence has been interested in *conditional logics* for *default reasoning* already from the '80s (see the work of J. Delgrande [6,7]) *counterfactual reasoning* (M. Ginsberg, [10]) and '*normality conditionals*' in nonmonotonic reasoning [2,5]. The reader is referred to the handbook article of J. Delgrande [8] for a broad overview of conditional logics for defeasible reasoning. The investigations on the intimate relation of conditional logics to nonmonotonic reasoning have been further triggered by the seminal work of S. Kraus, D. Lehmann and M. Magidor [14,16], whose framework (KLM) has become the 'industry standard' for nonmonotonic consequence relations. There exist various possible-worlds semantics for conditional logics (see [8,18,19]) and a connection to modal logic (known from D. Lewis' work [17]) which has been further explored by the modal construction of '*normality conditionals*' [5,15].

A logic of '*normality conditionals*' for default reasoning, attempts to pin down the principles governing the statements of the form '*if A, then normally B is the case*'. '*Normally*' is susceptible to a variety of interpretations. One is based on a '*normality*' ordering between possible worlds: $A \Rightarrow B$ is true if it happens that in the most '*normal*' (least *exceptional*) A-worlds, B is also true [5,15]. Another, more recent one [12] interprets '*normally*' as a '*majority*' quantifier: $A \Rightarrow B$ is true iff B is true in '*most*' A-worlds. Questions of '*size*' in preferential nonmonotonic reasoning have been firstly introduced by K. Schlechta [20].

A majority-based account of default conditionals, depends heavily on what counts as a 'majority' of alternative situations, what is a 'large' set of possible worlds. It is difficult to state a good definition that would work for both the finite and the infinite case; the notions of (weak) *filters* and (weak) *ultrafilters* that have been used capture the minimum requirements of such a notion [21]. In this paper, we experiment with a notion of '*overwhelming majority*', combined with the widely accepted intuition that $A \Rightarrow B$ means that $A \wedge B$ is more plausible than $A \wedge \neg B$. We define conditionals of this form to (essentially) mean that $A \wedge B$ is true is '*all, but finitely many*') points in the countable modal frame $(\omega, <)$ (the first infinite ordinal, strictly ordered under $<$), whose modal axiomatization (the normal modal logic **KD4LZ**) is known as the 'future' fragment of the temporal logic of discrete linear time [11,22]. This majority conditional is modally defined and this readily provides a decision procedure, as a modal translation of conditional formulas can be checked for validity in $(\omega, <)$ using any of the proof procedures known for **KD4LZ**. We examine the properties of this conditional, in particular with respect to the (conditional incarnation of the) '*conservative core*' of defeasible reasoning set by the KLM framework. The paradigm of '*overwhelming majority*' in our work is consistently represented with cofinite subsets of ω, with the sole exception of a conditional which is defined over cofinal subsets of ω. Then, we discuss the possibility of defining conditional over cofinite subsets of ω in the neighborhood semantics for conditional logics; we prove that the conditionals defined can be very weak, even compared to the conditionals introduced in [9]. Due to space limitations, proofs of the results are omitted; for more details and full proofs, the reader is referred to [13].

2 Background

We assume a language $\mathcal{L}$ of classical propositional logic, built upon the known *connectives* $\{\neg, \wedge, \vee, \rightarrow, \equiv\}$. The language $\mathcal{L}_\square$ of propositional modal logic extends $\mathcal{L}$ with a modal necessity operator $\square A$. The language $\mathcal{L}_\Rightarrow$ of propositional conditional logic extends $\mathcal{L}$ with a binary conditional connective $(A \Rightarrow B)$, interpreted for our purposes as 'A *normally implies* B'. We assume that the reader is acquainted with the basics of Modal Logic and Conditional Logic (see [4,18]). We are going to make use of the following fact (see [11,22]): it is well known that the frame $(\omega, <)$ of the natural numbers with their natural strict ordering is axiomatized by the logic $\mathbf{\Omega}$, where $\mathbf{\Omega}$ is an abbreviation for the normal modal logic **K4DLZ** [11, Ch. 8]. The logic $\mathbf{\Omega}$ has been investigated in the context of axiomatizing the '*future*' fragment of discrete linear time. We will extensively exploit below that $\vdash_\Omega A$ iff $(\omega, <) \models A$. Due to space limitations, we are not able to provide details on Conditional Logics and the KLM systems. Yet, all the axioms and rules mentioned, appear in the table to be found at the end of Sect. 3. The reader should keep in mind that we use the symbol $\rightarrow$ for the classical ('*material*') implication and $\Rightarrow$ for the '*majority-default*' conditional(s) defined.

3 '*Overwhelming Majority*' Conditionals

We wish to define (variants of) a default conditional of the form 'A *normally implies* B'. The fundamental question is to provide a concrete interpretation of the statement '*normally*'. Earlier approaches resort to '*normality*' orderings ([5,7,15]: $A \Rightarrow B$ is true iff B is true in the most normal A-worlds), and considerations of '*size*' ([12]: $A \Rightarrow B$ is true iff B is true in '*many*' ('*most*') A-worlds). In this paper, we design '*majority default*' conditionals based on this intuition - note that we consistently work with the infinite set ω of possible worlds:

- $A \Rightarrow B$ is an '*overwhelming majority*' conditional, in the sense that we consider as '*large*' the cofinite subsets of ω (and '*small*' the finite ones). Obviously, this is an (extreme, but) intuitively acceptable form of '*overwhelming majority*'.
- $A \Rightarrow B$ is true , either vacuously (if there are no '*many*' A-worlds) or essentially: iff $\|A \wedge B\|$ is much larger (it is a cofinite set) than $\|A \wedge \neg B\|$.

Throughout this section, we will be working with the set ω of countably many possible worlds, with the aim of providing different accounts of 'A *normally implies* B' $(A \Rightarrow B)$ as 'B *is true in all, but finitely many, A-worlds*'.

3.1 Conditionals Modally Defined over $(\omega, <)$

Our first approach is to define a '*majority*' conditional over the frame $(\omega, <)$ of natural numbers, strictly ordered under $<$. Conforming to the intuition(s) expressed above, we will define $(A \Rightarrow B)$ as shorthand for:

$$(A \Rightarrow B) \quad \equiv_{def} \quad \Diamond\square\neg A \vee \Diamond\square(A \wedge B)$$

The import of such a modal definition over $(\omega, <)$ is that either there do not exist '*many*' A-worlds (A settles down to be false, at some '*point*') or there exist '*many*' '*points*' in which $A \wedge B$ is true ($A \wedge B$ is true in a cofinite subset of ω). To state properly the conditional logic induced by this definition , we proceed to define the following translation of conditionals to the (mono)modal language $\mathcal{L}_\square$:

Definition 1. We recursively define the following translation $()^* : \mathcal{L}_\Rightarrow \to \mathcal{L}_\square$

   (i) $(p)^* = p$, if $p \in \Phi$ (p is a propositional variable)
  (ii) $(A \circ B)^* = (A)^* \circ (B)^*$ for $\circ \in \{\wedge, \vee, \to, \equiv\}$
 (iii) $(\neg A)^* = \neg(A)^*$
 (iv) $(A \Rightarrow B)^* = \Diamond\square\neg(A)^* \vee \Diamond\square(A^* \wedge B^*)$

We proceed to define the logic $\overrightarrow{\Omega}$ of '*majority consequence*' over $(\omega, <)$:

Definition 2 [Conditional Logic $\overrightarrow{\Omega}$]. The logic $\overrightarrow{\Omega}$ consists of all formulae $A \in \mathcal{L}_\Rightarrow$, such that:

$$A \in \overrightarrow{\Omega} \quad \text{iff} \quad (\omega, <) \models A^*$$

It is known that the logic $\Omega = \mathbf{K4DLZ}$ is the logic of (is determined by) the frame $(\omega, <)$ and thus it holds that $(\omega, <) \models A^*$ iff $\vdash_\Omega A^*$.

Fact 1. Let $\mathfrak{M}$ be a model of $\mathfrak{F} = (\omega, <)$ and $n \in \omega$ an arbitrary world. It follows that $\mathfrak{M}, n \models (A \Rightarrow B)$ iff one of the following holds:

 (i) $(\exists n_1 > n)(\forall n_2 > n_1)\ \mathfrak{M}, n_2 \models \neg A$
(ii) $(\exists n_3 > n)(\forall n_4 > n_3)\ \mathfrak{M}, n_4 \models A \wedge B$

Some comments on the definition of $\overrightarrow{\Omega}$ are in order. This model-theoretic modal definition of the conditional has the advantage that it is a clear '*majority*' definition, easy to understand, with an intuitively acceptable '*largeness*' condition. It captures '*cofinite*' subsets of ω in an easy manner, in contrast to the difficulty of capturing this axiomatically. Further on, and perhaps more important, a decision procedure readily emerges from the definition: to check whether a conditional $A \Rightarrow B$ is in $\overrightarrow{\Omega}$, simply check whether $(A \Rightarrow B)^*$ has a tableaux proof in $\mathbf{K4DLZ}$; such a proof procedure exists. On the other hand, the ordering in $(\omega, <)$ has not any clear '*preference*' meaning here.

Theorem 2. The logic $\overrightarrow{\Omega}$:

1. is closed under the rules **RCEA**, **RCK** and **RCEC**
2. contains the axioms **CUT**, **AC**, **CC**, **Loop**, **OR**, **CSO**, **CM**, **CA**, **Transitivity**, **Weak Transitivity** and **Weak Modus Ponens**

Proof. We provide a sketch for **Weak Transitivity**: We have to show that

$$\mathfrak{F} \models (A \Rightarrow B) \wedge (B \Rightarrow C) \Rightarrow (A \Rightarrow C)$$

Assume an arbitrary state $n \in \omega$ and $\mathfrak{M}$ a model of $\mathfrak{F}$. We have that $\mathfrak{M}, n \models (A \Rightarrow B) \wedge (B \Rightarrow C) \Rightarrow (A \Rightarrow C)$ iff one of the following holds:

(i) $(\exists n_1 > n)(\forall n_2 > n_1)\ \mathfrak{M}, n_2 \models \neg(A \Rightarrow B) \vee \neg(B \Rightarrow C)$, or
(ii) $(\exists n_3 > n)(\forall n_4 > n_3)\ \mathfrak{M}, n_4 \models (A \Rightarrow B) \wedge (B \Rightarrow C) \wedge (A \Rightarrow C)$

Let (i) be false, that is let $(\forall n_1 > n)(\exists n_2 > n_1)\ \mathfrak{M}, n_2 \models (A \Rightarrow B) \wedge (B \Rightarrow C)$ $(*)$. We will show that (ii) has to be true. By $(*)$ we have that $(\forall n_1 > n)(\exists n_2 > n_1)$ such that both the following disjunctions hold:

- $(\exists n_5 > n_2)(\forall n_6 > n_5)\ \mathfrak{M}, n_6 \models \neg A$ **or** $(\exists n_5 > n_2)(\forall n_6 > n_5)\ \mathfrak{M}, n_6 \models A \wedge B$
- $(\exists n_5 > n_2)(\forall n_6 > n_5)\ \mathfrak{M}, n_6 \models \neg B$ **or** $(\exists n_5 > n_2)(\forall n_6 > n_5)\ \mathfrak{M}, n_6 \models B \wedge C$

This means that one of the following must hold:

(a) $(\forall n_1 > n)(\exists n_5 > n_1)(\forall n_6 > n_5)\ \mathfrak{M}, n_6 \models (\neg A \wedge \neg B)$
(b) $(\forall n_1 > n)(\exists n_5 > n_1)(\forall n_6 > n_5)\ \mathfrak{M}, n_6 \models (\neg A \wedge B \wedge C)$
(c) $(\forall n_1 > n)(\exists n_5 > n_1)(\forall n_6 > n_5)\ \mathfrak{M}, n_6 \models (A \wedge B \wedge C)$

All of these cases give us that

$$(\forall n_1 > n)\ \mathfrak{M}, n_1 \models (A \Rightarrow B) \wedge (B \Rightarrow C) \wedge (A \Rightarrow C)$$

Consequently, we also have that

$$(\exists n_3 > n)(\forall n_4 > n_3)\ \mathfrak{M}, n_4 \models (A \Rightarrow B) \wedge (B \Rightarrow C) \wedge (A \Rightarrow C)$$

which is exactly (ii). So one of (i) or (ii) must hold, which means that

$$\mathfrak{M}, n \models (A \Rightarrow B) \wedge (B \Rightarrow C) \Rightarrow (A \Rightarrow C)$$

Since the world n and model $\mathfrak{M}$ were arbitrarily chosen, the proof is complete. ∎

Theorem 3. The logic $\overset{\Rightarrow}{\Omega}$:

1. is not closed under the rule **RCE**
2. does not contain the axioms **ID, CV, MP, MOD, CS, CEM, SDA, Monotonicity** and **Weak Monotonicity**

Observe that $\overset{\Rightarrow}{\Omega}$ does not contain the **ID** axiom. This might appear strange; after all '*reflexivity seems to be satisfied universally by any kind of reasoning based on some notion of consequence*' [14, p. 177]. Yet, in the same sense as observed in [14], conditionals that do not satisfy it '*probably express some notion of theory change*'. It seems that failure of **ID** is due to the unavoidable '*temporal*' flavour of $(\omega, <)$, whose ordering directly reminds the setting of discrete linear time. However, this seems appropriate for conditionals incorporating a notion of 'temporal' causation, in the form '*if X, then normally it should be the case that Y holds in the future*' - "*normally, a strong earthquake implies a permanent change in future building codes*". It is natural, however, to consider alternative modal definitions of the conditional connective that would enforce the validity of **ID**. In the full paper, we demonstrate that some plausible attempts to validate **ID** result into a monotonic conditional logic (see [13]).

An Alternative: Cofinal vs Cofinite in $(\omega, <)$. In this subsection, we discuss a possible alternative. Instead of working with the (obviously large) cofinite subsets of ω, we will attempt to work with cofinal subsets: $S \subseteq \omega$ is cofinal in ω iff for every $n \in \omega$ there exists an $s \in S$, such that $n < s$.

We proceed to define the conditional $(A \Rightarrow B)$ as follows:

$$(A \Rightarrow B) \quad \equiv_{def} \quad \Diamond\Box\neg A \vee \Box\Diamond(A \wedge B)$$

Definition 3 [Conditional Logic $\overrightarrow{\omega}$]. The logic $\overrightarrow{\omega}$ consists of all formulae $A \in \mathcal{L}_\Rightarrow$, such that:

$$A \in \overrightarrow{\omega} \quad \text{iff} \quad (\omega, <) \models A^* \quad \text{iff} \quad \vdash_{\mathbf{K4DLZ}} A^*$$

where A^* is the obvious translation defined similarly to Definition 1.

The logic $\overrightarrow{\omega}$ turns out to be quite interesting.

Theorem 4. The logic $\overrightarrow{\omega}$:

1. is closed under the rules **RCEA**, **RCEC** and **RCE**
2. contains the axioms **ID**, **CUT**, **Loop**, **OR**, **CV**, **CM**, **MOD**, **CEM** and **Weak Modus Ponens**

Theorem 5. The logic $\overrightarrow{\omega}$:

1. is not closed under the rule **RCK**
2. does not contain the axioms **AC**, **CC**, **CSO**, **MP**, **CA**, **CS**, **SDA**, **Transitivity**, **Weak Transitivity**, **Monotonicity** and **Weak Monotonicity**

3.2 Majority Conditionals over ω Equipped with Neighborhoods of Cofinite Subsets

In this section, we return to the original '*cofinite-as-large*' intuition and we take a more '*traditional*' approach. We resort to the minimal (Scott-Montague) semantics for conditionals introduced by Chellas, and we discuss variants of truth assignment to conditional statements in worlds whose neighborhoods contain cofinite (large) subsets of ω. Models in this section are based on a frame $\mathfrak{F} = (\omega, f)$, where

$$f : \omega \times 2^\omega \to 2^{2^\omega}$$

maps worlds ($n \in \omega$) and propositions, to neighborhoods of cofinite subsets of ω.

Definition 4 [Conditional Logic $\overrightarrow{\mathfrak{m}_1}$]. Let $\overrightarrow{\mathfrak{m}_1}$ be the logic consisting of all $A \in \mathcal{L}_\Rightarrow$ valid in $\mathfrak{F} = (\omega, f)$, where a conditional is evaluated as follows:
For a model $\mathfrak{M}$ over $\mathfrak{F}$, $\mathfrak{M}, n \models (A \Rightarrow B)$ iff either

(i) there exists $S \subseteq \|\neg A\|$ such that $S \in f(n, \|A\|)$, or
(ii) there exists $T \subseteq \|A \wedge B\|$ such that $T \in f(n, \|A\|)$

Theorem 6. The logic $\overrightarrow{\mathbf{m}}_1$:

1. is closed under the rules **RCEA** and **RCEC**
2. contains the axiom **CM**

Theorem 7. The logic $\overrightarrow{\mathbf{m}}_1$:

1. is not closed under the rules **RCK** and **RCE**
2. does not contain the axioms **ID**, **CUT**, **AC**, **CC**, **Loop**, **OR**, **CV**, **CSO**, **MP**, **MOD**, **CA**, **CS**, **CEM**, **SDA**, **Transitivity**, **Weak Transitivity**, **Monotonicity**, **Weak Monotonicity** and **Weak Modus Ponens**

Definition 5 [Conditional Logic $\overrightarrow{\mathbf{m}}_2$]. Let $\overrightarrow{\mathbf{m}}_2$ be the logic consisting of all $A \in \mathcal{L}_\Rightarrow$ valid in $\mathfrak{F} = (\omega, f)$, where a conditional is evaluated as follows:
For a model $\mathfrak{M}$ over $\mathfrak{F}$, $\mathfrak{M}, n \models (A \Rightarrow B)$ iff either

(i) $\|\neg A\| \in f(n, \|A\|)$, or
(ii) $\|A \wedge B\| \in f(n, \|A\|)$

Theorem 8. The logic $\overrightarrow{\mathbf{m}}_2$ is closed under the rules **RCEA** and **RCEC**

Theorem 9. The logic $\overrightarrow{\mathbf{m}}_2$:

1. is not closed under the rules **RCK** and **RCE**
2. does not contain any of the axioms **ID**, **CUT**, **AC**, **CC**, **Loop**, **OR**, **CV**, **CSO**, **CM**, **MP**, **MOD**, **CA**, **CS**, **CEM**, **SDA**, **Transitivity**, **Weak Transitivity**, **Monotonicity**, **Weak Monotonicity** and **Weak Modus Ponens**

For the last definition, let $\mathfrak{F} = (\omega, f)$, where

$$f : \omega \times 2^\omega \to 2^{2^\omega}$$

maps worlds ($n \in \omega$) and propositions, to neighborhoods of cofinite subsets of ω and both the following hold:

(i) If $S \in f(n, X)$ and $S \subseteq T$ then $T \in f(n, X)$
(ii) If $S, T \in f(n, X)$ then $S \cap T \in f(n, X)$

The function f is well defined, because the class of cofinite subsets of ω (and of any set, actually) is 'upwards' closed (under supersets) and closed under intersection.

Definition 6 [Conditional Logic $\overrightarrow{\mathbf{m}}_3$]. Let $\overrightarrow{\mathbf{m}}_3$ be the logic consisting of all $A \in \mathcal{L}_\Rightarrow$ valid in $\mathfrak{F} = (\omega, f)$, where a conditional is evaluated as follows:
For a model $\mathfrak{M}$ over $\mathfrak{F}$, $\mathfrak{M}, n \models (A \Rightarrow B)$ iff either

(i) $\|\neg A\| \in f(n, \|A\|)$, or
(ii) $\|A \wedge B\| \in f(n, \|A\|)$

Theorem 10. The logic $\overrightarrow{\mathfrak{m}}_3$: (i) is closed under the rules **RCEA**, **RCK** and **RCEC**, (ii) contains the axioms **CC** and **CM**

Theorem 11. The logic $\overrightarrow{\mathfrak{m}}_3$: (i) is not closed under the rule **RCE**, (ii) does not contain the axioms **ID**, **CUT**, **AC**, **Loop**, **OR**, **CV**, **CSO**, **MP**, **MOD**, **CA**, **CS**, **CEM**, **SDA**, **Transitivity**, **Weak Transitivity**, **Monotonicity**, **Weak Monotonicity** and **Weak Modus Ponens**

Table 1. Logics $\overrightarrow{\Omega}, \overrightarrow{\omega}, \overrightarrow{\mathfrak{m}}_i$ vs KLM systems and known Conditional Logics.

In the big table below, all the results of this paper are summarized and the position of the conditional logics defined can be easily identified. The logics defined are compared to some known logics from the literature to be related to the KLM systems, or have been proposed in Commonsense Reasoning. A 'tick' means that a logic possesses the axiom (or rule) and a shaded box, that it does not Table 1.

4 Conclusions

In this paper, we have worked on a majority-based account of normality conditionals, based on the intuition that a cofinite subset of ω is obviously much larger than its complement. The attempt of defining conditionals modally over the frame $(\omega, <)$ has the obvious advantage that its modal axiomatization directly leads to a (for instance, tableaux-based) decision procedure, through an obvious translation. The other direction of employing Scott-Montague type semantics with neighborhoods of cofinite subsets, demonstrates the flexibility of the approach, as even weak logics can be defined by tuning the truth definitions.

The expected difficulty of obtaining a complete axiomatization, is partly due to the fact that conditional logic lacks the sophisticated model-theoretic machinery of modal logics that allows to prove the completeness result for the logic of $(\omega, <)$ (p-morphisms, bulldozing, cluster analysis of transitive frames, etc.). The experimentation with cofinite sets as the guiding principle behind '*overwhelming majority*' is however very instructive, as it allows to delineate the core rules of such an approach.

It is interesting to check, as a question that readily emerges form this work, the nonmonotonic consequence relations that emerge from these conditionals and also try to place them exactly in the universe of conditional logics (e.g. [18]).

References

1. Allen, J.F., Fikes, R., Sandewall, E. (eds.) Proceedings of the 2nd International Conference on Principles of Knowledge Representation and Reasoning (KR 1991), 22–25 April 1991. Morgan Kaufmann, Cambridge (1991)
2. Bell, J.: The logic of nonmonotonicity. Artif. Intell. **41**(3), 365–374 (1990)
3. Besnard, P., Hunter, A. (eds.) Reasoning with Actual and Potential Contradictions, Handbook of Defeasible Reasoning and Uncertainty Management Systems, vol. 2. Kluwer Academic Publishers, Boston (1998)
4. Blackburn, P., de Rijke, M., Venema, Y.: Modal Logic. Cambridge Tracts in Theoretical Computer Science, vol. 53. Cambridge University Press, Cambridge (2001)
5. Boutilier, C.: Conditional logics of normality: a modal approach. Artif. Intell. **68**(1), 87–154 (1994)
6. Delgrande, J.P.: A first-order conditional logic for prototypical properties. Artif. Intell. **33**(1), 105–130 (1987)
7. Delgrande, J.P.: An approach to default reasoning based on a first-order conditional logic: revised report. Artif. Intell. **36**(1), 63–90 (1988)

8. Delgrande, J.P.: Conditional logics for defeasible reasoning. In: Besnard and Hunter [3], vol. 2, pp. 135–173 (1998)
9. Delgrande, J.P.: On a rule-based interpretation of default conditionals. Ann. Math. Artif. Intell. **48**(3–4), 135–167 (2006)
10. Ginsberg, M.L.: Counterfactuals. Artif. Intell. **30**(1), 35–79 (1986)
11. Goldblatt, R.: Logics of Time and Computation. CSLI Lecture Notes, vol. 7, 2nd edn. Center for the Study of Language and Information, Stanford University, Stanford (1992)
12. Jauregui, V.: Modalities, conditionals and nonmonotonic reasoning. Ph.D. thesis, Department of Computer Science and Engineering, University of New South Wales (2008)
13. Koutras, C.D., Rantsoudis, C.: In all, but finitely many, possible worlds: model-theoretic investigations on 'overwhelming majority' default conditionals. Technical report, February 2015. http://www.uop.gr/~ckoutras/KR-MajCond-Full.pdf
14. Kraus, S., Lehmann, D.J., Magidor, M.: Nonmonotonic reasoning, preferential models and cumulative logics. Artif. Intell. **44**(1–2), 167–207 (1990)
15. Lamarre, P.: S4 as the conditional logic of nonmonotonicity. In: Allen et al. [1], pp. 357–367
16. Lehmann, D.J., Magidor, M.: What does a conditional knowledge base entail? Artif. Intell. **55**(1), 1–60 (1992)
17. Lewis, D.K.: Counterfactuals. Blackwell, Oxford (1973)
18. Nute, D.: Topics in Conditional Logic. Kluwer, Boston (1980)
19. Olivetti, N., Pozzato, G.L., Schwind, C.: A sequent calculus and a theorem prover for standard conditional logics. ACM Trans. Comput. Logic **8**(4), 427–473 (2007)
20. Schlechta, K.: Defaults as generalized quantifiers. J. Logic Comput. **5**(4), 473–494 (1995)
21. Schlechta, K.: Filters and partial orders. Logic J. IGPL **5**(5), 753–772 (1997)
22. Segerberg, K.: Modal logics with linear alternative relations. Theoria **36**, 301–322 (1970)

Game Theory

The Robustness of Periodic Orchestrations in Uncertain Evolving Environments

Jorge Castro[1], Joaquim Gabarro[2]([✉]), Maria Serna[2], and Alan Stewart[3]

[1] LARCA Research Group, Computer Science Department,
UPC Barcelona, Barcelona, Spain
[2] ALBCOM Research Group, Computer Science Department,
UPC Barcelona, Barcelona, Spain
gabarro@lsi.upc.edu
[3] School of Computer Science, The Queen's University of Belfast,
Belfast, UK

Abstract. A framework for assessing the robustness of long-duration *repetitive orchestrations* in uncertain *evolving* environments is proposed. The model assumes that service-based evaluation environments are stable over *short* time-frames only; over longer periods service-based environments evolve as demand fluctuates and contention for shared resources varies. The behaviour of a short-duration orchestration E in a stable environment is assessed by an *uncertainty profile* $\mathcal{U}$ and a corresponding zero-sum angel-daemon game $\Gamma(\mathcal{U})$ [2]. Here the angel-daemon approach is extended to assess *evolving* environments by means of a subfamily of *stochastic games*. These games are called *strategy oblivious* because their transition probabilities are strategy independent. It is shown that the value of a strategy oblivious stochastic game is well defined and that it can be computed by solving a linear system. Finally, the proposed stochastic framework is used to assess the evolution of the Gabrmn IT system.

Keywords: Orchestrations · Uncertainty · Zero-sum games · Stochastic games

1 Introduction

Web services pervade modern life; commonplace examples include media and healthcare services. Complex applications can be (rapidly) built by interconnecting (or orchestrating) a set of underlying services. Load balancing, provisioning,

J. Gabarro and M. Serna are partially supported by funds from the Spanish Ministry for Economy and Competitiveness (MINECO) and the European Union (FEDER funds) under grant TIN2013-46181-C2-1-R (COMMAS) and also by SGR 2014:1137 (ALBCOM) from AGAUR, Generalitat de Catalunya. J. Castro is partially supported by the Spanish Ministry for Economy and Competitiveness (MINECO) and the European Union (FEDER funds) under grants TIN2011-27479-C04-03 (BASMATI) and TIN2014-57226-P (APCOM) and by SGR 2014:890 (MACDA) from AGAUR, Generalitat de Catalunya.

© Springer International Publishing Switzerland 2015
S. Destercke and T. Denoeux (Eds.): ECSQARU 2015, LNAI 9161, pp. 129–140, 2015.
DOI: 10.1007/978-3-319-20807-7_12

and failure modes are fundamental issues for the cloud computing community; during an execution of an application the performance of *some* component services may degrade because of over-demand. However, cloud providers try to balance work-loads across computing resources. The overall performance of an application is affected by the interplay between positive and negative (competing) environmental influences. One approach to making service-based systems resilient is to use *ad hoc* techniques, based on the wisdom and folklore of experienced engineers. The goal of this paper is use formal methods to reason about the resilience of long duration service-based systems.

In [2] orchestration games are constructed, with one player (the daemon) maliciously degrading a bounded number of services (to cause the maximum delay) and the other player (the angel) applying bounded elasticity to improve performance. Uncertainty profiles and strategic situations are used in [2] to characterise *stable* evaluation environments. Nash equilibria are used to characterise the performance and resilience of applications when subject to complex environmental influences. In this paper game theory is applied to more complex scenarios where patterns of environmental stress evolve throughout an application's execution.

In order to analyse a long duration application which *repeatedly* evaluates an orchestration E we propose an extended stochastic uncertainty model. In the model execution environments are assumed to remain stable during evaluations of E. However, the environment may evolve between any of the periodic evaluations because of fluctuations in demand. It is assumed that the number of evaluation environments is finite and that evolution follows a Markovian process. Under this hypothesis the evolution of the environment can be assessed by means of stochastic games in which the future is described by means of a lottery. Stochastic games [8] have been widely used to study the inter-temporal behaviour of "real" systems [3]. In a zero-sum stochastic game $\Gamma = \langle \Gamma^1, \ldots, \Gamma^\ell \rangle$ each state l is formed by two components a zero sum game and a lottery. In state l, a player engages in the zero-sum game and after moves probabilistically to the next state.

For analyzing periodic orchestrations, it seems sufficient to consider oblivious lotteries, where the probability of changing state depends only on the current state. We prove that (i) games in the family of (zero-sum) *strategy oblivious* stochastic games have a well defined value, in the discounted model, and (ii) a game value can be computed by solving a linear system. This result allows the proposed framework to be applied to analyse the behaviour of the Gabrmn system.

The paper is organised as follows. Section 2 introduces periodic orchestrations while Sect. 3 introduces zero-sum, stochastic and *strategy oblivious* games. Section 3 also provides techniques for assessing complex evolving scenarios (Theorem 2). In Sect. 4 we discuss the assessment of both short- and long-duration orchestrations. The behaviour of the Gabrmn system in an evolving environment is analysed in Sect. 5 . Finally, we draw some conclusions in Sect. 6.

2   Periodic Orchestrations

The language Orc [4,5] can be used to model the co-ordination of a set of loosely-coupled services. Orc has a well defined semantics [10,12] and so lends itself to the study of orchestration behaviour.

The simplest Orc expression is a service call. When called a service responds by publishing a result (for example a link to a web page). Three predefined services (or internal sites) are used in this paper: 0, 1 and $Rtimer(t)$. Service 0 never publishes; a call to $1(x)$ echoes back its input argument x; a call to $Rtimer(t)$ publishes a result after t time steps. Any two orchestrations P and Q can be composed using the operators:

- Sequential composition $P > x > Q(x)$: Initially P is evaluated: for each output v, published by P, an instance $Q(v)$ is invoked. If P publishes the stream of values, $v_1, v_2, \ldots v_n$, then orchestration $P > x > Q(x)$ publishes some interleaving of the set $\{Q(v_1), Q(v_2), \ldots, Q(v_n)\}$. The abbreviation $P \gg Q$ is used in situations where Q does not depend on x.
- Parallel composition $P \mid Q$: The independent orchestrations P and Q are executed in parallel; $P \mid Q$ publishes *some* interleaving of the values published by P and Q.
- Pruning $P(x) < x < Q$: Orchestrations P and Q are evaluated in parallel; P may become blocked by a dependency on x. The first result published by Q is bound to x, the remainder of Q's evaluation is terminated and evaluation of the blocked residual of P is resumed.

Consider the periodic computation $D = \big(E \mid (Rtimer(\tau) \gg D)\big)$ which repeatedly calls a short-duration orchestration E, say $E = (A \mid B) < x < (F \mid G)$, at time intervals τ. It is assumed that the environment of E remains stable during any evaluation. During a particular evaluation of E some underlying services may be degraded, because of excessive demand, while other services may benefit from environmental resilience. The precise nature of the environmental factors in play at any one moment in time is difficult to characterise in a quantitative way. A qualitative environmental characterisation can be given using an uncertainty profile [2]. This specifies potential positive and negative environmental influences (e.g. overdemand, elasticity). The combined effect of these influences on an evaluation of E can be assessed using game theory [2]. For a periodic evaluation the environmental influences may evolve from one time period to the next. The goal of this paper is to demonstrate how stochastic games can be used to analyse such evolving situations.

3   Preliminaries on Games

Zero-sum and stochastic zero-sum games are introduced below; Standard notation is used throughout: $\Delta(S)$ denotes the set of probability distributions over a finite set S. Zero-sum games can be used to model stable stressed environments.

Definition 1. *A two player zero-sum game is a strategic game described by the tuple* $\Gamma = \langle A_1, A_2, u \rangle$. A_1 *and* A_2 *are the set of eligible actions for player 1 and 2, respectively. The third component is a mapping* u *from* $A_1 \times A_2$ *to the rational numbers. An element* $(i, j) \in A_1 \times A_2$ *is called a strategy profile. The utility of strategy profile* (i, j) *is* $u(i, j)$, *for player 1, and* $-u(i, j)$, *for player 2. Utilities are rational numbers.*

A mixed strategy is a lottery on the set of eligible actions. Utility u can be extended over mixed strategy profiles. Given a mixed strategy profile $(\alpha, \beta) \in \Delta(A_1) \times \Delta(A_2)$ where $\alpha = (\alpha_1, \ldots, \alpha_n)$ and $\beta = (\beta_1, \ldots, \beta_m)$ then $u(\alpha, \beta) = \sum_{i,j} \alpha_i u(i, j) \beta_j$. The *value* of a zero-sum game Γ is defined as $\nu(\Gamma) = \max_{\alpha \in \Delta(A_1)} \min_{\beta \in \Delta(A_2)} u(\alpha, \beta)$. For any (mixed) Nash equilibrium (α, β) it is known that $u(\alpha, \beta) = \nu(\Gamma)$.

Example 1. The class of 2×2-zero sum games is well-known [6]. Consider games $\Gamma = (\{T, B\}, \{L, R\}, u)$ and $\Gamma' = (\{T, B\}, \{L, R\}, u')$ below with utilities u and u'.

	L	R
T	1/2	1
B	1	1/2

Γ

	L	R
T	3	3/2
B	3/2	3

Γ'

In a Nash equilibrium with full support $u(T, \beta) = u(B, \beta) = \nu(\Gamma)$ and $u(\alpha, L) = u(\alpha, R) = \nu(\Gamma)$. Thus $\alpha = \beta = 1/2$, $\nu(\Gamma) = 3/4$ and $\nu(\Gamma') = 9/4$ ☐

The following linear transformation result for zero-sum games is well-known:

Lemma 1. *Let* $\Gamma = (A_1, A_2, u)$ *and* $\Gamma' = (A_1, A_2, u')$ *be two zero-sum games with* $u'(i, j) = au(i, j) + b$, *for some* $a > 0$. *Then games* Γ *and* Γ' *have the same set of Nash equilibria and* $\nu(\Gamma') = a\nu(\Gamma) + b$.

Following [6,9] stochastic games are formally defined as:

Definition 2. *A two person stochastic game* $\Gamma = \langle \Gamma^1, \ldots, \Gamma^\ell \rangle$ *is a tuple of* ℓ *sub-games. Each sub-game (or state)* Γ^l *has form* $\Gamma^l = \langle game^l(\Gamma), lotteries^l(\Gamma) \rangle$. *Here* $game^l(\Gamma)$ *is a zero-sum game and* $lotteries^l(\Gamma)$ *determines the next game:*

- $game^l(\Gamma) = \langle A_1^l, A_2^l, u^l \rangle$ *where* $A_1^l = \{1, \cdots, n_l\}$, $A_2^l = \{1, \ldots, m_l\}$, *and*
- $lotteries^l(\Gamma) : A_1^l \times A_2^l \rightarrow \Delta(\{1, \ldots, \ell\})$.

When appropriate $game^l(\Gamma)$ and $lotteries^l(\Gamma)$ can be abbreviated to $game^l$ and $lotteries^l$.

Example 2. A stochastic game Γ can be represented by a bi-matrix for each state combining utility and lottery. For instance,

	L	R
T	$1/2, (1/3, 2/3)$	$1, (2/3, 1/3)$
B	$1, (2/3, 1/3)$	$1/2, (1/3, 2/3)$

Γ^1

	L	R
T	$3, (1/4, 3/4)$	$3/2, (3/4, 1/4)$
B	$3/2, (3/4, 1/4)$	$3, (1/4, 3/4)$

Γ^2

represents $\Gamma = \langle \Gamma^1, \Gamma^2 \rangle$ where $\mathsf{game}^1 = \Gamma$ and $\mathsf{game}^2 = \Gamma'$ are the games in Example 1 and, for instance, $\mathsf{lotteries}^1(\{T, L\}) = (1/3, 2/3)$. □

A stochastic game is played through so called *stationary strategies* [8]. A *stationary strategy* is a pair (α, β) formed by $\alpha = (\alpha^1, \ldots, \alpha^\ell)$ and $\beta = (\beta^1, \ldots, \beta^\ell)$ where, for any $1 \le l \le \ell$, $\alpha^l \in \Delta(A_1^l)$ and $\beta^l \in \Delta(A_2^l)$. Thus a stationary strategy comprises a mixed strategy profile for each game state. Lotteries are extended on mixed strategies as $\mathsf{lotteries}_k^l(\alpha^l, \beta^l) = \sum_{i,j} \alpha_i^l \mathsf{lotteries}_k^l(i, j) \beta_j^l$ where $\mathsf{lotteries}_k^l$ denotes the k component of $\mathsf{lotteries}^l$.

Example 3. A stationary strategy, for the game Γ given in Example 2, where player 1 selects T in game^1 and B in game^2 while player 2 chooses L in game^1 and R in game^2, is $((\alpha^1, \alpha^2), (\beta^1, \beta^2)) = (((1, 0), (0, 1)), ((1, 0), (0, 1)))$ □

A stochastic game defines a collection of never ending games, one for each initial (sub-game) state. In a game players are rewarded and use a joint lottery to determine the next state. The λ-*discounted reward* model, $0 < \lambda < 1$, is used to define a utility for a stationary strategy. Consider the game with initial state Γ^l and with a stationary strategy (α, β). In the λ-*discounted reward* model the total payoff for player 1 is computed solving $\mathfrak{P}_\lambda^l(\alpha, \beta) = \lambda u^l(\alpha^l, \beta^l) + (1 - \lambda) \sum_k \mathsf{lotteries}_k^l(\alpha^l, \beta^l) \mathfrak{P}_\lambda^k(\alpha, \beta)$. In the following $\Gamma[\lambda]$ denotes the stochastic game Γ with a discount factor λ.

Example 4. Consider the stochastic game $\Gamma[\lambda]$ with stationary strategy (α, β) from Example 3 where the game starts in state 1. Initially player 1 wins $\lambda/2$ (and player 2 loses $-\lambda/2$). The next game has discount factor $(1 - \lambda)$; Γ^1 is played with probability $1/3$ and Γ^2 with probability $2/3$. Let $\mathfrak{P}^1 = \mathfrak{P}^1(\alpha, \beta)$ and $\mathfrak{P}^2 = \mathfrak{P}^2(\alpha, \beta)$ be the discounted pay-offs of player 1, playing strategy (α, β), starting from Γ^1 and Γ^2, respectively. The recursive structure of $\Gamma[\lambda]$ gives rise to the following equations:

$$\mathfrak{P}^1 = \lambda \frac{1}{2} + (1 - \lambda)(\frac{1}{3}\mathfrak{P}^1 + \frac{2}{3}\mathfrak{P}^2), \quad \mathfrak{P}^2 = \lambda 3 + (1 - \lambda)(\frac{1}{4}\mathfrak{P}^1 + \frac{3}{4}\mathfrak{P}^2)$$

and so $\mathfrak{P}^1(\alpha, \beta) = (51 - 39\lambda)/2(11 + \lambda)$ and $\mathfrak{P}^2(\alpha, \beta) = (51 + 21\lambda)/2(11 + \lambda)$ □

Shapley showed that any stochastic game $\Gamma = \langle \Gamma^1, \ldots, \Gamma^\ell \rangle$ has optimal strategies and a unique value vector $\mathfrak{v} = (v^1, \ldots, v^\ell)$. Given the stochastic game Γ, a numerical vector $w = (w^1, \ldots, w^\ell)$ and a discount factor λ, he defined the zero sum games $\Gamma^l[\lambda, w] = \langle A_1^l, A_2^l, u^l[\lambda, w] \rangle$ where $u^l[\lambda, w](i, j) = \lambda u^l(i, j) + (1 - \lambda) \sum_{k=1}^\ell \mathsf{lotteries}_k^l(i, j) w^k$, and he proved the following theorem that characterizes $\mathfrak{v}$ as a fix point.

Theorem 1 ([8]). *Let $\Gamma = \langle \Gamma^1, \ldots, \Gamma^\ell \rangle$ be a stochastic game and let $0 < \lambda < 1$. Then $\mathfrak{v}(\Gamma[\lambda]) = v = (v^1, \ldots v^\ell)$ where v is the unique solution of the system $v^l = \nu(\Gamma^l[\lambda, v])$, $l = 1, \ldots, \ell$. One optimal stationary strategy for $\Gamma[\lambda]$ consists of playing an optimal strategy at node l for the one shot game $\Gamma^l[\lambda, v]$.*

Example 5. Let $w = (w^1, w^2)$. Then the zero-sum auxiliary games $\Gamma^1[\lambda, w]$ and $\Gamma^2[\lambda, w]$ below are derived for the stochastic games in Examples 2 and 4:

	L	R
T	$\lambda\frac{1}{2} + (1-\lambda)\left(\frac{1}{3}w^1 + \frac{2}{3}w^2\right)$	$1\lambda + (1-\lambda)\left(\frac{2}{3}w^1 + \frac{1}{3}w^2\right)$
B	$1\lambda + (1-\lambda)\left(\frac{2}{3}w^1 + \frac{1}{3}w^2\right)$	$\frac{1}{2}\lambda + (1-\lambda)\left(\frac{1}{3}w^1 + \frac{2}{3}w^2\right)$

$$\Gamma^1[\lambda, w]$$

	L	R
T	$3\lambda + (1-\lambda)\left(\frac{1}{4}w^1 + \frac{3}{4}w^2\right)$	$\frac{3}{2}\lambda + (1-\lambda)\left(\frac{3}{4}w^1 + \frac{1}{4}w^2\right)$
B	$\frac{3}{2}\lambda + (1-\lambda)\left(\frac{3}{4}w^1 + \frac{1}{4}w^2\right)$	$3\lambda + (1-\lambda)\left(\frac{1}{4}w^1 + \frac{3}{4}w^2\right)$

$$\Gamma^2[\lambda, w]$$

From Theorem 1 we have, $\mathfrak{v}(\Gamma[\lambda]) = v = (v^1, v^2)$ where $v^1 = \nu(\Gamma^1[\lambda, v])$ and $v^2 = \nu(\Gamma^2[\lambda, v])$. Using the mixed equilibria in Example 1 we have $v^1 = \frac{3}{4}\lambda + \frac{1}{2}(v^1 + v^2)(1 - \lambda)$ and $v^2 = \frac{9}{4}\lambda + \frac{1}{2}(v^1 + v^2)(1 - \lambda)$. Thus, $\mathfrak{v} = (v^1, v^2) = \left(\frac{1}{2}(3 - \frac{3}{2}\lambda), \frac{1}{2}(3 + \frac{3}{2}\lambda)\right)$ □

Oblivious-uncertainty provides a model of the future that is strategy-independent:

Definition 3. *A stochastic game $\Gamma = \langle \Gamma^1, \ldots, \Gamma^\ell \rangle$ is strategy oblivious if each state $1 \le l \le \ell$, lotteries^l is a constant function (the same value for all $(i, j) \in A_1^l \times A_2^l$).*

Given an oblivious game, let vgame be the vector containing the values of the zero-sum state games. Writing lotteries$^l = \mathfrak{l}^l$, the lotteries corresponding to the different states are given in the following LOTTERIES matrix:

$$\text{vgame} = \begin{pmatrix} \nu(\text{game}^1) \\ \vdots \\ \nu(\text{game}^\ell) \end{pmatrix}, \quad \text{LOTTERIES} = \begin{pmatrix} \mathfrak{l}^1 \\ \vdots \\ \mathfrak{l}^\ell \end{pmatrix} = \begin{pmatrix} \mathfrak{l}_1^1 & \cdots & \mathfrak{l}_\ell^1 \\ \vdots & & \vdots \\ \mathfrak{l}_1^\ell & \cdots & \mathfrak{l}_\ell^\ell \end{pmatrix}$$

Here LOTTERIES is a stochastic matrix (each row sums to 1) and $\mathfrak{l}_k^l$ denotes the probability of moving from state l to state k. Recall that a *stationary distribution* $\mathfrak{p} = (\mathfrak{p}_1, \cdots, \mathfrak{p}_\ell)$ is a distribution satisfying $\mathfrak{p} \cdot \text{LOTTERIES} = \mathfrak{p}$.

Theorem 2. *Let $\Gamma = \langle \Gamma^1, \ldots, \Gamma^\ell \rangle$ be a discounted strategy oblivious stochastic game, $0 < \lambda < 1$. Then:*

1. *The value vector $\mathfrak{v} = \mathfrak{v}(\Gamma[\lambda])$ satisfies $\mathfrak{v} = \lambda\, \text{vgame} + (1 - \lambda)\text{LOTTERIES} \cdot \mathfrak{v}$*
2. *The value vector $\mathfrak{v}$ is $\mathfrak{v} = \lambda\bigl(I - (1 - \lambda)\text{LOTTERIES}\bigr)^{-1}\text{vgame}$.*
3. *If $\mathfrak{p}$ is a stationary then $\mathfrak{p} \cdot \mathfrak{v} = \mathfrak{p} \cdot \text{vgame}$.*

In the general case, the non-linearity of the equations in Theorem 1 defining
$\mathfrak{v}(\Gamma[\lambda])$ makes it difficult to compute the exact value of a discounted stochastic
game. In fact, a stochastic game defined on rational data can have an irrational
value vector [11]. In the oblivious case the value vector $\mathfrak{v}$ can be expressed as
a linear system over values of local state games (Theorem 2). Thus, as the
computation of vgame can be reduced to linear programming, assuming strategy
obliviousness and rational data the result vector $\mathfrak{v}$ is kept within the rationals.

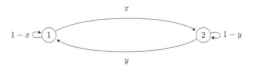

Fig. 1. A two state regular Markov chain.

Example 6. Let $\Gamma = \langle \Gamma^1, \Gamma^2 \rangle$ be a strategy oblivious stochastic game. The
matrix LOTTERIES corresponds to a 2 states Markov chain (see Fig. 1). Let

$$\text{LOTTERIES} = \begin{pmatrix} \mathfrak{l}_1^1 & \mathfrak{l}_2^1 \\ \mathfrak{l}_1^2 & \mathfrak{l}_2^2 \end{pmatrix} = \begin{pmatrix} (1-x) & x \\ y & (1-y) \end{pmatrix}, \ \mathfrak{p} = (\mathfrak{p}_1, \mathfrak{p}_2) = \left(\frac{y}{x+y}, \frac{x}{x+y} \right)$$

where $0 < x, y < 1$ and $\mathfrak{p}$ is a stationary distribution. Suppose that $\nu(\text{game}^1) = a$
and $\nu(\text{game}^2) = b$. The linear system derived from Theorem 2 is:

$$\begin{pmatrix} v^1 \\ v^2 \end{pmatrix} = \lambda \begin{pmatrix} a \\ b \end{pmatrix} + (1-\lambda) \begin{pmatrix} (1-x) & x \\ y & (1-y) \end{pmatrix} \begin{pmatrix} v^1 \\ v^2 \end{pmatrix}$$

4   An Assessment Model for Periodic Orchestrations

In this section an assessment model for orchestrations in stable environments [2]
is reviewed and extended to encompass periodic orchestrations in evolving environments.

Uncertainty Profiles and $\mathfrak{a}/\mathfrak{d}$-*games*. Let E be a non-recursive orchestration
which, when called, publishes a finite set of results and terminates. The environment for E is assumed to be uncertain but stable. Let $\alpha_+(E)$ be the set of sites
called by E (excluding 0). Let $\#s$ denote the cardinality of a set of sites s.
    The assessment of E under stress is undertaken by specifying those services
which have the potential to be affected by stress. An uncertainty profile $\mathcal{U}$ models
the *a priori* perception of orchestration behaviour under stress [2], providing a
model that lies between over-optimism and over-pessimism. A profile $\mathcal{U}$, fixes
two subsets of $\alpha_+(E)$, $\mathcal{A}$ and $\mathcal{D}$, together with the number of service failures
that can be expected to occur within both $\mathcal{A}$ and $\mathcal{D}$. The last component of $\mathcal{U}$
is a utility u function which measures resilience under a given type of stress.
Behaviour is analyzed by assuming that service failures in $\mathcal{A}$ (angelic services)
are selected to *cause the least amount of damage* whereas service failures in $\mathcal{D}$

(daemonic services) are selected to *maximise damage to the application*. The assessment of E goes though a zero-sum game $\Gamma(\mathcal{U})$, the $\mathfrak{a}/\mathfrak{d}$-game, providing an analysis of the competitive scenario [2]. Formally:

Definition 4 (Uncertainty Profile $\mathcal{U}$ and its Associated $\mathfrak{a}/\mathfrak{d}$-Game [2]).

- *An uncertainty profile for an orchestration E is a tuple $\mathcal{U} = \langle E, \mathcal{A}, \mathcal{D}, b_{\mathcal{A}}, b_{\mathcal{D}}, u \rangle$ where $\mathcal{A} \cup \mathcal{D} \subseteq \alpha_+(E)$, $b_{\mathcal{A}} \leq \#\mathcal{A}$, $b_{\mathcal{D}} \leq \#\mathcal{D}$ and $u(a,d) \geq 0$ is a utility function defined for all $a \subseteq \alpha_+(E)$, $d \subseteq \alpha_+(E)$.*
- *$\mathcal{U} = \langle E, \mathcal{A}, \mathcal{D}, b_{\mathcal{A}}, b_{\mathcal{D}}, u \rangle$ has an associated zero-sum angel-daemon game $\Gamma(\mathcal{U}) = \langle A_{\mathfrak{a}}, A_{\mathfrak{d}}, u \rangle$ with two players, $\mathfrak{a}$ (angel) and $\mathfrak{d}$ (daemon). Player $\mathfrak{a}$ selects a set with size $b_{\mathcal{A}}$ from $\mathcal{A}$: $A_{\mathfrak{a}} = \{a \subseteq \mathcal{A} \mid \#a = b_{\mathcal{A}}\}$. Player $\mathfrak{d}$ selects a set with size $b_{\mathcal{D}}$ from $\mathcal{D}$: $A_{\mathfrak{d}} = \{d \subseteq \mathcal{D} \mid \#d = b_{\mathcal{D}}\}$. Services in $\alpha_+(E) \setminus (a \cup d)$ remain reliable.*
- *The assessment $\nu(\mathcal{U})$ of an uncertainty profile $\mathcal{U}$ is defined to be the value of its associated angel-daemon $\nu(\Gamma(\mathcal{U}))$.*

Utility $u(a,d)$ measures the degree of resilience of E when $\mathfrak{a}$ "selects" services a and $\mathfrak{d}$ "selects" services d. Different utilities can be used to define different resilience measures. Three utilities with different weightings are shown:

$$u^o(a,d) = \frac{1}{2}\mathsf{out}(\mathsf{fail}_{a \cap d}(E)), u^r(a,d) = \frac{3}{2}\mathsf{out}(\mathsf{fail}_{d \setminus a}(E)), u^w(a,d) = \mathsf{out}(\mathsf{fail}_{a \cup d}(E))$$

Here the function $\mathsf{out}(\mathsf{fail}_f(E))$ returns the number of outputs published by E when services in the set f fail. In the *overloaded* environment, u^o, services selected by both $\mathfrak{a}$ and $\mathfrak{d}$ fail. In the *robust* environment, u^r, the angel has the capability to prevent its selected service from failing. In a failures-prone *weak* environment , u^w, neither $\mathfrak{a}$ or $\mathfrak{d}$ can avoid failures.

Example 7. $BigTwo = (G \mid A)$ can operate in $\mathcal{U}^o = \langle BigTwo, \{G, A\}, \{G, A\}, 1, 1, u^o \rangle$ describing an *overloaded* environment or in $\mathcal{U}^r = \langle BigTwo, \{G, A\}, \{G, A\}, 1, 1, u^r \rangle$ giving a *robust* environment or in $\mathcal{U}^w = \langle BigTwo, \{G, A\}, \{G, A\}, 1, 1, u^w \rangle$ givng a *weak* one. The games $\Gamma(\mathcal{U}^o)$, $\Gamma(\mathcal{U}^r)$ and $\Gamma(\mathcal{U}^w)$ are

	$\mathfrak{d}$	
$\mathfrak{a}$	$\{G\}$	$\{A\}$
$\{G\}$	1/2	1
$\{A\}$	1	1/2

$\Gamma(\mathcal{U}^o)$

	$\mathfrak{d}$	
$\mathfrak{a}$	$\{G\}$	$\{A\}$
$\{G\}$	3	3/2
$\{A\}$	3/2	3

$\Gamma(\mathcal{U}^r)$

	$\mathfrak{d}$	
$\mathfrak{a}$	$\{G\}$	$\{A\}$
$\{G\}$	1	0
$\{A\}$	0	1

$\Gamma(\mathcal{U}^w)$

Assessments are $\nu(\mathcal{U}^o) = 3/4$ and $\nu(\mathcal{U}^r) = 9/4$ (Example 1) and $\nu(\mathcal{U}^w) = 1/2$. $\qquad\square$

Uncertainty Profiles for Periodic Orchestrations. The assessment of the periodic orchestration is modelled using stochastic games. Possible execution environments of E are defined by uncertainty profiles.

Definition 5. *Let* $D = \big(E \mid (Rtimer(\mathtt{t}) \gg D)\big)$. *An* uncertainty profile *for* E *is a tuple* $\mathfrak{U} = \langle \mathcal{U}^1, \ldots, \mathcal{U}^\ell, \text{lotteries}^1, \ldots, \text{lotteries}^\ell \rangle$, *where, for each* $1 \leq i \leq \ell$, $\mathcal{U}^i$ *is an uncertainty profile over* E *and* $\text{lotteries}^i \in \Delta(\{1, \ldots, \ell\})$ *is collection of associated lotteries, one lottery for each strategy profile in the game* $\Gamma(\mathcal{U}^i)$. *Profile* $\mathfrak{U}$ *induces an associated stochastic* $\mathfrak{a}/\mathfrak{d}$ *game* $\Gamma(\mathfrak{U}) = \langle \Gamma^1, \ldots, \Gamma^\ell \rangle$ *where, for* $1 \leq i \leq \ell$, $\Gamma^l = \langle \Gamma(\mathcal{U}^l), \text{lotteries}^l \rangle$. *Let* $0 < \lambda < 1$ *be a discount value, if* $\mathfrak{v}(\Gamma(\mathfrak{U})[\lambda]) = (v^1, \ldots, v^\ell)$ *then the* assessment *of* D *under* $\mathfrak{U}$ *is defined as* $\nu(\mathfrak{U}) = v^1$.

Example 8. The orchestration $BigTwo^* = \big(BigTwo \mid (Rtimer(\mathsf{day}) \gg BigTwo^*)\big)$ is assessed by the uncertainty profile $\mathfrak{U} = \langle \mathcal{U}^o, \mathcal{U}^r, \text{lotteries}^o, \text{lotteries}^r \rangle$. Here tuples $\langle \Gamma(\mathcal{U}^o), \text{lotteries}^o \rangle$ and $\langle \Gamma(\mathcal{U}^r), \text{lotteries}^r \rangle$ correspond respectively to Γ^1 and Γ^2 components in Example 2. The associated stochastic game has been analyzed in Example 5 where it is shown that $v(\Gamma(\mathfrak{U})) = (\frac{1}{2}(3 - \frac{3}{2}\lambda), \frac{1}{2}(3 + \frac{3}{2}\lambda))$. Therefore the assessment of $BigTwo^*$ is $\frac{1}{2}(3 - \frac{3}{2}\lambda)$. □

5   Example: The **Gabrmn** System

Gabrmn is an IT system for managing clinical data generated from magnetic resonance spectra [2] . It comprises a number of sub-systems. Clinical data is stored in a sub-system *Databases*. Clinical applications, including *IDL*, are stored on server, *Apps*. A master server, *Proxy*, controls system behaviour. Email is a key service provided by servers *Mail* and *Mirror*; the sub-system $1(x) < x < (Mail \mid Mirror)$ has built-in redundancy. Service *Backup* allows system recovery to take place. Gabrmn is modelled in Orc as;

$$IT\_System = Proxy \gg \big((1(x) < x < (Mail \mid Mirror)) \mid Apps \mid Backup \mid Databases\big)$$

This expression is a stylized formalization developed after extensive discussion with the Gabrmn system manager (A. García) - see http://gabrmn.uab. es/. The number of outputs ($u^w = \mathsf{out}(\mathsf{fail}_{a \cup d})$) published by *IT_System* provides a measure of its "well-being" (maximum value 4). The long term behaviour of *IT_System* in stressed environments is modelled by the following stochastic game:

States. Taking $u^w = \mathsf{out}(\mathsf{fail}_{a \cup d})$, three different environments for Gabrmn are:

$$\mathcal{U}^1 = \langle IT\_System, \{Backup, Proxy, Mirror\}, \{Apps, Databases, Mail\}, 1, 1, u^w \rangle$$
$$\mathcal{U}^2 = \langle IT\_System, \{Apps, Mail, Mirror\}, \{Databases, Mail, Mirror\}, 1, 1, u^w \rangle$$
$$\mathcal{U}^3 = \langle IT\_System, \{Apps, Mail, Mirror\}, \{Databases, Mail, Mirror\}, 2, 1, u^w \rangle$$

Here a service fails if it is selected by either a or d. Profiles $\mathcal{U}^1$, $\mathcal{U}^2$, $\mathcal{U}^3$ induce games with valuations $\nu(\mathcal{U}^1) = \nu(\mathcal{U}^2) = 3$ and $\nu(\mathcal{U}^3) = 2$.

Evolution of the Environment. The parameterised uncertainty profile $\mathfrak{U}(x, y, z)$ models system evolution through environments $\langle \mathcal{U}^1, \mathcal{U}^2, \mathcal{U}^3 \rangle$ using an oblivious approach where

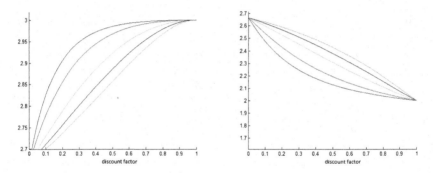

Fig. 2. Assessments v^1 (left) and v^3 (right) of $\mathfrak{U}$ with $x = y = z \in \{1, 0.75, 0.5, 0.25, 0.15\}$. In both figures the value 1 corresponds to the rightmost curve and 0.15 the the leftmost.

$$\text{vgame} = \begin{pmatrix} \nu(\mathcal{U}^1) \\ \nu(\mathcal{U}^2) \\ \nu(\mathcal{U}^3) \end{pmatrix} = \begin{pmatrix} 3 \\ 3 \\ 2 \end{pmatrix}, \ \text{LOTTERIES} = \begin{pmatrix} 1-x & x & 0 \\ 0 & 1-y & y \\ z & 0 & 1-z \end{pmatrix}$$

LOTTERIES models a perturbed round trip $1 \rightarrow 2 \rightarrow 3 \rightarrow 1$ with a probability to keep into the current state. The stochastic game $\Gamma(\mathfrak{U})$ where $\mathfrak{U} = \langle \mathcal{U}^1, \mathcal{U}^2, \mathcal{U}^3, \text{LOTTERIES} \rangle$ satisfies:

$$\mathfrak{v} = \lambda \begin{pmatrix} 1-(1-\lambda)(1-x) & -(1-\lambda)x & 0 \\ 0 & 1-(1-\lambda)(1-y) & -(1-\lambda)y \\ -(1-\lambda)z & 0 & 1-(1-\lambda)(1-z) \end{pmatrix}^{-1} \text{vgame}$$

This equation has been solved, using the Python **SymPy** library, to find the value vector $\mathfrak{v} = (v^1, v^2, v^3)$ for certain values of x, y and z and discount factors – see Fig. 2. Setting $x = 1$, $y = 1$ and $z = 1$ gives an environment with a deterministic full round trip (next is to $1 \rightarrow 2 \rightarrow 3 \rightarrow 1$). When $x = y = z$ the assessment v^1 increases monotonically as the probability of remaining in the first state increases (i.e. x decreases). As $\lambda \rightarrow 1$ the assessment v^1 in the discounted model is weighted towards today's performance ($\nu(\mathcal{U}^1) = 3$ – see Fig. 2 left). Fig. 2 right shows the assessment v^3, which corresponds to the game starting in the least reliable environment, $\mathcal{U}^3$: decreasing the probability of remaining in this state monotonically improves system performance. Similar results have been obtained for asymmetric case: $y = z$ and $x = y/2$.

6   Conclusions

The angel-daemon approach has been extended to assess periodic orchestrations in *evolving* environments. We have considered the subfamily of strategy oblivious stochastic games in which transition probabilities are independent of selected strategies. It has been shown that such games have well-defined valuations. The proposed framework has been used to assess the evolution of the Gabrmn IT system. We are in the process of identifying larger systems that can be cast naturally in our approach.

Our approach may go some way to answering a fundamental question of application developers: how can the resilience of service-based systems be assessed when some sub-components are subject to unpredictable forms of stress (e.g. contention for resources on a hypervisor)? Typically practitioners use ad hoc techniques, guided by their technical experience, to develop robust systems of micro-services. It is unclear how the uncertainty associated with a cloud (and services deployed therein) can be modelled realistically by using probabilistic techniques (because sudden surges in demand can occur, or the types of resource available may change in an unpredictable way). Here we provide a different approach which (partially) removes probabilities from the analysis of a natural strategic situation. Our approach provides a formal method for the analysis of an increasingly important class of architectures (until now analysed by trial-and-error techniques). We are working towards extending the approach by adding latency to the set of components that can be influenced by mixed-effect environmental influences.

The work reported here is complementary to that of [1,7] where the monotonicity of the QoS of web services is considered. One other possible line of future research is to extend the monotonicity properties of the assesments of non-recursive orchestrations [2] to periodic orchestrations.

References

1. Benveniste, A., Jard, C., Kattepur, A., Rosario, S., Thywissen, J.A.: QoS-aware management of monotonic service orchestrations. Formal Methods Syst. Des. **44**(1), 1–43 (2014)
2. Gabarro, J., Serna, M., Stewart, A.: Analysing web-orchestrations under stress using Uncertainty profiles. Comput. J. **57**(11), 1591–1615 (2014)
3. Levharit, D., Mirman, L.: The great fish war: an example using a dynamic cournot-nash solution. Bell J. Econ. **11**, 322–334 (1980)
4. Misra, J.: A programming model for the orchestration of web services. In: 2nd International Conference on Software Engineering and Formal Methods, SEFM 2004, pp. 2–11. IEEE (2004)
5. Misra, J., Cook, W.: Computation orchestration: a basis for wide-area computing. Softw. Syst. Model. **6**(1), 83–110 (2007)
6. Owen, G.: Game Theory, 3rd edn. Academic Press, Sant Diego (2001)
7. Rosario, S., Benveniste, A., Jard, C.: Flexible probabilistic QoS management of orchestrations. Int. J. Web Serv. Res. **7**(2), 21–42 (2010)
8. Shapley, L.: Stochatic games. In: PNAS, pp. 1095–1100 (1953)
9. Sorin, S.: New approaches and recent advances in two-person zero-sum repeated games. Ann. Int. Soc. Dyn. Games **7**, 67–93 (2005). Advances in Dynamic Games
10. Stewart, A., Gabarro, J., Keenan, A.: Reasoning about orchestrations of web services using partial correctness. Formal Aspects Comput. **25**, 833–846 (2013)

11. Vrieze, O.J.: Stochastic games, practical motivation and the orderfield property for special cases. In: Stochastic Games and Applications, 570 of NATO. Science, pp. 215–225 (2003)
12. Wehrman, I., Kitchin, D., Cook, W., Misra, J.: A timed semantics of Orc. Theor. Comput. Sci. **402**(2–3), 234–248 (2008)

Uncertainty in the Cloud: An Angel-Daemon Approach to Modelling Performance

Alan Stewart[1], Joaquim Gabarro[2]([⊠]), and Anthony Keenan[1]

[1] School of EEECS, The Queen's University of Belfast,
Belfast, Northern Ireland, UK
{a.stewart,a.keenan}@qub.ac.uk
[2] ALBCOM Research Group, Department of CS,
Barcelona Tech, Barcelona, Spain
gabarro@cs.upc.edu

Abstract. Uncertainty profiles are used to study the effects of contention within cloud and service-based environments. An uncertainty profile provides a qualitative description of an environment whose quality of service (QoS) may fluctuate unpredictably. Uncertain environments are modelled by strategic games with two agents; a daemon is used to represent overload and high resource contention; an angel is used to represent an idealised resource allocation situation with no underlying contention. Assessments of uncertainty profiles are useful in two ways: firstly, they provide a broad understanding of how environmental stress can effect an application's performance (and reliability); secondly, they allow the effects of introducing redundancy into a computation to be assessed.

Keywords: Uncertainty · Web-service · Orchestration · ORC · Cloud · Virtualization · Amazon EC2 · Resource contention · Performance · Reliability · Game theory

1 Introduction

In 1961 John McCarthy proposed a vision of service-based computing:

> "If computers of the kind I have advocated become the computers of the future, then computing may someday be organized as a public utility just as the telephone system is a public utility..."

The notion of service extends previous notions of programming through the addition of an interface through which users can access computing resources.

J. Gabarro is partially supported by funds from the Spanish Ministry for Economy and Competitiveness (MINECO) and the European Union (FEDER funds) under grant TIN2013-46181-C2-1-R (COMMAS) and also by SGR 2014:1137 (ALBCOM) from AGAUR, Generalitat de Catalunya.

S. Destercke and T. Denoeux (Eds.): ECSQARU 2015, LNAI 9161, pp. 141–150, 2015.
DOI: 10.1007/978-3-319-20807-7_13

There are many similarities between the service-based computation model and the established disciplines of sequential and parallel programming. Conventionally a state change is effected by an assignment statement $x := e$. The time take to execute this assignment is predictable and depends on the number of operations within e. In service-based computing state changes are effected through service calls. A service (hosted in the cloud, or elsewhere) may have less predictable performance behaviour than a conventional imperative program – the QoS of service-based systems are considered in detail in [1]. Some of the factors influencing the performance of applications in the cloud are:

1. the type of hardware supplied by a provider to host a (virtual) machine;
2. the number of other (applications running as) VMs on a shared resource;
3. the behaviour of a hypervisor [9] supervising the execution of a set of VMs;
4. the nature of competing applications (e.g. web services, computationally intensive applications);

In this paper *uncertain execution environments* are specified in a *qualitative* way, using a two-player strategic game. One player (the daemon $\eth$) represents destructive stress; $\eth$ tries to maximise damage to an orchestration E by distributing a fixed degree of environmental stress (e.g. resource contention) over E's services. In contrast the angel player $\mathfrak{a}$ represents the self-healing capability of a system; the angel makes a move by allocating "benevolent conditions" to a fixed number of E's services (e.g. advantageous hardware allocation, no resource contention). The Nash equilibria of the resulting game provides a broad picture of how orchestrations react to mixed environmental stress.

The paper is organised as follows. In Sect. 2 an overview of the Orc language [7] and examples of performance variability in the cloud are given; an abstract game-theoretic (angel daemon) stress model is constructed. In Sect. 3 a cloud-based matrix multiplication orchestration is developed. The performance of matrix multiplication on a range of machine deployments is assessed using Nash equilibria in Sect. 4[1]. In Sect. 5 it is shown how game theory can be used to assess the effectiveness of adding redundancy to orchestrations. In Sect. 6 the applicability of the approach to other application areas is examined – for example variant forms of Angel-Daemon game could be used to analyse the effects of stress on orchestration communications.

2   Orc and a Model of Uncertain Cloud Environments

The language Orc [7] can be used to specify service-based computations and workflows [2]. A service s may fail to respond (i.e. it is *silent*) when it is called in an unreliable environment. A reliable service publishes a single result. In complex scenarios a service may call on further services and so may cause *side effects* elsewhere. Orc contains a number of inbuilt services: 0 is always silent whereas $1(x)$ always publishes its argument x. Two Orc expressions E and F can be combined using the following operators:

---

[1] All equiliria of a two person zero-sum game are identical – such assessments could also be computed by using linear programming.

- Sequence $E > x > F(x)$: The orchestration E is evaluated: for each output v, published by E, an instance $F(v)$ is invoked. If E publishes the stream of values, $v_1, v_2, \ldots v_n$, then $E > x > F(x)$ publishes some interleaving of the set $\{F(v_1), F(v_2), \ldots, F(v_n)\}$. The abbreviation $E >> F$ is used in situations where F is independent of the publication value generated by E.
- Symmetric Parallelism $E \mid F$: The independent orchestrations E and F are executed in parallel; $E \mid F$ publishes *some* interleaving of the values published by E and F.
- Asymmetric parallelism $E(x) < x < F$: Orchestrations E and F are evaluated in parallel; E may become blocked by a dependency on x. The first result published by F is bound to x, the remainder of F's evaluation is terminated and evaluation of the blocked residue of E is resumed.

Example 1. Orchestration $Two(d) = (BBC(d)|CNN(d)) > x > Email(Bob, x)$ calls two news services in parallel on day d and sends the resulting publications, via an email service, to Bob. In contrast $One(d) = Email(Bob, x) < x < (BBC(d)|CNN(d))$ results in only one news summary for day d (the first available) being emailed to Bob.   □

Uncertain cloud environments can be modelled in Orc. The infrastructure as a service ($IaaS$) cloud model allows users to control underlying hardware resources. Consider the following $IaaS$ orchestration for multiplying two matrices, a and b:

$$P.provision(IMG) > MI > MI.deploy(MM) > MM_1 > MM_1(a, b)$$

Here a request is made to a provider P to supply a machine instance MI and configure it with an operating system image IMG; the machine instance is installed with a matrix multiply service MM; this service is then used to multiply the matrices a and b. The quality of service (QoS) realised by MM_1 depends on a number of environmental factors [1]. Typically $IaaS$ clouds contain a variety of *machine types*. Table 1 shows some of the CPUs on 2012 AWS EC2.

Table 1. A subset of CPUs available from AWS EC2 in 2012

Instance type	Model	Speed (GHz)	L1 Cache	L2 Cache	L3 Cache
m1.small	AMD Opteron 2218 HE	2.6	$2 \times 64\,$KB	$2 \times 1\,$MB	N/A
m1.small	Intel Xeon E5420	2.66	$4 \times 64\,$KB	$2 \times 6\,$MB	N/A
m1.small	Intel Xeon E5507	2.26	$4 \times 64\,$KB	$4 \times 256\,$KB	4 MB
c1.xlarge	Intel Xeon E5410 ($\times 2$)	2.333	$4 \times 64\,$KB	$2 \times 6\,$MB	N/A
c1.xlarge	Intel Xeon E5506 ($\times 2$)	2.133	$4 \times 64\,$KB	$4 \times 256\,$KB	4 MB
cc1.4xlarge	Intel Xeon X5570 ($\times 2$)	2.933	$4 \times 64\,$KB	$4 \times 256\,$KB	8 MB
cg1.xlarge					
cc2.8xlarge	Intel Xeon E5-2670 ($\times 2$)	2.6	$8 \times 64\,$KB	$8 \times 256\,$KB	20 MB

In practice the performance of an application may depend critically on the amount of cache available on its execution platform. The performance of the MM_1 service may be influenced by the type of hardware supplied by the provider P in response to the service call $P.provision(IMG)$. Secondly it is important from a performance point of view that the installed service MM be tuned for the hardware supplied at run-time. In [8] a repository of tuned BLAS[2] implementations is made available in order to achieve tuning. The performance of $MM_1(a, b)$ on a shared multicore architecture may be critically influenced by the volume of traffic on the multicore bus which connects cores to on-chip memory. The performance of an orchestration E in a stressful environment (such as a cloud) can be modelled by associating a delay function, $\delta(s)$, with each underlying service s, $s \in \alpha(E)$[3]. Consider a model incorporating both *overdemand (o)* and *elasticity (e)*: *Overdemand* (demonic behaviour) may cause service degradation (e.g. multi-tenancy leads to memory contention); *Elasticity* (angelic behaviour) includes the allocation of the best type of resource and the deployment of extra resources to support a service, when needed. A tuple $(\delta(s), \delta_o(s), \delta_e(s), \delta_{o+e}(s))$ is a *stress model* [4] which specifies the performance delays associated with a service s:

- $\delta(s)$ is the delay of s in unstressed situations;
- $\delta_o(s)$ is the delay associated with s when it is subject to *overdemand*;
- $\delta_e(s)$ is the delay associated with s under *angelic* conditions;
- $\delta_{o+e}(s)$ is the delay when *overdemand* and *angelic* conditions interact.

The constraints: $\delta_e(s) < \delta(s) < \delta_o(s)$, $\delta_e(s) < \delta_{o+e}(s) < \delta_o(s)$ are assumed. A *stress model* for an orchestration E is a set S of underlying service stress models $S = \{(\delta(s), \delta_o(s), \delta_e(s), \delta_{o+e}(s)) \mid s \in \alpha(E)\}$. Here orchestration performance in uncertain environments is assessed using a two-player game: one player, the daemon ($\eth$), has the potential to overload selected services and so increase delay (using the function δ_o). The other, the angel ($\mathfrak{a}$) has the potential to associate selected services with an idealised operating environment (δ_e). Stress-related performance delays for orchestrations are defined using two cost functions: $\Delta_{\max}(E)$ is the time taken for the generation of *all* publications of E and $\Delta_{\min}(E)$ is the time taken for the generation of the *first* publication. In the remainder of the paper we consider only pruning expressions of the form $E_3(x, y) < y < E_2 < x < E_1$ where the consumer E_3 is blocked until both producers E_1 and E_2 publish. Suppose that $[a, d]$ denotes the sets of services under the influence of $\mathfrak{a}$ and $\eth$, respectively. The delay associated with a service s is:

$$\Delta_{\min}(s)[a, d] = \Delta_{\max}(s)[a, d] = \begin{cases} \delta(s) & \text{if } s \notin a \wedge s \notin d. \\ \delta_o(s) & \text{if } s \in d \wedge s \notin a. \\ \delta_e(s) & \text{if } s \in a \wedge s \notin d. \\ \delta_{o+e}(s) & \text{if } s \in (a \cap d). \end{cases}$$

---

[2] Basic Linear Algebra Subprograms (BLAS) are a library of low-level subroutines that perform common linear algebra operations.

[3] $\alpha(E)$ denotes the set of services used in orchestration E – for example $\alpha(s_1(5)|s_2(8)) = \{s_1, s_2\}$, the two services used in the orchestration.

Orchestration delays are defined by:

$$\Delta_k(E_1 \mid E_2) = k\{\Delta_k(E_1), \Delta_k(E_2)\}, \quad \Delta_k(E_1 \gg E_2) = \Delta_k(E_1) + \Delta_k(E_2)$$
$$\Delta_k(s(x) < x < E) = \Delta_k(s) + \Delta_{\min}(E)$$
$$\Delta_k(s(x,y) < y < E_1 < x < E_2) = max\{\Delta_{\min}(E_1) \, , \, \Delta_{\min}(E_2)\} + \Delta_k(s)$$

where $k \in \{\min, \max\}$. Thus $\Delta_{min}(E_1 \mid E_2) = min\{\Delta_{min}(E_1), \Delta_{min}(E_2)\}$, the time taken for the system $E_1 \mid E_2$ to generate its first publication. Uncertainty profiles (with cost functions) are used to capture formally the behaviour of orchestrations in stressed environments [3,4]. The *uncertainty profile* $\mathcal{U} = \langle E, \mathcal{A}, \mathcal{D}, b_{\mathcal{A}}, b_{\mathcal{D}}, \Delta_{\max} \rangle$ specifies *qualitatively* a particular set of stress conditions for the orchestration E. Here $\mathcal{A} \cup \mathcal{D} \subseteq \alpha(E)$, $b_{\mathcal{A}} \leq \#\mathcal{A}$, $b_{\mathcal{D}} \leq \#\mathcal{D}$ and the cost function satisfies $\Delta_{\max}(E)[a, d] \geq 0$. Let $\alpha(E)$ denote the set of services used in E. In the profile:

- $\mathcal{A}$ and $\mathcal{D}$ denote the sets of services which can be influenced by $\mathfrak{a}$ and $\mathfrak{d}$, respectively. When stress can effect all services in E then $\mathcal{A} = \mathcal{D} = \alpha(E)$.
- Parameters $b_{\mathcal{A}}$ and $b_{\mathcal{D}}$ specify the number of services to suffer angelic and daemonic stress. For example, $(b_{\mathcal{A}}, b_{\mathcal{D}}) = (1, 1)$ exemplifies the weakest form of mixed stress while $(b_{\mathcal{A}}, b_{\mathcal{D}}) = (1, 2)$ is an unbalanced situation.
- The effect of stress on performance is measured by the cost function $\Delta_{\max}$.

Profile $\mathcal{U} = \langle E, \mathcal{A}, \mathcal{D}, b_{\mathcal{A}}, b_{\mathcal{D}}, \Delta_{\max} \rangle$ has an associated zero-sum *angel-daemon game* $\Gamma(\mathcal{U}) = \langle A_{\mathfrak{a}}, A_{\mathfrak{d}}, \Delta_{\max} \rangle$ with players $\mathfrak{a}$ (angel) and $\mathfrak{d}$ (daemon). Player $\mathfrak{a}$ selects $b_{\mathcal{A}}$ distinct stressed services from $\mathcal{A}$ giving the action set $A_{\mathfrak{a}} = \{a \subseteq \mathcal{A} \mid \#a = b_{\mathcal{A}}\}$. Player $\mathfrak{d}$ selects $b_{\mathcal{D}}$ distinct stressed services from $\mathcal{D}$ giving $A_{\mathfrak{d}} = \{d \subseteq \mathcal{D} \mid \#d = b_{\mathcal{D}}\}$. The set of combined actions $A = A_{\mathfrak{a}} \times A_{\mathfrak{d}}$ is called the *set of strategy profiles*. Given $\Gamma(\mathcal{U})$, player $\mathfrak{a}$ can "make a move" by selecting an action $a \in A_{\mathfrak{a}}$ (a is called a strategy). Likewise player $\mathfrak{d}$ can select an action $d \in A_{\mathfrak{d}}$. If both players select a strategy *independently* then the joint *strategy profile* is $s = (a, d)$. Players $\mathfrak{a}$ and $\mathfrak{d}$ have costs $\Delta_{\max}(E)[a, d]$ and $-\Delta_{\max}(E)[a, d]$, respectively. The angel player $\mathfrak{a}$ wishes to minimise an orchestration's cost delay whereas the daemon $\mathfrak{d}$ wishes to maximise it. Mixed strategies for players $\mathfrak{a}$ and $\mathfrak{d}$ are probability distributions $\alpha : A_{\mathfrak{a}} \to [0, 1]$ and $\beta : A_{\mathfrak{d}} \to [0, 1]$, respectively. A *mixed strategy profile* is a tuple (α, β) such that $\Delta_{\max}(E)[\alpha, \beta] = \sum_{(a,d) \in A_{\mathfrak{a}} \times A_{\mathfrak{d}}} \alpha(a) \Delta_{\max}(E)[a, d] \beta(d)$. Let $\Delta_{\mathfrak{a}}$ and $\Delta_{\mathfrak{d}}$ denote the set of mixed strategies for players $\mathfrak{a}$ and $\mathfrak{d}$, respectively. A pure strategy profile (a, d) is a special case of a mixed strategy profile (α, β) in which $\alpha(a) = 1$ and $\beta(d) = 1$. A mixed strategy profile (α, β) is a *Nash equilibrium* if for any $\alpha' \in \Delta_{\mathfrak{a}}$, $\Delta_{\max}(E)[\alpha, \beta] \leq \Delta_{\max}(E)[\alpha', \beta]$ and for any $\beta' \in \Delta_{\mathfrak{d}}$, $\Delta_{\max}(E)[\alpha, \beta] \geq \Delta_{\max}(E)[\alpha, \beta']$. A pure Nash equilibrium, PNE, is a Nash equilibrium (a, d) where a and d are pure strategies. The value of the zero-sum game $\Gamma(\mathcal{U})$ associated with the uncertainty profile $\mathcal{U}$ is denoted by $\nu(\mathcal{U})$ is $\nu(\mathcal{U}) = \min_{\alpha \in \Delta_{\mathfrak{a}}} \max_{\beta \in \Delta_{\mathfrak{d}}} \Delta_{\max}(E)[\alpha, \beta] = \max_{\beta \in \Delta_{\mathfrak{d}}} \min_{\alpha \in \Delta_{\mathfrak{a}}} \Delta_{\max}(E)[\alpha, \beta]$. Strategy (α, β) is a Nash equilibrium iff $\Delta_{\max}(E)[\alpha, \beta] = \nu(\mathcal{U})$.

3   Matrix Multiplication in the Cloud

A conventional block matrix multiplication (BMM) of an $p \times r$ block matrix A and a $r \times q$ block matrix B can be defined using the r-way partition: $C_{ij} = \sum_{k=1}^{r} A_{ik}B_{kj}$, $1 \leq i \leq p$, $1 \leq j \leq q$, where A_{ik} and B_{kj} denote the blocks of A and B. The case $p = q = r = 2$ is shown.

$$A = \begin{bmatrix} A_{11} & A_{12} \\ A_{21} & A_{22} \end{bmatrix} B = \begin{bmatrix} B_{11} & B_{12} \\ B_{21} & B_{22} \end{bmatrix} AB = \begin{bmatrix} (A_{11}B_{11} + A_{12}B_{21}) & (A_{11}B_{12} + A_{12}B_{22}) \\ (A_{21}B_{11} + A_{22}B_{21}) & (A_{21}B_{12} + A_{22}B_{22}) \end{bmatrix}$$

Suppose that the services MM and MA, for multiplying and adding small and medium sized matrices, are deployed in the cloud. For example, the Amazon EC2 m1.small instance has a 1.7 GB RAM capacity (enough to accommodate three 64-bit precision 8000×8000 matrices) while the EC2 c1.xlarge instance type has a 7 GB RAM capacity (enough to accommodate three 16000×16000 matrices). Matrices of larger size can be multiplied together by constructing a parallel BMM orchestration which generates *block* matrix-vector and dot-product subtasks.

$$BMM_{2\times2}([a, b, c, d], [e, f, g, h]) =$$
$$1([w, x, y, z]) < w < DP([a, b], [e, g]) < x < DP([a, b], [f, h])$$
$$< y < DP([c, d], [e, g]) < z < DP([c, d], [f, h])$$

Block dot products may be implemented either sequentially or in parallel:

$$SeqDP_{2\times2}([a, b], [c, d]) = MM(a, c) > m_1 > MM(b, d) > m_2 > MA(m_1, m_2)$$
$$DP_{2\times2}([a, b], [c, d]) = MA(m_1, m_2) < m_1 < MM(a, c) < m_2 < MM(b, d)$$

Refinement to an IaaS Orchestration. $BMM_{2\times2}$ can be refined to an orchestration which operates in the infrastructure as a cloud model ($IaaS$); here cloud hardware resources can be provisioned and managed *explicitly*. The IaaS-level orchestration below has in its argument list the name of a cloud provider, P, an operating system image, IMG, as well as the services MM and MA. The subsidiary orchestration DP_I uses P and IMG to provision two machines for each dot-product.

$$BMM_I([[A_{11}, A_{12}], [A_{21}, A_{22}], [B_{11}, B_{21}], [B_{12}, B_{22}]], P, IMG, MM, MA) =$$
$$1([[C_{11}, C_{21}], [C_{12}, C_{22}]])$$
$$< C_{11} < DP_I([A_{11}, A_{12}], [B_{11}, B_{21}], P, IMG, MM, MA)$$
$$< C_{12} < DP_I([A_{11}, A_{12}], [B_{12}, B_{22}], P, IMG, MM, MA)$$
$$< C_{21} < DP_I([A_{21}, A_{22}], [B_{11}, B_{21}], P, IMG, MM, MA)$$
$$< C_{22} < DP_I([A_{21}, A_{22}], [B_{12}, B_{22}], P, IMG, MM, MA)$$
$$DP_I([A_1, A_2], [B_1, B_2], P, IMG, MM, MA) =$$
$$M_1.deploy(MA) > MA_1 > MA_1(x, y)$$
$$< x < M_1.deploy(MM) > MM_1 > MM_1(A_1, B_1)$$
$$< y < M_2.deploy(MM) > MM_2 > MM_2(A_2, B_2)$$
$$< M_1 < P.provision(IMG) < M_2 < P.provision(IMG)$$

A Stress Model for BMM. Performance results for executing BMM on clusters of Amazon EC2 c1.xlarge instances (8 CPU cores per instance) are shown in Table 2:

Table 2. Average, minimum and maximum times (in seconds) for BMM

Matrix Size	Block Size	Instances Used	Avg	Min	Max
8000	8000	1	41 (m)	24	76
16000	16000	1	297.22	171	408
	8000	4	151.95	94	206
	8000	8	103.55	77	155

Times are calculated using 20 separate tests. Execution time is measured remotely from a client and includes internet latency. A stress model for BMM is constructed by mapping $\delta_e(MM)$ and $\delta_o(MM)$ onto the minimum and maximum execution times for MM, respectively. The data for the one instance 8000×8000 experiment is used to build a *qualitative* model[4]. Speed-up predictions made by the uncertainty model are upper-bounds on actual speed-ups [8] since latency is not taken into account. The following stress model S results:

$$\delta(MA) = \delta_{o+e}(MA) = a, \ \delta(MM) = \delta_{o+e}(MM) = m,$$
$$\delta_o(MA) = 2 * a, \ \delta_o(MM) = 2 * m, \ \delta_e(MA) = 0.5 * a, \ \delta_e(MM) = 0.5 * m$$

4 Assessing BMM Orchestrations Under Stress

The $IaaS$ model allows application developers to control directly the degree of parallelism employed by a cloud implementation. Three possible $IaaS$ deployment configurations for BMM are considered below:

- *single machine BMM*: The performance is *estimated* by the performance of a intra-machine deployment (sequential implementation) of $BMM_{2\times2}$.
- *dot product inter-machine virtualisation* (BMM_{SeqDP}): here a separate machine instance is allocated to each of the 4 dot products in BMM.
- *fully parallel inter-machine virtualisation* (BMM_I): here a separate machine instance is allocated to each of the 8 matrix multiplication services.

BLAS Routines and Intra-machine Virtualization. Matrix multiplication is implemented on a single machine instance using BLAS library calls. Performance is modelled using a *uniform stress model* where all services (on a single core) are subject to the same level of stress. The performance of sequential dot product in an environment with a stress level l, $l \in \{o, e, o + e\}$ is estimated by

---

[4] The cost of matrix multiplication etc. depend on the problem size. However, in order to simplify the analysis a fixed problem size is used.

$\Delta_l(SeqDP_{2\times2}) = 2\delta_l(MM) + \delta_l(MA)$. The performance of sequential $BMM_{2\times2}$ under mixed stress is estimated by $\Delta_{o+e}(BMM_{2\times2}) = 4\Delta_{o+e}(SeqDP_{2\times2}) = 4(2m + a)$ Since $m >> a$ then $\Delta_{o+e}(BMM_{2\times2}) \approx 8m$ (roughly in line with the experimental data for sequential matrix multiplication on 8000×8000 and 16000×16000 data – see Table 2).

Inter-machine Virtualization. A uniform stress model does not capture the uncertain nature of service-based environments where deployment may take place on independent machine instances. Orchestration BMM_{SeqDP} has independent machine instances allocated to each dot product:

$$BMM_{SeqDP}([a, b, c, d], [e, f, g, h]) =$$
$$1([w, x, y, z]) < w < SeqDP_1([a, b], [e, g]) < x < SeqDP_2([a, b], [f, h])$$
$$< y < SeqDP_3([c, d], [e, g]) < z < SeqDP_4([c, d], [f, h])$$

The profile $\mathcal{U} = \langle BMM_{SeqDP}, S, S, 1, 1, \Delta_{\max} \rangle$ where $S = \{SeqDP_1, \ldots, SeqDP_4\}$ models BMM_{SeqDP} under moderate balanced stress and gives rise to the game:

$\eth$

	DP_1	DP_2	DP_3	DP_4
DP_1	$2m + a$	$4m + 2a$	$4m + 2a$	$4m + 2a$
DP_2	$4m + 2a$	$2m + a$	$4m + 2a$	$4m + 2a$
DP_3	$4m + 2a$	$4m + 2a$	$2m + a$	$4m + 2a$
DP_4	$4m + 2a$	$4m + 2a$	$4m + 2a$	$2m + a$

The strategy $\alpha = \beta = (1/4, 1/4, 1/4, 1/4)$ is an equilibrium with delay $\Delta(\alpha, \beta) = \sum_{i,j} \alpha(DP_i)\beta(DP_j)\Delta(DP_i, DP_j) = 7(2m + a)/4 \approx 7m/2$. Table 2 shows that multiplication of matrices of size 16000×16000, takes $151.95 \approx 3.7m$ seconds.

Fully Parallel IaaS Deployment. In order to achieve high performance all MM instances in $BMM_{2\times2}$ are called in parallel (using $DP_{2\times2}$). The orchestration BMM_I has eight (parallel) instances of MM and four instances of MA. Thus $S = \{MM_1, \ldots, MM_8, MA_1, \ldots, MA_4\}$ is the set of services under the influence of stress. Profile $\mathcal{U} = \langle BMM_I, S, S, 1, 1, \Delta_{\max} \rangle$ provides a model of the behaviour of BMM_I in a mixed stress environment (where both angel and daemon have the capacity to influence a single service) and gives rise to the associated game

$\eth$

	MM_j	MA_l
MM_i	$(m + a) \lhd (i = j) \rhd (2m + a)$	$m + 2a$
MA_k	$2m + a/2$	$(m + a) \lhd (k = l) \rhd (m + 2a)$

$i, j \in \{1, \ldots, 8\}$ and $k, l \in \{1, \ldots, 4\}$

Here the notation $P \lhd b \rhd Q$ (denoting 'P if b else Q') is used to provide a compact description. If both players choose MM_1 then BMM_I will have performance

$m+a$; however if they choose different MM instances then performance degrades to $2m + a$ (a parallel computation is only as fast as its slowest component). When $m \geq 4a$, $\alpha = \beta = (1/8, 1/8, 1/8, 1/8, 1/8, 1/8, 1/8, 1/8, 0, 0, 0, 0)$ is a mixed equilibrium such that $\Delta(\alpha, \beta) = \frac{15}{8}m + a$. Thus mixed stress is predicted to degrade the performance of BMM_I from an optimum $m + a$ to $15m/8 + a$. In this case there is a discrepancy between experimental data ($\approx 2.5m$) and the game theory predication ($\approx \frac{15}{8}m$). However, the latter approach provides a much better performance estimate than a uniform stress model ($\approx m$).

5   Redundancy and Increased Stress Levels

In practice BMM orchestration deployments with 64 or more machine instances may have reliability issues due either to slow or non-responsive services [6]. The $\mathfrak{a}/\mathfrak{d}$ approach can be applied to reason about the use of redundancy to improve orchestration resilience. Service $DP_{2\times2}$ can be enhanced by the addition of duplicate multiplication services:

$$rdntMM\_DP_{2\times2}([a,b],[c,d]) =$$
$$MA(m_1, m_2) < m_1 < \big(1(m) < m < (MM_1(a,c) \mid MM_2(a,c))\big)$$
$$< m_2 < \big(1(m) < m < (MM_3(b,d)) \mid MM_4(b,d))\big)$$

Here MM_1, MM_2, MM_3, MM_4 are independent services. A mixed-stress profile for $rdntMM\_DP$ is $\mathcal{U}_{rdntMM\_DP} = \langle rdnt\_DP_{2\times2}\mathcal{S}, \mathcal{S}, 1, 1, \Delta_{\max}\rangle$ where $\mathcal{S} = \{MA, MM_1, MM_2, MM_3, MM_4\}$. The associated $\mathfrak{a}/\mathfrak{d}$-game has (MA, MA) as PNE with valuation $m+a$. Thus, it is predicted that adding redundancy improves performance of dot product from $3m/2 + a$ to $m + a$. Four $rdntMM\_DP$ can be incorporated within $BMM_{2\times2}$ in order to improve the overall QoS. This situation is assessed using the profile $\mathcal{U} = \langle rdntMM\_BMM_{2\times2}, \mathcal{S}, \mathcal{S}, 1, 1, \Delta_{\max}\rangle$ where $\mathcal{S} = \{MA_1, \ldots, MA_4, MM_1, \ldots, MM_{16}\}$. The resulting $\mathfrak{a}/\mathfrak{d}$-game has (MA, MA) as a PNE with valuation $m+a$ (compared to the estimated $15m/8+a$ for the normal implementation).

Dot product with in-built redundancy (above) can be analysed in a scenario with increased stress where the daemon influences two services whereas the angel can only moderate one. The situation is captured by the profile $\mathcal{U} = \langle rdntMM\_DP_{2\times2}, \mathcal{S}, \mathcal{S}, 1, 2, \Delta_{\max}\rangle$, $\mathcal{S} = \{MM_1, \ldots, MM_4, MA\}$. The associated game has no PNE. However mixed equilibria have valuations $3/2m + a$. Thus, additional stress causes dot product (with redundancy) to deteriorate from $m + a$ to $3/2m + a$. The behaviour of the full multiplication orchestration $rdntMM\_BMM_{2\times2}$ under increased stress can be analysed in a similar way using the profile $\mathcal{U} = \langle rdntMM\_BMM_{2\times2}, \mathcal{S}, \mathcal{S}, 1, 2, \Delta_{\max}\rangle$. Provided that $m \geq 4a$ the value of the $\mathfrak{a}/\mathfrak{d}$-game is $15m/8 + a$. Thus, additional stress is predicted to cause an approximate doubling in the execution time of $rdntMM\_BMM$.

6   Discussion

There are well established theories for estimating the performance of sequential and parallel computations with respect to the number of operations that are executed for a given size of input. Analysing performance in service-based environments is much more complex. A conventional orchestration cost model captures behaviour in favourable operating conditions. More generally, the behaviour of an orchestration is dependent on the current level of environmental stress and the resilience of underlying services. In this paper uncertainty profiles are used to model the competitive circumstances that arise when services are subject to the effects of both overdemand and elasticity. The model $a/\eth$-model provides an extra layer of understanding about the evaluation of complex orchestrations.

There is a reasonable correlation between the predictions made by the $a/\eth$-model and experimental data. It is important to remember that uncertainty profiles are *qualitative* descriptions of evaluation environments; $a/\eth$-games provide a broad picture of how stress affects orchestration behaviour. Our aim is to provide a framework in which designers can analyse the effects of resource contention on services and orchestrations (rather than having to rely on a trial-and-error approach). In the paper we demonstrate how $a/\eth$ performance parameters can be constructed from experimental data. Perhaps the usefulness of the model can be seen most clearly when analysing the stress resilience capabilities of a number of different forms of a workflow.

It is not clear how the $a/\eth$ approach *scales* with orchestration size. In general it may be difficult to calculate Nash equilibria for large irregular orchestrations. However, it should be noted that there are practical techniques for finding mixed equilibria of large games [5]. In this paper attention has been focused on the effect that resource contention can have on machine and orchestration performance.

References

1. Benveniste, A., Jard, C., Kattepur, A., Rosario, S., Thywissen, J.A.: Qos-aware management of monotonic service orchestrations. Formal Methods Syst. Des. **44**(1), 1–43 (2014)
2. Cook, W.R., Patwardhan, S., Misra, J.: Workflow patterns in Orc. In: Ciancarini, P., Wiklicky, H. (eds.) COORDINATION 2006. LNCS, vol. 4038, pp. 82–96. Springer, Heidelberg (2006)
3. Gabarro, J., Serna, M., Stewart, A.: Web services and *incerta spiriti*: a game theoretic approach to uncertainty. In: Liu, W. (ed.) ECSQARU 2011. LNCS, vol. 6717, pp. 651–662. Springer, Heidelberg (2011)
4. Gabarro, J., Serna, M., Stewart, A.: Analysing web-orchestrations under stress using uncertainty profiles. Comput. J. **57**(11), 1591–1615 (2014)
5. Jiang, A.X., Jain, M., Tambe, M.: Computational game theory for security and sustainability. JIP **22**(2), 176–185 (2014)
6. Keenan, A.: Orchestrating hight performance services: theory and practice. Ph.D. Thesis (2014)
7. Misra, J., Cook, W.R.: Computation orchestration: a asis for wide-area computing. Softw. Syst. Model. **6**(1), 83–110 (2007)
8. Harmer, T., Keenan, A., Stewart, A., Wright, p, Sun, Y.L., Perrott, R.: A constraints-based resource discovery model for multi-provider cloud environments. J. Cloud Comput. Adv. Syst. Appl. **1**, 1–14 (2012)
9. Waldspurger, C.A., Rosenblum, M.: I/O virtualization. Commun. ACM **55**(1), 66–73 (2012)

Game-Theoretic Resource Allocation with Real-Time Probabilistic Surveillance Information

Wenjun Ma, Weiru Liu, and Kevin McAreavey[✉]

School of EEECS, Queen's University Belfast, Belfast, UK
{w.ma,w.liu,kevin.mcareavey}@qub.ac.uk

Abstract. Game-theoretic security resource allocation problems have generated significant interest in the area of designing and developing security systems. These approaches traditionally utilize the Stackelberg game model for security resource scheduling in order to improve the protection of critical assets. The basic assumption in Stackelberg games is that a defender will act first, then an attacker will choose their best response after observing the defender's strategy commitment (e.g., protecting a specific asset). Thus, it requires an attacker's full or partial observation of a defender's strategy. This assumption is unrealistic in real-time threat recognition and prevention. In this paper, we propose a new solution concept (i.e., a method to predict how a game will be played) for deriving the defender's optimal strategy based on the *principle of acceptable costs of minimax regret*. Moreover, we demonstrate the advantages of this solution concept by analyzing its properties.

1 Introduction

Recently, the problem of allocating limited security resources for protecting critical infrastructure and the general public has attracted significant research interest. In the literature, most existing work deals with this problem in the Stackelberg game framework [10,14]. That is, a defender selects their strategy based on the assumption that an attacker can observe and understand the defender's strategy. As a result, the Stackelberg game framework mainly focuses on the effective scheduling of limited security resources through past experience or knowledge.

Example 1. *A surveillance system in an airport has detected that a person has been loitering in the shopping area excessively. A combination of metal detection and body-shape image capture at the entrance to the shopping area suggest that the person may be carrying a gun and a bag. Moreover, there are three critical assets in the shopping area: a Foreign Currency Exchange office, a Supermarket and a Jewelry Shop. Suppose there is currently only one security team available, where should the security team protect?*

In this example, using information obtained by the surveillance system and the event inference method in [7,15], we can infer the suspect's motivation,

© Springer International Publishing Switzerland 2015
S. Destercke and T. Denoeux (Eds.): ECSQARU 2015, LNAI 9161, pp. 151–161, 2015.
DOI: 10.1007/978-3-319-20807-7_14

e.g., detonating a bomb in a public place, carrying out a robbery, etc. Malevolent motivations such as these can be used to model subsequent attack preferences (e.g., a robber may be more likely to target a bank than a shopping mall, while a bomber may be more likely to target a shopping mall than a bank). Thus, we can make use of such motivations as indicators of different types of attacker. Given that there may be multiple potential targets for an attacker and that a defender has limited resources for protecting these targets, it is essential for the defender to determine which target an attacker is most likely to attack. This type of problem is called a Surveillance Driven Security Resource Allocation (SDSRA) problem.

Since, in SDSRA problems, security teams act after detecting a potential threat, it suggests that an attacker and a defender actually execute their actions simultaneously. This contrasts with the type of security games addressed in [14], where a security manager assigns a patrol schedule for the security team first and the attacker then makes their decision based on the observation of the defender's strategy. As a result, current solution concepts based on the Stackelberg game framework, such as the Strong Stackelberg equilibrium [14], robust non-equilibrium solutions [11] and worst-case approaches for interval uncertainty [4], are not well-suited for modelling SDSRA problems. Moreover, in such games, since an attacker cannot know a defender's payoff value as well as a defender's probability distribution over different attacker types (motivations), traditional solution concepts, such as the Bayes-Nash equilibrium [5], cannot handle these problems either. Therefore, a natural direction is to consider a new game framework and solution concept for handling these SDSRA problems.

In this paper, we propose a *principle of acceptable costs of minimax regret* for the SDSRA game model based on three assumptions: (i) influence of loss-aversion for each player; (ii) minimax regret and loss-aversion based strategy selection for each player; (iii) knowledge of payoff matrices.[1] With this principle, we propose a method to predict the strategy which will be selected by each type of attacker and to determine the defender's optimal strategy. Finally, we analyze the properties of this new solution concept to justify our framework and suggest a linear programming implementation. Our main contributions are as follows: (i) we extend the application of security games to the SDSRA problem; (ii) with our solution concept, we dynamically predict an attacker's target/goal based on information gathered and inferred from an intelligent surveillance system; (iii) according to an attacker's strategy, we flexibly determine a defender's optimal strategy by balancing the expected payoff for successful threat prevention and for unaffordable losses caused by failure; and (iv) we validate our method by analyzing its properties.

The rest of this paper is organized as follows: Sect. 2 introduces three assumptions underpinning the new solution concept for the SDSRA problem; Sect. 3 predicts the optimal mixed strategy for each possible type of attacker and analyzes the properties of our attacker strategy prediction method; Sect. 4 discusses the

---

[1] A defender's knowledge of both players' payoff matrices and an attacker's knowledge of their own payoff matrix.

selection of the optimal strategy for the defender; and Sect. 5 discusses related work and concludes the paper with future work proposals.

2   Rationalizability in SDSRA

When a security manager obtains real-time probabilistic surveillance information [15][2], we can describe the security game for SDSRA as follows:

Definition 1. *A security game of SDSRA is a 6-tuple of* $(N, \Theta, A, \Psi, M, U)$:

- $N = \{1, 2\}$, *where 1 stands for a defender and 2 stands for an attacker.*
- $\Theta = \{t_1, \ldots, t_n\}$: *set of potential types of an attacker.*
- $A = \{A_i \mid i = 1, 2\}$: A_i *is a pure strategies set of player i. Here, a pure strategy is an action executed by a player.*
- $\Psi = \{(a_k, b_l) \mid a_k \in A_1 \text{ and } b_l \in A_2\}$: *set of all pure strategy profiles.*
- $P = \{p(t) \mid p(t) \text{ is a probability value for each element } t \text{ of } \Theta\}$.
- $U = \{u_{i,t}(X) \mid i \in N, t \in \Theta, X \in \Psi\}$, $u_{i,t}(X)$ *is a payoffs function* $u_{i,t} : \Psi \to R\}$.

The probability distribution P and the defenders utilities (i.e., $u_{1,t}(X)$ *for each* $t \in \Theta$ *and* $X \in \Psi$) *are known only to the defender.*

For each player a mixed strategy s_i is a probability distribution over his set of pure strategies. The differences between the security game of SDSRA and the traditional security game are: (i) an attacker and a defender actually take their actions simultaneously; (ii) a defender's payoff value for each pure strategy profile is unknown by an attacker; (iii) an attacker is unlikely to know the defender's probability distribution over potential attacker types (motivations). The first difference is the reason that solution concepts for Stackelberg games are not applicable, while the second and the third differences are the reasons that the Bayes-Nash equilibrium is not applicable. As a result, we introduce a new solution concept, called the *principle of acceptable costs of minimax regret*, which exploits two factors in decision making under uncertainty: loss-aversion and regret[3]. These factors have been identified in the literature and have been observed in psychological experiments [6,12]. Similar to the idea of the rationalizability in the Nash equilibrium [9], we provide three constraints on players for our solution concept: **A1:** Each player considers the influence of loss-aversion (i.e., people's tendency to strongly prefer ensuring a sufficient minimum payoff rather than seeking potential maximum utility in decision making). **A2:** Each player minimizes their maximum regret based on their attitude towards loss-aversion and the strategic choices of others. **A3:** The attacker's payoffs matrix is known by the defender and each player knows his own payoff matrix.

---

[2] While surveillance information can be represented by some imprecise probability theories [7], due to space restrictions, in this paper we focus on probability theory.

[3] Regret is an emotion associated with decisions which yield undesirable outcomes.

Table 1. Aumann and maschler game

	A	B
A	1,0	0,1
B	0,3	1,0

Consider assumption **A1** first. This idea of loss-aversion has been discussed extensively in the literature. An example in [12] is, perhaps, the most well-known. Consider the game in Table 1, where player 1 is the row player and player 2 is the column player. Clearly, in this game, the payoffs for the unique Nash equilibrium $((\frac{3}{4}A, \frac{1}{4}B), (\frac{1}{2}A, \frac{1}{2}B))$ for each player can be guaranteed by their maximin strategy, i.e., $(\frac{1}{2}A, \frac{1}{2}B)$ for player 1 and $(\frac{1}{4}A, \frac{3}{4}B)$ for player 2. In the literature [3,12], many have argued over what strategy should be selected by each player: Nash equilibrium or maximin strategies? Some researchers, such as Harsanyi [3], have further argued that the players should indeed choose their maximin strategies, since the Nash equilibrium means a player would risk losing their maximin value without gaining a higher expected utility.

For Assumption **A2**, it means in our games players will minimize their maximum regret based on a threshold, rather that maximize their expect utility based on the correct subjective beliefs about another player's strategy. In fact, many behavioral studies (e.g., [1]) show that human decisions under uncertainty are strongly influenced by the emotion of regret. The *minimax regret* principle suggested in [13] says that a choice is admissible if this choice minimizes the maximum difference between the outcome of a choice and the best outcome that could have been obtained in a given state.

Finally, assumption **A3** is accepted by solution concepts in the Stackelberg game framework [14]. Such an assumption is more realistic than the Nash equilibrium concept when applied to real-world applications, since this concept assumes that all player strategies and all player payoffs are common knowledge. Hence, according to these assumptions, our solution concept should satisfy:

A player is willing to select a strategy with a lower maximum regret, after considering whether the minimum expected payoff of such a strategy is an acceptable reduction of their maximin expected payoff.

Actually, this principle has two advantages. Firstly, it avoids the overly pessimistic (worst case) approach of the maximin strategy. For example, suppose a lottery sells tickets for $1 with a 99 % chance of winning $5000, then the maximin strategy would reject the offer. Clearly this violates our intuition. In our principle, however, if losing $1 is acceptable to a player then this risk will be tolerated. Secondly, it avoids the potential for unaffordable losses resulting from the minimax regret strategy. For example, suppose a lottery sells tickets for $1000 with a 1 % chance of winning $5000, then the minimax regret strategy would always accept the offer. Clearly this violates our intuition also. In our principle, a player will consider whether $1000 is an acceptable loss and may or may not accept the offer. These advantages are useful in real-world security applications, since some losses are unaffordable (e.g., people's lives) while an overly pessimistic approach may mean that a player loses the chance to act.

3 Solution Concept for SDSRA Problem

First, we consider the prediction of the attacker's strategy. Formally, we have:

Definition 2. *Let $S_2 = \{s_2^1, \ldots, s_2^m, \ldots\}$ be a set of mixed strategies for the attacker, which each mixed strategy is a probability distribution over A_2. $\sigma_{2,t} \in [0,1]$ is the threshold of acceptable cost which an attacker of type t can tolerate and $a_t \in A_1$ is a pure strategy of a defender. Then the optimal strategy for the attacker of type t, denoted as $s_{2,t}^* \in S_2$, is given by:*

$$s_{2,t}^* = \operatorname{argmin}\{\bar{r}(s_2^i) \mid \bar{r}(s_2^i) = \max_{a_h}\{\max_{j \neq i} u_{2,t}(a_h, s_2^j) - u_{2,t}(a_h, s_2^i)\}\}, \tag{1}$$

where

$$\min_{a_s} u_{2,t}(a_s, s_2^i) \geq \max_{s_2^k}\min_{a_r} u_{2,t}(a_r, s_2^k) - \varsigma_{a,t}, \tag{2}$$

$$\varsigma_{a,t} = \sigma_{2,t}(\max_{s_2^k}\min_{a_r} u_{2,t}(a_r, s_2^k) - \min_{s_2^l}\min_{a_w} u_{2,t}(a_w, s_2^l)). \tag{3}$$

Equation 1 in Definition 2 means that an attacker will select, as their optimal strategy, a mixed strategy which can minimize their maximum regret. Hence, Eq. 2 limits the acceptable cost for a given attacker when adopting the minimax regret strategy. That is, the minimum expected utility of the strategy should be higher than an acceptable reduction of the maximin value. Equation 2 shows how to calculate the acceptable reduction, where $\varsigma_{a,t}$ denotes the maximum loss that a type t attacker might pay in a SDSRA security game. Moreover, $\sigma_{2,t}$ in Eq. 3 is determined by an attacker's type. That is, some attackers will accept a choice with a lower minimum utility in order to reduce the maximum regret, while some attacker will refuse a high loss of their minimum utility. In short, the higher the value of $\sigma_{2,t}$, the higher the tolerance for loss of the minimum utility. In real-world applications, $\sigma_{2,t}$ can be obtained for each type of attacker from historical data or from criminology experts. Clearly, different types of attackers will have different attitudes for loss of the minimum utility. For example, a politically motivated terrorist usually shows higher tolerance for loss of the minimum utility than a robber, who is normally more concerned about their own safety.

Now, we consider how to find an optimal strategy for the defender based on the optimal mixed strategy $s_{2,t}^*$ for each type of attacker and the probability distribution over the attacker's possible types. In contrast to traditional security games, in real-time surveillance systems a defender needs to decide how to act in order to prevent further actions from the attacker. As a result, since only one pure strategy will be adopted by one security resource of the defender, we only need to consider the minimax regret with respect to pure strategies. Thus, using the same idea as our principle of acceptable costs of minimax regret, we can select the optimal strategy for the defender by:

Definition 3. *Let $a_i \in A_1$ be a defender's pure strategy, Θ be the set of possible types of an attacker, $p(t)$ be the probability value of attacker type t, $\sigma_1 \in [0,1]$ be the threshold of acceptable cost that a defender can tolerate, and $s_{2,t}^*$ be the* *optimal mixed strategy for each type of attacker. Then the defender's optimal strategy, denoted as a*, is given by:*

$$a_1^* = \arg\max\{EU(a_i) \mid EU(a_i) = \sum_{t \in \Theta} p(t)u_{1,t}(a_i, s_{2,t}^*)\}, \qquad (4)$$

where

$$\min_{a_{2,t}} \sum_{t \in \Theta} p(t)u_{1,t}(a_i, a_{2,t}) \geq \max_{a_h} \min_{a_{2,t}} \sum_{t \in \Theta} p(t)u_{1,t}(a_h, a_{2,t}) - \varsigma_d, \qquad (5)$$

$$\varsigma_d = \sigma_1(\max_{a_h} \min_{a_{2,t}} \sum_{t \in \Theta} p(t)u_{1,t}(a_h, a_{2,t}) - \min_{a_l} \min_{a_{2,t}} \sum_{t \in \Theta} p(t)u_{1,t}(a_l, a_{2,t})). \qquad (6)$$

The reason we adopt the same formula as the maximum expected utility in Eq. (4) is that the defender already knows the attacker's optimal mixed strategy $s_{2,t}^*$ and the probability distribution over the attacker's possible types. As a result, according to Assumption 2 and Definition 2, the minimax regret strategy is the same as the maximum expected utility strategy for the defender. Moreover, since the attacker's strategy is based on a judgement of the attacker's payoff matrix, the threshold of acceptable cost assumption for each type of attacker, and imperfect information obtained by surveillance system, there is a chance that the attacker may play a different strategy than the strategy predicted by the defender. Thus, Eqs. (5) and (6) together guarantee the minimum expected utility for a given pure strategy is acceptable for the defender.

In fact, a security manager can fine-tune the value of σ_1 to reflect different (real-time) situations for different applications. In this way, our method is more flexible in balancing the possibility of unaffordable losses caused by the failure of prevention and the expected payoff for successfully preventing an attack.

4   Properties and Linear Programming

Since the correctness of the defender's optimal strategy in our method is based on a prediction of the attacker's strategy, we consider properties of Definition 2 to justify the attacker's strategy prediction method. Moreover, given these properties, the whole process in our solution concept can be interpreted as an optimization problem for which there exists efficient methods of computation.

Theorem 1. *The maximin strategy of an attacker for our SDSRA security game is an unique equalizer[4].*

Proof. Suppose $A_1 = \{a_1, \ldots, a_n\}$ is the set of defender's pure strategies; $\{q_1, \ldots, q_n\}$ is a set of probability values over the set of attacker's pure strategy $A_2 =$

---

[4] Formally, in a two-player game, a probability distribution p for the pure strategies of a given player i ($A_i = \{a_1, \ldots, a_n\}$) is an equalizer if and only if there exists $c \in \Re$ ($\Re$ is the set of real numbers) and any pure strategy b_j for their opponent, s.t. the following equation holds $\Sigma_{t=1}^n p(a_t)u_i(a_t, b_j) = c$.

$\{b_1, \ldots, b_n\}$. By the definition of an equalizer, our game has a unique equalizer if and only if for linear equations $Aq = u$, where

$$
A = \begin{bmatrix} u_2(a_1, b_1) & \cdots & u_2(a_1, b_n) \\ \vdots & \ddots & \vdots \\ u_2(a_n, b_1) & \cdots & u_2(a_n, b_n) \\ 1 & \cdots & 1 \end{bmatrix}, q = \begin{bmatrix} q_1 \\ \vdots \\ q_n \end{bmatrix}, u = \begin{bmatrix} c \\ \vdots \\ c \\ 1 \end{bmatrix},
$$

there exists a unique solution q. Thus, $rank(A) = n$. In other word, it requires: (i) no convex combination of some rows in A dominating convex combinations of other rows; (ii) the payoff matrix satisfies $|A_1| = |A_2| = n$. Since there does not exist any dominated strategy for the attacker, item (i) holds in our game. Hence, since the defender and attacker share the same set of targets, item (ii) also holds in our game. □

This theorem reveals that an attacker can always find a unique strategy that guarantees their expected payoff regardless of any mixed strategy of the defender.

Theorem 2. *In a SDSRA security game, the expected payoff of the maximin strategy will not be less than a completely mixed Bayes-Nash equilibrium.*

Proof. Since in a completely mixed bimatrix game, each player can guarantee the expected payoff from a completely mixed equilibrium by playing a maximin strategy if and only if such a strategy is an equalizer [12]. By Theorem 1, and the fact that a Bayesian game in which the type space is finite can be redefined as a normal form game in which the strategy space is finite dimensional [9], this result can be obtained directly. □

Since our games satisfy that no pure or mixed strategy of an attacker or defender is strictly or weakly dominated by a convex combination of their other strategies, Theorem 2 shows that in many cases, an attacker can guarantee that their expected payoff is not less than the completely mixed Bayes-Nash equilibrium by selecting a maximin strategy.

Theorem 3. *Suppose a_h is a pure strategy for the defender, b_k is a pure strategy for the attacker, then the maximin regret $\bar{r}_t(s_2^i)$ for the attacker's (of type t) strategy s_2^i in a SDSRA security game can also be obtained as follows:*

$$
\bar{r}_t(s_2^i) = \max_{a_h} \{ \max_{b_k} u_{2,t}(a_h, b_k) - u_{2,t}(a_h, s_2^i) \}
$$

Proof. Given the linearity of payoff functions and the fact that there does not exist any dominated strategy for the attacker, we obtain this result directly. □

This theorem means that we only need to consider the pure strategy of the attacker when considering the maximin regret strategy of the attacker.

Theorem 4. *Suppose a_h is a defender's pure strategy, b_k is an attacker's pure strategy, and the payoff value of successfully attacking each target is the same for an attacker with a given type t ($u_{2,t}(a_i, b_j) = u_{2,t}(a_s, b_r)$, $i \neq j$, $s \neq r$), then the minimax regret strategy is the same as the maximin strategy for the attacker.*

Proof. Suppose the maximin strategy for an attacker of a given type t is $\bar{s}_2$. By Theorem 1, for any defender's pure strategies a_i and a_s, we have $u_{2,t}(a_i, \bar{s}_2) = u_{2,t}(a_s, \bar{s}_2)$. Then, by Theorem 3 and $u_{2,t}(a_i, b_j) = u_{2,t}(a_s, b_r) > u_{2,t}(a_k, b_l)$, for any $i \neq j$, $s \neq r$, $k = l$,[5] we have

$$\bar{r}_t(\bar{s}_2) = u_{2,t}(a_h, b_k) - u_{2,t}(a_h, \bar{s}_2), \quad for \ any \ h \neq k.$$

Suppose there exists a minimax regret strategy $s_2^* \neq \bar{s}_2$, then we have $\bar{r}_t(s_2^*) \leq \bar{r}_t(\bar{s}_2)$. Given the uniqueness of the equalizer (Theorem 1) and $u_2(a_i, b_j) = u_2(a_s, b_r)$, $i \neq j$, $s \neq r$, we have $\bar{r}_t(s_2^*) \neq \bar{r}_t(\bar{s}_2)$. Moreover, by $\bar{r}_t(s_2^*) < \bar{r}_t(\bar{s}_2)$, for a given defender's pure strategy a_i, we have $u_{2,t}(a_i, b_k) - u_{2,t}(a_h, s_2^*) < u_{2,t}(a_i, b_k) - u_{2,t}(a_i, \bar{s}_2)$, $i \neq k$. Then, we have $u_{2,t}(a_h, s_2^*) > u_{2,t}(a_i, \bar{s}_2)$. Since $\bar{s}_2$ is a maximin strategy, there exists a pure strategy a_s, such that $u_{2,t}(a_s, s_2^*) < u_{2,t}(a_s, \bar{s}_2)$. So, we have $u_{2,t}(a_s, b_k) - u_{2,t}(a_s, s_2^*) > u_{2,t}(a_s, b_k) - u_{2,t}(a_s, \bar{s}_2)$, $s \neq k$. It violates our assumption that $\bar{r}_t(s_2^*) \leq \bar{r}_t(\bar{s}_2)$. So, $s_2^* = \bar{s}_2$.   □

Theorem 3 demonstrates that if the payoff value of successfully attacking each target is the same for an attacker with a given type, then he can choose their maximin strategy to guarantee their minimum payoff value as well as to reduce their maximum regret in our games. Also, the relationship between Definition 2 and the decision rule of minimax regret [13], as well as that of Γ-maximin [9] is as follows:

Theorem 5. *Let $\sigma_{2,t} \in [0, 1]$ be the threshold of acceptable cost that an attacker of type t can tolerate, and $s_{2,t}^*$ be the optimal strategy for attacker type t, according to the principle of acceptable costs of maximum regret:*

(i) if $\sigma_{2,t} = 1$, then $s_{2,t}^*$ is also an optimal choice according to the rule of minimax regret; and

(ii) if $\sigma_{2,t} = 0$, then $s_{2,t}^*$ is also an optimal choice according to the rule of Γ-maximin.

Proof. (i) From Eqs. (2) and (3) and the fact $\sigma_{2,t} = 1$, a mixed strategy s_2^i can be any element in the set of mixed strategies S_2. Then, from Eq. (1), $s_{2,t}^*$ is also an optimal choice according to the rule of minimax regret. (ii) From Eqs. (1), (2), and (3), with $\sigma_{2,t} = 0$, $s_{2,t}^*$ can only be an element with the maximin utility in the set of mixed strategies $S_{2,t}$. Thus, $s_{2,t}^*$ is also an optimal choice according to the Γ-maximin rule.   □

Actually, given Definitions 2 and 3 as well as Theorems 1 and 3, the whole process of finding a defender's optimal strategy based on the strategy selected by each possible type of attacker can be solved by two Linear Programs as follows[6]:

---

[5] $k = l$ means that both players select the same target (i.e., the attacker loses), while $i \neq j$ and $s \neq r$ mean that players select different targets (i.e., the attacker wins).

[6] Since a defender may have multiple available security resources, our Linear Programs will also consider this situation based on Definition 3.

$$\min_{\{q_j^t\}} \quad \overline{r}_{2,t}(\{q_j^t\})$$

$$\text{s.t.} \quad \overline{r}_{2,t}(\{q_j^t\}) \geq (u_{2,t}(a_h, b_k) - \sum_{i=1}^{n} q_j^t u_{2,t}(a_h, b_j))(\forall a_h, \forall b_k)$$

$$\sum_{j=1}^{n} q_j^t u_{2,t}(a_h, b_j) \geq (1 - \sigma_{2,t})C_{2,t} + \sigma_{2,t}V_{2,t} \quad (\forall a_h)$$

$$C_{2,t} = \sum_{l=1}^{n} \overline{q}_l^t u_{2,t}(a_s, b_k) \quad\quad (a_s \in A_1)$$

$$V_{2,t} = \min\{u_{2,t}(a_h, b_k)\} \quad\quad (\forall a_h, \forall b_k)$$

$$\sum_{j=1}^{n} q_j^t = 1, q_j^t \in [0, 1]$$

$$\max_{\{x_i\}} \quad \sum_{i=1}^{n}\sum_{j=1}^{n}\sum_{t\in\Theta} p(t)x_i u_{1,t}(a_i, b_j)q_j^t$$

$$\text{s.t.} \quad \sum_{i=1}^{n}\sum_{t\in\Theta} p(t)x_i u_{1,t}(a_i, b_j) \geq (1 - \sigma_1)C_1 + \sigma_1 V_1$$

$$C_1 = \max\{\sum_{t\in\Theta} p(t)u_{1,t}(a_i, b_j)\}$$

$$V_1 = \min\{\sum_{t\in\Theta} p(t)u_{1,t}(a_i, b_j)\}$$

$$\sum_{i=1}^{n} x_i^* = k, x_i^* \in \{0, 1\}$$

The first LP aims to find the mixed strategy selected by each possible type of attacker $\{q_t^j\}$ based on our principle while the second LP aims to find the defender's optimal strategy $\{x_i\}$. For the first LP, the objective function and the first constraint represent Eq. 1, the second, third and fourth constraints represent Eqs. 2 and 3 (where $\{\overline{q}_1^t, \ldots, \overline{q}_n^t\}$ is the probability distribution for a type t attacker's unique equalizer strategy), the fifth constraint limits the set $\{q_j^t\}$ as a probability distribution over the set of actions A_2. For the second LP, the objective function represents Eq. 4, the first, second and third constraints represent Eqs. 5 and 6, and the fourth constraint limits the strategies selected by a defender being a pure distribution over A_1 (that is, $p_i = 1$ or $p_i = 0$) and the amount of available security resources.

5   Conclusion

Related Work: Recently, security games have received increasing attention when aiming to solve security resource allocation problems [14]. Much of the work deals with this problem within the Stackelberg game framework [5,8,10]. That is, a defender commits to a strategy first and an attacker chooses their strategy based on the defender's commitment. The typical solution concept is the Strong Stackelberg Equilibrium, which assumes that an attacker will always break ties in favor of a defender in the case of indifference [5]. However, it is not always intuitive in real-world applications: how can an attacker observe the defender's strategy in a real-time, interactive environment? Thus, our work provides a more reasonable solution concept based on the principle of acceptable costs of minimax regret. On the other hand, in recent years there has been an increase in the deployment of intelligent surveillance systems, largely in response to the high demand for identifying and preventing threats for public safety, e.g., suspect object tracking [2] and anti-social behavior analysis [7]. However, to the best of our knowledge, little work of this kind focuses on how to allocate security resources to prevent possible attacks based on incomplete information in a surveillance system.

Conclusion: This paper proposed a new solution concept to handle SDSRA security games based on the principle of acceptable costs of minimax regret. Firstly, we discussed the rationalizability assumptions of our principle: loss-aversion, minimax regret, and knowledge of the payoff matrix. Then, based on this principle, we proposed a method to predict the attacker's strategy and to determine the optimal strategy for the defender. Finally, we validated our method with some properties and provided a Linear Program for our solution concept.

References

1. Chua, H.F., Gonzalez, R., Taylor, S.F., Welsh, R.C., Liberzon, I.: Decision-related loss: regret and disappointment. NeuroImage **47**(4), 2031–2040 (2009)
2. Gong, S., Loy, C., Xiang, T.: Security and surveillance. In: Moeslund, T.B., Hilton, A., Krüger, V., Sigal, L. (eds.) Visual Analysis of Humans, pp. 455–472. Springer, London (2011)
3. Harsanyi, J.C.: Rational Behaviour and Bargaining Equilibrium in Games and Social Situations. Cambridge University Press, Cambridge (1986)
4. Kiekintveld, C., Kreinovich, V.: Efficient approximation for security games with interval uncertainty. In: Proceedings of the AAAI Spring Symposium on Game Theory for Security, Sustainability, and Health GTSSH (2012)
5. Korzhyk, D., Yin, Z., Kiekintveld, C., Conitzer, V., Tambe, M.: Stackelberg vs. Nash in security games: an extended investigation of interchangeability, equivalence, and uniqueness. J. Artif. Intell. Res. **41**(2), 297–327 (2011)
6. Kuhnen, C.M., Knutson, B.: The neural basis of financial risk taking. Neuron **47**(5), 763–770 (2005)
7. Ma, J., Liu, W., Miller, P.: Event modelling and reasoning with uncertain information for distributed sensor networks. In: Deshpande, A., Hunter, A. (eds.) SUM 2010. LNCS, vol. 6379, pp. 236–249. Springer, Heidelberg (2010)
8. Ma, W., Luo, X., Liu, W.: An ambiguity aversion framework of security games under ambiguities. IJCAI **2013**, 271–278 (2013)

9. Osborne, M.J.: An Introduction to Game Theory. Oxford University Press, New York (2004)
10. Pita, J., Jain, M., Ordonez, F., Portway, C., Tambe, M., Western, C., Paruchuri, P., Kraus, S.: Using game theory for Los Angeles airport security. AI Mag. **30**(1), 43–57 (2009)
11. Pita, J., Jain, M., Tambe, M., Ordóñez, F., Kraus, S.: Robust solutions to stackelberg games: addressing bounded rationality and limited observations in human cognition. Artif. Intell. **174**(15), 1142–1171 (2010)
12. Pruzhansky, V.: Some interesting properties of maximin strategies. Int. J. Game Theory **40**(2), 351–365 (2011)
13. Savage, L.J.: The theory of statistical decision. J. Am. Stat. Assoc. **46**(253), 54–67 (1951)
14. Tambe, M.: Security and Game Theory: Algorithms, Deployed Systems Lessons Learned. Cambridge University Press, Cambridge (2011)
15. Wasserkrug, S., Gal, A., Etzion, O.: Inference of security hazards from event composition based on incomplete or uncertain information. IEEE Trans. Knowl. Data Eng. **20**(8), 1111–1114 (2008)

Belief Update

Belief Update Within Propositional Fragments

Nadia Creignou$^{(\boxtimes)}$, Raïda Ktari, and Odile Papini

Aix-Marseille Université, CNRS, LIF, LSIS, 163 av. de Luminy,
13288 Marseille, France
{Nadia.Creignou,Raida.Ktari,Odile.Papini}@univ-amu.fr

Abstract. Recently, belief change within the framework of fragments of propositional logic has gained attention. Previous works focused on belief revision, belief merging, and on belief contraction in the Horn fragment. The problem of belief update within the framework of fragments of propositional logic has been neglected so far. In the same spirit as a previous extension of belief revision to propositional fragments, we propose a general approach to define new update operators derived from existing ones such that the result of update remains in the fragment under consideration. Our approach is not limited to the Horn fragment but applicable to many fragments of propositional logic, like Horn, Krom and affine fragments. We study the logical properties of the proposed operators in terms of the KM's postulates satisfaction and highlight differences between revision and update in this context.

Keywords: Belief change · Belief update · Fragments of propositional logic · Knowledge representation and reasoning

1 Introduction

Belief update consists in incorporating into an agent's beliefs new information reflecting a change in her environment. The problematic of belief update first appeared in the domain of databases for updating deductive databases [14]. Significant links quickly emerged with works developed in artificial intelligence on belief change, especially on belief revision. Keller and Winslett [22], and later Katsuno and Mendelzon [21] allowed us to get a better understanding regarding the distinction between belief revision and belief update when they proposed a common framework to represent these operations. Belief revision happens when new information is introduced in a static environment, while belief update occurs in a changing environment. From a logical point of view, when the agent's beliefs are represented by a logical formula, revision makes the models of this formula evolve as a whole towards the closest models of new information. In contrast, update makes each model of this formula locally evolve towards the closest models of new information.

This work has received support from the French Agence Nationale de la Recherche, ASPIQ project reference ANR-12-BS02-0003.

S. Destercke and T. Denoeux (Eds.): ECSQARU 2015, LNAI 9161, pp. 165–174, 2015.
DOI: 10.1007/978-3-319-20807-7_15

Postulates characterizing the rational behavior of update operators have been proposed by Katsuno and Mendelzon (KM) [21] in the same spirit as the seminal AGM's postulates [1] for revision. Belief update gave rise to several studies, in most cases within the framework of propositional logic, and concrete belief update operators have been proposed mainly according to a semantic (model-based) point of view [3,7,8,11,12,15,16,18,23,29].

Many studies focused on belief change within the framework of propositional logic fragments, particularly on belief contraction [2,10,30] and belief revision [4,5,9,25,31]. However, as far as we know, the problem of belief update within fragments of propositional logic has not been addressed so far, except for complexity results in the Horn case [13,24].

The motivation of such a study is twofold. First, in many applications, the language is restricted *a priori*. For instance, a rule-based formalization of expert knowledge is much easier to handle for standard users. In case of update they expect an outcome in the same language. Second, some fragments of propositional logic allow for efficient reasoning methods, and then an outcome of update within such a fragment can be evaluated efficiently. It seems thus natural to investigate how known update operators can be refined such that the result of update remains in the fragment under consideration.

Let $\mathcal{L}'$ be a propositional fragment and given two formulas $\psi, \mu \in \mathcal{L}'$, the main obstacle hereby is that there is no guarantee that the outcome of an update, denoted by $\psi \diamond \mu$, remains in $\mathcal{L}'$ as well. Let, for example, $\psi = a$ and $\mu = \neg a \vee \neg b$, be two Horn formulas. Updating ψ by μ in using Forbus' [15] or Winslett's operator [28] results in a formula equivalent to $\phi = (a \vee b) \wedge (\neg a \vee \neg b)$, which is not a Horn formula and is not equivalent to any Horn formula (because its set of models is not closed under intersection, while this property characterizes Horn formulas, see [19])[1].

In order to overcome this problem we use the notion of refinement. A refinement adapts an operator defined in a propositional setting such that it can be applicable in a propositional fragment. The basic properties of a refinement are first to guarantee the outcome of the change operation to remain within the fragment and second to approximate the behavior of the original operator, in particular to keep the behavior of the original operator unchanged if the result already fits in the fragment. We characterize these refined operators in a constructive way.

This characterization allows us to study their logical properties in terms of satisfaction of the KM's postulates. We show that the basic KM's postulates (U1) − (U4) are preserved for any refinement for any fragment. We then study the limits of the preservation of the other postulates. For this we focus on the refinements of Forbus' and Winslett's operators within the Horn, Krom and affine fragments. All along this study we shed some light on subtle differences between update and revision.

---

[1] Note that in this example, revision and update do not coincide.

2   Preliminaries

2.1   Propositional Logic

Let $\mathcal{L}$ be the language of propositional logic build on an infinite countable set of variables (atoms) and equipped with standard connectives $\rightarrow$, $\oplus$, $\vee$, $\wedge$, $\neg$, and constants $\top$, $\bot$. A literal is an atom or its negation. A clause is a disjunction of literals. A clause is called *Horn* if at most one of its literals is positive; *Krom* if it consists of at most two literals. A $\oplus$-clause is defined like a clause but using exclusive - instead of standard - disjunction. We identify $\mathcal{L}_{Horn}$ (resp., $\mathcal{L}_{Krom}$, $\mathcal{L}_{affine}$) as the set of all formulas in $\mathcal{L}$ being conjunctions of Horn clauses (resp., Krom clauses, $\oplus$-clauses).

Let $\mathcal{U}$ be a finite set of atoms. An interpretation over $\mathcal{U}$ is represented either by a set $m \subseteq \mathcal{U}$ of atoms (corresponding to the variables set to true) or by its corresponding characteristic bit-vector of length $|\mathcal{U}|$. For any formula ϕ, let $\mathrm{Var}(\phi)$ denote the set of variables occurring in ϕ. As usual, if an interpretation m defined over $\mathcal{U}$ satisfies a formula ϕ such that $\mathrm{Var}(\phi) \subseteq \mathcal{U}$, we call m a model of ϕ. By $\mathrm{Mod}(\phi)$ we denote the set of all models (over $\mathcal{U}$) of ϕ. A formula ψ is *complete* over $\mathcal{U}$ if it has exactly one model over $\mathcal{U}$. Moreover, $\psi \models \phi$ if $\mathrm{Mod}(\psi) \subseteq \mathrm{Mod}(\phi)$ and $\psi \equiv \phi$ if $\mathrm{Mod}(\psi) = \mathrm{Mod}(\phi)$. For fragments $\mathcal{L}' \subseteq \mathcal{L}$, we use $T_{\mathcal{L}'}(\psi) = \{\phi \in \mathcal{L}' \mid \psi \models \phi\}$.

2.2   Characterizable Fragments of Propositional Logic

Let $\mathcal{B}$ be the set of Boolean functions $\beta \colon \{0,1\}^k \rightarrow \{0,1\}$ with $k \geqslant 1$, that are *symmetric* (i.e. for all permutations σ, $\beta(x_1, \ldots, x_k) = \beta(x_{\sigma(1)}, \ldots, x_{\sigma(k)})$), and 0- and 1-*reproductive* (i.e. for every $x \in \{0,1\}$, $\beta(x, \ldots, x) = x$). Examples of such functions are: The binary AND function denoted by $\wedge$, the ternary MAJORITY function, $\mathrm{maj}_3(x, y, z) = 1$ if at least two of the variables x, y, and z are set to 1, and the ternary XOR function $\oplus_3(x, y, z) = x \oplus y \oplus z$.

Recall that we consider interpretations also as bit-vectors. We thus extend Boolean functions to interpretations by applying coordinate-wise the original function. So, if $m_1, \ldots m_k \in \{0,1\}^n$, then $\beta(m_1, \ldots m_k)$ is defined by $(\beta(m_1[1], \ldots m_k[1]), \ldots, \beta(m_1[n], \ldots m_k[n]))$, where $m[i]$ is the i-th coordinate of the interpretation m.

The next definition gives a general formal definition of closure.

Definition 1. *Given a set $\mathcal{M} \subseteq 2^{\mathcal{U}}$ of interpretations and $\beta \in \mathcal{B}$, we define $Cl_\beta(\mathcal{M})$, the closure of $\mathcal{M}$ under β, as the smallest set of interpretations that contains $\mathcal{M}$ and that is closed under β, i.e. if $m_1, \ldots, m_k \in Cl_\beta(\mathcal{M})$, then $\beta(m_1, \ldots, m_k) \in Cl_\beta(\mathcal{M})$.*

For instance it is well-known that the set of models of any Horn formula is closed under $\wedge$, and actually this property characterizes Horn formulas.

Definition 2. *Let $\beta \in \mathcal{B}$. A set $\mathcal{L}' \subseteq \mathcal{L}$ of propositional formulas is a β-fragment (or a* characterizable fragment*) if: (i) For all $\psi \in \mathcal{L}'$, $\mathrm{Mod}(\psi) = Cl_\beta(\mathrm{Mod}(\psi))$. (ii) For all $\mathcal{M} \subseteq 2^{\mathcal{U}}$ with $\mathcal{M} = Cl_\beta(\mathcal{M})$ there exists $\psi \in \mathcal{L}'$ with $\mathrm{Mod}(\psi) = \mathcal{M}$. (iii) If $\phi, \psi \in \mathcal{L}'$ then $\phi \wedge \psi \in \mathcal{L}'$.*

Well-known fragments of propositional logic are $\mathcal{L}_{Horn}$ which is an $\wedge$-fragment, $\mathcal{L}_{Krom}$ which is a maj_3-fragment and $\mathcal{L}_{affine}$ which is $\oplus_3$-fragment [19,27].

2.3   Update

Belief update consists in incorporating into an agent's beliefs new information reflecting a change in her environment. More formally, an update operator, denoted by $\diamond$, is a function from $\mathcal{L} \times \mathcal{L}$ to $\mathcal{L}$ that maps two formulas ψ (the initial agent's beliefs) and μ (new information) to a new formula $\psi \diamond \mu$ (the updated agent's beliefs). We recall the KM's postulates for belief update [20].

Let $\psi, \psi_1, \psi_2, \mu, \mu_1, \mu_2 \in \mathcal{L}$.

(U1) $\psi \diamond \mu \models \mu$.
(U2)   If $\psi \models \mu$, then $\psi \diamond \mu \equiv \psi$.
(U3)   If ψ and μ are satisfiable then so is $\psi \diamond \mu$.
(U4)   If $\psi_1 \equiv \psi_2$ et $\mu_1 \equiv \mu_2$, then $\psi_1 \diamond \mu_1 \equiv \psi_2 \diamond \mu_2$.
(U5) $(\psi \diamond \mu) \wedge \phi \models \psi \diamond (\mu \wedge \phi)$.
(U6)   If $(\psi \diamond \mu_1) \models \mu_2$ and $(\psi \diamond \mu_2) \models \mu_1$, then $\psi \diamond \mu_1 \equiv \psi \diamond \mu_2$.
(U7)   If ψ is complete, then $(\psi \diamond \mu_1) \wedge (\psi \diamond \mu_2) \models \psi \diamond (\mu_1 \vee \mu_2)$.
(U8) $(\psi_1 \vee \psi_2) \diamond \mu \equiv (\psi_1 \diamond \mu) \vee (\psi_2 \diamond \mu)$.
(U9)   If ψ is complete and $(\psi \diamond \mu) \wedge \phi$ is satisfiable, then $\psi \diamond (\mu \wedge \phi) \models (\psi \diamond \mu) \wedge \phi$.

These postulates have been discussed in several papers (see for example [18]). The postulates (U1), (U4) and (U5) directly correspond to the belief revision postulates (R1), (R4) and (R5) respectively. The postulate (U2) differs from (R2), the latter stating that if $\psi \wedge \mu$ is satisfiable then $\psi \diamond \mu \equiv \psi \wedge \mu$. A consequence of (U2) for update is that once an inconsistency is introduced in the initial beliefs there is no way to eliminate it [20]. Note that this is not the case for belief revision. Furthermore, (U3) is a weaker version of (R3). The latter states that if μ is satisfiable then so is $\psi \diamond \mu$, while in order to ensure the consistency of the result of update (U3) requires an additional condition, namely that the initial beliefs be consistent as well. The postulates (U6), (U7) and (U8) are specific to update operators. Finally, (U9) is a weaker version of (R6), it is similar but restricted to complete formulas ψ.

Katsuno and Mendelzon provided a representation theorem [20] stating that a revision operator corresponds to a set of preorders on interpretations. More formally, for all $\psi, \mu \in \mathcal{L}$ and for $\leqslant_\psi$ a preorder on interpretations satisfying certain conditions [20], a revision operator satisfying the AGM postulates is defined by $\mathrm{Mod}(\psi \circ \mu) = min(\mathrm{Mod}(\mu), \leqslant_\psi)$. Similarly, they provided a representation theorem for update [21]. More formally, for all $m \in Mod(\psi)$, $\mu \in \mathcal{L}$ and for $\leqslant_m$ a preorder on interpretations satisfying certain conditions [21], an update operator satisfying the KM's postulates is defined by $\mathrm{Mod}(\psi \diamond \mu) = \bigcup_{m \in \mathrm{Mod}(\psi)} min(\mathrm{Mod}(\mu), \leqslant_m)$.

These representation theorems pinpoint the differences between revision and update. Update stems from a point-wise minimization, model by model of ψ, while revision stems from a global minimization on all the models of ψ. Update operators, for each model m of ψ, select the closest set of models of μ, while revision operators select the set of models of μ which are the closest to the set of models of ψ. Note that when there exists only one model of ψ revision and update coincide.

Forbus' operator was introduced in [15] in the context of qualitative physics. This operator is analogous to Dalal's revision operator [6] and measures minimality change by cardinality of model change. More formally, let ψ and μ be two propositional formulas, and m and m' be two interpretations, $m \Delta m'$ denotes the symmetric difference between m and m' and $|\Delta|_m^{min}(\mu)$ denotes the minimum number of variables in which m and a model of μ differ and is defined as $min\{|m \Delta m'| : m' \in \text{Mod}(\mu)\}$. Forbus' operator is now defined as: $\text{Mod}(\psi \diamond_F \mu) = \bigcup_{m \in \text{Mod}(\psi)} \{m' \in \text{Mod}(\mu) : |m \Delta m'| = |\Delta|_m^{min}(\mu)\}$. This operator satisfies (U1) − (U8) [20] and (U9) [18].

Winslett's operator, also called *PMA (Possible Models Approach)* [28] was introduced for reasoning about actions and change. This operator is analogous to Satoh's revision operator [26] and interprets minimal change in terms of set inclusion instead of cardinality on model difference. More formally, $\Delta_m^{min}(\mu)$ denotes the minimal difference between m and a model of μ ans is defined as $min_{\subseteq}(\{m \Delta m' : m' \in \text{Mod}(\mu)\})$. Winslett's operator is now defined as: $\text{Mod}(\psi \diamond_W \mu) = \bigcup_{m \in \text{Mod}(\psi)} \{m' \in \text{Mod}(\mu) : m \Delta m' \in \Delta_m^{min}(\mu)\}$. This operator satisfies (U1) − (U8) [20] but does not satisfy (U9).

In this paper we are interested in update operators which are tailored for certain fragments. We say that $\diamond$ satisfies the postulates (Ui) ($i \in \{1, \ldots, 9\}$) in a fragment $\mathcal{L}' \subseteq \mathcal{L}$ if these postulates hold when restricted to formulas from $\mathcal{L}'$.

3   Refinements of Operators

A study on how existing belief change operators can be adapted to fit into fragments of propositional logic was initiated in [5]. In the same spirit: Given an update operator $\diamond$ and a fragment $\mathcal{L}'$ of propositional logic, how can $\diamond$ be adapted (or refined) to a new operator $\blacklozenge$ such that for all $\psi, \mu \in \mathcal{L}'$, also $\psi \blacklozenge \mu \in \mathcal{L}'$?[2]

As in [5] few natural desiderata for such refined operators can be stated.

Definition 3. *Let $\mathcal{L}'$ be a fragment of propositional logic and $\diamond : \mathcal{L} \times \mathcal{L} \to \mathcal{L}$ an update operator. We call an operator $\blacklozenge : \mathcal{L}' \times \mathcal{L}' \to \mathcal{L}'$ a $\diamond$-refinement for $\mathcal{L}'$ if it satisfies the following properties, for each $\psi, \psi', \mu, \mu' \in \mathcal{L}'$: (i) Consistency: $\psi \blacklozenge \mu$ is satisfiable if and only if $\psi \diamond \mu$ is satisfiable. (ii) Equivalence: If $\psi \diamond \mu \equiv \psi' \diamond \mu'$, then $\psi \blacklozenge \mu \equiv \psi' \blacklozenge \mu'$. (iii) Containment: $T_{\mathcal{L}'}(\psi \diamond \mu) \subseteq T_{\mathcal{L}'}(\psi \blacklozenge \mu)$. (iv) Invariance: If $\psi \diamond \mu \in \mathcal{L}'$, then $T_{\mathcal{L}'}(\psi \blacklozenge \mu) = T_{\mathcal{L}'}(\psi \diamond \mu)$.*

In [5] the authors defined such refined operators in the context of revision through the notion of β-mapping as defined below. We can do the same for update.

---

[2] There exist update operators that are well-adapted for any characterisable fragment, i.e. that provide a result in the fragment, for instance Hegner's operator and more generally dependence based update operators [18].

Definition 4. *Given $\beta \in \mathcal{B}$, we define a β-mapping, f_β, as an application from sets of models into sets of models, $f_\beta : 2^{2^\mathcal{U}} \longrightarrow 2^{2^\mathcal{U}}$, such that for every $\mathcal{M} \subseteq 2^\mathcal{U}$:*
(1) $Cl_\beta(f_\beta(\mathcal{M})) = f_\beta(\mathcal{M})$, i.e., $f_\beta(\mathcal{M})$ is closed under β. (2) $f_\beta(\mathcal{M}) \subseteq Cl_\beta(\mathcal{M})$.
(3) If $\mathcal{M} = Cl_\beta(\mathcal{M})$, then $f_\beta(\mathcal{M}) = \mathcal{M}$. (4) If $\mathcal{M} \neq \varnothing$, then $f_\beta(\mathcal{M}) \neq \varnothing$.

Definition 5. *Let $\diamond : \mathcal{L} \times \mathcal{L} \longrightarrow \mathcal{L}$ be an update operator and $\mathcal{L}' \subseteq \mathcal{L}$ a β-fragment of classical logic with $\beta \in \mathcal{B}$. For a β-application f_β, we denote with $\diamond^{f_\beta} : \mathcal{L}' \times \mathcal{L}' \longrightarrow \mathcal{L}'$ the operator for $\mathcal{L}'$ defined as $\mathrm{Mod}(\psi \diamond^{f_\beta} \mu) := f_\beta(\mathrm{Mod}(\psi \diamond \mu))$. The class $[\diamond, \mathcal{L}']$ contains all operators $\diamond^{f_\beta}$ where f_β is a β-mapping.*

Interestingly (and as in [5], since update operators as revision operators apply to a pair of formulas and return a formula) this class actually captures all refinements we had in mind.

Proposition 6. *Let $\diamond : \mathcal{L} \times \mathcal{L} \longrightarrow \mathcal{L}$ be an update operator and $\mathcal{L}' \subseteq \mathcal{L}$ a characterizable fragment of classical logic. Then, $[\diamond, \mathcal{L}']$ is the set of all $\diamond$-refinements for $\mathcal{L}'$.*

Hence, β-mappings will allow us to define a variety of refined update operators. A natural objective is now to study how these refined update operators behave with respect to satisfaction of KM's postulates, and how update differs from revision in this context. We will consider in particular two β-mappings, namely the closure Cl_β and Min_β defined as follows.

Definition 7. *Let $\beta \in \mathcal{B}$ and suppose that $\leqslant$ is a fixed linear order on the set $2^\mathcal{U}$ of interpretations. We define the function Min_β as $\mathrm{Min}_\beta(\mathcal{M}) = \mathcal{M}$ if $Cl_\beta(\mathcal{M}) = \mathcal{M}$, and $\mathrm{Min}_\beta(\mathcal{M}) = \min_\leqslant(\mathcal{M})$ otherwise.*

For $\mathcal{L}'$ a β-fragment and $\diamond$ an update operator, the corresponding operators $\diamond^{Cl_\beta}$ and $\diamond^{\mathrm{Min}_\beta}$ are thus respectively given as $\mathrm{Mod}(\psi \diamond^{Cl_\beta} \mu) = Cl_\beta(\mathrm{Mod}(\psi \diamond \mu))$ and $\mathrm{Mod}(\psi \diamond^{\mathrm{Min}_\beta} \mu) = \mathrm{Min}_\beta(\mathrm{Mod}(\psi \diamond \mu))$.

Example 8. Let $\psi, \mu \in \mathcal{L}_{Horn}$, such that $\mathrm{Mod}(\psi) = \{\{a,b,c\}, \{a,b,c,d,e\}\}$, and $\mathrm{Mod}(\mu) = \{\{b,c\}, \{c,d\}, \{a,b,d\}, \{c\}, \{d\}, \{b\}, \varnothing\}$. We have $\mathrm{Mod}(\psi \diamond_F \mu) = \{\{b,c\}, \{a,b,d\}\}$ and $\mathrm{Mod}(\psi \diamond_W \mu) = \{\{b,c\}, \{c,d\}, \{a,b,d\}\}$. We obtain $\mathrm{Mod}(\psi \diamond_F^{Cl_\wedge} \mu) = Cl_\wedge(\mathrm{Mod}(\psi \diamond_F \mu)) = \{\{b,c\}, \{a,b,d\}, \{b\}\}$ and $\mathrm{Mod}(\psi \diamond_W^{Cl_\wedge} \mu) = Cl_\wedge(\mathrm{Mod}(\psi \diamond_W \mu)) = \{\{b,c\}, \{c,d\}, \{a,b,d\}, \{b\}, \{c\}, \{d\}, \varnothing\}$.
　　Consider the following order over interpretations: $\{c,d\} < \{b,c\} < \{a,b,d\}$. We thus get $\mathrm{Mod}(\psi \diamond_F^{\mathrm{Min}_\wedge} \mu) = \mathrm{Min}_\wedge(\mathrm{Mod}(\psi \diamond_F \mu)) = \{\{b,c\}\}$ and $\mathrm{Mod}(\psi \diamond_W^{\mathrm{Min}_\wedge} \mu) = \mathrm{Min}_\wedge(\mathrm{Mod}(\psi \diamond_W \mu)) = \{\{c,d\}\}$.

4　Postulates

Proposition 9. *Let $\diamond$ be an update operator and $\mathcal{L}' \subseteq \mathcal{L}$ a characterizable fragment. For $i = 1, \ldots, 4$, if $\diamond$ satisfies postulate (Ui), then so does any refinement of this operator in $\mathcal{L}'$, $\blacklozenge \in [\diamond, \mathcal{L}']$.*

Proof. Suppose $\mathcal{L}'$ is a β-fragment. Thus we can assume that $\blacklozenge \in [\diamond, \mathcal{L}']$ is an operator of the form $\diamond^{f_\beta}$ where f_β is a suitable β-mapping. Since postulates (U1) and (U4) are exactly the same postulates as (R1) and (R4), and since satisfaction of (U3) follows from satisfaction of (R3), according to [5, Proposition 6] we only have to deal with (U2). By definition $\text{Mod}(\psi \blacklozenge \mu) = f_\beta(\text{Mod}(\psi \diamond \mu))$. Since $\diamond$ satisfies postulate (U2), if $\psi \models \mu$, then $\psi \diamond \mu \equiv \psi$, i.e. $\text{Mod}(\psi \diamond \mu) = \text{Mod}(\psi)$. Therefore, $f_\beta(\text{Mod}(\psi \diamond \mu)) = f_\beta(\text{Mod}(\psi))$. Since $\psi \in \mathcal{L}'$, $f_\beta(\text{Mod}(\psi)) = \text{Mod}(\psi)$. Thus, $\psi \blacklozenge \mu \equiv \psi$.

A natural question is whether there exist refined update operators that satisfy more postulates.

In the following, it is implicit that within $\mathcal{L}_{Horn}$ (resp. $\mathcal{L}_{Krom}$, $\mathcal{L}_{affine}$) a β-mapping is a $\wedge$-mapping (resp., maj_3-mapping, $\oplus_3$-mapping).

Proposition 10. *The refined update operators* $\diamond_F^{Cl_\beta}$, $\diamond_F^{\text{Min}_\beta}$, $\diamond_W^{Cl_\beta}$ *and* $\diamond_W^{\text{Min}_\beta}$ *violate postulate (U5) in any* $\mathcal{L}' \in \{\mathcal{L}_{Horn}, \mathcal{L}_{Krom}, \mathcal{L}_{affine}\}$.

Proof. We give the proof in detail for the refinement by Min_β, for $\diamond \in \{\diamond_F, \diamond_W\}$ and $\mathcal{L}' \in \{\mathcal{L}_{Horn}, \mathcal{L}_{Krom}\}$. Let ψ, μ and ϕ in $\mathcal{L}_{Horn}$ (resp. $\mathcal{L}_{Krom}$) such that $\text{Mod}(\psi) = \{\{a, b, c, d, e, f\}, \{b, c, d, e, f\}\}$, $\text{Mod}(\mu) = \{\varnothing, \{c\}, \{a, b\}, \{c, d\}, \{e, f\}, \{a, b, c\}\}$, $\text{Mod}(\phi) = \{\{a, b\}, \{c, d\}, \{e, f\}, \varnothing\}$. Observe that since these sets of models are closed under $\wedge$ (resp. under maj_3) such formulas exist. Consider the following order $\{a, b\} < \{c, d\} < \{e, f\} < \{a, b, c\}$. On the one hand we obtain $\text{Mod}(\psi \diamond \mu) = \{\{c, d\}, \{e, f\}, \{a, b, c\}\}$, and thus $\text{Mod}(\psi \diamond^{\text{Min}_\beta} \mu) = \{\{c, d\}\}$. Therefore, $\text{Mod}((\psi \diamond^{\text{Min}_\beta} \mu) \wedge \phi) = \{\{c, d\}\}$. On the other hand, $\text{Mod}(\psi \diamond (\mu \wedge \phi)) = \{\{a, b\}, \{c, d\}, \{e, f\}\}$, thus $\text{Mod}(\psi \diamond^{\text{Min}_\beta} (\mu \wedge \phi)) = \{\{a, b\}\}$. It is then clear that $(\psi \diamond^{\text{Min}_\beta} \mu) \wedge \phi \not\models \psi \diamond^{\text{Min}_\beta} (\mu \wedge \phi)$, thus proving that $\diamond_F^{\text{Min}_\beta}$ and $\diamond_W^{\text{Min}_\beta}$ violate postulate (U5) in $\mathcal{L}_{Horn}$ and $\mathcal{L}_{Krom}$.

Remark 11. Let us emphasize that this result shows a difference between revision and update. Indeed, let us recall that Forbus' operator can be considered as the update counterpart of Dalal's revision operator. The refinements of these two operators by the function Min_β show a different behavior: While in [5] it was proven that $\diamond_D^{\text{Min}_\beta}$ satisfies (R5), the above proposition shows that $\diamond_F^{\text{Min}_\beta}$ violates (U5).

For the postulate (U9) we obtain a rather general negative result, which is similar to the result obtained for (R6) in the context of revision (but which nevertheless requires new examples to be proven, since we need complete formulas).

Proposition 12. *Let* $\diamond \in \{\diamond_F, \diamond_W\}$ *and* $\mathcal{L}' \in \{\mathcal{L}_{Horn}, \mathcal{L}_{Krom}, \mathcal{L}_{affine}\}$. *Then any refined operator* $\blacklozenge \in [\diamond, \mathcal{L}']$ *violates postulate (U9) in* $\mathcal{L}'$.

The status of the postulate (U6) is less clear than the ones we have investigated so far. Indeed the two following propositions show that the satisfaction of (U6) depends on the β-mapping that is used to define the refinement.

Proposition 13. *Let* $\diamond$ *be an update operator and* $\mathcal{L}'$ *a* β*-fragment. If* $\diamond$ *satisfies (U6), then so does the refined operator* $\diamond^{Cl_\beta}$ *in* $\mathcal{L}'$.

Proof. Suppose that $(\psi \diamond^{Cl_\beta} \mu_1) \models \mu_2$ and $(\psi \diamond^{Cl_\beta} \mu_2) \models \mu_1$. Thus, $Cl_\beta(\text{Mod}(\psi \diamond \mu_1)) \subseteq \text{Mod}(\mu_2)$ and $Cl_\beta(\text{Mod}(\psi \diamond \mu_2)) \subseteq \text{Mod}(\mu_1)$. Moreover, $\text{Mod}(\psi \diamond \mu_1) \subseteq$

$Cl_\beta(\mathrm{Mod}(\psi \diamond \mu_1))$ and also $\mathrm{Mod}(\psi \diamond \mu_2) \subseteq Cl_\beta(\mathrm{Mod}(\psi \diamond \mu_2))$. Therefore, $\mathrm{Mod}(\psi \diamond \mu_1) \subseteq \mathrm{Mod}(\mu_2)$ and $\mathrm{Mod}(\psi \diamond \mu_2) \subseteq \mathrm{Mod}(\mu_1)$. Since $\diamond$ satisfies (U6), we get $\psi \diamond \mu_1 \equiv \psi \diamond \mu_2$. According to the equivalence property cited in Definition 3, we have finally $\psi \diamond^{Cl_\beta} \mu_1 \equiv \psi \diamond^{Cl_\beta} \mu_2$.

Proposition 14. *The refined operators $\diamond_F^{\mathrm{Min}_\beta}$ and $\diamond_W^{\mathrm{Min}_\beta}$ violate postulate (U6) in any $\mathcal{L}' \in \{\mathcal{L}_{Horn}, \mathcal{L}_{Krom}, \mathcal{L}_{affine}\}$.*

Proof. Let $\diamond \in \{\diamond_F, \diamond_W\}$. We give a full proof for the fragment $\mathcal{L}_{Horn}$. Let $\psi, \mu_1, \mu_2 \in \mathcal{L}_{Horn}$ with $\mathrm{Mod}(\psi) = \{\{b\}, \{a, b, c, d\}\}$, $\mathrm{Mod}(\mu_1) = \{\{a\}, \{a, b\}, \{a, c\}, \{a, b, c, e\}\}$ and $\mathrm{Mod}(\mu_2) = \{\{a, b\}, \{a, b, c, e\}\}$. Suppose that $\{a, b\} < \{a, c\} < \{a, b, c, e\}$. On the one hand, we have $\mathrm{Mod}(\psi \diamond \mu_1) = \{\{a, b\}, \{a, c\}, \{a, b, c, e\}\}$ which is not closed under $\wedge$. Thus, $\mathrm{Mod}(\psi \diamond^{\mathrm{Min}_\wedge} \mu_1) = \mathrm{Min}_\wedge(\{\{a, b\}, \{a, c\}, \{a, b, c, e\}\}) = \{\{a, b\}\} \subseteq \mathrm{Mod}(\mu_2)$. On the other hand, we have $\mathrm{Mod}(\psi \diamond \mu_2) = \{\{a, b\}, \{a, b, c, e\}\}$, a set of models closed under $\wedge$. Consequently, $\mathrm{Mod}(\psi \diamond^{\mathrm{Min}_\wedge} \mu_2) = \{\{a, b\}, \{a, b, c, e\}\} \subseteq \mathrm{Mod}(\mu_1)$. But, $\psi \diamond^{\mathrm{Min}_\wedge} \mu_1 \not\equiv \psi \diamond^{\mathrm{Min}_\wedge} \mu_2$, thus proving that $\diamond_F^{\mathrm{Min}_\beta}$ and $\diamond_W^{\mathrm{Min}_\beta}$ violate the postulate (U6) in $\mathcal{L}_{Horn}$.

Now observe that (U7) and (U8) are not applicable in our study since they use disjunction of formulas while our fragments are not closed under disjunction (given μ_1 and μ_2 in $\mathcal{L}'$, $\mu_1 \vee \mu_2$ does not necessarily belong to $\mathcal{L}'$). However, it would be interesting to study whether these postulates hold in the special case where $\mu_1 \vee \mu_2$ (respectively $\psi_1 \vee \psi_2$) is equivalent to a formula in the fragment.

Actually, the most uncontroversial postulate (U8) in the context of full propositional logic is not appropriate to the study of update operators that provide results within a characterizable fragment. Indeed, the union of closed sets of models obtained after having considered independently each model of the formula representing the belief set, has no reason to be a closed set of models. However, note that by construction our refined operators first compute the result obtained through an original operator. Therefore, starting from an update operator that satisfies (U8) the models of the formula will equally contribute to the update. So at least the spirit is preserved, even if of course one has to perform a post-processing in order to remain in the fragment. Moreover for the refinement by the closure Cl_β it is easy to prove that for all formulas ψ and μ in $\mathcal{L}'$, $T_{\mathcal{L}'}(\psi \diamond^{Cl_\beta} \mu) = T_{\mathcal{L}'}(\psi \diamond \mu)$. Therefore if $\diamond$ can be considered as an update operator, then so can $\diamond^{Cl_\beta}$ in $\mathcal{L}'$.

5   Conclusion

In this paper we investigated belief update within the framework of propositional fragments, a belief change operation which has been neglected so far. We proposed a general constructive approach to define new update operators derived from existing ones such that the result of the update remains in the fragment under consideration. Then, we studied the logical properties of theses refined update operators. We showed that any refined update operator preserves the basic KM's update postulates (U1) – (U4) for any fragment. We then focused on Forbus' and Winslett's update operators, within Horn, Krom and affine fragments. While in this paper we presented only two β-mappings, Cl_β and Min_β, we also investigated less drastic ones. We showed that all the proposed refinements violate the postulate (U5). This result is very interesting since it highlights a difference between revision and update. An interesting issue is whether this postulate is indeed violated by any refined update operator. Regarding the postulate (U6) the situation is less clear since the refinement by the closure preserves this postulate, while the other studied refinements do not. It would be interesting to characterize the refined operators that preserve it. We also showed that none of the refinements of Forbus' and Winslett's operators satisfies the postulate (U9).

A natural extension of this work is to study update when only the formula representing the belief set is in the fragment, but not new information, that is operators from $\mathcal{L}' \times \mathcal{L}$ to $\mathcal{L}'$. Our approach can handle this extension. It allows us to define refined update operators, which - contrary to revision where the second postulate (R2) is problematic - satisfy the first four basic postulates (it is sufficient to use β-mappings f_β that are contracting, i.e. such that for all $\mathcal{M}$, $f_\beta(\mathcal{M}) \subseteq \mathcal{M}$, e.g. Min_β). Moreover, in this context the postulate (U7) makes sense and it would be worth investigating it. Another interesting issue is how to reformulate the postulate (U8) so that it is adapted to fragments (as it was done for postulates for belief revision [9] and belief merging [17] in the Horn fragment). Besides, future work will be dedicated to the study of the computational complexity of the refined update operators. Finally, we plan to continue our study in exploring systematically other belief change operations, including belief contraction.

References

1. Alchourrón, C.E., Gärdenfors, P., Makinson, D.: On the logic of theory change: partial meet contraction and revision functions. J. Symb. Log. **50**, 510–530 (1985)
2. Booth, R., Meyer, T.A., Varzinczak, I.J., Wassermann, R.: On the link between partial meet, kernel, and infra contraction and its application to Horn logic. J. Artif. Intell. Res. (JAIR) **42**, 31–53 (2011)
3. Boutilier, C.: A unified model of qualitative belief change: a dynamical systems perspective. Artif. Intell. **98**(1–2), 281–316 (1998)
4. Cadoli, M., Scarcello, F.: Semantical and computational aspects of Horn approximations. Artif. Intell. **119**(1–2), 1–17 (2000)
5. Creignou, N., Papini, O., Pichler, R., Woltran, S.: Belief revision within fragments of propositional logic. J. Comput. Syst. Sci. **80**(2), 427–449 (2014)
6. Dalal, M.: Investigations into theory of knowledge base revision. In: Proceedings of AAAI, St. Paul, Minnesota, pp 449–479 (1988)
7. del Val, A., Shoham, Y.: A unified view of belief revision and update. J. Log. Comput. **4**(5), 797–810 (1994)
8. Delgrande, J.P., Jin, Y., Pelletier, F.J.: Compositional belief update. CoRR, abs/1401.3431 (2014)
9. Delgrande, J.P., Peppas, P.: Belief revision in Horn theories. Artif. Intell. **218**, 1–22 (2015)

10. Delgrande, J.P., Wassermann, R.: Horn clause contraction functions. J. Artif. Intell. Res. (JAIR) **48**, 475–511 (2013)
11. Doherty, P., Lukaszewicz, W., Madalinska-Bugaj, E.: The pma and relativizing minimal change for action update. Fundam. Inform. **44**(1–2), 95–131 (2000)
12. Dubois, D., Prade, H.: Belief revision and updates in numerical formalisms: an overview, with new results for the possibilistic framework. In: Proceedings of IJCAI, pp. 620–625 (1993)
13. Eiter, T., Gottlob, G.: On the complexity of propositional knowledge base revision, updates, and counterfactuals. Artif. Intell. **57**(2–3), 227–270 (1992)
14. Fagin, R., Ullman, J.D., Vardi, M.Y.: On the semantics of updates in databases. In: The second ACM SIGACT SIGMOD, pp. 352–365 (1983)
15. Forbus, K.D.: Introducing actions into qualitative simulation. In: Proceedings of IJCAI, pp. 1273–1278 (1989)
16. Friedman, N., Halpern, J.Y.: Modeling belief in dynamic systems, part II: revision and update. J. Artif. Intell. Res. (JAIR) **10**, 117–167 (1999)
17. Haret, A.: Merging in the Horn fragment. Master's thesis, TU Wien (2014)
18. Herzig, A., Rifi, O.: Propositional belief base update and minimal change. Artif. Intell. **115**(1), 107–138 (1999)
19. Horn, A.: On sentences which are true of direct unions of algebras. J. Symb. Log. **16**, 14–21 (1951)
20. Katsuno, H., Mendelzon, A.O.: Propositional knowledge base revision and minimal change. Artif. Intell. **52**(3), 263–294 (1991)
21. Katsuno, H., Mendelzon, A.O.: On the difference between updating a knowledge base and revising it. In: Gärdenfors, P. (ed.) Belief Revision, pp. 183–203. Cambridge University Press, Cambridge (1992)
22. Keller, A.M., Winslett, M.: On the use of an extended relational model to handle changing incomplete information. IEEE Trans. Softw. Eng. **11**(7), 620–633 (1985)
23. Lang, J.: Belief update revisited. In: Proceedings of IJCAI, pp. 2517–2522 (2007)
24. Liberatore, P., Schaerf, M.: Belief revision and update: complexity of model checking. J. Comput. Syst. Sci. **62**(1), 43–72 (2001)
25. Van De Putte, F.: Prime implicates and relevant belief revision. J. Log. Comput. **23**(1), 109–119 (2013)
26. Satoh, K.: Nonmonotonic reasoning by minimal belief revision. In: Proceedings of FGCS, Tokyo, pp. 455–462 (1988)
27. Schaefer, T.J.: The complexity of satisfiability problems. In: Proceedings of STOC, pp. 216–226 (1978)
28. Winslett, M.: Reasoning about action using a possible models approach. In: Proceedings of AAAI, pp. 89–93 (1988)
29. Zhang, Y., Foo, N.Y.: Updates with disjunctive information: from syntactical and semantical perspectives. Comput. Intell. **16**(1), 29–52 (2000)
30. Zhuang, Z.Q., Pagnucco, M.: Entrenchment-based Horn contraction. J. Artif. Intell. Res. (JAIR) **51**, 227–254 (2014)
31. Zhuang, Z.Q., Pagnucco, M., Zhang, Y.: Definability of Horn revision from Horn contraction. In: Proceedings of IJCAI (2013)

Private Expansion and Revision in Multi-agent Settings

Thomas Caridroit[(✉)], Sébastien Konieczny, Tiago de Lima,
and Pierre Marquis

CRIL, CNRS and Université d' Artois, Lens, France
{caridroit,konieczny,delima,marquis}@cril.fr

Abstract. AGM belief change aims at modeling the evolution of an agent's beliefs about its environment. In many applications though, a set of agents sharing the same environment must be considered. For such scenarios, beliefs about other agents' beliefs must be taken into account. In this work, we study private expansion and revision operators in such a multi-agent setting. More precisely, we investigate the changes induced by a new piece of information made available to one agent in the set. We point out an adaptation of AGM expansion and revision postulates to this setting, and present expansion and revision operators.

1 Introduction

Belief change aims at finding adequate ways to make the beliefs of an agent evolve when she faces new evidence. The main theoretical framework for belief change is AGM (Alchourrón-Gärdenfors-Makinson) theory and its developments [1,13,14]. In most works on belief revision, the belief set of the agent consists of beliefs about the environment (the world), and is represented by a set of formulas in classical logic. However, in many applications, an agent is not alone in her environment, but shares it with other agents, who also have beliefs. Beliefs about the beliefs of other agents is an important piece of information, in order to make the best decisions and to perform the best actions. Using beliefs on beliefs of other agents is for instance crucial in game theory [5,6,18,22]. The most common logical tools for representing beliefs on beliefs of other agents are epistemic logics. So belief change in epistemic logics is an important issue. There exist some works on the connections between epistemic logics and belief change theory. However most of them study how to encode belief change operators within models with accessibility relations representing plausibility levels, which guide the revision process [8,10,21,23]. Here, we are interested in another connection between epistemic logics and belief change theory that is closer to the AGM approach. Our objective is to design operators that change the beliefs of the agents in standard $KD45_n$ models. This task is more complicated than in the standard AGM framework, because, in a multi-agent context, the new pieces of evidence can take different forms. For instance, a new piece of evidence can be either observed/transmitted/available to every agent or only to

© Springer International Publishing Switzerland 2015
S. Destercke and T. Denoeux (Eds.): ECSQARU 2015, LNAI 9161, pp. 175–185, 2015.
DOI: 10.1007/978-3-319-20807-7_16

some of them. This kind of issue has already been studied in epistemic logics with announcements, where public and private announcements lead to distinct belief changes [4,24]. We use the terms "public change" and "private change" in the following. A public change is a change that is produced by a piece of evidence available to every agent. In this case, we are in the standard AGM case, and we can use the standard AGM machinery in order to define adequate belief change operators. A private change is a change that is produced by a piece of evidence available to one agent only. This means that the beliefs of this agent must change, whereas the beliefs of the other ones remain unchanged. In this case, we cannot directly apply AGM operators. Specific operators are required and this is what we present in this work. More precisely the aim of this paper is to define and study a multi-agent belief change setting, where the beliefs of the agents are encoded by a $KD45_n$ model. We consider private change, so a given agent receives some new piece of evidence, and one wants to define the new $KD45_n$ model that represents the new epistemic situation. We consider only objective pieces of evidence, i.e., evidences about the environment (world). The problem of considering change by subjective pieces of evidence, i.e., evidences about the beliefs of other agents, is more difficult and is left for future work. We study both expansion and revision. For each case, we provide a translation of AGM postulates for the multi-agent setting, and some specific operators. The rest of the paper is as follows. First, we give some formal preliminaries about $KD45_n$ models and AGM belief change theory. Then, we translate the AGM postulates for expansion to the multi-agent setting. In the next sections, we present a particular expansion operator, we translate the AGM postulates for revision, and we point out a family of revision operators. Finally we discuss some related works before concluding. For space reasons we cannot give the proofs, they can be found in the corresponding technical report [11].

2   Preliminaries

We consider a propositional language L_0 built up from a finite set of propositional variables P and the usual connectives. $\bot$ and $\top$ represent respectively contradiction and tautology. Let K be a belief set (i.e., a deductively closed set of formulas) and let φ be a formula. $K + \varphi$ denotes the expansion of K by φ, which is the new belief set obtained by adding φ to K. And $K * \varphi$ denotes the revision of K by φ. Alchourrón, Gärdenfors and Makinson [1,14] pointed out some postulates for the expansion and revision of belief sets. These postulates logically encode the constraints expected on the behaviour of expansion/revision operators. Several representation theorems in terms of maximal consistent sets [1], plausibility relations on formulas [14], or plausibility relations on worlds exist [17], allowing to define operators with the expected properties. We are interested here in a framework with several agents, each of them having her own beliefs about the state of the world and about the beliefs of the other agents.. This requires the use of epistemic logic. Formally, let $A = \{1, \dots, n\}$ be a finite set of agents. We consider the language L containing the propositional language L_0 plus one belief operator B_i for each agent $i \in A$. In addition, we sometimes use B_i^k to abbreviate a sequence of k operators B_i (i.e., $B_i^0 \varphi$ abbreviates φ and $B_i^{k+1}\varphi$ abbreviates $B_i B_i^k \varphi$, for $k \geq 0$.) A formula of the form $B_i\varphi$ is read 'agent i believes that φ is true'. Formulas in L_0 are also called objective formulas, while subjective formulas are formulas which are not objective. In order to give the right interpretation to our formulas, especially, to the operators B_i, we use the standard system $KD45_n$ for n-agent doxastic logic [12]. Such a system consists of the set of formulas in L that can be derived using some axioms and inference rules. The same set of validities can be captured using a semantic approach. The most common one is based on Kripke models.

Definition 1 (Kripke Model). *A Kripke model is a tuple $\langle W, R, V \rangle$ where $W \neq \emptyset$ is a set of possible worlds, $R = \{R_i \mid i \in A\}$, with R_i a binary accessibility relation for agent i that is serial, transitive and Euclidean, and $V : W \to 2^P$ is a valuation function. For each world $w \in W$, $V(w)$ is the set of propositional variables which are true at w. A pointed Kripke model is a pair (M, w), where $M = \langle W, R, V \rangle$ is a Kripke model and $w \in W$ is the real world.*

$R_i(w)$ denotes the set of possible worlds that are accessible from w for agent i, that is, $R_i(w) = \{w' \mid (w, w') \in R_i\}$. We note $(M, w) \models \varphi$ the fact that the formula φ is satisfied at the world w in the model M. This notion is defined using the usual satisfaction relation such that $(M, w) \models B_i\varphi$ iff $\forall w' \in W$ if $(w, w') \in R_i$ then $(M, w') \models \varphi$. We use $\|\varphi\|_M$ to denote the set of possible worlds of M that satisfy φ, that is, $\|\varphi\|_M = \{w : w \in W \text{ and } (M, w) \models \varphi\}$. Two pointed Kripke models may satisfy the same set of formulas, and are then considered equivalent. It is known that if two pointed Kripke models are bisimilar[1] (noted $(M, w) \underline{\leftrightarrow} (M', w')$), then they are equivalent. A pointed $KD45_n$ model (M, w) represents a set of n belief sets $K_i^{(M,w)}$, one for each agent $i \in A$, where $K_i^{(M,w)} = \{\varphi \mid (M, w) \models B_i\varphi\}$. We also define the objective belief set of agent i (i.e., what i believes about the state of the world). This is the set $O_i^{(M,w)} = K_i^{(M,w)} \cap L_0$. In the following, for simplicity reasons, we make the assumption that the new piece of evidence is a consistent formula. Making a change by an inconsistent formula is allowed by AGM postulates, but is not of much interest in practical applications. Furthermore, the axiom **D** forbids inconsistent beliefs.

3   Private Expansion

Our goal in this section is to provide an extension of the AGM postulates to a multi-agent setting. We focus on private expansion operators: only one agent increases her beliefs, on a private announcement, the beliefs of other agents as well as the higher order beliefs remain unchanged. Let us denote the result of the private expansion of the model (M, w) by the objective formula φ for agent a as the model $(M, w) +_a \varphi = (M', w') = (\langle W', R', V' \rangle, w')$. The AGM postulates for expansion can be rewritten as follows:

---

[1] For the definition, see [9].

(E_n0) $V'(w') = V(w)$
(E_n1) If $(M, w) \not\models B_a \neg \varphi$ then $(M, w) +_a \varphi \in KD45_n$
(E_n2) $(M, w) +_a \varphi \models B_a \varphi$
(E_n3) $(M, w) \models B_i \psi$ iff $(M, w) +_a \varphi \models B_i \psi$, for $i \neq a$
(E_n4) If $(M, w) \not\models B_a \neg \varphi$ then $(M, w) \models B_a^k B_i \psi$ iff $(M, w) +_a \varphi \models B_a^k B_i \psi$, for
    $i \neq a$ and $k \geq 1$
(E_n5) If $(M, w) \models B_a \psi$ then $(M, w) +_a \varphi \models B_a \psi$
(E_n6) If $(M, w) \models B_a \varphi$ then $(M, w) +_a \varphi \rightleftharpoons (M, w)$
(E_n7) If $(M_1, w_1) \models B_i \psi$ implies $(M_2, w_2) \models B_i \psi$ then
    $(M_1, w_1) +_a \varphi \models B_i \chi$ implies $(M_2, w_2) +_a \varphi \models B_i \chi$
(E_n8) For all (M', w'), if (M', w') satisfies (E_n1)–(E_n7) then $(M, w) +_a \varphi \models B_a \psi$
    implies $(M', w') \models B_a \psi$

Most of these postulates are a translation of AGM ones for $KD45_n$ models. The other ones mostly translate the fact that the only things that change are the beliefs of agent a about the state of the world. (E_n0) says that the true world does not change: as usual in belief revision the world does not change,[2] it is only the beliefs of the agents that evolve. (E_n1) says that, in the event that new piece of information does not contradict the beliefs of the agent, after the private expansion, the model remains $KD45_n$. Indeed, when the expansion is done by a formula that contradicts the beliefs of the agent, the result infringes the axiom **D** for the agent. The model is therefore no longer $KD45_n$. In fact, it may happen that the model is not $KD45_n$ if the agent a makes an expansion by a formula that contradicts her current beliefs. (E_n2) is the success postulate. It states that after the private expansion by φ, the agent a believes φ. Postulate (E_n3) states that the beliefs of all agents except a do not change. Postulate (E_n4) states that the beliefs of the agent a about other agents do not change. These two postulates can be seen as an adaptation of Parikh relevant revision postulates in this multi-agent setting [19]. Postulates (E_n5) and (E_n6) ensure that if φ is already believed by agent a then the private expansion does not change anything, so the resulting model is bisimilar to the initial one. Postulate (E_n7) is the translation of the monotonicity property. It states that, if a model allows more inferences than another one, then the expansion of the first one allows more inferences than the expansion of the second one. Postulate (E_n8) is the minimality postulate. It states that the result of the expansion of the model by φ is a minimal belief change. These postulates imply that:

Proposition 1. *There is a unique (up to modal equivalence) private expansion operator satisfying (E_n0)–(E_n8).*

The following proposition shows that our private expansion operator is closely related to the AGM expansion operator.

Proposition 2. *Let $+_a$ be the private expansion operator for a satisfying postulates (E_n0)–(E_n8). The $+$ operator defined by $O_a^{(M,w)} + \varphi = O_a^{(M,w)+_a\varphi}$ is the AGM expansion operator (i.e., it satisfies $(K+1)$–$(K+6)$ [1]).*

---

[2] When the world evolves, one has to use update [15,16].

4   A Private Expansion Operator

Let us now give a constructive definition of the private expansion operator characterized in the previous section. In the remainder of this paper, we use as a notation for the newly created worlds (due to expansion or revision) v_w^e. This notation means that the world v_w^e is a "copy" of the world w (this copy is essential to avoid losing the higher-order beliefs of the agent who performs the expansion or the revision of her beliefs) and having the valuation e.

Definition 2. Expansion of (M, w_0) **by** φ **for agent** a. Let $(M, w_0) = (\langle W, R, V \rangle, w_0)$ be a $KD45_n$ pointed model, and φ be a consistent objective formula (i.e., $\varphi \in L_0$). We define the private expansion of (M, w_0) by φ for agent a as $(M, w_0) +_a \varphi = (\langle W', R', V' \rangle, w_0')$, such that:

- $E = \{V(w) \mid w \in R_a(w_0) \cap \|\varphi\|_M\}$
- $W' = W \cup W^\varphi \cup \{w_0'\}$ where
    - $W^\varphi = \bigcup\limits_{w \in R_a(w_0)} W_w^\varphi$ and $\quad W_w^\varphi = \bigcup\limits_{e \in E} \{v_w^e\}$
- $R_a' = R_a \cup R_a^\varphi \cup R_a^0$ where
    - $R_a^\varphi = \{(w_1^\varphi, w_2^\varphi) \mid w_1^\varphi, w_2^\varphi \in W^\varphi\}$
    - $R_a^0 = \{(w_0', w^\varphi) \mid w^\varphi \in W^\varphi\}$
- $R_i' = R_i \cup R_i^{\overrightarrow{\varphi}} \cup R_i^0$, for $i \neq a$, where
    - $R_i^{\overrightarrow{\varphi}} = \{(v_w^e, w') \mid wR_iw' \text{ and } v_w^e \in W^\varphi\}$, for $i \neq a$
    - $R_i^0 = \{(w_0', w) \mid (w_0, w) \in R_i\}$, for $i \neq a$
- $V'(w) = V(w)$, for $w \in W$
- $V'(v_w^e) = e$, for $v_w^e \in W^\varphi$
- $V'(w_0') = V(w_0)$

When the agent a expands her beliefs, the model must change in order to represent these new beliefs, but the beliefs of other agents should remain unchanged. The new set of possible worlds W' contains all possible worlds of the initial model plus a new real world w_0' and a set of worlds W^φ representing the new beliefs of a. The set W^φ contains a copy of each world in $R_a(w_0)$ which does not contradict φ. The new accessibility relation R_a' contains the initial relation R_a and the set R_a^0. The set R_a^0 consists of pairs (w_0', w^φ) where $w^\varphi \in W^\varphi$, thus modifying the beliefs of the agent performing the expansion. The set R_a^φ consists of the pairs $(w_1^\varphi, w_2^\varphi) \in W^\varphi$. The worlds in W^φ thus form a clique, because they are equally plausible for the agent performing the expansion. Each accessibility relation R_i', for $i \neq a$, contains the initial relation R_i and the sets R_i^0 and $R_i^{\overrightarrow{\varphi}}$. The set R_i^0 consists of all pairs (w_0', w) such that $(w_0, w) \in R_i$, thus preserving the beliefs of agents not performing expansion and higher-order beliefs of all agents. The set $R_i^{\overrightarrow{\varphi}}$ consists of pairs (v_w^e, w'), where $v_w^e \in W^\varphi$ such that $(w, w') \in R_i$, thus keeping higher-order beliefs of the agent performing the expansion. We can now show that:

Proposition 3. The operator $+$ satisfies (E_n0)–(E_n8).

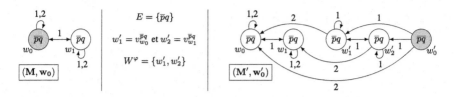

Fig. 1. $(M, w_0) +_1 q$

As a direct consequence of Proposition 1, we know that this operator is the unique private expansion operator. Let us now illustrate the behaviour of this private expansion operator on a simple example.

Example 1. Consider the KD45$_n$ model (M, w_0) of Fig. 1. In this situation, agent 1 believes $\neg p$ and she believes that agent 2 also believes $\neg p$. Agent 2 believes $\neg p \wedge \neg q$, and she believes that agent 1 believes $\neg p$. After the expansion by q, agent 1 must believe $\neg p \wedge q$. The obtained model (M', w_0') is reported as well on Fig. 1. The world having the valuation $\neg p \wedge q$ has to be duplicated in order to keep the higher-order beliefs of agent 1. Contrastingly, the beliefs of agent 2 remain unchanged, so in particular she still believes that agent 1 believes $\neg p$.

5   Private Revision

Let us turn now to the definition of private revision operators. These operators behave like expansion when there is no inconsistency between the beliefs of the agent and the new piece of evidence, but, unlike expansion, do not trivialize when this is not the case.

Let us denote the result of the private revision of the model (M, w) by the objective formula φ for agent a to be the model $(M, w) \star_a \varphi = (M', w') = (\langle W', R', V' \rangle, w')$. The AGM postulates for revision can be rewritten as follows:

$(R_n 0)$ $V'(w') = V(w)$
$(R_n 1)$ $(M, w) \star_a \varphi \in \text{KD45}_n$
$(R_n 2)$ $(M, w) \star_a \varphi \models B_a \varphi$
$(R_n 3)$ $(M, w) \models B_i \psi$ iff $(M, w) \star_a \varphi \models B_i \psi$, for $i \neq a$
$(R_n 4)$ $(M, w) \models B_a^k B_i \psi$ iff $(M, w) \star_a \varphi \models B_a^k B_i \psi$, for $i \neq a$
$(R_n 5)$ If $(M, w) \star_a \varphi \models B_i \psi$ then $(M, w) +_a \varphi \models B_i \psi$
$(R_n 6)$ If $(M, w) \not\models B_a \neg \varphi$, then $(M, w) +_a \varphi \leftrightharpoons (M, w) \star_a \varphi$
$(R_n 7)$ If $(M^1, w^1) \leftrightharpoons (M^2, w^2)$ and $\models \varphi \equiv \psi$, then $(M^1, w^1) \star_a \varphi \leftrightharpoons (M^2, w^2) \star_a \psi$
$(R_n 8)$ If $(M, w) \star_a (\varphi \wedge \psi) \models B_i \chi$ then $((M, w) \star_a \varphi) +_a \psi \models B_i \chi$
$(R_n 9)$ If $(M, w) \star_a \varphi \not\models B_a \neg \psi$, then $((M, w) \star_a \varphi) +_a \psi \models B_i \chi$ implies $(M, w) \star_a (\varphi \wedge \psi) \models B_i \chi$.

$(R_n 1)$ ensures that the model obtained after a revision is still a KD45$_n$ model. $(R_n 2)$ is the success postulate, it states that φ is believed by a after the revision. $(R_n 3)$ states that the beliefs of all agents except a do not change. $(R_n 4)$ states that the beliefs of the agent a about other agents do not change. These two postulates can be seen as an adaptation of Parikh relevant revision postulates in this multi-agent setting [19]. (R_n5) and (R_n6) state that when the new piece of evidence is consistent with the beliefs of the agent, revision is just expansion. (R_n7) is an irrelevance of syntax postulate, stating that if two formulas are logically equivalent, then they lead to the same revision results. (R_n8) and (R_n9) state when the revision by a conjunction can be obtained by a revision followed by an expansion. Let us now show that the revision operators satisfying those postulates are conservative extensions of the usual AGM belief revision operators:

Proposition 4. *Let $\star_i$ be an revision operator satisfying postulates (R_n0)–(R_n9). The $\star$ operator defined as $O_i^{(M,w)} \star \varphi = O_i^{(M,w)\star_i\varphi}$ is an AGM revision operator (i.e., it satisfies $(K*1)$–$(K*8)$ [1]).*

6   A Family of Private Revision Operators

Let us now define a family of private revision operators. These operators are defined similarly to the expansion operator of the previous section, but in the cases when the new piece of evidence is inconsistent with the current beliefs of the agent they use a classical AGM belief revision operator $\circ$ in order to compute the new beliefs of the agent.

Definition 3. *Revision of (M, w_0) by φ for agent a. Let $(M, w_0) = (\langle W, R, V \rangle, w_0)$ be a $KD45_n$ model, let φ be a consistent objective formula (i.e., $\varphi \in L_0$), and let $\circ$ be an AGM revision operator. We define the private revision of (M, w_0) by φ for agent a (with revision operator $\circ$) as $(M, w_0) \star_a^\circ \varphi = (\langle W', R', V' \rangle, w_0')$, such that:*

- *if $R_a(w_0) \cap \|\varphi\|_M \neq \emptyset$*
  - *then $E = \{V(w) \mid w \in R_a(w_0) \cap \|\varphi\|_M\}$*
  - *else $E = \{e \mid e \subseteq P \text{ and } e \models O_a^{(M,w_0)} \circ \varphi\}$*
- *$W' = W \cup W^\varphi \cup \{w_0'\}$ where*
  - *$W^\varphi = \displaystyle\bigcup_{w \in R_a(w_0)} W_w^\varphi \qquad$ and $\qquad W_w^\varphi = \displaystyle\bigcup_{e \in E} \{v_w^e\}$*
- *$R_a' = R_a \cup R_a^\varphi \cup R_a^0$ where*
  - *$R_a^\varphi = \{(w_1^\varphi, w_2^\varphi) \mid w_1^\varphi, w_2^\varphi \in W^\varphi\}$*
  - *$R_a^0 = \{(w_0', w^\varphi) \mid w^\varphi \in W^\varphi\}$*
- *$R_i' = R_i \cup R_i^{\overrightarrow{\varphi}} \cup R_i^0$ for $i \neq a$, where*
  - *$R_i^{\overrightarrow{\varphi}} = \{(v_w^e, w') \mid wR_iw', v_w^e \in W^\varphi\}$ for $i \neq a$*
  - *$R_i^0 = \{(w_0', w) \mid (w_0, w) \in R_i\}$ for $i \neq a$*
- *$V'(w) = V(w)$ for $w \in W$*
- *$V'(v_w^e) = e$ for $v_w^e \in W^\varphi$*
- *$V'(w_0') = V(w_0)$*

The construction of the revised model is similar to the construction of the expanded model discussed earlier. Only the new set of worlds W^φ is different: if the new information φ is considered possible by agent a, she performs an expansion, otherwise, each of the worlds of the new set W^φ has as valuation a (propositional) model of the new information φ.

Let us now show that these operators exhibit the expected logical properties:

Proposition 5. *The operators $\star_a^\circ$ satisfy $(R_n 0)$–$(R_n 9)$.*

Let us now illustrate the behaviour of these private revision operators on a simple example.

Example 2. We consider the model (M, w_0) of Fig. 2, where agent 1 believes $\neg x \wedge \neg y$ and believes that agent 2 believes $x \wedge y$. Agent 2 believes $x \wedge y$ and believes that agent 1 believes $x \leftrightarrow y$. After the revision by $x \wedge y$, agent 1 must believe $x \wedge y$. Whereas the beliefs of agent 2 remain unchanged. The obtained model (M', w_0') is reported as well in Fig. 2. In this example, agent 1 uses Dalal's AGM revision operator $\circ_D$ [17]. We can observe that the revised model obtained using Definition 3 may not be minimal. Nevertheless, a minimal model can be obtained via a bisimulation contraction. Here, this leads to the model (M'', w_0').

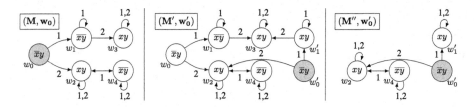

Fig. 2. $(M'', w_0') \cong (M, w_0) \star_1^{\circ_D} (x \wedge y)$

Our approach to private revision can be encoded in a formalism called dynamic epistemic logic [7]. To provide such an encoding, we need event models with assignments, as proposed in [25]. The idea is, for a given formula φ, to create a specific event model such that its execution simulates the revision by φ. An event model is a structure $N = \langle S, T, \text{pre}, \text{pos} \rangle$, where S is a non-empty set of possible events; $T = \{T_i : i \in A\}$, where T_i is a binary accessibility relation for agent i; pre : $S \to L$ is a function that returns, for each possible event $s \in S$, a formula in L representing its pre-condition; and pos : $S \to (P \to \{\top, \bot\})$ is a function that returns, for each possible event $s \in S$, its post-condition. The post-condition is an assignment of propositional variables to $\top$ or $\bot$. Thus, pos is used to reset the valuations after the execution of the events. A pointed event model is a pair (N, s), where $s \in S$ is the actual event. The product of (M, w) by (N, s) is a new pointed model $(M^N, w.s)$ where $M^N = \langle W^N, R^N, V^N \rangle$, $W^N = \{w.s \mid M, w \models \text{pre}(s)\}$, $R^N = \{(w.s, w'.s') : (w, w') \in R_a \text{ and } (s, s') \in T_a\}$ and $V^N(w) = \{p \mid \text{pos}(w)(p) = \top\}$.

In the sequel, we show that the revision of Definition 3 is equivalent to a specific model product. More precisely, $(M, w_0) \star_a^\circ \varphi$ and $(M^{N^{\star_a^\circ}}, w.s_0)$ are bisimilar, where:

- $S = \{s_0, s_\top\} \cup \{s_w^e \mid v_w^e \in W^\varphi\}$
- $T_a = \{(s_0, s_w^e) \mid v_w^e \in W^\varphi\} \cup \{(s_{w_1}^{e_1}, s_{w_2}^{e_2}) \mid v_{w_1}^{e_1}, v_{w_2}^{e_2} \in W^\varphi\} \cup \{(s_\top, s_\top)\}$
- $T_i = \{(s_0, s_\top), (s_\top, s_\top)\} \cup \{(s_w^e, s_\top) \mid v_w^e \in W^\varphi\}$, for $i \neq a$
- $\mathrm{pre}(s_0) = \bigwedge\limits_{p \in V(w_0)} p \wedge \bigwedge\limits_{p \in P \setminus V(w_0)} \neg p$
- $\mathrm{pre}(s_w^e) = \bigwedge\limits_{p \in V(w)} p \wedge \bigwedge\limits_{p \in P \setminus V(w)} \neg p$
- $\mathrm{pre}(s_\top) = \top$
- $\mathrm{pos}(s_w^e)(p) = \begin{cases} \top, & \text{if } e \models p \\ \bot, & \text{if } e \not\models p \end{cases}$
- $\mathrm{pos}(s_0) = \mathrm{pos}(s_\top) = \emptyset$

The event model here is somewhat similar to the one we could make for expansion. A main difference is that the clique of possible events s_w^e is replaced by a single possible event s_φ with $\mathrm{pre}(s_\varphi) = \varphi$ and $\mathrm{pos}(s_\varphi) = \emptyset$.

Proposition 6. $((M, w_0) \star_a^\circ \varphi) \rightleftharpoons (M^{N^{\star_a^\circ}}, w_0.s_0)$.

7 Related Work

As explained in the introduction, there are some works on the connections between epistemic logics and belief change theory, but most of them study how to encode belief change operators within an epistemic model [8,10,21,23]. Basically the problem is to try to perform belief revision within the epistemic model. Contrastingly, we study in this work how to perform belief revision (and expansion) on a $KD45_n$ model, representing the beliefs of a group of agents. In the same vein, in [20] the authors study what they call revision of $KD45_n$ models due to communication between agents: some agents (publicly) announce (part of) their beliefs. Their model is closer to expansion than to true revision, and concerns only subjective beliefs. In [15] the authors study action progression in multi-agent belief structures. Their work is mainly about the effects of actions using update, but they also briefly mention the problem of revision by objective formulas. Their construction is related to the one we point out, but they do not study the properties of the operators they considered. Finally the closest work to our own one is the study of private expansion and revision made by Aucher [2–4]. The difference is that Aucher considers an internal model of the problem, i.e., a model of the situation viewed from each agent, so he does not use a $KD45_n$ model for modeling the system, but one internal model by agent. He uses a notion of multi-agent possible worlds in order to compute the result of the revision, so the result of the revision is a set of such multi-agent worlds, whereas in this work we work with $KD45_n$ models, and we obtain a unique $KD45_n$ model as result of a revision. It is easy to find a translation between internal models and $KD45_n$ models, so one can look at the technical details between the expansion and revision operators we present in this work and the one proposed (on internal models) by Aucher [2–4]. Concerning expansion, it turns out that the two operations are equivalent (that is not surprising since we proved that there is only one rational expansion operator). First, note that it is possible to obtain an internal model I_M for agent $a \in N$ from any KD45$_n$ model (M, w_0). Indeed, it suffices to consider the set formed of models (M^k, w^k) generated from each w^k such that $w^k \in R_a(w_0)$. Similarly, it is possible to obtain an internal event model I_N for agent $a \in A$ from the event model (N, s_0). Now, it is easy to see that the internal model for a obtained from the product of (M, w_0) by (N, s_0) is the same as the product of I_M by I_N. Concerning revision the situation is different. Aucher allows revision by subjective formulas and compute distances between the corresponding (epistemic) models. We are interested here only by revision with objective formulas. In this particular case Aucher's revision does not allow the agent concerned by the private revision to choose, among the models of the objective formulas, the ones that are the most plausible. This is problematic since it is one of the main goals of belief revision to make such a selection. We can do that thanks to the underlying AGM revision operators in the definition of the private revision operator. So our private revision result implies (usually strictly) the result given by Aucher's revision.

8   Conclusion

In this paper we investigate the problem of belief change in a multi-agent context. More precisely we study private expansion and revision of KD45$_n$ models by objective formulas. We present a set of postulates for expansion and revision close to the classical AGM ones for the single agent case. We also define specific expansion and revision operators and show that they satisfy the properties pointed out. As future work we plan to consider different extensions of this work. The first issue to be considered is the problem of private change by subjective formulas. For expansion the method will be quite similar to the one we described here for objective formulas. But for revision the subjective case is both more complicated and richer than the revision by objective formulas, due to the minimality of change requirement. In fact some interesting metrics can be defined and used to define minimal change for revision. Another issue we want to address is group change. The idea is that the new evidence is not given privately to only one agent, but to a group of agents. This case straightforwardly includes private change and public change as special cases. So it is clearly the most general framework. Interaction between the agents adds interesting additional problems, since each agent of the group will have to revise her beliefs about the beliefs of the other agents of the group receiving the same observation.

References

1. Alchourrón, C.E., Gärdenfors, P., Makinson, D.: On the logic of theory change: partial meet contraction and revision functions. J. Symb. Log. **50**, 510–530 (1985)
2. Aucher, G.: Perspectives on belief and change. Ph.D. thesis, Université Paul Sabatier; University of Otago (2008)

3. Aucher, G.: Generalizing AGM to a multi-agent setting. Log. J. IGPL **18**(4), 530–558 (2010)
4. Aucher, G.: Private announcement and belief expansion: an internal perspective. J. Log. Comput. **22**(3), 451–479 (2012)
5. Aumann, R.J.: Agreeing to disagree. Ann. Stat. **4**(6), 1236–1239 (1976)
6. Aumann, R.J.: Interactive epistemology I: knowledge. Int. J. Game Theory **28**(3), 263–300 (1999)
7. Baltag, A., Moss, L.S.: Logics for epistemic programs. Synthese **139**, 165–224 (2004). Knowledge. Rationality & Action 1–60, 2004
8. Baltag, A., Smets, S.: Dynamic belief revision over multi-agent plausibility models. In: Proceedings of LOFT 2006, pp. 11–24 (2006)
9. Blackburn, P., de Rijke, M., Venema, Y.: Modal Logic. Cambridge University Press, Cambridge (2001)
10. Board, O.: Dynamic interactive epistemology. Games Econ. Behav. **49**(1), 49–80 (2004)
11. Caridroit, T., Konieczny, S., de Lima, T., Marquis, P.: Private expansion and revision in multi-agent settings. Technical Report (2015). http://www.cril.fr/~caridroit/ECSQARU15_PERMAS.pdf
12. Fagin, R., Halpern, J.Y., Moses, Y., Vardi, M.: Reasoning About Knowledge. The MIT Press, Cambridge (1995)
13. Fermé, E.L., Hansson, S.O.: AGM 25 years - twenty-five years of research in belief change. J. Philos. Log. **40**(2), 295–331 (2011)
14. Gärdenfors, P.: Knowledge in Flux. MIT Press, Cambridge (1998)
15. Herzig, A., Lang, J., Marquis, P.: Action progression and revision in multiagent belief structures. In: Proceedings of NRAC 2005 (2005)
16. Katsuno, H., Mendelzon, A.O.: On the difference between updating a knowledge base and revising it. In: Proceedings of KR 1991, pp. 387–394 (1991)
17. Katsuno, H., Mendelzon, A.O.: Propositional knowledge base revision and minimal change. Artif. Intell. **52**, 263–294 (1991)
18. Pacuit, E., Roy, O.: Epistemic foundations of game theory. In: Stanford Encyclopedia of Philosophy (2014)
19. Parikh, R.: Beliefs, belief revision, and splitting languages. In: Logic, Language and Computation, vol. 2, pp. 266–278. Center for the Study of Language and Information, Stanford (1999)
20. Tallon, J.-M., Vergnaud, J.-C., Zamir, S.: Communication among agents: a way to revise beliefs in KD45 kripke structures. J. Appl. Non-Classical Log. **14**(4), 477–500 (2004)
21. van Benthem, J.: Dynamic logic for belief revision. J. Appl. Non-Classical Log. **14**, 129–155 (2004)
22. van Benthem, J.: Logic in Games. MIT Press, Cambridge (2014)
23. van Ditmarsch, H.P.: Prolegomena to dynamic logic for belief revision. Synthese **147**(2), 229–275 (2005)
24. van Ditmarsch, H.P., van der Hoek, W., Kooi, B.: Dynamic Epistemic Logic. Springer, Amsterdam (2008)
25. van Ditmarsch, H.P., van der Hoek, W., Kooi, B.P.: Dynamic epistemic logic with assignment. In: Proceedings of AAMAS 2005, pp. 141–148. ACM (2005)

Contraction in Propositional Logic

Thomas Caridroit[(⊠)], Sébastien Konieczny, and Pierre Marquis

CRIL, CNRS, Université d'Artois, Lens, France
{caridroit,konieczny,marquis}@cril.fr

Abstract. The AGM model for the revision and contraction of belief sets provides rationality postulates for each of the two cases. In the context of finite propositional logic, Katsuno and Mendelzon pointed out postulates for the revision of belief bases which correspond to the AGM postulates for the revision of beliefs sets. In this paper, we present postulates for the contraction of propositional belief bases which correspond to the AGM postulates for the contraction of belief sets. We highlight the existing connections with the revision of belief bases in the sense of Katsuno and Mendelzon thanks to Levi and Harper identities and present a representation theorem for operators of contraction of belief bases.

1 Introduction

Belief change has been studied for many years in philosophy, databases, and artificial intelligence. The AGM model, named after its three initiators Carlos Alchourrón, Peter Gärdenfors and David Makinson, is the main formal framework for modeling belief change [1]. Its key concepts and constructs have been the subject of significant developments [5,6,13]. Alchourrón, Gärdenfors and Makinson pointed out some postulates and representation theorems thereby establishing the basis for a framework suited to the belief change issue when beliefs are expressed using the language of any Tarskian logic. Tarskian logics consider abstract consequence relations, that satisfy inclusion, monotony and idempotence (and the AGM framework adds also to them the supraclassicality, compacity and deduction conditions).

Katsuno and Mendelzon [11] presented a set of postulates for revision operators in the framework of finite propositional logic and a representation theorem in terms of faithful assignments.[1] This representation theorem is important because it is at the origin of the main approaches to iterated belief revision [4].

Revision and contraction operators are closely related, as reflected by Levi and Harper identities. These identities can be used to define contraction operators from revision operators and vice versa. So the existence of work on contraction in the context of finite propositional logic might be expected. However, as far as we know, this issue has not been investigated.

The objective of this paper is to define operators of propositional contraction matching Katsuno and Mendelzon's revision operators and to check that these

---

[1] Such assignments correspond to a specific case of Grove's systems of spheres [7].

© Springer International Publishing Switzerland 2015
S. Destercke and T. Denoeux (Eds.): ECSQARU 2015, LNAI 9161, pp. 186–196, 2015.
DOI: 10.1007/978-3-319-20807-7_17

operators offer the expected properties. In the following, we present a set of postulates for contraction operators in the framework of finite propositional logic, and establish a corresponding representation theorem. The obtained results are not very surprising, but they are new nevertheless, and they appear as a first important step in the study of iterated contraction.

The rest of the paper is organized as follows. In Sect. 2, some formal preliminaries are presented. In Sect. 3, the AGM and KM frameworks for belief contraction and revision are recalled. In Sect. 4, a connection between belief sets and belief bases is pointed out. In Sect. 5, we define postulates that a contraction operator on belief bases should satisfy. In Sect. 6 the correspondence between contraction of belief sets and contraction of belief bases is investigated; we check, using Levi and Harper identities, that there is a connection between propositional revision operators satisfying Katsuno and Mendelzon postulates and propositional contraction operators satisfying our postulates. Section 7 gives a representation theorem for the contraction of belief bases. We conclude and discuss some perspectives for future work in Sect. 8. For space reasons, several proofs are not included, they can be found in the corresponding technical report [3].

2   Preliminaries

We consider a finite propositional language L built up from a (finite) set of symbols P and the usual connectives. $\bot$ (resp. $\top$) is the Boolean constant `false` (resp. `true`). Formulas are interpreted in the standard way, and $Cn(\varphi) = \{\psi \in L \mid \varphi \vdash \psi\}$ denotes the deductive closure of $\varphi \in L$.

A belief base is a set of propositional formulas $\{\varphi_1, \ldots, \varphi_n\}$. We suppose in this paper that a belief base is represented by $\varphi = \varphi_1 \wedge \ldots \wedge \varphi_n$ (This is a usual harmless assumption xhen one supposes irrelevance of syntax[2] (cf. postulate (C5)).

A belief set K is a deductively closed set of formulas. Obviously one can associate with any belief base φ a belief set that is the set of all its consequences $K = Cn(\varphi)$.

If φ is a formula, then $Mod(\varphi)$ denotes the set of its models. Conversely if M is a set of interpretations, then α_M denotes the formula (unique, up to logical equivalence) the models of which are those of M.

Given a preorder (i.e., a reflexive and transitive relation) $\leq_\varphi$ over the set of interpretations, $<_\varphi$ is its strict part defined by $I <_\varphi J$ if and only if $I \leq_\varphi J$ and $J \not\leq_\varphi I$ and $\simeq_\varphi$ is the associated equivalence relation defined by $I \simeq_\varphi J$ if and only if $I \leq_\varphi J$ and $J \leq_\varphi I$. $\min(X, \leq_\varphi)$ denotes the set of minimal elements of X for $\leq_\varphi$, i.e., $\min(X, \leq_\varphi) = \{x \in X \mid \nexists y \in X \text{ such that } y <_\varphi x\}$.

3   AGM and KM Belief Revision and Contraction

Alchourrón, Gärdenfors and Makinson [1,5] pointed out the following postulates for the contraction of belief sets. These postulates are formulated in a very

---

[2] Note that in some works the term "belief base" is just used for syntax-dependent belief change [8]. Here this term denotes a non-deductively closed set of formulas (as in [11]).

general framework, but here we limit the discussion to the case of finite propositional logic. Given a belief set K and a formula μ, $K \div \mu$ denotes the contraction of K by μ. $+$ is the expansion operator, the result it gives is just the set of consequences of the union of the two theories (i.e. $K + \mu = Cn(K \cup \{\mu\})$).

(K ÷ 1) $K \div \mu$ is a belief set
(K ÷ 2) $K \div \mu \subseteq K$
(K ÷ 3) If $\mu \notin K$, then $K \div \mu = K$
(K ÷ 4) If $\nvdash \mu$, then $\mu \notin K \div \mu$
(K ÷ 5) If $\mu \in K$, then $K \subseteq (K \div \mu) + \mu$
(K ÷ 6) If $\mu \equiv \beta$, then $K \div \mu = K \div \beta$
(K ÷ 7) $(K \div \mu) \cap (K \div \beta) \subseteq K \div (\mu \wedge \beta)$
(K ÷ 8) If $\mu \notin K \div (\mu \wedge \beta)$, then $K \div (\mu \wedge \beta) \subseteq K \div \mu$

See [5] for detailed explanations on these postulates (we will comment their propositional counterpart later). Alchourrón, Gärdenfors and Makinson also provided postulates $((\mathbf{K} \star \mathbf{1}) - (\mathbf{K} \star \mathbf{8}))$ for belief revision. We will focus on their propositional counterpart proposed by Katsuno and Mendelzon [11]. But let us first recall that AGM belief revision and belief contraction are closely related. Actually every belief revision operator induces a belief contraction one, and vice versa:

(Levi Identity) $K \star \mu = (K \div \neg\mu) + \mu$
(Harper Identity) $K \div \mu = K \cap (K \star \neg\mu)$

Let us now recall the Katsuno and Mendelzon propositional counterpart to belief revision postulates and their representation theorem in terms of faithful assignment [11]. Let φ and μ be two propositional formulas where φ represents the current belief base of the agent and μ is the new piece of information (i.e., the change formula). The revision of φ by μ, denoted by $\varphi \circ \mu$, must satisfy the following postulates [11]:

(R1) $\varphi \circ \mu \vdash \mu$
(R2) If $\varphi \wedge \mu$ is consistent, then $\varphi \circ \mu \equiv \varphi \wedge \mu$
(R3) If μ is consistent, then $\varphi \circ \mu$ is consistent
(R4) If $\varphi_1 \equiv \varphi_2$ and $\mu_1 \equiv \mu_2$, then $\varphi_1 \circ \mu_1 \equiv \varphi_2 \circ \mu_2$
(R5) $(\varphi \circ \mu) \wedge \psi \vdash \varphi \circ (\mu \wedge \psi)$
(R6) If $(\varphi \circ \mu) \wedge \psi$ is consistent, then $\varphi \circ (\mu \wedge \psi) \vdash (\varphi \circ \mu) \wedge \psi$

A representation theorem is a way to associate with a set of postulates a constructive approach to build the corresponding family of operators. Katsuno and Mendelzon presented such a theorem in terms of faithful assignment, which associates with each belief base a pre-order that ranks the interpretations from the most plausible ones to the least plausible ones.

Definition 1. *A faithful assignment is a mapping that associates with any belief base φ a pre-order $\leq_\varphi$ on the set of all interpretations such that:*

1. If $I \models \varphi$ and $J \models \varphi$, then $I \simeq_\varphi J$
2. If $I \models \varphi$ and $J \nvDash \varphi$, then $I <_\varphi J$
3. If $\varphi \equiv \varphi'$, then $\leq_\varphi = \leq_{\varphi'}$

Theorem 1 [11]. *A revision operator* $\circ$ *satisfies the postulates (R1)-(R6) if and only if there exists a faithful assignment that associates with each belief base* φ *a total pre-order* $\leq_\varphi$ *such that*

$$Mod(\varphi \circ \mu) = min(Mod(\mu), \leq_\varphi)$$

4   From Belief Sets to Belief Bases

Our purpose is now to define contraction operators on belief bases in the framework of finite propositional logic. Let φ and μ be two formulas. $\varphi - \mu$ denotes the contraction of φ by μ, which is the new formula obtained by removing the piece of beliefs μ from the (consequences of the) belief base φ of the agent.

In order to relate AGM belief set contraction and our notion of propositional belief base contraction, we first have to formalize the link between belief sets and belief bases.

Proposition 1 shows that a belief set is always the deductive closure (C_n) of a belief base:

Proposition 1. *For any belief set* K, *there is a belief base* φ_K *such that* $K = Cn(\varphi_K)$ *and conversely, for any belief base* φ, *there is a belief set* $K_\varphi = Cn(\varphi)$.

Indeed, Cn is a bijection from E to F where F is the set of belief sets and E is the set of belief bases considered up to logical equivalence. Thus, for a belief base φ, the notation $K_\varphi = Cn(\varphi)$ and for a belief set K, the notation $\varphi_K = Cn^{-1}(K)$ are safe.

On this ground a correspondence between AGM contraction operators on belief sets and the contraction operators on belief bases can be established:

Definition 2. *Given a contraction operator on belief sets* $\div$, *the operator* $-_{(\div)}$ *on belief bases is defined by:* $\varphi -_{(\div)} \mu = \varphi_{K_\varphi \div \mu}$. *Conversely, given a contraction operator on belief bases* $-$, *the operator* $\div_{(-)}$ *on belief sets is defined by:* $K \div_{(-)} \mu = K_{\varphi_K - \mu}$.

Finally, the following proposition shows that if we use a contraction operator on belief sets $\div$ to define, via Definition 2, a contraction operator on belief bases $-_{(\div)}$, then the contraction operator on belief sets defined via Definition 2 is the initial contraction operator $\div$ (and vice versa):

Proposition 2. *We have* $-_{(\div_{(-)})} = -$. *Similarly we have* $\div_{(-_{(\div)})} = \div$

Let a contraction operator $\div$ on belief sets and $-$ a contraction operator on belief bases. The operators $\div$ and $-$ are said to correspond to each other if $\div = \div_{(-)}$ and $- = -_{(\div)}$.

5   Postulates for Propositional Contraction

We now define the following set of postulates for contraction of propositional belief bases:

(C1) $\varphi \vdash \varphi - \mu$

(C2) If $\varphi \nvdash \mu$, then $\varphi - \mu \vdash \varphi$

(C3) If $\varphi - \mu \vdash \mu$, then $\vdash \mu$

(C4) If $\varphi \vdash \mu$, then $(\varphi - \mu) \wedge \mu \vdash \varphi$

(C5) If $\varphi_1 \equiv \varphi_2$ and $\mu_1 \equiv \mu_2$, then $\varphi_1 - \mu_1 \equiv \varphi_2 - \mu_2$

(C6) $\varphi - (\mu \wedge \beta) \vdash (\varphi - \mu) \vee (\varphi - \beta)$

(C7) If $\varphi - (\mu \wedge \beta) \nvdash \mu$, then $\varphi - \mu \vdash \varphi - (\mu \wedge \beta)$

The intuitive meaning of these postulates is as follows: (C1) ensures that after contraction, no new information is added to the belief base. (C2) indicates that if μ is not deducible from φ, then no change is made during the contraction. (C3) ensures that the only possibility for the contraction of φ by μ to fail is that μ is a tautology. (C4) says us that the conjunction of the contraction of φ by μ and μ gives a propositional formula which is equivalent to φ (the converse implication is a consequence of (C1)). (C5) reflects the principle of independence of syntax. (C6) and (C7) express the minimality of change for the conjunction. (C6) says that the contraction by a conjunction always implies the disjunction of the contractions by the conjuncts. (C7) says that if μ has not been removed during the contraction by $\mu \wedge \beta$, then the contraction by μ must imply the contraction by the conjunction.

The following proposition shows that the contraction operators satisfying postulates (C1)-(C7) correspond to the contraction operators satisfying the AGM postulates (K÷1)-(K÷8).

Proposition 3. *Let* $\div$ *be a contraction operator on belief sets and* $- (= -_{(\div)})$ *its corresponding operator on belief bases. Then* $\div$ *satisfies (K÷1)-(K÷8) if and only if* $-$ *satisfies (C1)-(C7).*

Furthermore, it turns out that the contraction of φ by a conjunction $(\mu \wedge \beta)$ can have only three different outcomes (up to logical equivalence). Such a trichotomy result is similar to the one in the classical AGM framework [5].

Proposition 4. *In the presence of (C1)-(C5), (C6) and (C7) are equivalent to (Tri):*

$$(\textbf{\textit{Tri}}) \quad \varphi - (\mu \wedge \beta) \equiv \begin{cases} \varphi - \mu \text{ or} \\ \varphi - \beta \text{ or} \\ (\varphi - \mu) \vee (\varphi - \beta) \end{cases}$$

In fact, looking at the proof of this proposition, we also know that if $\varphi - (\mu \wedge \beta) \vdash \beta$, then $\varphi - (\mu \wedge \beta) \equiv \varphi - \mu$. This means that when β is more entenched (i.e., more important/plausible) than μ, then when we are asked to remove $\mu \wedge \beta$ if we prefer to keep β (and to remove μ), then the contraction by the conjunction is exactly the contraction by μ alone.

6   A Correspondence Between Contraction and Revision

Now that we have defined postulates for contraction operators on belief bases, we can check that the contraction operators satisfying these postulates correspond to revision operators in the sense of Katsuno and Mendelzon [11].

We first show that Levi and Harper identities hold also in this propositional setting. We note $\circ_{(-)}$ the revision operator on belief bases defined from $-$ via Levi identity and $-_{(\circ)}$ the contraction operator on belief bases defined from $\circ$ via Harper identity.

Definition 3. *Levi and Harper identities for belief bases can be expressed as follows:*

$$\varphi \circ_{(-)} \mu \equiv (\varphi - \neg\mu) \wedge \mu \qquad\qquad \textbf{\textit{(Levi identity)}}$$
$$\varphi -_{(\circ)} \mu \equiv \varphi \vee (\varphi \circ \neg\mu) \qquad\qquad \textbf{\textit{(Harper identity)}}$$

Operators obtained by means of these identities satisfy the expected properties:

Proposition 5. *If the contraction operator* $-$ *satisfies (C1)-(C5) then the revision operator* $\circ$ $(= \circ_{(-)})$ *defined using Levi identity satisfies (R1)-(R4). Furthermore if (C6) is satisfied by* $-$*, then (R5) is satisfied by* $\circ$*, and if (C7) is satisfied by* $-$*, then (R6) is satisfied* $\circ$*.*

Therefore, the KM revision operators for propositional belief bases can be defined using Levi identity from the contraction operators for propositional belief bases we have introduced. Reciprocally, contraction operators for propositional belief bases can be defined using Harper identity, from KM revision operators for belief bases.

Proposition 6. *If the revision operator* $\circ$ *satisfies (R1)-(R4) then the contraction operator* $-$ $(= -_{(\circ)})$ *defined using Harper identity satisfies (C1)-(C5). Furthermore, if (R5) is satisfied by* $\circ$*, then (C6) is satisfied by* $-$ *and if (R6) is satisfied by* $\circ$*, then (C7) is satisfied by* $-$*.*

The following proposition shows that if we use a revision operator $\circ$ to define, via Harper identity, a contraction operator $-_{(\circ)}$, then the revision operator defined via Levi identity, from $-_{(\circ)}$ is the initial revision operator $\circ$. The other way around, if we use a contraction operator $-$ to define, via Levi identity a revision operator $\circ_{(-)}$, then the contraction operator defined via Harper identity from $\circ_{(-)}$ is the initial contraction operator $-$.

Proposition 7

$-$ *if $\circ$ is a revision operator, then* $\circ_{(-_{(\circ)})} = \circ$
$-$ *if $-$ is a contraction operator, then* $-_{(\circ_{(-)})} = -$

Our postulates for contraction of belief bases are thus in close correspondence with the revision postulates for belief bases defined by Katsuno and Mendelzon.

7   Representation Theorem

Let us now check that we can state a representation theorem for contraction within the framework of finite propositional logic, which is a counterpart of the representation theorem of Katsuno and Mendelzon for revision.

Lemma 1. *Let* − *be a contraction operator satisfying (C1)-(C7).*

$$\text{If } \alpha_{\{I\}} \nvdash \varphi \text{ then } \varphi - \neg\alpha_{\{I\}} \equiv \varphi \vee \alpha_{\{I\}}$$

This lemma indicates that if a formula α, with only one model, does not imply a formula φ, then the contraction of φ by the negation of α is equivalent to the disjunction of φ and α.

The idea of the representation theorem is to express the set of models of the contraction of a base φ by a change formula μ as the union of the models of φ and of the minimal counter-models of μ with respect to $\leq_\varphi$.

Theorem 2. *A contraction operator* − *satisfies the postulates* **(C1)-(C7)** *if and only if there exists a faithful assignment that associates with each belief base* φ *a total pre-order* $\leq_\varphi$ *on the set of all interpretations such that*

$$Mod(\varphi - \mu) = Mod(\varphi) \cup min(Mod(\neg\mu), \leq_\varphi)$$

Proof. The only-if part of the proof consists mainly in checking the **(C1)-(C7)** properties. For space reasons we focus only on the if part which is more tricky. Let − be a contraction operator which satisfies the postulates (C1) to (C7).

For each formula φ, we define a total pre-order $\leq_\varphi$ using the operator − : $\forall I, I'$ two interpretations, we define the relation $\leq_\varphi$ by $I \leq_\varphi I'$ if and only if $I \in Mod(\varphi - \neg\alpha_{\{I,I'\}})$.

We first show that $\leq_\varphi$ is a total pre-order.

- **Total:** let I and I' be two interpretations. As $\alpha_{\{I,I'\}}$ has at least one model, $\neg\alpha_{\{I,I'\}}$ has at least one counter-model. We deduce that $\nvdash \neg\alpha_{\{I,I'\}}$, which allows us to conclude from (C3) that $\varphi - \neg\alpha_{\{I,I'\}} \nvdash \neg\alpha_{\{I,I'\}}$. So we know that there is $J \in Mod(\varphi - \neg\alpha_{\{I,I'\}})$ such that $J \in Mod(\alpha_{\{I,I'\}}) = \{I, I'\}$. Therefore, either $I \in Mod(\varphi - \neg\alpha_{\{I,I'\}})$ and thus $I \leq_\varphi I'$, or $I' \in Mod(\varphi - \neg\alpha_{\{I,I'\}})$ and thus $I' \leq_\varphi I$. Hence $\leq_\varphi$ is total.
- **Reflexive:** Every binary relation which is total necessarily is reflexive.
- **Transitive:** Suppose that $I \leq_\varphi J$ and $J \leq_\varphi L$. Let us consider the case when I, J and L are pairwise distinct, and none of them is a model of φ. Indeed, in the remaining case when at least two of them are equal, transitivity is trivially satisfied. If one of them is a model of φ, then the result also trivially holds by (C1). Indeed, if $L \models \varphi$, then by the assumptions and (C1) we deduce that I and J are also models of φ. Similarly, if $J \models \varphi$, then by (C1) $I \models \varphi$. And if $I \models \varphi$ then by construction $I \leq_\varphi I'$ forall I', so especially for $I' = L$.

  So now let us consider the general case. Towards a contradiction, suppose $I \nleq_\varphi L$. As $\leq_\varphi$ is total, we have $L <_\varphi I$, therefore $L \models \varphi - \neg\alpha_{\{I,L\}}$ and $I \nvDash \varphi - \neg\alpha_{\{I,L\}}$. By (Tri) we have that $\varphi - \neg\alpha_{\{I,J,L\}} \equiv \varphi - \neg\alpha_{\{I,L\}}$ or $\varphi - \neg\alpha_{\{I,J,L\}} \equiv \varphi - \neg\alpha_{\{J\}}$ or $\varphi - \neg\alpha_{\{I,J,L\}} \equiv (\varphi - \neg\alpha_{\{I,L\}}) \vee (\varphi - \neg\alpha_{\{J\}})$.
  - Case (1) $\varphi - \neg\alpha_{\{I,J,L\}} \equiv \varphi - \neg\alpha_{\{I,L\}}$. From (C6) we have that $\varphi - \neg\alpha_{\{I,L\}} \vdash \varphi - \neg\alpha_{\{I\}} \vee \varphi - \neg\alpha_{\{L\}} \equiv \varphi \vee \alpha_{\{I\}} \vee \alpha_{\{L\}}$. Since $J \nvDash \varphi \vee \alpha_{\{I\}} \vee \alpha_{\{L\}}$, we have $J \nvDash \varphi - \neg\alpha_{\{I,L\}}$, so $J \nvDash \varphi - \neg\alpha_{\{I,J,L\}}$. Since $L \models \varphi - \neg\alpha_{\{I,J,L\}}$ and $L \nvDash \neg\alpha_{\{J,L\}}$, we deduce that $\varphi - \neg\alpha_{\{I,J,L\}} \nvdash \neg\alpha_{\{J,L\}}$. So by (C7) we have that $\varphi - \neg\alpha_{\{J,L\}} \vdash \varphi - \neg\alpha_{\{I,J,L\}}$. As $J \nvDash \varphi - \neg\alpha_{\{I,J,L\}}$, we have $J \nvDash \varphi - \neg\alpha_{\{J,L\}}$, which means by definition that $J \nleq_\varphi L$. Contradiction.

- Case (2) $\varphi - \neg\alpha_{\{I,J,L\}} \equiv \varphi - \neg\alpha_{\{J\}} \equiv \varphi \vee \alpha_{\{J\}}$. This means in particular that $I \not\models \varphi - \neg\alpha_{\{I,J,L\}}$ and $J \models \varphi - \neg\alpha_{\{I,J,L\}}$. So we know that $\varphi - \neg\alpha_{\{I,J,L\}} \not\vdash \neg\alpha_{\{I,J\}}$. So by (C7) we have that $\varphi - \neg\alpha_{\{I,J\}} \vdash \varphi - \neg\alpha_{\{I,J,L\}}$. As $I \not\models \varphi - \neg\alpha_{\{I,J,L\}}$, we have $I \not\models \varphi - \neg\alpha_{\{I,J\}}$, which means by definition that $I \not\leq_\varphi J$. Contradiction.
- Case (3) $\varphi - \neg\alpha_{\{I,J,L\}} \equiv (\varphi - \neg\alpha_{\{I,L\}}) \vee (\varphi - \neg\alpha_{\{J\}}) \equiv (\varphi - \neg\alpha_{\{I,L\}}) \vee (\varphi \vee \alpha_{\{J\}})$. This equivalence implies that $J \models \varphi - \neg\alpha_{\{I,J,L\}}$, $L \models \varphi - \neg\alpha_{\{I,J,L\}}$, and $I \not\models \varphi - \neg\alpha_{\{I,J,L\}}$. Since $J \models \varphi - \neg\alpha_{\{I,J,L\}}$ and $J \not\models \neg\alpha_{\{I,J\}}$, we deduce that $\varphi - \neg\alpha_{\{I,J,L\}} \not\vdash \neg\alpha_{\{I,J\}}$. So by (C7) we have that $\varphi - \neg\alpha_{\{I,J\}} \vdash \varphi - \neg\alpha_{\{I,J,L\}}$. As $I \not\models \varphi - \neg\alpha_{\{I,J,L\}}$, we have $I \not\models \varphi - \neg\alpha_{\{I,J\}}$, which means by definition that $I \not\leq_\varphi J$. Contradiction.

We have shown that $\leq_\varphi$ is a total, reflexive and transitive relation. It is therefore a total pre-order. Then we show that the mapping $\varphi \mapsto \leq_\varphi$ is a faithful assignment.

- The third condition (if $\varphi_1 \equiv \varphi_2$, then $\leq_{\varphi_1} = \leq_{\varphi_2}$) comes from (C5). Indeed, if $\varphi_1 \equiv \varphi_2$ then $\varphi_1 - \neg\alpha_{\{I_1,I_2\}} \equiv \varphi_2 - \neg\alpha_{\{I_1,I_2\}}$, hence $I_1 \leq_{\varphi_1} I_2$ iff $I_1 \leq_{\varphi_2} I_2$, so $\leq_{\varphi_1} = \leq_{\varphi_2}$.
- The first condition comes from (C1): $\varphi \vdash \varphi - \neg\mu$, so if $I_1 \in Mod(\varphi)$ then $I_1 \in Mod(\varphi - \neg\alpha_{\{I_1,I_2\}})$ and if $I_2 \in Mod(\varphi)$ then $I_2 \in Mod(\varphi - \neg\alpha_{\{I_1,I_2\}})$. So by definition, we have $I_1 \leq_\varphi I_2$ and $I_2 \leq_\varphi I_1$, hence $I_1 \simeq_\varphi I_2$.
- Let us now show that the second condition (if $I_1 \models \varphi$ and $I_2 \not\models \varphi$ then $I_1 <_\varphi I_2$) is satisfied. From the definition of $\leq_\varphi$ and (C1), we can deduce from $I_1 \models \varphi$ that $I_1 \leq_\varphi I_2$. It remains to show that $I_2 \not\leq_\varphi I_1$. We consider two cases:
  - If $\varphi \vdash \neg\alpha_{\{I_1,I_2\}}$, then we have $\varphi \vdash \neg\alpha_{\{I_1\}} \wedge \neg\alpha_{\{I_2\}}$. So, in particular, $\varphi \vdash \neg\alpha_{\{I_1\}}$, which contradicts the fact that $I_1 \models \varphi$, showing that this case is impossible.
  - If $\varphi \not\vdash \neg\alpha_{\{I_1,I_2\}}$, then, from (C2), $\varphi - \neg\alpha_{\{I_1,I_2\}} \vdash \varphi$. We therefore deduce that $I_2 \not\vdash \varphi - \neg\alpha_{\{I_1,I_2\}}$, hence $I_2 \not\leq_\varphi I_1$.

The second condition for the assignment to be faithful is checked.

Finally, it remains to show that

$$Mod(\varphi - \mu) = Mod(\varphi) \cup min(Mod(\neg\mu), \leq_\varphi).$$

We consider two cases:

- If $\varphi \not\vdash \mu$, then from (C1) and (C2), $Mod(\varphi - \mu) = Mod(\varphi)$. Furthermore, $\exists I \in Mod(\varphi)$ such that $I \in Mod(\neg\mu)$. The second condition on faithful assignment allows us to deduce that $min(Mod(\neg\mu), \leq_\varphi) \subseteq Mod(\varphi)$. The conclusion follows.
- If $\varphi \vdash \mu$, then we assume $\not\vdash \mu$ without loss of generality. Indeed, if $\vdash \mu$ then $Mod(\varphi - \mu) = Mod(\varphi) \cup min(Mod(\neg\mu), \leq_\varphi)$ is trivially deduced from (C1) and (C4), which shows that $\varphi - \mu \vdash \varphi \vee \neg\mu$ since $Mod(\neg\mu) = \emptyset = min(Mod(\neg\mu), \leq_\varphi)$ when μ is valid. (C4) allows us to deduce that $Mod(\varphi - \mu) \subseteq Mod(\varphi) \cup min(Mod(\neg\mu), \leq_\varphi)$. Given an interpretation I such that $I \models \varphi - \mu$, we can deduce from (C4) that $I \models \varphi$ or $I \models \neg\mu$.

- If $I \models \varphi$, then directly $I \in Mod(\varphi) \cup min(Mod(\neg\mu), \leq_\varphi)$.
- If $I \models \neg\varphi$ and $I \models \neg\mu$, then we want to show that $I \in min(Mod(\neg\mu), \leq_\varphi)$. Towards a contradiction, suppose that there exists an interpretation $J \models \neg\mu$ such that $J <_\varphi I$. By definition of faithful assignment, we have $I \nvdash \varphi - (\neg\alpha_{\{I,J\}})$. In addition, we know that $I \models \neg\mu$ and $J \models \neg\mu$, so $\mu \vdash \neg\alpha_{\{I,J\}}$. Therefore there exists β such that $I \models \beta$, $J \models \beta$ and $\mu \equiv (\neg\alpha_{\{I,J\}}) \wedge \beta$. By (C6), $\varphi - \mu \vdash (\varphi - (\neg\alpha_{\{I,J\}})) \vee (\varphi - \beta)$, we also know that $\varphi - (\neg\alpha_{\{I,J\}} \vee \neg\beta) \nvdash \neg\alpha_{\{I,J\}}$ by (C3). By (C6) and (C7), we have $\varphi - \mu \equiv \varphi - \neg\alpha_{\{I,J\}}$. This contradicts our assumption, $I \nvdash \varphi - \neg\alpha_{\{I,J\}}$.

Subsequently we have $Mod(\varphi - \mu) \subseteq Mod(\varphi) \cup min(Mod(\neg\mu), \leq_\varphi)$. Let us show now that $Mod(\varphi) \cup min(Mod(\neg\mu), \leq_\varphi) \subseteq Mod(\varphi - \mu)$.

- If $I \in Mod(\varphi)$, then since from (C1), we have $\varphi \vdash \varphi - \mu$, we conclude that $I \in Mod(\varphi - \mu)$.
- Suppose now that $I \notin Mod(\varphi)$ and $I \in min(Mod(\neg\mu), \leq_\varphi)$ and suppose that $I \notin Mod(\varphi - \mu)$. In this case, $min(Mod(\neg\mu), \leq_\varphi)$ is not empty, which means that $\nvdash \mu$. So, from (C3), $\varphi - \mu \nvdash \mu$. We can deduce that $\exists J \in Mod(\varphi - \mu)$ such that $J \in Mod(\neg\mu)$.

  Let us consider the two possible cases: $J \in Mod(\varphi)$ and $J \notin Mod(\varphi)$. If $J \in Mod(\varphi)$, then by the second condition of the faithful assignment we have that $J <_\varphi I$. But as $J \in Mod(\neg\mu)$, this means that $I \notin min(Mod(\neg\mu), \leq_\varphi)$. Contradiction. If $J \notin Mod(\varphi)$, then we have that $J \in Mod(\varphi - \mu)$ and $I \notin Mod(\varphi-\mu)$. So $\varphi - \mu \nvdash \neg\alpha_{\{I,J\}}$, hence by (C7) we have that $\varphi - \neg\alpha_{\{I,J\}} \vdash \varphi - \mu$. As $I \notin Mod(\varphi - \mu)$, we have $I \notin Mod(\varphi - \neg\alpha_{\{I,J\}})$. Then by definition (and (C3)) this means that $J <_\varphi I$. But we also know that $J \in Mod(\neg\mu)$, so this implies that $I \notin min(Mod(\neg\mu), \leq_\varphi)$. Contradiction. □

Note that a similar construction has been used in [14] for the contraction of Horn belief sets.[3]

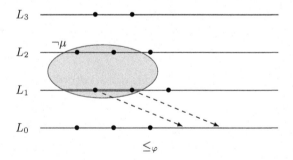

Fig. 1. Contraction of φ by μ

We illustrate the representation theorem on Fig. 1. The interpretations (depicted as dots) are located at different levels L_i, two interpretations at the

---

[3] We thank a reviewer for pointing this paper to us.

same level are equally plausible (i.e., $I \simeq_\varphi J$) and an interpretation I appearing at a lower level than another J is strictly more plausible (i.e., $I <_\varphi J$). The interpretations appearing at the lowest level (L_0) are the models of the belief base φ.

When φ is contracted by μ, the result consists of all models of φ to which are added to the most plausible models of $\neg\mu$ according to the pre-order of plausibility $\leq_\varphi$ associated with φ by the faithful assignment. This represents the minimal change required for not implying μ any longer. These interpretations are located at L_1 on Fig. 1. The minimal interpretations of $\neg\mu$ (at L_1) are added next to the interpretations of φ (at L_0).

8   Conclusion and Perspectives

In this paper we investigated belief contraction in the framework of finite propositional logic. The aim was, like in Katsuno and Mendelzon work for revision, to define postulates for contraction operators. We have checked that the operators of contraction characterized by our postulates correspond to the revision operators characterized by Katsuno and Mendelzon postulates. We have also given a representation theorem in terms of faithful assignment.

The aim of this work was to ensure that the translation of the AGM contraction in the finite propositional framework offers the expected properties. This is more than a technical exercice, since this step is necessary to define iterated contraction operators, which is the main perspective of this work. Indeed, the translation by Katsuno and Mendelzon of the AGM postulates is the basis of the study of iterated revision operators following Darwiche and Pearl [2,4,10,12]. There has been very few work on iterated contraction: to the best of our knowledge, only one paper [9] addresses this problem, but in a different framework from the one of Darwiche and Pearl. Defining "Darwiche and Pearl"-like iterated contraction operators will be a first step in the investigation of the relationships between [9] and [4].

References

1. Alchourrón, C.E., Gärdenfors, P., Makinson, D.: On the logic of theory change: Partial meet contraction and revision functions. J. Symbolic Logic **50**(2), 510–530 (1985)
2. Booth, R., Meyer, T.A.: Admissible and restrained revision. J. Artif. Intell. Res. (JAIR) **26**, 127–151 (2006)
3. Caridroit, T., Konieczny, S., Marquis, P.: Contraction in propositional logic, Technical report (2015). http://www.cril.fr/~caridroit/ECSQARU15_Contraction.pdf
4. Darwiche, A., Pearl, J.: On the logic of iterated belief revision. Artif. Intell. **89**(1–2), 1–29 (1997)
5. Gärdenfors, P.: Knowledge in Flux: Modeling the Dynamics of Epistemic States. MIT Press, Bradford Books, Cambridge (1988)

6. Gärdenfors, P., Makinson, D.: Revisions of knowledge systems using epistemic entrenchment. In: Proceedings of the 2nd Conference on Theoretical Aspects of Reasoning about Knowledge (TARK 1988), pp. 83–95 (1988)
7. Grove, A.: Two modellings for theory change. J. Phil. Logic **17**, 157–170 (1988)
8. Hansson, S.: A Textbook of Belief Dynamics. Kluwer Academic Publishers, NewYork (1999)
9. Hild, M., Spohn, W.: The measurement of ranks and the laws of iterated contraction. Artif. Intell. **172**(10), 1195–1218 (2008)
10. Jin, Y., Thielscher, M.: Iterated belief revision, revised. Artif. Intell. **171**(1), 1–18 (2007)
11. Katsuno, H., Mendelzon, A.O.: Propositional knowledge base revision and minimal change. Artif. Intell. **52**(3), 263–294 (1992)
12. Konieczny, S., Pino Pérez, R.: Improvement operators. In: Proceedings of the 11th International Conference on Principles of Knowledge Representation and Reasoning (KR 2008), pp. 177–187, 16–19 September 2008
13. Rott, H.: Belief contraction in the context for the general theory of rational choice. J. Symbolic Logic **58**(4), 1426–1450 (1993)
14. Zhuang, Z. Q., Pagnucco, M.: Model based horn contraction. In: Proceedings of the 13th International Conference on Principles of Knowledge Representation and Reasoning (KR 2012), 10–14 June 2012

Classification

Multi-classifiers of Small Treewidth

Arnoud Pastink[(✉)] and Linda C. van der Gaag

Department of Information and Computing Sciences,
Utrecht University, Utrecht, The Netherlands
{A.J.Pastink,L.C.vanderGaag}@uu.nl

Abstract. Multi-dimensional Bayesian network classifiers are becoming quite popular for multi-label classification. These models have the advantage of a high expressive power, but may induce a prohibitively high runtime of classification. We argue that the high runtime burden originates from their large treewidth. Thus motivated, we present an algorithm for learning multi-classifiers of small treewidth. Experimental results show that these models have a small runtime of classification, without loosing accuracy compared to unconstrained multi-classifiers.

1 Introduction

Multi-dimensional Bayesian network classifiers [9], or multi-classifiers for short, constitute an increasingly popular approach to multi-label classification. While these models have the advantage of a high expressive power, they may come associated with a high runtime of classification. Especially for large sets of instances to be classified and in applications in which instances are to be classified instantaneously, can this high runtime burden prove prohibitive. Although various researchers addressed the classification time of multi-classifiers and designed learning algorithms giving reasonable runtime properties in general [4,7], available algorithms do not come with any actual guarantees on classification time.

In this paper, we argue that the high runtime complexity of multi-classifiers can be attributed to their tendency to have a large treewidth. Motivated by this observation, we present an algorithm for learning multi-classifiers of small treewidth. The algorithm bounds treewidth not by imposing general topological constraints, but by iteratively monitoring treewidth of partially constructed classifiers in a branch-and-bound approach. As a result, our algorithm retains much of the expressive power of the multi-classifier framework and is expected to result in good-quality models for efficient classification. Experiments on various data sets in fact show that the classifiers learned with our algorithm perform comparably, in terms of classification accuracy, to multi-classifiers of unbounded treewidth. Our results further show that by bounding treewidth a huge reduction, up to a factor 400, of the runtime complexity of classification is achieved.

The paper is organised as follows. In Sect. 2 we introduce our notational conventions and review multi-classifiers. In Sect. 3 we address the relationship between multi-classifiers and treewidth. Earlier research addressing the runtime of multi-classifiers is reviewed in Sect. 4. In Sect. 5 we present our algorithm for

© Springer International Publishing Switzerland 2015
S. Destercke and T. Denoeux (Eds.): ECSQARU 2015, LNAI 9161, pp. 199–209, 2015.
DOI: 10.1007/978-3-319-20807-7_18

learning multi-classifiers of small treewidth. In Sect. 6 we report results achieved with our algorithm on various multi-label data sets. The paper is rounded off with our conclusions and directions for future work in Sect. 7.

2   Preliminaries

We consider a finite non-empty set $\mathbf{V}$ of discrete random variables, in which each variable $V_i \in \mathbf{V}$ takes its value from a finite set of states. The joint state space for a subset $\mathbf{S} \subseteq \mathbf{V}$ is the Cartesian product of the sets of states of the separate variables in $\mathbf{S}$; we use $\kappa_{\mathbf{S}}$ to denote the size of this joint state space. Given our focus on classification, we assume that the set $\mathbf{V}$ is partitioned into a set $\mathbf{C} = \{C_1, \ldots, C_n\}$, $n \geq 1$, of class variables and a set $\mathbf{X} = \{X_1, \ldots, X_m\}$, $m \geq 1$, of feature variables, with $\mathbf{C} \cup \mathbf{X} = \mathbf{V}$ and $\mathbf{C} \cap \mathbf{X} = \varnothing$. A joint state of the feature variables $\mathbf{X}$ is referred to as a feature vector and is denoted by $\mathbf{x}$; a joint state $\mathbf{c}$ of the class variables $\mathbf{C}$ is called a class vector. A pair $(\mathbf{c}, \mathbf{x})$ is termed an instance over $\mathbf{V}$. We further assume a (multi-)set $\mathcal{D}$ of instances over $\mathbf{V}$, which is partitioned into a training set $\mathcal{D}^{tr} = \{(\mathbf{c}_1, \mathbf{x}_1), \ldots, (\mathbf{c}_k, \mathbf{x}_k)\}$, $k \geq 1$, and a set of test instances $\mathcal{D}^{te} = \{(\mathbf{c}_1, \mathbf{x}_1), \ldots, (\mathbf{c}_l, \mathbf{x}_l)\}$, $l \geq 1$.

A multi-classifier over the random variables $\mathbf{V}$ is a Bayesian network of restricted topology over $\mathbf{V}$ [9]. Its set of arcs A is partitioned into three subsets:

- $A_{\mathbf{C}} \subseteq \mathbf{C} \times \mathbf{C}$ includes the arcs among the class variables, and the subgraph induced by $A_{\mathbf{C}}$ is called the class subgraph;
- $A_{\mathbf{X}} \subseteq \mathbf{X} \times \mathbf{X}$ contains the arcs among the feature variables, and the subgraph induced by $A_{\mathbf{X}}$ is called the feature subgraph;
- $A_{\mathbf{CX}} \subseteq \mathbf{C} \times \mathbf{X}$ includes the arcs from a class variable to a feature variable, and the subgraph induced by $A_{\mathbf{CX}}$ is called the bridge subgraph.

In this paper, we focus on multi-classifiers in which each class variable has at most one class variable parent, a feature variable has at most p class parents, and the feature subgraph is either empty or a forest-structured graph.

Classification of a feature vector $\mathbf{x}$ amounts to finding a class vector $\mathbf{c}$ that maximizes the posterior probability given $\mathbf{x}$, that is, it amounts to finding

$$\operatorname*{argmax}_{\mathbf{c} \in \mathbf{C}} \{\Pr(\mathbf{c} \mid \mathbf{x})\}$$

The performance of a multi-classifier is estimated from the accuracy of its classifications for a set $\mathcal{D}^{te}$ of test instances $(\mathbf{c}_i, \mathbf{x}_i)$. For each feature vector $\mathbf{x}_i$, a most likely class vector $\hat{\mathbf{c}}_i$ is computed from the classifier and compared with the true class vector $\mathbf{c}_i$ of the instance. Performance is now expressed by two metrics. The global accuracy acc_G of the classifier given the testset $\mathcal{D}^{te}$ is defined as:

$$acc_G(\mathcal{D}^{te}) = \frac{1}{|\mathcal{D}^{te}|} \cdot \sum_{(\mathbf{c}_i, \mathbf{x}_i) \in \mathcal{D}^{te}} \delta(\mathbf{c}_i, \hat{\mathbf{c}}_i)$$

where $\delta(\mathbf{c}_i, \hat{\mathbf{c}}_i)$ equals 1 if $\mathbf{c}_i = \hat{\mathbf{c}}_i$ and 0 otherwise. This metric serves to measure the proportion of (complete) class vectors that are predicted correctly. The Hamming metric measures the proportion of class variables for which a correct prediction is made. The Hamming accuracy acc_H of the classifier is defined as:

$$acc_H(\mathcal{D}^{te}) = \frac{1}{|\mathcal{D}^{te}|} \cdot \sum_{(\mathbf{c}_i, \mathbf{x}_i) \in \mathcal{D}^{te}} \left(\frac{1}{n} \cdot \sum_{i=1}^{n} \delta(\hat{c}_{ij}, c_{ij}) \right)$$

where c_{ij} is the state of the j-th class variable in the i-th test instance, and $\delta(\hat{c}_{ij}, c_{ij})$ equals 1 if $\hat{c}_{ij} = c_{ij}$ and 0 otherwise.

Multi-classifiers are usually learned from a (multi-)set of instances. The objective then is to construct a classifier from the training instances that performs well on the test data and allows good classification of yet unseen instances. In this paper, we take a score-based approach to learning. Each possible graphical structure is assigned a numerical score which describes how well the structure fits the training data. To this end, we employ the BDeu score [5], which conveniently decomposes as a sum of BDeu scores per variable:

$$\mathrm{BDeu}(G) = \sum_{V_i \in \mathbf{C} \cup \mathbf{X}} \mathrm{BDeu}(V_i, \mathrm{pa}(V_i))$$

where G is the graphical structure under consideration, V_i is a variable in G and $\mathrm{pa}(V_i)$ are its parents. For a variable V_i, the BDeu score given its parents equals:

$$\mathrm{BDeu}(V_i, \mathrm{pa}(V_i)) = \sum_{j=1}^{q_i} \left[\log \frac{\Gamma(\alpha_{ij})}{\Gamma(\alpha_{ij} + n_{ij})} + \sum_{k=1}^{|V_i|} \log \frac{\Gamma(\alpha_{ijk} + n_{ijk})}{\Gamma(\alpha_{ijk})} \right]$$

where n_{ijk} is the number of training instances in which the variable V_i is in state k and its parents are in their j-th joint state, and $n_{ij} = \sum_k n_{ijk}$; q_i is the number of joint states of the parents of V_i. With an equivalent sample size of α, we get that $\alpha_{ij} = \frac{\alpha}{q_i}$ and $\alpha_{ijk} = \frac{\alpha_{ij}}{|V_i|}$, where $|V_i|$ is the number of states of V_i. Upon learning, the goal now is to maximise the BDeu score with respect to the training data, subject to the structural constraints imposed.

The class subgraph of a multi-classifier can be learned independently from its feature and bridge subgraphs [9]. If the feature subgraph is known to be empty, then the bridge subgraph can be learned optimally by selecting the best scoring parent set per feature variable [7]. If the feature subgraph is non-empty however, the bridge subgraph cannot be learned independently from the feature subgraph. To arrive at optimality with respect to the BDeu score, the bridge and feature subgraphs should then be learned simultaneously. We note that simply selecting the best scoring parent set per feature variable would now not necessarily result in a valid multi-classifier as acyclicity would not be guaranteed.

In this paper, we adapt an existing approach to learning extended tree augmented naive Bayesian classifiers (ETANs) in general [6], to learning the combined bridge and feature subgraph of a multi-classifier. First a feature subgraph is learned on a copy $\mathbf{X}'$ of the set of feature variables $\mathbf{X}$. The BDeu scores for the variables in $\mathbf{X}'$ are established from those for $\mathbf{X}$ by collapsing the scores of the parent sets that include class variables. More specifically, for each variable $X_i' \in \mathbf{X}'$ the following BDeu scores are established:

$$\mathrm{BDeu}(X_i', \varnothing) = \max_{\mathbf{S} \subseteq \mathbf{C}} \mathrm{BDeu}(X_i, \mathbf{S})$$

$$\mathrm{BDeu}(X_i', X_j') = \max_{\mathbf{S} \subseteq \mathbf{C}} \mathrm{BDeu}(X_i, \mathbf{S} \cup \{X_j\})$$

Using a standard Bayesian network learner [1] or a modified version of the ETAN-algorithm [6], we now learn feature subgraph on $\mathbf{X}'$, where each feature variable X_i' is allowed at most one parent. For each variable X_i', the chosen parent X_j' (or the empty parent set) is then expanded to the parent set of the original score. The result is a combined bridge and feature subgraph with maximal BDeu score given the structural constraints of the multi-classifier.

3   Multi-classifiers and Treewidth

Computing a class vector of highest posterior probability from a multi-classifier given a specific feature vector, is equal to solving the most probable explanation (MPE) problem. This MPE problem is known to be NP-hard in general [12], and remains NP-hard even for binary networks in which both the indegree and the outdegree of all variables is at most two [12]. The MPE problem can be solved in polynomial time however, for networks of bounded treewidth.

We briefly revisit the importance of the concept of treewidth in Bayesian networks in general. Current algorithms for probabilistic inference build upon a junction-tree representation of a network. To construct such a representation, the network's graphical structure G is first moralised by adding edges between all pairs of parents of a variable and subsequently dropping directions. The moralised graph is then triangulated by adding edges to make it chordal, that is, to render a graph in which any cycle of four or more variables has a shortcut. A tree-decomposition of the triangulated graph G_T now is a tree $\mathcal{T}_G$ such that:

- each node $Cl_i \in \mathcal{T}_G$ corresponds with a maximal clique in G_T, and vice versa;
- for every i, j, k, if node Cl_j lies on the path from Cl_i to Cl_k in $\mathcal{T}_G$, then $Cl_i \cap Cl_k \subseteq Cl_j$.

The width of the tree-decomposition $\mathcal{T}_G$ of G is equal to $\max_i \{ |Cl_i| - 1 \mid Cl_i \in \mathcal{T}_G \}$, where $|Cl_i|$ is the number of variables in the i-th clique. The treewidth of the graphical structure G of a network now is equal to the minimum width over all tree-decompositions of its moralised graph, and is denoted by $\tau(G)$.

Current inference algorithms for Bayesian networks in general pass messages through a junction-tree representation of a network [10], which embeds for its graphical structure a tree-decomposition of the network's original graph. The processing time of a single clique in the junction tree is proportional to the size of the clique's state space. Only if this size is bounded by a constant for all

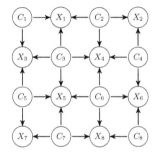

Fig. 1. A 4×4 grid multi-classifier

cliques, can inference be performed efficiently. We note that if the treewidth is bounded, a bounded state space per variable suffices for feasible inference.

The treewidth of a multi-classifier in general is not bounded by a constant, not even if the indegree and outdegree of all variables are small. As an example, we consider a multi-classifier constructed from a generalised $n \times n$ chessboard; the classifier for $n = 4$ is depicted in Fig. 1. Each black tile of the chessboard is represented by a class variable, and each white tile is captured by a feature variable; for each adjacent pair of tiles, an arc is added from the associated class variable to the feature variable. The resulting multi-classifier has empty class and feature subgraphs; the number of parents per feature variable is at most four. The treewidth of this classifier is n [2], which shows that even simple multi-classifiers can have a prohibitively large treewidth and, hence, a high classification runtime.

4   Related Work

The runtime of classification with a multi-classifier having been addressed before, we briefly review earlier work on reducing the computational burden involved.

The property of class-bridge decomposability for multi-classifiers was introduced to allow a divide-and-conquer strategy for classification. If a classifier is class-bridge decomposable, its graphical structure decomposes, given a feature vector, into multiple components defined by the bridge subgraph; classification then is performed in each component separately. The treewidth of such a classifier is equal to the maximum treewidth of its individual components. Heuristic algorithms have been designed for learning class-bridge decomposable multi-classifiers [4]. Since these algorithms do not address treewidth explicitly, the treewidth of a class-bridge decomposable multi-classifier may still be prohibitively large. The algorithm in fact does not give any guarantee on the runtime complexity of classification with the learned classifier.

Corani *et al.* [7] learn sparse multi-classifiers. The class subgraphs of their classifiers are forests, and the bridge subgraphs are learned optimally by taking the best scoring parent set per feature variable, given an empty feature subgraph. Despite their sparsity, the treewidth of the resulting classifiers may be quite large and bounded only by the total number of class variables.

Learn a multi-classifier of treewidth at most k:

---

1. Learn an optimal forest-structured class subgraph;
2. Search the space of all possible bridge subgraphs, maintaining a branch-and-bound tree of partial multi-classifiers. While the branch-and-bound tree has unvisited nodes, perform the following steps:
   2.1 Take the next partial multi-classifier P from the branch-and-bound tree;
   2.2 Add a new feature variable with its best-scoring parent set to P;
   2.3 **if** BDeu$(P) <$ lowerbound **then**
       − Stop expanding P, and go to Step 2.1;
   2.4 **if** $\tau(P) > k$ **then**
       − Replace the current parent set by the next one, and go to Step 2.3;
   2.5 **else**
       − Add each remaining feature variable to P, and insert into the search tree;
       − Update the lower bound if applicable;
3. Optionally, learn a forest-structured feature subgraph.

Fig. 2. An algorithm for learning multi-classifiers of treewidth at most k

5   Learning Multi-classifiers of Small Treewidth

Our algorithm for learning multi-classifiers of small treewidth takes a branch - and-bound approach to systematically searching the space of all graphical structures for one with highest BDeu score given a treewidth of at most k. Since a large treewidth can be induced by just the bridge subgraph of such a classifier, the algorithm focuses on this subgraph. The algorithm is summarised in Fig. 2.

Step 1: The algorithm starts by learning an optimal forest-structured graph over the class variables; to this end any standard algorithm can be used [8]. The learned subgraph is then fixed for the remainder of the learning process.

Step 2: Given the learned class subgraph, the algorithm builds a bridge subgraph by iteratively adding feature variables to the partially constructed multi-classifier. The algorithm computes to this end, for each such variable, the BDeu scores of all its possible parent sets. After adding a new feature variable and its current best-scoring parent set, the algorithm compares the BDeu score of the partial multi-classifier so far against a lower bound.

An initial lower bound on the BDeu score of the classifier to be learned is established by finding the best single class parent for each feature variable, and taking the score of the resulting forest of naive Bayesian classifiers. When joined with the class subgraph from Step 1, the resulting classifier has treewidth one, and hence constitutes a feasible solution. To compare the BDeu score of a partially constructed multi-classifier against the lower bound, this partial classifier needs to be extended to a multi-classifier with all feature variables involved. To this end, the algorithm adds the best parent set for each yet remaining feature variable; we note that this completed classifier may be infeasible as its treewidth may be larger than k. The BDeu score of the completed classifier thus is an upper bound on the score which can be attained by the current partial multi-classifier.

If the score of the partial multi-classifier so far is smaller than the lower bound, the current branch of the branch-and-bound tree is abandoned. If the BDeu score is larger than the lower bound, the algorithm verifies that the treewidth of the classifier does not yet exceed k. Computing the treewidth of a partial multi-classifier being its most intensive task, the algorithm minimises the number of computations involved. Since the feature subgraph of a partial multi-classifier is empty, each feature variable X_i is connected with class parents only. After moralisation therefore, X_i and its parents constitute a (maximal) clique. From this property, we have that [3]:

$$\tau(P) = \max\{d, \tau(P \setminus \{X_i\})\}$$

where $\tau(P)$ is the treewidth of the multi-classifier so far, and d is the indegree of X_i; $P \backslash \{X_i\}$ is the graphical structure obtained by moralising P and subsequently removing X_i. From this property we find that the treewidth of the partial classifier P can be computed from the moralised subgraph of class variables only. If the treewidth of the partial multi-classifier exceeds k, the current branch of the branch-and-bound tree is abandoned. Otherwise, the associated node in the tree is expanded by adding the next feature variable; if its BDeu-score exceeds the current lower bound moreover, this bound is updated.

Step 3: In an optional post-processing step, the algorithm adds a forest-structured feature subgraph to the classifier. Given the learned class and bridge subgraphs, the algorithm greedily inserts arcs that serve to increase the overall BDeu score of the multi-classifier yet keep its treewidth smaller than k.

Although Step 1 of the learning algorithm yields an optimal class subgraph and Step 2 results in an optimal bridge subgraph given this class subgraph, the algorithm is not guaranteed to yield a multi-classifier of highest BDeu score. Since the class subgraph resulting from Step 1 may affect the treewidth of the model under construction, a multi-classifier with another, non-optimal class subgraph could have a higher BDeu score.

6   Experiments

We conducted a number of experiments with our algorithm for learning multi-classifiers of small treewidth. Before reporting the results obtained, we first discuss the general set-up of our experiments.

6.1   Data Sets and Baseline Characteristics

For our experiments, we used the data sets listed in Table 1; these sets are commonly used for multi-label classification. In a pre-processing step, numerical variables were discretised into four bins of equal size. We further performed feature selection to remove any irrelevant features. Since feature selection for multi-classifiers is an open problem, we used to this end the approach by Corani et al. [7], performing correlation-based feature selection per class variables and retaining the union of all selected feature variables.

Table 1. Data set properties, the treewidth (τ) of the unconstrained multi-classifier, and the baseline performance of the associated constant classifiers.

Data set	Training	Test	Classes	Features	Selected	τ	acc_H	acc_G
Emotions	391	202	6	72	19	3	0.67	0.11
Scene	1211	1196	6	294	119	4	0.82	0.16
Yeast	1500	917	14	103	39	4	0.77	0.10
Genbase	465	199	27	1186	72	7	0.95	0.27
Medical	645	333	45	1449	342	18	0.97	0.17
Enron	1123	579	53	1001	243	13	0.94	0.067

Prior to the experiments with our learning algorithm, we established baseline accuracies for the various data sets. For computing a baseline Hamming accuracy, a constant classifier was constructed which returns for each class variable separately the value that appears most often in the training set; for a baseline global accuracy, the constant classifier returns the class vector that appears most often. The baseline accuracies thus obtained are reported in Table 1. We further learned multi-classifiers without any restrictions on treewidth, allowing at most three parents per feature variable for reasons of feasibility. The treewidths of the resulting classifiers are also reported in Table 1. Since the treewidths of the multi-classifiers learned from the data sets Emotions, Scene and Yeast proved small, we decided to exclude these data sets from our further experiments.

We then studied the performance of our learning algorithm, both with and without using the option to add a feature subgraph to the multi-classifier under construction. The global and Hamming accuracies established from the test sets for the learned multi-classifiers were compared against those obtained from the classifiers without any restrictions on treewidth. All multi-classifiers were learned under the topological constraints introduced in Sect. 2. The BDeu scores were computed with GOBNILP [1], with an equivalent sample size of $\alpha = 5$. The software for our algorithm was written in Java.

6.2   Results

Although experiments were run with various small τ values, we report the results obtained with $\tau = 3$ only; the results with other small treewidths were similar.

The accuracies established from the respective test sets for the learned multi-classifiers are summarised in Table 2; the table also reports the accuracies of the classifiers that were learned without any bounds on treewidth. For each data set we used a Wilcoxon signed-rank test with $p < 0.05$ on both Hamming and global accuracy to detect significantly better performance of either type of classifier. With the Medical data set, the global accuracy of the unconstrained multi-classifier proved to be significantly better than that of the classifier of small treewidth. No further significant differences in performance were found. The total state space sizes κ of the junction-tree representations of the learned classifiers are also reported in Table 2. For the Enron and Medical data sets specifically,

Table 2. Accuracies of multi-classifiers with unbounded and small treewidth (τ) respectively, and the total state space size (κ) of the associated junction trees.

	Empty feature subgraph				Forest-structured feature subgraph			
Data set	τ	κ	acc_H	acc_G	τ	κ	acc_H	acc_G
Genbase	7	3396	0.999	0.965	13	142828	0.998	0.960
	3	1492	0.999	0.970	3	1520	0.999	0.970
Medical	18	2204040	0.987	**0.622**	36	$6.6 \cdot 10^{11}$	0.988	0.622
	3	5700	0.987	0.586	3	6048	0.987	0.595
Enron	13	82292	0.945	0.138	34	$1.8 \cdot 10^{9}$	0.946	0.130
	3	3996	0.945	0.143	3	4456	0.946	0.147

the differences in state space size between the small-treewidth classifier and the classifier of unbounded treewidth are quite large. By constraining treewidth, a reduction of the state space size by a factor 20 for Enron and by almost a factor 400 for Medical is achieved, indicating a major reduction of classification time. We further used the option to learn an additional forest-structured feature subgraph for our multi-classifiers, keeping treewidth within the same $\tau = 3$ bound. We compared the accuracies found with the learned classifiers against those obtained from similar multi-classifiers of unbounded treewidth. Table 2 reports the results obtained. Again applying, per data set, a Wilcoxon signed-rank test with $p < 0.05$ on both types of accuracy, revealed no significant differences. With respect to the differences in total state space size, the table shows again that by constraining treewidth major reductions of classification time are achieved.

The experimental results summarised in Table 2 suggest that adding a forest-structured feature subgraph to a learned multi-classifier does not significantly improve its performance. This finding may be explained by the fundamental property of Bayesian networks that direct probabilistic influences dominate over induced ones [11]. We consider as an example the simple network structure in Fig. 3 on the left, and study the influence of the feature variable X_q on the class variable C_j. Now, if an arc is added from X_p to X_q as shown in the figure on the right, entering a feature vector will induce an intercausal influence between X_p and C_j. This influence is known to be dominated by the direct influence from X_q on C_j. As it further tends to be weak, the induced influence in fact is not likely to cause large shifts in the probability distribution over the class variables.

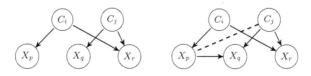

Fig. 3. The effect of an induced intercausal influence

7   Conclusions

Attributing their often high classification time to their large treewidth, we designed a branch-and-bound algorithm for learning multi-classifiers of small treewidth. For various well-known multi-label data sets, we showed that the performance of the resulting treewidth-constrained classifiers does not differ significantly from that of multi-classifiers without any bounds on treewidth. Our experimental results further showed that by constraining treewidth, major reductions of the runtime of classification are achieved. In future research, we will conduct a deeper study of the performance of our treewidth-constrained classifiers compared to unbounded multi-classifiers, especially in view of more informative feature subgraphs. We will further investigate whether our learning algorithm can be improved from a computational point of view to bring real-world application of multi-classifiers within closer reach.

References

1. Bartlett, M., Cussens, J.: Advances in Bayesian network learning using integer programming. In: Nicholson, A., Smyth, P. (eds.) Proceedings of the 29th Conference on Uncertainty in Artificial Intelligence, pp. 182–191. AUAI Press (2013)
2. Bodlaender, H.L.: A partial k-arboretum of graphs with bounded treewidth. Theoret. Comput. Sci. **209**(1), 1–45 (1998)
3. Bodlaender, H.L., Koster, A.M., Van den Eijkhof, F., Van der Gaag, L.C.: Preprocessing for triangulation of probabilistic networks. In: Breese, J., Koller, D. (eds.) Proceedings of 17th Conference on Uncertainty in Artificial Intelligence, pp. 32–39. Morgan Kaufmann (2001)
4. Borchani, H., Bielza, C., Larrañaga, P.: Learning CB-decomposable multi-dimensional Bayesian network classifiers. In: Myllymaki, P., Roos, T., Jaakkola, T. (eds.) Proceedings of the 5th European Workshop on Probabilistic Graphical Models. pp. 25–32 (2010)
5. Buntine, W.: Theory refinement on Bayesian networks. In: Bonissone, P., D'Ambrosio, B., Smets, P. (eds.) Proceedings of the 7th Conference on Uncertainty in Artificial Intelligence, pp. 52–60. Morgan Kaufmann (1991)
6. de Campos, C.P., Cuccu, M., Corani, G., Zaffalon, M.: Extended tree augmented naive classifier. In: van der Gaag, L.C., Feelders, A.J. (eds.) PGM 2014. LNCS, vol. 8754, pp. 176–189. Springer, Heidelberg (2014)
7. Corani, G., Antonucci, A., Mauá, D.D., Gabaglio, S.: Trading off speed and accuracy in multilabel classification. In: van der Gaag, L.C., Feelders, A.J. (eds.) PGM 2014. LNCS, vol. 8754, pp. 145–159. Springer, Heidelberg (2014)
8. Edmonds, J.: Optimum branchings. J. Res. Natl. Bur. Stan. B **71**(4), 233–240 (1967)
9. Van der Gaag, L.C., De Waal, P.R.: Multi-dimensional Bayesian network classifiers. In: Studeny, M., Vomlel, J. (eds.) Proceedings of the 3rd European Workshop on Probabilistic Graphical Models, pp. 107–114 (2006)
10. Lauritzen, S.L., Spiegelhalter, D.J.: Local computations with probabilities on graphical structures and their application to expert systems. J. Roy. Stat. Soc. **50**(2), 157–224 (1988)

11. Renooij, S., Van der Gaag, L.C., Parsons, S.: Propagation of multiple observations in QPNs revisited. In: Van Harmelen, F. (ed.) Proceedings of the 15th European Conference on Artificial Intelligence. pp. 665–669 (2002)
12. Shimony, S.E.: Finding MAPs for belief networks is NP-hard. Artif. Intell. **68**(2), 399–410 (1994)

Balanced Tuning of Multi-dimensional Bayesian Network Classifiers

Janneke H. Bolt[✉] and Linda C. van der Gaag

Department of Information and Computing Sciences, Utrecht University,
P.O. Box 80.089, 3508 TB Utrecht, The Netherlands
{j.h.bolt,l.c.vandergaag}@uu.nl

Abstract. Multi-dimensional classifiers are Bayesian networks of restricted topological structure, for classifying data instances into multiple classes. We show that upon varying their parameter probabilities, the graphical properties of these classifiers induce higher-order sensitivity functions of restricted functional form. To allow ready interpretation of these functions, we introduce the concept of balanced sensitivity function in which parameter probabilities are related by the odds ratios of their original and new values. We demonstrate that these balanced functions provide a suitable heuristic for tuning multi-dimensional Bayesian network classifiers, with guaranteed bounds on the changes of all output probabilities.

1 Introduction

The family of multi-dimensional Bayesian network classifiers (MDCs) was introduced to generalise one-dimensional classifiers to application domains that require instances to be classified into multiple dimensions [6,9]. An MDC includes multiple class variables and multiple feature variables, which are connected by a bipartite graph directed from the class variables to the feature variables. Classifying a data instance amounts to computing the joint probability distribution over the class variables given the instance's features, and returning the most likely joint class combination. MDCs enjoy a growing interest as a suitable tool for multi-dimensional classification [1,4].

Like more traditional classifiers, multi-dimensional Bayesian network classifiers are typically learned from data. Tailored algorithms are available for fitting MDCs to the joint probability distributions reflected in the data at hand. While often available data prove suboptimal already for constructing a one-dimensional classifier, any skewness properties of the joint or conditional distributions over the class variables will prove especially problematic for learning multi-dimensional classifiers. Expert knowledge, for example of expected classifications, can then be instrumental in correcting unwanted biases by careful tuning of the parameter probabilities of the learned classifier.

Tuning the parameters of a multi-dimensional classifier requires detailed insight in the effects of changing their values on the classifier's output probabilities. For Bayesian networks in general, the technique of sensitivity analysis

© Springer International Publishing Switzerland 2015
S. Destercke and T. Denoeux (Eds.): ECSQARU 2015, LNAI 9161, pp. 210–220, 2015.
DOI: 10.1007/978-3-319-20807-7_19

has evolved as a practical tool for studying the effects of changes in a network's parameter probabilities. Research so far has focused on one-way sensitivity analyses in which a single parameter is varied. The effects of systematic variation of multiple parameters have received far less attention, mostly due to the computational burden of establishing the functions describing these effects. A recent exception is [2] in which an efficient algorithm for studying the effects of multiple changes, within a fixed interval, on an established MPE is given. For tuning the parameters of a multi-dimensional classifier however, more detailed insights in the effects of simultaneously varying multiple parameters is preferred or even necessary.

In this paper, we present an elegant method for tuning the output probabilities of a multi-dimensional Bayesian network classifier by simultaneous parameter adjustment. We begin by showing that the topological properties of an MDC induce higher-order sensitivity functions of restricted functional form which can be established efficiently. By employing a carefully balanced scheme of parameter adjustment, such a function is reduced to an insightful single-parameter balanced sensitivity function which can be readily exploited as a suitable heuristic for tuning. The heuristic is shown to incur changes within guaranteed bounds in all output probabilities over the class variables, thereby providing global insight in the change in the network's output distributions.

The paper is organised as follows. In Sect. 2 we review multi-dimensional classifiers, and sensitivity functions of Bayesian networks in general. In Sect. 3 we derive the general form of a higher-order sensitivity function for MDCs. In Sect. 4, the concept of balanced sensitivity function is introduced; we describe how such a function is used for effective parameter tuning in a multi-dimensional classifier and prove bounds on the changes induced in all output probabilities. Section 5 illustrates the basic idea of balanced parameter tuning by means of an example, and Sect. 6 concludes the paper.

2 Preliminaries

We briefly review multi-dimensional classifiers and thereby introduce our notations. We further describe higher-order sensitivity functions for Bayesian networks in general.

2.1 Bayesian Networks and Multi-dimensional Classifiers

We consider a set of random variables $\mathbf{V} = \{V_1, \ldots, V_m\}$, $m \geq 1$. We will use v_i to denote an arbitrary value of V_i; we will write v and $\bar{v}$ for the two values of a binary variable V. A joint value assignment to $\mathbf{V}$ is indicated by $\mathbf{v}$. In the sequel, we will use V_i and $\mathbf{V}$ also to indicate the set of possible value assignments to V_i and $\mathbf{V}$, respectively.

A Bayesian network is a graphical model of a joint probability distribution Pr over a set of random variables $\mathbf{V}$. Each variable from $\mathbf{V}$ is represented by a node in a directed acyclic graph, and vice versa; (in-)dependencies between the variables are, as far as possible, captured by the graph's set of arcs according to the well-known d-separation criterion [7]. Each variable $V_i \in \mathbf{V}$ further has associated a set of conditional probability distributions $\Pr(V_i \mid \pi_{V_i})$, where π_{V_i} denotes the set of parents of V_i in the graph; the separate probabilities in these distributions are termed the network's parameters. The joint probability distribution $\Pr$ now factorises over the network's graph as

$$\Pr(\mathbf{V}) = \prod_{V_i \in \mathbf{V}} \Pr(V_i \mid \pi_{V_i})$$

where V_i and π_{V_i} take their value assignments compatible with $\mathbf{V}$. We will use $\sim$ and $\nsim$ to indicate compatibility and incompatibility of value assignments, respectively.

A multi-dimensional classifier now is a Bayesian network of restricted topology. Its set of variables is partitioned into a set $\mathbf{C}$ of class variables and a set $\mathbf{F}$ of feature variables, and its digraph does not allow the feature variables to have class children [6,9]. An MDC is used to assign a joint value assigment, or instance, $\mathbf{f}$ to a most likely combination of class values $\mathbf{c}$, that is, it is used to establish $\text{argmax}_{\mathbf{c}} \Pr(\mathbf{c} \mid \mathbf{f})$. In this paper we focus specifically on classifiers without any direct relationships between their class variables, yet in which no further topological assumptions are made; we will denote such classifiers by $MDC(\mathbf{C}, \mathbf{F})$. For a feature variable $F_i \in \mathbf{F}$, we will use $\mathbf{F}_{F_i} = \mathbf{F} \cap \pi_{F_i}$ to denote its set of feature parents, and $\mathbf{C}_{F_i}$ to denote its parents from $\mathbf{C}$. Specific value assignments to these sets are indicated by $\mathbf{f}_{F_i}$ and $\mathbf{c}_{F_i}$ respectively.

2.2 Sensitivity Functions of Bayesian Networks

Upon systematically varying multiple parameter probabilities $\mathbf{x} = \{x_1, \ldots, x_n\}$, $n \geq 1$, of a Bayesian network in general, a higher-order sensitivity function results which expresses an output probability $\Pr(\mathbf{y} \mid \mathbf{e})$ of interest in terms of these parameters $\mathbf{x}$. More specifically, the result is a function of the following form:

$$\Pr(\mathbf{y} \mid \mathbf{e})(\mathbf{x}) = \frac{\sum_{\mathbf{x}_k \in \mathcal{P}(\mathbf{x})} \left(c_k \cdot \prod_{x_i \in \mathbf{x}_k} x_i \right)}{\sum_{\mathbf{x}_k \in \mathcal{P}(\mathbf{x})} \left(d_k \cdot \prod_{x_i \in \mathbf{x}_k} x_i \right)}$$

where $\mathcal{P}(\mathbf{x})$ is the powerset of the set of network parameters $\mathbf{x}$ and where the constants c_k, d_k are determined by the non-varied network parameters. We will use $\mathbf{x}^{\mathbf{o}} = \{x_1^o, \ldots, x_n^o\}$ to indicate the original values of the parameters $\mathbf{x}$ in the network under study, $\Pr^o$ to indicate original probabilities, that is, probabilities computed with the original values of all parameters involved, and O^o to indicate original odds.

Upon varying a parameter x_j for a variable V_i, the other parameters of the same conditional distribution over V_i are co-varied to let the distribution sum to 1. In the most commonly used co-variation scheme, these parameters are varied proportionally with x_j. Since other schemes may also be appropriate [8], we will formulate our results in the sequel without assuming any specific scheme of co-variation.

3   The n-way Sensitivity Function of an MDC

Establishing a higher-order sensitivity function for a Bayesian network in general is computationally expensive, as the number of additive terms involved, and hence the number of constants to be computed, can be exponential in the number of parameters being varied. In this section, we show that, due to its restricted topological structure and dedicated use, a multi-dimensional classifier allows more ready calculation of the n-way sensitivity functions for its output probabilities. We show more specifically, that an output probability $\Pr(\mathbf{c}\,|\,\mathbf{f})$ for a given $\mathbf{c}$ can be expressed in terms of the original output probability and the original and new values of all parameters compatible with the instance $\mathbf{f}$. The form of the sensitivity function is given in the proposition below; the proofs of all propositions in this paper are provided in the appendix.

Proposition 1. *Let $MDC(\mathbf{C}, \mathbf{F})$ be a multi-dimensional classifier as defined above. Let $\mathbf{f}$ be an instance of $\mathbf{F}$, and let $\mathbf{x} = \{x_1, \ldots, x_n\}$, $n \geq 1$, be the set of network parameters compatible with $\mathbf{f}$. Then, for all $\mathbf{c} \in \mathbf{C}$,*

$$\Pr(\mathbf{c} \mid \mathbf{f})(\mathbf{x}) = \frac{\Pr^o(\mathbf{c} \mid \mathbf{f}) \cdot \prod\limits_{x_i \sim \mathbf{c}, x_j \nsim \mathbf{c}} x_i \cdot x_j^o}{\sum\limits_{\mathbf{c}^* \in \mathbf{C}} \left(\Pr^o(\mathbf{c}^* \mid \mathbf{f}) \cdot \prod\limits_{x_i \sim \mathbf{c}^*, x_j \nsim \mathbf{c}^*} x_i \cdot x_j^o \right)}$$

The sensitivity function $\Pr(\mathbf{c}\,|\,\mathbf{f})(\mathbf{x})$ stated above includes all parameters of the feature variables which are compatible with the instance $\mathbf{f}$ to be classified. The parameters $\Pr(f_i' \mid \pi_{F_i})$ of a feature variable F_i with f_i' incompatible with $\mathbf{f}$ do not occur in the function since these parameters are not involved directly in the computation of the output probability: upon variation of such a parameter, the output probability is affected only indirectly by the co-variation of $\Pr(f_i \mid \pi_{F_i})$ with $f_i \sim \mathbf{f}$. Without loss of generality, we thus include just the parameters compatible with $\mathbf{f}$, which implies that the proposition holds for any co-variation scheme used for the parameters of the feature variables. Also all parameters $\Pr(c_i)$ of a class variable C_i are included in the sensitivity function. These parameters cannot be varied freely however, as their sum should remain 1. By assuming a specific co-variation scheme, we could have included the dependent parameters implicitly, as with the feature parameters. By their explicit inclusion, however, the function is independent of the co-variation scheme used for the class parameters and can be further tailored to a specific scheme upon practical application.

Although the function stated above includes all parameters compatible with the instance to be classified, it is easily adapted to a sensitivity function involving only a subset of these parameters: since each parameter is included exactly once in each term of the fraction, either by its original value x^o or as a variable x, any non-varied parameter cancels out. The sensitivity function is also readily adapted to output probabilities $\Pr(\mathbf{c} \mid \mathbf{g})$ with $\mathbf{G} \subset \mathbf{F}$, provided there are no observed feature variables with unobserved feature parents. The parameters of the unobserved feature variables then should simply be excluded.

The sensitivity function stated in Proposition 1 reveals that an output probability of a multi-dimensional classifier changes monotonically with specific parameter adjustments. Proposition 2 details this property of monotonicity.

Proposition 2. *Let $MDC(\mathbf{C}, \mathbf{F})$ be a classifier as before, and let $\Pr(\mathbf{c} \mid \mathbf{f})$ be its output probability of interest. Let $\mathbf{x} = \{x_1 \ldots, x_n\}$, $n \geq 1$, be the parameters of $MDC(\mathbf{C}, \mathbf{F})$ compatible with $\mathbf{f}$, and let $\mathbf{x}'$, $\mathbf{x}^*$ be two sets of values for these parameters. Then,*

$$x_i' \leq x_i^* \text{ for all } x_i \sim \mathbf{c} \text{ and } x_j' \geq x_j^* \text{ for all } x_j \nsim \mathbf{c} \Leftrightarrow \Pr(\mathbf{c} \mid \mathbf{f})(\mathbf{x}') \leq \Pr(\mathbf{c} \mid \mathbf{f})(\mathbf{x}^*)$$

The proposition states that by increasing the parameters in $\mathbf{x}$ compatible with $\mathbf{c}$ and decreasing the incompatible ones, the output probability of the class combination $\mathbf{c}$ increases. Such a parameter change will be called monotone with respect to the output probability $\Pr(\mathbf{c}|\mathbf{f})$. We note that the monotonicity property of a parameter change provides information about the direction in which the separate parameters need to be adjusted to arrive at the intended effect on the output probability. The following corollary states that this probability takes its maximum at the parameters' extreme values.

Corollary 1. *Let $MDC(\mathbf{C}, \mathbf{F})$, $\Pr(\mathbf{c} \mid \mathbf{f})$ and $\mathbf{x}$ be as before. The sensitivity function $\Pr(\mathbf{c} \mid \mathbf{f})(\mathbf{x})$ attains its maximum at $x_i = 1$ for all $x_i \sim \mathbf{c}$ and $x_j = 0$ for all $x_j \nsim \mathbf{c}$. A similar property holds for the minimum of the function.*

4   Balanced Tuning of MDCs

In the previous section we showed that the output probability $\Pr(\mathbf{c} \mid \mathbf{f})$ of a multi-dimensional classifier changes monotonically given a monotone parameter adjustment. While this property indicates the direction in which parameters have to be adjusted, it does not yet suggest the amount of adjustment for arriving at the intended output. We now introduce for this purpose the concept of a balancing scheme for parameter adjustment. A balancing scheme governs a simultaneous change in all parameters x involved, by amounts defined by their odds ratios $\frac{x^o \cdot (1-x)}{(1-x^o) \cdot x}$. Balancing the parameters of a classifier constitutes a simple and generally applicable approach to parameter tuning; we will show moreover that the approach comes with guaranteed bounds on the changes of all possible output probabilities. We now first define the concept of balancing scheme.

Definition 1. *Let $x, y \in \langle 0, 1 \rangle$ be parameters of an MDC, and let x^o and y^o be their original values. We say that a scheme for parameter adjustment balances y positively with x if $\frac{x^o \cdot (1-x)}{(1-x^o) \cdot x} = \frac{y^o \cdot (1-y)}{(1-y^o) \cdot y}$; it balances y negatively with x if $\frac{x^o \cdot (1-x)}{(1-x^o) \cdot x} = \frac{(1-y^o) \cdot y}{y^o \cdot (1-y)}$.*

An important property of a balancing scheme for parameter adjustment is that, if a parameter x is varied over the full value range $\langle 0, 1 \rangle$, then the parameter y covers the full range $\langle 0, 1 \rangle$ as well, that is, the range of possible values of y is not constrained by balancing y with x; this property is illustrated for $x^o = 0.7$

and $y^o = 0.8$ in Fig. 1. We note that we assume that a balancing scheme does not adjust deterministic parameters and that non-deterministic parameters will not adopt deterministic values.

Building upon balancing schemes, we now define a balanced sensitivity function[1].

Definition 2. *Let* $\Pr(\mathbf{c}\,|\,\mathbf{f})$ *be the output probability of an MDC as before, and let* $\mathbf{x} = \{x_1, \ldots, x_n\}$, $n \geq 1$, *be its parameters compatible with* $\mathbf{f}$. *A balanced sensitivity function for* $\Pr(\mathbf{c} \mid \mathbf{f})$ *is a function* $\Pr(\mathbf{c} \mid \mathbf{f})(x_i)$ *in a single parameter* $x_i \in \mathbf{x}$, *with all parameters* $x_j \in \mathbf{x}$ *balanced with* x_i.

A balanced function $\Pr(\mathbf{c} \mid \mathbf{f})(x_i)$ is the intersection of the n-way function $\Pr(\mathbf{c} \mid \mathbf{f})(\mathbf{x})$ with the (curved) surface defined by the balancing scheme. It takes the following form:

$$\Pr(\mathbf{c} \mid \mathbf{f})(x_i) = \frac{c_0 + c_1 \cdot x_i^1 + \ldots + c_m \cdot x_i^m}{d_0 + d_1 \cdot x_i^1 + \ldots + d_m \cdot x_i^m}$$

where the constants c_j, d_j again are determined by the non-varied parameters, each x_i^k is a multiplicative term of degree k, and m is the number of probability tables from which the parameters are chosen. As an example, Fig. 2 depicts the two-way sensitivity function $\Pr(cd\,|\,fgh)(x, y)$ of the MDC from Fig. 3, in the two parameters $x = \Pr(f\,|\,c)$ and $y = \Pr(g\,|\,cd)$. The figure further depicts the two surfaces determining the balanced sensitivity functions in x and in y separately, that are derived from the two-way function given a positive and a negative balancing scheme for the two parameters.

A balanced sensitivity function provides insight in the effects of varying multiple parameter probabilities according to a balanced scheme of adjustment. For a required change in the output probability of interest $\Pr(\mathbf{c} \mid \mathbf{f})$, the amount by which the parameter x_i is to be adjusted is readily established; the balanced scheme of adjustment then enforces the other parameter probabilities to be adjusted accordingly. To guarantee that the balanced sensitivity function covers the same value range for the output probability as the underlying n-way function, all parameters have to be balanced monotonically with the output probability of interest.

Given a (not necessarily monotone) balanced change, the changes incurred in all output probabilities over the class variables are bounded, in terms of the odds ratio of the original and new probabilities, as stated in the following proposition.

Proposition 3. *Let* $MDC(\mathbf{C}, \mathbf{F})$ *be a multi-dimensional classifier and let* $\mathbf{G} \subseteq \mathbf{F}$. *Let parameters* $\mathbf{x}$ *be balanced with the parameter* x *and let* $\alpha \geq 1$ *be such that either* $\frac{x \cdot (1-x^o)}{(1-x) \cdot x^o} = \alpha$ *or* $\frac{(1-x) \cdot x^o}{x \cdot (1-x^o)} = \alpha$. *Then,*

$$\frac{1}{\alpha^k} \leq \frac{O(\mathbf{C} \mid \mathbf{G})(x)}{O^o(\mathbf{C} \mid \mathbf{G})} \leq \alpha^k$$

---

[1] In earlier research, we introduced the related concept of *sliced sensitivity function* [3] which specifies an output probability of a Bayesian network in n linearly related parameters.

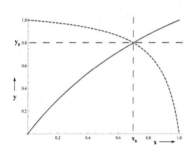

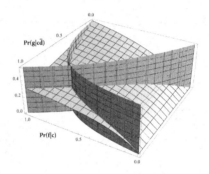

Fig. 1. Positively (solid line) and negatively (dashed line) balanced parameters x and y, with $x^o = 0.7$ and $y^o = 0.8$.

Fig. 2. A two-way sensitivity function in $x = \Pr(f|c)$, $y = \Pr(g\,|\,c\bar{d})$, and the surfaces defining the balanced sensitivity functions with $x^o = 0.7$ and $y^o = 0.8$.

where $k = s + 2 \cdot t$, with s the number of probability tables from which just a single parameter is in $\mathbf{x}$ and t the number of tables with two or more parameters in $\mathbf{x}$.

Although the bounds stated above are not strict, they do give insight in the overall perturbation of the classifier's output distributions.

The idea of measuring the distance between two probability distributions by their odds ratio was introduced before by Chan and Darwiche [5]. More specifically, they proposed a measure which strictly bounds the odds ratio of an arbitrary probability of interest. Given changes in just a single probability table, their bounds are readily computed from just those changes; computing these bounds given multiple parameter changes however, is computationally expensive in general.

5   Tuning an Example Multi-dimensional Classifier

We consider the example classifier from Fig. 3 and its output probability of interest $\Pr(cd \mid fgh)$. With the original parameter values, we find that $\Pr(cd \mid fgh) = 0.29$. Now suppose that domain experts indicate that this probability should be 0.40, and that we would like to arrive at this value by adjusting the parameters $x = \Pr(f\,|\,c)$, $y = \Pr(g\,|\,c\bar{d})$ and $z = \Pr(h\,|\,g\bar{d})$. By Proposition 1, we find the sensitivity function:

$$\Pr(cd|fgh)(x,y,z) = \frac{p_1^o \cdot x \cdot y^o \cdot z^o}{p_1^o \cdot x \cdot y^o \cdot z^o + p_2^o \cdot x \cdot y \cdot z + p_3^o \cdot x^o \cdot y^o \cdot z^o + p_4^o \cdot x^o \cdot y^o \cdot z}$$
$$= \frac{0.94 \cdot x}{0.94 \cdot x + 3.47 \cdot x \cdot y \cdot z + 0.25 + 1.39 \cdot z}$$

where $p_1^o = \Pr^o(cd \mid fgh)$, $p_2^o = \Pr^o(c\bar{d} \mid fgh)$, $p_3^o = \Pr^o(\bar{c}d \mid fgh)$ and $p_4^o = \Pr^o(\bar{c}\bar{d}\,|\,fgh)$. From this higher-order function, we now derive a balanced

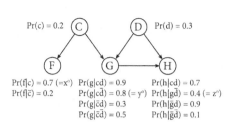

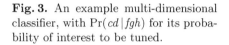

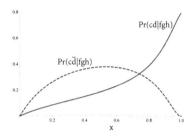

Fig. 3. An example multi-dimensional classifier, with $\Pr(cd\,|\,fgh)$ for its probability of interest to be tuned.

Fig. 4. Balanced functions for $\Pr(cd\,|\,fgh)$ and $\Pr(c\bar{d}\,|\,fgh)$, given a monotone balancing scheme for x, y, z with respect to $\Pr(cd\,|\,fgh)$.

sensitivity function $\Pr(cd\,|\,fgh)(x)$ by appropriately balancing the parameters y and z with x. Since $x \sim \Pr(cd\,|\,fgh)$, $y \nsim \Pr(cd\,|\,fgh)$ and $z \nsim \Pr(cd\,|\,fgh)$, we balance both y and z negatively with x, to guarantee that the output probability retains the same value range as with the corresponding higher-order sensitivity function. We find the balanced function

$$\Pr(cd\mid fgh)(x) = \frac{0.15 \cdot x - 0.184 \cdot x^2 + 0.05 \cdot x^3}{0.26 + 0.23 \cdot x - 1.07 \cdot x^2 + 0.59 \cdot x^3}$$

which is depicted in Fig. 4. The expert-provided value 0.4 for $\Pr(cd\mid fgh)$ is attained at $x = 0.81$; the other parameters then take the values $y = 0.69$ and $z = 0.27$. The value α of the adjustment is 1.83. As we changed a single parameter from three CPTs, we find that $[1/\alpha^k, \alpha^k] = [0.16, 6.10]$. In addition to the monotonically balanced sensitivity function $\Pr(cd\mid fgh)(x)$, the figure also depicts the function $\Pr(c\bar{d}\mid fgh)(x)$ found with the same balancing scheme for the parameters x, y, z. Since this scheme is non-monotone for $\Pr(c\bar{d}\mid fgh)$, the resulting balanced function is no longer monotone.

To attain the desired output probability $\Pr(cd\mid fgh) = 0.40$, also another combination of parameters can be varied. Varying other parameter combinations will generally result in another α and hence in other bounds on the changes in all output probabilities. For example, the desired probability is also found with $\Pr(f\mid\bar{c}) = 0.11$, $\Pr(g\mid\bar{c}d) = 0.34$ and $\Pr(h\mid cd) = 0.82$. For this parameter combination $\alpha = 1.97$ is found, from which the interval $[1/\alpha^k, \alpha^k] = [0.13, 7.60]$ is established. In uncertainty of the actual changes therefore, the first tuning option is preferred.

6   Conclusions

Motivated by the observation that available data sets often prove problematic for learning multi-dimensional classifiers, we presented an elegant method for tuning their parameter probabilities based on expert-provided information. We showed that the topological properties and dedicated use of an MDC induce higher-order sensitivity functions of restricted functional form which can be established efficiently. We further designed a scheme of balanced parameter adjustment, by which a higher-order sensitivity function is reduced to an insightful single-parameter function which is readily exploited as a suitable heuristic for tuning. The heuristic was shown to incur changes within guaranteed bounds in all output probabilities over the class variables. Although not strict, these bounds do give insight in the changes in the classifier's output distributions which are incurred by balanced adjustment of different sets of parameters. In our future research, we would like to study these bounds with the aim of further tightening them. We also plan to study optimality properties of balancing parameter probabilities by their odds ratios in view of the odds-ratio based measure on the output.

The tuning method developed in this paper does not as yet provide for selecting parameters for tuning. Parameter selection may be based upon various considerations. An example criterion may be to select parameters which give the smallest changes in the output distribution as a whole, as was already suggested in our example. Yet, parameters may also be selected based on the sizes of the samples from which they were estimated originally. We plan to investigate the effects of these and other criteria in various real-world applications of multi-dimensional network classifiers.

Acknowledgements. This work was supported by the Netherlands Organisation for Scientific Research.

Appendix

Proof of Proposition 1. Let $MDC(\mathbf{C}, \mathbf{F})$ be a multi-dimensional classifier as before. Writing the output probability $\Pr(\mathbf{c} \mid \mathbf{f})$ for a given $\mathbf{c}$ and $\mathbf{f}$ as $\Pr(\mathbf{c} \mid \mathbf{f}) = (\Pr(\mathbf{f} \mid \mathbf{c}) \cdot \Pr(\mathbf{c})) / (\sum_{\mathbf{C}} \Pr(\mathbf{f} \mid \mathbf{C}) \cdot \Pr(\mathbf{C}))$, and including terms involving the original probability values $\Pr^o(\mathbf{c} \mid \mathbf{f})$ and $\Pr^o(\mathbf{c})$, results in

$$\Pr(\mathbf{c}|\mathbf{f}) = \frac{\left(\frac{\Pr(\mathbf{f}|\mathbf{c})\cdot\Pr(\mathbf{c})\cdot\Pr^o(\mathbf{f}|\mathbf{c})\cdot\Pr^o(\mathbf{c})}{\Pr^o(\mathbf{f})\cdot\Pr^o(\mathbf{f}|\mathbf{c})\cdot\Pr^o(\mathbf{c})}\right)}{\left(\sum_{\mathbf{C}}\frac{\Pr(\mathbf{f}|\mathbf{C})\cdot\Pr(\mathbf{C})\cdot\Pr^o(\mathbf{f}|\mathbf{C})\cdot\Pr^o(\mathbf{C})}{\Pr^o(\mathbf{f})\cdot\Pr^o(\mathbf{f}|\mathbf{C})\cdot\Pr^o(\mathbf{C})}\right)} = \frac{\left(\frac{\Pr^o(\mathbf{c}|\mathbf{f})\cdot\Pr(\mathbf{f}|\mathbf{c})\cdot\Pr(\mathbf{c})}{\Pr^o(\mathbf{f}|\mathbf{c})\cdot\Pr^o(\mathbf{c})}\right)}{\left(\sum_{\mathbf{C}}\frac{\Pr^o(\mathbf{C}|\mathbf{f})\cdot\Pr(\mathbf{f}|\mathbf{C})\cdot\Pr(\mathbf{C})}{\Pr^o(\mathbf{f}|\mathbf{C})\cdot\Pr^o(\mathbf{C})}\right)}$$

Rearranging its summands into a single fraction gives for the denominator

$$\frac{\sum_{\mathbf{c}^*\in\mathbf{C}}\left(\Pr^o(\mathbf{c}^* \mid \mathbf{f}) \cdot \Pr(\mathbf{f} \mid \mathbf{c}^*) \cdot \Pr(\mathbf{c}^*) \cdot \prod_{\mathbf{C}\backslash\mathbf{c}^*} \Pr^o(\mathbf{f} \mid \mathbf{C}) \cdot \Pr^o(\mathbf{C})\right)}{\prod_{\mathbf{C}}\Pr^o(\mathbf{f} \mid \mathbf{C}) \cdot \Pr^o(\mathbf{C})}$$

where $\mathbf{C}\backslash\mathbf{c}^*$ is used to denote the set of all joint assignments to $\mathbf{C}$ except $\mathbf{c}^*$. Substitution and simplification now gives

$$
\begin{aligned}
\Pr(\mathbf{c}\mid\mathbf{f}) &= \frac{\Pr^o(\mathbf{c}\mid\mathbf{f})\cdot\Pr(\mathbf{f}\mid\mathbf{c})\cdot\Pr(\mathbf{c})\cdot\prod_{\mathbf{C}\backslash\mathbf{c}}\Pr^o(\mathbf{f}\mid\mathbf{C})\cdot\Pr^o(\mathbf{C})}{\sum_{\mathbf{c}^*\in\mathbf{C}}\Pr^o(\mathbf{c}^*\mid\mathbf{f})\cdot\Pr(\mathbf{f}\mid\mathbf{c}^*)\cdot\Pr(\mathbf{c}^*)\cdot\prod_{\mathbf{C}\backslash\mathbf{c}^*}\Pr^o(\mathbf{f}\mid\mathbf{C})\cdot\Pr^o(\mathbf{C})} \\[2mm]
&= \frac{\Pr^o(\mathbf{c}\mid\mathbf{f})\cdot\prod_i\Pr(f_i\mid\mathbf{c},\mathbf{f}_{F_i})\cdot\Pr(\mathbf{c})\cdot\prod_{\mathbf{C}\backslash\mathbf{c}}\prod_i\Pr^o(f_i\mid\mathbf{C})\cdot\Pr^o(\mathbf{C})}{\sum_{\mathbf{c}^*\in\mathbf{C}}\left(\Pr^o(\mathbf{c}^*\mid\mathbf{f})\cdot\prod_i\Pr(f_i\mid\mathbf{c}^*,\mathbf{f}_{F_i})\cdot\Pr(\mathbf{c}^*)\cdot\prod_{\mathbf{C}\backslash\mathbf{c}^*}\prod_i\Pr^o(f_i\mid\mathbf{C},\mathbf{f}_{F_i})\cdot\Pr^o(\mathbf{C})\right)}
\end{aligned}
$$

in which we used that $\Pr(\mathbf{f}\mid\mathbf{c})=\prod_i\Pr(f_i\mid\mathbf{c},\mathbf{f}_{F_i})$ with $f_i,\mathbf{f}_{F_i}\sim\mathbf{f}$, and that $\Pr(\mathbf{c})=\prod_j\Pr(c_j)$ with $c_j\sim\mathbf{c}$. We then find that

$$
\Pr(\mathbf{c}\mid\mathbf{f})(\mathbf{x})=\frac{\Pr^o(\mathbf{c}\mid\mathbf{f})\cdot\prod_{x_i\sim\mathbf{c},x_j\not\sim\mathbf{c}}x_i\cdot x_j^o}{\sum_{\mathbf{c}^*\in\mathbf{C}}\left(\Pr^o(\mathbf{c}^*\mid\mathbf{f})\cdot\prod_{x_i\sim\mathbf{c}^*,x_j\not\sim\mathbf{c}^*}x_i\cdot x_j^o\right)} \qquad \square
$$

Proof of Proposition 2. For the one-way sensitivity function describing the output probability $\Pr(\mathbf{c}\mid\mathbf{f})$ of an MDC in a parameter $x\sim\mathbf{c}$, we have that $\Pr(\mathbf{c}\mid\mathbf{f})(x)=(x\cdot r)/(x\cdot s+t)$, where $r,s,t\geq 0$ since these constants arise from multiplication and addition of probabilities. The function's first derivative equals $\Pr(\mathbf{c}\mid\mathbf{f})'(x)=(r\cdot t)/(s\cdot x+t)^2$, which is always positive. Irrespective of the values of the other parameters in the classifier therefore, an increase in value of $x\sim\mathbf{c}$ will result in an increase of $\Pr(\mathbf{c}\mid\mathbf{f})$. Similarly, the output probability increases with a decrease in value of $x\not\sim\mathbf{c}$. $\qquad\square$

Proof of Proposition 3. Let $MDC(\mathbf{C},\mathbf{F})$, $\mathbf{G}$ and $\mathbf{x}$ be as stated in the proposition, and let $\mathbf{H}$ be such that $\mathbf{H}=\mathbf{F}\backslash\mathbf{G}$. We first show that the proposition holds for any value combination $\mathbf{c}\in\mathbf{C}$ given a fixed instance $\mathbf{f}$. Using Proposition 1 we find that

$$
O(\mathbf{c}\mid\mathbf{f})(\mathbf{x})=\frac{\Pr(\mathbf{c}\mid\mathbf{f})(\mathbf{x})}{1-\Pr(\mathbf{c}\mid\mathbf{f})(\mathbf{x})}=\frac{\Pr^o(\mathbf{c}\mid\mathbf{f})\cdot\prod_{x_i\sim\mathbf{c},x_j\not\sim\mathbf{c}}x_i\cdot x_j^o}{\sum_{\mathbf{c}^*\in\mathbf{C}\backslash\mathbf{c}}\left(\Pr^o(\mathbf{c}^*\mid\mathbf{f})\cdot\prod_{x_i\sim\mathbf{c}^*,x_j\not\sim\mathbf{c}^*}x_i\cdot x_j^o\right)}
$$

from which we find

$$
\frac{O(\mathbf{c}\mid\mathbf{f})(\mathbf{x})}{O^o(\mathbf{c}\mid\mathbf{f})}=\frac{\sum_{\mathbf{c}^*\in\mathbf{C}\backslash\mathbf{c}}\left(\Pr^o(\mathbf{c}^*\mid\mathbf{f})\cdot\prod_{x_i\sim\mathbf{c},x_j\not\sim\mathbf{c}}x_i\cdot x_j^o\right)}{\sum_{\mathbf{c}^*\in\mathbf{C}\backslash\mathbf{c}}\left(\Pr^o(\mathbf{c}^*\mid\mathbf{f})\cdot\prod_{x_i\sim\mathbf{c}^*,x_j\not\sim\mathbf{c}^*}x_i\cdot x_j^o\right)}
$$

and hence

$$
\min_{\mathbf{c}^*\in\mathbf{C}\backslash\mathbf{c}}\frac{\prod_{x_i\sim\mathbf{c},x_j\not\sim\mathbf{c}}x_i\cdot x_j^o}{\prod_{x_i\sim\mathbf{c}^*,x_j\not\sim\mathbf{c}^*}x_i\cdot x_j^o}\leq\frac{O(\mathbf{c}\mid\mathbf{f})(\mathbf{x})}{O^o(\mathbf{c}\mid\mathbf{f})}\leq\max_{\mathbf{c}^*\in\mathbf{C}\backslash\mathbf{c}}\frac{\prod_{x_i\sim\mathbf{c},x_j\not\sim\mathbf{c}}x_i\cdot x_j^o}{\prod_{x_i\sim\mathbf{c}^*,x_j\not\sim\mathbf{c}^*}x_i\cdot x_j^o}
$$

If $\mathbf{x}$ includes all parameters of the classifier, from each probability table exactely two parameters will not cancel out from the fraction $(\prod_{x_i \sim \mathbf{c}, x_j \propto \mathbf{c}} x_i \cdot x_j^o) / (\prod_{x_i \sim \mathbf{c}^*, x_j \propto \mathbf{c}^*} x_i \cdot x_j^o)$. For each such parameter x, the fraction includes either $\frac{x}{x^o}$ or $\frac{x^o}{x}$. Now, for $\alpha \geq 1$, we have that $\frac{x}{x^o}, \frac{x^o}{x} \in [1/\alpha, \alpha]$. With a balanced sensitivity function therefore, the minimum of the fraction equals $1/\alpha^k$ and the maximum is α^k, where k is two times the number of probability tables. If $\mathbf{x}$ includes just a subset of the classifier's parameters, we find that $k = s + 2 \cdot t$, where s is the number of probability tables from which just a single parameter is in $\mathbf{x}$ and t is the number of tables with two or more parameters in $\mathbf{x}$.

For an instance $\mathbf{f}' \propto \mathbf{f}$, we find $\Pr(\mathbf{c} \,|\, \mathbf{f}')$ by replacing (some of) the parameters in the fraction above by their proportional co-variant, which gives $\frac{1-x}{1-x^o}$ or its reciprocal. Since for $\alpha \geq 1$, these fractions are in $[1/\alpha, \alpha]$ as well, the proof above generalises to all instances in $\mathbf{F}$. For a partial instance $\mathbf{g}$ we have that $\Pr(\mathbf{C} \,|\, \mathbf{g}) = \sum_{\mathbf{H}} \Pr(\mathbf{C} \,|\, \mathbf{g}, \mathbf{H}) \cdot \Pr(\mathbf{H} \,|\, \mathbf{g})$. Since $(O(\mathbf{C} \,|\, \mathbf{gH}))/(O^o(\mathbf{C} \,|\, \mathbf{gH})) \in [1/\alpha^k, \alpha^k]$ and $\sum_{\mathbf{H}} \Pr(\mathbf{H} \,|\, \mathbf{g}) = 1$, we further find that $(O(\mathbf{C} \,|\, \mathbf{g}))/(O^o(\mathbf{C} \,|\, \mathbf{g})) \in [1/\alpha^k, \alpha^k]$ for all $\mathbf{g} \in \mathbf{G}$. $\qquad\square$

References

1. Bielza, C., Li, G., Larrañaga, P.: Multi-dimensional classification with Bayesian networks. Int. J. Approximate Reasoning **52**, 705–727 (2011)
2. De Bock, J., de Campos, C.P., Antonucci, A.: Global sensitivity analysis for MAP inference in graphical models. In: Ghahramani, Z., Welling, M., Cortes, C., Lawrence, N.D., Weinberger, K.Q. (eds.) Advances in Neural Information Processing Systems, vol. 27, pp. 2690–2698 (2014)
3. Bolt, J.H., Renooij, S.: Local sensitivity of Bayesian networks to multiple parameter shifts. In: van der Gaag, L.C., Feelders, A.J. (eds.) PGM 2014. LNCS, vol. 8754, pp. 65–80. Springer, Switzerland (2014)
4. Borchani, H., Bielza, C., Toro, C., Larrañaga, P.: Predicting human immunodeficiency virus inhibitors using multi-dimensional Bayesian network classifiers. Artif. Intell. Med. **57**, 219–229 (2013)
5. Chan, H., Darwiche, A.: A distance measure for bounding probabilistic belief change. Int. J. Approximate Reasoning **38**, 149–174 (2005)
6. van der Gaag, L.C., de Waal, P.R.: Multi-dimensional Bayesian network classifiers. In: Vomlel, J., Studený, M. (eds.) Proceedings of the Third European Workshop in Probabilistic Graphical Models, pp. 107–114 (2006)
7. Pearl, J.: Probabilistic Reasoning in Intelligent Systems: Networks of Plausible Inference. Morgan Kaufmann Publishers, Palo Alto (1988)
8. Renooij, S.: Co-variation for sensitivity analysis in Bayesian networks: properties, consequences and alternatives. Int. J. Approximate Reasoning **55**, 1022–1042 (2014)
9. de Waal, P.R., van der Gaag, L.C.: Inference and learning in multi-dimensional Bayesian network classifiers. In: Mellouli, K. (ed.) ECSQARU 2007. LNCS (LNAI), vol. 4724, pp. 501–511. Springer, Heidelberg (2007)

A New View of Conformity and Its Application to Classification

Myriam Bounhas[1,2]([envelope]), Henri Prade[3,4], and Gilles Richard[3]

[1] LARODEC Laboratory, ISG de Tunis, Tunis, Tunisia
myriam_bounhas@yahoo.fr
[2] Emirates College of Technology, Abu Dhabi, UAE
[3] IRIT, Université Paul Sabatier, 118 Route de Narbonne,
31062 Toulouse Cedex 09, France
{prade,richard}@irit.fr
[4] QCIS, University of Technology, Sydney, Australia

Abstract. The paper discusses a new way of estimating the conformity of an item, described in terms of Boolean-valued features, with respect to a class of items. A usual view of conformity is to compare, feature by feature, the item value with the corresponding distribution of values observed over the class. Then combining the comparison results for the different features yields a global conformity measure. In this paper, the item is rather compared to triples of elements taken in the class: it is checked if the item conforms, over a maximal number of features, to the majority of the elements in each triple. Based on the idea that a new item should be allocated the class to which it conforms the most, a simple classification algorithm is proposed. Experiments on a set of benchmarks show that it is competitive with classical methods.

1 Introduction

The conformity of a new item x wrt an existing set of items $\mathcal{C}$ is generally viewed in terms of the agreement of each feature value of x with the distribution of the values for this feature among the items constituting the set $\mathcal{C}$. All items are described in terms of a common set of relevant features. The distribution of each feature (or more generally each group of features) is usually probabilistic and then based on the histogram of the observed values. However, if the set $\mathcal{C}$ is rather defined in intention (e.g. the set of *recent* and *cheap* items) by means of more or less desirable values for the features (considered individually or jointly), then possibility distributions may be used, and the conformity of an item x wrt a set $\mathcal{C}$ may be viewed as a fuzzy pattern matching problem [4,5].

In the above views, the conformity is estimated by confronting a feature-based description of the new item x with a representation of the set $\mathcal{C}$ in terms of feature distributions. The *conformity measure* is then expressed in terms of conditional probabilities or possibilities. Then, in a classification problem, given the conformity measure of x wrt classes, x is allocated to the one maximizing this number. *Conformal predictors* [10] offer a renewed, formal, expression of

© Springer International Publishing Switzerland 2015
S. Destercke and T. Denoeux (Eds.): ECSQARU 2015, LNAI 9161, pp. 221–232, 2015.
DOI: 10.1007/978-3-319-20807-7_20

this principle. Roughly speaking, with a conformal predictor, a new item x is associated to the class that maximizes the proportion (or p-value) of elements in the class "stranger"(i.e. with a lower conformity) than x.

In this paper, in the case of Boolean features, we adopt a slightly different view, where the evaluation of the conformity relies on a local view: an item is all the more conforming to a set $\mathcal{C}$ that it conforms to a maximum number of small subsets of $\mathcal{C}$. The paper is organized as follows. In Sect. 2, a new way of estimating the conformity of an item wrt a set of items is advocated. It is based on judging if for each feature the value of the item is identical to the one of the majority over a maximum number of triples taken from the considered set. On this basis a classification algorithm is implemented, where the new item is allocated to the class to which it conforms the most in the above sense. Using the same conformity measure, another algorithm is proposed with a cross-conformal flavor [12], where we use p-values (i.e. the proportions of items with lower conformity measure than the current one). The 2 algorithms are experimented on several classification benchmarks. Results competitive with standard approaches are reported in Sect. 4. Moreover the simple conformity-based algorithm seems to obtain results that are comparable to the one based on p-values, with a lower computational complexity.

2   Evaluating Conformity

In this section, after briefly examining a common view of conformity in terms of majority among a whole class, we advocate another way of judging conformity on the basis of majority inside triples.

Let us introduce some notations. $\mathcal{C}$ denotes a set of items known to belong to the same class C. Each element in $\mathcal{C}$ is supposed to be described by a Boolean vector of n feature values. Namely, $x \in \mathcal{C}$ and $x = (x_1, \cdots, x_n)$ and $\forall i, x_i \in \{0, 1\}$. Let $d = (d_1, \cdots, d_n)$ be a new item, for which we want to evaluate the conformity with $\mathcal{C}$.

2.1   Usual View of Conformity

In the classical Bayesian view, we have $Prob(C|d) = \frac{1}{Z} \times Prob(C) \times \prod_{i=1}^{n} Prob(d_i|C)$ assuming that the n features are independent. The evidence Z depends only on d, $Prob(C)$ reflects some characteristics of C such as its size, and $\prod_{i=1}^{n} Prob(d_i|C)$ evaluates the conformity of $d = (d_1, \cdots, d_n)$ with $\mathcal{C}$. But under some conditional independence assumptions, this probability can be rewritten as a weighted product of $Prob(d_i|C)$, i.e. the conditional probability to get value d_i for feature i in the class C. Usually, $Prob(d_i|C)$ is estimated as the frequency of elements having value d_i for feature i in the whole class C. Thus, the expression of $Prob(C|d)$ involves the product of $Prob(C)$ with a kind of conjunctive combination expressed by the product of the proportion of elements of $\mathcal{C}$ identical to d for each feature i. A counterpart of this evaluation exists in the setting of possibility theory [2]. In the case of Boolean features, let $p(\mathcal{C}, i)$

be the proportion of the majority value for feature i in $\mathcal{C}$. Then, an elementary estimation of $Prob(C|\boldsymbol{d})$ is

$$\frac{1}{Z} \times Prob(C) \times \prod_{i \in M} p(\mathcal{C}, i) \times \prod_{j \in \overline{M}} (1 - p(\mathcal{C}, j))$$

where $M \subseteq \{1, \cdots, n\}$ is the subset of features where $\boldsymbol{d}$ is conform to the majority in $\mathcal{C}$, and $\overline{M}$ is the complementary subset where $\boldsymbol{d}$ is not conform to the majority. The idea of conformity in this approach is thus related to the notion of majority wrt the *whole* set $\mathcal{C}$ itself. In the following, we investigate the idea of judging conformity wrt *a collection of smaller subsets* of $\mathcal{C}$ and provide some empirical evidence in favor of this idea.

2.2   A View of Conformity Based on Triples

We suggest here to consider this majority with regard to the smallest sets where a strict majority always appears. In the case of Boolean values (1 and 0), the smallest subsets are clearly triples. Let $\boldsymbol{a}$, $\boldsymbol{b}$, $\boldsymbol{c}$ be three elements in $\mathcal{C}$, and let a, b, c be the values of their component corresponding to a particular feature i. Then, in a Boolean world, there are two possibilities, either $a = b = c$, or two of the three are equal. In both cases, a strict majority takes place. Let m denote the majority value. Now consider the newcomer $\boldsymbol{d}$ with value d for feature i. Either $d = m$, and m remains the majority value in $\{a, b, c, d\}$, or $d \neq m$, and *there is no longer any majority in* $\{a, b, c, d\}$ (two values are equal to 1 and two values to 0). Only with the first case, d conforms to the majority.

Note that if we consider *larger* subsets in $\mathcal{C}$, even with only 4 elements rather than 3, it becomes possible that the newcomer increases the minority, without changing the majority. Indeed, the majority value that may be shared by 3 elements in the 4-elements subset will then remain unchanged in the 5-elements subset resulting from the arrival of a fifth element whatever its value. A similar phenomenon takes place if we start with larger subsets in $\mathcal{C}$ having 5 elements or more. So we are losing a distinctive property of 3-elements subsets which have a different majority behavior depending if d conforms or not to the majority in the 3-elements subset. *This means that triples are the only subsets such that adding an item that does not conform to the triple majority destroys the majority.* Thus, 3-elements subsets are able to clearly discriminate, among different d those that conform to the majority of the triple.

The idea of conformity just described may receive a logical reading, by defining it as $Even(a, b, c, d)$:

$$Even(a, b, c, d) =_{def} H_4(a, b, c, d) \vee Eq(a, b, c, d)$$

where $Eq(a, b, c, d) =_{def} (d = a) \wedge (d = b) \wedge (d = c)$ and $H_4(a, b, c, d)$ is such that:

$H_4(a, b, c, d) = 1$
    if $(a, b, c, d) \in \{(1, 1, 0, 1), (1, 0, 1, 1), (0, 1, 1, 1), (0, 0, 1, 0), (0, 1, 0, 0), (1, 0, 0, 0)\}$

$H_4(a, b, c, d) = 0$ otherwise.

As can be seen, $H_4(a, b, c, d) = 1$ if and only if there is an *intruder* value in $\{a, b, c, d\}$ which is not d. It is worth noticing that $H_4(a, b, c, d)$ has been recently identified as one of the four existing heterogeneous logical proportions that are quaternary connectives built on the basis of the comparison of similarity and dissimilarity indicators pertaining to pairs (a, b), and (c, d). A completely different type of logical proportions, called homogeneous, includes analogical proportions that have also been proved suitable for classification task [1,3,7]. See [8] for an introduction to homogeneous and heterogeneous logical proportions. The situations where $Even(a, b, c, d) = 1$ exactly cover the two cases already mentioned where d is identical to the majority value in the triple $\{a, b, c\}$, namely either $a = b = c$, or two of the three are equal to d. So the fact that d joins $\{a, b, c\}$, when $Even(a, b, c, d) = 1$, leaves the resulting subset as *even* as it was, hence the name, and in fact the majority is reinforced by the arrival of d. Note also that $Even(a, b, c, d)$ is left unchanged by any permutation of $\{a, b, c\}$. This means that the ordering inside triples does not matter. Besides, $Even(a, b, c, d) = Even(\overline{a}, \overline{b}, \overline{c}, \overline{d})$ where $\overline{x} = 1$ if $x = 0$ and $\overline{x} = 0$ if $x = 1$, expressing that $Even(a, b, c, d)$ does not depend on the way the information is encoded.

If we want to evaluate to what extent a vector d conforms with a set $\mathcal{C}$ for a feature i, we have clearly to consider all the triples $\{a, b, c\}$ in $\mathcal{C}$ (or in practice a large representative subset of all the triples). This leads to use the definition of $Even(a, b, c, d)$ as a basic brick to define a global evenness-measure $Even(\mathcal{C}, d_i)$ of d wrt $\mathcal{C}$ for feature i:

$$Even(\mathcal{C}, d_i) = \Sigma_{(a,b,c) \in \mathcal{C}^3} Even(a_i, b_i, c_i, d_i).$$

It should be clear that the stronger the majority in $\mathcal{C}$ in favor of a particular value for a feature i, the larger the number of triples $\{a_i, b_i, c_i\}$ such that $Even(a_i, b_i, c_i, d_i) = 1$ when d_i is in conformity with this majority. Observe also that if there is only one exceptional value, distinct of all the other values all equal to m for feature i in $\mathcal{C}$, then for *all* the triples in $\mathcal{C}$ $Even(a_i, b_i, c_i, d_i) = 1$ if $d_i = m$. If there are two values different from m, then this still holds, except for $|\mathcal{C}| - 2$ triples. Thus high values of $Even(\mathcal{C}, d_i)$ reflect that there are few exceptions in $\mathcal{C}$, distinct from d_i, regarding the value of feature i. Moreover, it can be checked that if we add to $\mathcal{C}$ an element d such as $Even(a_i, b_i, c_i, d_i) = 1$ for *all* triples, thus building a new subset $\mathcal{C}' = \mathcal{C} \cup \{d\}$, then $Even(a'_i, b'_i, c'_i, d'_i) = 1$ will be preserved for all triples in $\mathcal{C}'$ wrt a new comer d'.

In order to measure to what extent a vector d conforms to $\mathcal{C}$, we have to consider all features. This leads to define

$$Even(\mathcal{C}, d) =_{def} \Sigma_{i=1}^{n} Even(\mathcal{C}, d_i)$$

Clearly, $Even(\mathcal{C}, d)$ is all the greater as there does not exist many features where d behaves as an intruder for a larger number of triples. Then, the larger $Even(\mathcal{C}, d)$, the better d conforms to $\mathcal{C}$. However, note the independence assumption underlying the latter summation, where all features are considered individually.

2.3   Normalization

Clearly, $Even(\mathcal{C}, d_i)$ belongs to $[0, \binom{|\mathcal{C}|}{3}]$, and $Even(\mathcal{C}, \boldsymbol{d})$ to $[0, n \cdot \binom{|\mathcal{C}|}{3}]$. Thus, it may seem natural to normalize by dividing $Even(\mathcal{C}, d_i)$ by $\binom{|\mathcal{C}|}{3}$. This leads to

$$Even^*(\mathcal{C}, \boldsymbol{d}) = \frac{1}{\binom{|\mathcal{C}|}{3}} Even(\mathcal{C}, \boldsymbol{d}).$$

where $Even^*(\mathcal{C}, \boldsymbol{d}) \in [0, n]$.

But, we have to remember the Bayesian lesson where the conformity is multiplied by the prior $Prob(C)$, for acknowledging the fact that for the same level of conformity, we should favor the largest class. This is not taken into account by $Even^*(\mathcal{C}, \boldsymbol{d})$. $Prob(C)$ is usually taken as $|\mathcal{C}|/N$ where N is the total number of elements in the training set. Besides, since $\binom{|\mathcal{C}|}{3}$ has the same order of magnitude as $|\mathcal{C}|^3$ for large classes, $Even^*(\mathcal{C}, \boldsymbol{d})$ may be estimated as

$$Even^{**}(\mathcal{C}, \boldsymbol{d}) = \frac{1}{|\mathcal{C}|^2} Even(\mathcal{C}, \boldsymbol{d}).$$

As we understand from this discussion, the formula $Even(a, b, c, d)$ can be used as a building block for defining a conformity measure of a new item d with respect to a set $\mathcal{C}$. In the following section, we briefly recall how a conformity (or non-conformity) measure can be used as the underlying concept to build up valid machine learning algorithms. Since it would be too time-consuming to consider all the triples in a set $\mathcal{C}$, we restrict one of the elements of the triples to be among the k nearest neighbors of $\boldsymbol{d}$ (some experiments have shown that this does not lead to significant difference on the results). So the order of magnitude of the number of triples is now $k \cdot |\mathcal{C}|^2$ rather than $|\mathcal{C}|^3$. So the conformity measure that will be used in practice is (we omit the division by k since it is a constant):

$$Even^{***}(\mathcal{C}, \boldsymbol{d}) =_{def} \frac{1}{|\mathcal{C}|} \Sigma_{i=1}^n \Sigma_{(a,b)\in\mathcal{C}^2, \ c \text{ is a } k \text{ nearest neighbor of } d} \ Even(a_i, b_i, c_i, d_i).$$

Since the conformity measure has to be maximized, we may focus on triples for which $\boldsymbol{d}$ is an intruder for at most $n - l$ features, where $l = 0, 1, \cdots$. Then, instead of keeping all the triples, we can just choose a threshold $l \in [0, n]$, and consider only the triples $(\boldsymbol{a}, \boldsymbol{b}, \boldsymbol{c})$ in $\mathcal{C}$ where $\Sigma_{i\in[1,n]} Even(a_i, b_i, c_i, d_i) \geq l$.

Thus, we see that $Even^{***}(\mathcal{C}, \boldsymbol{d})$ may be considered as a conformity measure in the sense given in [9, 11]. In the next section, we briefly recall how a conformity (or non-conformity) measure can be used as the underlying concept to build up classifiers.

3   Conformal Predictors

Conformal predictions provide solid foundations to design machine learning algorithm, with sound theoretical properties. We may refer to [11] for a deep analysis of this framework and to [10] for a comprehensive tutorial. We just recall here the philosophy of conformal prediction. The main tool to build up such a predictor is the concept of *non conformity* or *conformity* measure. Roughly speaking, the non-conformity $nonConf(S, z)$ of a given element z to an existing set S of observed data is a real number measuring to what extend z can be considered as an outsider w.r.t. the elements of S. The dual concept is the conformity measure, which can be build from a non-conformity measure by combining with a decreasing function such as: $conf(S, z) = \frac{1}{nonConf(S,z)}$, or $conf(S, z) = -nonConf(S, z)$. A lot of options are available. As soon as we have such a measure (let us say a conformity measure) at our disposal, a natural idea, when it comes to predict a new value among a set Z of candidate values, having already observed S, is to consider that the most suitable candidate z is the one maximising its conformity with S, i.e., something like $z_0 = argmax_{z \in Z} conf(S, z)$. Unfortunately, as these measures, both conformity and non conformity, are a matter of taste and provide a kind of absolute value which can be changed with the scale of the initial measure, it is much more clever to consider, for each element z the proportion of elements in S that are less conform than z: the larger this proportion, the better z conforms to S and the better z as a candidate to be the next element in S. This proportion is called the p-value of z wrt S.

Starting from a training set TS of already observed elements, the final option to build up a conformal predictor is

- to compute, for each element $s \in TS$, $conf(TS \setminus \{s\} \cup \{z\}, s)$,
- then $p\text{-value}(TS, z) = \frac{|\{s \in TS | conf(TS \setminus \{s\} \cup \{z\}, s) \leq conf(TS, z)\}|}{|TS| + 1}$

The most suitable candidate is now: $z_0 = argmax_z p\text{-value}(TS, z)$. One of the most outstanding properties of conformal predictors is the fact that, instead of simply giving flat predictions, they provide a confidence measure of the given prediction. In this paper, we do not deal with this aspect of conformal predictors.

In classification, a new item z has to be associated with a class and the previous definitions still apply but considering now an element as a pair (z, l_z) where l_z is the label of z. This leads to the basic procedure defining a conformal classifier as follows:

for each label $l \in C$ (C is a set of labels or classes)

- compute $p\text{-value}(TS, (z, l)) = \frac{|\{s \in TS | conf(TS \setminus \{s\} \cup \{(z,l)\}, s) \leq conf(TS, (z,l))\}|}{|S|}$
- allocate to z the label $l_0 = argmax_l \ p\text{-value}(TS, (z, l))$

Roughly speaking, we allocate to z the label which makes it to conform the best to the corresponding class. It is quite clear that, despite its elegant theoretical results, this framework leads to very processing intensive algorithms and are only practical for small data sets. As such, they have to be optimized and we recall below a way to perform such an optimization as it has been described by [12].

3.1   Other Types of Conformity-Based Predictors

Looking for more computationally efficient algorithms, inductive conformal predictors and cross conformal predictors have been designed in [9,12]. The main idea is to split the initial training set and to introduce a new way to compute the p-values.

- Regarding inductive conformal predictors, TS is split into a pure training set S and a disjoint calibration set C such that $S \cup C = TS$. Then a new calculation of the p-values is given still leading to valid predictors.
- Cross conformal predictors are inspired by the cross-validation method where the training set TS is split into a finite set of folds. A more sophisticated p-value definition is given. Unfortunately, the theoretical properties of these cross-conformal predictors have still to be investigated as they do not exactly follow the initial conformal framework: their validity is more an empirical observation rather than a mathematical fact.

Our approach is inspired by the cross-conformal approach but does not follow the exact scheme. Still, the training set TS is split into non overlapping subsets Y_i: in the case of classification, the simplest option is to consider a partition of TS via the classes and $C_j = \{s \in TS | label(s) = j\}$.

Given a new item z to be classified, when allocating to z a candidate label l, we just compute p-value$(C_l, (z, l)$ instead of computing a p-value wrt the whole training set TS. This is a way to drastically reduce the time complexity of the initial procedure. We give below the main lines of our classification procedure in Algorithm 1 with $conf(C, d) = Even^{***}(C, d)$, for fixed values of k and l (see the end of Sect. 2).

Algorithm 1.

Input: a training set TS of examples $z = (x, cl(x))$
a new item d, a conformity measure $conf$
Algo:
Partition TS into sets C of examples having the same label cl. // cl is the label of the class C
for each C **do**
  Compute $conf(C, d)$ i.e. the conformity measure of d w.r.t. C.
  For each $z \in C$, compute $\alpha_z = conf(C \cup \{d\} \setminus \{z\}, z)$
  Compute p-value$(C, d) = \frac{|\{z \in C \cup \{d\} | \alpha_z \leq conf(C, d)\}|}{|C| + 1}$
end for
$cl(d) = argmax_{label(C)}\{p\text{-value}(C, d)\}$
Output: $cl(d)$

Algorithm 2.

Input: a training set TS of examples $z = (x, cl(x))$
a new item d, the conformity measure $Even^{***}(C, d)$, for fixed values of k and l
Algo:
Partition TS into sets C of examples having the same label cl.
for each C **do**
  Compute $Even(C, d)$
end for
$cl(d) = argmax_{label(C)}\{Even(C, d)\}$
Output: $cl(d)$

3.2   Another Simplified Option

Despite we have reduced the set of explored elements, our predictors are still very resource-consuming, just because a lot of numbers have to be computed in order to get a single p-value. A more simple option is just to compute the evenness measure such as defined in the previous section, (instead of computing the real p-values). This leads to a procedure described in Algorithm 2.

Both Algorithms 1 and 2 have been implemented, using our evenness measure as a conformity measure. Results of experiments are described in the next section.

4   Experimentations and Discussion

This section provides experimental results for the two "conformity"-based classifiers. The experimental study is based on several data sets selected from the U.C.I. machine learning repository [6] where we focus on classification problems involving categorical attributes only:

- Balance and Car are multiple classes databases.
- Voting, Spect, Monk1, Monk2, Monk3 data sets are binary class problems. Monk3 has noise added (in the training set only).
- Voting and Spect data sets contain only binary attributes. Voting dataset has missing attribute values.

All non binary attributes are encoded in the Boolean setting so that to be handled in this context. A brief description of these data sets is given in Table 1. In terms of protocol, we apply a standard 10 folds cross-validation technique and we run our tests for the two conformity-based classifiers described with Algorithms 1 and 2.

In Table 2, we provide mean accuracies and standard deviations for the two proposed classifiers for different values of k and l (k being the number of nearest neighbors of d, l refers to the number of attributes i of d such that d_i belongs to a majority). The first two columns correspond to the results of Algorithm 1

Table 1. Description of datasets

Datasets	Instances	Nominal Att.	Binary Att.	Classes
Balance	625	4	20	3
Car	743	6	21	4
TicTacToe	405	9	27	2
Voting	435	-	16	2
Spect Heart	267	-	22	2
Monk1	432	6	15	2
Monk2	432	6	15	2
Monk3	432	6	15	2

Table 2. Results for the two classifiers

Datasets		Algo1		Algo2	
	k	$\ell = n$	$\ell = n - 1$	$\ell = n$	$\ell = n - 1$
Balance	1	79.99±3.19	81.78±4.71	79.0±4.3	86.1±2.5
	3	82.53± 3.32	81.64±3.39	82.2±3.6	87.4±1.7
	5	83.36±2.7	82.25±3.16	83.1±3.4	**88.0±1.1**
Car	1	87.6±2.61	87.05 ±3.61	91.2±3.4	88.9±4.3
	3	90.7±3.35	89.65±3.21	91.7±2.8	89.0±4.1
	5	91.51±3.27	90.32±2.43	**92.0±2.7**	90.6±4.4
Tic Tac Toe	1	80.31±5.45	82.07±5.57	82.55±5.76	86.78±5.75
	3	81.07±6.45	85.01±5.6	83.54±6.13	87.47±4.61
	5	82.78±4.84	**88.45±3.75**	84.51±5.37	88.21±4.247
Voting	1	93.1±3.8	93.1±3.8	94.5±2.8	94.7±3.0
	3	94.5±3.9	94.5±3.9	94.9±2.7	94.9±3.1
	5	94.5±3.9	94.5±3.9	**95.2±2.7**	95.2±3.0
Spect	1	83.9±2.2	79.5±2.0	83.2±4.79	76.9±5.8
	3	79.4±3.9	79.1±2.0	84.0±3.3	76.6±6.0
	5	79.4±3.9	79.5±2.0	**84.3±4.0**	76.6±6.0
Monk1	1	99.5±0.9	99.5±0.9	**100**	**100**
	3	99.5±0.9	98.8±1.9	**100**	**100**
	5	99.5±0.9	99.3±1.1	**100**	**100**
Monk2	1	44.0±5.6	34.8±6.7	50.7±5.6	47.2±4.6
	3	48.4±5.2	33.1±6.4	54.8±5.26	54.9±4.3
	5	52.8±5.8	35.7±6.6	57.8±4.9	**61.8±4.7**
Monk3	1	**100**	99.8±0.7	**100**	**100**
	3	99.5±1.4	99.3±1.4	**100**	99.3±1.5
	5	99.8±0.7	99.1±1.5	**100**	99.3±1.5

and the two second columns correspond to Algorithm 2. The best results are highlighted in bold.

In order to evaluate the efficiency of these classifiers, we compare their accuracies to off-the-shelves classifiers. Table 3 includes classification results with SVM, k-Nearest Neighbors IBk for k=1, k=10, JRip (an optimized propositional rule learner) and the standard Naive Bayes (NB). Accuracy results are obtained using the free implementation of Weka software.

From Table 2, we can make the following comments:

- The "conformity"-based classifier described by Algorithm 2 exhibits results as good as the ones of Algorithm 1 for all datasets for $l = n$.
- For $l = n - 1$, the "conformity"-based classifier is less efficient than the p-value classifier for dataset "Spect.", more efficient for datasets "Balance" and "Monk2" and has equivalent results for other datasets. For a given d to be

Table 3. Results for well-known classifiers

Datasets	SVM	IBk (k=1, k=10)	JRIP	NB	Algo2 (k=5,l=n)
Balance	90	83, 83	76	91	83
Car	91	92, 92	91	86	**92**
Tic Tac Toe	100	98, 93	95	79	84
Voting	96	93, 92	95	90	95
Spect	81	75, 81	81	79	**84**
Monk1	75	100, 100	98	75	**100**
Monk2	67	44 , 64	73	60	58
Monk3	100	100, 99	100	97	**100**

classified, if there are many *irrelevant* items z (such that $\alpha_z = 0$ for many classes) used to compute the p-value in Algorithm 1, this may perturb the classification. Since Algorithm 2 uses $Even(\mathcal{C}, \boldsymbol{d})$ to measure the class conformity, it seems to be less sensitive to irrelevant data.

- The two algorithms achieve the best classification rates if $l = n$. This means that the classifiers are likely to be more accurate when the classification is made on the basis of triples for which *all* attributes of d belongs to a majority. However, for some datasets such as Balance and Monk2, the classifier needs to consider more levels l when it is difficult to satisfy the constraint $\Sigma_{i\in[1,n]}Even(a_i, b_i, c_i, d_i) \geq l$ for $l = n$ or even $l = n-1$. Thus, we also tested smaller levels of l and for "Balance" and "Monk2" data sets, we get an accuracy respectively equal to 90.1 ± 1.74 and 67.13 ± 0.61 with Algorithm 2 for $l = n-3$.
- Algorithm 2 exhibits good results in spite of implementing a simplified procedure (whose complexity is much less than the one of Algorithm 1).
- The classification success of the classifier for Balance and Car (which have multiple classes) suggests its ability to deal with multiple class data sets.
- If we analyze results in Table 3, we note that the two proposed classifiers perform as well as the best known algorithms like SVM on many datasets. In particular, Algorithm 2, with a large k works as well as any other classifiers for data sets Balance (for $l = n-3$), Spect., Monk1 and Monk3 (for $l = n$), and reaches results similar to SVM for Monk2 dataset (for $l = n-3$).
- If we compare our results to the Naive Bayes classifier (NB), it is clear that the "conformity"-based classifier outperforms the NB for all datasets, except Monk2, and Balance where our classifiers perform worse.
- However, "conformity"-based classifiers seem to be less efficient when dealing with the Monk2 and Tic Tac Toe data sets. Regarding Monk2, it is known that the underlying function ("having exactly two attributes with value 1") is more complicated than the functions underlying Monk1 and Monk3, and involves all the attributes (while in the two other functions only 3 attributes among 6 are involved in the hidden function). We suspect that the existence of a large discontinuity in the classification of data (a nearest neighbor $\boldsymbol{d}$ of

c will not generally be labeled with the same class $cl(c)$) may be too difficult to apprehend using the conformity measure. For Tic Tac Toe, we also notice that all attributes are involved in the classification function. Moreover, this data set contains the largest number of attributes among all datasets which may require a larger sample for an accurate prediction.

These experiments empirically confirm our initial intuition that working with subsets of triples instead of the whole set $\mathcal{C}$ may be of interest.

Lastly, although one may find a flavor of conformal prediction [11] in the two proposed approaches, the way we use the evenness measure, which may be viewed as a conformity measure, is quite different from conformal predictors. Moreover, the way we compute the p-values for a class in Algorithm 1 only considers examples belonging to this specific class. Although this is computationally less costly than in conformal predictors, Algorithm 1 remains a resource-consuming algorithm.

5   Conclusion

This paper has proposed a new way to evaluate the conformity of an item with respect to a set, which is based on the consideration of 3-elements subsets that enable us to discriminate the situations where the item is in conformity with the majority of the values in the subsets. By cumulating these elementary evaluations on triples, we have shown that it is possible to build a meaningful conformity measure. This measure has proved its effectiveness for designing simple classifiers that get competitive results on classical benchmark datasets.

References

1. Bayoudh, S., Miclet, L., Delhay, A.: Learning by analogy: a classification rule for binary and nominal data. In: Proceedings of the International Joint Conference on Artificial Intelligence IJCAI 2007, pp. 678–683 (2007)
2. Bounhas, M., Mellouli, K., Prade, H., Serrurier, M.: Possibilistic classifiers for numerical data. Soft Comput. **17**(5), 733–751 (2013)
3. Bounhas, M., Prade, H., Richard, G.: Analogical classification: a new way to deal with examples. In: 21st European Conference on Artificial Intelligence, ECAI 2014, 18–22 August 2014. Frontiers in Artificial Intelligence and Applications, vol. 263, pp. 135–140. IOS Press, Prague, Czech Republic (2014)
4. Cayrol, M., Farreny, H., Prade, H.: Fuzzy pattern matching. Kybernetes **11**, 103–116 (1982)
5. Dubois, D., Grabisch, M., De Mouzon, O., Prade, H.: A possibilistic framework for single-fault causal diagnosis under uncertainty. Int. J. Gen. Syst. **30**, 167–192 (2001)
6. Mertz, J., Murphy, P.: Uci repository of machine learning databases (2000). ftp://ftp.ics.uci.edu/pub/machine-learning-databases
7. Miclet, L., Bayoudh, S., Delhay, A.: Analogical dissimilarity: definition, algorithms and two experiments in machine learning. JAIR **32**, 793–824 (2008)

8. Prade, H., Richard, G.: Homogenous and heterogeneous logical proportions. IfCoLog J. Logics Appl. **1**(1), 1–51 (2014)
9. Saunders, C., Gammerman, A.J., Vovk, V.: Computationally efficient transductive machines. In: Arimura, H., Sharma, A.K., Jain, S. (eds.) ALT 2000. LNCS (LNAI), vol. 1968, pp. 325–333. Springer, Heidelberg (2000)
10. Shafer, G., Vovk, V.: A tutorial on conformal prediction. J. Mach. Learn. Res. **9**, 371–421 (2008)
11. Vovk, V., Gammerman, A., Saunders, C.: Machine-learning applications of algorithmic randomness. In: International Conference on Machine Learning, pp. 444–453 (1999)
12. Vovk, V.: Cross-conformal predictors. Annals Math. Artif. Intell. (2014)

Inconsistency

Using Shapley Inconsistency Values for Distributed Information Systems with Uncertainty

John Grant[1] and Anthony Hunter[2]([✉])

[1] Department of Computer Science and UMIACS, University of Maryland,
College Park, MD 20742, USA
[2] Department of Computer Science, University College London, Gower Street,
London WC1E 6BT, UK
anthony.hunter@ucl.ac.uk

Abstract. We study the problem of analyzing inconsistency in a distributed information system where the reliability of the sources is taken into account. We model uncertainty by assigning a probability to each source. This yields a definition of the expected inconsistency of the system. We also extend this with the use of Shapley values for determining the responsibility of each formula to inconsistency. Then we use the Shapley inconsistency values to assign an expected blame to each formula. From this we define the concept of weakness of a formula which represents the degree to which it should be deleted to resolve the inconsistency of the system.

1 Introduction

The general problem that we consider in this paper is the aggregation of information from multiple distributed sources (e.g. databases, information from the web, etc.). As a user, we ask queries of the sources and as a result we get answers. We do not control the sources, and we cannot change them. Our primary concern is to evaluate the answers we get back from the sources by considering the inconsistency between them with respect to integrity constraints that we may have.

We let $(K_1, ..., K_n)$ denote a tuple of sources of information, where each K_i is a set of formulae. We do not necessarily know the contents of each K_i; however, we can query each source. We assume that we have a priori a set of integrity constraints based on the context. Suppose we ask a question Q, and we get the answer A_i from source i (i.e. $K_i \vdash A_i$). We assume each A_i is a nonempty set of facts (i.e. a set of atoms or propositional letters). Then, for any question Q, there is an answer tuple $(A_1, ..., A_n)$. We do not formalize the query process in this paper, and so our starting point is the set of integrity constraints and the answer tuple.

S. Destercke and T. Denoeux (Eds.): ECSQARU 2015, LNAI 9161, pp. 235–245, 2015.
DOI: 10.1007/978-3-319-20807-7_21

Example 1. Suppose we are searching the web on information about Paris. From source 1, we get the facts listed in A_1 below, and from source 2, we get the facts listed in A_2. So for that query, we have the answer tuple (A_1, A_2) where

$$A_1 = \{\texttt{population(7million)}, \texttt{medianage(45)}\}$$
$$A_2 = \{\texttt{population(4million)}, \texttt{averagesalary(23KEuro)}\}$$

We assume first-order predicate logic for our language for integrity constraints; however, we will rewrite the integrity constraints to suit what might appear in the answer tuples. Thus, $\forall x \forall y (\texttt{population}(x) \wedge \texttt{population}(y) \rightarrow x = y)$ might be an integrity contraint for the first example. In this example we will use the instantiated version as $\neg\texttt{population(7million)} \vee \neg\texttt{population(4million)}$. So we will assume that each integrity constraint is a disjunction of negated atoms and write it as A_0.

Given an answer tuple $(A_1, ..., A_n)$ and the corresponding set of integrity constraints A_0, we will be interested in the consistency of $\cup_{i=0}^{n} A_i$, that is, whether $\cup_{i=0}^{n} A_i \vdash \perp$ where $\vdash$ denotes the classical consequence relation and $\perp$ stands for falsity. Thus, Example 1 with the given integrity constraint is inconsistent.

Given an answer tuple, and a set of integrity constraints, we want to be able to resolve inconsistencies by removing facts from answers. Our goal is to find the formulae that are for some good reasons the best to eliminate in order to restore consistency. To support this process, we will use measures of inconsistency. We will review these in the next section, but essentially, they assess the number of conflicts, the inter-connectedness of conflicts, the proportion of the information that is in conflict, etc.

In order to help analyse the conflict, we will also take the reliability of the sources of information into account. Let P be a function that assigns a value in $[0, 1]$ to each source $i \in \{1, .., n\}$. We assume that $P(i)$ denotes the probability that a randomly selected formula in A_i is correct based on previous performance by the source where the previous performance is determined from the correctness of previous answers when checked by an oracle/expert/etc. We also assign $P(A_0) = 1$, that is, all integrity constraints are known to be correct.

We formalize a novel approach to analyzing inconsistency by using probabilistic information about sources of information in conjunction with measures of inconsistency.

2   Background to Measuring Inconsistency

We assume a propositional language $\mathcal{L}$ of formulae composed from a set of atoms $\mathcal{A}$ and the logical connectives $\wedge$, $\vee$, $\neg$. A knowledgebase K is a finite set of formulae. We let $\vdash$ denote the classical consequence relation, and write $K \vdash \perp$ to denote that K is inconsistent. $\mathcal{R}^{\geq 0}$ is the set of nonnegative real numbers.

For a knowledgebase K, $\mathsf{MI}(K)$ is the set of minimal inconsistent subsets of K. $\mathsf{Free}(K)$ is the set of formulae not involved in any inconsistency and $\mathsf{Problematic}(K)$ is $K \setminus \mathsf{Free}(K)$. For one of the inconsistency measures we will use we define a semantics that uses Priest's three valued logic (3VL) [7] with the classical two valued semantics augmented by a third truth value, B (for both), denoting inconsistency. The truth values for the connectives are defined in the following table.

α	T	T	T	B	B	B	F	F	F
β	T	B	F	T	B	F	T	B	F
$\alpha \vee \beta$	T	T	T	T	B	B	T	B	F
$\alpha \wedge \beta$	T	B	F	B	B	F	F	F	F
$\neg\alpha$	F	F	F	B	B	B	T	T	T

An interpretation i is a function that assigns to each atom in K one of the three truth values: $i : \mathsf{Atoms}(K) \to \{F, B, T\}$. For an interpretation i the atoms that are assigned the truth value B represent the inconsistency for which we obtain $\mathsf{Conflictbase}(i) = \{\alpha \mid i(\alpha) = B\}$. A model of K is an interpretation where no formula is assigned the truth value F: $\mathsf{Models}(K) = \{i \mid$ for all $\phi \in K, i(\phi) = T$ or $i(\phi) = B\}$ Then, as a measure of inconsistency for K we define $\mathsf{Contension}(K) = \mathsf{Min}\{|\mathsf{Conflictbase}(i)| \mid i \in \mathsf{Models}(K)\}$. So the contension gives the minimal number of atoms that must be assigned B in order to get a 3VL model of K.

Example 2. For $K = \{a, \neg a, a \vee b, \neg b\}$, there are two models of K, i_1 and i_2, where $i_1(a) = B$, $i_1(b) = B$, $i_2(a) = B$, and $i_2(b) = F$. Therefore, $\mathsf{Conflictbase}(i_1) = 2$ and $\mathsf{Conflictbase}(i_2) = 1$. Hence, $\mathsf{Contension}(K) = 1$.

An inconsistency measure assigns a nonnegative real value to every knowledgebase. We assume several requirements for inconsistency measures [4]. The conditions ensure that all and only consistent knowledgebases get measure 0, the measure is monotonic for subsets, the removal of a formula that does not participate in an inconsistency leaves the measure unchanged, and the addition of a logically weaker formula cannot lead to a larger inconsistency than the addition of a logically stronger formula.

Definition 1. *An inconsistency measure $I : \mathcal{K} \to \mathcal{R}^{\geq 0}$ is a function such that the following four conditions hold $\forall K, K' \in \mathcal{K}_\mathcal{L}$, $\forall \alpha, \beta \in \mathcal{L}$.*

- *Consistency: $I(K) = 0$ iff K is consistent.*
- *Monotony: $I(K \cup K') \geq I(K)$.*
- *Free Formula Independence: If α is a free formula of K, then $I(K) = I(K \setminus \{\alpha\})$.*
- *Dominance: If $\alpha \vdash \beta$ and $\alpha \nvdash \perp$, then $I(K \cup \{\alpha\}) \geq I(K \cup \{\beta\})$.*

There are many inconsistency measures in the literature but we will just focus on two in this paper (where K is a knowledgebase): $I_C(K) = |\mathsf{MI}(K)|$ is the inconsistency measure that counts the number of inconsistent subsets of K [3,4]; and

$I_B(K) = \mathsf{Contension}(K)$ is the inconsistency measure that counts the minimum number of atoms that need to be assigned B amongst the 3VL models of K [1,2,5].

We wish to compute the blame of each formula towards inconsistency. For this purpose we use a given inconsistency measure as the payoff function defining a game in coalitional form, and then use the Shapley value to compute the part of the inconsistency that can be imputed to each formula of the belief base [4]. Consider a game with players $1, \ldots, n$ whose utility function u assigns a nonnegative value to each coalition $C \subseteq \{1, \ldots, n\}$ such that if $C_1 \subseteq C_2$ then $u(C_1) \leq u(C_2)$. The Shapley value calculates each player's contribution to the utility of the coalitions the player joins in an optimal way. In our framework, following [4], we have a knowledgebase $K = \{\alpha_1, \ldots, \alpha_N\}$. The "utility" is the inconsistency measure; so for this purpose, the larger the inconsistency, the larger the utility of a set of formulae. The Shapley inconsistency value is defined as follows.

Definition 2. *The* **Shapley Inconsistency Value** *(SIV), denoted S_I, is the Shapley value of the coalitional game defined by the basic inconsistency measure I, where $|K| = n$, $|C| = c$, and $\alpha \in K$, as follows.*

$$S_I^\alpha(K) = \sum_{C \subseteq K} \frac{(c-1)!(n-c)!}{n!}(I(C) - I(C \setminus \{\alpha\}))$$

Clearly, the only subsets of K that need to be considered are the ones where removing a formula changes the inconsistency measure, that is, the inconsistent sets. It will be convenient in the examples to first calculate the part of the formula that does not refer to the inconsistency measure for each inconsistent set C. We write $f(C) = \frac{(c-1)!(n-c)!}{n!}$. Hence, $S_I^\alpha(K) = \sum_{C \subseteq K} f(C)(I(C) - I(C \setminus \{\alpha\}))$.

Example 3. Let $K' = \{a, b, \neg a, \neg a \vee \neg b\}$. The subsets of K' for which removing a formula may change the inconsistency are: $C_1 = \{a, b, \neg a, \neg a \vee \neg b\}$ $C_2 = \{a, b, \neg a\}$ $C_3 = \{a, b, \neg a \vee \neg b\}$ $C_4 = \{a, \neg a, \neg a \vee \neg b\}$ $C_5 = \{a, \neg a\}$ Then $f(C_1) = \frac{3!}{4!} = \frac{1}{4}$, $f(C_2) = f(C_3) = f(C_4) = f(C_5) = \frac{2!}{4!} = \frac{1}{12}$. $I_C(C_1) = 2, I_C(C_i) = 1$ for $2 \leq i \leq 5$ and $I_B(C_i) = 1$ for $1 \leq i \leq 5$. We obtain $S_{I_C}^a(K) = \frac{2}{4} + \frac{4}{12} = \frac{5}{6}$; $S_{I_C}^{\neg a}(K) = \frac{1}{4} + \frac{1}{4} = \frac{1}{2}$; $S_{I_C}^b(K) = S_{I_C}^{\neg a \vee \neg b} = \frac{1}{4} + \frac{1}{12} = \frac{1}{3}$. $S_{I_B}^a(K) = \frac{1}{4} + \frac{4}{12} = \frac{7}{12}$; $S_{I_B}^{\neg a}(K) = \frac{3}{12} = \frac{1}{4}$; $S_{I_B}^b(K) = S_{I_B}^{\neg a \vee \neg b} = \frac{1}{12}$.

There are some interesting developments of Shapley values for inconsistency (see for example [6]), but there has been no consideration of the probabilistic uncertainty associated with an inconsistency measure.

3   Uncertainty of Sources for Answer Tuples

There are many issues in managing distributed information. In this paper, we consider a specific problem of handling answer tuples as defined next. We assume that $\mathcal{A}$ denotes the set of atoms (propositional letters or ground predicates) in the language.

Definition 3. *Let* $\{1,\ldots,n\}$ *be the names for sources of information. An* **answer tuple***, denoted* $T = (A_1,\ldots,A_n)$*, is a tuple where for each* A_i*,* $1 \leq i \leq n$*,* $A_i \subseteq \mathcal{A}$*.*

An answer tuple, by itself, is never inconsistent. The inconsistency that occurs is the result of a set of integrity constraints that we assume is given a priori. We write A_0 for this set that contains formulae, each of which is a disjunction of negated atoms in $\mathcal{A}$. We say that T is inconsistent if $\bigcup_{i=0}^{n}(A_i) \vdash \perp$. Otherwise T is consistent. We will use the following subsidiary definitions: For the elements of T, $\mathsf{Elem}(T) = \bigcup_{i=1}^{n} A_i$; for the candidates of T, $\mathsf{Cand}(T) = \{S | S \subseteq \mathsf{Elem}(T)\}$.

To handle the issue of the reliability of the sources, we assume that a probability assignment is available for each source. Such an assignment may have been learnt from previous performance of sources, or obtained by some subjective judgment. We deal separately with the set of integrity constraints, A_0; basically we treat them as having probability 1.

Definition 4. *Let* $\{1,...,n\}$ *be the names for sources of information. A* **probability assignment to sources***, denoted* P*, is a function* $P : \{1,...,n\} \rightarrow [0,1]$*.*

Given the probability assignment to sources, together with an answer tuple $T = (A_1,...,A_n)$, we have further information to prefer some subsets of $\mathsf{Elem}(T)$ over others. To illustrate our concerns, we consider some scenarios next.

- At one extreme, suppose the probability is $P(i) = 0$ for each $i \in \{1,..,n\}$, then we need to consider only one candidate for the combination, which is $\emptyset$, since we believe that none of the formulae should be in the combination.
- At the other extreme, suppose the probability is $P(i) = 1$ for each $i \in \{1,..,n\}$, then we need to consider only one candidate for the combination, which is $\mathsf{Elem}(T)$, since we believe all should be in the combination.
- Between these two extremes, there may be multiple options for the combination. For example, suppose we have two sources, with the answers $A_1 = \{a\}$ and $A_2 = \{b\}$, while $A_0 = \{\neg a \vee \neg b\}$. Let $P(1) = 0.5$ and $P(2) = 0.5$. Then, there are four candidates for the combination to consider (i.e. $\mathsf{Cand}(T) = \{\{a,b\},\{a\},\{b\},\{\}\}$), each with probability of 0.25, with the first candidate ($\{a,b\}$) being inconsistent.

The next step is to find the probability of each candidate. Consider that the sources may have different probability assignments and an atom may appear in several sets A_i. Suppose, for example, that the atom a appears in A_1 and A_2. Then, when we consider a candidate, such as $\{a,b\}$, we must consider all different cases where a was in A_1 but not in A_2, or a was in A_2 but not in A_1, or it was in both. As we need to take care of all of these cases, we start with a renaming where each atom is renamed using a superscript to indicate its source. So a in A_1 becomes a^1 and a in A_2 becomes a^2. We write r for this renaming and for answer tuple $T = (A_1,\ldots,A_n)$ we obtain $r(T) = (r(A_1),\ldots,r(A_n))$, where each $r(A_i)$ is obtained from A_i by adding the superscript i to each atom, that is, for $A_i = \{a,b,c\}$, $r(\{a,b,c\}) = \{a^i,b^i,c^i\}$. The inverse operator r^{-1} removes the subscripts. Thus if C' is a candidate of $r(T)$, then $r^{-1}(C')$ (which is a set, hence duplicates are removed) is a candidate of T.

We compute the probability of a candidate C' of $r(T)$ as follows. Let $y_i = |A_i| = |A'_i|$ and suppose that C' contains x_i elements from A'_i. We say that $(x_1, \ldots, x_n)$ is the generator of C' and write $Gen(C') = \{(x_1, \ldots, x_n)\}$. Using the renaming r, each candidate of $r(T)$ has a unique generator. Then computing the probability of a candidate C' of T' we get $P(C') = \prod_{i=1}^{n} P(i)^{x_i} \times (1 - P(i))^{y_i - x_i}$. Now suppose that C is a candidate of T. There may be several candidates C' of $r(T)$ such that $r^{-1}(C') = C$. Let $C_r = \{C' | r^{-1}(C') = C\}$. Then $P(C) = \sum_{C' \in C_r} P(C')$. We also write $Gen(C) = \{(x_1, \ldots, x_n) | (x_1, \ldots, x_n) \in Gen(C')$ and $C' \in C_r\}$. From this we obtain

$$P(C) = \sum_{(x_1, \ldots, x_n) \in \mathsf{Gen}(C)} P(1)^{x_1} \times (1 - P(1))^{(y_1 - x_1)} \times \ldots \times P(n)^{x_n} \times (1 - P(n))^{(y_n - x_n)}$$

Example 4. To illustrate the calculation of the probability distribution over candidates, we consider an example with $A_0 = \{\neg a \vee \neg c\}$ where $T = (A_1, A_2)$ with $A_1 = \{a, b\}$ and $A_2 = \{c\}$. Let the probability assignment for sources be $P(1) = 4/5$ and $P(2) = 2/3$. Here, $\mathsf{Cand}(T) = \wp(\{a, b, c\})$. In this example, for each candidate there is a unique generator because each atom appears in just one source's answer. For each candidate, we give the generator, and the probability for the candidate, in Table 1.

For a fact $\alpha \in \mathsf{Elem}(T)$, we have an a priori probability that it is true. This is the sum of the probability of each candidate that contains it. We denote this probability by the function $P : Atoms \rightarrow [0, 1]$, where $P(\alpha) = \sum_{C \in \mathsf{Cand}(T) \text{ s.t. } \alpha \in C} P(C)$.

Proposition 1. *For* $T = (A_1, \ldots, A_n)$, $\sum_{C \in \mathsf{Cand}(T)} P(C) = 1$.

The next proposition shows that if an atom that is an element of an answer tuple is removed, the probability of each candidate of the new answer tuple is the sum of the probabilities of the candidate and the candidate obtained by adding the atom.

Table 1. Calculations for Example 4

Candidate	Generator	Probability of candidate
$\{a, b, c\}$	$(2, 1)$	$4/5 \times 4/5 \times 2/3 = 32/75$
$\{a, b\}$	$(2, 0)$	$4/5 \times 4/5 \times 1/3 = 16/75$
$\{a, c\}$	$(1, 1)$	$4/5 \times 1/5 \times 2/3 = 8/75$
$\{a\}$	$(1, 0)$	$4/5 \times 1/5 \times 1/3 = 4/75$
$\{b, c\}$	$(1, 1)$	$1/5 \times 4/5 \times 2/3 = 8/75$
$\{b\}$	$(1, 0)$	$1/5 \times 4/5 \times 1/3 = 4/75$
$\{c\}$	$(0, 1)$	$1/5 \times 1/5 \times 2/3 = 2/75$
$\{\}$	$(0, 0)$	$1/5 \times 1/5 \times 1/3 = 1/75$

Proposition 2. *Let* $T = (A_1, \ldots, A_n)$, P *be a probability assignment over sources, and* $\alpha \in \mathsf{Elem}(T)$. *Let* $T' = (A_1 \setminus \{\alpha\}, \ldots, A_n \setminus \{\alpha\})$ *(where if* $A_i \setminus \{\alpha\} = \emptyset$, *it is omitted from* T'*) and write* P' *for the (same) probability assignment over sources for* T'. *Let* $C' \in \mathsf{Cand}(T')$. *Then* $P'(C') = P(C') + P(C' \cup \{\alpha\})$.

In the next section, we use the set of candidates to define a notion of expected inconsistency of a set of answers that is based on the probability distribution over the candidates.

4   Expected Inconsistency of a Set of Formulae

We can measure the inconsistency of each candidate (using any inconsistency measure that is appropriate), and then aggregate the inconsistency measure for the combination as follows.

Definition 5. *Let* I *be an inconsistency measure,* $T = (A_1, ..., A_n)$ *an answer tuple, and* P *a probability distribution over the sources. The* **expected inconsistency** *of* T *with respect to* I, *denoted* $E_{I,P}(T)$, *is* $E_{I,P}(T) = \sum_{C \in \mathsf{Cand}(T)} P(C) \times I(C)$.

Example 5. To illustrate the definitions so far, consider the case where $A_0 = \{\neg a \vee \neg c, \neg b \vee \neg d\}$, $A_1 = \{a, b\}$ $A_2 = \{c, d\}$, $P(1) = 0.5$, and $P(2) = 0.5$. So $T = (A_1, A_2)$, and the set of candidates $\mathsf{Cand}(T)$ is the following

$$\{a, b, c, d\} \ \{a, c, d\} \ \{b, c, d\} \ \{c, d\} \ \{a, b, c\} \ \{a, c\} \ \{b, c\} \ \{c\}$$
$$\{a, b, d\} \quad \{a, d\} \quad \{b, d\} \quad \{d\} \quad \{a, b\} \quad \{a\} \quad \{b\} \quad \{\}$$

Let $I = I_C$ or $I = I_B$. The numbers are the same for both measures. Hence, we obtain $I(\{a, b, c, d\}) = 2$, and for the remaining 6 inconsistent sets C', $I(C') = 1$. For each $C \in \mathsf{Cand}(T)$, $P(C) = 1/16$. Therefore, $E_{I,P}(T) = \frac{1}{16}(2 + (6 \times 1)) = \frac{8}{16} = \frac{1}{2}$.

So expected inconsistency takes into account the inconsistency measure as well as the probabilities of the sources and hence the candidates.

Proposition 3. *For* $T = (A_1, ..., A_n)$, *and an inconsistency measure* I, *if each source* i *is such that* $P(i) = 1$, *then* $E_{I,P}(T) = I(\bigcup_{i=0}^{n} A_i)$.

Proposition 4. *For* $T = (A_1, ..., A_n)$, *and an inconsistency measure* I, *if each source* i *is such that* $P(i) = 0$, *then* $E_{I,P}(C) = 0$ *for all* $C \in \mathsf{Cand}(T)$.

Proposition 5. *For an answer tuple* $T = (A_1, ..., A_n)$, *an inconsistency measure* I, *and a probability distribution* P, $E_{I,P}(T) \leq I(\mathsf{Elem}(T))$.

Proposition 6. *Let* $T = (A_1, \ldots, A_n)$, I *be an inconsistency measure, and* P *be a probability assignment and* $T' = (A_1 \setminus \{\alpha\}, \ldots, A_n \setminus \{\alpha\})$ *(if* $A_i \setminus \{\alpha\} = \emptyset$, *it is omitted from* T'*). Then* $E_{I,P}(T) \geq E_{I,P}(T')$.

Whilst the proposal for expected inconsistency is in terms of answer tuples, it is a trivial revision of the definition for expected inconsistency (i.e. Definition 5) to enable it to handle arbitrary knowledgebases of classical logic. Expected inconsistency is a simple extension of the approach of inconsistency measures. Intuitively, it involves discounting inconsistency that is unlikely to occur. So for instance, a small inconsistency that it very likely to occur can be worse than a large inconsistency that is unlikely to occur.

5   Expected Blame of a Formula

We use the Shapley Inconsistency Values of Definition 2 to ascribe the proportion of blame to each formula. Our definition of expected blame for an atom is the weighted sum of the blame for the atom in each candidate containing the atom.

Definition 6. *Let I be an inconsistency measure, $T = (A_1, ..., A_n)$ an answer tuple, and P a probability assignment. The **expected blame** of α in T with respect to I and P, denoted $B_{I,P}^{\alpha}(T)$, is $B_{I,P}^{\alpha}(T) = \sum_{C \in \mathsf{Candidates}(T)} P(C) \times S_I^{\alpha}(C)$.*

Example 6. Consider $A_0 = \{\neg a \vee \neg b, \neg b \vee \neg c\}$, $A_1 = \{a\}$, $A_2 = \{b\}$, and $A_3 = \{c\}$, where $P(1) = 1$, $P(2) = 0.8$, and $P(3) = 0.5$. There are 4 candidates with non-zero probability: $C_1 = \{a, b, c\}$, $C_2 = \{a, b\}$, $C_3 = \{a, c\}$, and $C_4 = \{a\}$, where $P(C_1) = P(C_2) = 0.4$ and $P(C_3) = P(C_4) = 0.1$. We do the calculation separately for I_C and I_B.

- For $I = I_C$, The Shapley values are as follows: $S_I^a(C_1) = S_I^c(C_1) = S_I^a(C_2) = S_I^b(C_2) = 0.5$ and $S_I^b(C_1) = 1$. All other Shapley values are 0. Next we compute the expected blames: $B_{I,P}^a(T) = (0.4 \times 0.5) + (0.4 \times 0.5) = 0.4$, $B_{I,P}^b(T) = (0.4 \times 1) + (0.4 \times 0.5) = 0.6$, and $B_{I,P}^c(T) = (0.4 \times 0.5) = 0.2$.
- For $I = I_B$, The Shapley values are as follows; $S_I^a(C_1) = S_I^c(C_1) = \frac{1}{6}$ $S_I^a(C_2) = S_I^b(C_2) = 0.5$ and $S_I^b(C_1) = \frac{2}{3}$. All other Shapley values are 0. Next we compute the expected blames: $B_{I,P}^a(T) = (0.4 \times \frac{1}{6}) + (0.4 \times 0.5) = \frac{4}{15}$, $B_{I,P}^b(T) = (0.4 \times \frac{2}{3}) + (0.4 \times 0.5) = \frac{7}{15}$, and $B_{I,P}^c(T) = (0.4 \times \frac{1}{6}) = \frac{1}{15}$.

In both cases the blame for b is highest because it is involved in all the miminal inconsistent subsets, and the blame for a is higher than the blame for c because the probability of a is higher than c.

The probability assigned to a source directly affects the blame attributed to any atom given by that source. As formalized next, if α is given by a single source, the blame for α increases as the probability assigned to the source of α increases.

Proposition 7. *Let $T = (A_1, ..., A_n)$, and I be an inconsistency measure. Suppose that atom α appears in only one source as an answer, say A_1. Let P_1 and P_2 be probability assignments such that $P_1(1) \leq P_2(1)$ and $P_1(i) = P_2(i)$ for $i > 1$. Then $B_{I,P_1}^{\alpha}(T) \leq B_{I,P_2}^{\alpha}(T)$.*

In the following theorem, the first three properties are a restatement in this logical framework of the properties of the Shapley value: the distribution property states that the inconsistency values of the formulae sum to the total amount of expected inconsistency in the answer tuple; the symmetry property ensures that with equal probabilities only the amount of inconsistency brought by a formula matters for computing the expected blame; the minimality property expresses that a formula that is not embedded in any contradiction (i.e. does not belong to any minimal inconsistent subset) will not be blamed by the Shapley inconsistency values; and the dominance property states that logically stronger formulae bring (potentially) more conflicts.

Theorem 1. *Let I be basic inconsistency measure, and let P be a probability assignment to sources. Every expected blame value $B_{I,P}$ satisfies:*

- *Distribution: $E_{I,P}(T) = \sum_{\alpha \in \mathsf{Elements}(T)} B_{I,P}^{\alpha}(T)$*
- *Symmetry: If $\alpha, \beta \in \mathsf{Elem}(T)$*
  and for all $S \in \mathsf{Cand}(T)$ such that $\alpha \notin S$ and $\beta \notin S$,
  $$P(S \cup \{\alpha\}) = P(S \cup \{\beta\}) \text{ and } I(S \cup \{\alpha\}) = I(S \cup \{\beta\})$$
  then $B_{I,P}^{\alpha}(T) = B_{I,P}^{\beta}(T)$.
- *Minimality: If α is a free formula of T, then $B_{I,P}^{\alpha}(T) = 0$*
- *Dominance: If $\alpha \vdash \beta$ and $\alpha \not\vdash \bot$, then $B_{I,P}^{\alpha}(T) \geq B_{I}^{\beta}(T)$*

Expected blame is an extension of the approach of Shapley inconsistency values to the case of probabilities assigned to sources. Intuitively, it involves discounting blame that is unlikely to occur. So, for instance, blame for a small inconsistency that is very likely to occur can be greater than blame for a larger inconsistency unlikely to occur.

6   Weakness of a Formula

Given an inconsistent answer tuple $(A_1, ..., A_n)$, we want to resolve some of the inconsistency by deleting an individual formula. We will use the blame of each formula, but using only blame is not enough. We need to use separately the probability of the formula to obtain a reasonable answer for determining the best formula to delete. There is an interplay between the inconsistency caused by a formula, and the uncertainty of the formula. To illustrate, consider the following example.

Example 7. Let $A_0 = \{\neg a \vee \neg b\}$, $A_1 = \{a\}$, and $A_2 = \{b\}$. In this case, for any I and P, $B_{I,P}^a(T) = B_{I,P}^b(T)$, but if $P(1) > P(2)$, then we would be more inclined to delete b as it has the same blame for the inconsistency, but the belief in it is lower.

Recall that in Sect. 3 we defined the probability of each fact. So now, we start with the Shapley value for each formula, and weight it by a function of the probability of the formula. We will consider the weighting function as a parameter that can be chosen by the user of the system. As an example of a weighting function, let $F(\alpha) = 1 - P(\alpha)$, because we prefer to delete formulae whose probability is small. It is certainly possible to consider other weighting functions. For example, let $F_1(\alpha) = k \times (1 - P(\alpha))$ for some number k. However, this merely expands or shrinks the difference between the weights but does not change the weight order. Another possibility is to use a step function, such as the following: $F_2(\alpha) = 4$ if $P(\alpha) = 0$, $F_2(\alpha) = 3$ if $0 < P(\alpha) \leq 0.5$, $F_2(\alpha) = 2$ if $0.5 < P(\alpha) < 1$, and $F_2(\alpha) = 1$ if $P(\alpha) = 1$. Such a function blurs the distinction between probabilities within a certain range. Hence, we will continue working with F as defined above.

Definition 7. *Let I be an inconsistency measure, $T = (A_1, ..., A_n)$ an answer tuple, $\alpha \in \mathsf{Elem}(T)$, P a probability function over sources, and F the weighting function. The **weakness** of α in T with respect to I and P, is $W^\alpha_{I,P}(T) = F(\alpha) \times B^\alpha_{I,P}(T)$.*

Our goal is to use this definition of weakness, to reduce $B^\alpha_{I,P}(T)$ and $P(\alpha)$ to a single value for α which represents the degree to which we should delete it. The higher the degree of weakness (i.e. the greater the product of the weight and the blame for inconsistency for the formula), the greater the degree to which we should delete it.

Example 8. Let $A_0 = \{\neg a \vee \neg b\}$, $A_1 = \{a\}$, and $A_2 = \{b\}$. There is only one inconsistent candidate: $\{a, b\}$. For $I = I_C$ or $I = I_B$, the Shapley values are $S^a_I(T) = 0.5$ and $S^b_I(T) = 0.5$. We will use $F(\alpha) = 1 - P(\alpha)$ as the weighting function and consider the following scenarios for the probabilities for $P(1)$ and $P(2)$.

- $P(1) = 0.8$, $P(2) = 0.2$. Hence, $P(a) = 0.8$ and $P(b) = 0.2$. So, $W^a_I(T) = 0.1$ and $W^b_I(T) = 0.4$. Delete b.
- $P(1) = 0.6$ and $P(b) = 0.8$, Hence, $P(a) = 0.6$ and $P(b) = 0.8$. So, $W^a_I(T) = 0.2$ and $W^b_I(T) = 0.1$. Delete a.
- $P(1) = 0.5$ and $P(b) = 0.5$, Hence, $P(a) = 0.5$ and $P(b) = 0.5$. So, $W^a_I(T) = W^b_I(T) = 0.25$. As the probability of a and b is the same, there is no preference between deleting a or b.

Example 9. Continuing with Example 6 where we already computed the blames, we obtain the following weaknesses: When $I = I_C$, $W^a_{I,P}(T) = 0$, $W^b_{I,P}(T) = 0.12$, and $W^c_{I,P}(T) = 0.1$; And when $I = I_B$, $W^a_{I,P}(T) = 0$, $W^b_{I,P}(T) = \frac{7}{15}$, and $W^c_{I,P}(T) = \frac{1}{30}$. Note how close the weaknesses of b and c are for I_C. The reason is that while b has higher blame, it also has higher probability and hence smaller weight. However, for I_B the blame is so much higher for b than for c that the higher probability does not compensate enough to make the weights close.

Proposition 8. *For $T = (A_1, ..., A_n)$, an inconsistency measure I, and a probability assignment over sources P, if $P(i) = 1$ for each source, then $W^\alpha_{I,P}(T) = 0$ for all $\alpha \in \mathsf{Elem}(T)$.*

The concept of weakness combines blame and the probability of the source that provides a fact. So if we try to resolve inconsistency by deleting some formulae, it is reasonable to start with the weakest one. Our examples illustrate the appropriateness of using this concept.

7   Summary and Future Work

We believe that this is the first paper that studies measuring inconsistency in the context where the uncertainty of the source of a formula is taken into account. We do not define a new inconsistency measure; our work applies to and combines with any given inconsistency measure. For such a measure we define the expected inconsistency of the answers based on the probabilities of the sources. We also define the expected blame of a formula and show that this definition has several useful properties. Finally, we combine blame with uncertainty to define the weakness of each formula, thereby providing a method to resolve inconsistencies by removing the weakest formulae.

In the future we plan to study additional properties of both expected blame and weakness. We will also consider the mechanism of inconsistency resolution in this framework, distinguishing between internal resolution (using weakness) and external resolution, where, in the latter case, we may request additional information from an outside source before deletion. Finally, we will consider how to measure the quality of the inconsistency resolution process.

References

1. Grant, J., Hunter, A.: Measuring inconsistency in knowledgebases. J. Intell. Inf. Syst. **27**, 159–184 (2006)
2. Hunter, A.: Measuring inconsistency in knowledge via quasi-classical models. In: Proceedings of the National Conference on Artificial Intelligence (AAAI 2002), pp. 68–73. MIT Press (2002)
3. Hunter, A., Konieczny, S.: Approaches to measuring inconsistent information. In: Bertossi, L., Hunter, A., Schaub, T. (eds.) Inconsistency Tolerance. LNCS, vol. 3300, pp. 191–236. Springer, Heidelberg (2005)
4. Hunter, A., Konieczny, S.: On the measure of conflicts: shapley inconsistency values. Artif. Intell. **174**, 1007–1026 (2010)
5. Konieczny, S., Lang, J., Marquis, P.: Quantifying information and contradiction in propositional logic through epistemic actions. In: Proceedings of the 18th International Joint Conference on Artificial Intellignce (IJCAI 2003), pp. 106–111 (2003)
6. Mu, K., Liu, W., Jin, Z.: Measuring the blame of each formula for inconsistent prioritized knowledge bases. J. Logic Comput. **22**(3), 481–516 (2012)
7. Priest, G.: Logic of paradox. J. Philos. Logic **8**, 219–241 (1979)

Consistency-Based Reliability Assessment

Laurence Cholvy[1]([⊠]), Laurent Perrussel[2], William Raynaut[1,2],
and Jean-Marc Thévenin[2]

[1] ONERA Toulouse, Toulouse, France
laurence.cholvy@onera.fr
[2] IRIT-Université Toulouse 1 Capitole, Toulouse, France
{laurent.perrussel,william.raynaut,jean-marc.thevenin}@irit.fr

Abstract. This paper addresses the question of assessing the relative reliability of unknown information sources. We propose to consider a phase during which the consistency of information they report is analysed, whether it is the consistency of each single report, or the consistency of a report w.r.t. some trusted knowledge or the consistency of different reports together. We adopt an axiomatic approach by first giving postulates which characterize how the resulting reliability preorder should be; then we define a family of operators for building this preorder and demonstrate that it satisfies the proposed postulates.

1 Motivation

Techniques for merging raw information have been studied in an extensive way. These techniques usually assume that all information provided by the sources (i.e. agents) should be considered as a whole. Two different approaches have been studied: the first one considers sources in an equal way and has led to merging techniques such as majority, arbitration merging or distance-based merging for solving conflict between contradicting information [5,6,9]. The second one distinguishes sources through a reliability criterion. Taking sources reliability into account provides rationales for discounting or ignoring pieces of information whose source is not considered as sufficiently reliable. Some promote a quantitative model of reliability: information sources are associated with a reliability level represented by a number used by the merging operator. According to the belief function theory, the reliability level of a source is a number between 0 and 1. This number is then used by the discounting rule in order to weaken the importance of information provided by this source [13]. Some others promote a qualitative approach to reliability and consider that information sources are ranked according to their reliability. This order or pre-order is then used by the merging operator. In [3], the author defines a merging operator which assumes that the sources are totally ordered : if s is said to be more reliable than s' and together provide contradicting information, then information provided by s is privileged; while information provided by s' which does not contradict information of s is also considered as acceptable. The same idea is followed by [10] for reasoning about more complex beliefs and in [12] for revising a belief base.

© Springer International Publishing Switzerland 2015
S. Destercke and T. Denoeux (Eds.): ECSQARU 2015, LNAI 9161, pp. 246–256, 2015.
DOI: 10.1007/978-3-319-20807-7_22

All previous works assume that the reliability of the sources is given as a parameter (quantitative or qualitative): they do not address the question of how to build up this reliability.

This paper addresses this key question. We adopt a qualitative point of view to reliability representation: the relative reliability of information sources is represented by a total preorder. We focus on the question of estimating this reliability preorder in the following context: sources are unknown (no extra information about them is available) and information provided by the sources is only qualitative (i.e., statements). We propose to consider a phase, before the information merging phase, during which information sources are observed in order to obtain a reliability preorder. We consider that during this phase, the most important is to analyse the consistency of information reported by the different sources, be it the consistency of each single report, or the consistency of a report w.r.t. some trusted knowledge, or the consistency of different reports together.

This paper is organized as follows. Section 2 presents preliminary definitions. Postulates which axiomatically characterize the reliability preorders are given in Sect. 3. Section 4 describes a generic operator building such preorders and demonstrate that it satisfies the postulates. Examples of operators are given in Sect. 5. Finally, Sect. 6 concludes the paper.

2 Preliminaries

Let A be a finite set of agents; let L be a propositional logic defined over a finite set of propositional letters and propositional constants $\top$ and $\bot$. An interpretation m is a mapping from the set of formulas of L to the set of truth values $\{0, 1\}$ so that $m(\top) = 1$ and $m(\bot) = 0$. The set of all interpretations is denoted M. Interpretation m is *a model* of formula F iff $m(F) = 1$. *Tautologies* are formulas which are interpreted by 1 in any interpretation. We write $\models F$ when F is a tautology. A formula is *consistent* iff it has at least one model.

Let $\leq$ be a total preorder on A representing the relative reliability of agents: $a \leq b$ stands for b is at least as reliable as a. $GT(a, \leq) = \{x \in A \setminus \{a\} : a \leq x\}$ is the set of agents which are as least as reliable as a. Let $a \in A$, $\leq_1$ be a total preorder on A and $\leq_2$ a total preorder on $A \setminus \{a\}$; $\leq_1$ *is compatible with* $\leq_2$ iff $\forall x \forall y \ x \leq_2 y \Longrightarrow x \leq_1 y$.

In the following, raw information is a *communication* consisting of a pair associating an agent and a statement:

- *A communication set on A* is a set of pairs $< a, \varphi >$ where $a \in A$ and φ is a formula of L. $< a, \varphi >$ means that agent a has reported φ.
- Let Ψ be a communication set on A. $Ag(\Psi) = \{a \in A, \exists \varphi \ < a, \varphi > \in \Psi\}$.
- Given a communication set Ψ, we define *the communication set of a* as $\Psi_a = \{< a, \varphi > | < a, \varphi > \in \Psi\}$ and the communication of a set of agents C as

$$\Psi(C) = \bigcup_{a \in C} \Psi_a$$

The *report* associated to some Ψ represents the content of the communication:

$$\mathsf{Report}(\Psi) = \begin{cases} \bigwedge_{<a,\varphi>\in\Psi} \varphi & \text{if } \Psi \neq \emptyset \\ \top & \text{otherwise} \end{cases}$$

- Let Ψ and Ψ' be two communication sets on A. Ψ and Ψ' are *equivalent* iff for any agent a in A: $\models \mathsf{Report}(\Psi_a) \leftrightarrow \mathsf{Report}(\Psi'_a)$. That is, a's report in Ψ is equivalent to a's report in Ψ'. We write $\Psi \equiv \Psi'$. Obviously $\Psi \equiv \Psi'$ iff $\forall C \subseteq A \ \Psi(C) \equiv \Psi'(C)$

- Let Ψ and Ψ' be two communication sets on A. Ψ and Ψ' are *weakly equivalent* iff for any agent a in A, $\exists b, \exists c \in A$ such that $\models \mathsf{Report}(\Psi_a) \leftrightarrow \mathsf{Report}(\Psi'_b)$ and $\models \mathsf{Report}(\Psi'_a) \leftrightarrow \mathsf{Report}(\Psi_c)$. That is, we relax here the constraint that report of agent a should be equivalent both in Ψ and Ψ'; instead we only require some other agent, possibly different from a, report equivalent information. We write $\Psi \rightleftharpoons \Psi'$. Obviously $\Psi \equiv \Psi'$ iff $\forall C \subseteq A \ \Psi(C) \rightleftharpoons \Psi'(C)$

2.1 *IC*-Contradictory Communication Sets

Consistency of reports will be evaluated with respect to some integrity constraint IC, a consistent formula of L. IC has to be viewed as information taken for granted or certain. Let us now revisit the classical notion of minimal inconsistent set w.r.t. communication sets. Formally, let Ψ be a set of communications on A:

- Ψ is *IC-contradictory* iff $\mathsf{Report}(\Psi) \wedge IC$ is inconsistent; otherwise Ψ is *IC*-consistent.
- Ψ is *minimal IC-contradictory* iff Ψ is *IC*-contradictory and no strict subset of Ψ is *IC*-contradictory.
- $\Psi \perp IC$ denotes *the set of minimal IC-contradictory subsets of Ψ.*
- $A^\perp = \cup_{F\in\Psi\perp IC} Ag(F)$ is the set of agents which have reported a piece of information which belongs to some minimal *IC*-contradictory communication set. Notice that $A^\perp \neq \emptyset$ iff Ψ is *IC*-contradictory.

Example 1. Consider agents a, b, c, d and propositional letters p, q, r, s. Assume $IC = \neg(p \wedge q)$ and $\Psi = \{< a, p >, < a, r >, < b, q >, < c, \neg r >, < d, s >\}$. The minimal *IC*-contradictory subsets of Ψ are $E_1 = \{< a, p >, < b, q >\}$ and $E_2 = \{< c, \neg r >, < a, r >\}$. Thus $A^\perp = \{a, b, c\}$.

Example 2. Consider now agents a, b and propositional letters p, q. Assume $IC = p$ and $\Psi = \{< a, \neg p \wedge q >, < b, \neg q >\}$. The *IC*-contradictory subsets of Ψ are $E_1 = \{< a, \neg p \wedge q >\}$ and $E_2 = \{< a, \neg p \wedge q >, < b, \neg q >\}$ but only E_1 is minimal. Thus $A^\perp = \{a\}$.

This last example shows that $A^\perp$ is not the set of *all* agents which bring some contradiction. $A^\perp$ is to be seen as the set of agents which prevent the consistency of Ψ i.e. if communications of agents of $A^\perp$ are ignored, Ψ becomes *IC*-consistent. I.e., $\Psi \setminus A^\perp$ is *IC*-consistent (but not necessarily maximal consistent).

2.2   *IC*-Conflicting Agents

We go further for revisiting the notion of minimal inconsistent set by considering set of agents rather than set of statements. This set helps us to identify the sources which are related to inconsistent report.

- Let $C \subseteq A$. C is *IC-conflicting* iff $\mathsf{Report}(\Psi(C)) \wedge IC$ is inconsistent.
- C is *minimal IC-conflicting* iff it is *IC*-conflicting and no strict subset of C is *IC*-conflicting.

Example 3. Let's consider the previous example. $\{a, b, c, d\}$ is *IC*-conflicting. $\{a, b\}$ and $\{a, c\}$ are minimal *IC*-conflicting.

We can show that the union of minimal *IC*-conflicting subsets of A is included in $A^{\perp}$. But the reverse is not true: consider $IC = \neg q$ and $\Psi = \{< a, p >, < b, \neg p >, < b, q >\}$. $A^{\perp} = \{a, b\}$ while the only minimal *IC*-conflicting subset of agents is $\{b\}$.

3   Assessing Reliability

The following postulates define in an axiomatic way that reliability assessment should be rooted in the notion of contradiction occurring in a set of communications.

Given a set of agents A, an integrity constraint IC and a communication set Ψ, the total preorder representing the relative reliability of agents in A is denoted $\Gamma^{IC,A}(\Psi)$. The operator Γ, which defines this relative reliability preorder is characterized as follows:

P1 $\Gamma^{IC,A}(\Psi)$ is a total preorder on A.
P2 If $\Psi \equiv \Psi'$ then $\Gamma^{IC,A}(\Psi) = \Gamma^{IC,A}(\Psi')$.
P3 If $\models IC \leftrightarrow IC'$ then $\Gamma^{IC,A}(\Psi) = \Gamma^{IC',A}(\Psi)$.
P4 If $\models \mathsf{Report}(\Psi_a)$ then $\Gamma^{IC,A}(\Psi)$ is compatible with $\Gamma^{IC,A\setminus\{a\}}(\Psi \setminus \Psi_a)$.
P5 If A is not *IC*-conflicting then $\Gamma^{IC,A}(\Psi)$ is the equality preorder.
P6 If A is *IC*-conflicting then $A \setminus A^{\perp} \subseteq GT(a, \Gamma^{IC,A}(\Psi))$ for any $a \in A^{\perp}$.
P7 If $\{a_1, ..., a_k\}$ $(k \geq 2)$ is a minimal *IC*-conflicting subset of agents, then
$\exists i \; \forall j \; j \neq i, \; GT(a_j, \Gamma^{IC,A}(\Psi)) \subset GT(a_i, \Gamma^{IC,A}(\Psi))$.

Postulate **P1** specifies that the expected result is a total preorder. **P2** and **P3** deal with syntax independence. More precisely, if we consider two equivalent communication sets or if we consider two equivalent *IC* formulas, then we get the same total preorder on agents. **P4** states that an agent which reports a tautology or which reports no information has no influence on the relative reliability of other agents. **P5**, **P6** and **P7** focus on consistency of information provided by agents in A. Postulate **P5** considers the case when A is not *IC*-conflicting (i.e. Ψ set is not *IC*-contradictory). In such a case, the sources are considered as equally reliable. **P6** and **P7** consider the cases when A is *IC*-conflicting. According to **P6**, any agent reporting a piece of information belonging to some minimal IC-contradictory communication set is considered as less reliable than any other agent which have not. According to **P7**, if some agents are minimally IC-conflicting, then at least one of these agents is strictly less reliable than the others. This is inline with our understanding of reliability: if some agents are equally reliable, then after merging we will believe, with the same strength, information they will provide. However, it is generally assumed [4,11] that graded belief satisfies a modal logic axiom which states that beliefs should be consistent: that is, two contradictory pieces of information cannot be believed with the same strength. Consequently, agents who are involved in a minimal IC-conflicting set cannot be equally reliable.

4   Operator Assessing Reliability

In this section, we propose a generic operator which builds the reliability preorder of agents by taking into account their contribution to inconsistencies.

4.1   Contribution of Agents to Inconsistencies

We start by introducing a measure to quantify the inconsistency degree of communication sets w.r.t. some IC. This measure is adapted from the one proposed in [8] for measuring inconsistency of sets of formulas.

Definition 1. *A syntax weak-independent IC-inconsistency measure is a function I_{IC} which associates any communication set Ψ with a positive real number $I_{IC}(\Psi)$ so that:*

- **Consistency** : $I_{IC}(\Psi) = 0$ iff Ψ is IC-consistent.
- **Monotony** : $I_{IC}(\Psi \cup \Psi') \geqslant I_{IC}(\Psi)$
- **Dominance** : for all ϕ and ψ, if $IC \wedge \phi \models \psi$ and $IC \wedge \phi$ is consistent, then $I_{IC}(\Psi \cup \{< a, \phi >\}) \geqslant I_{IC}(\Psi \cup \{< b, \psi >\})$ for any $a, b \in A$.
- **Free formula independence** : If $< a, \phi >$ is free (it does not belong to any minimal IC-contradictory subset of $\Psi \perp IC$), then $I_{IC}(\Psi) = I_{IC}(\Psi \setminus \{< a, \phi >\})$.
- **Syntax weak-independence** :
  1. for all IC' if $\models IC \leftrightarrow IC'$ then $I_{IC}(\Psi) = I_{IC'}(\Psi)$
  2. for all Ψ' if $\Psi \rightleftharpoons \Psi'$ then $I_{IC}(\Psi) = I_{IC}(\Psi')$

The consistency property states that the measure of inconsistency of a communication set is null iff this communication set is not IC-contradictory. The monotony property says that the measure of inconsistency of a communication set does not decrease if we add more communications in this set. The dominance property states that logically stronger reports bring potentially more contradictions. The free formula independence property states that adding a report that does not cause any contradiction cannot change the consistency measure of the communication set. Finally, the syntax weak-independence says that the measure of inconsistency of a communication set does not depend on the syntax on the integrity constraints. It also says that two weakly equivalent communication sets get the same measure of inconsistency.

Notice that $I_{IC}(\emptyset) = 0$ since $\mathsf{Report}(\emptyset) = \top$.

Proposition 1. *Let Ψ be a communications set on A, IC an integrity constraint and $a \in A$. If $a \notin A^{\perp}$ then $I_{IC}(\Psi_a) = 0$. The reverse is not true.*

Next we consider a function for measuring how much an agent contributes to the IC-inconsistency of a communication set. The contribution of an agent to the fact that Ψ is IC-contradictory is defined as the Shapley value and measures the importance of this agent in a coalitional game defined by function I_{IC} [8].

Definition 2. *Consider a set of agents A, a communication set Ψ on A, an integrity constraint IC and a syntax weak-independent IC-inconsistency measure I_{IC}. Function $Cont_{\Psi}^{I_{IC}}$ associates any agent a with a positive real number $Cont_{\Psi}^{I_{IC}}(a)$ so that:*

$$Cont_{\Psi}^{I_{IC}}(a) = \sum_{\substack{C \subseteq A \\ C \neq \emptyset}} \frac{(|C| - 1)!(|A| - |C|)!}{|A|!} (I_{IC}(\Psi(C)) - I_{IC}(\Psi(C \setminus \{a\})))$$

Proposition 2. *Let Ψ be a communications set on A, IC an integrity constraint and $a \in A$. Then, $a \notin A^{\perp} \implies Cont_{\Psi}^{I_{IC}}(a) = 0$. The reverse is not true.*

Given the function $Cont_{\Psi}^{I_{IC}}$, one can obviously define a total preorder on A as follows:

Definition 3. *Let a and b be two agents of A.*

$$a \leq_{Cont_{\Psi}^{I_{IC}}} b \quad \text{iff} \quad Cont_{\Psi}^{I_{IC}}(a) \geq Cont_{\Psi}^{I_{IC}}(b)$$

This defines the reliability as follows: a source is considered strictly more (resp, equally) reliable than another iff its contribution to the global inconsistency is stricty smaller than (resp equal to) the contribution of the other. But, unfortunately, this preorder does not satisfy the seven postulates, as shown in the following.

Proposition 3. $\leq_{Cont_{\Psi}^{I_{IC}}}$ *satisfies* **P1–P6** *but does not satisfy* **P7**.

To prove that $\leq_{Cont_{\Psi}^{I_{IC}}}$ does not satisfy **P7**, just consider $\Psi = \{< a, p >, < b, \neg p > \}$ and $IC = true$. $\{a, b\}$ is a *minimal IC-conflicting* set of agents but however, $a =_{Cont_{\Psi}^{I_{IC}}} b$.

As a consequence, we have to find another way to buid operators for reliability assessment. This is the purpose of the following paragraph.

4.2 $\Gamma^{I_{IC}}$ Operator

Definition 4. *Consider a set of agents A, a communication set on A, Ψ, an integrity constraint IC and a given syntax weak-independent IC-inconsistency measure I_{IC}. The operator $\Gamma^{I_{IC}}$ for assessing reliability is defined by:*

1. $X \leftarrow A$
2. $E \leftarrow \Psi \perp IC$
3. $\leq \leftarrow \{a \leq b \mid a, b \in A\}$
4. **while** $E \neq \emptyset$ **do**
   (a) *Deterministically choose* $a \in Ag(\cup_{F \in E} F)$ *which maximizes* $Cont_\Psi^{I_{IC}}(a)$
   (b) $X \leftarrow X \setminus \{a\}$
   (c) $E \leftarrow E \setminus \{F \in E \mid a \in Ag(F)\}$
   (d) $\leq \leftarrow \leq \setminus \{b \leq a \mid b \in X\}$
5. **return** $\leq$

In the previous algorithm, X is the set of agents which has to be ordered, E is the set of minimal IC-contradictory subsets of Ψ which contain communications of agents in X. $\leq$ is the reliability pre-order and $a \leq b$ stands for b is at least as reliable as a. First Lines 1–3 initialize the variables: X is initialized as A, E contains all the minimal IC-contradictory subsets of Ψ and $\leq$ is equality. Then according to lines (4) and (a)–(d), the operator chooses one agent a among those which maximally contribute to the IC-contradiction of Ψ, removes a from X, deletes from E all the subsets which contains some communication of a, and updates $\leq$ so that a is no more reliable than agents in X. This is done until E is empty. Notice that line (a) expresses a deterministic choice, such as lexicographic order.

Example 4. Consider agents a, b, c, d and propositional letters p, q, r. Consider $\Psi = \{< a, p >, < b, q >, < c, \neg q >, < d, r >\}$ and $IC = \neg r$. Consequently, $\Psi \perp IC = \{\{< b, q >, < c, \neg q >\}, \{< d, r >\}\}$. Assume that:

$$Cont_\Psi^{I_{IC}}(a) < Cont_\Psi^{I_{IC}}(b) = Cont_\Psi^{I_{IC}}(c) < Cont_\Psi^{I_{IC}}(d)$$

Assume a lexicographic order for choice. First, Lines 1–3 sets X, E and $\leq$ as follows:

$$X = \{a, b, c, d\} \quad E = \{\{< b, q >, < c, \neg q >\}, \{< d, r >\}\}$$
$$\leq \, = \{a = b = c = d\}$$

Next, first iteration chooses "d" at step (a) and we get:

$$X = \{a, b, c\} \quad E = \{\{< b, q >, < c, \neg q >\}\}$$
$$\leq \, = \{d < a = b = c\}$$

Lexicographic order entails that the 2nd iteration chooses "b":

$$X = \{a, c\} \quad E = \emptyset$$
$$\leq \, = \{d < b < a = c\}$$

As $E = \emptyset$, the algorithm stops and returns the pre-order: $d < b < a = c$.

The following propositions show that ranks are coherent with the inconsistency measure. That is, the more an agent is inconsistent, the less it is reliable:

Proposition 4. *Let Ψ be a communications set on A and IC an integrity constraint. Let $\leq$ be the preorder given by operator $\Gamma_1^{I_{IC}}$. For any two agents a and $b \in A$:*

$$\text{If } Cont_\Psi^{I_{IC}}(a) \geqslant Cont_\Psi^{I_{IC}}(b) \text{ then } a \leq b$$

We have the immediate following corollary:

Corollary 1. *If $a \notin A^\perp$ then for all $b \in A$, $b \leq a$.*

The opposite direction of previous proposition can only be considered for strict order. This is due to the choice step *(a)*: an agent may maximize the consistency measure but may not be chosen; agents may then be considered with same rank of reliability as agents getting a lower measure related to their contribution to inconsistency. In the previous example, $a = c$ while $Cont_\Psi^{I_{IC}}(a) < Cont_\Psi^{I_{IC}}(c)$.

Proposition 5. *Let Ψ be a communications set on A and IC an integrity constraint. Let $\leq$ be the preorder given by operator $\Gamma_1^{I_{IC}}$. For any two agents a and $b \in A$:*

$$\text{If } a < b \text{ then } Cont_\Psi^{I_{IC}}(a) \geq Cont_\Psi^{I_{IC}}(b)$$

The two previous propositions show that the choice step plays a crucial role in the behavior in the operator. Indeed this choice enforces the satisfaction of postulate **P7**.

Theorem 1. *Consider a set of agents A, a communication set on A, Ψ, an integrity constraint IC and a syntax weak-independent IC-inconsistency measure I_{IC}. $\Gamma^{I_{IC}}$ operators satisfy postulates **P1-P7**.*

5   Examples of Inconsistency Measures

Let us now detail two possible inconsistency measures which allow us to build two reliability assessment operators. These two measures are based on the ones proposed by [8]. The first measure is inspired by the drastic distance:

Definition 5 (Drastic Measure). *Let Ψ be a set of communications on A and IC a consistent formula. The drastic inconsistency measure I_d^{IC} is defined by:*

$$I_d^{IC}(\Psi) = \begin{cases} 0 & \text{if } \Psi \text{ is } IC\text{-consistent} \\ 1 & \text{otherwise} \end{cases}$$

Theorem 2. *I_d^{IC} is a syntax weak-independent inconsistency measure.*

Then $\Gamma_d^{I^{IC}}$ is a good candidate to assess reliability.

Example 5. Consider agents a, b, c, d and propositional letters p, q, r. Consider $\Psi = \{< a, p \wedge q >, < b, q >, < c, \neg q >, < d, r >\}$ and $IC = \neg r$. Then we get: $Cont_{\Psi}^{I_d^{IC}}(a) = \frac{1}{12}$ $Cont_{\Psi}^{I_d^{IC}}(b) = \frac{1}{12}$ $Cont_{\Psi}^{I_d^{IC}}(c) = \frac{3}{12}$ $Cont_{\Psi}^{I_d^{IC}}(d) = \frac{7}{12}$. Operator $\Gamma^{I^{IC}}$ returns $d < c < a = b$

Let us now consider a second measure which is more refined than Drastic measure. The measure is based on minimal inconsistency communication sets and the intuition is that the degree of inconsistency is proportional to the number of inconsistent subsets. The measure has to take care of our syntax-based perspective: to avoid syntactic biases, the measure considers the whole set of communications given by an agent.

Definition 6 (Minimal Inconsistent Subsets Measure). *Let Ψ be a set of communications on A and IC a consistent formula. The inconsistency measure I_{MI}^{IC} based on the number of minimal IC-contradictory subset is defined as:*

$$I_{MI}^{IC}(\Psi) = \left| \left(\bigcup_{a \in Ag(\Psi)} < a, \mathsf{Report}(\Psi_a) > \right) \perp IC \right|$$

Theorem 3. *I_{MI}^{IC} is a syntax weak-independent inconsistency measure.*

Then $\Gamma^{I_{MI}^{IC}}$ is a good candidate to assess reliability. Let's illustrate this second measure on the same example.

Example 6. Consider agents a, b, c, d and propositional letters p, q, r. Consider $\Psi = \{< a, p \wedge q >, < b, q >, < c, \neg q >, < d, r >\}$ and $IC = \neg r$. Then we get: $Cont_{\Psi}^{I_{MI}^{IC}}(a) = \frac{1}{2}$ $Cont_{\Psi}^{I_{MI}^{IC}}(b) = \frac{1}{2}$ $Cont_{\Psi}^{I_{MI}^{IC}}(c) = 1$ $Cont_{\Psi}^{I_{MI}^{IC}}(d) = 1$. Notice that the contributions of c and d are equal. According to these contributions $\Gamma^{I_{MI}^{IC}}$ return either $d < c < a = b$ or $c < d < a = b$ depending on the deterministic choice.

6   Conclusion

This work proposes to assess the relative reliability of some information sources by analysing the consistency of information they report, whether it be the consistency of each single report, or the consistency of a report as regard to some trusted knowledge or the consistency of different reports together. We have given some postulates stating what the relative reliability preorder should be. Then we have introduced a generic operator for building such preorder which is parametrized by a function for measuring the inconsistency of the information reported. We prove that this generic operator agrees with the postulates.

This framework may be extended in several ways. First, inconsistency measures should deserve more attention. Recent work on this topic [1,7] shows promising results such as giving a weight to the inconsistency itself. A second issue concerns our key principle relying assessment considering only inconsistency: the more agent is connected to inconsistency, the less it is reliable. The reverse notion, might then also be considered for assessing the reliability. In other words, how can we "reward" an agent which is never inconsistent. The third issue concerns the one shot dimension of the assessment process: iteration should be possible and reliability assessment should then be viewed as a refinement process. In that case, the key issue is to set rationales for changing reliability from $a < b$ to $b < a$. Finally, it must be noticed that if one has already some partial information about the reliability of the agents (for instance, one knows that agent a is more reliable than b but has no idea about c reliability) then the process described in this paper is not applicable as is: in this case, we could achieve reliability assessment by combining that preorder with the one produced by the operator $\Gamma^{I_{IC}}$. For future work, we plan to study these agregation operators.

As we can see the proposed framework offers numerous perspectives and our aim is to take advantage of its flexibility for going further.

Acknowledgements. We sincerely thank the anonymous reviewers whose questions helped us to improve the paper.

References

1. Besnard, P.: Revisiting Postulates for Inconsistency Measures. In: Proceedings of JELIA 2014, Funchal, Portugal, September 2014
2. Borja Macías, V., Pozos Parra, P.: Model-based belief merging without distance measures. In: Proceedings of AAMAS 2007, Honolulu, USA, May 2007
3. Cholvy, L.: Reasoning about merged information. In: Handbook of Defeasible Reasoning and Uncertainty Management, vol. 1. Kluwer Publishers (1998)
4. Demolombe, R., Liau, C.-J.: A logic of graded trust and belief fusion. In: Proceedings of the 4th Workshop on Deception, Fraud and Trust in Agent Societies, Montréal, Québec (2001)
5. Benferhat, S., Dubois, D., Kaci, S., Prade, H.: Possibilistic merging and distance-based fusion of propositional information. Ann. Math. Artif. Intell. **34**(1–3), 217–252 (2002)
6. Everaere, P., Konieczny, S., Marquis, P.: Disjunctive merging: Quota and Gmin merging operators. Artif. Intell. **174**(12–13), 824–849 (2010)
7. Grant, J., Hunter, A.: Distance-based measures of inconsistency. In: Proceedings of ECSQARU 2013, Utrecht, The Netherlands (2013)
8. Hunter, A., Konieczny, S.: On the measure of conflicts: Shapley Inconsistency Values. Artif. Intell. **174**(14), 1007–1026 (2010)
9. Konieczny, S., Pino Pérez, R.: Merging information under constraints: a logical framework. J. Logic Comput. **12**(5), 773–808 (2002)
10. Liau, C.-J.: A modal logic framework for multi-agent belief fusion. ACM Trans. Comput. Logic **6**(1), 124–174 (2005)
11. Laverny, N., Lang, J.: From knowldege-based programs to graded belief-based programs, Part I: on-line reasoning. In: Synthese, vol. 147, pp. 277–321, Springer (2005)

12. Lorini, E., Perrussel, L., Thévenin, J.-M.: A modal framework for relating belief and signed information. In: Leite, J., Torroni, P., Ågotnes, T., Boella, G., van der Torre, L. (eds.) CLIMA XII 2011. LNCS, vol. 6814, pp. 58–73. Springer, Heidelberg (2011)
13. Shafer, G.: A Mathematical Theory of Evidence. Princeton University Press, Princeton (1976)

Handling Revision Inconsistencies: Towards Better Explanations

Fabian Schmidt[1]($\boxtimes$), Jörg Gebhardt[1], and Rudolf Kruse[2]

[1] ISC Gebhardt, Celle, Germany
schmidt@isc-gebhardt.de
[2] Otto-von-Guericke University, Magdeburg, Germany

Abstract. When dealing with complex knowledge, inconsistencies become a big problem. Due to the complexity of modern knowledge systems, usually a manual elimination of inconsistencies by a domain expert is preferable, since automated systems are most of the time not able to properly model and use the domain knowledge of an expert. In order to eliminate an inconsistency correctly, with respect to the specific domain, an expert needs a proper understanding of that inconsistency respectively the components that constitute it. Especially in our focus area of inconsistencies that occur during the revision of probability distributions, creating useful explanations is in most cases still a manual and hence expensive effort. In this work we discuss how to automatically create groupings of partitions created by revision assignments and how explanations can benefit from those grouped partitions.

1 Introduction

One important aspect of managing knowledge is the need to react to changes in beliefs quickly and frequently. Methods have been developed to adapt knowledge to new beliefs. In order to adapt knowledge properly, the **principle of minimal change** [10] should be respected. This principle states that no changes are to be made to the knowledge base that are not necessary to incorporate given new beliefs. This means the knowledge base after the incorporation of the new beliefs should be the closest knowledge base to the original one, in an information theoretic sense. The **revision operation** has been introduced as belief change operation that applies new beliefs respecting the principle of minimal change [7]. Further properties a revision operation should satisfy have been formulated as postulates in [1,3]. How to approach revision algorithmically has been outlined in [5] and computational considerations have been made in [12]. This work focusses on the revision of probability distributions. In this field the revision operation has been successfully implemented for Markov networks [6,8]. Markov networks are a member of a class of so called graphical models [2,11,13,17], which are techniques to decompose high-dimensional probability spaces into a number of smaller low-dimensional probability spaces.

The growing complexity and interconnectedness of knowledge bases and increasing number of new beliefs lead almost inevitably to inconsistencies. Inconsistencies in knowledge bases however, pose a threat to the usability of any

© Springer International Publishing Switzerland 2015
S. Destercke and T. Denoeux (Eds.): ECSQARU 2015, LNAI 9161, pp. 257–266, 2015.
DOI: 10.1007/978-3-319-20807-7_23

knowledge system and should consequently be addressed. Handling inconsistencies is a multi-facet problem. In this work we focus on the handling of inconsistencies during the revision of probability distributions. Different important aspects of that problem have been introduced in [15]. Furthermore, two types of inconsistencies and a revision control algorithm have been described in [9].

One important aspect of handling inconsistencies properly is to try to eliminate them. Two types of elimination can be differentiated: the first type is the automated elimination during the revision; the second type is the manual elimination by domain experts that normally happens after the revision operation. In order to manually eliminate inconsistencies, domain experts need to gain a proper understanding of the underlying contradictions at the core of inconsistencies. Therefore, the creation of meaningful explanations for inconsistencies is important. Different components of explanations have been described in [14]. Furthermore, one automated method for creating explanations has been proposed in [15]. In that approach, a minimal explaining set of revision assignments is determined and used as explanation. In this work, we will discuss the grouping of partitions created by revision assignments and how they can be used to create easier to understand explanations that also work with more complex problems.

In Sect. 2 of this paper, we will formally introduce the revision operation, the revision factor and revision inconsistencies. Section 3 then discusses the grouping of partitions. Additionally, we will introduce our example application and present some test results. In Sect. 4, we conclude our work and give some ideas for further research.

2   Fundamentals

In this section we will describe revision assignments, the revision operation, the revision factor and what inconsistencies are in that context.

2.1   The Revision Operation

This paper focusses on the revision of probability distributions and we therefore define it in this context.

As mentioned before, the goal of (probabilistic) revision is to compute a posterior probability distribution which satisfies given new distribution conditions, only accepting a minimal change of the quantitative interaction structures of the underlying prior distribution.

More formally, in our setting, a revision operation (see [6,9]) operates on a joint probability distribution $P(V)$ on a set $V = \{X_1, ..., X_n\}$ of variables with finite domains $\Omega(X_i)$, $i = 1, ..., n$. The purpose of the operation is to adapt $P(V)$ to new sets of beliefs. The beliefs are formulated in a so-called **revision structure** $\Sigma = (\sigma_s)_{s=1}^S$. This structure consists of **revision assignments** σ_s, each of which is referred to a (conditional) assignment scheme $(R_s|K_s)$ with a **context scheme** K_s, $K_s \subseteq V$, and a **revision scheme** R_s, where $\varnothing \neq R_s \subseteq V$ and $K_s \cap R_s = \varnothing$. The pair $(P(V), \Sigma)$ is called **revision problem**.

For example, in the revision assignment $(NAV=nav1|\ Country=France) :=$ 0.2, which sets the probability for the navigation system $nav1$ in the country $France$ to 0.2, the context scheme K_s is $\{Country\}$ and the revision scheme R_s is $\{NAV\}$.

Revision assignments partition the probability space with respect to their context and revision schemes. Expanding on the previous example, suppose there are five different values for the variable NAV and three revision assignments, namely:

$$\sigma_1 \overset{Def}{=} [(NAV = nav1|Country = France) := 0.2]$$

$$\sigma_2 \overset{Def}{=} [(NAV = nav2|Country = France) := 0.25]$$

$$\sigma_3 \overset{Def}{=} [(NAV = nav3|Country = France) := 0.3]$$

The revision assignments create the partitions $\{nav1\}$, $\{nav2\}$, and $\{nav3\}$ for the domain $\Omega(NAV)$ in the context of $Country=France$. Since the probabilities of those three assignments do not sum up to 1, they also together create a fourth partition containing $\{nav4, nav5\}$. We will use this type of partitions later for our grouping approach.

The result of the revision, and solution to the revision problem, is a probability distribution $P_\Sigma(V)$ which

- satisfies the revision assignments (the postulated new probabilities)
- preserves the probabilistic interaction structure as far as possible.

By preserving the interaction structure we mean that, except from the modifications induced by the revision assignments in Σ, all probabilistic dependencies of $P(V)$ are preserved. This requirement ensures that modifications are made according to the principle of minimal change.

It can be proven (see, i.e. [6]) that in case of existence, the solution of the revision problem $(P(V), \Sigma)$ is uniquely defined. This solution can be determined using iterative proportional fitting [17]. Starting with the initial probability distribution, this process adapts the initial probability distribution iteratively, one revision assignment at the time, and converges to a limit distribution that solves the revision problem, given there are no inconsistencies.

2.2   Revision Factors

In each iteration of the iterative proportional fitting process, partitions as explained earlier are multiplied with a so called **revision factor** in order to incorporate the current revision assignment. Consider a single revision assignment $\sigma^* \overset{Def}{=} P^*(\rho_s|\kappa_s)$ of a new probability for $\rho_s|\kappa_s$, with ρ_s and κ_s being single partitions.

With respect to the concept of minimal change, revising $P(V)$ by σ^* leads to the probability distribution $P_{rev}(V)$ which satisfies the condition $P_{rev}(\rho_s|\kappa_s) = P^*(\rho_s|\kappa_s)$ and $P_{rev}(V - K_s - R_s, \kappa_s, \rho_s) = P(V - K_s - R_s, \kappa_s, \rho_s)$.

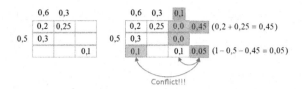

Fig. 1. Inner inconsistency

Using the general rule for factorisation, we obtain

$$P_{rev}(V - K_s - R_s, \kappa_s, \rho_s) = P_{rev}(V - K_s - R_s | \kappa_s, \rho_s) P_{rev}(\rho_s | \kappa_s) P_{rev}(\kappa_s)$$
$$= P(V - K_s - R_s | \kappa_s, \rho_s) P^*(\rho_s | \kappa_s) P(\kappa_s)$$
$$= \frac{P^*(\rho_s | \kappa_s)}{P(\rho_s | \kappa_s)} P(V - K_s - R_s, \kappa_s, \rho_s),$$

where $\frac{P^*(\rho_s | \kappa_s)}{P(\rho_s | \kappa_s)}$ describes the revision factor.

In case of a solvable revision problem $(P(V), \Sigma)$ those factors converge towards one as the revision operation converges.

2.3 Inconsistencies in the Context of the Revision Operation

In case of inconsistencies, the revision will oscillate between multiple limit distributions. In the worst case there are as many limit distributions as there are revision assignments where each limit distribution satisfies the incorporation of one revision assignment. Furthermore, the revision factors will also be oscillating between different values in order to transfer the probabilities from one limit distribution to another one.

Inconsistencies have been analysed in [9] and two types of inconsistencies of revision problems have been distinguished:

Inner consistency of a revision structure Σ is given, if and only if a probability distribution exists that satisfies the revision assignments of Σ; otherwise we refer to **inner inconsistencies** of Σ.

In Fig. 1, a simple example is shown where the given revision assignments already lead to an inconsistency without the consideration of the underlying interaction structure. The filled entries in the left table represent the revision assignments. In the right table consequences for the rest of the table are shown and one conflict is highlighted.

Given that Σ has the property of inner consistency, it is still possible that due to the zero probabilities of $P(V)$ the revision problem $(P(V), \Sigma)$ is not solvable, since a modification of the interaction structure of $P(V)$ would be necessary in order to satisfy the given revision assignments. Therefore, a second type of inconsistency is defined as follows:

Given that Σ has the property of inner consistency, the revision problem $(P(V), \Sigma)$ shows the property of **outer inconsistency**, if and only if there is no solution to this revision problem.

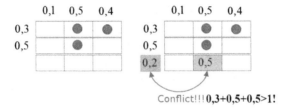

Fig. 2. Outer inconsistency

Figure 2 illustrates an outer inconsistency. In the left table again the numbers represent revision assignments. This time there are additional circles representing zero values that cannot be changed during the revision operation. As before, the right table shows consequences for the remaining table entries as well as an inconsistency.

For the purpose of creating explanations, we now know that there are two potential sources of contradictions. Namely, the revision structure Σ and the interaction structure of $P(V)$, or more precisely its zero-values.

3   Explaining Revision Inconsistencies

In the case of inconsistency the revised distribution P_{rev} does not exist. After cancelling the revision we obtain P_{appr}, a distribution that approximates P_{rev}. Due to the inconsistency there exists at least $\sigma \in \Sigma$ where $P_{appr}(\sigma) \neq P^*(\sigma)$. In order to support the manual elimination of inconsistencies, our explanations aim to highlight the core contradiction that caused $P_{appr}(\sigma^*) \neq P^*(\sigma^*)$ for one chosen revision assignment σ^*. In previous works we proposed a minimal explaining set of revision assignments that together constitute the contradiction as described in [15] as explanation. Such set is effective as long as the number of elements in it is moderately small, or the explained inconsistency doesn't spread over too many dimensions. With an increasing number of participating variables and items in the set, explanations get more and more incomprehensible. Therefore, even after the introduction of an automated method for finding minimal explaining sets, there are still requests for manual analysis of inconsistencies, because the automatically created explanation is not sufficient.

We identified two aspects that most manually created explanations cover, and are currently not incorporated into our automated system: A relevant extract of the interaction structure as well as a meaningful grouping of partitions, created by the revision assignments. In this work, we focus on the automated acquisition of meaningful groupings of partitions.

3.1   Grouping

Grouping together partitions, created by the revision structure Σ, has two positive effects on explanations. First, it reduces the number of elements presented to a domain expert. And second, it magnifies the core feature of the interaction structure that contributes to an inconsistency. To visualise this effect, Fig. 3 shows the interaction structure between two variables. On the left side the original interaction structure is shown. The right side presents the condensed version after the manual grouping of partitions. Relations between the groups of elements are more clearly visible on the right side.

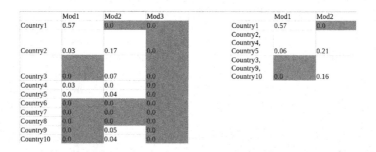

Fig. 3. Left: original interaction structure, right: interaction structure after manual grouping

The biggest challenge when grouping elements automatically is to find a suitable similarity measure in order to decide which elements should be grouped. For the grouping of partitions created by revision assignments, we found that the revision factor can be used. The revision factor is applied to partitions created by the revision structure in every iteration of the revision operation in order to adapt probabilities according to the specified revision structure. During the revision operation very often partitions that would be grouped together by a data analysis expert, are adapted with the same or very similar revision factors. The revision factor converges for every partition once the revision operation converges. In the case that the revision converges towards exactly one limit distribution (and hence does not show inconsistencies), the revision factors will converge towards one. Otherwise, the revision factors will differ and provide a suitable similarity measure. The fact that they are converging means that we can use them as a base for further analysis, and in our case as a measure of similarity.

One of the most common class of methods to group objects by similarity are clustering algorithms. In order to choose a suitable algorithm from that class we have to analyse our grouping problem. In general, we are interested in a result that has the least possible number of clusters, but still explains the chosen inconsistency. The exact number of clusters is unknown and most likely changes between problems. Another aspect is the number of elements we need to cluster. In our case we are dealing with somewhere between a couple of hundred to a couple of thousand revision assignments. However, that number can usually already drastically be reduced before starting the clustering. We decided to use hierarchical clustering [4, 16], since the hierarchy provides us with an easy method

	mod1	mod2	mod3	mod4	mod5	revision factor
nav1	0,1443	0,0134	0,0000	0,0000	0,0000	1,0857
nav2	0,0000	0,0000	0,0800	0,2200	0,0000	0,8000
nav3	0,0037	0,0014	0,0000	0,0000	0,0000	1,0857
nav4	0,4519	0,0352	0,0000	0,0000	0,0000	1,0857
nav5	0,0000	0,0000	0,0000	0,0000	0,0379	1,0857
nav6	0,0000	0,0000	0,0000	0,0000	0,0121	1,0857
revision factor	0,9211	0,9211	1,2500	1,2500	0,9211	

Grouped

	mod1+mod2+mod5	mod3+mod4
~(nav2)	0,7000	0,0000
nav2	0,0000	0,3000

Fig. 4. Above: original interaction structure, below: interaction structure after automated grouping by revision factors

to progressively test groupings with an increasing number of clusters until we found the best solution.

The resulting algorithm groups partitions that are derived from the revision structure Σ and clusters them using the revision factors that are observed when the revision operation converges. The result is a set of groupings of partitions that can then be used to create a more concise view on the relevant part of the interactions structure of the resulting probability distribution P_{rev}.

The grouping created in Fig. 3 could technically be achieved by deriving it from the interaction structure. However, this is a very simple example we choose to illustrate the effect of grouping. In real applications, the interaction structure is only one component that influences the similarity between different partitions. The clustering of partitions using the revision factors is able to also find similarity between structurally different partitions. Furthermore, partitions that look structurally similar in certain projections might indeed have differences caused by higher level dependencies that remain hidden during a structural analysis of a given projection.

Figure 4 shows an example where using revision factors finds groupings that would not have been visible through structural analysis alone. When analysing the structure of the table above, one would find three partitions for the variable NAV. Namely {nav1,nav3,nav4}, {nav2}, and {nav5,nav6}. Similarly for the variable MODEL: {mod1,mod2}, {mod3,mod4}, and {mod5}. However, the analysis of the revision factors revealed that there is an even more concise grouping shown in the table below.

For those reasons structural analysis in general only gives a partial view on the picture. Another aspect is that the interaction structure is relatively static as it does not change during the revision, except from the changes induced by the revision structure. On the other hand, revision factors change dynamically in every iteration of the revision and hence reflect the dynamics of the revision operation to a certain degree. In this way, even dependencies that are not visible in a given projection are considered. This is especially important since manual analysis, most of the time, is restricted to schemes that the data analysis expert considers important. Furthermore, in case of inconsistencies the way the revision factors change already gives certain insight into the nature of inconsistencies.

All the mentioned properties of the grouping of partitions using the revision factor as a similarity measure lead to groupings that can be used to provide a concise explanation for a given inconsistency.

3.2   Application

The presented approach is tested at the Volkswagen Group in their system for estimating part demands and managing capacities for short- and medium-term forecasts, called EPL (EigenschaftsPLanung: item planning). The system combines several heterogeneous input sources such as rules describing buildable vehicle specifications, production history reflecting customer preferences, and market forecasts leading to stipulations of modified item rates, and capacity restrictions that are modelled as revision assignments. Those sources are fused into Markov Networks and the revision operation is then used to estimate the part demands. More details of the modelling of EPL can be found in [6,7]. EPL is currently the biggest industrial application for Markov networks. Using EPL the demands for more than a hundred different model groups from multiple car manufacturers of the Volkswagen Group are estimated every week. In case of the VW Golf– being Volkswagens most popular car class–there are about 200 item families with typically 4 to 8 (but up to 150) values each, that together fully describe a car to be produced, and many of these families can directly be chosen by the customer.

3.3   Experimental Results

In our productive system we are currently using an explanation based on a minimal explaining set of revision assignments as described in [15]. Compared with that approach we achieved two improvements by using the presented clustering method. First, we reduced the number of elements needed to explain an inconsistency (see 1). Second, we achieved some significant performance improvements since we are not searching for a minimal explaining set of revision assignments.

Each example comes from a different model group and planning inconsistency. In all the provided examples the clustering algorithm finds an explanation with less elements faster than the algorithm we were using previously. The last example in Table 1 is an extreme case. Even with an optimised version of the original algorithm, the problem is practically not explainable as 680 revision assignments in the explaining set are hard to understand. Furthermore, with 3 h and 50 min of processing time, the problem is probably faster analysed manually. The clustering algorithm still finds 169 clusters which are similarly hard to understand. However, reaching this result in just 7.5 min instead of 3 h and 50 min, means we can resort to a manual analysis significantly earlier. The three examples were chosen to show results for problems with different complexity.

Table 1. Example reduction of the computation time and number of elements in the explanation when using clustering to group partitions

Example	1	2	3
time using the minimal explaining set algorithm	0.807 s	4.027 s	3h49 min
# revision assignments in the minimal set	10	8	680
time using clustering method	0.229 s	1.996 s	7.5 min
# clusters	3	5	169

Although the clustering algorithm finds smaller explanations faster, the type of explanation is slightly different compared to a minimal explaining set of revision assignments and in most cases relies on the dependency structure to understand what the clusters actually mean. The minimal explaining alone is enough to understand simple problems. However, for more complex inconsistencies the clustering algorithm becomes the better choice.

4 Conclusion

The maintenance of knowledge is one of the most important topics in our current times. Aside from the storage and retrieval of knowledge, adapting it to ever changing business environments is one of the biggest challenges. Methods like the revision operation have been introduced in order to suit the need for proper adaptation of knowledge according to new beliefs. However, with more complex knowledge and longer lists of changed beliefs, inconsistencies are practically unavoidable and need to be handled appropriately. One aspect of handling inconsistencies is their elimination which requires their understanding. In order to help domain experts to understand inconsistencies, explaining them is an essential part of the elimination process. In this work we introduced the idea of grouping partitions created by revision assignments as a method to create more concise explanations while at the same time we save valuable processing time. Our experiments showed a significant improvement in both categories but also revealed some areas for future research.

In this paper, as well as in our previous works, it became quite apparent that providing explanations without the corresponding excerpt of the dependency structure reduces the understandability of an explanation considerably. However, identifying and presenting the relevant parts of the structure, is a non-trivial task even for data analysis experts. In order to improve the expressiveness of automatically created explanations, we are interested in finding and presenting those excerpts of the structure in an automated manner as well.

References

1. Alchourrón, C.E., Gärdenfors, P., Makinson, D.: On the logic of theory change: Partial meet contraction and revision functions. J. Symbolic Log. **50**(02), 510–530 (1985)

2. Borgelt, C., Steinbrecher, M., Kruse, R.: Graphical Models - Representations for Learning, Reasoning and Data Mining. Wiley, Chichester (2009)
3. Darwiche, A.: On the logic of iterated belief revision. Artif. Intell. **89**(1–2), 1–29 (1997)
4. Defays, D.: An efficient algorithm for a complete link method. Comput. J. **20**(4), 364–366 (1977)
5. Gabbay, D.: Controlled revision - an algorithmic approach for belief revision. J. Logic Comput. **13**(1), 3–22 (2003)
6. Gebhardt, J., Borgelt, C., Kruse, R., Detmer, H.: Knowledge revision in markov networks. Mathware Soft Comput. **11**(2–3), 93–107 (2004)
7. Gebhardt, J., Detmer, H., Madsen, A.L.: Predicting parts demand in the automotive industry-an application of probabilistic graphical models. In: Proceedings of the International Joint Conference on Uncertainty in Artificial Intelligence (2003)
8. Gebhardt, J., Klose, A., Detmer, H., Ruegheimer, F., Kruse, R.: Graphical models for industrial planning on complex domains. In: del la Riccia, G, e.a. (ed.) Decision Theory and Multi-Agent Planning, pp. 131–143. No. 482 in CISM Courses and Lectures. Springer (2006)
9. Gebhardt, J., Klose, A., Wendler, J.: Markov network revision: on the handling of inconsistencies. In: Moewes, C., Nürnberger, A. (eds.) Computational Intelligence in Intelligent Data Analysis. SCI, vol. 445, pp. 153–165. Springer, Heidelberg (2013)
10. Gärdenfors, P.: Knowledge in Flux: Modeling the Dynamics of Epistemic States. MIT Press, Cambridge (1988)
11. Kruse, R., et al.: Computational Intelligence. A Methodological Introduction. Springer, London (2013)
12. Nebel, B.: Base revision operations and schemes: representation, semantics and complexity. In: Proceedings of the 11th ECAI 1994, Amsterdam, The Netherlands, pp. 341–345. Wiley (1994)
13. Pearl, J.: Probabilistic Reasoning in Intelligent Systems: Networks of Plausible Inference. Morgan Kaufmann, San Mateo (1991)
14. Schmidt, F., Gebhardt, J., Kruse, R.: Handling revision inconsistencies: creating useful explanations. In: HICSS-48, Proceedings, 5–8 January 2015, Koloa, Kauai, HI, USA, pp. 1–8. IEEE Computer Society (2015)
15. Schmidt, F., Wendler, J., Gebhardt, J., Kruse, R.: Handling inconsistencies in the revision of probability distributions. In: Pan, J.-S., Polycarpou, M.M., Woźniak, M., de Carvalho, A.C.P.L.F., Quintián, H., Corchado, E. (eds.) HAIS 2013. LNCS, vol. 8073, pp. 598–607. Springer, Heidelberg (2013)
16. Sibson, R.: Slink: An optimally efficient algorithm for the single-link cluster method. Comput. J. **16**(1), 30–34 (1973)
17. Whittaker, J.: Graphical Models in Applied Multivariate Statistics. Wiley, New York (1990)

On Measuring Inconsistency Using Maximal Consistent Sets

Meriem Ammoura[1,2], Badran Raddaoui[1], Yakoub Salhi[1](✉),
and Brahim Oukacha[2]

[1] CRIL - CNRS UMR 8188, University Artois, 62307 Lens Cedex, France
meriem.am21@gmail.com, {raddaoui,salhi}@cril.fr
[2] LAROMAD - University Mouloud Mammeri, Tizi Ouzou, Algeria
oukachabrahim@yahoo.fr

Abstract. An important problem in knowledge-based systems is inconsistency handling. This problem has recently been attracting a lot of attention in AI community. In this paper, we tackle the problem of evaluating the amount of conflicts in knowledge bases, and provide a new fine grained inconsistency measure, denoted MCSC, based on maximal consistent sets. In particular, it is suitable in systems where inconsistency results from multiple consistent sources. We show that our measure satisfies several rational postulates proposed in the literature. Moreover, we provide an encoding in integer linear programming for computing MCSC.

1 Introduction

In classical logics, the principle of explosion is a law which states that any formula can be deduced from a contradiction using the inference process. This principle means that the inference process alone in classical logic does not allow to reason under inconsistency. To remedy this problem, several approaches have been proposed in the literature, such as argumentation theory, paraconsistent logics, belief revision, etc. The main goal of these approaches is to deal with inconsistency as an informative concept. In the same vein, inconsistency measures have been introduced in order to be used in analyzing inconsistency. In the literature, an inconsistency measure is defined as a function that associates a value to each knowledge base [1]. Several inconsistency measures have been proposed in the literature (e.g. [1–8]), and it has been shown that they are suitable for various applications such as e-commerce protocols [9], software specifications [10], belief merging [5], news reports [11], requirements engineering [1], integrity constraints [12], databases [13], ontologies [14], semantic web [14], network intrusion detection [15], and multi-agent systems [8].

In [1], Hunter and Konieczny have proposed four axiomatic properties that any inconsistency measure should satisfy. Namely, the properties of consistency, monotony, free-formula independence, and dominance. However, in a recent article [16], Besnard has provided objections to the axiomatic properties of free-formula independence and dominance. Indeed, the author has pointed out in

© Springer International Publishing Switzerland 2015
S. Destercke and T. Denoeux (Eds.): ECSQARU 2015, LNAI 9161, pp. 267–276, 2015.
DOI: 10.1007/978-3-319-20807-7_24

his article undesirable consequences of these properties, such as ignoring certain conflicts, and has provided alternative properties in order to avoid these consequences.

Inconsistency is often measured by quantifying its origin in a monodimensional way, such as the number of minimal inconsistent subsets. However, no value alone can capture the multiple aspects of inconsistency. Indeed, inconsistency in a knowledge base may result from several reasons and has to be measured in a multi-dimensional way. For instance, let us consider the knowledge base $K = \{p, \neg p \wedge q, \neg p \wedge r, \neg p \wedge s\}$. Clearly, the inconsistency of K results from the conflict between the formula p and the subformula $\neg p$ in the other formulæ. If we use the inconsistency measure I_{LP_m} defined in [4] and based on Priest's three-valued logic [17], then we can capture the conflict between a and $\neg a$ ($I_{LP_m}(K) = 1$). However, since I_{LP_m} consider K as a single formula, it does not reveal the fact that there are three conflicts between the formulæ of K. To this end, one can use the measure I_{MI} [1] defined as the number of minimal inconsistent subsets of K ($I_{MI}(K) = 3$). The measure I_{MI} is not more informative than I_{LP_m} and conversely, but the two measures provide information about incomparable facets of inconsistency. In other words, two measures are not necessarily comparable in the sense that one is better than the other, they can capture incomparable aspects that constitute inconsistency. We think that Besnard's objections to the properties of free-formula independence and dominance may be used to argue in this sense. For instance, the property of free-formula independence has a sense when we do not consider the internal structure of the formulæ in a knowledge base. Indeed, it simply means that adding a new formula which is not involved in a conflict does not change the amount of inconsistency.

In this work, we introduce an inconsistency measure, denoted MCSC, by following an approach based on the use of maximal consistent subsets. This approach consists in considering that the inconsistency of a knowledge base is a consequence of the fact that its pieces of information are received from ignored multiple consistent sources, where each possible source is identified by a consistent subset of formulæ. In this context, the degree of conflict of a knowledge base can be seen as the smallest number of pieces of information that cannot be shared by possible sources covering all the elements of this base. Clearly, computing this value can be performed by considering only the possible sources identified by the maximal consistent subsets since the objective consists in minimizing the number of non shared pieces of information.

We show that our inconsistency measure satisfies several desirable properties proposed in the literature, such as Free Formula Independence and Superadditivity. We also provide properties of bounds on MCSC. Then, we study the relationship between our measure and the inconsistency metric proposed in [18]. This study comes from the fact that these two measures satisfy a fundamental property, called Independent MIS-additivity. Finally, we show that our measure can be formulated as an integer linear program by providing an encoding allowing its computation.

2   Formal Setting

In this section, we define the syntax and the semantics of propositional logic. Let Prop be a countably set of propositional variables. We use the letters p, q, r, etc. to range over Prop. The set of *propositional formulæ*, denoted Form, is defined inductively started from Prop, the constant $\bot$ denoting absurdity, the constant $\top$ denoting true, and using the logical connectives $\neg$, $\wedge$, $\vee$, $\rightarrow$. Notationally, we use the greek letters ϕ, ψ to represent formulæ. Given a syntactic object S, we use $\mathcal{P}(S)$ to denote the set of propositional variables appearing in S. For a set S, we denote by $|S|$ its cardinality.

A *Boolean interpretation* $\mathcal{I}$ of a formula ϕ is defined as a function from $\mathcal{P}(\phi)$ to $\{0, 1\}$ (0 corresponds to *false* and 1 to *true*). It is inductively extended to propositional formulæ as usual. A formula ϕ is consistent if there exists a Boolean interpretation $\mathcal{I}$ of ϕ such that $\mathcal{I}(\phi) = 1$. ϕ is *valid* or *a theorem*, if every Boolean interpretation is a model of ϕ.

It is worth noticing that we can restrict the language to the connectives $\neg$ and $\wedge$, since we have the following equivalences: $\phi \vee \psi \equiv \neg(\neg\phi \wedge \neg\psi)$ and $\phi \rightarrow \psi \equiv \neg\phi \vee \psi$. A *knowledge base* K is a finite set of propositional formulæ.

Definition 1. *Let K be a knowledge base. M is a minimal inconsistent subset (MIS) of K iff (i) $M \subseteq K$, (ii) $M \vdash \bot$ and (iii) $\forall\phi \in M$, $M \setminus \{\phi\} \nvdash \bot$.*

We denote by $MISes(K)$ the set of all minimal inconsistent subsets of K.

Definition 2. *Let K be a knowledge base and M a subset of K. M is a maximal consistent subset (MCS) of K iff (i) $M \subseteq K$, (ii) $M \nvdash \bot$, (iii) $\forall\phi \in K \setminus M$, $M \cup \{\phi\} \vdash \bot$.*

We denote by $MCSes(K)$ the set of all maximal consistent sets of K.

Definition 3. *Let K be a knowledge base and ϕ a knowledge in K. ϕ is a free knowledge in K iff $\phi \notin M$ for every $M \in MISes(K)$.*

We use $Free(K)$ to denote the set of free knowledge in K.

In recent years, inconsistent data reasoning has seen a revival in interest because of number of challenges in terms of collecting, modelling, representing, and querying the information. In this context, various logic-based approaches have been proposed in the literature for quantifying the amount of inconsistency. Therefore, several properties have been defined to characterize such measures. More specifically, in [1] the authors propose axiomatic properties that any inconsistency measure should satisfy. An inconsistency measure I is called a *basic inconsistency measure* if it satisfies the following properties, for all knowledge bases K and K', and for all formulæ ϕ and ψ:

- *Consistency*: $I(K) = 0$ iff K is consistent;
- *Monotony*: $I(K) \leq I(K \cup K')$;
- *Free Formula Independence*: if $\phi \in free(K)$, then $I(K) = I(K \setminus \{\phi\})$;
- *Dominance*: if $\phi \vdash \psi$ and $\phi \nvdash \bot$, then $I(K \cup \{\psi\}) \leq I(K \cup \{\phi\})$.

It is worth noticing that Besnard has provided in [16] objections on the properties of free formula independence and dominance. In particular, the objection to the property of free formula independence comes from the fact that a free formula may be involved in a conflict and in this case it has to increase the amount of inconsistency. Let us consider, for instance, the following knowledge base proposed in [16]: $K = \{p \wedge r, q \wedge \neg r, \neg p \vee \neg q\}$. The knowledge base K has a single minimal inconsistent subset $M = \{p \wedge r, q \wedge \neg r\}$ and, consequently, $\neg p \vee \neg q$ is a free-formula in K. Using the property of free-formula independence, we should have $I(M) = I(K)$. However, p and q are compatible and $p \wedge q$ is contradicted by the free-formula $\neg p \vee \neg q$. Consequently, one can consider that K contains more conflicts than M and in this case the free-formula independence property fails. Let us note that to detect whether free-formulæ are involved in a conflict, we have to consider the internal structure of formulæ.

We agree with Besnard's objections in the sense that it is not suitable to require Hunter and Konieczny's basic properties for any inconsistency measure. However, we think that inconsistency is a multi-dimensional concept and a single inconsistency measure is insufficient to capture all the information about the amount of inconsistency. In this context, to capture certain aspects that constitute inconsistency, we need inconsistency measures satisfying Hunter and Konieczny's properties. In particular, aspects which are not related to internal structure of formulæ in knowledge bases.

3   MCS-Cover Based Inconsistency Measure

In this section, we introduce a new inconsistency measure, denoted $MCSC$, which is based on the use of the MCSes. Intuitively, the main idea behind $MCSC$ is in considering that the inconsistency is due to the fact that the information are often received from ignored multiple consistent information sources. In this context, the degree of conflict corresponds to the smallest number of knowledges that cannot be shared by possible information sources. The possible information sources are characterized by the consistent subsets. Since our aim is to minimize non shared knowledges, we only consider the possible information sources characterized by the MCSes.

Let us first define the following fundamental concepts that will be useful in the sequel.

Definition 4 (MCS-Cover). *Let K be a knowledge base. A MCS-cover $\mathcal{C}$ of K is a subset of $MCSes(K)$ such that $\bigcup_{S \in \mathcal{C}} S = K$.*

Let us consider, for instance, the knowledge base $K = \{\neg p \vee \neg q, \neg p \vee \neg r, \neg q \vee \neg r, p, q, r\}$. The following two sets are MCS-covers of K: $\mathcal{C}_1 = \{\{\neg p \vee \neg q, \neg p \vee \neg r, \neg q \vee \neg r, p\}, \{p, q, r\}\}$, $\mathcal{C}_2 = \{\{\neg p \vee \neg q, \neg p \vee \neg r, \neg q \vee \neg r, p\}, \{\neg p \vee \neg q, \neg p \vee \neg r, q, r\}\}$.

We now define a preorder relation on the MCS-covers of a given knowledge base, denoted $\succeq$. Let K be a knowledge base. For all $\mathcal{C}$ and $\mathcal{C}'$ two MCS-covers of K, $\mathcal{C} \succeq \mathcal{C}'$ if and only if $|\bigcap_{S \in \mathcal{C}} S| \geqslant |\bigcap_{S' \in \mathcal{C}'} S'|$. Let us consider again the previous example. We have $\mathcal{C}_2 \succeq \mathcal{C}_1$ since $|\{\neg p \vee \neg q, \neg p \vee \neg r, \neg q \vee \neg r, p\} \cap \{p, q, r\}| = 1$ and $|\{\neg p \vee \neg q, \neg p \vee \neg r, \neg q \vee \neg r, p\} \cap \{\neg p \vee \neg q, \neg p \vee \neg r, q, r\}| = 2$.

Definition 5 (Normal MCS-Cover). *Let K be a knowledge base and $\mathcal{C}$ an MCS-cover of K. Then, $\mathcal{C}$ is a normal MCS-cover if $\mathcal{C}'$ is not an MCS-cover for every $\mathcal{C}' \subset \mathcal{C}$.*

Definition 6 (Maximum MCS-Cover). *Let K be a knowledge base and $\mathcal{C}$ a MCS-cover of K. Then, $\mathcal{C}$ is said to be a maximum MCS-cover of K if it is normal and $\forall \, \mathcal{C}'$ MCS-cover of K, $\mathcal{C} \succeq \mathcal{C}'$. We denote by $\lambda(K)$ the value $|\bigcap_{S \in \mathcal{C}} S|$.*

Definition 7 (MCSC). *Let K be a knowledge base. The inconsistency measure of K, denoted $MCSC(K)$, is defined as follows: $MCSC(K) = |K| - \lambda(K)$.*

Regarding the previous example of knowledge base, we have $MCSC(K) = 4$ since $\mathcal{C}_2$ is a maximum MCS-cover.

We now provide a generalization of the inconsistency measure MCSC. The base idea consists in associating a weight to each formula in a knowledge base representing the degree of its relevance. In this context, the inconsistency value corresponds to the smallest weight of non shared knowledge.

Given a knowledge base K, we define a weight function W of K as a function from K to $\mathbb{N}^*$.

Definition 8 (Weighted Maximum MCS-Cover). *Let K be a knowledge base, W a weight function of K and $\mathcal{C}$ a MCS-cover of K. Then, $\mathcal{C}$ is said to be a weighted maximum MCS-cover of K w.r.t. W if it is normal and $\sum_{\phi \in \bigcap_{M \in \mathcal{C}} M} W(\phi) \geqslant \sum_{\phi \in \bigcap_{M \in \mathcal{C}'} M} W(\phi)$ for every MCS-cover $\mathcal{C}'$. We denote by $\lambda(K, W)$ the value $\sum_{\phi \in \bigcap_{M \in \mathcal{C}} M} W(\phi)$.*

Definition 9 (WMCSC). *Let K be a knowledge base and W a weight function of K. The inconsistency measure of K, denoted $WMCSC(K, W)$, is defined as follows: $MCSC(K) = |K| - \lambda(K, W)$.*

Clearly, WMCSC can be seen as a generalization of MCSC. Indeed, by using a weight function W giving the weight 1 to every formula in the knowledge base K, we get $WMCSC(K, W) = MCSC(K)$. Let us note that there are several ways to define a weight function of a knowledge base from the structure of its formulæ. For instance, the weight of a formula may be defined as the number of propositional variables occurring in it. Intuitively, this means that the importance of a knowledge depends on the number of pieces of information which are binded by it.

4 Properties of MCSC Measure

In the section, we describe some important properties of the inconsistency measure $MCSC$. We first show that it satisfies the properties of consistency, monotony, free formula independence, and a weak form of the property of dominance. Then, we show that our measure satisfies also the property of super-additivity.

Proposition 1. *MCSC measure satisfies Consistency, Monotony and Free Formula Independence.*

Proof. Consistency. Let K be a consistent knowledge base. Then, $\{K\}$ is the unique maximum MCS-cover of K ($\lambda(K) = |K|$). Hence, $MCSC(K) = 0$.

Monotony. Proposition 3 can be seen as a generalization of Monotony.

Free Formula Independence. Let K be a knowledge base and ϕ a free formula in K. Let $\mathcal{C} = \{S_1, \ldots, S_n\}$ be a maximum MCS-cover of $K \setminus \{\phi\}$. Since $\phi \in Free(K)$, $S_i \cup \{\phi\} \nvdash \bot$ holds for every $1 \leqslant i \leqslant n$. Thus, $\{S_1 \cup \{\phi\}, \ldots, S_n \cup \{\phi\}\}$ is a maximum MCS-cover of K and we obtain $\lambda(K) = \lambda(K \setminus \{\phi\}) + 1$. As a consequence, $MCSC(K) = |K| - \lambda(K) = |K \setminus \{\phi\}| + 1 - \lambda(K \setminus \{\phi\}) - 1 = MCSC(K \setminus \{\phi\})$.

Proposition 2. *Let K be a knowledge base and ϕ and ψ two formulæ such that $\phi \nvdash \bot$ and $\phi \vdash \psi$. If $\phi \notin K$ or $\psi \in K$, then $MCSC(K \cup \{\psi\}) \leq MCSC(K \cup \{\phi\})$.*

Proof. Let $\mathcal{C}$ be a maximum MCS-cover of $K \cup \{\phi\}$. We consider w.l.o.g. that $\psi \notin K$ since $MCSC$ satisfies the property of monotony. Clearly, by replacing in $\mathcal{C}$ the formula ϕ with ψ we obtain a set of satisfiable subsets of $K \cup \{\psi\}$. As a consequence, we have $\lambda(K \cup \{\psi\}) \geqslant \lambda(K \cup \{\phi\})$. Thus, we obtain $MCSC(K \cup \{\psi\}) = |K \cup \{\psi\}| - \lambda(K \cup \{\psi\}) \leqslant |K \cup \{\phi\}| - \lambda(K \cup \{\phi\}) = MCSC(K \cup \{\phi\})$.

Let us note that $MCSC$ does not satisfy Dominance. Consider for instance the knowledge base $K = \{p \wedge (p \rightarrow q), \neg q\}$. We have $p \wedge (p \rightarrow q) \nvdash \bot$, $p \wedge (p \rightarrow q) \vdash q$ and $\lambda(K) = 0$. Moreover, $\lambda(K \cup \{q\}) = 0$ holds. Then, we have $MCSC(K \cup \{q\}) = 3 > MCSC(K \cup \{p \wedge (p \rightarrow q)\}) = 2$.

Other rational postulates than those of the basic system have been proposed in the literature. In particular, we consider the following additivity properties introduced in [1, 19]:

- *Super-additivity*: if $K \cap K' = \emptyset$, then $I(K \cup K') \geqslant I(K) + I(K')$.
- *MIS-additivity*: if $MISes(K) = MISes(K') \uplus MISes(K'')$, then $I(K) = I(K') + I(K'')$.

One can easily see that Super-additivity is a generalization of Monotony.

Proposition 3. *MCSC measure satisfies Super-additivity.*

Proof. Let K and K' be two knowledge bases such that $K \cap K' = \emptyset$ and $\mathcal{C}$ a maximum MCS-cover of $K \cup K'$. Clearly, for all $S \in MCSes(K \cup K')$, there exist $S' \in MCSes(K)$ and $S'' \in MCSes(K')$ such that $S \subseteq S' \cup S''$. Then, there exist MCS-covers $\mathcal{C}'$ and $\mathcal{C}''$ of K and K' respectively such that $\bigcap_{S \in \mathcal{C}} S \subseteq (\bigcap_{S' \in \mathcal{C}'} S') \cup (\bigcap_{S \in \mathcal{C}''} S'')$. As a consequence, we have $\lambda(K \cup K') \leqslant \lambda(K) + \lambda(K')$. Therefore, $MCSC(K \cup K') \geqslant MCSC(K) + MCSC(K')$ holds.

In the following proposition, we show that $MCSC$ measure satisfies a property generalizing Super-additivity.

Proposition 4. *Given two knowledge bases K and K', we have:*

$$MCSC(K \cup K') \geqslant MCSC(K) + MCSC(K') - |K \cap K'|.$$

Proof. We have, for all $S \in MCSes(K \cup K')$, $S' = S \cap K$ and $S'' = S \cap K'$ are both consistent. Let $\mathcal{C} = \{S_1, \ldots, S_n\}$ be a maximum MCS-cover of $K \cup K'$. Then, $\mathcal{C}' = \{S_1 \cap K, \ldots, S_n \cap K\}$ and $\mathcal{C}'' = \{S_1 \cap K', \ldots, S_n \cap K'\}$ are sets of consistent subsets. Moreover, $\bigcap_{S \in \mathcal{C}} S = (\bigcap_{S' \in \mathcal{C}'} S') \cup (\bigcap_{S'' \in \mathcal{C}''} S'')$. Thus, $\lambda(K \cup K') \leqslant \lambda(K) + \lambda(K')$ holds and, consequently, $MCSC(K \cup K') \geqslant |K \cup K'| - \lambda(K) - \lambda(K')$ holds. Since $|K \cup K'| = |K| + |K'| - |K \cap K'|$, we deduce that $MCSC(K \cup K') \geqslant MCSC(K) + MCSC(K') - |K \cap K'|$.

It is worth noticing that $MCSC$ does not satisfy MIS-additivity. Consider, for instance, $K = \{a, b, \neg a \wedge \neg b\}$, $K_1 = \{a, \neg a \wedge \neg b\}$ and $K_2 = \{b, \neg a \wedge \neg b\}$. It is easy to see that $MCSC(K) = 3$, $MCSC(K_1) = 2$ and $MCSC(K_2) = 2$. We have $MISes(K) = MISes(K_1) \uplus MISes(K_2)$, but $MCSC(K) \neq MCS(K_1) + MCS(K_2)$.

Proposition 5. *Given a knowledge base K, $MCSC(K) \leqslant |K| - |Free(K)|$.*

Proof. This property is a direct consequence of the fact that, for all $S \in MCSes(K)$, $Free(K) \subseteq S$.

Proposition 6. *Given a minimal inconsistent set of formulæ K such that $|K| > 1$, we have $MCSC(K) = 2$.*

Proof. Let $K = \{\phi_1, \ldots, \phi_n\}$ be a minimal inconsistent set such that $n > 1$. Then, $S = \{\phi_1, \ldots, \phi_{n-1}\}$ and $S' = \{\phi_2, \ldots, \phi_n\}$ are MCSes of K, and $\{S, S'\}$ are an MCS-cover of K. Then, $MCSC(K) \leqslant n - (n - 2) = 2$ holds. Let us assume that $MCSC(K) = 1$. Then, there exist S and S' in $MCSes(K)$ such that $S \neq S'$ and $|S \cap S'| \geqslant n - 1$. Thus, $|S| = |S'| = n$ holds and we get a contradiction. Therefore, we obtain $MCSC(K) = 2$.

5   Relationship Between $MCSC$ and I_{CC} Measures

In this section, we study the relationship between our inconsistency measure and an existing one, denoted I_{CC}, introduced recently by Jabbour et al. in [18]. This study comes from the fact that the two metrics $MCSC$ and I_{CC} satisfy both a fundamental property, called Independent MIS-additivity. Firstly, we introduce the measure I_{CC} as follows. Given a knowledge base K, a MIS-decomposition of K is a pair $\langle \{K_1, \ldots, K_n\}, K' \rangle$ satisfying the following properties: (i) $(\bigcup_{i=1}^{n} K_i) \cap K' = \emptyset$; (ii) $K_i \vdash \bot$ for every $1 \leqslant i \leqslant n$; (iii) $K_i \cap K_j = \emptyset$ for every $1 \leqslant i \neq j \leqslant n$; (iv) $MISes(\bigcup_{i=1}^{n} K_i) = \uplus_{i=1}^{n} MISes(K_i)$.

Given a knowledge base K, $I_{CC}(K) = n$ if there is a MIS-decomposition $\langle D, K' \rangle$ where $|D| = n$, and there is no MIS-decomposition $\langle D', K'' \rangle$ such that

$|D'| > n$. In this case, $\langle D, K' \rangle$ is called *maximum MIS-decomposition*. Intuitively, this measure can be seen as the maximum number of MISes that can be isolated by removing formulæ from the knowledge base.

Definition 10 (Independent MIS-Additivity). *Let I be an inconsistency measure. Then, I satisfies the property of independent MIS-additivity[1] iff, for all knowledge bases K and K', if $MISes(K \cup K') = MISes(K) \uplus MISes(K')$ and $(\bigcup_{M \in MISes(K)} M) \cap (\bigcup_{M \in MISes(K')} M) = \emptyset$, then $I(K \cup K') = I(K) + I(K')$.*

Proposition 7. *MCSC measure satisfies the property of independent MIS-additivity.*

Proof. Let K, K_1 and K_2 be knowledge bases such that $MISes(K) = MISes(K_1) \uplus MISes(K_2)$ and, for all $M \in MISes(K_1)$ and $M' \in MISes(K_2)$, $M \cap M' = \emptyset$. We denote K', K_1' and K_2' the sets $\bigcup_{M \in MISes(K)} M$, $\bigcup_{M \in MISes(K_1)} M$ and $\bigcup_{M \in MISes(K_2)} M$ respectively. Let us note that $K' = K_1' \uplus K_2'$. Using the property of free formula independence, we have $MCS(K) = MCS(K')$, $MCS(K_1) = MCS(K_1')$ and $MCS(K_2) = MCS(K_2')$. Then, using the properties of super-additivity, we have $MCSC(K) \geqslant MCS(K_1) + MCS(K_2)$. Let $S \in MCSes(K_1')$ and $S' \in MCSes(K_2')$. Since $(\bigcup_{M \in MISes(K_1)} M) \cap (\bigcup_{M \in MISes(K_2)} M) = \emptyset$, $S \cup S'$ is a consistent set in K'. Then, using the fact that $K' = K_1' \uplus K_2'$, we have $\lambda(K') \geqslant \lambda(K_1') + \lambda(K_2')$ and, consequently, $MCSC(K') \leqslant MCSC(K_1') + MCSC(K_2')$. Thus, $MCSC(K) \leqslant MCSC(K_1) + MCSC(K_2)$ holds. Therefore, we get $MCSC(K) = MCSC(K_1) + MCSC(K_2)$. ∎

Proposition 8. *Given a knowledge base K, we have $MCSC(K) \geqslant 2 \times I_{CC}(K)$.*

Proof. The property is a consequence of Super-additivity and Proposition 6. ∎

We now show that $MCSC$ allows to distinguish knowledge bases which are not distinguishable by I_{CC}. Consider, for instance, the two knowledge bases $K_1 = \{p \wedge q, p \wedge r, \neg p\}$ and $K_2 = \{p \wedge q, \neg p\}$. Then, $MISes(K_1) = \{\{p \wedge q, \neg p\}, \{p \wedge r, \neg p\}\}$ and $MISes(K_2) = \{\{p \wedge q, \neg p\}\}$. Hence, we have clearly $I_{CC}(K_1) = I_{CC}(K_2) = 1$. Furthermore, $\mathcal{C}_1 = \{\{p \wedge q, p \wedge r\}, \{\neg p\}\}$ and $\mathcal{C}_2 = \{\{p \wedge q\}, \{\neg p\}\}$ are maximum MCS-covers of K_1 and K_2 respectively. As a consequence, $\lambda(K_1) = \lambda(K_2) = 0$. Thus, $MCSC(K_1) = 3$ and $MCSC(K_2) = 2$ hold.

Conversely, consider the knowledge bases $K_3 = \{p \wedge q_1, p \wedge q_2, \neg p, r, \neg r\}$ and $K_4 = \{p \wedge q_1, p \wedge q_2, p \wedge q_3, p \wedge q_4, \neg p\}$. Then, $\langle \{\{p \wedge q_1, p \wedge q_2, \neg p\}, \{r, \neg r\}\}, \emptyset \rangle$ and . $\langle \{\{p \wedge q_1, p \wedge q_2, p \wedge q_3, p \wedge q_4, \neg p\}\}, \emptyset \rangle$ are maximum MIS-decompositions of K_3 and K_4 respectively and, consequently, $I_{CC}(K_3) = 2$ and. $I_{CC}(K_3) = 1$ hold. Moreover, $\{\{p \wedge q_1, p \wedge q_2, r\}, \{\neg p, \neg r\}\}$ and $\{\{p \wedge q_1, p \wedge q_2, p \wedge q_3, p \wedge q_4\}, \{\neg p\}\}$ are maximum MCS-covers of K_3 and K_4 respectively. Thus, we obtain $MCSC(K_3) = MCSC(K_4) = 5$.

The previous examples show that $MCSC$ allows to distinguish knowledge bases which are not distinguishable by I_{CC} and vice versa. As a consequence, these measures do not capture the same facets in measuring inconsistency.

---

[1] In the original paper, this property is called *enhanced additivity*.

6   Integer Linear Programming Formulation

In this section, we show that our measure can be formulated as an integer linear program (ILP) by providing an encoding defined mainly from the set of the MCSes of a knowledge base. To do this, each variable used in our encoding is binary (a 0-1 variable) and corresponds to either a formula or an MCS. The constraints are defined so that the objective consists in maximizing the function corresponding to the sum of the variables associated to formulæ.

Variables. We associate a binary variable X_ϕ having as domain $\{0, 1\}$ to each formula ϕ in K. We also associate a binary variable Y_M having as domain $\{0, 1\}$ to each MCS M of K.

The integer linear program ILP-MCSC(K) is as follows:

$$minimize \quad |K| - \sum_{\phi \in K} X_\phi$$
$$\text{subject to:}$$

$$\sum_{M : \phi \in M} Y_M \geqslant 1 \; for \; all \; \phi \in K \tag{1}$$

$$X_\phi + Y_M \leqslant 1 \; for \; all \; \phi \in K \; and \; M \in MCSes(K) \; with \; \phi \notin M \tag{2}$$

Proposition 9 (Soundness). *Given a knowledge base K and a solution S of ILP-MCSC(K), then $MCSC(K) = |K| - |\{\phi \in K \mid S(X_\phi) = 1\}|$.*

Proof. Each solution S_1 of the linear inequality (1) means that the set $\mathcal{C} = \{M \in MCSes(K) \mid S_1(Y_M) = 1\}$ is an MCS-cover of K. Moreover, each solution S_2 of the linear inequality (2) means that $\{\phi \in K \mid S_2(X_\phi) = 1\} \subseteq \bigcap_L M$ where $L = \{M \in MCSes(K) \mid S_2(Y_M) = 1\}$. Thus, since minimizing $|K| - \sum_{\phi \in K} X_\phi$ corresponds to maximizing $\sum_{\phi \in K} X_\phi$, we have $\lambda(K) = |\{\phi \in K \mid S(X_\phi) = 1\}|$. As a consequence, $MCSC(K) = |K| - |\{\phi \in K \mid S(X_\phi) = 1\}|$ holds.

7   Conclusion and Perspectives

Several approaches for measuring inconsistency have been proposed in the literature. In this paper, we proposed an original approach based on the use of maximal consistent sets. The basic idea consists in considering the conflict of a knowledge base as a consequence of the use of multiple consistent information sources. We showed that our inconsistency measure satisfies several desired rational properties. We also proposed an encoding in integer linear programming for its computation.

As a future work, we intend to investigate complexity issues related to our framework. We also plan to define algorithms for the problem of MCSC computation and conduct experimental evaluations.

References

1. Hunter, A., Konieczny, S.: On the measure of conflicts: Shapley inconsistency values. Artif. Intell. **174**(14), 1007–1026 (2010)
2. Grant, J.: Classifications for inconsistent theories. Notre Dame J. Formal Logic **19**(3), 435–444 (1978)
3. Knight, K.: Measuring inconsistency. J. Philos. Logic **31**(1), 77–98 (2002)
4. Konieczny, S., Lang, J., Marquis, P.: Quantifying information and contradiction in propositional logic through test actions. In: IJCAI, pp. 106–111 (2003)
5. Qi, G., Liu, W., Bell, D.A.: Measuring conflict and agreement between two prioritized belief bases. In: IJCAI, pp. 552–557 (2005)
6. Mu, K., Liu, W., Jin, Z.: A general framework for measuring inconsistency through minimal inconsistent sets. Knowl. Inf. Syst. **27**(1), 85–114 (2011)
7. Grant, J., Hunter, A.: Distance-based measures of inconsistency. In: van der Gaag, L.C. (ed.) ECSQARU 2013. LNCS, vol. 7958, pp. 230–241. Springer, Heidelberg (2013)
8. Hunter, A., Parsons, S., Wooldridge, M.: Measuring inconsistency in multi-agent systems. Kunstliche Intelligenz **28**, 169–178 (2014)
9. Chen, Q., Zhang, C., Zhang, S.: A verification model for electronic transaction protocols. In: Yu, J.X., Lin, X., Lu, H., Zhang, Y. (eds.) APWeb 2004. LNCS, vol. 3007, pp. 824–833. Springer, Heidelberg (2004)
10. Martinez, A.B.B., Arias, J.J.P., Vilas, A.F.: On measuring levels of inconsistency in multi-perspective requirements specifications. In: PRISE 2004, pp. 21–30 (2004)
11. Hunter, A.: How to act on inconsistent news: ignore, resolve, or reject. Data Knowl. Eng. **57**(3), 221–239 (2006)
12. Grant, J., Hunter, A.: Measuring inconsistency in knowledgebases. J. Intell. Inf. Syst. **27**(2), 159–184 (2006)
13. Martinez, M.V., Pugliese, A., Simari, G.I., Subrahmanian, V.S., Prade, H.: How dirty is your relational database? an axiomatic approach. In: Mellouli, K. (ed.) ECSQARU 2007. LNCS (LNAI), vol. 4724, pp. 103–114. Springer, Heidelberg (2007)
14. Zhou, L., Huang, H., Qi, G., Ma, Y., Huang, Z., Qu, Y.: Measuring inconsistency in dl-lite ontologies. In: Web Intelligence, pp. 349–356 (2009)
15. McAreavey, K., Liu, W., Miller, P., Mu, K.: Measuring inconsistency in a network intrusion detection rule set based on snort. Int. J. Semant. Comput. **5**(3), 281–322 (2011)
16. Besnard, P.: Revisiting postulates for inconsistency measures. In: Fermé, E., Leite, J. (eds.) JELIA 2014. LNCS, vol. 8761, pp. 383–396. Springer, Heidelberg (2014)
17. Priest, G.: Minimally inconsistent LP. Stud. Logica. **50**, 321–331 (1991)
18. Jabbour, S., Ma, Y., Raddaoui, B.: Inconsistency measurement thanks to mus decomposition. In: AAMAS, pp. 877–884 (2014)
19. Thimm, M.: Inconsistency measures for probabilistic logics. Artif. Intell. **197**, 1–24 (2013)

Graphical Models

On the Analysis of Probability-Possibility Transformations: Changing Operations and Graphical Models

Salem Benferhat[1,2], Amélie Levray[1,2](✉), and Karim Tabia[1,2]

[1] University of Lille Nord de France, 59000 Lille, France
{benferhat,levray,tabia}@cril.univ-artois.fr
[2] UArtois, CRIL UMR CNRS 8188, 62300 Lens, France

Abstract. Representing and reasoning with uncertain information is a common topic in Artificial Intelligence. In this paper, we focus on probability-possibility transformations in the context of changing operations and graphical models. Existing works mainly propose probability-possibility transformations satisfying some desirable properties. Regarding the analysis of the behavior of these transformations with respect to changing operations (such as conditioning and marginalization), only few works addressed such issues. This paper concerns the commutativity of transformations with respect to some reasoning tasks such as marginalization and conditioning. Another crucial issue addressed in this paper is the one of probability-possibility transformations in the context of graphical models, especially the independence of events and variables.

Keywords: Probability-possibility transformations · Marginalization · Conditioning · Graphical models

1 Introduction

Several frameworks exist for representing and reasoning with uncertain information. Probability and possibility theories are among the most commonly used. Probability theory is the oldest theory dealing with uncertainty and frequentist setting. The early works involving probability and possibility theories were devoted to estalishing connections between these two frameworks (as in [12,15,19]). These works are mostly interested in finding desirable properties to satisfy and then proposing transformations that guarantee these properties. An example of such desirable properties is the consistency principle used to preserve as much information as possible.

Probability-possibility transformations are useful in many ways. For instance, an example of propagating probabilistic (stochastic) and possibilistic information in risk analysis is provided in [1]. Another motivation is the fact that probabilities are more suitable in a frequentist setting, but this requires a large number of data, and when data is not available in sufficient quantities then the possibilistic

S. Destercke and T. Denoeux (Eds.): ECSQARU 2015, LNAI 9161, pp. 279–289, 2015.
DOI: 10.1007/978-3-319-20807-7_25

setting can fill this lack as in [13]. Another motivation for probability-possibility transformations is to use existing tools (e.g. algorithms and software) developed in one setting rather than developing everything from scratch.

In this paper, we deal with probability-possibility transformations with respect to reasoning tasks and graphical models. On that matter, a few works have been published. In [18], the author address the commutativity of probability-possibility transformations with respect to some reasoning tasks. The authors in [16] study some issues related to transforming Bayesian networks into possibilistic networks. In [5], the authors deal with transforming probability intervals into other uncertainty settings. Note that in this paper, we are only interested in transformations from probability distributions into possibility distributions. Given a distribution encoding some uncertain information, be it possibilistic or probabilistic, we are supposed to be able to reason about events of interest. In this work, we are interested in studying complementary issues such as preserving marginalization, conditioning and independence relations. We analyze these issues when the available information is encoded by means of distributions or in a compact way in the form of graphical models. We show that there is no transformation from the probabilistic into the possibilistic setting that guarantee most of the reasoning tasks dealt with in this work. For instance, regarding preserving marginalization, we show that no transformation can preserve the relative order of arbitrary events even if it preserves the relative order of interpretations. When transforming probabilistic graphical models, the order of interpretations cannot be preserved neither. Before presenting our results, let us first recall some concepts and present some existing probability-possibility transformations.

2   A Refresher on Probability and Possibility Theories and Graphical Models

Probability theory is a well-known and widely used uncertainty framework. One of the building blocks of this setting is the one of probability distribution p assigning a probability degree to each elementary state of the world. Probability theory is ruled by Kolmogorov's axioms (non negativity, normalization and additivity) and usually have two main interpretations (namely, the frequentist and subjective interpretations). Among the alternative uncertainty theories, possibility theory [8,19] is a well-known one. It is based on the notion of possibility distribution π which maps every state ω_i of the world Ω (the universe of discourse) to a degree in the interval $[0, 1]$ expressing a partial knowledge over the world. By convention, $\pi(\omega_i)=1$ expresses that ω_i is totally possible, while $\pi(\omega_i)=0$ means that this world is impossible. Note that possibility degrees are interpreted either (i) *qualitatively* (in min-based possibility theory) where only the "ordering" of the values is important, or *quantitatively* (in product-based possibility theory) where the possibilistic scale $[0, 1]$ is quantitative as in probability theory. One of the main difference between probability theory and possibility theory is that the former is additive while the latter is maxitive ($\Pi(\phi\cup\psi)=\max(\Pi(\phi), \Pi(\psi)) \; \forall\phi, \psi\subseteq\Omega$).

Conditioning is an important belief change operation concerned with updating the current beliefs encoded by a probability or a possibility distribution when a completely sure event (evidence) is observed. While there are several similarities between the quantitative possibilistic and the probabilistic frameworks (conditioning is defined in the same way following the so-called Dempster rule of conditioning), the qualitative one is significantly different. Note that the two definitions of possibilistic conditioning satisfy the condition: $\forall \omega \in \phi$, $\pi(\omega) = \pi(\omega|\phi) \otimes \Pi(\phi)$ where $\otimes$ is either the product or min-based operator. In the quantitative setting, the product-based conditioning is defined as follows:

$$\pi(w_i|_p\phi) = \begin{cases} \frac{\pi(w_i)}{\Pi(\phi)} & \text{if } w_i \in \phi; \\ 0 & \text{otherwise.} \end{cases} \tag{1}$$

Conditioning in the qualitative setting is defined as follows [11]:

$$\pi(w_i|_m\phi) = \begin{cases} 1 & \text{if } \pi(w_i) = \Pi(\phi) \text{ and } w_i \in \phi; \\ \pi(w_i) & \text{if } \pi(w_i) < \Pi(\phi) \text{ and } w_i \in \phi; \\ 0 & \text{otherwise.} \end{cases} \tag{2}$$

Working directly with uncertainty (probability or possibility) distributions is not convenient in terms of spatial and temporal complexity. Indeed, the distribution size can become too large to be stored and manipulated. This is why belief graphical models [4] have been developed. They represent uncertain information in a more compact way, and multiple tools have been developed for inference.

Bayesian Networks. A Bayesian network [4] is specified by:

- *A graphical component* with vertices and edges forming a directed acyclic graph (DAG). Each vertice represents a variable A_i of the modeled problem and the edges encode independence relationships among variables.
- *A quantitative component*, where every variable A_i is associated with a local probability distribution $p(A_i|par(A_i))$ for A_i in the context of its parents, denoted $par(A_i)$.

A Bayesian network encodes a joint probability distribution using the following chain rule:

$$P(A_1, ..., A_n) = \prod_{i=1}^{n} P(A_i|par(A_i)) \tag{3}$$

Bayesian networks are not only used to represent information but also to reason with it. Many algorithms for exact and approximate inferences exist for probabilistic graphical models [4].

Possibilistic Networks. A possibilistic network [3] is also specified by a graphical and a numeric component where the local tables are possibility distributions. The chain rule is defined as follows:

$$\pi(A_1, ..., A_n) = \otimes_{i=1..n}\pi(A_i|par(A_i)) \tag{4}$$

where $\otimes$ is either the product or min-based operator (namely, $\otimes = \min$ or $\otimes = *$). Unless otherwise stated, all that follows is valid in both the quantitative or qualitative possibilistic settings.

3 Probability-Possibility Transformations

In this section, we first review the main principles of probability-possibility transformations. In particular, since probability and possibility theories represent different kinds of uncertainty, there is a need to focus on the concept of consistency coined by Zadeh [19] and redefined by many authors like Dubois and Prade [7].

3.1 Basic Principles for Probability-Possibility Transformations

The first principle that transformations tried to satisfy is due to Zadeh [19]:

Zadeh Consistency Principle. Zadeh [19] measures the consistency between a probability and possibility distribution as follows:

$$C_z(\pi, p) = \sum_{i=1..n} \pi(\omega_i) * p(\omega_i). \tag{5}$$

where p and π are a probability and a possibility distributions respectively over a set of n worlds. It intuitiveley captures the fact that *"A high degree of possibility does not imply a high degree of probability, and a low degree of probability does not imply a low degree of possibility"*. The computed consistency degree is questionable [7,12] in the sense that two resulted possibility distributions can have the same consistency degree but do not contain the same amount of information.

Dubois and Prade Consistency Principle. Dubois and Prade [7] defined three postulates allowing to define the optimal transformation [7] which always exist and it is unique.

- *Consistency condition* states that for each event (i.e. a set of worlds) $\phi \subseteq \Omega$, $P(\phi) \leq \Pi(\phi)$. Here, the obtained possibility distribution should dominate the probability distribution.
- *Preference preservation*: $\forall (\omega_1, \omega_2) \in \Omega^2$, $p(\omega_1) \geq p(\omega_2)$ iff $\pi(\omega_1) \geq \pi(\omega_2)$. Intuitively, if two worlds are ordered in a given way in p, then π should preserve the same order.
- *Maximum specificity principle*: This principle requires to search for the most specific possibility distribution that satisfies the two above conditions. Let π_1 and π_2 be two possibility distributions, π_1 is said to be more specific than π_2 if $\forall \omega_i \in \Omega$, $\pi_1(\omega_i) \leq \pi_2(\omega_i)$.

3.2 Transformation Rules

Many probability-possibility transformations have been proposed in the literature. We cite the *Optimal transformation* (OT) [7], *Klir transformation* (KT) [12], *Symmetric transformation* (ST) [10], and *Variable transformation* (VT) [14]. The optimal transformation (*OT*) guarantees the most specific possibility distribution that satisfies Dubois and Prade's consistency principle. It is defined as follows:

$$\pi(\omega_i) = \sum_{j/p(\omega_j) \leq p(\omega_i)} p(\omega_j). \tag{6}$$

Note that there exist transformations from the possibilistic setting into the probabilistic one [10] and into other uncertainty frameworks [5].

4 Transformations and Changing Operations

Our purpose in this paper is to study the commutativity of transformations on reasoning tasks. In [18], the author was the first to study this question but his focus was only if the resulted distributions are *identical*. He showed that there is no transformation satisfying commutativity of transformations with respect to operations like conditioning and marginalization. We use $\triangleright(p)=\pi$ to denote the transformation from a probability distribution into possibility distribution satisfying Dubois and Prade preference preservation principle. In the following, we study the commutativity of transformations with respect to (i) the order of arbitrary events and (ii) two changing operators that are marginalization and conditioning. We focus on these two issues especially for useful practical uses of transformations. In fact, among the most used queries in probabilistic models, we find MPE queries (searching for the most plausible explanations) and MAP (where given some observations, the objective is to find the most plausible values of some variables of interest) [4]. For instance, let $p(ABC)$ be a probability distribution over three binary variables A, B and C. Let $C=0$ be an observation. MPE querry would be "which is the most probable interpretation for $p(A, B, C=0)$". MAP querry would be "which is the most probable set of interpretations for $p(A, B|C=0)$". To answer such queries using probability-possibility transformations, it is necessary to study the commutativity of transformations with respect to the marginalization and conditioning operations.

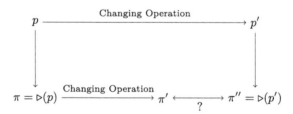

Fig. 1. Commutativity of operations

We consider operations on distributions as depicted on Fig. 1. On one hand we obtain a possibility distribution by first applying an operation then the transformation, and on the other hand we obtain the possibility distribution by first transforming the probability distribution then applying the corresponding operation in the possibilistic setting. Our objective is to compare these distributions and see if they encode the same order.

We first consider the operation of marginalization which consists in building the marginal distributions from a joint distribution.

4.1 Marginalization and Transformations: Preservation of the Order of Arbitrary Events

As said in the previous section, one of the principles of Dubois and Prade requires that the order of interpretations must be preserved, but nothing is said regarding arbitrary events (sets of interpretations). For instance, is it enough for a transformation to preserve the order of interpretations to preserve the order of arbitrary events? Proposition 1 states that there is no probability-possibility transformation preserving the order of events.

Proposition 1. *Let ▷ be a probability-possibility transformation operation (or function)[1]. Then there exists a probability distribution p, $\phi \subseteq \Omega$, $\psi \subseteq \Omega$, with $\phi \neq \psi$, and $\pi = {\triangleright}(p)$ such that*

$$P(\phi) < P(\psi) \text{ holds but } \Pi(\phi) < \Pi(\psi) \text{ does not hold.}$$

The reason of loosing the strict order is due to the difference in behavior of the additivity axiom in the probabilistic setting and the maxitivity axiom of the possibilistic setting. As a consequence of Proposition 1, if the universe of discourse Ω is a cartesian product of a set of variable domains, then the marginalization over variables will not preserve the relative order of events after the transformation operation.

4.2 Conditioning and Transformations: Preservation of the Order of Arbitrary Events

The question here is *"is the order of interpretations and arbitrary events preserved if we apply conditionning before or after transformation?"*.

Proposition 2 states that the order of elementary interpretations after conditioning is preserved if the used transformation preserves the order of interpretations.

Proposition 2. *Let $\phi \subseteq \Omega$ be an evidence. Let ▷ be a probability-possibility transformation, p' be a probability distribution obtained by conditioning p by ϕ, $\pi'' = {\triangleright}(p')$ and π' is the possibility distribution obtained by conditioning $\pi = {\triangleright}(p)$ by ϕ. Then, $\forall \omega_i, \omega_j \in \Omega$, $\pi'(\omega_i) < \pi'(\omega_j)$ iff $\pi''(\omega_i) < \pi''(\omega_j)$.*

Proposition 2 is valid using both the product or min-based conditioning.

As a consequence of Proposition 2, if one is interested in MPE queries, then the answers of such queries are exactly the same if we condition then transform or first transform then condition. However, because of the loss of the order of events when marginalizing (see Proposition 1), then the answers to MAP queries will not be the same.

4.3 Independence Relations and Transformations

When dealing with uncertain and incomplete information, the notion of independence[2] is very important. This subsection checks if the independence relation

---

[1] ▷ is always assumed to satisfy Dubois and Prade consistency and preference preservation principle.

[2] Let α, ϕ and ψ be three arbitrary events, in probability theory (resp. possibility theory), ϕ is said to be independent of ψ in the context of α iff $P(\phi|\psi, \alpha) = P(\phi|\alpha)$ (resp. $\Pi(\phi|\psi, \alpha) = \Pi(\phi|\alpha)$).

between events is preserved. Of course, the concept of independence is linked to the one of conditioning and marginalization. Proposition 3 states that there is no transformation operation ▷ that preserves the independence relations.

Proposition 3. *Let ϕ, ψ and $\alpha \subseteq \Omega$ be three events. Let ▷ be a probability-possibility transformation operation. Then there exist a probability distribution p and $\pi = {\vartriangleright}(p)$ such that*

$$P(\phi|\psi\alpha) = P(\phi|\alpha) \text{ but } \Pi(\phi|_\otimes\psi\alpha) \neq \Pi(\phi|_\otimes\alpha)$$

In Proposition 3, $|_\otimes$ denotes either the product or min-based conditioning operator. As a consequence, we can state that the independence of variables is not preserved either. This represents a major issue especially if one applies transformations to graphical models which are based on the concept of conditional independence relations.

5   Graphical Models and Transformations

Let us first define a transformation of a probabilistic graphical model into a possibilistic one. We transform a Bayesian network into a possibilistic network as follows (as in [16]):

Definition 1. *Let $\mathcal{BN}$ be a Bayesian network over a set of variables $A=\{A_1,..,A_n\}$, $\mathcal{PN}$ be a possibilistic network over the same set of variables A. $\mathcal{PN}$ is obtained by a transformation operation ▷ defined as follows:*

- *The graphical component of $\mathcal{PN}$ is the same graph as the one of the Bayesian network $\mathcal{BN}$.*
- *The numerical component of $\mathcal{PN}$ is such that every local probability table $p(A_i|par(A_i))$ is transformed with ▷ into $\pi(A_i|par(A_i)) = {\vartriangleright}(p(A_i|par(A_i)))$.*

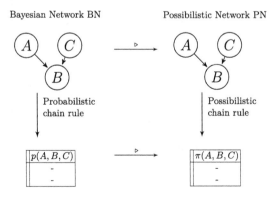

Fig. 2. Belief graphical model transformation

The advantage of transforming a graphical model using Definition 1 is preserving independence relations, while computationally it is less consuming to transform a set of local tables than a whole joint distribution. The problem now is that there is no guarantee that the order of interpretations and events is preserved in the obtained possibilistic network and its underlying joint distribution. Figure 2 illustrates the issue of transforming a Bayesian network into a possibilistic one.

Let us now check if the order of interpretations induced by $p_{\mathcal{BN}}$ (the joint distribution encoded by the Bayesian network $\mathcal{BN}$) is preserved in the obtained joint possibility distribution $\pi_{\mathcal{PN}}$ (the joint distribution encoded by the possibilistic network $\mathcal{PN}$). Proposition 4 answers this question.

Proposition 4. *Let $\triangleright$ be a probability-possibility transformation. Then there exist a Bayesian network $\mathcal{BN}$, $\omega_1 \in \Omega$ and $\omega_2 \in \Omega$ where:*

$$\pi'(\omega_1) < \pi'(\omega_2) \text{ does not imply } \pi''(\omega_1) < \pi''(\omega_2)$$

where: i) $\pi'(\omega) = \triangleright(p(\omega))$ and p is the joint distribution induced by $\mathcal{BN}$ and ii) π'' is the joint distribution induced by $\mathcal{PN}$ using Definition 1.

Example 1. Let $\mathcal{BN}$ be the Bayesian network of Fig. 3 over two disconnected variables A and B. Note that the probability distribution $p(A)$ in $\mathcal{BN}$ is a permutation[3] of the probability distribution $p(B)$. Hence, the transformation of $p(A)$ and $p(B)$ by $\triangleright$ gives $\pi(A)$ and $\pi(B)$ where $\pi(B)$ is also a permutation of $\pi(A)$. In this example, since $\triangleright$ is assumed to preserve the order of interpretations, we have $1 > \alpha_1 > \alpha_2 > \alpha_3$. The probability and possibility degrees of interpretations $a_1 b_1$ and $a_2 b_2$ are

- $p(a_1 b_1) = 0.4 * 0.15 = 0.06$
- $p(a_2 b_2) = 0.2 * 0.2 = 0.04$ then, $p(a_1 b_1) > p(a_2 b_2)$ (a)

- $\pi(a_1 b_1) = \alpha_3$
- $\pi(a_2 b_2) = \alpha_2$ then, $\pi(a_1 b_1) < \pi(a_2 b_2)$ (b)

From (a) and (b) one can see that the relative order of interpretations is reversed whatever is the used transformation in the ordinal setting. In the same way, in the quantitative setting, the relative order of interpretations can not be preserved by any transformation.

A	$p(A)$	$\pi(A)$
a_1	0.4	1
a_2	0.2	α_2
a_3	0.25	α_1
a_4	0.15	α_3

$\textcircled{A}$ $\textcircled{B}$

B	$p(B)$	$\pi(B)$
b_1	0.15	α_3
b_2	0.2	α_2
b_3	0.25	α_1
b_4	0.4	1

Fig. 3. Example of Bayesian-possibilistic network transformation.

---

[3] The permutation property of probability-possibility transformations is discussed in [18].

6   Related Works and Discussions

This paper dealt with some issues about probability-possibility transformations especially those regarding reasoning tasks and graphical models. We showed that there is no transformation that can preserve the order of arbitrary events through some reasoning operations like marginalization. As for the independence of events and variables, we showed that there is no transformation that preserves the independence relations. When the uncertain information is encoded by means of graphical models, we showed that no transformation can preserve the order of interpretations and events.

In the literature, there are two works in particular that dealt with the issues of our work. First, in [16] the authors studied transformation of Bayesian networks into possibilistic networks. They extend the definition of the consistency principle to preserve the order of interpretations and the distributions obtained after a transformation. Note that in this work, the authors focused mostly on certain existing transformations such as OT and ST while our work deal with all the transformations preserving the order of interpretations. The second work close to ours [18] addressed the commutativity of transformation with respect to some operations but its aim was to show that the obtained distributions are not identical. In our work, we are actually interested in the commutativity but only regarding the order of interpretations and events. Some of these issues were dealt with in the context of fuzzy interval analysis [9].

An interesting question is whether there exist particular probability distributions p such that the transformation operation $\triangleright$ preserves the relative ordering between interpretations after marginalisation. A first natural idea is uniform probability distributions. Any transformation $\triangleright$ should preserve normalisation which results in an uniform possibility distribution (where each state is associated to the possibility's degree of (1). Consequently, any event will have a possibility's degree of 1, meaning that there will not be a reversal in the order of interpretation on marginals distributions for example. Another kind of probability distributions is called "atomic bond system" [17] or big-stepped or lexicographic [2,6] probability distributions p defined by: $\forall \omega_i \in \Omega$, $p(\omega_i) > \sum\{p(\omega_j) : \omega_j \in \Omega$ and $p(\omega_j) < p(\omega_i)\}$. Clearly, if p is a big-stepped distribution then the transformation operation $\triangleright$ preserves the ordering between interpretations after marginalisation. Note however that for both particular cases (uniform and big-stepped distribution) the ordering between non-elementary events is not preserved.

It is known that probability-possibility transformations suffer from loss of information as we move from an additive framework to a qualitative or semi-qualitative framework. But the impact on the reasoning was not yet completely studied. The results we obtained confirm that there is a loss of information at several levels regarding reasoning. But this does not mean we can do nothing with transformations. In particular, responses to MPE queries are not affected by the transformations. Which is not the case for the MAP queries unfortunately. As future works, we will study MAP inference in credal networks (based on sets of probabilities and known for their high computational complexity in comparison to Bayesian or possibilistic networks) by transforming them into possibilistic networks. This can provide good and efficient approximations for MAP inference with a better computational cost. Other open questions concern the commutativity of transformations with other definitions of conditioning and independence in the possibilistic setting.

Acknowledgements. This work is done with the support of a CNRS funded project PEPS FaSciDo 2015 called MAPPOS.

References

1. Baudrit, C., Couso, I., Dubois, D.: Joint propagation of probability and possibility in risk analysis: towards a formal framework. Int. J. Approximate Reasoning **45**(1), 82–105 (2007)
2. Benferhat, S., Dubois, D., Prade, H.: Possibilistic and standard probabilistic semantics of conditional knowledge bases. J. Log. Comput. **9**(6), 873–895 (1999)
3. Borgelt, C., Kruse, R.: Learning possibilistic graphical models from data. IEEE. Trans. Fuzzy Syst. **11**(2), 159–172 (2003)
4. Darwiche, A.: Modeling and Reasoning with Bayesian Networks. Cambridge University Press, Cambridge (2009)
5. Destercke, S., Dubois, D., Chojnacki, E.: Transforming probability intervals into other uncertainty models. In: 5th EUSFLAT Conference, 11–14 September 2007, Ostrava, Czech Republic. Regular Sessions, vol. 2, pp. 367–373 (2007)
6. Dubois, D., Fargier, H., Prade, H.: Ordinal and probabilistic representations of acceptance. J. Artif. Int. Res. **22**(1), 23–56 (2004)
7. Dubois, D., Foulloy, L., Mauris, G., Prade, H.: Probability-possibility transformations, triangular fuzzy sets, and probabilistic inequalities. Reliable Comput. **10**(4), 273–297 (2004)
8. Dubois, D., Prade, H.: Possibility Theory: An Approach to Computerized Processing of Uncertainty. Plenum Press, New York (1988)
9. Dubois, D., Prade, H.: Random sets and fuzzy interval analysis. Fuzzy Sets Syst. **42**(1), 87–101 (1991). DP165
10. Dubois, D., Prade, H., Sandri, S.: On possibility/probability transformations. In: Fuzzy Logic, pp. 103–112 (1993)
11. Hisdal, E.: Conditional possibilities independence and non interaction. Fuzzy Sets Syst. **1**(4), 283–297 (1978)
12. Klir, G.J., Geer, J.F.: Information-preserving probability- possibility transformations: Recent developments. In: Fuzzy Logic, pp. 417–428 (1993)
13. Masson, M.-H., Denoeux, T.: Inferring a possibility distribution from empirical data. Fuzzy Sets Syst. **157**(3), 319–340 (2006)
14. Billaudel, P., Mouchaweh, M.S., Bouguelid, M.S., Riera, B.: Variable probability-possibility transformation, 417–428, September 2006
15. Prade, H., Dubois, D.: Random Sets and Fuzzy Interval Analysis. Fuzzy Sets Syst. **42**(1), 87–101. Elsevier North-Holland, Inc., Amsterdam (1991)
16. Slimen, Y.B., Ayachi, R., Amor, N.B.: Probability-Possibility Transformation: Application to Bayesian and Possibilistic Networks. In: Masulli, F. (ed.) WILF 2013. LNCS, vol. 8256, pp. 122–130. Springer, Heidelberg (2013)
17. Snow, P.: Standard probability distributions described by rational default entailment (1996)

18. Sudkamp, T.: On probability-possibility transformations. Fuzzy Sets Syst. **51**, 73–81 (1992)
19. Zadeh, L.A.: Fuzzy sets as a basis for a theory of possibility. Fuzzy Sets Syst. **100**, 9–34 (1999)

Computing Concise Representations of Semi-graphoid Independency Models

Stavros Lopatatzidis[1,2](✉) and Linda C. van der Gaag[1,2]

[1] SYSTeMS Research Group, Ghent University,
Technologiepark-Zwijnaarde 914, 9052 Zwijnaarde, Belgium
stavros.lopatatzidis@ugent.be
[2] Department of Information and Computing Sciences, Utrecht University,
Princetonplein 5, 3584 CC Utrecht, The Netherlands
L.C.vanderGaag@uu.nl

Abstract. The conditional independencies from a joint probability distribution constitute a model which is closed under the semi-graphoid properties of independency. These models typically are exponentially large in size and cannot be feasibly enumerated. For describing a semi-graphoid model therefore, a more concise representation is used, which is composed of a representative subset of the independencies involved, called a basis, and letting all other independencies be implicitly defined by the semi-graphoid properties; for computing such a basis, an appropriate algorithm is available. Based upon new properties of semi-graphoid models in general, we introduce an improved algorithm that constructs a smaller basis for a given independency model than currently existing algorithms.

1 Introduction

Many are the mathematical models consisting of random variables over which joint probability distributions are defined. Among these are the well-known probabilistic graphical models [2–5]. The practicability of computing probabilities of interest from these models derives from the explicit representation of the independency relation among their variables. Independency relations embedded in joint probability distributions and their representation have therefore been subjects of extensive studies.

Pearl and his co-researchers were among the first to formalise properties of probabilistic independency in an axiomatic system [5]. The axioms from this system are known as the semi-graphoid axioms, and the independency relation of any joint probability distribution has been shown to adhere to these axioms. The semi-graphoid axioms are often looked upon as derivation rules for generating new independencies from a basic set of independencies. Any set of independencies that is closed under finite application of these rules is then called a semi-graphoid independency model.

Semi-graphoid independency models in general are exponentially large in size. Representing them by enumeration of their element independencies therefore is

S. Destercke and T. Denoeux (Eds.): ECSQARU 2015, LNAI 9161, pp. 290–300, 2015.
DOI: 10.1007/978-3-319-20807-7_26

not feasible in practice. Studený was the first to propose a more concise representation of an independency model, based on the semi-graphoid axioms [6,7]. The idea is to explicitly enumerate a representative subset of independencies, called a basis, from a semi-graphoid model and let all other independencies be defined implicitly through the derivation rules. Studený designed an efficient algorithm for computing such a basis for a semi-graphoid independency model from a given starting set of independencies, which was later improved by Baioletti and his co-researchers [1].

In this paper, we revisit the representation of semi-graphoid independency models, and show that the subset of independencies that have to be represented explicitly, can be further reduced in size. We introduce the new notion of maximal non-symmetric basis for this purpose, with an associated algorithm for its computation. The practicability of our algorithm for computing more concise representations of semi-graphoid independency models is demonstrated by means of an example independency model.

The paper is organised as follows. We provide some preliminaries on semi-graphoid models in Sect. 2, and review concise representations of such models in Sect. 3. Our notion of maximal non-symmetric basis and our associated algorithm are detailed in Sect. 4. The paper ends with our concluding observations in Sect. 5.

2   Semi-graphoid Independency Models

We briefly review semi-graphoid independency models [5,7], and thereby introduce our notations. We consider a finite, non-empty set S of random variables. A *triplet* over S is a statement of the form $\langle A, B \mid C \rangle$, where $A, B, C \subseteq S$ are mutually disjoint subsets of S with $A, B \neq \varnothing$; we will use $X = A \cup B \cup C$ to refer to the triplet's set of variables. A triplet $\langle A, B \mid C \rangle$ states that the sets of variables A and B are mutually independent given the set C; in view of a joint probability distribution Pr over S, the triplet thus states that $\Pr(A, B \mid C) = \Pr(A \mid C) \cdot \Pr(B \mid C)$. The set of all triplets over S is denoted as $S^{(3)}$. A set of triplets now constitutes a semi-graphoid independency model if it satisfies the four so-called semi-graphoid properties stated in the following definition.

Definition 1. *A semi-graphoid independency model is a subset of triplets $J \subseteq S^{(3)}$ which satisfies the following properties:*

G1: *if $\langle A, B \mid C \rangle \in J$, then $\langle B, A \mid C \rangle \in J$* (Symmetry)
G2: *if $\langle A, B \mid C \rangle \in J$, then $\langle A, B' \mid C \rangle \in J$ for any non-empty subset $B' \subseteq B$* (De-composition)
G3: *if $\langle A, B_1 \cup B_2 \mid C \rangle \in J$ with $B_1 \cap B_2 = \varnothing$, then $\langle A, B_1 \mid C \cup B_2 \rangle \in J$* (Weak Union)
G4: *if $\langle A, B \mid C \cup D \rangle \in J$ and $\langle A, C \mid D \rangle \in J$, then $\langle A, B \cup C \mid D \rangle \in J$* (Contraction)

The semi-graphoid properties of independency are often viewed, and referred to, as derivation rules for generating new triplets from a given set of triplets.

Given a starting set of triplets $J \subseteq S^{(3)}$ and a designated triplet $\theta \in S^{(3)}$, we write $J \vdash^* \theta$ if the triplet θ can be derived from J by finite application of the semi-graphoid rules G1–G4. The *closure* of J, denoted by $\overline{J}$, then is the set of all triplets $\theta \in S^{(3)}$ such that $J \vdash^* \theta$.

3   Representing Semi-graphoid Independency Models

Semi-graphoid independency models typically are exponentially large in size, and representing them by enumeration of their element triplets is not feasible in practice. Studený was the first to propose a more concise representation of a semi-graphoid model, based on the semi-graphoid derivation rules [7]. The idea is to explicitly capture only a subset of triplets from a model, called its *basis*, and let all other triplets be defined implicitly through the derivation rules. In Sect. 3.1 we review the basic notions in Studený's representation; in Sect. 3.2 we describe the associated algorithm.

3.1   Derivational Relations Among Triplets

We begin by defining the notion of *dominance* which underlies the representation of semi-graphoid models proposed by Studený [7].

Definition 2. *Let $J \subseteq S^{(3)}$ be a semi-graphoid independency model, and let G2s and G3s be the following derivation rules over J:*

G2s: *if $\langle A,B \,|\, C \rangle \in J$, then $\langle A',B \,|\, C \rangle \in J$ for any non-empty subset $A' \subseteq A$*
G3s: *if $\langle A_1 \cup A_2,B \,|\, C \rangle \in J$ with $A_1 \cap A_2 = \varnothing$, then $\langle A_1,B \,|\, C \cup A_2 \rangle \in J$*

Now, let $\theta_i \in J$, $i = 1,2$. If θ_1 can be derived from θ_2 by finite application of the rules G2–G3 and G2s–G3s, we say that θ_1 is dominated by θ_2, *denoted $\theta_1 \prec \theta_2$. A triplet which is not dominated by any other triplet in J, is called* dominant in J.

The notion of dominance pertains to a single triplet and the triplets that can be derived from it by means of the rules G2–G3 and G2s–G3s; we note that the latter pair of rules serve to incorporate the property of symmetry into the derivational relation. Necessary and sufficient conditions have been formulated for dominance of a triplet [7].

   Similar to Studený's notion of dominance, Baioletti *et al.* [1] introduced the notion of *g-inclusion* for describing the derivational relation between triplets, as defined below.

Definition 3. *Let $J \subseteq S^{(3)}$ be a semi-graphoid independency model and let $\theta_i \in J$, $i = 1,2$. Then, θ_1 is* g-included in θ_2, *denoted $\theta_1 \sqsubseteq \theta_2$, if θ_1 can be derived from θ_2 by finite application of the rules G1–G3. A triplet θ is called* maximal in J *if it is not g-included in any other triplet τ from J with $\tau \neq \theta, \theta^T$ where the transpose θ^T is obtained from θ by means of the symmetry rule G1.*

Also for g-inclusion of a triplet necessary and sufficient conditions have been stated [1].

The definitions of dominance and g-inclusion show that the two notions are closely related. More specifically, for any two triplets θ_1, θ_2 with $\theta_1 \neq \theta_2, \theta_2^T$, the following property holds: $\theta_1 \sqsubseteq \theta_2$ if and only if $\theta_1 \prec \theta_2$ or $\theta_1 \prec \theta_2^T$. The difference between the two notions is that, while the notion of dominance incorporates symmetry through the symmetrical counterparts of the decomposition and weak union rules, the notion of g-inclusion involves symmetry through the symmetry rule itself. We note that by explicitly including the rule of symmetry, any triplet is g-included in its symmetric transpose; in contrast, a triplet is not dominated by its transpose.

The notions of dominance and g-inclusion are readily extended to triplet sets.

Definition 4. *Let* $J_i \subseteq S^{(3)}$, $i = 1, 2$, *be semi-graphoid independency models. Then,*

- *J_1 is g-included in J_2, denoted by $J_1 \sqsubseteq J_2$, if for each triplet $\theta \in J_1$ there exists a triplet $\theta' \in J_2$ such that $\theta \sqsubseteq \theta'$;*
- *J_1 is dominated by the set J_2, denoted by $J_1 \prec J_2$, if for each triplet $\theta \in J_1$, there exists a triplet $\theta' \in J_2$ such that $\theta \prec \theta'$.*

3.2   Computing a Basis for a Semi-graphoid Model

Since dominated triplets are derived from other triplets, they do not convey any additional information about the original model and thus are not required explicitly for its representation. As a consequence, it is possible to select a subset of triplets from an independency model which captures the same information as the entire model itself; such a subset is called a *basis* of the original model. Studený now showed that the subset of all dominant triplets constitutes such a basis for a semi-graphoid independency model, and thereby arrived at a concise model representation. For computing the subset of dominant triplets, he constructed a dedicated operator, which is defined as follows [7].

Definition 5. *Let* $J \subseteq S^{(3)}$. *For all triplets* $\theta_i = \langle A_i, B_i \mid C_i \rangle \in J$ *with* $X_i = A_i \cup B_i \cup C_i$, $i = 1, 2$, *the gc-operator is defined as:*

$$gc(\theta_1, \theta_2) = \langle A_1 \cap A_2, (B_2 \backslash C_1) \cup (B_1 \cap X_2) \mid C_1 \cup (A_1 \cap C_2) \rangle$$

if a valid triplet, and $gc(\theta_1, \theta_2) = $ *undefined otherwise.*

Studený showed that if the gc-operator is applied to two triplets θ_1, θ_2 to result in a valid triplet θ, then this triplet θ dominates all elements from the triplet set obtained from applying the rules G1–G4 to θ_1, θ_2. A slightly stronger result than Studený's original one is stated in the following lemma by Baioletti *et al.* [1].

Lemma 1. *Let* $J \subseteq S^{(3)}$. *Let* $\theta_i = \langle A_i, B_i \mid C_i \rangle \in J$ *with* $X_i = A_i \cup B_i \cup C_i$, $i = 1, 2$, *and let* $gc(\theta_1, \theta_2)$ *be as in Definition 5. Furthermore, let the triplet set* $H_{G4}(\theta_1, \theta_2) = \{\tau \mid$ *there exist triplets* $\theta_1' \prec \theta_1 \in J$, $\theta_2' \prec \theta_2 \in J$ *such that* $\theta_1', \theta_2' \vdash_{G4} \tau\}$. *Then,*

- $H_{G4}(\theta_1, \theta_2) = \varnothing$ if and only if at least one of the following conditions is not met:
  (a) $A_1 \cap A_2 \neq \varnothing$;
  (b) $C_1 \subseteq X_2$ and $C_2 \subseteq X_1$;
  (c) $B_2 \backslash C_1 \neq \varnothing$;
  (d) $B_1 \cap X_2 \neq \varnothing$;
  (e) $|(B_2 \backslash C_1) \cup (B_1 \cap X_2)| \geq 2$;
- if $H_{G4}(\theta_1, \theta_2) \neq \varnothing$, then $gc(\theta_1, \theta_2) \in H_{G4}(\theta_1, \theta_2)$ and $\tau \prec gc(\theta_1, \theta_2)$ for any other triplet τ from $H_{G4}(\theta_1, \theta_2)$.

The lemma states that the gc-operator indeed constructs dominant triplets [6]. The conditions (a)–(e) mentioned in the lemma constitute all conditions under which the contraction rule G4 can be applied to triplets which are dominated by θ_1, θ_2.

Building upon the gc-operator, Studený designed an algorithm for generating, from a starting set of triplets, all dominant triplets of a semi-graphoid model [7]; the algorithm thereby establishes a basis for the model. The algorithm takes the starting triplet set for its input and adds any symmetric triplet which is not yet included. It then applies the gc-operator to any pair of triplets for which the conditions (a)–(e) from Lemma 1 hold, and adds the result to the basis under construction. Subsequently, all dominated triplets are removed. These steps are re-iterated until the basis no longer changes.

In the first step, Studený's algorithm adds all symmetric triplets to the original starting set, to enhance it for all possible applications of the contraction rule G4. Based upon this observation, Baioletti et al. [1] generalised the contraction rule to a new rule G4* which does not require the symmetric triplets to be added explicitly to the basis under construction. The new derivation rule states for any semi-graphoid model $J \subseteq S^{(3)}$:

$$G4^*: \text{if } \theta_1, \theta_2 \in J, \text{ then } GC(\theta_1, \theta_2) \subseteq J$$

where $GC(\theta_1, \theta_2) = \{gc(\theta_1, \theta_2), gc(\theta_1, \theta_2^T), gc(\theta_1^T, \theta_2), gc(\theta_1^T, \theta_2^T)\}$. The generalised rule thus constructs not just the single triplet from applying the contraction rule to θ_1, θ_2, but those from applying the rule to all combinations involving transposes as well.

By finite application of the G4* rule to a starting set J, a triplet set results. This set is related to the closure of J as stated in the following lemma [1].

Lemma 2. Let $J \subseteq S^{(3)}$ and let $\overline{J}$ be its closure. Let J^{G4^*} be the set of all triplets that are derived from J by the derivation rule G4*. Then, $J^{G4^*} \subseteq \overline{J}$ and $\overline{J} \sqsubseteq J^{G4^*}$.

The property $J^{G4^*} \subseteq \overline{J}$ stated in the lemma expresses that application of the derivation rule G4* does not yield any triplets which are not in the closure of the starting set J; the property $\overline{J} \sqsubseteq J^{G4^*}$ implies that all triplets from $\overline{J}$ are represented in J^{G4^*} through g-inclusion. The lemma thus states that finite application of G4* serves to generate essentially the same information from the set J as finite application of G1–G4.

Although any triplet from the closure $\overline{J}$ is g-included in the triplet set J^{G4^*} which results from application of the G4* derivation rule, this latter set does not constitute a concise basis for the model at hand as it may include several redundant triplets. To reduce the set J^{G4^*} in size without losing information, it is restricted to its subset of maximal triplets. We define the notion of maximal triplet set for triplet sets in general.

Definition 6. *Let $J \subseteq S^{(3)}$. A* maximal triplet set *of J is a subset $J_{/\sqsubseteq}$ of triplets such that $J_{/\sqsubseteq} = \{\theta \in J \mid$ there is no $\theta' \in J$ with $\theta' \neq \theta, \theta^T$ such that $\theta \sqsubseteq \theta'\}$.*

For a starting set J, a maximal triplet set of its closure $\overline{J}$ contains the same independency information as the closure itself and hence constitutes a basis for the semi-graphoid model at hand. The following lemma now holds for maximal triplet sets of the closure $\overline{J}$ and of the triplet set J^{G4^*} constructed from the starting set J by application of the G4* derivation rule, respectively.

Lemma 3. *Let $J \subseteq S^{(3)}$, and let $\overline{J}_{/\sqsubseteq}$ and $J^{G4^*}_{/\sqsubseteq}$ be maximal triplet sets as defined above. Then, $\overline{J}_{/\sqsubseteq} \sqsubseteq J^{G4^*}_{/\sqsubseteq}$ and $J^{G4^*}_{/\sqsubseteq} \sqsubseteq \overline{J}_{/\sqsubseteq}$.*

The lemma implies that any maximal triplet sets of the closure $\overline{J}$ and of the set J^{G4^*} share exactly the same information, even though the two maximal sets may differ. Computing the basis of a semi-graphoid independency model thereby amounts to computing the maximal triplet set $J^{G4^*}_{/\sqsubseteq}$ of the set of triplets which results from finite application of the G4* rule. The algorithm to this end starts with the initial triplet set J_0, and computes in each iteration the triplet set $J_k = J_{k-1} \cup \bigcup \{GC(\theta_1, \theta_2) \mid \theta_1, \theta_2 \in J_{k-1}\}$, removing dominated triplets between iterations, until $J_k = J_{k-1}$; for ease of reference, we will refer to this algorithm for computing a basis as the Studený–Baioletti algorithm.

4   Improved Basis Computation

In this section, we present our improved algorithm for basis computation. Like the Studený–Baioletti algorithm, our algorithm is based on application of the gc-operator, yet incorporates several new notions. These notions serve to improve the algorithm's efficiency on the one hand and the size of the established basis on the other hand. In Sect. 4.1 we state necessary conditions for identifying triplets to which the gc-operator can never be applied. In Sect. 4.2, we further argue that symmetric triplets need not be added or kept throughout the computations. In Sect. 4.3, we present our adapted derivation rule and summarise our algorithm for basis computation; Sect. 4.4 illustrates the potential of our algorithm by means of an example.

4.1   Excluding Triplets from Computation

The Studený–Baioletti algorithm for basis computation builds on the gc-operator, and on application of the G4* derivation rule more specifically. A starting set however, may include triplets for which can be established apriori that they will not give any results by the derivation rule. The following lemma identifies such triplets.

Lemma 4. *Let $J \subseteq S^{(3)}$ and let $\theta = \langle A,B \,|\, C \rangle \in J$. If for each $\theta' = \langle A',B' \,|\, C' \rangle \in J$ with $\theta' \neq \theta, \theta^T$ at least one of the following conditions holds:*

(a) $C \not\subseteq X'$
(b) $A \cap (A' \cup B') = \varnothing$ and $B \cap (A' \cup B') = \varnothing$
(c) $(A \cup B) \backslash C' = \varnothing$ and $(A' \cup B') \backslash C = \varnothing$
(d) $(A \cup B) \cap X' = \varnothing$ and $(A' \cup B') \cap X = \varnothing$

then $J^{G4^*} \backslash \{\theta, \theta^T\} = (J \backslash \{\theta, \theta^T\})^{G4^*}$, that is, finite application of G4 to J yields no valid triplets from applying the gc-operator to θ or θ^T.*

Proof (Sketch). We recall that application of G4* to a pair of triplets θ, θ' produces the sets $GC(\theta, \theta')$ and $GC(\theta', \theta)$. These sets are non-empty only if the gc-operator yields at least one valid triplet, that is, if at least one of the conditions stated in Lemma 1 holds. For $gc(\theta, \theta') = \langle A \cap A', (B' \backslash C) \cup (B \cap X') \,|\, C \cup (A \cap C') \rangle$, for example, it is now easily shown that, if one of the conditions (a)–(d) above is satisfied, then at least one of the conditions from Lemma 1 does not hold and $gc(\theta, \theta')$ is undefined. Similar results hold for all other triplets θ'' from J or generated from J by applying the gc-operator.   □

We conclude that any triplet θ to which Lemma 4 applies, can be safely set aside from the computations and be added to the resulting basis.

4.2   Maintaining a Non-Symmetric Basis

We recall that the first step of Studený's original algorithm was to add all symmetric triplets to the starting set to cover all possible applications of the contraction rule G4. In the reformulation of the algorithm by Baioletti *et al.*, these applications are covered through the G4* derivation rule, thereby forestalling the need to explicitly add all symmetric transposes to the starting set. Application of the gc-operator upon constructing the sets $GC(\theta_1, \theta_2)$ and $GC(\theta_2, \theta_1)$ for two triplets θ_1, θ_2, however, may introduce transposes in a basis under construction. From the definition of maximal triplet set, we note that such a set may contain both a triplet θ and its transpose θ^T. Once introduced, both triplets may thus be carried throughout further computations and both end up in the computed basis. We will now show that by removing symmetric transposes from a maximal triplet set, a set of triplets results which shares the same information as a maximal triplet set of the full closure of the starting set and hence still constitutes a basis. We begin by defining the notion of *maximal non-symmetric triplet set*.

Definition 7. *Let $J \subseteq S^{(3)}$. A maximal non-symmetric triplet set of J is a maximal triplet set $J_{/\sqsubseteq n}$ of J such that for every triplet $\theta \in J_{/\sqsubseteq n}$ we have that $\theta^T \notin J_{/\sqsubseteq n}$.*

From the definition of maximal non-symmetric triplet set it is readily seen that the properties $J_{/\sqsubseteq n} \sqsubseteq J_{/\sqsubseteq}$ and $J_{/\sqsubseteq} \sqsubseteq J_{/\sqsubseteq n}$ hold, since for every triplet θ we have that $\theta \sqsubseteq \theta^T$ and $\theta^T \sqsubseteq \theta$. By taking the maximal non-symmetric triplet set of the set J^{G4^*} and building upon Lemma 3 moreover, we derive the following lemma which states that the set $J^{G4^*}_{/\sqsubseteq n}$ shares the exact same information as the maximal non-symmetric triplet set of the closure of the independency model at hand.

Lemma 5. *Let $J \subseteq S^{(3)}$, and let $\overline{J}_{/\sqsubseteq n}$ and $J^{G4^*}_{/\sqsubseteq n}$ be as defined above. Then, it holds that $\overline{J}_{/\sqsubseteq n} \sqsubseteq J^{G4^*}_{/\sqsubseteq n}$ and $J^{G4^*}_{/\sqsubseteq n} \sqsubseteq \overline{J}_{/\sqsubseteq n}$.*

From the lemma we conclude that a maximal non-symmetric triplet set of the set J^{G4^*} constitutes an appropriate basis for the model defined by the starting set J. We can now exploit the property that this basis will not include any symmetric triplet pairs, already during its construction. Let $J^- \subseteq \overline{J}$ be an intermediate basis computed in some iteration of the algorithm, from which we are to remove all dominated triplets. If the set J^- includes triplets θ', θ and θ^T with $\theta \prec \theta'$, then the triplet θ will be removed, yet θ^T will be kept since $\theta^T \nprec \theta'$. We are guaranteed that in some later iteration of the algorithm, the triplet θ^T will be removed, since in terms of g-inclusion it holds that $\theta, \theta^T \sqsubseteq \theta'$. By using g-inclusion instead of dominance as a criterion for removing triplets from intermediate bases therefore, the triplet θ^T is removed immediately and not unnecessarily carried throughout the computations. We note however that, if an intermediate basis includes the two dominant triplets θ, θ^T, one of these triplets needs to be retained in the basis under construction, even though the two triplets are mutually g-included.

4.3 An Improved Algorithm for Basis Computation

Building upon the properties introduced above, we detail in this section our improved algorithm for basis computation. Like the Studený –Baioletti algorithm, our algorithm builds in essence on application of the G4* derivation rule. To reduce the computational burden involved in applying the rule however, we use a dedicated representation for pairs of triplets and an accordingly adapted derivation rule. We recall that the Studený –Baioletti algorithm computes the two triplet sets $GC(\theta_1, \theta_2)$ and $GC(\theta_2, \theta_1)$ for each pair of triplets θ_1, θ_2 from an intermediate basis. During these computations, the gc-operator is applied eight times. Eight times therefore, the conditions for the operator to yield a valid triplet are evaluated. We now propose a representation of the triplet pair by means of which this number of evaluations is reduced.

Definition 8. *Let $\theta_i = \langle A_i, B_i \mid C_i \rangle \in S^{(3)}$, $i = 1, 2$. We say that the triplet pair $\{\theta_1, \theta_2\}$ is in* normal form *if*

$$\theta_1 = \langle A_A \cup A_B \cup A_C \cup A_X, B_A \cup B_B \cup B_C \cup B_X \mid C_A \cup C_B \cup C_C \cup C_X \rangle$$
$$\theta_2 = \langle A_A \cup B_A \cup C_A \cup A_Y, A_B \cup B_B \cup C_B \cup B_Y \mid A_C \cup B_C \cup C_C \cup C_Y \rangle$$

where $A_A = (A_i \cap A_j)$, $A_B = (A_i \cap B_j)$, $A_C = (A_i \cap C_j)$, $A_X = (A_i \setminus X_j)$, $A_Y = (A_j \setminus X_i)$ and the other subsets are defined analogously. The pair $\{\theta_1, \theta_2\}$ is in almost normal form *if it is in normal form and $C_X = C_Y = \emptyset$.*

From the definition above, we note that if a pair of triplets $\{\theta_1, \theta_2\}$ is in normal form, then each of the eight potential triplets from the set $CG(\theta_1, \theta_2) \cup CG(\theta_2, \theta_1)$

is generated simply by manipulating the subsets identified in the representation. For example, the potential triplet $gc(\theta_1, \theta_2)$ is equal to $\langle A_A, A_B \cup B_B \cup B_Y \cup B_A \cup B_C \mid C_A \cup C_B \cup C_C \cup C_X \cup A_C \rangle$. The other potential triplets are generated analogously from the same representation, thereby avoiding the necessity of finding properly dominated triplets and their transposes for the application of the gc-operator. From the definition of normal form, we further note that a pair of triplets $\theta_i = \langle A_i, B_i \mid C_i \rangle \in S^{(3)}$, $i = 1, 2$, can be brought in almost normal form only if the conditions $C_i \subseteq X_j$ and $C_j \subseteq X_i$ are met. As these conditions constitute also a necessary condition for generating a valid triplet upon applying the gc-operator to the two triplets or its transposes, we are guaranteed that if two triplets cannot be represented in almost normal form, they cannot yield any dominant triplets upon applying the operator. Formulating a pair of triplets in (almost) normal form amounts to establishing the various subsets involved and then verifying whether the equalities stated in the definition hold.

Based upon the above representation, we now re-formulate the G4* derivation rule into the similar yet more efficient G4+ rule:

$$\text{G4}^+ \colon \text{if } \theta_1, \theta_2 \in J, \text{ then } J^+(\theta_1, \theta_2) \subseteq J$$

where $J^+(\theta_1, \theta_2) = GC(\theta_1, \theta_2) \cup GC(\theta_2, \theta_1)$ with $GC(\theta_i, \theta_j)$, $i, j = 1, 2$, $i \neq j$, computed as described above.

Our improved algorithm for basis computation now builds upon application of this G4+ derivation rule. The algorithm is summarised in Fig. 1. The algorithm takes a starting triplet set J and identifies, through a call to the function *NonApplicable*, all triplets which can be safely set aside during the basis computation; the function verifies to this end the conditions stated in Lemma 4. It then starts the basis computation with the resulting initial basis J_0. In each iteration k, it establishes the set N_k of triplets which are newly generated by the G4+ rule from a triplet θ_1 from the current basis J_{k-1} and a triplet θ_2 from the set

---

Algorithm for Computing a Non-Symmetric Basis for J

1: **function** *Non-SymmetricBasis*(J)
2:     $A \leftarrow NonApplicable(J)$
3:     $J_0 \leftarrow J \backslash A$
4:     $N_0 \leftarrow J \backslash A$
5:     $k \leftarrow 0$
6:     **repeat**
7:         $k \leftarrow k + 1$
8:         $N_k := \bigcup_{\theta_1 \in J_{k-1}, \theta_2 \in N_{k-1}} J^+(\theta_1, \theta_2)$
9:         $J_k \leftarrow FindNonSymmetricMaximal(J_{k-1} \cup N_k)$
10:    **until** $J_k = J_{k-1}$
11:    **return** $J_k \cup A$
12: **end function**

Fig. 1. Our improved algorithm for computing a non-symmetric basis.

of triplets N_{k-1} which were generated in the previous iteration. The algorithm establishes the new basis J_k for the next iteration by taking the maximal non-symmetric triplet set of $J_{k-1} \cup N_k$. The function *FindNonSymmetricMaximal* removes to this end all triplets which are g-included in another triplet unequal to its transpose and in addition removes one of the elements from any remaining triplet set $\{\theta, \theta^T\}$. We would like to note that the most important difference of our algorithm with the Studený -Baioletti algorithm lies in this function *FindNonSymmetricMaximal*.

4.4   An Example

By means of an example, we demonstrate that our algorithm indeed improves on the Studený –Baioletti algorithm for basis computation, in terms of the size of the resulting basis. We take a starting set J composed of the following triplets:

$$\langle \{5\},\{6\} \mid \varnothing \rangle \qquad \langle \{1,2\},\{3,4\} \mid \{6\} \rangle \qquad \langle \{2,3\},\{1,4\} \mid \{5\} \rangle$$
$$\langle \{1,2\},\{3,4\} \mid \{5\} \rangle \qquad \langle \{3\},\{1,4\} \mid \{2,5\} \rangle$$

and compute a basis for the semi-graphoid model $\overline{J}$, by means of both algorithms; in Fig. 2, we report, for each algorithm, the number of triplets included in the sets N_k, J_{k-1} and J_k for each iteration k. Our algorithm computed the following basis:

$$\langle \{5\},\{6\} \mid \varnothing \rangle \qquad \langle \{1,2\},\{3,4\} \mid \{6\} \rangle \qquad \langle \{1,3\},\{2,4\} \mid \{5\} \rangle$$
$$\langle \{2,3\},\{1,4\} \mid \{5\} \rangle \qquad \langle \{2\},\{1,3,4\} \mid \{5\} \rangle \qquad \langle \{1\},\{2,3,4\} \mid \{5\} \rangle$$
$$\langle \{4\},\{1,2,3\} \mid \{5\} \rangle \qquad \langle \{1,2\},\{3,4\} \mid \{5\} \rangle \qquad \langle \{3\},\{1,2,4\} \mid \{5\} \rangle$$

The algorithm set aside, from the actual basis computations, the two triplets $\langle \{5\},\{6\} \mid \varnothing \rangle$ and $\langle \{1,2\},\{3,4\} \mid \{6\} \rangle$, since to these triplets Lemma 4 applies. As a consequence, the algorithm enters the basis computations with a starting set of three triplets. From the actual basis computations, a set of seven maximal non-symmetric triplets resulted; to this set, the two triplets mentioned above were added, and the algorithm returned a basis of nine triplets. The basis constructed by the Studený –Baioletti algorithm included a total of 12 triplets. In addition to the triplets found by our algorithm, the constructed basis included the triplets $\langle \{2,4\},\{1,3\} \mid \{5\} \rangle$, $\langle \{1,4\},\{2,3\} \mid \{5\} \rangle$ and $\langle \{3,4\},\{1,2\} \mid \{5\} \rangle$. We note that these three triplets are the symmetric transposes of triplets already included in the basis. Our algorithm thus resulted in a smaller basis and in fact had smaller intermediate bases to consider in each step of the iteration.

The Studený -Baioletti algorithm				Our improved algorithm		
k	N_k	J_{k-1}	J_k	k	N_k	J_{k-1}	J_k
1	13	5	9	1	11	3	6
2	18	9	12	2	16	6	7
3	18	12	12	3	16	7	7

Fig. 2. Some statistics of running the Studený –Baioletti algorithm and our algorithm for basis computation, on the example independency model.

5 Conclusions

We revisited the representation of semi-graphoid independency models and showed that their basis can be further reduced in size. We introduced the new notion of maximal non-symmetric triplet set, which allows removal of symmetric triplets from a basis under construction. We further improved upon the state-of-the-art algorithm for basis construction by showing that particular triplets can be excluded from the computations involved. In our future research, we will investigate the use of our new notion of basis for constructing graphical representations of independency. We will further focus on graphoid models and investigate whether these models equally allow a new notion of triplet set to reduce representation size.

Acknowledgments. The authors would like to thank Peter de Waal for verifying the main results of the reported research and the referees for their helpful comments.

References

1. Baioletti, M., Busanello, G., Vantaggi, B.: Conditional independence structure and its closure: inferential rules and algorithms. Int. J. Approximate Reasoning **50**, 1097–1114 (2009)
2. Dawid, A.P.: Separoids: a mathematical framework for conditional independence and irrelevance. Ann. Math. Artif. Intell. **32**, 335–372 (2001)
3. de Campos, L.M., Castellano, J.G.: Bayesian network learning algorithms using structural restrictions. Int. J. Approximate Reasoning **45**, 233–254 (2007)
4. Lauritzen, S.L.: Graphical Models. Oxford University Press, New York (1996)
5. Pearl, J.: Probabilistic Reasoning in Intelligent Systems: Networks of Plausible Inference. Morgan Kaufmann, San Francisco (1988)
6. Studený, M.: Semigraphoids and structures of probabilistic conditional independence. Ann. Math. Artif. Intell. **21**, 71–98 (1997)
7. Studený, M.: Complexity of structural models. In: Prague Conference on Information Theory, Statistical Decision Functions and Random Processes (1998)

Learning Structure in Evidential Networks from Evidential DataBases

Narjes Ben Hariz[(✉)] and Boutheina Ben Yaghlane

LARODEC Laboratory, Institut Supérieur de Gestion de Tunis,
Le Bardo, Tunisia
narjes.benhariz@gmail.com

Abstract. Evidential networks have gained a growing interest as a good tool fusing belief function theory and graph theory to analyze complex systems with uncertain data. The graphical structure of these models is not always clear, it can be fixed by experts or constructed from existing data. The main issue of this paper is how to extract the graphical structure of an evidential network from imperfect data stored in evidential databases.

1 Introduction

Data in real-world problems are generally characterized by different forms of imperfection: imprecision, uncertainty and/or inconsistency. Many theories have been proposed to deal with this problem of imperfection, one of the most popular is the belief function theory. It is a general framework that handles both partial and total ignorance and offers interesting rules for combining evidence.

Based on this theory, evidential networks are considered as a powerful and flexible tool for modeling complex systems by combining belief function theory and graph theory. Among the most popular evidential graphical models are the evidential networks with conditional belief functions proposed by Xu et al. [23] and the directed evidential networks with conditional belief functions proposed by Ben Yaghlane et al. [4].

As in Bayesian networks, evidential networks are based on two parts: the qualitative part represented by a directed acyclic graph and the quantitative part including a set of parameters modeled by conditional belief functions. The graphical structure of these networks is not always clear, specially in real complex systems. Therefore, a good way for constructing this structure is to estimate it from data.

We address in this paper the issue of learning structure in evidential networks from evidential databases, by extending the classical methods widely used for learning structure in Bayesian networks to the belief functions framework. More precisely, we are interested in generalizing learning methods based on tests of independency, including for example the algorithms proposed by Pearl and Verma [22] and the algorithms proposed by Spirtes et al. [20]. Our learning process is based on evidential chi-square test $E\chi_2$, a generalization of the statistical chi-square test in the belief functions framework.

© Springer International Publishing Switzerland 2015
S. Destercke and T. Denoeux (Eds.): ECSQARU 2015, LNAI 9161, pp. 301–311, 2015.
DOI: 10.1007/978-3-319-20807-7_27

The rest of the paper is organized as follows: we first recall some basic concepts of belief function theory and evidential databases, then we present briefly evidential networks and a short review of the most important algorithms used for learning structure in Bayesian networks. In the main part of the paper, we present our learning process and the evidential chi-square independency test. In the last part of the paper we more explain our approach by an illustrative example.

2   Belief Function Theory and Evidential DataBases

The belief function theory, evidence theory or also Dempster-Shafer theory [17,19], is a mathematical framework commonly used for handling imperfection in data. In the following, we present briefly some theoretical aspects of evidence theory and we introduce databases based on this theory.

2.1   Basic Concepts of Belief Function Theory

Let $N = \{N_1, ..., N_n\}$ be a set of random variables.

Definition 1. *Each variable N_i takes its values from a set of exclusive and exhaustive elements called the frame of discernment and denoted by Ω_{N_i}.*

Definition 2. *We denote by $2^{\Omega_{N_i}}$ the set of all subsets (propositions or events) from Ω_{N_i}.*

Definition 3. *The degree of belief accorded exactly to a proposition A, is called the basic belief assignment or a mass function (bba). It is a mapping from $2^{\Omega_{N_i}}$ to $[0,1]$ such that:*

$$\sum_{A \subseteq \Omega} m^{\Omega}(A) = 1 \tag{1}$$

Definition 4. *Any event $A \in \Omega_{N_i}$ with $m^{\Omega_{N_i}}(A) > 0$ is called a focal element, and the set of all these elements is denoted by $F(m^{\Omega_{N_i}})$.*

Definition 5. *Let $m^{\Omega_{N_i}}[B](A)$ denote the conditional basic belief assignment of A given B, it is defined by Dempster's rule of conditioning:*

$$m^{\Omega_{N_i}}[B](A) = \sum_{C \subseteq \overline{B}} m^{\Omega_{N_i}}(A \cup C), \tag{2}$$

where $\bar{B}$ is the complement of the proposition B.

More details about the rules of conditioning in the belief function theory can be found in [18,21].

2.2   Evidential DataBases

An Evidential DataBase (EDB) is a database storing data with different forms of imperfection: certain, probabilistic, possibilistic, missing and/or evidential data, modeled in the belief functions framework. More details and examples about this notion can be found in [1,8].

Definition 6. *Let $EDB(L, C)$ denote an evidential database with L lines (records) and C columns (variables), each variable N_i define its possible values in a frame of discernment denoted by Ω_{N_i}.*

Definition 7. *Let V_{lc} be the evidential value of cell in the lth line and c^{th} column, V_{lc} is defined by a mass function m_{lc} from $2^{\Omega_{N_i}}$ to $[0, 1]$ such as:*

$$m_{lc}^{\Omega_{N_i}}(\emptyset) = 0 \; and \sum_{A \subseteq \Omega_{N_i}} m_{lc}^{\Omega_{N_i}}(A) = 1 \tag{3}$$

3   Evidential Networks

Evidential networks or belief function networks are graphical models based on the belief functions framework for modeling uncertainty. These models are considered as a generalization of Bayesian networks for handling different types of uncertainty and taking into account both total and partial ignorance.

Among the most popular evidential graphical models Directed EVidential Networks with conditional belief functions (DEVNs) proposed by Ben Yaghlane et al. [4] and Evidential Networks with Conditional belief functions (ENCs) proposed by Xu et al. [23]. DEVNs are developed to extend ENCs for handling n-ary relations between variables.

As in probabilistic networks, evidential graphical models are based essentially on two parts: the qualitative part describing the graphical structure of the network and the quantitative part describing the conditional dependencies between variables.

3.1   Qualitative Part

ENCs and DEVNs have the same graphical structure which is similar to the graphical structure of Bayesian networks (BNs). This structure is modeled by a Directed Acyclic Graph (DAG) $G = (N, E)$ characterized essentially by a set of nodes $N = \{N_1, ..., N_x\}$ representing the different variables of the problem and a set of edges $E = \{E_1, ..., E_y\}$ coding conditional dependencies between variables.

It is important to note that the graphical properties and concepts of a DAG are maintained in evidential networks including conditional independency criterions such as the d-separation, the converging connection (also called v-structure) and the CPDAG (Completed Partially Directed Acyclic Graph). More details about these notions can be found in [3,14].

3.2   Quantitative Part

The quantitative level is represented by a set of parameters θ modeled by conditional belief functions. Each node N_i in an evidential network is a representation of a random variable taking its values on a frame of discernment Ω_{N_i}. Each root node is associated with an a priori mass function, other nodes are associated with a conditional mass function. DEVNs are more flexible then ENCs in modeling conditional beliefs. In DEVNs the conditional mass function can be defined in two manners: per edge or per child node.

In this paper we are interested in the qualitative part of evidential networks. As both ENCs and DEVNs have the same qualitative part we adopt for the rest of the paper a general notation for evidential networks (ENs).

4   Learning Structure in Bayesian Networks

Learning the graphical structure of Bayesian networks from data remains an interesting topic of research. In this section we present a short overview of the literature on learning Bayesian network structure, more details can be found in [10,12,13].

The structure learning methods in BNs are grouped on three essential families:

Constrained based methods. These methods are based on the test of the conditional dependencies between variables in order to build the requested graph.

Score based methods. The main idea of these methods is to find the best structure from the search space of possible DAGs by maximizing a scoring function.

Hybrid methods. Combine constrained based methods and score based methods in order to deal with more complex problems.

In this work we will mainly interest on the methods based on testing the conditional dependencies between variables. The majority of these methods follow the same approach which is based on three steps:

① Build an undirected graph according to a statistical test.
② Detect the V-structures.
③ Get a CPDAG by propagating some edges orientation.

This family of methods includes two principal groups of algorithms:

- The algorithms proposed by Pearl and Verma [15,22] such as IC and IC*. The main idea of these algorithms is to start from an empty graph and try to add edges between dependent variables according to the result of the statistical test.
- The algorithms proposed by Spirtes, Glymour and Scheines [20] such as SGS and PC. These algorithms are based also on a statistical test to delete edges between independent variables from a complete graph.

One of the most statistical tests commonly used for measuring the conditional independency between variables in learning structure algorithms is the chi-square (χ^2) test. This metric will be generalized in the next section for dealing with uncertain data.

5   Learning Structure in Evidential Networks

In this part, we focus on the main purpose of this paper which is how to build the graphical part of an evidential network from data stored in evidential databases.

As we mentioned previously, we are interested in this work in generalizing the constrained based methods, the extension of the other methods of structure learning will be the object of further works.

5.1   Evidential Independency Test

The idea of extending the statistical tests of independency (essentially the χ^2 test) to the belief function theory comes from the principle of the generalization of the maximum likelihood estimation to the evidence framework originally introduced in [7] and applied to learn parameters in evidential networks in [2].

As in probability theory these tests are based on a relation between the observed data and the expected one.

Let us consider X and Y two variables, and Z a set of variables from our $EDB(L, C)$.

Definition 8. *The evidential observed values corresponding respectively to X and Y and to X and Y given Z, denoted by EO_{xy} and $EO_{xy|z}$, are defined by the following equations:*

$$EO_{xy} = \sum_{l=1}^{L} m_{lc}^{\Omega_X}(X = x) * m_{lc}^{\Omega_Y}(Y = y) \tag{4}$$

$$EO_{xy|z} = \sum_{l=1}^{L} m_{lc}^{\Omega_X}(X = x) * m_{lc}^{\Omega_Y}(Y = y) * \prod_{j} m_{lcj}^{\Omega_{Z_j}}(Z_j = z_j) \tag{5}$$

Definition 9. *Let EE_{xy} and $EE_{xy|z}$ denote the evidential expected values such that:*

$$EE_{xy} = \frac{\sum_{l=1}^{L} m_{lc}(X = x) * \sum_{l=1}^{L} m_{lc}(Y = y)}{L} \tag{6}$$

$$EE_{xy|z} = \frac{\sum_{l=1}^{L} m_{lc}(X = x) * \prod_{j} m_{lcj}^{\Omega_{Z_j}}(Z_j = z_j) * \sum_{l=1}^{L} m_{lc}(Y = y) * \prod_{j} m_{lcj}^{\Omega_{Z_j}}(Z_j = z_j)}{\sum_{l=1}^{L} \prod_{j} m_{lcj}^{\Omega_{Z_j}}(Z_j = z_j)} \tag{7}$$

Definition 10. *The evidential test of independency between the two variables X and Y is defined as follows:*

$$E\chi^2_{XY} = \sum_{x=1}^{2^{\Omega_X}-1} \sum_{y=1}^{2^{\Omega_Y}-1} \frac{(EO_{xy} - EE_{xy})^2}{EE_{xy}} \tag{8}$$

with a degree of freedom $df = ((2^{\Omega_X} - 1) - 1)((2^{\Omega_Y} - 1) - 1)$.

The two variables X and Y are considered independent if the value of $E\chi^2_{XY}$ is less than the critical value in the chi-squared distribution.

Definition 11. *The conditional evidential test of independency between the two variables X and Y in the context of Z is defined as follows:*

$$E\chi^2_{XY|Z} = \sum_{x=1}^{2^{\Omega_X}-1} \sum_{y=1}^{2^{\Omega_Y}-1} \sum_{z=1}^{2^{\Omega_Z}-1} \frac{(EO_{xy|z} - EE_{xy|z})^2}{EE_{xy|z}} \tag{9}$$

with a degree of freedom $df = ((2^{\Omega_X} - 1) - 1)((2^{\Omega_Y} - 1) - 1)\prod_j(2^{\Omega_{Z_j}} - 1)$.

The two variables X and Y are said independent in the context of Z if the value of $E\chi^2_{XY|Z}$ is less than the critical value in the chi-squared distribution.

The principle of the extension of the χ^2 test can be also used for generalizing other statistical tests such as the likelihood ratio (G^2) test or even the score functions based on the likelihood principle, in order to generalize score based and hybrid algorithms.

It must be emphasized that, the $E\chi^2$ test has the same major limitation of the classical χ^2 test. This test become inappropriate when the number of variables is high and the amount of data is not sufficient. In probability theory Spirates et al. propose an heuristic to overcome this drawback: if the degree of freedom is higher than $\frac{L}{10}$ the two variables are considered dependent.

In the evidence theory this problem is even more serious, as we consider in the calculation process the power set of each variable. Thus we propose, in this case, to calculate the degree of freedom according to the focal elements of each variable as follows: $df' = (|F(m^{\Omega_X})| - 1)(|F(m^{\Omega_Y})| - 1)$.

If the problem persists, then the hypothesis of Spirtes et al. can be applied.

5.2   Learning Approach

The generalization of the χ^2 test in the belief function framework will be the core of our learning process. In fact, our goal is to estimate the different dependency relations between variables from an $EDB(L, C)$ using the $E\chi^2$ test, in order to get the $DAG(N, E)$ that most closely matches the data. This approach is based on two main steps:

① Test the different independency relations between variables:
  - Calculate the evidential observed values using Eqs. (4) and (5).
  - Calculate the evidential expected values using Eqs. (6) and (7).
  - Test the dependency between variables according to the $E\chi^2$ test measured using Eqs. (8) and (9).

② Apply a learning structure algorithm based on independency tests:
- Build an undirected graph according to $E\chi^2$: delete edges between independent variables if we started with a complete graph or add edges between dependent variables if we started with an empty graph.
- Detect the V-structures according to the calculated $E\chi^2$ test.
- Propagate edges to get a CPDAG representing the sought DAG.

Note that, a possible simplification in the first step of our approach is to consider only focal elements for each variable, in order to reduce the number of values that must be calculated in the $E\chi^2$ test. In this case we consider df' as a degree of freedom.

This approach generalizes any constrained based method classically used for estimating the graphical structure of a Bayesian network.

It will be also interesting to compare our learning approach using the $E\chi^2$ test and other independency tests dedicated to uncertain data such as the independency tests proposed in [16].

6   Illustrative Example

To further explain the details of our learning method, we introduce in this section an illustrative example based on the classical problem Asia Chest Clinic first described in [11]. Table 1 presents a part from an EDB corresponding to the latter problem.

Our problem includes eight variables $\{A, S, T, L, B, O, X, D\}$ having the power sets, respectively: $\{a, \bar{a}, a\cup\bar{a}\}$; $\{s, \bar{s}, s\cup\bar{s}\}$; $\{t, \bar{t}, t\cup\bar{t}\}$; $\{l, \bar{l}, l\cup\bar{l}\}$; $\{b, \bar{b}, b\cup\bar{b}\}$; $\{o, \bar{o}, o\cup\bar{o}\}$; $\{x, \bar{x}, x\cup\bar{x}\}$ and $\{d, \bar{d}, d\cup\bar{d}\}$.

Note that in the EDB a is denoted by 0, $\bar{a}$ is denoted by 1 and $a\cup\bar{a}$ is denoted by $\{0, 1\}$. All other propositions are denoted by the same way.

The first step of our approach is to test dependency between variables. In the following we give some calculation details of the evidential chi-square test applied to the variables T and O using 20 instances from our EDB (represented in Table 1).

- $EO_{to} = \sum_{l=1}^{20} m_{lc}^{\Omega_T}(T=t) * m_{lc}^{\Omega_O}(O=o) = 1*1+1*1+1*0.3+1*1+1* 0.4+1*1 = 4.7$
- By the same manner we get:
  $EO_{t\bar{o}} = 5.3\ EO_{to\bar{o}} = 1\ EO_{\bar{t}o} = 4.99\ EO_{\bar{t}\bar{o}} = 2.41\ EO_{\bar{t}o\bar{o}} = 1.6\ EO_{t\bar{t}o} = 0$
  $EO_{t\bar{t}\bar{o}} = 0\ EO_{t\bar{t}o\bar{o}} = 0$
- $EE_{to} = \frac{\sum_{l=1}^{20} m_{lc}(T=t) * \sum_{l=1}^{20} * m_{lc}(O=o)}{20} = \frac{11*(0.21+1+1+1+0.3+1+1+0.4+0.2+1)}{20} = 3.91$
- Applying the same formula:
  $EE_{t\bar{o}} = 5.65\ EE_{to\bar{o}} = 1.43\ EE_{\bar{t}o} = 3.19\ EE_{\bar{t}\bar{o}} = 2.63\ EE_{\bar{t}o\bar{o}} = 1.17\ EE_{t\bar{t}o} = 0$
  $EE_{t\bar{t}\bar{o}} = 0\ EE_{t\bar{t}o\bar{o}} = 0$
- $E\chi^2_{TO} = [\frac{(EO_{to}-EE_{to})^2}{EE_{to}}] + ... + [\frac{(EO_{t\bar{t}o\bar{o}}-EE_{t\bar{t}o\bar{o}})^2}{EE_{t\bar{t}o\bar{o}}}] = 2.52$
- $df = ((2^2 - 1) - 1) * ((2^2 - 1) - 1) = 4$

Table 1. EDB corresponding to the Asia Chest Clinic problem

A	S	T	L	B	O	X	D
0	0	1	0	0	0(0.21)1(0.79)	0	1
0	0	0	1	0	1	1	1
0(0.5)1(0.5)	0	0	{0,1}	0	0	1	0
1	0	1	0	0	1	1	0
0	0	1	0	0	1	1	1
0	0	1	0	0	0	0	0
{0,1}	0	0	1	0	0	1	1
0	0	0	0	0	0(0.3)1(0.7)	0	0
0(0.22){0,1}(0.78)	0	1	0	0	{0,1}	1	1
0	0	1	0	0	1(0.9){0,1}(0.1)	1	1
0(0.2){0,1}(0.8)	0	1	{0,1}	1	0	1	1
0	0	0	1	0	0	0	1
0	0	0	1	0	1	0	1
0(0.1)1(0.2){0,1}(0.7)	0	0	0	0	{0,1}	1	1
0	0	0	1	0	0(0.4)1(0.6)	0	0
1	0	1	0	0	0(0.2)1(0.3){0,1}(0.5)	0	0
1(0.45){0,1}(0.55)	0	0	0	0	0	1	1
1	0	1	1	0	1	1	1
0	0	0	0	0	1	0	1
0(0.36){0,1}(0.64)	0	0	0	0	1	1	1

Note that, when dealing with perfect data such as the case of variables S, T, B, X and D, the $E\chi^2$ give the same result as the classical χ^2 test.

Assuming that $\alpha = 5\%$, the critical value according to the chi-squared distribution is equal to 9.488 which is higher then the value of the calculated test $E\chi^2_{TO}$. According to this result, the two variables T and O are independent. However, we should note that the obtained value of $E\chi^2_{TO}$ is not significant, because the amount of data considered in this example is very small.

After finishing the different calculation steps and applying the PC algorithm, the result of the evidential learning process from the whole data set is presented in Fig. 1.

Phase 1, phase 2 and phase 3 represent the different iterations of the first step of the PC algorithm which is building an undirected graph by eliminating edges between independent variables from the complete graph, corresponding to the Asia network.

The next step in the learning process is to detect the different v-structures in the obtained undirected graph using the calculated $E\chi^2$ test in order to build a CPDAG modeling the required DAG.

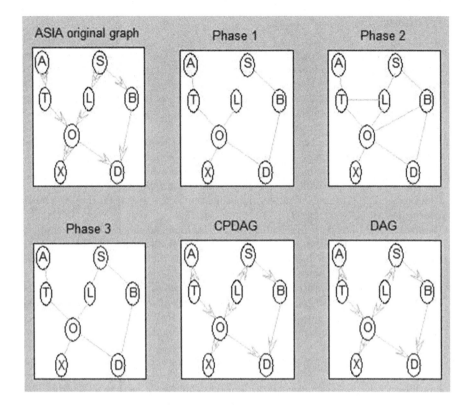

Fig. 1. Result of the evidential learning process

The last step will be then to pass from the CPDAG to the final network as shown in Fig. 1, the algorithm of the construction of a DAG from a CPDAG is detailed in [5].

7   Conclusion

A constrained based approach for learning evidential networks structure from evidential data has been proposed. This approach generalizes the classical constrained based methods usually used for learning structure in BNs by extending the statistical χ^2 test to the belief function framework in order to deal with different types of imperfection in data.

In the future works, we will tend to investigate different horizons:

– Extend score based methods to deal with evidence data.
– Develop detailed experimental results and compare the efficiency of structure learning approaches in the evidence framework.

References

1. Bach Tobji, M.A., Ben Yaghlane, B., Mellouli, K.: A new algorithm for mining frequent itemsets from evidential databases. In: Proceedings of Information Processing and Management of Uncertainty (IPMU 2008), pp. 1535–1542, Malaga (2008)
2. Ben Hariz, N., Ben Yaghlane, B.: Learning parameters in directed evidential networks with conditional belief functions. In: Cuzzolin, F. (ed.) BELIEF 2014. LNCS, vol. 8764, pp. 294–303. Springer, Heidelberg (2014)
3. Ben Yaghlane, B.: Uncertainty Representation and Reasoning in Directed Evidential Networks. P.hD. thesis, Institut Supérieur de Gestion de Tunis (2002)
4. Ben Yaghlane, B., Mellouli, K.: Inference in directed evidential networks based on the transferable belief model. IJAR **48**(2), 399–418 (2008)
5. Chickering, D.: Optimal structure identification with greedy search. J. Mach. Learn. Res. **3**, 507–554 (2002)
6. Dempster, A.P., Laird, N.M., Rubin, D.B.: Maximum likelihood from incomplete data via the EM algorithm. J. Roy. Stat. Soc. Ser. B **39**, 1–38 (1977)
7. Denœux, T.: Maximum likelihood estimation from uncertain data in the belief function framework. Knowl. Data Eng. **25**, 113–119 (2013)
8. Hewawasam, K., Premaratne, K., Subasingha, S., Shyu, M.-L.: Rule mining and classifcation in imperfect databases. In: Proceedings of the 8th International Conference on Information Fusion, vol. 1, pp. 661–668, Philadelphia (2005)
9. Jordan, M.: Learning in Graphical Models. Kluwer Academic Publisher, New York (1998)
10. Krause, P.J.: Learning probabilistic networks. Knowl. Eng. Rev. **13**(4), 321–351 (1998)
11. Lauritzen, S.L., Spiegelhalter, D.J.: Local computation with probabilities and graphical structures and their application to expert systems. J. Roy. Stat. Soc. B **50**, 157–224 (1988)
12. Naim, P., Wuillemin, P.H., Leray, P., Pourret, O., Becker, A.: Réseaux Bayésiens. Eyrolles, Paris (2004)
13. Neapolitan, R.: Learning Bayesian Networks. Prenctice Hall, New York (2003)
14. Pearl, J.: Probabilistic Reasoning in Intelligent Systems: Networks of Plausible Inference. Morgan Kaufmann, New York (1988)
15. Pearl, J., Verma, T.: A theory of inferred causation. In: Allen, J., Fikes, R., Sandewall, E. (eds.) Proceedings of the Second International Conference on Knowledge Representation and Reasoning, pp. 441–452. Morgan Kaufmann, New York (1991)
16. Petitrenaud, S.: Independence tests for uncertain data with a frequentist method. In: Proceedings of the 5th International Conference on Soft Methods in Probability and Statistic (SMPS 2010), pp. 519–526 (2010)
17. Shafer, G.: A Mathematical Theory of Evidence. Princeton University Press, Princeton (1976)
18. Smets, P.: Jeffrey's rule of conditioning generalized to belief functions. In: Proceedings of the Ninth international conference on Uncertainty in artificial intelligence (UAI 1993), pp. 500–505, Washington (1993)
19. Smets, P., Kennes, R.: The transferable belief model. Artif. Intell. **66**, 191–234 (1994)
20. Spirtes, P., Glymour, C., Scheines, R.: Causation, Prediction, and Search. Springer-Verlag, New York (2000)

21. Tang, Y., Zheng, J.: Dempster conditioning and conditional independence in evidence theory. In: Australian Conference on Artificial Intelligence, vol. 3809, pp. 822–825, Sydney (2005)
22. Verma, T., Pearl, J.: Equivalence and synthesis of causal models. In: Proceedings of Sixth Conference on Uncertainty in Artifcial Intelligence, pp. 220–227 (1990)
23. Xu, H., Smets, Ph.: Evidential reasoning with conditional belief functions. In: Heckerman, D., et al. (eds.) Proceedings of Uncertainty in Artificial Intelligence (UAI 1994), pp. 598–606, Seattle (1994)

Evaluating Product-Based Possibilistic Networks Learning Algorithms

Maroua Haddad[1,2]([✉]), Philippe Leray[2], and Nahla Ben Amor[1]

[1] LARODEC Laboratory ISG, Université de Tunis, Tunis, Tunisia
maroua.haddad@gmail.com, nahla.benamor@gmx.fr
[2] LINA-UMR CNRS 6241, University of Nantes, Nantes, France
philippe.leray@univ-nantes.fr

Abstract. This paper proposes a new evaluation strategy for *product-based* possibilistic networks learning algorithms. The proposed strategy is mainly based on sampling a possibilistic networks in order to construct an imprecise data set representative of their underlying joint distribution. Experimental results showing the efficiency of the proposed method in comparing existing possibilistic networks learning algorithms is also presented.

1 Introduction

Researches devoted to graphical models handle a classical form of data which consists in precise information and at most handle missing data. This is due to the fact that most of these works are defined in the probabilistic framework which represents a well-founded normative framework for knowledge representation and reasoning with uncertain but *precise* data. However, in real world applications, we are often faced to more sophisticated imperfect data. In such situation, probability theory does not remain the adequate framework, hence, the birth of several other uncertainty theories such as the case of possibility theory [1]. Consequently, alternative graphical models have been proposed to reason with this form of imperfect data such as possibilistic networks. Despite the multitude of research endeavors concerning propagation in possibilistic networks, e.g. [2,3], the problem of learning such networks from data remains very limited. Moreover, existing methods [4–6] do not propose a convincing evaluation process since most of them has been limited by the lack of an accurate and standard validation procedure. This paper proposes a new evaluation strategy for *product-based* possibilistic networks learning algorithms based on sampling. Such an approach is commonly used for probabilistic graphical models and especially in the evaluation of Bayesian networks learning algorithms, but, it raises several difficulties when applied to possibilistic networks as it will be detailed in this paper. This paper is organized as follows: Sect. 2 gives a brief introduction to possibility theory. Section 3 defines possibilistic networks and discusses their learning from data. Section 4 details our proposed evaluation strategy to possibilistic networks learning algorithms. Section 5 is dedicated to the experimental results.

© Springer International Publishing Switzerland 2015
S. Destercke and T. Denoeux (Eds.): ECSQARU 2015, LNAI 9161, pp. 312–321, 2015.
DOI: 10.1007/978-3-319-20807-7_28

2   Brief Recall on Possibility Theory

This section recalls elementary notions of possibility theory [7] and points out the notion of possibility distribution estimation. Let $V = \{X_1, ..., X_n\}$ be a set of variables such that $D_1, ..., D_n$ are their respective domains and let x_{ik} be an instance of X_i, i.e. each $x_{ik} \in D_i$ corresponds to a state (a possible value) of X_i. The agents knowledge (state set) of X_i can be encoded by a possibility distribution $\pi(X_i)$ corresponding to a mapping from the universe of discourse D_i to the unit interval [0,1]. For any state $x_{ik} \in D_i$, $\pi(x_{ik}) = 1$ means that x_{ik} realization is totally possible $\pi(x_{ik}) = 0$ means that x_{ik} is an impossible state. It is generally assumed that at least one state x_{ik} is totally possible and π is then said to be normalized. Extreme cases of knowledge are presented by *complete knowledge*, i.e. $\exists x_{ik} \in D_i$ s.t. $\pi(x_{ik}) = 1$ and $\forall x_{ij} \in D_i$ s.t. $x_{ij} \neq x_{ik}, \pi(x_{ij}) = 0$ and *total ignorance*, i.e. $\forall x_{ik} \in D_i, \pi(x_{ik}) = 1$ (all values in D_i are possible). The definition of a possibility distribution could be generalized to a set of variables V defined on the universe of discourse $\Omega = D_1 \times ... \times D_n$ encoded by π. π corresponds to a mapping from Ω to the unit interval [0,1]. ω is called interpretation or event and is denoted by a tuple $(x_{1k}, ..., x_{nl})$. $\omega[X_i]$ is the value of X_i in ω.

Possibility theory is based on minimum specificity principle. More precisely, let π and π' be two possibility distributions, π is said to be more specific (more informative) than π' iff $\forall x_{ik} \in D_i, \pi(x_{ik}) \leq \pi'(x_{ik})$. Given a possibility distribution π, we can define for any subset $A \subseteq D_i$ two dual measures: possibility measure $\Pi(A) = \max_{x_{ik} \in A} \pi(x_{ik})$ and necessity measure $N(A) = 1 - \Pi(\bar{A})$ where Π assesses at what level A is consistent with our knowledge represented by π whereas N evaluates at what level $\bar{A}$ is impossible.

The particularity of the possibilistic scale is that it can be interpreted in two ways. First, it can be interpreted in an ordinal manner which means that possibility degrees reflect only a specific order between possible values. Second, the possibilistic scale can be interpreted in a numerical way meaning that possibility degrees make sense in the ranking scale. These two interpretations induce two definitions of possibilistic conditioning which consists in reviewing a possibility distribution by a new certain information ϕ, an interpretation of $\Phi \subseteq V$. The *product-based* conditioning is defined by:

$$\pi(\omega|_* \phi) = \begin{cases} \frac{\pi(\omega)}{\Pi(\phi)} & if \ \omega[\Phi] = \phi \\ 0 & otherwise. \end{cases} \tag{1}$$

While the *min-based* conditioning is defined by:

$$\pi(\omega \mid_{min} \phi) = \begin{cases} 1 & if \ \pi(\omega) = \Pi(\phi) \ and \ \omega[\Phi] = \phi \\ \pi(\omega) & if \ \pi(\omega) < \Pi(\phi) \ and \ \omega[\Phi] = \phi \\ 0 & otherwise. \end{cases} \tag{2}$$

One crucial notion when sampling networks, is the estimation of possibility distribution from generated data sets. In the numerical interpretation,

Joslyn [8] has proposed a possibility distribution estimation method from imprecise data using possibilistic histograms. Moreover, he discusses the non-specificity of obtained possibility distributions in some particular cases such as certain and consistent data sets (for more details see [8]). Let $\mathcal{D}_i = \{d_i^{(l)}\}$ be a dataset relative to a variable X_i, $d_i^{(l)} \in \mathcal{D}_i$ (resp. $d_i^{(l)} \subseteq \mathcal{D}_i$) if data are precise (resp. imprecise). The number of occurrences of each $x_{ik} \in \mathcal{D}_i$, denoted by N_{ik}, is the number of times x_{ik} appears in $\mathcal{D}_i$: $N_{ik} = |\{l \text{ s.t. } x_{ik} \in d_i^{(l)}\}|$. The non-normalized estimation $\hat{\pi}^{nn}(x_{ik})$ is expressed as follows:

$$\hat{\pi}^{nn}(x_{ik}) = \frac{N_{ik}}{N} \tag{3}$$

where N is the number of observations in $\mathcal{D}_i$. N is equal (resp. lower or equal) to the sum of N_{ik} if data are precise (resp. imprecise). Equation 3 could be defined as a set of variables $X_i, X_j, ...X_w$. In this case, N_{ik} becomes $N_{ik,jl,...,wp} = N(\{x_{ik}x_{jl}...x_{wp}\} \subseteq \mathcal{D}_{ijw})$.

3   Learning Possibilistic Networks

3.1   Definition of Possibilistic Networks

Possibilistic networks [9] represent the possibilistic counterpart of Bayesian networks [10] having similarly two components: a *graphical component* composed of a DAG which encodes a set of independence relations (i.e. each variable $X_i \in V$ is conditionally independent of its non-descendent given its parents) and a *numerical component* corresponding to the set of conditional possibility distributions relative to each node $X_i \in V$ in the context of its parents, denoted by $Pa(X_i)$, i.e. $\pi(X_i|Pa(X_i))$. The two definitions of the possibilistic conditioning lead naturally to two different ways to define possibilistic networks: product-based possibilistic networks based on the product-based conditioning expressed by Eq. 1. These models are theoretically and algorithmically close to Bayesian networks. In fact, these two models share the graphical component, i.e. the DAG and the product operator in the computational process. This is not the case of qualitative based on min-based conditioning defined by Eq. 2 that represents a different semantic. In both cases, possibilistic networks are a compact representation of possibility distributions. More precisely, the joint possibility distribution could be computed by the possibilistic chain rule expressed as follows:

$$\pi_\otimes(X_1, ..., X_n) = \otimes_{i=1..n}\pi(X_i \mid_\otimes Pa(X_i)) \tag{4}$$

where $\otimes$ corresponds to the product operator (*) for quantitative possibilistic networks and to the minimum operator (min) for qualitative possibilistic networks. In the remaining, we focus on *product-based* possibilistic networks. Figure 1 represents an example of a *product-based* possibilistic network with four ternary variables.

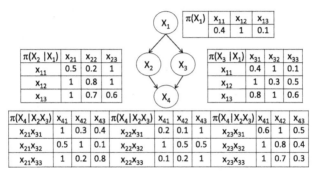

Fig. 1. Example of a product-based possibilistic network

3.2 Possibilistic Networks Structure Learning

By analogy to Bayesian networks, structure learning methods could be categorized into three families: constraint-based, score-based and hybrid methods. In the possibilistic case, Gebhardt and Kruse have proposed a score-based method handling imprecise data [5]. Borgelt et al. [4] have proposed possibilistic versions of two learning methods initially proposed to Bayesian networks: K2 and maximum weight spanning tree handling, also, imprecise data. Sangüesa et al. [6] have proposed two hybrid learning methods from precise data: the first one learns trees and the second one learns the more general structure of DAGs. Most of attempts to learn possibilistic networks are direct adaptations of learning methods initially proposed for Bayesian networks ignoring also parameters learning problem. Moreover, all these works have been proposed before advances made concerning possibilistic networks as independence models leading to use contrary hypothesis: a numerical operator (*) in the conditioning and an ordinal operator (min) in the conditional independence relation.

3.3 Possibilistic Networks Parameters Learning

Parameters learning of Bayesian networks is performed satisfying *maximum entropy* principle [11]. The possibilistic analog of the latter corresponds to minimum specificity. By analogy to Bayesian networks, learning possibilistic networks parameters consists in estimating possibility distributions according to minimum specificity principle [12], i.e. estimating the least specific possibility distributions. As far as we know, parameters learning has not been studied yet and existing learning methods compute possibility distributions using either Eq. 3 as done in [4,5] or probability possibility transformations [13] as done in [6].

4 Evaluating Learning Algorithms

Probabilistic graphical models learning methods, in particular Bayesian networks, are tested using randomly generated networks (synthetic) or networks that have been used in real systems, so that the structure of the network is

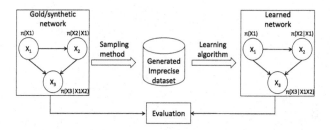

Fig. 2. Evaluation process of possibilistic networks learning algorithms

known and can serve as a rigorous gold standard e.g. Asia and Insurance networks. In the probabilistic case, evaluating learning algorithm is ensured using the following process: we select an arbitrary Bayesian network either a synthetic one or a gold standard from which we generate a data set using Forward Sampling algorithm [14]. Then, we try to recover the initial network using a learning algorithm and we compare the initial network with the learned one.

None of the existing possibilistic networks learning methods has proposed a formal evaluation strategy and each existing work has proposed its evaluation measure whose values are difficult to interpret. In the following, we propose to transpose the evaluation strategy proposed in the probabilistic case to the possibilistic one in order to evaluate a possibilistic networks learning algorithm as shown by Fig. 2.

4.1 Generating Possibilistic Networks

In the possibilisic case, there are currently no publicly available possibilistic networks used in real systems and could be used as gold standard. We propose either to generate randomly a possibilistic network or to transform a gold Bayesian network to a possibilistic one. Generating a random possibilistic network consists in generating its two components. Concerning the graphical component, we could use any method proposed in the context of Bayesian networks such as [15]. For the numerical component, we propose to generate random values from [0,1] for each distribution satisfying normalization property, i.e. at least one of states degrees is equal to 1. We can, also, transform a Bayesian network to a possibilistic one retaining the same structure and performing a probability possibility transformation on its distributions, e.g. [13], on its probability distributions.

4.2 Sampling Possibilistic Networks

Once the possibilistic network is generated, we want to generate an imprecise dataset representative of its possibility distributions. To the best of our knowledge, there is no possibilistic networks sampling method. However, two approaches have been proposed [16,17] to sample one variable and are based on α-cut notion expressed as follows:

$$\alpha - \mathrm{cut}_{X_i} = \{x_{ik} \in D_i \text{ s.t. } \pi(x_{ik}) \geq \alpha\} \tag{5}$$

where α is randomly generated from [0,1].

The epistemic sampling method proposed by Guyonnet et al. in [17] focuses on the generation of imprecise data by returning all values of α-cut_{X_i} for any variable X_i. In fact, it returns a nested random set which represents the state of knowledge about the sampled variable X_i. Chanas and Nowakowski proposed another method in [16] which is dedicated to the generation of precise data from the pignistic probability distribution by returning a single value uniformly chosen from α-cut_{X_i}.

In this paper, we propose to generalize the variable sampling method proposed in [17] to possibilistic networks. This choice is justified by the fact that this method generates a more generic form of imperfect data i.e. imprecise data. The sampling process constructs a database of N (predefined) observations by instantiating all variables in V w.r.t. their possibility distributions. Obviously, variables are most easily processed w.r.t. a topological order, since this ensures that all parents are instantiated. Instantiating a parentless variable corresponds to computing its α-cut. Instantiating a conditioned variable corresponds to computing also its α-cut but given its sampled parents values. This could not be directly applied to conditional possibility distribution which is composed of more than one distribution depending on the number of the values of its sampled parents. To instantiate a conditioned variable X_i s.t. $Pa(X_i) = A)$, we compute α-cut from $\pi(X_i|Pa(X_i) = A)$, computed as follows:

$$\pi(X_i|Pa(X_i) = A) = \max_{a_i \in A} \pi(X_i|a_i)\pi(a_i) \tag{6}$$

Example 1. Let us consider the possibilistic network in Fig. 1. The topological order is X_1, X_2, X_3, X_4. Applying the described sampling process we obtain:

1. X_1: $\alpha = 0.3$, α-$cut_{X_1} = \{x_{11}, x_{12}\}$.
2. X_2: $\alpha = 0.9$
   (a) $\pi'(x_{21}) = max(0.4 * 0.5, 1 * 1) = 1$, $\pi'(x_{22}) = max(0.4 * 0.2, 1 * 0.8) = 0.8$, $\pi'(x_{23}) = max(0.4 * 1, 1 * 1) = 1$.
   (b) α-$cut_{X_2} = \{x_{21}, x_{23}\}$.
3. X_3: $\alpha = 0.7$
   (a) $\pi'(x_{31}) = max(0.4 * 0.4, 1 * 1) = 1$, $\pi'(x_{32}) = max(0.4 * 1, 1 * 0.3) = 0.4$, $\pi'(x_{33}) = max(0.4 * 0.1, 1 * 0.5) = 0.5$.
   (b) α-$cut_{X_3} = \{x_{31}\}$.
4. X_4: $\alpha = 0.2$
   (a) $\pi'(x_{41}) = max(1*1*1, 1*1*0.6) = 1$, $\pi'(x_{32}) = max(1*1*0.3, 1*1*1) = 1$, $\pi'(x_{33}) = max(1 * 1 * 0.4, 1 * 1 * 0.5) = 0.5$.
   (b) α-$cut_{X_4} = \{x_{41}, x_{42}, x_{43}\}$.

The obtained observation is then $(\{x_{11}, x_{12}\}, \{x_{21}, x_{23}\}, \{x_{31}\}, \{x_{41}, x_{42}, x_{43}\})$. We repeat the process to obtain N samples.

4.3   Evaluation Measures

An evaluation measure assesses learned possibilistic networks quality and quantify the efficiency of the learning method graphically or numerically. We could evaluate learning algorithms graphically by comparing the initial and the learned possibilistic networks structures using graphical evaluation measures proposed in the context of Bayesian networks, e.g. sensitivity (ratio of edges correctly identified in the learned network), specificity (ratio of edges correctly identified as not belonging in the learned network) and editing distance (number of operations required to transform a learned possibilistic network structure into the initial one. For more details, see [18,19]. Note that, it is necessary to take into account Markov equivalence properties when computing these measures. In fact, we should compute editing distance between equivalence class representatives and sensitivity and specificity of DAGs skeletons i.e. without edges orientation or DAGs v-structure (in the form $X_i \longrightarrow X_j \longleftarrow X_k$).

Learning algorithms could be evaluated numerically by comparing the initial network and the learned one using a possibilistic dissimilarity measure between their joint possibility distribution as done by KL divergence in the probabilistic case. Such a measure has been proposed to compare two possibility distributions π and π' defined in D_i s.t. $\pi(x_{ik}) \geq \pi'(x_{ik}) \forall x_{ik} \in D_i$ [4]. This hypothesis is restrictive for comparing two possibilistic networks. However, we can use the possibilistic similarity measure proposed in [20] which is expressed by:

$$Aff(\pi_0, \pi_l) = 1 - \frac{\kappa * d(\pi_0, \pi_l) + \lambda * Inc(\pi_0, \pi_l)}{\kappa + \lambda} \tag{7}$$

Information affinity is based on two quantities: inconsistency degree $Inc(\pi_0, \pi_l) = 1 - \max_{\omega_i \in \Omega}\{\pi_0(\omega_i) \wedge \pi_l(\omega_i)\}$ ($\wedge$ can be taken as min or product operator[1]) and Manhattan distance i.e. $d(\pi_0, \pi_l) = \frac{\sum_{l=1}^{m} |\pi_0(\omega_i) - \pi_l(\omega_i)|}{m}$, where $\kappa > 0$ and $\lambda > 0$.

KL divergence and information affinity involve heavy computing if the number of variables increases. This can be explained by the fact that they involve all $\omega \in \Omega$. For KL divergence, we can compute an approximation to it, but, for information affinity, such approximation has not been studied yet.

5 Experimental Study

This section proposes an experimental study having two main purposes. The first set of experiments evaluates the efficiency of the proposed sampling method to generate an imprecise data set representative of a given possibilistic network. The second set of experiments illustrates the whole proposed evaluation strategy on main existing possibilistic learning algorithms in literature. These experiments were ran on the following platform: 2.30 GHz Intel(R) Core (TM) i5-2410M with 8 Go of memory.

---

[1] Using the min operator instead of the product means that we give less importance to the inconsistency degree.

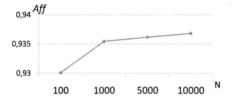

Fig. 3. Information affinity between π_0 and π_l w.r.t the number of data (average over 100 experiments)

5.1 Evaluation of the Proposed Sampling Method

The first set of experiments evaluates the efficiency of our sampling method. We study the convergence of the joint possibility distribution computed from generated data using Eq. 3, denoted by π_0, to the theoretical one, i.e. computed using Eq. 4, denoted by π_0. Specifically, we generate synthetic data sets containing 100, 1000, 5000 and 10000 observations from 100 randomly generated possibilistic networks composed of nb nodes where nb is randomly generated in [5,10]. In order to compare π_0 and π_l, we measure the similarity between the two possibility distributions using Information Affinity (Eq. 7) and we take $\lambda = \kappa = 1$ and $\wedge$ is the min operator. Figure 3 presents information affinity values between π_0 and π_l. Each value is the average of results of the 100 experiments carried out with a standard deviation around 0.04. Figure 3 shows that the information affinity grows relatively smoothly with the number of observations, as expected. This is an obvious result because when we increase the number of observations, the data set becomes more informative and representative of the joint possibility distribution, i.e. most possible ω_i appears more frequently, less possible appears less frequently and so on until reaching the least possible ω_i or impossible ω_i. Consequently, we deflate considerably the gap between the initial possibility distribution and the learned one. Note that in all experiments if $\pi_0(\omega_i) = 1$, then, $\pi_l(\omega_i) = 1$, i.e. the proposed sampling method conserves the most possible interpretation.

5.2 Illustration of the Evaluation Strategy

In the second set of experiments, we generate 100 data sets of 100, 1000, 5000 and 10000 observations from the famous Asia network [21] (8 nodes and 8 edges). This network is a probabilistuc one, so in order to adapt it to our possibilistic context, we apply *optimal probability possibility transformation* [13] on its conditional probability distributions. Then, we apply existing possibilistic learning structure algorithms which handle imprecise data, i.e. the possibilistic adaptation of k2 (πK2), maximum weight spanning tree (πMWST) [4] and greedy search (πGS) [5]. In the current work, πK2 [4] and πMWST are tested using two scores, namely, *possibilistic mutual information* (d_{mi}) and *possibilistic χ^2 measure* (d_{χ^2}) and πK2 treats variables in a predefined order (we generate 5 orders in each experiment and we retain the best structure). πGS uses expected non specificity as score and begins with the class of all directed graphs w.r.t V that

Table 1. Editing distance, specificity and sensitivity of learned structures

	Editing distance			
N	100	1000	5000	10000
πGS	17,23+/-1,2	17,3+/-1,3	17,22+/-1,4	17,28+/-1,2
πMWST+d_{χ^2}	12,65 +/- 0,8	11,81 +/- 1,2	11,97 +/- 1	11,98 +/- 1
πMWST+ d_{mi}	12,97 +/- 0,3	11,84 +/- 1,4	10,09 +/- 0,5	10 +/- 0
πK2+d_{χ^2}	9,75 +/- 1,3	10,89 +/- 1,4	10,52 +/- 1,2	10,52 +/- 1,1
πK2+ d_{mi}	8,12 +/- 0,3	9,52 +/- 1,4	10,55 +/- 1,3	10,65 +/- 1,3
	Specificity			
N	100	1000	5000	10000
πGS	0,35+/-0,03	0,34+/-0,03	0,35+/-0,03	0,34+/-0,03
πMWST+d_{χ^2}	0,8 +/- 0,03	0,84 +/- 0,04	0,83 +/- 0,02	0,83 +/- 0,02
πMWST+ d_{mi}	0,79 +/- 0,01	0,83 +/- 0,05	0,9 +/- 0,01	0,9 +/- 0,01
πK2+d_{χ^2}	0,89 +/- 0,07	0,81 +/- 0,04	0,82 +/- 0,04	0,82 +/- 0,04
πK2+ d_{mi}	0,98 +/- 0,02	0,9 +/- 0,07	0,84 +/- 0,05	0,83 +/- 0,05
	Sensitivity			
N	100	1000	5000	10000
πGS	0,68+/-0,09	0,69+/-0,08	0,7+/-0,09	0,7+/-0,08
πMWST+d_{χ^2}	0,27 +/- 0,06	0,34 +/- 0,1	0,32 +/- 0,06	0,31 +/- 0,06
πMWST+ d_{mi}	0,25 +/- 0,02	0,35 +/- 0,1	0,49 +/- 0,04	0,5 +/- 0
πK2+d_{χ^2}	0,06 +/- 0,02	0,16 +/- 0,08	0,19 +/- 0,06	0,18 +/- 0,06
πK2+ d_{mi}	0,01 +/- 0,03	0,08 +/- 0,03	0,12 +/- 0,07	0,13 +/- 0,06

satisfy the condition $|Pa(X_i)| \leq 1$ for all $X_i \in V$ and we, also, ran it five times retaining the best learned structure. Then, we compute editing distance between equivalence class representatives, skeleton sensitivity and specificity between the learned and the initial structures. Table 1 shows the average of obtained results. We can see that πGS scoring function seems to be less interesting than the ones used by πK2 and πMWST which has not been previously established. Such a result clearly deserves more investigations but it is not the purpose of the present paper.

6   Conclusion

Despite the similarities between Bayesian networks and possibilistic ones and especially those based on the product operator (since they share the same graphical component and even same computations in the propagation process), working with possibility distributions highlights several difficulties when dealing with the learning task. This paper proposes a new evaluation strategy for *product-based* possibilistic networks learning algorithms. The proposed method provides several means to assess learned networks quality, i.e. we could use two families of evaluation measures: graphical ones to compare networks structures and information affinity to compute similarity between learned and initial distributions.

The proposed evaluation strategy presents a clear experimental framework. Thereby, it will be interesting to realize now a comparative and intensive study of existing possibilistic networks algorithms to evaluate score functions quality, learned networks quality and execution time. Future work concerns an approximation of the numerical evaluation measure information affinity in order to make its use possible in complex domains involving a huge number of variables.

References

1. Dubois, D.: Possibility theory and statistical reasoning. Comput. Stat. Data Anal. **51**(1), 47–69 (2006)
2. Benferhat, S., Smaoui, S.: Hybrid possibilistic networks. Int. J. Approximate Reasoning **44**(3), 224–243 (2007)
3. Ayachi, R., Ben Amor, N., Benferhat, S.: A generic framework for a compilation-based inference in probabilistic and possibilistic networks. Inf. Sci. **257**, 342–356 (2014)
4. Borgelt, C., Steinbrecher, M., Kruse, R.: Graphical models: Representations for Learning, vol. 704. Reasoning and Data Mining. Wiley, Chichester (2009)
5. Gebhardt, J., Kruse, R.: Learning possibilistic networks from data. In: International Workshop on Artificial Intelligence and Statistics, pp. 233–244 (1996)
6. Sangüesa, R., Cabós, J., Cortes, U.: Possibilistic conditional independence: a similarity-based measure and its application to causal network learning. Int. J. Approximate Reasoning **18**(1), 145–167 (1998)
7. Dubois, D., Prade, H.: Possibility theory: qualitative and quantitative aspects. In: Smets, P. (ed.) Quantified Representation of Uncertainty and Imprecision, vol. 1, pp. 169–226. Springer, Netherlands (1998)
8. Joslyn, C.: Towards an empirical semantics of possibility through maximum uncertainty. In: International Fuzzy Systems Association: Artificial Intelligence, pp. 86–89 (1991)
9. Fonck, P.: Propagating uncertainty in a directed acyclic graph. In: Information Processing and Management of Uncertainty Conference, vol. 92, pp. 17–20 (1992)
10. Pearl, J.: Probabilistic Reasoning in Intelligent Systems: Networks of Plausible Inference. Morgan Kaufmann, San Mateo (1988)
11. Herskovits, E., Cooper, G.F.: An entropy-driven system for construction of probabilistic expert systems from databases. In: UAI 1990, pp. 117–128. Elsevier (1991)
12. Klir, G.J.: Uncertainty and Information: Foundations of Generalized Information Theory. Wiley, Hoboken (2005)
13. Dubois, D., Prade, H., Sandri, S.: On possibility/probability transformations. In: Lowen, R., Roubens, M. (eds.) Fuzzy logic, vol. 12, pp. 103–112. Springer, Netherlands (1993)
14. Henrion, M.: Propagating uncertainty in Bayesian networks by probabilistic logic sampling. In: Uncertainty in Artificial Intelligence, pp. 149–164 (1986)
15. Xiang, Y., Miller, T.: A well-behaved algorithm for simulating dependence structures of Bayesian networks. IJAM **1**, 923–932 (1999)
16. Chanas, S., Nowakowski, M.: Single value simulation of fuzzy variable. Fuzzy Sets Syst. **25**(1), 43–57 (1988)
17. Guyonnet, D., Bourgine, B., Dubois, D., Fargier, H., Côme, B., Chilès, J.P.: Hybrid approach for addressing uncertainty in risk assessments. J. Environ. Eng. **129**(1), 68–78 (2003)
18. Tsamardinos, I., Brown, L.E., Aliferis, C.F.: The max-min hill-climbing Bayesian network structure learning algorithm. Mach. learn. **65**(1), 31–78 (2006)
19. Shapiro, L.G., Haralick, R.M.: A metric for comparing relational descriptions. Pattern Anal. Mach. Intell. **7**(1), 90–94 (1985)
20. Jenhani, I., Ben Amor, N., Elouedi, Z.: Decision trees as possibilistic classifiers. Int. J. Approximate Reasoning **48**(3), 784–807 (2008)
21. Lauritzen, S.L., Spiegelhalter, D.J.: Local computations with probabilities on graphical structures and their application to expert systems. J. Roy. Stat. Soc. **50**, 157–224 (1988)

Bayesian Networks

Every LWF and AMP Chain Graph Originates from a Set of Causal Models

Jose M. Peña[⊠]

ADIT, IDA, Linköping University, 58183 Linköping, Sweden
jose.m.pena@liu.se

Abstract. This paper aims at justifying LWF and AMP chain graphs by showing that they do not represent arbitrary independence models. Specifically, we show that every chain graph is inclusion optimal wrt the intersection of the independence models represented by a set of directed and acyclic graphs under conditioning. This implies that the independence model represented by the chain graph can be accounted for by a set of causal models that are subject to selection bias, which in turn can be accounted for by a system that switches between different regimes or configurations.

1 Introduction

Chain graphs (CGs) are graphs with possibly directed and undirected edges, and no semidirected cycle. They have been extensively studied as a formalism to represent independence models. CGs extend Bayesian networks (BNs), i.e. directed and acyclic graphs (DAGs), and Markov networks, i.e. undirected graphs. Therefore, they can model symmetric and asymmetric relationships between the random variables of interest. This was actually one of the main reasons for developing them. However, unlike Bayesian and Markov networks whose interpretation is unique, there are three main interpretations of CGs as independence models: The Lauritzen-Wermuth Frydenberg (LWF) interpretation [12,16], the multivariate regression (MVR) interpretation [6,7], and the Andersson-Madigan-Perlman (AMP) interpretation [1,17]. A fourth interpretation has been proposed in [9] but it has not been studied sufficiently and, thus, it will not be discussed in this paper. It should be mentioned that any of the three main interpretations can represent independence models that cannot be represented by the other two interpretations [37].

Along with other reasons, DAGs can convincingly be justified by the fact that each of them represents a causal model. Whether this is an ontological model is still debated. However, it is widely accepted that the causal model is at least epistemological and thus worth studying [24]. Of the three main interpretations of CGs, however, only MVR CGs have a convincing justification: Since MVR CGs are a subset of maximal ancestral graphs without undirected edges, every MVR CG represents the independence model represented by a DAG under marginalization [35, Theorem 6.4]. That is, every MVR CG can be accounted for by

S. Destercke and T. Denoeux (Eds.): ECSQARU 2015, LNAI 9161, pp. 325–334, 2015.
DOI: 10.1007/978-3-319-20807-7_29

a causal model that is partially observed. Unfortunately, LWF and AMP CGs cannot be justified in the same manner because (i) LWF and AMP CGs can represent independence models that cannot be represented by maximal ancestral graphs [35, Sect 9.4], and (ii) maximal ancestral graphs can represent all the independence models represented by DAGs under marginalization and conditioning [35, Theorem 4.18]. In other words, LWF and AMP CGs can represent independence models that cannot be represented by any DAG under marginalization and conditioning. Of course, LWF and AMP CGs can be justified by the fact that they improve the expressivity of DAGs, i.e. they can represent more independence models than DAGs [26]. However, this is a weak justification unless those independence models are not arbitrary but induced by some class of knowledge representatives within some uncertainty calculus of artificial intelligence, e.g. the class of probability distributions [39, Sect 1.1]. This is exactly what the authors of [17, 27, 28, 40] do by showing that every LWF and AMP CG is faithful to some probability distribution. However, this does not strengthen much the justification unless these probability distributions are not arbitrary but they represent meaningful systems or phenomena. This is exactly what the authors of [15] do. In particular, the authors show that every LWF CG includes the independence model induced by the equilibrium probability distribution of a dynamic model with feed-back. The downside of this justification is that the equilibrium distribution may not be reached in finite time and, thus, it may not coincide with the distribution that represents the behaviour of the dynamic model at any finite time point. Therefore, there is no guarantee that the CG includes the independence model induced by the latter, which is the goal. The authors are aware of this and state that their justification should better be understood as an approximated one. Another work in the same vein is [11], whose authors show that some LWF CGs are inclusion minimal wrt the result of temporal aggregation in a DAG representing a spatio-temporal process. Unfortunately, the authors do not show whether their result holds for every LWF CG. Yet another work along the same lines is [31], whose author shows that every AMP CG is faithful to the independence model represented by a DAG under marginalization and conditioning. It is worth noting that the DAG contains deterministic nodes, because the result does not hold otherwise [34]. Finally, the author of [38] presents the following justification of LWF CGs. Each connectivity component of a LWF CG models an area of expertise. The undirected edges in the connectivity component indicate lack of independencies in the area of expertise. The directed edges in the CG indicate which areas of expertise are prerequisite of which other areas. However, the author does not describe how the independencies in the local models of the areas of expertise get combined to produce a global model of the domain, and how this model relates to the one represented by the CG.

In this work, we show that every LWF and AMP CG G is inclusion optimal wrt the intersection of the independence models represented by a set of DAGs under conditioning. In other words, we show that (i) the independencies represented by G are a subset of theintersection, and (ii) the property (i) is not satisfied by any CG that represents a proper superset of the independencies represented by G. Note that if there exists a CG that is faithful to the intersection, then that CG is inclusion optimal. In general, several inclusion optimal CGs exist and they do not necessarily represent the same independence model. Therefore, in principle, one prefers the inclusion optimal CGs that represent the largest number of independencies. However, finding any such CG seems extremely difficult, probably NP-complete in the light of the results in [29]. Thus, one is typically content with finding any inclusion optimal CG. An example of this are the algorithms for learning inclusion optimal BNs [5, 22] and LWF CGs [32]. This is also why we are content with showing in this paper that every LWF and AMP CG is inclusion optimal wrt the intersection of the independence models represented by a set of DAGs under conditioning. The intersection can be thought of as a consensus independence model, in the sense that it contains all and only the independencies upon which all the DAGs under conditioning agree. We elaborate further on the term consensus in the paragraph below. The fact that every LWF and AMP CG originates from a set of DAGs under conditioning implies that the independence model represented by the former can be accounted for by a set of causal models that are subject to selection bias, which in turn can be accounted for by a system that switches between different regimes or configurations. Two examples of such a system are the progression of a disease through different stages, and the behaviour of a broker alternating between looking for buying and selling opportunities. We have recently introduced a new family of graphical models aiming at modeling such systems [2, 3]. In summary, we provide an alternative justification of LWF and AMP CGs that builds solely on causal models and does not involve equilibrium distributions or deterministic nodes, which may seem odd to some readers. Our hope is that this strengthens the case of LWF and AMP CGs as a useful representation of the independence models entailed by causal models.

Before we proceed further, it is worth discussing the relationship between our justification of LWF and AMP CGs and belief aggregation. First, recall that a BN is an efficient representation of a probability distribution. Specifically, a BN consists of structure and parameter values. The structure is a DAG representing an independence model. The parameter values specify the conditional probability distribution of each node given its parents in the BN structure. The BN represents the probability distribution that results from the product of these conditional probability distributions. Moreover, the probability distribution satisfies the independence model represented by the BN structure. Belief aggregation consists in obtaining a group consensus probability distribution from the probability distributions specified by the individual members of the group. Probably, the two most commonly used consensus functions are the weighted arithmetic and geometric averages. The authors of [25] show that belief aggregation is problematic when the consensus and the individual probability distributions are represented as BNs. Specifically, they show that even if the group members agree on the BN structure, there is no sensible consensus function that always returns a probability distribution that can be represented as a BN whose structure is equivalent to the agreed one [25, Proposition 2]. The only exception to this negative result is when the individual BN structures are decomposable and the consensus function is the weighted geometric average [25, Sects 3.3-3.4]. However, the authors also point out that this negative result does not invalidate the arguments of those who advocate preserving the agreed independencies, e.g. [13] and [33, Sect 8.12]. It simply indicates that a different approach to belief aggregation is needed in this case. They actually mention one such approach that consists in performing the aggregation in two steps: First, find a consensus BN structure that preserves as many of the agreed independencies as possible and, second, find consensus parameter values for the consensus BN structure. The first step has received significant attention in the literature [8, 18–20, 23]. A work that studies both steps is [4].[1] We have also studied both steps [10, 29]. The two step approach described above is also suitable when some of the group members are able to contribute with a BN structure but not with parameter values. This scenario is not unlikely given that people typically find easier to gather qualitative than quantitative knowledge.

Our justification of LWF and AMP CGs implicitly advocates preserving the agreed independencies, because the DAGs in the justification are combined through the intersection of the independence models that they represent and, thus, the agreed independencies are kept. As shown above, this is a sensible advocation. Therefore, in this paper we make use of it to propose a sensible justification of LWF and AMP CGs. The DAGs in our justification are hand-picked to ensure that the combination thereof produces the desired result. This raises the question of how to combine a set of arbitrary DAGs under marginalization and conditioning into a LWF or AMP CG. In this paper, we also investigate this question. Ideally, we would like to find a LWF or AMP CG that is inclusion optimal wrt the intersection of the independence models represented by the DAGs under marginalization and conditioning. Unfortunately, this problem seems extremely hard. So, we actually study a simpler version of it. Note that this problem corresponds to the first step of the approach to belief aggregation described above. The second step, i.e. combining the parameter values associated to the DAGs, is beyond the scope of this paper.

The rest of the paper is organized as follows. In Sect. 2, we introduce some preliminaries and notation. In Sect. 3, we present our justification of LWF and AMP CGs. In Sect. 4, we discuss how to combine arbitrary DAGs into a LWF or AMP CG. We close with some discussion in Sect. 5.

2   Preliminaries

In this section, we review some concepts from graphical models that are used later in this paper. Unless otherwise stated, all the graphs in this paper are defined over a finite set V. Moreover, they are all simple, i.e. they contain at most one edge between any pair of nodes. The elements of V are not distinguished from

---

[1] Unfortunately, we could not get access to this work. So, we trust the description of it made in [25, Sect 3.5].

singletons. The set operators union, intersection and difference are given equal precedence in the expressions. The term maximal is always wrt set inclusion.

If a graph G contains an undirected or directed edge between two nodes V_1 and V_2, then we write that $V_1 - V_2$ or $V_1 \rightarrow V_2$ is in G. The parents of a set of nodes X of G is the set $pa_G(X) = \{V_1 | V_1 \rightarrow V_2$ is in G, $V_1 \notin X$ and $V_2 \in X\}$. The children of X is the set $ch_G(X) = \{V_1 | V_1 \leftarrow V_2$ is in G, $V_1 \notin X$ and $V_2 \in X\}$. The neighbors of X is the set $ne_G(X) = \{V_1 | V_1 - V_2$ is in G, $V_1 \notin X$ and $V_2 \in X\}$. The boundary of X is the set $bd_G(X) = ne_G(X) \cup pa_G(X)$. The adjacents of X is the set $ad_G(X) = ne_G(X) \cup pa_G(X) \cup ch_G(X)$. A route between a node V_1 and a node V_n in G is a sequence of (not necessarily distinct) nodes $V_1, \ldots, V_n$ st $V_i \in ad_G(V_{i+1})$ for all $1 \leq i < n$. If the nodes in the route are all distinct, then the route is called a path. A route is called undirected if $V_i - V_{i+1}$ is in G for all $1 \leq i < n$. A route is called descending if $V_i \rightarrow V_{i+1}$ or $V_i - V_{i+1}$ is in G for all $1 \leq i < n$. A route is called strictly descending if $V_i \rightarrow V_{i+1}$ is in G for all $1 \leq i < n$. The descendants of a set of nodes X of G is the set $de_G(X) = \{V_n |$ there is a descending path from V_1 to V_n in G, $V_1 \in X$ and $V_n \notin X\}$. The strict ascendants of X is the set $san_G(X) = \{V_1 |$ there is a strictly descending path from V_1 to V_n in G, $V_1 \notin X$ and $V_n \in X\}$. A route $V_1, \ldots, V_n$ in G is called a semidirected cycle if $V_n = V_1$, $V_1 \rightarrow V_2$ is in G and $V_i \rightarrow V_{i+1}$ or $V_i - V_{i+1}$ is in G for all $1 < i < n$. A chain graph (CG) is a graph whose every edge is directed or undirected st it has no semidirected cycles. Note that a CG with only directed edges is a directed and acyclic graph (DAG), and a CG with only undirected edges is an undirected graph (UG). A set of nodes of a CG is connected if there exists an undirected path in the CG between every pair of nodes in the set. A connectivity component of a CG is a maximal connected set. We denote by $co_G(X)$ the connectivity component of the CG G to which a node X belongs. A chain α is a partition of V into ordered subsets, which we call blocks. We say that a CG G and a chain α are consistent when (i) for every edge $X \rightarrow Y$ in G, the block containing X precedes the block containing Y in α, and (ii) for every edge $X - Y$ in G, X and Y are in the same block of α. Note that the blocks of α and the connectivity components of G may not coincide, but each of the latter must be included in one of the former.

Let X, Y, Z and W denote four disjoint subsets of V. An independence model M is a set of statements of the form $X \perp_M Y | Z$, meaning that X is independent of Y given Z. Moreover, M is called graphoid if it satisfies the following properties: Symmetry $X \perp_M Y | Z \Rightarrow Y \perp_M X | Z$, decomposition $X \perp_M Y \cup W | Z \Rightarrow X \perp_M Y | Z$, weak union $X \perp_M Y \cup W | Z \Rightarrow X \perp_M Y | Z \cup W$, contraction $X \perp_M Y | Z \cup W \wedge X \perp_M W | Z \Rightarrow X \perp_M Y \cup W | Z$, and intersection $X \perp_M Y | Z \cup W \wedge X \perp_M W | Z \cup Y \Rightarrow X \perp_M Y \cup W | Z$. Moreover, M is called compositional graphoid if it is a graphoid that also satisfies the composition property $X \perp_M Y | Z \wedge X \perp_M W | Z \Rightarrow X \perp_M Y \cup W | Z$. By convention, $X \perp_M \emptyset | Z$ and $\emptyset \perp_M Y | Z$.

We now recall the semantics of LWF and AMP CGs. A section of a route ρ in a LWF CG is a maximal undirected subroute of ρ. A section $V_2 - \ldots - V_{n-1}$ of ρ is a collider section of ρ if $V_1 \rightarrow V_2 - \ldots - V_{n-1} \leftarrow V_n$ is a subroute of ρ.

Moreover, ρ is said to be Z-open with $Z \subseteq V$ when (i) every collider section of ρ has a node in Z, and (ii) no non-collider section of ρ has a node in Z.

A node B in a route ρ in an AMP CG G is called a triplex node in ρ if $A \to B \leftarrow C$, $A \to B - C$, or $A - B \leftarrow C$ is a subroute of ρ. Note that maybe $A = C$ in the first case. Note also that B may be both a triplex and a non-triplex node in ρ. Moreover, ρ is said to be Z-open with $Z \subseteq V$ when (i) every triplex node in ρ is in Z, and (ii) every non-triplex node in ρ is outside Z.[2]

Let X, Y and Z denote three disjoint subsets of V. When there is no Z-open route in a LWF or AMP CG G between a node in X and a node in Y, we say that X is separated from Y given Z in G and denote it as $X \perp_G Y | Z$. The independence model represented by G, denoted as $I(G)$, is the set of separations $X \perp_G Y | Z$. In general, $I(G)$ is different depending on whether G is interpreted as a LWF or AMP CG. However, if G is a DAG or UG, then $I(G)$ is the same under the two interpretations. Given a CG G and two disjoint subsets L and S of V, we denote by $[I(G)]_L^S$ the independence model represented by G under marginalization of the nodes in L and conditioning on the nodes in S. Specifically, $X \perp_G Y | Z$ is in $[I(G)]_L^S$ iff $X \perp_G Y | Z \cup S$ is in $I(G)$ and $X, Y, Z \subseteq V \setminus L \setminus S$.

We say that a CG G includes an independence model M if $I(G) \subseteq M$. Moreover, we say that G is inclusion minimal wrt M if removing any edge from G makes it cease to include M. We say that a CG G_α is inclusion minimal wrt an independence model M and a chain α if G_α is inclusion minimal wrt M and G_α is consistent with α. We also say that a CG G is inclusion optimal wrt an independence model M if $I(G) \subseteq M$ and there exists no other CG H st $I(G) \subset I(H) \subseteq M$.

Finally, a subgraph of a CG G is a CG whose nodes and edges are all in G. The subgraph of a CG G induced by a set of its nodes X is the CG over X that has all and only the edges in G whose both ends are in X. A complex in a LWF CG is an induced subgraph of it of the form $V_1 \to V_2 - \ldots - V_{n-1} \leftarrow V_n$. A triplex in an AMP CG is an induced subgraph of it of the form $A \to B \leftarrow C$, $A \to B - C$, or $A - B \leftarrow C$.

3 Justification of LWF and AMP CGs

The theorem below shows that every LWF or AMP CG G is inclusion optimal wrt the intersection of the independence models represented by some DAGs under conditioning. The DAGs are obtained as follows. First, we decompose G into a DAG G_D and an UG G_U, i.e. G_D contains all and only the directed edges in G, and G_U contains all and only the undirected edges in G. Then, we construct a DAG G_S from G_U by replacing every edge $X - Y$ in G_U with $X \to S_{XY} \leftarrow Y$. The nodes S_{XY} are called selection nodes. Let S denote all the selection nodes in G_S. Note that G_D and G_U are defined over the nodes V, but G_S is defined over the nodes $V \cup S$. The proofs of all the theorems in this paper can be found in the extended version of this paper that is available at the authors' website.

---

[2] See [17, Remark 3.1] for the equivalence of this and the standard definition of Z-open route for AMP CGs.

Theorem 1. *The LWF or AMP CG G is inclusion optimal wrt $I(G_D) \cap [I(G_S)]_\emptyset^S$.*

Unfortunately, the LWF or AMP CG G may not be faithful to $I(G_D) \cap [I(G_S)]_\emptyset^S$. To see it, let G be $A \to B - C \leftarrow D$. Then, $A \perp D | B \cup C$ is in $I(G_D) \cap [I(G_S)]_\emptyset^S$ but not in $I(G)$. We doubt that one can prove (and so strengthen our justification) that every LWF or AMP CG is faithful to the intersection of the independence models represented by some DAGs under conditioning. However, it is true that the decomposition of G into G_D and G_U is not the only one that allows us to prove that G is inclusion optimal wrt to the intersection of the independence models represented by some DAGs under conditioning. For instance, we can also prove this result if G is decomposed into a set of DAGs and UGs st none of them has more than one edge, or if G is decomposed into a set of CGs st none of them has a subgraph of the form $A \to B - C$. We omit the proofs. In any case, this does not change the main message of this work, namely that LWF and AMP CGs can be justified on the sole basis of causal models. Having said this, we prefer the original decomposition because it is not completely arbitrary: G_D represents the relationships in G that are causal, and G_U those that are non-causal and need to be explained through conditioning.

Finally, note that the LWF or AMP CG G may not be the only inclusion optimal CG wrt $I(G_D) \cap [I(G_S)]_\emptyset^S$. To see it, let G be $A \to B - C \leftarrow D$. Then, any LWF or AMP CG that has the same adjacencies as G is inclusion optimal wrt $I(G_D) \cap [I(G_S)]_\emptyset^S$. Some of these other inclusion optimal CGs may even be preferred instead of G according to some criteria (e.g. number of independencies represented, or number of directed and/or undirected edges). However, G is preferred according to an important criterion: It is the only one that has all and only the strictly ascendant relationships (i.e. direct and indirect causal relationships) between two nodes in V that exist in G_D and G_S.

4   Combining Arbitrary DAGs into a LWF or AMP CG

In this section, we study the opposite of the problem above. Specifically, let $G_1, \ldots, G_r$ denote r arbitrary DAGs, where any G_i is defined over the nodes $V \cup L_i \cup S_i$ and it is subject to marginalization of the nodes in L_i and conditioning on the nodes in S_i. We would like to find a LWF or AMP CG that is inclusion optimal wrt $\bigcap_{i=1}^r [I(G_i)]_{L_i}^{S_i}$. However, this seems to be an extremely hard problem. So, we study a simpler version of it in which we are only interested in those CGs that are consistent with a chain α. Then, our goal becomes to find an inclusion minimal LWF or AMP CG wrt $\bigcap_{i=1}^r [I(G_i)]_{L_i}^{S_i}$ and α. The prior knowledge of α represents our a priori knowledge on which nodes may be causally related and which nodes may be non-causally related. The latter determine the blocks of α, and the former the ordering of the blocks in α. The theorems below solve our problem. Specifically, they give a constructive characterization of the unique LWF (respectively AMP) CG that is inclusion minimal wrt a graphoid (respectively compositional graphoid) and a chain. Note that any $I(G_i)$ is a compositional graphoid [36, Theorem 1]. Moreover, it is easy to verify that any $[I(G_i)]_{L_i}^{S_i}$ is also a compositional graphoid and, thus, $\bigcap_{i=1}^{r}[I(G_i)]_{L_i}^{S_i}$ is also a compositional graphoid. Thus, the theorems below apply to our problem.

Theorem 2. *Let M denote an independence model, and α a chain with blocks $b_1, \ldots, b_n$. If M is a graphoid, then there exits a unique LWF CG G_α that is inclusion minimal wrt M and α. Specifically, for each node X of each block b_i of α, $bd_{G_\alpha}(X)$ is the smallest subset of $\bigcup_{j=1}^{i} b_j \setminus X$ st $X \perp_M \bigcup_{j=1}^{i} b_j \setminus X \setminus bd_{G_\alpha}(X)|bd_{G_\alpha}(X)$.*

Theorem 3. *Let M denote an independence model, and α a chain with blocks $b_1, \ldots, b_n$. If M is a compositional graphoid, then there exits a unique AMP CG G_α that is inclusion minimal wrt M and α. Specifically, consider the blocks in α in reverse order and perform the following two steps for each of them. First, for each node X of the block b_i, $ne_{G_\alpha}(X)$ is the smallest subset of $b_i \setminus X$ st $X \perp_M b_i \setminus X \setminus ne_{G_\alpha}(X)|\bigcup_{j=1}^{i-1} b_j \cup ne_{G_\alpha}(X)$. Second, for each node X of the block b_i, $pa_{G_\alpha}(X)$ is the smallest subset of $\bigcup_{j=1}^{i-1} b_j$ st $X \perp_M V \setminus X \setminus de_{G_\alpha}(X) \setminus pa_{G_\alpha}(X)|pa_{G_\alpha}(X)$.*[3]

5   Discussion

The purpose of this paper has been to justify LWF and AMP CGs by showing that they do not represent arbitrary independence models. Unlike previous justifications, ours builds solely on causal models and does not involve equilibrium distributions or deterministic nodes, which may seem odd to some readers. Specifically, for any given LWF or AMP CG, we have imagined a system that switches between different regimes or configurations, and we have shown that the given CG represents the different regimes jointly. To do so, we have assumed that each of the regimes can be represented by a causal model. We have also assumed that the causal models may be subject to selection bias. In other words, we have assumed that each of the regimes can be represented by a DAG under conditioning.

In this paper, we have also studied the opposite of the problem above, namely how to combine a set of arbitrary DAGs under marginalization and conditioning into a consensus LWF or AMP CG. We have shown how to do it optimally when the consensus CG must be consistent with a given chain. The chain may represent our prior knowledge about the causal and non-causal relationships in the domain at hand. In the future, we would like to drop this requirement. We would also like to find parameter values for the consensus CG by combining the parameter values associated to the given DAGs.

Acknowledgments. This work is funded by the Center for Industrial Information Technology (CENIIT) and a so-called career contract at Linköping University, and by the Swedish Research Council (ref. 2010-4808).

---

[3] Note that $de_{G_\alpha}(X)$ for any $X \in b_i$ is known when the second step for b_i starts, because $ne_{G_\alpha}(X)$ for any $X \in \bigcup_{j=i}^{n} b_j$ and $pa_{G_\alpha}(X)$ for any $X \in \bigcup_{j=i+1}^{n} b_j$ have already been identified.

References

1. Andersson, S.A., Madigan, D., Perlman, M.D.: Alternative Markov properties for chain graphs. Scand. J. Stat. **28**, 33–85 (2001)
2. Bendtsen, M., Peña, J.M.: Gated Bayesian networks. In: Proceedings of the 12th Scandinavian Conference on Artificial Intelligence, pp. 35–44 (2013)
3. Bendtsen, M., Peña, J.M.: Learning Gated Bayesian networks for algorithmic trading. In: van der Gaag, L.C., Feelders, A.J. (eds.) PGM 2014. LNCS, vol. 8754, pp. 49–64. Springer, Heidelberg (2014)
4. Bonduelle, Y.: Aggregating expert opinions by resolving sources of disagreement. Ph.D. thesis, Stanford University (1987)
5. Chickering, D.M., Meek, C.: Finding optimal Bayesian networks. In: Proceedings of the 18th Conference on Uncertainty in Artificial Intelligence, pp. 94–102 (2002)
6. Cox, D.R., Wermuth, N.: Linear dependencies represented by chain graphs. Stat. Sci. **8**, 204–218 (1993)
7. Cox, D.R., Wermuth, N.: Multivariate Dependencies - Models - Analysis and Interpretation. Chapman & Hall, London (1996)
8. del Sagrado, J., Moral, S.: Qualitative combination of Bayesian networks. Int. J. Intell. Syst. **18**, 237–249 (2003)
9. Drton, M.: Discrete chain graph models. Bernoulli **15**, 736–753 (2009)
10. Etminani, K., Naghibzadeh, M., Peña, J.M.: DemocraticOP: a democratic way of aggregating Bayesian network parameters. Int. J. Approximate Reasoning **54**, 602–614 (2013)
11. Ferrandiz, J., Castillo, E., Sanmartin, P.: Temporal aggregation in chain graph models. J. Stat. Planning Infer. **133**, 69–93 (2005)
12. Frydenberg, M.: The chain graph Markov property. Scand. J. Stat. **17**, 333–353 (1990)
13. Laddaga, R.: Lehrer and the consensus proposal. Synthese **36**, 473–477 (1977)
14. Lauritzen, S.L.: Graphical Models. Oxford University Press, Oxford (1996)
15. Lauritzen, S.L., Richardson, T.S.: Chain graph models and their causal interpretations. J. Roy. Stat. Soc. B **64**, 321–361 (2002)
16. Lauritzen, S.L., Wermuth, N.: Graphical models for associations between variables, some of which are qualitative and some quantitative. Annu. Stat. **17**, 31–57 (1989)
17. Levitz, M., Perlman, M.D., Madigan, D.: Separation and completeness properties for AMP chain graph Markov models. Ann. Stat. **29**, 1751–1784 (2001)
18. Matzkevich, I., Abramson, B.: The topological fusion of Bayes nets. In: Proceedings of the 8th Conference on Uncertainty in Artificial Intelligence, pp. 191–198 (1992)
19. Matzkevich, I., Abramson, B.: Some complexity considerations in the combination of Belief networks. In: Proceedings of the 9th Conference on Uncertainty in Artificial Intelligence, pp. 152–158 (1993)
20. Matzkevich, I., Abramson, B.: Deriving a minimal I-Map of a belief network relative to a target ordering of its nodes. In: Proceedings of the 9th Conference on Uncertainty in Artificial Intelligence, pp. 159–165 (1993)
21. Maynard-Reid II, P., Chajewska, U.: Agregating learned probabilistic beliefs. In: Proceedings of the 17th Conference in Uncertainty in Artificial Intelligence, pp. 354–361 (2001)
22. Nielsen, J.D., Kočka, T., Peña, J.M.: On local optima in learning Bayesian networks. In: Proceedings of the 19th Conference on Uncertainty in Artificial Intelligence, pp. 435–442 (2003)

23. Nielsen, S.H., Parsons, S.: An application of formal argumentation: fusing Bayesian networks in multi-agent systems. Artif. Intell. **171**, 754–775 (2007)
24. Pearl, J.: Causality: Models, Reasoning, and Inference. Cambridge University Press, Cambridge (2000)
25. Pennock, D.M., Wellman, M.P.: Graphical models for groups: belief aggregation and risk sharing. Decis. Anal. **2**, 148–164 (2005)
26. Peña, J.M.: Approximate counting of graphical models via MCMC. In: Proceedings of the 11th International Conference on Artificial Intelligence and Statistics, pp. 352–359 (2007)
27. Peña, J.M.: Faithfulness in chain graphs: the discrete case. Int. J. Approximate Reasoning **50**, 1306–1313 (2009)
28. Peña, J.M.: Faithfulness in chain graphs: the Gaussian case. In: Proceedings of the 14th International Conference on Artificial Intelligence and Statistics, pp. 588–599 (2011)
29. Peña, J.M.: Finding consensus Bayesian network structures. J. Artif. Intell. Res. **42**, 661–687 (2011)
30. Peña, J.M.: Learning AMP chain graphs under faithfulness. In: Proceedings of the 6th European Workshop on Probabilistic Graphical Models, pp. 251–258 (2012)
31. Peña, J.M.: Marginal AMP chain graphs. Int. J. Approximate Reasoning **55**, 1185–1206 (2014)
32. Peña, J.M., Sonntag, D., Nielsen, J.D. An inclusion optimal algorithm for chain graph structure learning. In: Proceedings of the 17th International Conference on Artificial Intelligence and Statistics, pp. 778–786 (2014)
33. Raiffa, H.: Decision Analysis: Introductory Lectures on Choices under Uncertainty. Addison-Wesley, Reading (1968)
34. Richardson, T.S.: Chain Graphs and Symmetric Associations. In: Learning in Graphical Models, pp. 231–260 (1998)
35. Richardson, T., Spirtes, P.: Ancestral graph Markov models. Ann. Stat. **30**, 962–1030 (2002)
36. Sadeghi, K., Lauritzen, S.L.: Markov properties for mixed graphs. Bernoulli **20**, 676–696 (2014)
37. Sonntag, D., Peña, J.M.: Chain graph interpretations and their relations. In: van der Gaag, L.C. (ed.) ECSQARU 2013. LNCS, vol. 7958, pp. 510–521. Springer, Heidelberg (2013)
38. Studený, M.: Bayesian networks from the point of view of chain graphs. In: Proceedings of the 14th Conference on Uncertainty in Artificial Intelligence, pp. 496–503 (1998)
39. Studený, M.: Probabilistic Conditional Independence Structures. Springer, Heidelberg (2005)
40. Studený, M., Bouckaert, R.R.: On chain graph models for description of conditional independence structures. Ann. Stat. **26**, 1434–1495 (1998)

Factorization, Inference and Parameter Learning in Discrete AMP Chain Graphs

Jose M. Peña[⊠]

ADIT, IDA, Linköping University, 58183 Linköping, Sweden
jose.m.pena@liu.se

Abstract. We address some computational issues that may hinder the use of AMP chain graphs in practice. Specifically, we show how a discrete probability distribution that satisfies all the independencies represented by an AMP chain graph factorizes according to it. We show how this factorization makes it possible to perform inference and parameter learning efficiently, by adapting existing algorithms for Markov and Bayesian networks. Finally, we turn our attention to another issue that may hinder the use of AMP CGs, namely the lack of an intuitive interpretation of their edges. We provide one such interpretation.

1 Introduction

Chain graphs (CGs) are graphs with possibly directed and undirected edges, and no semidirected cycle. They have been extensively studied as a formalism to represent independence models, because they can model symmetric and asymmetric relationships between random variables. There are three different interpretations of CGs as independence models: The Lauritzen-Wermuth-Frydenberg (LWF) interpretation [6], the multivariate regression (MVR) interpretation [3], and the Andersson-Madigan-Perlman (AMP) interpretation [1]. No interpretation subsumes another [1,11].

In this paper, we focus on AMP CGs. Despite being much more expressive than Markov and Bayesian networks [10], AMP CGs have not enjoyed much success in the literature or in practice. We believe this is due to mainly two reasons. First, it is not known how to perform inference and parameter learning for AMP CGs efficiently, because it is not known how to factorize a probability distribution that satisfies all the independencies represented by an AMP CG. Compare this situation to that of LWF CGs, where such a factorization exists [4, Theorem 4.1] and thus inference can be performed efficiently [2, Sect. 6.5]. Second, AMP CGs do not appeal to intuition: Whereas the directed edges in a Bayesian network may be interpreted as causal relationships and the undirected edges in a Markov network as correlation relationships, it is not clear how to combine these two interpretations to produce an intuitive interpretation of the edges in an AMP CG.

In this paper, we address the two problems mentioned above. First, we introduce a factorization for AMP CGs and show how it makes it possible to perform

© Springer International Publishing Switzerland 2015
S. Destercke and T. Denoeux (Eds.): ECSQARU 2015, LNAI 9161, pp. 335–345, 2015.
DOI: 10.1007/978-3-319-20807-7_30

inference and parameter learning efficiently, by adapting existing algorithms for Markov and Bayesian networks. Second, we propose an intuitive interpretation of the edges in an AMP CG. We start with some notation and definitions.

2 Preliminaries

Unless otherwise stated, all the graphs and probability distributions in this paper are defined over a finite set of discrete random variables V. We use uppercase letters to denote random variables and lowercase letters to denote their states. The elements of V are not distinguished from singletons. If a graph G contains an undirected or directed edge between two nodes V_1 and V_2, then we write that $V_1 - V_2$ or $V_1 \rightarrow V_2$ is in G. The parents of a set of nodes X of G is the set $Pa_G(X) = \{V_1|V_1 \rightarrow V_2$ is in G, $V_1 \notin X$ and $V_2 \in X\}$. The adjacents of X is the set $Ad_G(X) = \{V_1|V_1 \leftarrow V_2$, $V_1 \rightarrow V_2$ or $V_1 - V_2$ is in G, $V_1 \notin X$ and $V_2 \in X\}$. A route between a node V_1 and a node V_n in G is a sequence of (not necessarily distinct) nodes $V_1, \ldots, V_n$ st $V_i \in Ad_G(V_{i+1})$ for all $1 \leq i < n$. If the nodes in the route are all distinct, then the route is called a path. A route is called descending if $V_i \rightarrow V_{i+1}$ or $V_i - V_{i+1}$ is in G for all $1 \leq i < n$. A route is called strictly descending if $V_i \rightarrow V_{i+1}$ is in G for all $1 \leq i < n$. The descendants of a set of nodes X of G is the set $De_G(X) = \{V_n|$ there is a descending route from V_1 to V_n in G, $V_1 \in X$ and $V_n \notin X\}$. The non-descendants of X is the set $Nd_G(X) = V \backslash X \backslash De_G(X)$. The strict ascendants of X is the set $Sa_G(X) = \{V_1|$ there is a strictly descending route from V_1 to V_n in G, $V_1 \notin X$ and $V_n \in X\}$. A route $V_1, \ldots, V_n$ in G is called a cycle if $V_n = V_1$. Moreover, it is called a semidirected cycle if $V_n = V_1$, $V_1 \rightarrow V_2$ is in G and $V_i \rightarrow V_{i+1}$ or $V_i - V_{i+1}$ is in G for all $1 < i < n$. An AMP chain graph (AMP CG) is a graph whose every edge is directed or undirected st it has no semidirected cycles. An AMP CG with only directed edges is called a directed and acyclic graph (DAG), whereas an AMP CG with only undirected edges is called an undirected graph (UG). A set of nodes of an AMP CG G is connected if there exists a route in the CG between every pair of nodes in the set st all the edges in the route are undirected. A connectivity component of G is a maximal (wrt set inclusion) connected set of nodes. The connectivity components of G are denoted as $Cc(G)$, whereas $Cc_G(X)$ denotes the connectivity component to which the node X belongs. A set of nodes of G is complete if there exists an undirected edge between every pair of nodes in the set. The complete sets of nodes of G are denoted as $Cs(G)$. A clique of G is a maximal (wrt set inclusion) complete set of nodes. The cliques of G are denoted as $Cl(G)$. The subgraph of G induced by a set of its nodes X, denoted as G_X, is the graph over X that has all and only the edges in G whose both ends are in X.

We now recall the semantics of AMP CGs. A node B in a path ρ in an AMP CG G is called a triplex node in ρ if $A \rightarrow B \leftarrow C$, $A \rightarrow B - C$, or $A - B \leftarrow C$ is a subpath of ρ. Moreover, ρ is said to be Z-open with $Z \subseteq V$ when

- every triplex node in ρ is in $Z \cup Sa_G(Z)$, and
- every non-triplex node B in ρ is outside Z, unless $A - B - C$ is a subpath of ρ and $Pa_G(B) \backslash Z \neq \varnothing$.

Let X, Y and Z denote three disjoint subsets of V. When there is no Z-open path in an AMP CG G between a node in X and a node in Y, we say that X is separated from Y given Z in G and denote it as $X \perp_G Y | Z$. The independence model represented by G is the set of separations $X \perp_G Y | Z$. The independence model represented by G under marginalization of some nodes $L \subseteq V$ is the set of separations $X \perp_G Y | Z$ with $X, Y, Z \subseteq V \setminus L$. Finally, we denote by $X \perp_p Y | Z$ that X is independent of Y given Z in a probability distribution p. We say that p is Markovian wrt an AMP CG G when, for all X, Y and Z disjoint subsets of V, if $X \perp_G Y | Z$ then $X \perp_p Y | Z$.

3   Factorization

A probability distribution p is Markovian wrt an AMP CG G iff the following three properties hold for all $C \in Cc(G)$ [1, Theorem 2]:

- C1: $C \perp_p Nd_G(C) \setminus Cc_G(Pa_G(C)) | Cc_G(Pa_G(C))$.
- C2: $p(C | Cc_G(Pa_G(C)))$ is Markovian wrt G_C.
- C3*: For all $D \subseteq C$, $D \perp_p Cc_G(Pa_G(C)) \setminus Pa_G(D) | Pa_G(D)$.

Then, C1 implies that p factorizes as

$$p = \prod_{C \in Cc(G)} p(C | Cc_G(Pa_G(C))).$$

The authors of [1, p. 50] note that if p were strictly positive and G were a LWF CG, then each conditional distribution above would factorize further into a product of potentials over certain subsets of the nodes in $C \cup Pa_G(C)$, as shown in [4, Theorem 4.1]. However, the authors state that no such further factorization appears to hold in general if G is an AMP CG. We show that this is not true if p is strictly positive. Specifically, C2 together with [6, Theorems 3.7 and 3.9] imply that

$$p(C | Cc_G(Pa_G(C))) = \prod_{K \in Cs(G_C)} \varphi(K, Cc_G(Pa_G(C))).$$

However, one can show that $\varphi(K, Cc_G(Pa_G(C)))$ is actually a function of $K \cup Pa_G(K)$, i.e. $\varphi(K, Cc_G(Pa_G(C))) = \varphi(K, Pa_G(K))$. It suffices to recall from the proof of [6, Theorem 3.9] how $\varphi(K, Cc_G(Pa_G(C)))$ can be obtained from $p(C | Cc_G(Pa_G(C)))$, a method also known as canonical parameterization [5, Sect. 4.4.2.1]. Specifically, let $\phi(K, Cc_G(Pa_G(C))) = \log \varphi(K, Cc_G(Pa_G(C)))$. Choose a fixed but arbitrary state k_* of K. Then,

$$\phi(k, Cc_G(Pa_G(C))) = \sum_{q \subseteq k} (-1)^{|k \setminus q|} \log p(q, \bar{q}_* | Cc_G(Pa_G(C)))$$

where $\bar{q}_*$ denotes the elements of k_* corresponding to the elements of $K \setminus Q$. Now, note that $p(q, \bar{q}_* | Cc_G(Pa_G(C))) = p(q, \bar{q}_* | Pa_G(K))$ by C3*, because $Q \subseteq K$. Then, $\varphi(K, Cc_G(Pa_G(C)))$ is actually a function of $K \cup Pa_G(K)$.

Putting together the results above, we have that p factorizes as

$$p = \prod_{C \in Cc(G)} \prod_{K \in Cs(G_C)} \varphi(K, Pa_G(K)) = \prod_{C \in Cc(G)} \prod_{K \in Cl(G_C)} \psi(K, Pa_G(K)). \quad (1)$$

Note that the well-known factorizations induced by DAGs and UGs (see [6, Sect. 3.2.1 and 3.2.2]) are special cases of Eq. 1.

4   Parameter Learning

The factorization in Eq. 1 enables us to perform parameter learning for AMP CGs efficiently by deploying the iterative proportional fitting procedure (IPFP) [8, Sect. 19.5.7], which returns the maximum likelihood estimates of the entries of the potentials for some given data. Specifically, we first simplify further the factorization by multiplying its potentials until no potential domain is included in another potential domain. Let $Q_1, \ldots, Q_n$ denote the potential domains in the resulting factorization. Note that each domain Q_i is of the form $K \cup Pa_G(K)$ with $K \in Cl(G_C)$ and $C \in Cc(G)$. Then, we run the IPFP per se:

> 1 For each potential $\psi(Q_i)$
> 2   Set $\psi^0(Q_i) = 1$
> 3 Repeat until convergence
> 4   For each potential $\psi^t(Q_i)$
> 5   Set $\psi^{t+1}(Q_i) = \psi^t(Q_i) \frac{p_e(Q_i)}{p^t(Q_i)}$

where $p^t = \prod_{i=1}^n \psi^t(Q_i)$, and p_e is the empirical probability distribution over V obtained from the given data.

5   Inference

The factorization in Eq. 1 also enables us to perform inference in AMP CGs efficiently by deploying the algorithm for inference in DAGs developed by [7], and upon which most other inference algorithms build. Specifically, we start by transforming G into its moral graph G^m by running the procedure below. This procedure differs from the one in [7], because G is an AMP CG and not a DAG. In any case, the moralization procedure in [7] is a special case of the procedure below.

> 1 Set $G^m = G$
> 2 For each connectivity component $C \in Cc(G)$
> 3   For each clique $K \in Cl(G_C)$
> 4   Add the edge $X \to Y$ to G^m for all $X \in Pa_G(K)$ and $Y \in K$
> 5   Add the edge $X - Y$ to G^m for all $X, Y \in Pa_G(K)$ st $X \neq Y$
> 6 Replace all the directed edges in G^m with undirected edges

The reason of why G^m has the edges it has will become clear later. We continue by transforming G^m into a triangulated graph G^t, and sorting its cliques to satisfy the so-called running intersection property. The procedure below accomplishes these two objectives. An UG is triangulated when every cycle in it contains a chord, i.e. an edge between two non-consecutive nodes in the cycle. The cliques of a triangulated graph can be ordered as $Q_1, \ldots, Q_n$ so that for all $1 < j \leq n$, $Q_j \cap (Q_1 \cup \ldots \cup Q_{j-1}) \subseteq Q_i$ for some $1 \leq i < j$. This is known as the running intersection property (RIP).

1 Set $G^t = G^m$
2 Repeat until all the nodes in G^t are marked
3   Select an unmarked node in G^t with the largest number of marked neighbours
4   Mark the node and make its marked neighbours form a complete set in G^t by adding undirected edges
5   Save the node plus its marked neighbours as a candidate clique
6 Remove every candidate clique that is included in another
7 Label every clique with the last iteration that marked one of its nodes
8 Sort the cliques in ascending order of their labels

Finally, let $Q_1, \ldots, Q_n$ denote the ordering of the cliques of G^t returned by the procedure above. Let $S_j = Q_j \cap (Q_1 \cup \ldots \cup Q_{j-1})$ and $R_j = Q_j \setminus S_j$. Note that for every $K \in Cl(G_C)$ with $C \in Cc(G)$, there is some Q_i st $K \cup Pa_G(K) \subseteq Q_i$, because the moralization procedure above made $K \cup Pa_G(K)$ a complete set in G^m and thus in G^t. Then,

$$p(V) = \prod_{C \in Cc(G)} \prod_{K \in Cl(G_C)} \psi(K, Pa_G(K)) = \prod_{i=1}^{n} \phi(Q_i) \tag{2}$$

and thus

$$p(V) = f([Q_1 \cup \ldots \cup Q_{n-1}] \setminus S_n, S_n) g(S_n, R_n)$$

and thus

$$R_n \perp_p [Q_1 \cup \ldots \cup Q_{n-1}] \setminus S_n | S_n$$

by [6, p. 29], and thus

$$p(V) = p(Q_1 \cup \ldots \cup Q_{n-1}) p(R_n | Q_1 \cup \ldots \cup Q_{n-1}) = p(Q_1 \cup \ldots \cup Q_{n-1}) p(R_n | S_n). \tag{3}$$

Note also that

$$p(Q_1 \cup \ldots \cup Q_{n-1}) = \sum_{r_n} p(Q_1 \cup \ldots \cup Q_{n-1}, r_n) = [\prod_{i=1}^{n-1} \phi(Q_i)] \sum_{r_n} \phi(S_n, r_n). \tag{4}$$

Then, Eqs. 2-4 imply that

$$p(R_n | S_n) = \phi(Q_n) / \sum_{r_n} \phi(S_n, r_n).$$

Note that $S_n \subseteq Q_j$ for some $1 \leq j < n$ by the RIP. Then, we replace $\phi(Q_j)$ with $\phi(Q_j) \sum_{r_n} \phi(S_n, r_n)$, after which Eq. 4 implies that

$$p(Q_1 \cup \ldots \cup Q_{n-1}) = \prod_{i=1}^{n-1} \phi(Q_i).$$

We repeat the steps above for $p(Q_1 \cup \ldots \cup Q_{n-1})$ and so we obtain $p(R_i|S_i)$ for all $1 \leq i \leq n$. Now, note that $S_1 = \varnothing$ and, thus, $p(Q_1) = p(R_1|S_1)$. Moreover, since $S_2 \subseteq Q_1$ by the RIP, then

$$p(S_2) = \sum_{q_1 \setminus s_2} p(S_2, q_1 \setminus s_2)$$

and thus

$$p(Q_2) = p(R_2|S_2)p(S_2).$$

We repeat the steps above for $Q_3, \ldots, Q_n$ and so we obtain $p(Q_i)$ for all $1 \leq i \leq n$. To obtain $p(Q_i|o)$ where o denotes some observations or evidence, we first remove all the entries of $\phi(Q_j)$ that are inconsistent with o for all $1 \leq j \leq n$, then we repeat the steps above to get $p(Q_i, o)$ and, finally, we normalize by $p(o) = \sum_{q_i} p(q_i, o)$. To obtain $p(X|o)$ where $X \not\subseteq Q_i$ for all $1 \leq i \leq n$, we compute $p(x, o)$ for all x as if $\{x, o\}$ were the observations and, then, we normalize by $p(o) = \sum_x p(x, o)$.

6   Error AMP CGs

So far in this article, we have shown how an AMP CG factorizes a probability distribution, and how this helps in performing parameter learning and inference efficiently. We believe that our findings solve some computational issues that have hindered the use of AMP CGs in practice. In this section, we turn our attention to another issue that may have also hindered the use of AMP CGs, namely the lack of an intuitive interpretation of their edges. Whereas the directed edges in a DAG may be interpreted as causal relationships and the undirected edges in an UG as correlation relationships, it is not clear how to combine these two interpretations to produce an intuitive interpretation of the edges in an AMP CG. We propose here a way to do it by adapting to discrete AMP CGs the interpretation for Gaussian AMP CGs presented in [1, Sect.5] and further studied in [9, Sect. 3]. Specifically, we propose to interpret the directed edges in an AMP CG as causal relationships. In other words, the parents of a node represent its causal mechanism. We propose to assume that this mechanism is deterministic but it may sometimes work erroneously. We propose to interpret the undirected edges in the AMP CG as the correlation structure of the errors of the causal mechanisms of the different nodes. To show the validity of this interpretation, we will first modify the AMP CG by adding a deterministic node for each original node to represent explicitly the occurrence or not of an error in

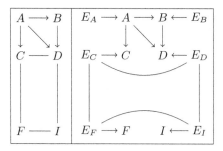

Fig. 1. An AMP CG and its corresponding EAMP CG.

its causal mechanism and, then, we will show that the original and the modified AMP CGs are equivalent in some sense. We call the modified CG an error AMP (EAMP) CG. Since an EAMP CG is an AMP CG with deterministic nodes, we discuss these first.

6.1   AMP CGs with Deterministic Nodes

We say that a node X of an AMP CG is determined by some $Z \subseteq V$ when $X \in Z$ or X is a function of Z in each probability distribution that is Markovian wrt the CG. In that case, we also say that X is a deterministic node. We use $D(Z)$ to denote all the nodes that are determined by Z. From the point of view of the separations in an AMP CG, that a node outside the conditioning set of a separation is determined by it, has the same effect as if the node were actually in the conditioning set. We extend accordingly the definition of separation for AMP CGs to the case where deterministic nodes may exist. Given an AMP CG G, a path ρ in G is said to be Z-open when

- every triplex node in ρ is in $D(Z) \cup Sa_G(D(Z))$, and
- no non-triplex node B in ρ is in $D(Z)$, unless $A - B - C$ is a subpath of ρ and $Pa_G(B) \setminus D(Z) \neq \varnothing$.

6.2   EAMP CGs

The EAMP CG H corresponding to an AMP CG G is an AMP CG over $V \cup E$, where E denotes the error nodes. Specifically, there is an error node $E_X \in E$ for every node $X \in V$, and it represents whether an error in the causal mechanism of X occurs or not. We set $Pa_H(X) = Pa_G(X) \cup E_X$ to represent that E_X is part of the causal mechanism of X in H. This causal mechanism works as follows: If $E_X = 0$ (i.e. no error) then $pa_G(X)$ determines the state of X to be the distinguished state $x_*^{pa_G(X)}$, else X may take any state but the distinguished one. The undirected edges in H are all between error nodes, and they represent the correlation structure of the error nodes. Specifically, the undirected edge $E_X - E_Y$ is in H iff the undirected edge $X - Y$ is in G. Note that the error nodes are never observed, i.e. they are latent. The procedure below formalizes the transformation just described. See Fig. 1 for an example.

1 Set $H = G$
2 For each node $X \in V$
3   Add the node E_X and the edge $E_X \rightarrow X$ to H
4 Replace every edge $X - Y$ in H st $X, Y \in V$ with an edge $E_X - E_Y$

Now, consider a probability distribution $p(V, E)$ that is Markovian wrt the EAMP CG H. Then,

$$p(V, E) = p(V|E)p(E) = [\prod_{X \in V} p(X|Pa_G(X), E_X)]p(E) \qquad (5)$$

by C1 and C3*. Moreover, in order for the causal mechanism of X in H to match the description above, we restrict $p(X|Pa_G(X), E_X)$ to be of the following form:

$$p(X|pa_G(X), E_X) = \begin{cases} 1 & \text{if } E_X = 0 \text{ and } X = x_*^{pa_G(X)} \\ 0 & \text{if } E_X = 0 \text{ and } X \neq x_*^{pa_G(X)} \\ q(X|pa_G(X)) & \text{if } E_X = 1 \end{cases} \qquad (6)$$

where $q(X|pa_G(X))$ is an arbitrary conditional probability distribution with the only constraints that $q(X|pa_G(X)) = 0$ if $X = x_*^{pa_G(X)}$, and $q(X|pa_G(X)) > 0$ otherwise. The first constraint follows from the description above of the causal mechanism of X in H, whereas the second is necessary for $p(V)$ being strictly positive. Note that E_X is determined by $Pa_G(X) \cup X$. Specifically, if $X = x_*^{pa_G(X)}$ then $E_X = 0$, else $E_X = 1$. Then, E is determined by V. Hereinafter, when we say that a probability distribution is Markovian wrt an EAMP CG, it should be understood that it also satisfies the constraint in Eq. 6.

We assume that $p(E)$ is strictly positive, as a way to ensure that $p(V)$ is strictly positive. This together with the fact that $p(E)$ is Markovian wrt H_E, which follows from $p(V, E)$ being Markovian wrt H, implies that $p(E)$ factorizes as shown in Eq. 1 and, thus, Eq. 5 becomes

$$p(V, E) = [\prod_{X \in V} p(X|Pa_G(X), E_X)][\prod_{E_C \in Cc(H_E)} \prod_{E_K \in Cl(H_{E_C})} \phi(E_K)]. \qquad (7)$$

Thus, it is clear that the EAMP CG H can be interpreted as we wanted: Each node is controlled by the causal mechanism specified in the AMP CG G, the mechanism is deterministic if no error occurs and it is random otherwise, and the errors of the different mechanisms obey the correlation structure specified in G. To see the last point, note that $E_C \in Cc(H_E)$ iff $C \in Cc(G)$, and $E_K \in Cl(H_{E_C})$ iff $K \in Cl(G_C)$. Thus, H somehow keeps the structural information in G. To make this claim more specific, note that the independence model represented by G coincides with that represented by H under marginalization of the error nodes which, recall from above, are latent [9, Theorem 1].[1] Recall that the independence model represented by H can be read off as shown in Sect. 6.1. Note that that the independence model represented by G coincides with that represented by H under marginalization of the error nodes implies that the probability distribution resulting from marginalizing E out of a distribution $p(V, E)$ that is Markovian wrt to H is Markovian wrt G and, thus, it factorizes as shown in Eq. 1. Specifically, recall that E is determined by V and, thus, $p(V, E)$ is actually a function of V. Then, it suffices to set each potential $\psi(K, Pa_G(K))$ in Eq. 1 equal to the following product of the terms in Eq. 7:

$$\psi(K, Pa_G(K)) = [\prod_{X \in K} p(X|Pa_G(X), E_X)]\phi(E_K)$$

bearing in mind that if X belongs to several cliques K, then $p(X|Pa_G(X), E_X)$ is assigned to only one (any) of the potentials $\psi(K, Pa_G(K))$. For instance, the following is a valid assignment for the AMP and EAMP CGs in Fig. 1:

$$
\begin{array}{ll}
\psi(A) & = p(A|E_A)\phi(E_A) \\
\psi(B, A) & = p(B|A, E_B)\phi(E_B) \\
\psi(C, D, A, B) & = p(C|A, E_C)\phi(E_C, E_D)
\end{array}
\quad
\begin{array}{ll}
\psi(C, F, A) & = p(F|E_F)\phi(E_C, E_F) \\
\psi(D, I, A, B) & = p(D|A, B, E_D)\phi(E_D, E_I) \\
\psi(F, I) & = p(I|E_I)\phi(E_F, E_I)
\end{array}
$$

Unfortunately, the opposite of the last result above does not hold. That is, not every probability distribution that factorizes according to an AMP CG coincides with the marginal of a distribution that is Markovian wrt the corresponding EAMP CG. To see it, let G be the AMP CG $A \rightarrow B - C$. Let H be the EAMP CG corresponding to G, i.e. $E_A \rightarrow A \rightarrow B \leftarrow E_B - E_C \rightarrow C$. Consider a probability distribution $p(A, B, C, E_A, E_B, E_C)$ that is Markovian wrt H. Since

---

[1] Unlike in this work, V is a Gaussian random variable in [9]. However, that is irrelevant in the proof of [9, Theorem 1]. The proof builds upon the following two properties which, as we show, also hold for the framework in this work:

- A node $E_X \in E$ is determined by some $Z \subseteq V$ iff $Pa_G(X) \cup X \subseteq Z$. The if part follows from the fact shown above that E_X is determined by $Pa_G(X) \cup X$. To see the only if part, assume to the contrary that Z determines E_X but $Pa_G(X) \cup X \nsubseteq Z$. Then, $X \notin Z$ or there is some $Y \in Pa_G(X) \setminus Z$. If $X \notin Z$, then let H' be the EAMP CG H' over $V \cup E$ whose only edge is $E_X \rightarrow X$, and let p' be a probability distribution that is Markovian wrt H'. Note that E_X is a function of just X in p'. If $X \in Z$, then let H' have the edges $E_X \rightarrow X \leftarrow Y \leftarrow E_Y$, and let p' be Markovian wrt H' st $x_*^{y_0} \neq x_*^{y_1}$. Note that E_X is a function of just $X \cup Y$ in p'. Note also that in either case p' is Markovian wrt H, because H' is a subgraph of H. Note also that in neither case E_X is a function of Z in p'. This contradicts that Z determines E_X.
- A node $X \in V$ is determined by some $Z \subseteq V$ iff $X \in Z$. The if part is trivial. To see the only if part, note that X is determined by Z only if $X \in Z$ or E_X is determined by Z. However, E_X is determined by Z only if $X \in Z$ by the previous property.

as shown above $\{E_A, E_B, E_C\}$ is determined by $\{A, B, C\}$, Eq. 7 implies that

$$\frac{p(a_0, b_*^{a_0}, C)}{p(a_1, b_*^{a_1}, C)} = \frac{p(a_0|E_A)p(b_*^{a_0}|a_0, E_B)p(C|E_C)\phi(E_A)\phi(E_B, E_C)}{p(a_1|E_A)p(b_*^{a_1}|a_1, E_B)p(C|E_C)\phi(E_A)\phi(E_B, E_C)} = \frac{p(a_0|E_A)\phi(E_A)}{p(a_1|E_A)\phi(E_A)} \tag{8}$$

because both $\{a_0, b_*^{a_0}\}$ and $\{a_1, b_*^{a_1}\}$ determine that $E_B = 0$, which implies that $p(b_*^{a_0}|a_0, E_B) = p(b_*^{a_1}|a_1, E_B) = 1$. Now, consider a probability distribution $p'(A, B, C)$ that factorizes according to G. Then, Eq. 1 implies that

$$\frac{p'(a_0, b_*^{a_0}, C)}{p'(a_1, b_*^{a_1}, C)} = \frac{\psi(a_0)\psi(a_0, b_*^{a_0}, C)}{\psi(a_1)\psi(a_1, b_*^{a_1}, C)}. \tag{9}$$

Note that the ratio in Eq. 9 is a function of C whereas the ratio in Eq. 8 is not. Therefore, $p(A, B, C) \neq p'(A, B, C)$ in general.

Finally, note that every node $X \in V$ in an EAMP CG H forms a connectivity component on its own. Therefore, the factorization in Eq. 7 is actually of the same form as the factorization in Eq. 1. This comes as no surprise because, after all, H is an AMP CG over $V \cup E$.

7   Discussion

We have addressed some issues that may hinder the use of AMP CGs in practice. We hope that the results reported in this paper help others to deploy AMP CGs in practical applications. Specifically, we have shown how a discrete probability distribution that is Markovian wrt an AMP CG factorizes according to it. We have also shown how this factorization makes it possible to perform inference and parameter learning efficiently. Finally, we have provided an intuitive interpretation of AMP CGs that sheds some light on what the different edges may mean. Unfortunately, the interpretation provided is not perfect, i.e. not every probability distribution that factorizes according to an AMP CG coincides with the marginal of a distribution that is Markovian wrt the corresponding EAMP CG. We are working to solve this problem. We are also working on proving the opposite of the result in Sect. 3, i.e. proving that every probability distribution that factorizes according to an AMP CG is Markovian wrt it.

Acknowledgments. This work is funded by the Swedish Research Council (ref. 2010-4808), and by a so-called career contract at Linköping University.

References

1. Andersson, S.A., Madigan, D., Perlman, M.D.: Alternative Markov Properties for Chain Graphs. Scand. J. Stat. **28**, 33–85 (2001)
2. Cowell, R.G., Dawid, P., Lauritzen, S.L., Spiegelhalter, D.J.: Probabilistic Networks and Expert Systems. Springer, Hiedelberg (1999)
3. Cox, D.R., Wermuth, N.: Multivariate Dependencies - Models Analysis and Interpretation. Chapman and Hall, London (1996)

4. Frydenberg, M.: The Chain Graph Markov Property. Scand. J. Stat. **17**, 333–353 (1990)
5. Koller, D., Friedman, N.: Probabilistic Graphical Models. MIT Press, Cambridge (2009)
6. Lauritzen, S.L.: Graphical Models. Oxford University Press, Cambridge (1996)
7. Lauritzen, S.L., Spiegelhalter, D.J.: Local computations with probabilities on graphical structures and their application to expert systems. J. Roy. Stat. Soc. B **50**, 157–224 (1988)
8. Murphy, K.P.: Machine Learning: A Probabilistic Perspective. MIT Press, Cambridge (2012)
9. Peña, J.M.: Marginal AMP chain graphs. Int. J. Approximate Reasoning **55**, 1185–1206 (2014)
10. Sonntag, D.: On expressiveness of the AMP chain graph interpretation. In: van der Gaag, L.C., Feelders, A.J. (eds.) PGM 2014. LNCS, vol. 8754, pp. 458–470. Springer, Heidelberg (2014)
11. Sonntag, D., Peña, J.M.: Chain Graph Interpretations and their Relations Revisited. International Journal of Approximate Reasoning (to appear)

A Differential Approach for Staged Trees

Christiane Görgen, Manuele Leonelli[(✉)], and James Q. Smith

Department of Statistics, The University of Warwick,
Coventry CV4 7AL, UK
{c.gorgen,m.leonelli,j.q.smith}@warwick.ac.uk

Abstract. Symbolic inference algorithms in Bayesian networks have now been applied in a variety of domains. These often require the computation of the derivatives of polynomials representing probabilities in such graphical models. In this paper we formalise a symbolic approach for staged trees, a model class making it possible to visualise asymmetric model constraints. We are able to show that the probability parametrisation associated to trees has several advantages over the one associated to Bayesian networks. We then continue to compute certain derivatives of staged trees' polynomials and show their probabilistic interpretation. We are able to determine that these polynomials can be straightforwardly deduced by compiling a tree into an arithmetic circuit.

1 Introduction

The notion of probabilistic graphical models has been successfully established [10]. In particular, Bayesian networks (BNs) [13] have proved to provide an intuitive qualitative framework, based on various conditional independence constraints [8], as well as a computationally efficient inferential tool [11].

Probabilistic inference in BNs has been characterised in the literature not only using numerical approaches but also symbolic methods, where probabilities are treated as unknown quantities [5,7]. Symbolic approaches like these provide a natural framework around which to perform various sensitivity analyses. It has only recently been recognised that a variety of such probabilistic queries can be answered by computing derivatives of polynomials representing the model's probabilities [7]. In [7] it is further shown that the computational burden of calculating these polynomials can be reduced through an arithmetic circuit (AC) representation.

Symbolic methods have proved useful in BNs (e.g. [5]), although these techniques do come with a considerable computational cost. In this paper we study a different class of models called *staged trees* [18,19] where such difficulties are eased. We demonstrate that the *interpolating* polynomial [7,15] associated to a staged tree can be straightforwardly deduced by simply looking at the structure of the underlying graph. This is because the parametrisation associated to these models is more intuitive than the one of BNs.

It has been shown that in fact discrete BNs are a special case of the class of staged tree models [2,18,19]. The latter have the advantage over BNs of

© Springer International Publishing Switzerland 2015
S. Destercke and T. Denoeux (Eds.): ECSQARU 2015, LNAI 9161, pp. 346–355, 2015.
DOI: 10.1007/978-3-319-20807-7_31

being able to explicitly represent asymmetric (conditional independence) constraints and relations between functions of random variables, explicitly modelling information which is only present in the probability structure of a BN model. Importantly, polynomials arising from this more general class of models have an interesting algebraic structure which is not necessarily homogeneous and multilinear as in the BN case. We are able to demonstrate that a probabilistic semantic can be attributed to the partial derivatives of interpolating polynomials. In addition, these can also be used to represent various causal assumptions under the Pearlean causal paradigm [14]. Typically, because of the wide variety of possible hypotheses they embody, staged trees are necessarily models over much smaller state spaces than BNs. Since this is the main computational issue for symbolic approaches associated with BNs, it follows that trees can be very practical for investigating inferential queries.

The polynomials of staged trees can be computed by compiling them into ACs just as for BNs. As noted in [12], the presence of asymmetries simply entails setting equal to zero some terms in the polynomial associated with a model with no such asymmetries. Therefore, the AC of a staged tree has often a substantially smaller number of leaves. Together with the point above this means that, when using a symbolic approach for our model class, computations and inferential challenges are therefore eased.

2 Staged Tree Models

In this paper, as in [17, 19], we focus on graphical models represented by trees. We examine *event trees* $T = (V, E)$, directed rooted trees where each inner vertex $v \in V$ has at least two children. In this context, the sample space of the model corresponds to the *set of root-to-leaf paths* in the graph and each directed path, which is a sequence of edges $r = (e \mid e \in E(r))$, for $E(r) \subset E$, has a meaning in the modelling context. To every edge $e \in E$ we associate a *primitive probability* $\theta(e) \in (0, 1)$ such that on each *floret* $\mathcal{F}(v) = (v, E(v))$, where $E(v) \subseteq E$ is the set of edges emanating from $v \in V$, the primitive probabilities sum to unity. The probability of an atom is then simply the product of primitive probabilities along the edges of its path: $\pi_\theta(r) = \prod_{e \in E(r)} \theta(e)$. After [6, 19] we define:

Definition 1. *Let* $\theta_v = (\theta(e) \mid e \in E(v))$ *be the vector of primitive probabilities associated to the floret* $\mathcal{F}(v)$, $v \in V$, *in a tree* $T = (V, E)$. *A staged tree is an event tree as above where, for some* $v, w \in V$, *the floret probabilities are identified* $\theta_v = \theta_w$. *Then,* $w, v \in V$ *are in the same stage.*

Setting floret probabilities equal can be thought of as representing conditional independence information. If vertices are linked to random variables [19, 20] their edges are associated with a projection of the model's sample space. Two vertices are thus in the same stage if they have the same (conditional) distribution over their edges. When drawing a tree, vertices in the same stage are assigned the same colour in order to have a visual counterpart for that information.

Staged trees are flexible representations for many discrete models. They are capable of representing all conditional independence hypotheses within discrete BNs, whilst at the same time being more flexible in expressing modifications of these, as we will see below. In particular, the graphical complexity is made up for by the extra expressiveness of these models [19]. In this paper, although the associated *Chain Event Graph (CEG)* is more convenient for displaying information in a staged tree model, we will stick to the latter graphs when representing their algebraic features.

Example 1. For the purposes of this short paper, we consider the following simplification of a real system described in [19]. A binary model is designed to explain a possible unfolding of the following events in a cell culture: a cell finds itself in a benign or hostile environment, the level of activity within this might be high or low, and if the environment is hostile then a cell might either survive or die.

We can model this narrative using a BN on three variables: the state of the environment is represented by Y_0 taking values in $\mathbb{Y}_0 = \{\text{hostile}, \text{benign}\}$, cell activity is measured by Y_1 as $\mathbb{Y}_1 = \{\text{high}, \text{low}\}$ and viability via Y_2 with $\mathbb{Y}_2 = \{\text{die}, \text{survive}\}$. Then $\mathbb{Y} = (\mathbb{Y}_0, \mathbb{Y}_1, \mathbb{Y}_2)$ is the model space.

If we argue that a high or low level of activity is independent of the environment being hostile or benign and that whether or not a cell dies does not depend on its activity, then our model corresponds to the collider BN in (1), stating that $Y_0 \perp\!\!\!\perp Y_1$ and $Y_0 \not\perp\!\!\!\perp Y_1 \mid Y_2$.

$$Y_0 \longrightarrow Y_2 \longleftarrow Y_1 \tag{1}$$

Observe that this graphical representation, though storing all conditional independence constraints between the Y_i variables, does not inform us about all of the assumptions above. It forces us to retain information which is meaningless in our context, as for instance the atom $\omega = (\text{benign}, \text{high}, \text{die}) \in \mathbb{Y}$ which has probability zero. The representation of (1) in terms of a staged tree $\mathcal{T}_{\text{BN}}$ in Fig. 1, where each root-to-leaf path represents one $\omega \in \mathbb{Y}$, is therefore large. As the number of variables gets larger, the percentage of information not described through the graph can increase dramatically.

The apparent symmetries in this representation are typical for event trees induced by BNs: all paths are of the same length and the stage structure (colouring) depends on the distance of a vertex from the root. Keeping in mind the assumptions made in our model, for example that there is no cell damage in a benign environment, we notice that the lower part of the tree in Fig. 1 does not contain any valuable information. There is even more redundancy if we add an extra level of complexity to the model, for instance by assessing the constitution of a surviving cell—which is meaningless if a unit has died. Thus, the model at hand is a context specific BN rather than a BN (see e.g. [19]), and there is a strong case for using a staged tree model.

We call the state space of our improved graphical model

$$\mathbb{X}_{\mathcal{T}} = \{\omega_1 = (\text{hostile, high, die}), \dots, \omega_8 = (\text{benign, low})\},$$

which is the set of all meaningful unfoldings of events. It is canonically identified with the set of root-to-leaf paths of an event tree $\mathcal{T} = (V, E)$,

$$R_{\mathcal{T}} = \{r_1 = (e_{01}, e_{11}, e_{31}), r_2 = (e_{01}, e_{11}, e_{32}), \ldots, r_8 = (e_{02}, e_{22})\},$$

where we reduce the vertex set of $\mathcal{T}_{\mathrm{BN}}$ to $V = \{v_0, v_1, \ldots, v_{10}\}$ and the edges are $E = \{e_{01}, e_{02}, \ldots, e_{42}\}$, with e_{ij} corresponding to the jth edge emanating from v_i, for fitting i and j.

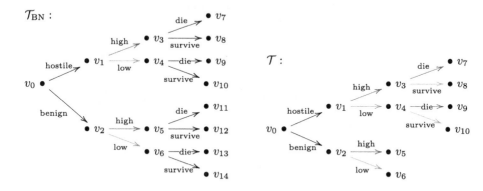

Fig. 1. A staged tree $\mathcal{T}_{\mathrm{BN}}$ representation of the BN in (1) of Example 1.

Fig. 2. An asymmetric staged tree $\mathcal{T}$ representing the context specific information of the BN in (1) of Example 1.

Following this approach, we obtain the staged tree $\mathcal{T}$ in Fig. 2. This new representation is far more expressive than the BN itself and less cluttered than the BN's tree $\mathcal{T}_{\mathrm{BN}}$, whilst conveying the same information: the colouring expresses the given conditional independence assumptions that can also be read from the BN. For instance, by colouring the edges in $E(v_1)$ and $E(v_2)$ in the same manner, we visualise equality of the probability labels

$$\begin{aligned}\theta(e_{11}) = \theta(e_{21}) \text{ or } P(Y_1 = \text{high}|Y_0 = \text{hostile}) = P(Y_1 = \text{high}|Y_0 = \text{benign}),\\ \theta(e_{12}) = \theta(e_{22}) \text{ or } P(Y_1 = \text{low}|Y_0 = \text{hostile}) = P(Y_1 = \text{low}|Y_0 = \text{benign}).\end{aligned} \quad (2)$$

The same procedure is applied on the edges of v_7, v_9 and v_8, v_{10}.   □

Having understood the advantages of a staged tree over a BN, we now present a symbolic approach to calculate probabilities in this type of models. Following concepts introduced in [15] in the context of designed experiments, we define:

Definition 2. *Let $\mathcal{T} = (V, E)$ be a staged tree with primitive probabilities $\theta(e)$, $e \in E$, and set of root-to-leaf paths $R_{\mathcal{T}}$. We call $\Lambda(e) = \{r \in R_{\mathcal{T}} \mid e \in E(r)\}$ an edge-centred event, and set $\lambda_e(r)$, for $e \in E$, to be an indicator of $r \in \Lambda(e)$. We call*

$$c_{\mathcal{T}}(\theta, \lambda) = \sum_{r \in R_{\mathcal{T}}} \pi_{\theta}(r) \prod_{e \in E(r)} \lambda_e(r) = \sum_{r \in R_{\mathcal{T}}} \prod_{e \in E(r)} \lambda_e(r)\theta(e)$$

the interpolating polynomial of $\mathcal{T}$.

The interpolating polynomial is a sum of atomic probabilities with indicators for certain conditional events happening or not happening. Even though all these unknowns sum to one, in our symbolic approach we treat them just like indeterminates. We will report in [9] some recent results that use interpolating polynomials to characterise when two staged trees are statistically equivalent.

We now look at this model class from an algebraic point of view. As seen in Example 1, the sample space of a BN with vertex set $\{Y_1, \ldots, Y_n\}$, $Y_i \in \mathbb{Y}_i$, $i = 1, \ldots, n$, gives rise to an event tree where each root-to-leaf path $r \in R_T$ is associated to an atom $\omega \in \mathbb{Y}_1 \times \ldots \times \mathbb{Y}_n$ and is hence of length n. By definition, $P(\omega) = \pi_\theta(r) = \prod_{r \in E(r)} \theta(e)$ and therefore the interpolating polynomial of a BN is a sum of monomials each of which is of degree $2n$ and so *homogeneous*. Moreover, the stage structure of a BN tree as in Fig. 1 is such that no two vertices along the same directed path are in the same stage, in fact stages exist only along *orthogonal cuts* [20]. Thus in particular, the interpolating polynomial of a BN is also *multilinear*, that is linear in all components. Note that, although in this paper we consider Bayesian subjective probabilities only, other representations of uncertainty in directed graphical models entertain similar multilinear structures (see e.g. [1]).

Note that the indicators $\lambda_e(r)$ on the edges $e \in E(r)$ are associated to the (conditional) event represented by e, having probability $\theta(e)$. This notation is apparently redundant, but will turn out to be useful in Sect. 3. We observe that this redundancy is one of the great advantages of a staged tree: whilst [7] needs to compute conditional probabilities of all *compatible parent structures* of an event, which is a rather obscure concept in a symbolic framework, and [5] computes the product space of any indeterminates' combination regardless of their meaning, a tree visualisation of our model gives us the necessary structure immediately: events can be simply read from the paths in the graph. Recently, [12] developed an algorithm which automatically computes only the required monomials in BN models. Although this makes computations more efficient the parametrisation in [12] is still not as transparent as the one associated to trees.

Example 2. Recall the model analysed in Example 1. Ignoring the equalities implied by the stage structure, the interpolating polynomial of a model represented by the BN in (1) or the tree in Fig. 1 equals

$$
\begin{aligned}
c_{\mathrm{BN}}(\theta) = \ & \theta_{01}\theta_{11}\theta_{31} + \theta_{01}\theta_{11}\theta_{32} + \theta_{01}\theta_{12}\theta_{41} + \theta_{01}\theta_{12}\theta_{42} \\
& + \theta_{02}\theta_{21}\theta_{51} + \theta_{02}\theta_{22}\theta_{52} + \theta_{02}\theta_{22}\theta_{61} + \theta_{02}\theta_{22}\theta_{62},
\end{aligned}
\tag{3}
$$

where we simplified our notation to $\theta_{ij} = \theta(e_{ij})$ for each i, j. We also omitted for ease of notation the indicator functions on all terms. This polynomial has been simply read from the event tree by first multiplying over all primitive probabilities along one root-to-leaf path, and then summing over all of these paths. This is a lot easier done using Fig. 1 than in (1), where we would have had to sum over compatible parent configurations, which could have not been read directly from a DAG. Observe that here, as outlined above, c_{BN} is homogeneous of degree 3. The number of terms equals the number of paths in the tree representation.

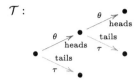

$\mathcal{T}:$

Fig. 3. The staged tree of a repeated coin toss with interpolating polynomial (7).

Conversely, the more adequate improved model without meaningless terms or terms with probability zero has the interpolating polynomial

$$c(\theta) = \theta_{01}\theta_{11}\theta_{31} + \theta_{01}\theta_{11}\theta_{32} + \theta_{01}\theta_{12}\theta_{41} + \theta_{01}\theta_{12}\theta_{42} + \theta_{02}\theta_{21} + \theta_{02}\theta_{22}. \quad (4)$$

This is a lot easier to handle than c_{BN} but still conveys exactly the same information. When plugging in the conditional independence constraints as in (2), we obtain the interpolating polynomial of the staged tree in Fig. 2 as:

$$c_{\mathcal{T}}(\theta) = \theta_{01}\theta_{11}\theta_{31} + \theta_{01}\theta_{11}\theta_{32} + \theta_{01}\theta_{12}\theta_{31} + \theta_{01}\theta_{12}\theta_{32} + \theta_{02}\theta_{11} + \theta_{02}\theta_{12}, \quad (5)$$
$$= \theta_{01}(\theta_{11}(\theta_{31} + \theta_{32}) + \theta_{12}(\theta_{31} + \theta_{32})) + \theta_{02}(\theta_{11} + \theta_{12}), \quad (6)$$

where we substituted $\theta_{1j} = \theta_{2j}$ and $\theta_{3j} = \theta_{4j}$, for $j = 1, 2$. This is now inhomogeneous but still multilinear, and it has total degree 3 with individual monomial terms having degree 2 or 3. Notice that $c_{\mathcal{T}}$ can be easily factorised in (6) by simply following the structure of the underlying graph [9]. In [4], polynomials of this type are called *factored*. This representation entails great computational advantages since the compilation into an AC is almost instantaneous. Whilst for BNs the factored representation might be difficult to obtain, it comes almost for free in tree models.

We observe that the graphical simplicity of a staged tree model in comparison to an uncoloured tree or a BN is also reflected algebraically: the polynomial in (5) has fewer indeterminates than the one in (4) and a lot fewer than the polynomial associated to a tree which is derived from a BN in (3). This is because in the BN the redundancy of atoms gives rise to redundant terms. □

Observe that, although the interpolating polynomial of the staged tree in Example 2 is multilinear, the concept of stages allows for enough flexibility to construct models where this is not the case. Suppose we are interested in a situation where we flip a coin and repeat this experiment only if the first outcome is heads. This is depicted graphically by the coloured tree in Fig. 3. The interpolating polynomial of this model is non-homogeneous and not multilinear:

$$c_{\mathcal{T}}(\theta, \tau, \lambda, \lambda') = \lambda^2\theta^2 + \lambda\lambda'\theta\tau + \lambda'\tau, \quad (7)$$

for $\theta + \tau = 1$ and indicators λ of 'heads' and λ' of 'tails'. Again, this algebraic structure and model type cannot, without significant obscuration, be expressed in terms of a BN. If the polynomial is multilinear, we call our model *square-free*. The focus of this paper lies on these.

By construction, Theorem 1 of [7] holds for a staged tree interpolating polynomial:

Lemma 1. *For any event A represented by a set of root-to-leaf paths R_A in a staged tree $\mathcal{T}$, we know that*

$$P(A) = \sum_{r \in R_A} \pi_\theta(r) = \sum_{r \in R_A} \prod_{e \in E(r)} \lambda_e(r)\theta(e) = c_{\mathcal{T}}(\theta, \lambda|_{R_A}),$$

where $\lambda|_{R_A}$ indicates that $\lambda_e(r) = 1$ for all $e \in E(r)$ with $r \in R_A$, and else zero.

We are therefore able to symbolically compute the probability of any event associated to a tree.

Example 3. In the notation of Examples 1 and 2, suppose we are interested in calculating the probability of death of a cell. This is captured by the event $A = \{x \in \mathbb{X}_{\mathcal{T}} \mid x_3 = \text{die}\}$. Thus $R_A = \Lambda(e_{31}) \cup \Lambda(e_{41}) = \{r_1, r_2\}$ corresponds to all root-to-leaf paths going through an edge labelled 'die' which translates in summing all terms in (5) which include the label θ_{31}. Therefore, again omitting the λ indicators, $P(A) = \sum_{r \in R_A} \pi_\theta(r) = \theta_{01}\theta_{11}\theta_{31} + \theta_{01}\theta_{12}\theta_{31}$. $\square$

3   The Differential Approach

We are now able to provide a probabilistic semantic, just as [7] for BNs, to the derivatives of polynomials associated to staged trees. For ease of notation we let in this section $\lambda_e = \lambda_e(r)$.

Proposition 1. *For equally coloured edges $e \in E$ and an event A represented by the root-to-leaf paths R_A, the following results hold:*

$$P(\Lambda(e)|A) = \frac{1}{c_{\mathcal{T}}(\theta, \lambda|_{R_A})} \frac{\partial c_{\mathcal{T}}(\theta, \lambda|_{R_A})}{\partial \lambda_e}, \quad P(\Lambda(e), A) = \theta(e)\frac{\partial c_{\mathcal{T}}(\theta, \lambda|_{R_A})}{\partial \theta(e)}, \quad (8)$$

where $\Lambda(e)$ is an edge-centred event.

All the probabilities in (8) are equal to zero whenever $e \notin E(r)$ for all $r \in R_A$. Notice that the derivatives of tree polynomials have the exact same interpretation of the ones of BNs as in [7]. Here we restricted our attention to square-free staged trees but analogous results hold in the generic case: each monomial with indeterminate λ_e and $\theta(e)$ of degree higher than one would need to be differentiated a number of times equal to the degree of that indeterminate.

Proposition 2. *In the notation of Proposition 1, we have that for $e, e_1, e_2 \in E$:*

$$P(\Lambda(e_1), \Lambda(e_2) \mid A) = \frac{1}{c_{\mathcal{T}}(\theta, \lambda|_{R_A})} \frac{\partial^2 c_{\mathcal{T}}(\theta, \lambda|_{R_A})}{\partial \lambda_{e_1} \partial \lambda_{e_2}}, \quad (9)$$

$$P(\Lambda(e_1), \Lambda(e_2), A) = \theta(e_1)\theta(e_2)\frac{\partial c_{\mathcal{T}}(\theta, \lambda|_{R_A})}{\partial \theta(e_1)\partial \theta(e_2)}, \quad (10)$$

$$P(A \mid \Lambda(e)) = \frac{\partial^2 c_{\mathcal{T}}(\theta, \lambda|_{R_A})}{\partial \theta(e)\partial \lambda_e}. \quad (11)$$

It is an easy exercise to deduce from Proposition 2 the probabilistic meaning of higher order derivatives.

The above propositions demonstrate that the results of [7] are transferable to the class of staged trees. In addition we are able to derive that in the staged tree model class derivatives can be associated to causal propositions in the sense of the Perlean concept of causal intervention on trees, as formalised in [21]. Note that such a result does not hold in general for the polynomials describing BN probabilities.

Proposition 3. *Suppose the staged tree is believed to be causal as in [18]. Then under the notation of Proposition 2,*

$$P(A \parallel \Lambda(e)) = \frac{\partial^2 c_T(\theta, \lambda|_{R_A})}{\partial \theta_e \partial \lambda_e} \tag{12}$$

is the probability of the event A when the system is forced to go through edge e.

Note that all the quantities in (8)–(12) can be used in sensitivity analysis, for instance by investigating the changes in probability estimates when the system is set to be in a certain scenario of interest.

Example 4. We now compute a set of derivatives on the interpolating polynomial c_T in (5) with respect to λ_{31} and θ_{31} to perform probabilistic inference over the event A that a cell dies, as in Example 3. Thus, we consider the edge $e = (v_3, v_7)$ and

$$\frac{1}{c_T(\theta, \lambda|_{R_A})} \frac{\partial c_T(\theta, \lambda|_{R_A})}{\partial \lambda_e} = \frac{\theta_{01}\theta_{11}\theta_{31} + \theta_{01}\theta_{12}\theta_{31}}{\theta_{01}\theta_{11}\theta_{31} + \theta_{01}\theta_{12}\theta_{31}} = 1, \tag{13}$$

$$\theta(e) \frac{\partial c_T(\theta, \lambda|_{R_A})}{\partial \theta(e)} = \theta_{13}(\theta_{01}\theta_{11} + \theta_{01}\theta_{12}) = P(A), \tag{14}$$

$$\frac{\partial^2 c_T(\theta, \lambda|_{R_A})}{\partial \theta(e) \partial \lambda_e} = \theta_{01}\theta_{11} + \theta_{01}\theta_{12}. \tag{15}$$

Observe that (13) is equal to unity since every path associated to the event A must go through e. From the same argument follows that (14) is equal to $P(A)$. Equation (15) is a simple consequence of Bayes' theorem, which can be checked algebraically. □

4 Trees as Circuits

The previous sections have introduced a comprehensive symbolic inferential toolbox for trees, based on the computation of the interpolating polynomial and its derivatives. In [7] it is shown that an efficient method to compute such polynomials is by representing them as an *AC*. This is a DAG whose leaves are the indeterminates and the inner nodes are labelled by multiplication and summation operations. The *size* of the circuit equals its number of edges.

ACs of staged tree polynomials are smaller in size than the ones associated to BNs for two reasons: first, a tree might have fewer root-to-leaf paths

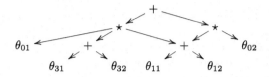

Fig. 4. The arithmetic circuit of the model represented in Example 2, yielding (5).

(as in Example 1); second, there can be less indeterminates because unfoldings with probability zero are not included in the model and coloured labels further decrease the number of indeterminates. Therefore, in asymmetric settings we can expect computations to be much faster for trees than for BNs.

A major problem in the compilation of BN polynomials consists in the identification of the AC of smallest size. This usually entails the computation of the BN's jointree and the application of more complex algorithms [7]. We note here that in tree models this is straightforward since the interpolating polynomial is naturally factored.

Example 5. Recall the interpolating polynomial of the staged tree from Example 2. We notice that (6) can be rewritten as $c_T(\theta) = \theta_{01}(\theta_{11} + \theta_{12})(\theta_{31} + \theta_{31}) + \theta_{02}(\theta_{11} + \theta_{12})$.

This gives us the AC in Fig. 4 where leaves with the same parent are labelled by primitive probabilities from the same floret, and labels belonging to leaves in the tree are first summed in the AC. It is easy to deduce that the AC associated to the BN's polynomial in (3) would be much larger than the one in Fig. 4. We note also that, whilst all the ACs deriving from BNs in [7] are trees, ours is more generally a DAG. This is a consequence of the more flexible stage structure of generic staged trees than the one of trees depicting BNs.   □

5   Discussion

Staged tree models, whilst representing a much larger model class than discrete BNs, have proven to have a much more intuitive symbolic representation. We have been able to show that in this framework polynomial derivatives have a probabilistic semantic which is of use in sensitivity analysis. Our parametrisation further led to computational advantages because of the almost automatic compilation into an AC.

Importantly, this paper relates the symbolic definition of discrete BNs to the one of generic trees via the notion of an interpolating polynomial introduced in Definition 2. We can therefore now start investigating classes of models that are defined only symbolically, since the interpolating polynomial is able to capture all the probabilistic information of the model. This can then lead to the definition of new models that in general cannot be depicted by a graph.

In addition, the recognition that the probabilities associated to certain statistical models have a polynomial form started a whole new area of research called *algebraic statistics* [16]. We are now developing results which apply new exciting methodologies from this subject to staged tree models. We are also starting to develop computer algebra methods to work with trees that exploit the symbolic definition of the model we provided here and that will facilitate the use of such models in practical applications. The examples we work with are of course larger than those presented here (see [2,3]) and provide the framework for sensitivity analyses in important areas of application.

References

1. Antonucci, A., de Campos, C.P., Huber, D., Zaffalon, M.: Approximating Credal Network Inferences by Linear Programming. In: van der Gaag, L.C. (ed.) ECSQARU 2013. LNCS, vol. 7958, pp. 13–24. Springer, Heidelberg (2013)
2. Barclay, L.M., Hutton, J.L., Smith, J.Q.: Refining a Bayesian network using a Chain Event Graph. Int. J. Approx. Reason. **54**, 1300–1309 (2013)
3. Barclay, L.M., Hutton, J.L., Smith, J.Q.: Chain event graphs for informed missingness. Bayesian Anal. **9**(1), 53–76 (2014)
4. Brandherm, B., Jameson, A.: An extension of the differential approach for Bayesian network inference to dynamic Bayesian networks. Int. J. Intell. Syst. **19**(8), 727–748 (2004)
5. Castillo, E., Gutiérrez, J.M., Hadi, A.S.: A new method for efficient symbolic propagation in discrete Bayesian Networks. Networks **28**(1), 31–43 (1996)
6. Cowell, R.G., Smith, J.Q.: Causal discovery through MAP selection of stratified Chain Event Graphs. Electron. J. Stat. **8**, 965–997 (2014)
7. Darwiche, A.: A differential approach to inference in Bayesian networks. J. ACM **50**(3), 280–305 (2003)
8. Dawid, A.P.: Conditional independence in statistical theory. J. Roy. Stat. Soc. B **41**(1), 1–31 (1979)
9. Görgen, C., Smith, J.Q.: Equivalence Classes of Chain Event Graph Models. In preparation
10. Jordan, M.I.: Graphical models. Stat. Sci. **19**(1), 140–155 (2004)
11. Lauritzen, S.L., Spiegelhalter, D.J.: Local computations with probabilities on graphical structures and their application to expert systems. J. Roy. Stat. Soc. B **50**, 157–224 (1988)
12. Leonelli, M., Smith, J.Q., Riccomagno, E.: Using computer algebra for the symbolic evaluation of discrete influence diagrams. Technical report, CRISM (2015)
13. Pearl, J.: Probabilistic Reasoning in Intelligent Systems: Networks of Plausible Inference. Morgan Kaufmann, San Francisco (1988)
14. Pearl, J.: Causality: Models, Reasoning and Inference. Cambridge University Press, Cambidge (2000)
15. Pistone, G., Riccomagno, E., Wynn, E.P.: Gröbner bases and factorisation in discrete probability and Bayes. Stat. Comput. **11**, 37–46 (2001)
16. Riccomagno, E.: A short history of algebraic statistics. Metrika **69**(2–3), 397–418 (2009)
17. Shafer, G.: The Art of causal Conjecture. MIT Press, Cambridge (1996)
18. Smith, J.Q.: Bayesian Decision Analysis: Principles and Practice. Cambridge University Press, Cambridge (2010)
19. Smith, J.Q., Anderson, P.E.: Conditional independence and Chain Event Graphs. Artif. Intell. **172**, 42–68 (2008)
20. Thwaites, P.A., Smith, J.Q.: Separation theorems for Chain Event Graphs. CRiSM 11–09 (2011)
21. Thwaites, P.A., Smith, J.Q., Riccomagno, E.: Causal analysis with Chain Event Graphs. Artif. Intell. **174**, 889–909 (2010)

CPD Tree Learning Using Contexts as Background Knowledge

Gerard Ramstein[✉] and Philippe Leray

LINA, DUKe Research Group, 44306 Nantes, France
{gerard.ramstein,philippe.leray}@univ-nantes.fr

Abstract. Context specific independence (CSI) is an efficient means to capture independencies that hold only in certain contexts. Inference algorithms based on CSI are capable to learn the Conditional Probability Distribution (CPD) tree relative to a target variable. We model motifs as specific contexts that are recurrently observed in data. These motifs can thus constitute a domain knowledge which can be incorporated into a learning procedure. We show that the integration of this prior knowledge provides better learning performances and facilitates the interpretation of local structure.

Keywords: Context specific independence · CPD tree · Bayesian network

1 Introduction

Our work falls within the framework of context-specific independence (CSI) [1]. It has been shown that the identification of context-specific relationships within probabilistic relational models constitutes a powerful tool to discover local structures, i.e. interactions that hold on the studied domain. In many applications, conditional independence relationships are true only in specific contexts. A context is a partial configuration of variables that alone induces an effect on a target variable. In diagnosis for instance, in spite of the variety of human symptoms, a small subset of them may suffice to infer a disease. This restrained set of symptoms forms an example of context. Contexts are valuable pieces of information that can be collected as background knowledge. Recurrent contexts observed over distinct datasets form motifs that can be exploited to discover unexpected associations between previous studies and a new experiment. This is specially the case when the same causes induce different effects (i.e. the same motif affects distinct target variables; for example, a symptom set is shared over previously unrelated diseases). The problem of learning local structure has already been addressed, notably in [2]. This paper outlines the use of prior domain knowledge for inferring local structures. From a general point of view, incorporating prior domain knowledge into learning algorithms can greatly enhance their performances. Another advantage is that this strategy enables the user to identify recurrent motifs in his own dataset. We discuss in Sect. 2 some related work

© Springer International Publishing Switzerland 2015
S. Destercke and T. Denoeux (Eds.): ECSQARU 2015, LNAI 9161, pp. 356–365, 2015.
DOI: 10.1007/978-3-319-20807-7_32

for incorporating knowledge into learning procedures. Section 3 introduces some basic concepts associated to domain knowledge and local structure. In Sect. 4, we propose a method for learning local structure from previously acquired motifs. This strategy is evaluated through experimental results that are presented in Sect. 5. Concluding remarks and future work are given in Sect. 6.

2   Related Work

The identification of CSI in Bayesian networks [1] provides compact data structures for representing probabilistic information. In [2], the authors have proposed CPD trees to express context independencies. Other alternative models have been suggested, such as Recursive Probability Trees (RPTs) [3]. RPTs are a generalization of probability trees that can hold potentials in a factorized way. Factorization yields a more compact representation, but the flexibility of RPTs makes the discovery of motifs more complex. CPD trees have then been adopted for this preliminary work. The incorporation of prior knowledge in BN learning algorithms has already been investigated. In [4], the authors exploit an ontology by translating concepts and relations into a BN structure. Ontology-based construction of BNs requires the existence of a formal representation of a specific domain, which is not guaranteed. Rather than a global formal approach, we suggest to infer local structure from a collection of motifs, from which a small subset is expected to be consistent with the investigated data. Our strategy, which rather consists in assembling fragmented pieces of information, has also been tackled in [5]. This work is more an attempt to represent general types of reasoning and does not exploit CSIs. Other approaches address the issue of updating a knowledge base (KB) according to new evidence. In [6], a cyclic approach has been proposed, which incorporates causal discoveries and ontology evolution. Some authors suggest to tune a KB when conflicts have been detected [7]. Contrary to these works, our paper assumes the existence of a well-formed KB of motifs and examines the impact of its incorporation into learning algorithms. A data mining inspired approach [8] proposes to reveal interesting attribute sets using BN as background knowledge. If one models motifs as itemsets, this approach shares some similarities with our work, since it combines BN and itemsets. However, it differs in the fact that we guide BN construction using motifs rather than the opposite.

3   Concepts Related to the Notion of Local Structure

3.1   Context-Specific Independence

A variable assignment (*VA*) is a couple (X, x), noted $(X = x)$, where X is a random variable and x the value taken by X. A *context* **c** generalizes this concept to a set of variables $\mathbf{C} = \{C_1, \ldots, C_n\}$. A context will be represented in extension as follows: $\mathbf{c} = (C_1 = c_1, \ldots, C_n = c_n)$. The notion of context is generally used to define a set of conditions reducing the interaction between a variable and its parents. For instance, a meteorological context including heavy rain will strongly affect the probability that a tennis match will be played.

As pointed out in [2], the notion of context provides an explicit representation of the local structure. Contexts also yield a simpler encoding of the real complexity of the underlying interactions. To capture this local structure, we introduce a formal foundation for the concept of context. Following definition of *context-specific independence* (CSI) due to [1], let $\mathbf{X}, \mathbf{Y}, \mathbf{Z}, \mathbf{C}$ be four disjoint sets of variables. $\mathbf{X}$ and $\mathbf{Y}$ are independent given $\mathbf{Z}$ in context $\mathbf{C} = \mathbf{c}$ if

$$P(\mathbf{X}|\mathbf{Z}, \mathbf{c}, \mathbf{Y}) = P(\mathbf{X}|\mathbf{Z}, \mathbf{c}) \text{ whenever } P(\mathbf{Y}, \mathbf{Z}, \mathbf{c}) > 0.$$

3.2   Conditional Probability Distribution Tree

The conventional representation of conditional probability distribution (CPD) takes the form of a table indexed by all possible values of the set of parents. Consequently, a CPD table has $2^{|\mathbf{S}|}$ rows, where $|\mathbf{S}|$ is the number of parents. As explained in [2], such tabular representation is locally exponential and largely overestimates the actual complexity of the involved interactions. An alternative representation exploiting the concept of context defined above is the *CPD tree*. This notion designates a tree whose leaves represent the distribution of the target variable and whose internal nodes represent the parents branching over their values. A tree *path* is an ordered list of *VAs* corresponding to the path from the root towards a given node. A path will be denoted as follows: $[X_1 = x_1, \ldots, X_n = x_n]$. Note that we use brackets for ordered lists and parenthesis for unordered lists such as contexts and motifs. Inducing a CPD tree from a dataset can be performed using learning procedures such as greedy hill climbing [2], using an approach that has been designed for learning decision trees.

4   Learning Local Structures from Motifs

Our objective is to build a CPD tree from a list of motifs collected in a KB=$\{m_k\}$ where $m_k = (X_1^k = x_1^k, \ldots, X_{n_k}^k = x_{n_k}^k)$. A *motif* is a context that is considered as relevant. The interestingness of a motif can be explicitly stated by experts or be related to its recurring nature over different datasets. In this latter case, the same motif has been observed in many situations, but *not necessarily over the same target variable*: in the previous example of meteorological context, the same cause may affect different outdoor games, such as baseball. Due to their similarity, the same notation will be used for contexts and motifs.

In this section, we first propose an extended version of the concept of CPD tree. Then, we present a learning algorithm from data, using an existing KB and based on two phases: the first one constructs a maximally expanded CPD tree and the second one trims this candidate tree. These two steps are described, as well as a Tabu search extracting an optimal subset of motifs from a given KB.

4.1   Extended Definitions for CPD Tree Learning

We propose to extend the concept of CPD tree by introducing a categorization of its leaves. A leaf represents a CPD associated to a particular configuration (assignment of a variable set). Two situations may arise: either this configuration reveals an remarkable context impacting the target variable, or it is only the consequence of the construction of alternative paths. We call *M-leaf* a leaf associated to a specific context. The prefix M indicates that this leaf may be the evidence for a motif. A M-leaf is graphically represented by symbol $\triangle$. The second type is called a *D-leaf* and is represented by symbol $\square$. This type corresponds to a *default* probability distribution shared by all the D-leaves. We introduce this category to express the absence of a particular context. It presents two advantages: simplification of the encoding of the local structure (all default leaves share the same distribution parameters); better identification of specific interactions (paths leading to a M-leaf). To illustrate these concepts, let consider a voluntary simplified example of a network dedicated to medical diagnosis. Our target variable is associated to heart rate measurement (denoted H), in association with a restricted list of symptoms: chest pain (P), cough (C), indigestion (I) and fatigue (F). The parent set of H is $\mathbf{S} = \{P, C, I, F\}$. All the members of $\mathbf{S}$ are random variables that can take two values: 0(false) and 1(true). In our example, heart rate depends only on a reduced number of symptoms related to a specific disease. Figure 1 shows an example of extended CPD tree that could have be learned from an actual dataset. Note that this tree presents five leaves, but only reveals two interesting features: $\triangle_1$ (bradycardia due to hypothyroidism); $\triangle_2$ (tachycardia due to pulmonary embolism). In our oversimplified example, D-leaves $(\square_1, \square_2, \square_3)$ reflect the fact that patients which are not suffering from either hypothyroidism or pulmonary embolism tend to have a normal heart rate. While a CPD table would require 16 rows for variable H, a CPD tree can be summarized into two paths and three parameters (distribution related to bradycardia, tachycardia, and normal heart rate).

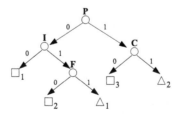

Fig. 1. Example of an extended CPD tree

We state that a motif is retrieved in an inferred CPD tree $\mathcal{T}$ if there exist at most one path π of $\mathcal{T}$ for which the two following conditions are met : (i) π leads to a M-leaf; (ii) π contains p, that is every VA in p exists in π. Finally, one needs to introduce the concept of *consistency*. A motif p is said to be consistent with a path π if the following rule applies: for any $VA = (X = x)$ in π such as

X exists in p, then its assignment in p is x. Similarly, two motifs are said to be consistent if all their common variables also share the same assignment.

4.2 Inference of CPD Trees

The proposed method for inferring CPD trees follows the standard approach of heuristic search. Our learning algorithm attempts to search for the local structure which best fits a dataset according to a scoring function. The term $score(\mathcal{T},D)$ denotes the score related to an expended CPD tree $\mathcal{T}$ and a dataset D (the Bayesian information criterion scoring function has been applied in our experiments). Our algorithm exploits a knowledge base KB and starts with an initial tree $\mathcal{T}$ consisting in a unique node, labeled as D-leaf. This initialization assumes that D does not contain any motif.

> **procedure learnCPDtree($\mathcal{T}$,D,KB)**
> 1.   hasChanged=**false**
> 2.   Leaves=getAllLeaves($\mathcal{T}$)
> 3.   **For each** leaf $\mathcal{L}$ in Leaves **do**
> 4.   UKB=update(KB,$\mathcal{L}$)
> 5.   if UKB $\neq \emptyset$ then
> 6. $\mathcal{T}$=grow($\mathcal{T}$,$\mathcal{L}$,D,UKB)
> 7.   hasChanged=**true**
> 8.   **end**
> 9.   **end**
> 10.   **if** hasChanged **then** learnCPDtree($\mathcal{T}$,D,KB)
> **end.**

Procedure *learnCPDtree* first collects all the leaves of $\mathcal{T}$ (*line 2*). These nodes represent potential locations for growing the CPD tree, using the internal method *grow*. The *update* function (*line 4*) returns an updated version of KB that contains the remaining constraints that apply when node $\mathcal{L}$ has been reached. To illustrate this point, let us return to the example of Fig. 1 and suppose that our initial KB is $\{(C = 1, P = 1), (I = 1, F = 1)\}$. The update of KB for a current node consists into two actions:

- removal of all the motifs from KB that are not consistent with the actual path. For instance, if this latter is $[P = 0]$ (node marked I in Fig. 1), then motif $(C = 1, P = 1)$ has to be removed.
- removal of all VAs that have already met the conditions expressed by a motif. For instance path $[P = 0, I = 1]$ (node marked F) contains a VA ($I = 1$) that has already been visited. Then, motif $(I = 1, F = 1)$ must be updated into $(F = 1)$.

If UKB is not empty, function *grow* is called (*line 6*). The aim of *grow* is to replace a current leaf $\mathcal{L}$ by a new node. Finally, the procedure *learnCPDtree* is recursively called as long as the tree can been expanded (*line 10*).

function grow$((\mathcal{T},\mathcal{L},\text{D},\text{KB})$
1.   pbest=bestPattern$(\mathcal{L},\text{D},\text{KB})$
2.   vabest=bestVariableAssignment$(\mathcal{L},\text{D},\text{pbest})$
3. $\mathcal{T}'$=addNode$(\mathcal{T},\mathcal{L},\text{vabest})$
4.   return $\mathcal{T}'$
end.

Function *grow* is the core of the tree building. Firstly, it searches for the motif *pbest* that achieves the local maximum score when placed at node $\mathcal{L}$ (*line 1*). We estimated that growing the tree node by node is a better approach than replacing a leaf by a branch (i.e. a whole motif). This strategy yields a more accurate node assignment and provides a more compact tree representation. This is the reason why we select from *pbest* the variable assignment *vabest* = (*vbest* = *ibest*) that achieves the highest score (*line 2*). $\mathcal{L}$ is replaced by a new node $\mathcal{N}$ denoted by *vbest* (*line 3*). By nature, any interior node of a CPD tree possesses a set of outgoing arcs to its children, each one associated with a unique variable assignment. Therefore, a child is added to $\mathcal{N}$ for the arc corresponding to assignment *ibest*. This particular child is a M-leaf; the remaining children are labeled as D-leaves. Since *learnCPDtree* replaces leaves by interior nodes, these labels are updated as long as the tree grows. Note that multiple and possibly interleaved motifs may appear in the same path π, as long as they are consistent.

This algorithm generates a maximally expanded tree, in order to circumvent the problem of local maxima (see [9] for a justification). In a second phase, the tree is trimmed in a bottom-up fashion, using procedure *trimCPDtree*. This method is based on a selection of the node to be pruned (*line 1*). Function *cut* then replaces the node by a leaf $\mathcal{L}$ and creates a new tree $\mathcal{T}'$ (*line 3*). The type of $\mathcal{L}$, either M-leaf or D-leaf, is determined by testing the score of $\mathcal{T}'$ for both options and by selecting the option achieving the highest score. This new tree is then compared to $\mathcal{T}$. If the trimmed tree obtains a better score, it is retained (*line 4*). Finally, this procedure is recursively called as long as a pruning node is available (*line 5*).

procedure trimCPDtree$(\mathcal{T},D,\text{KB})$
1.   node=selectNode$(\mathcal{T})$
2.   **if** *node* $\neq NIL$ **then**
3. $\mathcal{T}'$=cut$(\mathcal{T},\text{node})$
4.   **if** score$(\mathcal{T}',D)$ > score$(\mathcal{T},D$) **then** $\mathcal{T}=\mathcal{T}'$
5.   trimCPDtree$(\mathcal{T},D,\text{KB})$
          end.
end.

Procedure *selectNode* defines the best location for pruning $\mathcal{T}$. This selection can only be performed if a set of candidate nodes has already been determined. For this purpose, during the previous growing phase, all the nodes have been marked by an additional boolean label *prune* indicating if it can be pruned or not. The following rules were applied:

– a branch can be removed at node $\mathcal{N}$ if it corresponds to the beginning of a new motif. This property can be easily detected by comparing an original motif m to its updated version. If motif m starts at $\mathcal{N}$, then $prune(\mathcal{N}) = true$,
– a node $\mathcal{N}$ that has been created as D-leaf is labeled as $prune(\mathcal{N}) = true$,
– a node $\mathcal{N}$ that does not meet the two previous conditions is labeled as $prune(\mathcal{N}) = false$.

Function *selectNode* returns the node which is the most appropriate cutting point in $\mathcal{T}$. As previously said, the trimming strategy operates in a bottom-up manner. Therefore, our method searches for the nodes $\mathcal{N}$ verifying $prune(\mathcal{N})$ and retains the node having the maximal depth in the tree (in case of ex-aequo, one candidate node is chosen at random). The label *prune* of this node is set to false, in order to reduce the candidate list. When no more candidates remain, *selectNode* returns NIL.

4.3   Motif Selection Using Tabu Search

The inference method presented above is capable to reconstruct a CPD tree from the exact list of motifs that are effectively concealed in a dataset D. From a practical point of view, one can only assume that some motifs in a knowledge base may be effectively retrieved in D. The existence of false positives degrades the performances of our learning procedure. In fact, even if our trimming method reduces the presence of false positives in inferred CPD trees, it cannot eliminate all of them. For instance, the first motif selected in the growing phase cannot be trimmed without the removal of all the motifs that follows it. Therefore, we adopted a Tabu method [10] to eliminate false positives. This technique aims at defining which motif in KB must be retained as input of our previously described inference algorithm. In our adaptation of Tabu search, a *solution* S represents the subset of motifs extracted from KB that will be retained for our inference method. This latter then estimates an optimal tree $\mathcal{T}$ according only to the subset S. From this outcome, $score(\mathcal{T},D)$ can be computed as the measure of the fitness of the solution S. A solution can be modeled as a boolean vector of size n, where n is the number of motifs in KB. The ith motif is retained if its boolean value is set to true. The optimization algorithm starts with an initial empty solution, assuming that D does no contain any motifs. Neighbors of the current candidate are then generated to find a more adequate solution based on the same list of motifs, except some random mutations (in our implementation, a neighbor contains 1 to 5 boolean changes in relation to the current solution). Note that the trimming procedure is still needed, since Tabu search only defines the optimal motif list, but does not prevent a given motif to be present in multiple occurrences in the inferred tree.

5   Experimental Results

To evaluate the relevance of using a knowledge base for inferring local structure, we performed multiple experiments with various settings. The parent variables are all binary and the target variable is continuous. We simulated datasets encompassing a certain number of motifs of different sizes. For comparison purpose, we adopted two methods. The first one (further referred as *standard* method) discovered new motifs without any a priori knowledge. This learning procedure was based on the method described in [2]. The second one (further referred as *motif-based* method) was our technique exploiting a knowledge base of motifs.

5.1 Experimental Setup

Our experiments were carried out using the following methodology:

- Generation of a golden reference which is a random extended CPD tree containing motifs of different sizes. The total number of variables has been set to 100 for all experiments. We controlled the complexity of the golden reference by defining two random parameters: the number n of motifs; the size s_m of each motif (number of variables composing the motif m). Both n and s_m followed a uniform law on a predefined interval. Three ranges have been fixed for n: $[1, 3]$, $[4, 6]$ and $[7, 10]$. Similarly, we specified three ranges for s_m: $[2, 4]$, $[5, 7]$ and $[8, 10]$. The combination of these intervals defined nine complexity groups. For each of these groups, 20 random extended CPD tree were generated.
- Extraction of a list L_T of true positive motifs from the generated CPD tree.
- Generation of a random dataset using L_T. All the generated datasets contain the same number of instances set to 20,000. An instance of a dataset is determined from a particular leaf of the generated CPD tree. Firstly, one randomly selects the type of the leaf (proportion of two-thirds for M-leaf; one-third for D-leaf). Secondly, a leaf of the same type is randomly selected. By definition, all the variables belonging to the path towards this leaf have specific values. Only the remaining variables are not constrained and are randomly assigned. Thirdly, the value of the target variable must be defined. For a D-leaf, the value follows a default normal distribution ($\mu = 0$, $\sigma = 1$). For each M-leaf, an arbitrary index i has been attributed and the value follows a normal law ($\mu_i = 3 + i$, $\sigma_i = 0.1$).
- Creation of a KB of motifs belonging to the golden reference as well as false motifs. The proportion of false motifs issued from L_T has been set to 90 %. False motifs have been randomly generated from the initial list of variables, so that (i) they observed a comparable complexity (i.e. motif size) in relation to the true motifs; (ii) they were not a subset of any true motif.
- Inference of CPD trees using standard as well as motif-based methods.
- Performance comparison based on precision and recall of the extracted motifs, as well as the compactness of the learned CPD trees.

5.2 Results

Both standard and motif-based methods are capable to retrieve relevant motifs. These method achieve a precision of 1 in respectively 91.5 % and 95.1 % of the cases. These good results may be chiefly attributed to the high separability of the original motif distributions. Conversely, the sensitivity was generally more contrasted: a recall of 1 was obtained in only 26.3 % of the cases for the standard method, compared to 62.7 % for our method. Likewise, recall scores were lower for the first method (mean=0.49), compared to the second one (mean=0.90). Figure 2 details the influence of data complexity on the sensitivity. The number of motifs impacts on the recall performance for both methods, but more specifically on the standard one. As expected, motif-based method is also more robust with regards to motif size. Another advantage of our method is that it strongly reduces the complexity of the inferred trees. Our procedure induces a tree complexity (number of nodes) that is comparable to that of the golden reference (t-test p-value of 0.32). This is clearly not the case for the standard approach which tends to build large trees (mean relative increase of 34 %), making the interpretation of the inferred motifs much more difficult.

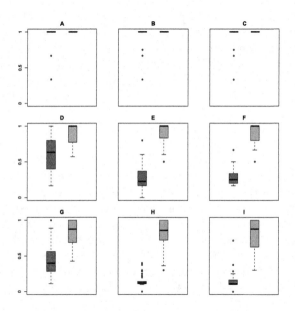

Fig. 2. Recall performances. Rows correspond to the followings ranges of n: $[1,3]$ (top), $[4,6]$ (middle) and $[7,10]$(bottom). Columns correspond to the following ranges of s_p: $[2,4]$(left), $[5,7]$(middle) and $[8,10]$(right). For each figure, left (resp. right) box plot corresponds to the standard (resp. motif-based) method.

6   Conclusion and Future Work

In this paper,we have proposed a new approach to discover local structure using a priori knowledge defined by a set of "interesting" motifs. We have shown that the incorporation of such motifs greatly improves learning procedures aiming at inferring CPD trees, leading to better performances and tree compactness. The same concept also provides an efficient means to interpret new datasets. Recurrent trends could thus be revealed, allowing experts to investigate new connections and to infer some common causes for previously unassociated phenomenons. There is room for substantial improvement in the current implementation. If the proposed strategy has proven to be efficient for retrieving known motifs, it is not capable in its current form to discover new motifs that are not a mere combination of predefined ones. To address this shortcoming, a hybrid approach could be investigated, that would associate discovery of new motifs and discrimination between known and new motifs. Another line of future work concerns the definition and the consistency of our knowledge base. We have only considered the information relative to motifs, assuming that the variable domain is stable during the motif acquisition process. In many situations, datasets may contain distinct sets of variables, due to incomplete or incremental experimental designs. Therefore, a context must be associated with its background, that is the variable set in which the context independency has been observed. Finally, we intend to apply our prototype to real-world problems. Functional genomics is a research field that is particularly well adapted for that purpose: public databases gather a vast amount of gene-related data collected from various sources. This information needs to be analyzed in a systematic way and we believe that motif-based approaches would help biologists to make unexpected links between separate studies.

Acknowledgments. This work was supported by the GRIOTE Bioinformatics Research Project of Pays de la Loire Region, France.

References

1. Boutilier, C., Friedman, N., Goldszmidt, M., Koller, D.: Context-specific independence in Bayesian networks. pp. 115–123 (1996)
2. Friedman, N., Goldszmidt, M.: Learning Bayesian networks with local structure. In: Learning in Graphical Models, pp. 252–262. MIT Press (1996)
3. Cano, A., Gómez-Olmedo, M., Moral, S., Pérez-Ariza, C.B.: Recursive probability trees for Bayesian Networks. In: Meseguer, P., Mandow, L., Gasca, R.M. (eds.) CAEPIA 2009. LNCS, vol. 5988, pp. 242–251. Springer, Heidelberg (2010)
4. Fenz, S., Tjoa, A.M., Hudec, M.: Ontology-based generation of Bayesian networks. In: Barolli, L., Xhafa, F., Hsu, H.-H. (eds.) CISIS, pp. 712–717. IEEE Computer Society, Washington, D.C (2009)
5. Neil, M., Fenton, N., Nielson, L.: Building large-scale Bayesian networks. Knowl. Eng. Rev. **15**, 257–284 (2000)
6. Ben Messaoud, M., Leray, P., Ben Amor, N.: A Serendipitous strategy for learning causal Bayesian Networks using ontologies. In: Liu, W. (ed.) ECSQARU 2011. LNCS, vol. 6717, pp. 182–193. Springer, Heidelberg (2011)
7. Eugene Jr., S., Qi, G., Eunice, E.S.: Bayesian knowledge base tuning. Int. J. Approximate Reasoning **54**(8), 1000–1012 (2013)
8. Jaroszewicz, S., Scheffer, T., Simovici, D.A.: Scalable pattern mining with Bayesian networks as background knowledge. Data Min. Knowl. Discov. **18**(1), 56–100 (2009)
9. Quinlan, J.R., Rivest, R.L.: Inferring decision trees using the minimum description length principle. Inf. Comput. **80**(3), 227–248 (1989)
10. Glover, F., Laguna, M.: Tabu Search. Kluwer Academic Publishers, Boston (1997)

Relevance of Evidence in Bayesian Networks

Michelle Meekes, Silja Renooij[✉], and Linda C. van der Gaag

Utrecht University, Utrecht, The Netherlands
meekes.michelle@gmail.com, {s.renooij,l.c.vandergaag}@uu.nl

Abstract. For many inference tasks in Bayesian networks, computational efforts can be restricted to a relevant part of the network. Researchers have studied the relevance of a network's variables and parameter probabilities for such tasks as sensitivity analysis and probabilistic inference in general, and identified relevant sets of variables by graphical considerations. In this paper we study relevance of the evidence variables of a network for such tasks as evidence sensitivity analysis and diagnostic test selection, and identify sets of variables on which computational efforts can focus. We relate the newly identified sets of relevant variables to previously established relevance sets and address their computation compared to these sets. We thereby paint an overall picture of the relevance of various variable sets for answering questions concerning inference and analysis in Bayesian network applications.

1 Introduction

Bayesian networks have become increasingly popular for decision support in a range of application domains. Capturing general domain knowledge, Bayesian networks owe much of their strength to their ability to derive probability distributions for individual problem instances, given the evidence available from that instance. In view of practical applications however, decision makers should have insight not just in the established probability distributions themselves but in their robustness as well. This observation has motivated researchers to develop techniques for this purpose. The sensitivity of a network's output probabilities to inaccuracies in its parameters can be studied using a parameter sensitivity analysis [2]. A sensitivity-to-evidence analysis allows studying the contribution of specific observations to the output of interest and investigating the effects of changing or removing a particular observation [4]. Algorithms developed for these types of analysis typically rely on (multiple) propagations throughout a network, and hence incur high computational costs.

To relieve the computational burden of probabilistic inference with a Bayesian network, the runtime efforts of computing an output probability of interest can be focused on a relevant part of the network, which depends on the target variables and the specific set of observed variables at hand [3]. This relevant part can to a large extent be identified from graphical considerations only. For example, d-separated nodes and barren nodes are readily identified from a network's graph (we refer to [3] for an overview of available methods) and subsequently pruned without affecting the computed output distribution [1].

© Springer International Publishing Switzerland 2015
S. Destercke and T. Denoeux (Eds.): ECSQARU 2015, LNAI 9161, pp. 366–375, 2015.
DOI: 10.1007/978-3-319-20807-7_33

Although the concept of relevance has been studied for probabilistic inference in general, it has hardly been addressed in the context of the analyses mentioned above. An exception is the concept of parameter sensitivity set which was introduced to describe the set of variables to which a parameter sensitivity analysis can be restricted [2]. In this paper we will study the relevance of various sets of network variables for answering questions related to evidence, such as sensitivity-to-evidence analyses and test-selection procedures. Where previous relevance studies often focused on a single output variable, we consider in this paper the more general case of a set of target variables; the insights developed will therefore be relevant to MAP and MPE studies as well [7]. We will define three new sets of relevant nodes and show how these relate to existing relevance sets; we further show that these sets can be efficiently determined from a network by graphical considerations only. We thereby provide an overall view of the relevance of both known and newly defined sets of nodes, for answering various types of question related to practical applications of Bayesian networks.

The paper is organised as follows. In Sect. 2 we present some preliminaries. Section 3 introduces our new sets of relevant and irrelevant nodes. In Sect. 4 we show how to efficiently establish these sets, and illustrate their possible application. The paper ends with our concluding remarks in Sect. 5.

2   Preliminaries

A Bayesian network is a concise representation of a joint probability distribution Pr over a set of random variables [5]. It consists of a directed acyclic graph $G = (\mathbf{V}_G, \mathbf{A}_G)$, which captures the random variables as nodes and their interdependencies through arcs; in the sequel we will use the term node to refer to nodes and variables alike. The network further includes a set of conditional probabilities for its parameters, which jointly define the distribution Pr through:

$$\Pr(\mathbf{V}_G) = \prod_{V_i \in \mathbf{V}_G} \Pr(V_i \mid \pi(V_i))$$

where $\pi(V_i)$ denotes the parent set of V_i in the graph. The factorisation of the distribution Pr derives from the well-known concept of d-separation which provides a semantics for the network's graph [8]. For any three disjoint sets of nodes $\mathbf{X}, \mathbf{Y}, \mathbf{Z} \subset \mathbf{V}_G$, the set $\mathbf{Z}$ is said to d-separate the sets $\mathbf{X}$ and $\mathbf{Y}$ in G, written $\langle \mathbf{X} | \mathbf{Z} | \mathbf{Y} \rangle_G^d$, if there do not exist any active chains between $\mathbf{X}$ and $\mathbf{Y}$ given evidence for $\mathbf{Z}$. A chain between two nodes is active if each of its head-to-head nodes is either observed or has an observed descendant, and none of its other nodes are observed. The variables captured by d-separated nodes are considered probabilistically independent.

For computing probabilities of interest from a Bayesian network, general inference algorithms have been designed which derive their efficiency from the d-separation properties of a network's graphical structure. In view of these properties, researchers have studied the computation of an output distribution $\Pr(\mathbf{T} \mid \mathbf{e})$ for a set $\mathbf{T}$ of target nodes given evidence $\mathbf{e}$, and identified sets of nodes whose parameter probabilities are not involved in establishing this distribution. Two well-known examples of such sets are the set of nodes d-separated from $\mathbf{T}$ given $\mathbf{E}$, denoted $DSep(\mathbf{T}, \mathbf{E})$, and the set $Barren(\mathbf{T}, \mathbf{E})$ of barren nodes, where a barren node is a node in $\mathbf{V}_G \backslash (\mathbf{T} \cup \mathbf{E})$ without descendants, or with barren descendants only. These sets of nodes are efficiently established through the Bayes-ball algorithm [9], which runs on the network's graph and does not require probabilistic inference. After pruning these nodes from the graph, a minimal computationally equivalent subgraph results from which the output distribution can be established [1].

3   Defining Sets of (Ir)relevant Nodes

Inspired by the well-known concept of parameter sensitivity set and its role in reducing the computational burden of a parameter sensitivity analysis [2], we develop the concept of evidence sensitivity set as the set of nodes for which a change in observed value, or a change in observational status, may affect a posterior probability distribution of interest.

3.1   Parameter and Evidence Sensitivity Sets

Parameter sensitivity analysis is a well-known technique for studying the possible effects of inaccuracies in the parameter probabilities of a Bayesian network [2]. To reduce the computational burden involved, such an analysis is typically restricted to the parameters of a network which, based upon graphical considerations, cannot be discarded as uninfluential. The concept of parameter sensitivity set was introduced to identify the nodes to which these possibly influential parameter probabilities apply [2]. We briefly review this concept, generalising it to marginal output distributions $\Pr(\mathbf{T} \mid e)$ for sets of target nodes $\mathbf{T}$.

Definition 1. *Let $G = (\mathbf{V}_G, \mathbf{A}_G)$ be the digraph of a Bayesian network. Let $\mathbf{T} \subset \mathbf{V}_G$, $\mathbf{T} \neq \varnothing$, be a set of target nodes and let $\mathbf{E} \subset \mathbf{V}_G \setminus \mathbf{T}$ be a set of evidence nodes in G. The parameter sensitivity set for $\mathbf{T}$ given $\mathbf{E}$ is the set*

$$ParSens(\mathbf{T}, \mathbf{E}) = \{X \in \mathbf{V}_G \mid \neg \langle \{P_X\} | \mathbf{E} | \mathbf{T} \rangle_{G^*}^d \}$$

where G^* is the parented graph of G in which each node X has an additional auxiliary parent P_X.

As described by Coupé and Van der Gaag [2], the parent nodes P_X used for defining the parameter sensitivity set can be viewed as capturing the uncertainty in the parameters for the node X. If this uncertainty is not d-separated from the target nodes, it may affect their probability distribution. The authors proved that a sensitivity analysis can be restricted to this parameter sensitivity set.

While a parameter sensitivity analysis addresses the effects of inaccuracies in a network's parameters, a sensitivity-to-evidence analysis focuses on the effects of changes in the observation entered for a node or in a node's observational status [4]. Similar to the parameter sensitivity set, we now develop the concept of evidence sensitivity set as the set of nodes to which an evidence sensitivity analysis can be restricted. We begin by distinguishing between two types of evidence sensitivity set. The given-evidence sensitivity set consists of all observed nodes for which a change in value or in observational status may affect the probability distribution of interest. While the given-evidence sensitivity set includes observed nodes only, the potential-evidence sensitivity set comprises all yet *unobserved* evidence nodes for which obtaining evidence may affect the output distribution. We define the evidence sensitivity sets more formally.

Definition 2. *Let* $G, \mathbf{T}, \mathbf{E}$ *be as before. Then,*

- *the given-evidence sensitivity set for* $\mathbf{T}$ *given* $\mathbf{E}$ *is the set*

$$GivEvSens(\mathbf{T}, \mathbf{E}) = \{X \in \mathbf{E} \mid \neg\langle\{X\}|\mathbf{E}\backslash\{X\}|\mathbf{T}\rangle_G^d\}$$

- *the potential-evidence sensitivity set for* $\mathbf{T}$ *given* $\mathbf{E}$ *is the set*

$$PotEvSens(\mathbf{T}, \mathbf{E}) = \mathbf{T} \cup \{X \in \mathbf{V}_G \setminus \mathbf{E} \mid \neg\langle\{X\}|\mathbf{E}|\mathbf{T}\rangle_G^d\}$$

- *the evidence sensitivity set for* $\mathbf{T}$ *given* $\mathbf{E}$ *is the set*

$$EvSens(\mathbf{T}, \mathbf{E}) = GivEvSens(\mathbf{T}, \mathbf{E}) \cup PotEvSens(\mathbf{T}, \mathbf{E})$$

We note that the given-evidence sensitivity set contains only nodes from the set $\mathbf{E}$ of observed nodes. If such a node $X \in \mathbf{E}$ is not d-separated from a target node given the remaining evidence, then X and $\mathbf{T}$ may be conditionally dependent, and any change in or removal of the observation for X may affect the output probabilities $\Pr(\mathbf{T} \mid \mathbf{e})$. The potential-evidence sensitivity set on the other hand, contains only nodes which are yet *unobserved*. The given-evidence sensitivity set and the potential-evidence sensitivity set thus are disjoint. If an unobserved node $X \notin \mathbf{E}$ is not d-separated from a target node given the available evidence, then X and $\mathbf{T}$ may be conditionally dependent, and entering an observation for X may affect the probabilities $\Pr(\mathbf{T} \mid \mathbf{e})$. Although we could assume that nodes in the target set will never be observed, we include $\mathbf{T}$ in the potential-evidence sensitivity set since observations for nodes in $\mathbf{T}$ most likely affect the probability distribution over the set of target nodes. We further note that all sensitivity sets are defined for a specific $\mathbf{T}$ and $\mathbf{E}$ and may therefore change upon adding or removing an observation. The dynamics involved may then be more complex than just moving nodes between the various sensitivity sets.

Our new concept of evidence sensitivity set is closely related to the concept of parameter sensitivity set, yet is different. The following proposition shows in fact that the parameter sensitivity set is a subset of the evidence sensitivity set.

Proposition 1. *Let* $G, \mathbf{T}, \mathbf{E}$ *be as before. Then,*

(i) $\mathbf{T} \subseteq ParSens(\mathbf{T}, \mathbf{E})$*;*
(ii) $ParSens(\mathbf{T}, \mathbf{E}) \cap \mathbf{E} \subseteq GivEvSens(\mathbf{T}, \mathbf{E})$*;*
(iii) $ParSens(\mathbf{T}, \mathbf{E})\backslash\mathbf{E} \subseteq PotEvSens(\mathbf{T}, \mathbf{E})$*.*

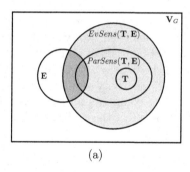 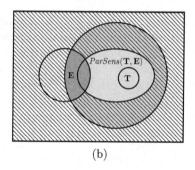

(a)   (b)

Fig. 1. The relations between the various sets. (a) The light grey area indicates the potential-evidence sensitivity set, whereas the dark grey constitutes the given-evidence sensitivity set; (b) the hatched area represents all nodes that can be pruned, i.e. d-separated nodes, barren nodes and irrelevant evidence nodes

Proof

(i) We consider adding an auxiliary parent P_T to a target node $T \in \mathbf{T}$. Since P_T and T are directly connected, we have that $\neg \langle \{P_T\}|\mathbf{E}|\rangle_{G^*}^d$. Therefore, $T \in ParSens(\mathbf{T}, \mathbf{E})$ by definition.

(ii) We consider a node $X \in ParSens(\mathbf{T}, \mathbf{E}) \cap \mathbf{E}$. Since $X \in \mathbf{E}$, the auxiliary parent P_X has active chains only to other parents of X. Since $X \in ParSens(\mathbf{T}, \mathbf{E})$, at least one such parent Y must have an active chain to a target node. As a result, X cannot be d-separated from $\mathbf{T}$ given $\mathbf{E} \backslash \{X\}$.

(iii) We consider a node $X \in ParSens(\mathbf{T}, \mathbf{E}) \backslash \mathbf{E}$. Since P_X is not d-separated from $\mathbf{T}$ given $\mathbf{E}$ in G^*, there must be an active chain from X to $\mathbf{T}$ in G. $\square$

A schematic summary of the above properties is given in Fig. 1(a). The dark grey area represents the intersection of the sensitivity sets with the set of observed nodes $\mathbf{E}$; this area thus coincides with the given-evidence sensitivity set. The light grey area constitutes the potential-evidence sensitivity set; the diagram shows that the set of target nodes is a subset of this set.

3.2 Ignoring Irrelevant Evidence Nodes

The concept of computationally equivalent subgraph was introduced to describe a subgraph of a Bayesian network, with its associated parameters, from which the correct output distribution over the network's target variables can be established. Although the minimal computationally equivalent subgraph identified by Baker and Boult [1], contains no nodes $X \notin \mathbf{T} \cup \mathbf{E}$ that can be pruned, it may contain evidence nodes that are d-separated from the target nodes given the remaining evidence, that is, it may contain evidence nodes outside $GivEvSens(\mathbf{T}, \mathbf{E})$. The identified subgraph thus is not minimal in the sense that no proper subgraph exists from which the output distribution can be correctly established. For the sake of completeness, we define the set of irrelevant evidence nodes and explicitly state the property that these nodes cannot affect the output distribution.

Definition 3. *Let* $G, \mathbf{T}, \mathbf{E}$ *be as before. Then, the irrelevant evidence set for* $\mathbf{T}$ *given* $\mathbf{E}$ *equals*

$$IrrEv(\mathbf{T}, \mathbf{E}) = \{E \in \mathbf{E} \mid \langle \{E\} | \mathbf{E} \backslash \{E\} | \mathbf{T} \rangle_G^d \}$$

The irrelevant evidence nodes together constitute a set of nodes whose parameter probabilities indeed are not required for computing $\Pr(\mathbf{T} \mid \mathbf{E})$.

Proposition 2. *Let* $G, \mathbf{T}, \mathbf{E}$ *be as before. Then,* $\Pr(\mathbf{T} \mid \mathbf{E}) = \Pr(\mathbf{T} \mid \mathbf{E} \backslash IrrEv$ $(\mathbf{T}, \mathbf{E}))$.

Proof. Assuming that $\Pr(\mathbf{E})$ is strictly positive, the proposition is proven by repeated application of the intersection property of independence relations. □

From the above property we conclude that the minimal computationally equivalent subgraph can be further pruned by removing all nodes from $IrrEv(\mathbf{T}, \mathbf{E})$. Moreover, since $IrrEv(\mathbf{T}, \mathbf{E}) = \mathbf{E} \setminus GivEvSens(\mathbf{T}, \mathbf{E})$, the proposition also shows that $\Pr(\mathbf{T} \mid \mathbf{E})$ can indeed be correctly computed by restricting the set of evidence nodes to $GivEvSens(\mathbf{T}, \mathbf{E})$.

3.3   Relating the Different Sets

We now establish the relationship between the various sensitivity sets and well-known types of irrelevant node.

Proposition 3. *Let* $G, \mathbf{T}, \mathbf{E}$ *be as before. Then,*

(i) $DSep(\mathbf{T}, \mathbf{E}) = V_G \setminus (EvSens(\mathbf{T}, \mathbf{E}) \cup \mathbf{E})$;
(ii) $Barren(\mathbf{T}, \mathbf{E}) = PotEvSens(\mathbf{T}, \mathbf{E}) \setminus ParSens(\mathbf{T}, \mathbf{E})$;

Proof

(i) The set $DSep(\mathbf{T}, \mathbf{E})$ contains all nodes $X \in V_G \backslash (\mathbf{T} \cup \mathbf{E})$ such that $\langle \{X\} | \mathbf{E} | \mathbf{T} \rangle_G^d$. By definition, this set equals $\mathbf{V}_G \setminus (PotEvSens(\mathbf{T}, \mathbf{E}) \cup \mathbf{E})$, and corresponds with the white area *outside* the circles in Fig. 1(a).
(ii) Barren nodes are unobserved nodes that are not d-separated from the target nodes given the evidence, yet are not involved in the computation of the output distribution over these nodes; once observed however (directly or indirectly), barren nodes can become computationally relevant. □

For computing the output distribution $\Pr(\mathbf{T} \mid \mathbf{E})$ over the target nodes $\mathbf{T}$ of a Bayesian network, we can safely prune all nodes from $DSep(\mathbf{T}, \mathbf{E}) \cup Barren(\mathbf{T}, \mathbf{E}) \cup IrrEv(\mathbf{T}, \mathbf{E})$. From the above proposition we find that this set equals:

$$\mathbf{V}_G \setminus (ParSens(\mathbf{T}, \mathbf{E}) \cup (\mathbf{E} \backslash IrrEv(\mathbf{T}, \mathbf{E})))$$,

where $\mathbf{E} \backslash IrrEv(\mathbf{T}, \mathbf{E})$ equals $GivEvSens(\mathbf{T}, \mathbf{E})$. We can therefore prune all nodes from $\mathbf{V}_G$ except those in $ParSens(\mathbf{T}, \mathbf{E}) \cup GivEvSens(\mathbf{T}, \mathbf{E})$; this set of nodes is illustrated in Fig. 1(b).

4   Identifying (Ir)relevant Nodes

Many Bayesian network properties can be recognised just by inspecting the network's graph. Core d-separation statements, for example, can be verified in time linear to the size of the graph. A well-known algorithm for this purpose is the *Bayes-ball algorithm* [9]. Although this algorithm was not designed for establishing sensitivity sets as defined in the previous section, we will demonstrate that the information maintained by the algorithm suffices for identifying these sets. We will subsequently illustrate all concepts introduced in this paper, as well as their potential use, by means of an example.

4.1   Bayes-Ball for Sensitivity Sets

The Bayes-ball algorithm was designed to identify various sets of relevant and irrelevant nodes. The algorithm explores the graph of a Bayesian network in view of an output distribution $\Pr(\mathbf{T} \mid \mathbf{E})$ over its target nodes. It starts from these target nodes and "bounces a ball" through the graph, respecting d-separation properties. Visited nodes are marked as such, and in addition get a top or bottom mark when their parents or children, respectively, are scheduled for a visit. Initially, all target nodes are marked on top and at the bottom; evidence nodes, if visited, can receive a top mark only. After exploring the graph, the algorithm establishes the following sets of nodes, based on the marks received:

- $N_i(\mathbf{T} \mid \mathbf{E}) = \{X \in \mathbf{V}_G \mid X \text{ is not marked at the bottom}\}$;
- $N_p(\mathbf{T} \mid \mathbf{E}) = \{X \in \mathbf{V}_G \mid X \text{ is marked on top}\}$;
- $N_e(\mathbf{T} \mid \mathbf{E}) = \{X \in \mathbf{E} \mid X \text{ is marked as visited}\}$.

The set $N_i(\mathbf{T} \mid \mathbf{E})$, termed the set of *irrelevant nodes*, includes all d-separated nodes [9]. We note that the algorithm includes all evidence nodes in the set of irrelevant nodes as well. Evidence nodes in general are not irrelevant to the computation at hand, however, with the exception of nodes in $IrrEv(\mathbf{T}, \mathbf{E})$. The set $N_p(\mathbf{T} \mid \mathbf{E})$, called the set of *requisite probability nodes*, includes the nodes whose parameters are needed for the computation of the output probability; we note that the adjective 'requisite' refers to the node's parameter probabilities. The set $N_e(\mathbf{T} \mid \mathbf{E})$, coined the set of *requisite observation nodes*, includes the evidence nodes whose value is required for the computations. A computationally equivalent subgraph for the computations can now be obtained from the original Bayesian network by pruning all nodes outside the set $N_p(\mathbf{T} \mid \mathbf{E}) \cup N_e(\mathbf{T} \mid \mathbf{E})$.

The sensitivity sets defined and reviewed in the previous section can be readily identified from the information recorded by the Bayes-ball algorithm as stated in the following proposition; for a formal proof of the proposition, we refer to [6].

Proposition 4. *Let $G, \mathbf{T}, \mathbf{E}$ be as before. Consider running Bayes-ball on G with respect to $\Pr(\mathbf{T} \mid \mathbf{E})$. Then,*

- *$ParSens(\mathbf{T}, \mathbf{E}) = \{X \in \mathbf{V}_G \mid X \text{ is marked on top}\}$;*
- *$GivEvSens(\mathbf{T}, \mathbf{E}) = \{X \in \mathbf{E} \mid X \text{ is marked as visited}\}$;*

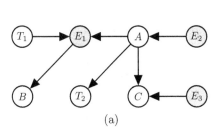
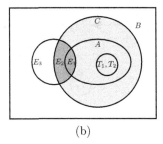

$$(a) \qquad\qquad\qquad\qquad (b)$$

Fig. 2. (a) The digraph of the example Bayesian network, and (b) the sensitivity sets for $Pr(\mathbf{T} \mid \mathbf{E})$

- $PotEvSens(\mathbf{T}, \mathbf{E}) = \{X \in \mathbf{V}_G \mid X \text{ is marked at the bottom}\};$
- $IrrEv(\mathbf{T}, \mathbf{E}) = \{X \in \mathbf{E} \mid X \text{ is not marked as visited}\}.$

The proposition reveals that the different sensitivity sets identified in the previous section actually provide alternative semantics for the three Bayes-ball sets:

- $N_i(\mathbf{T} \mid \mathbf{E}) = \mathbf{V}_G \setminus PotEvSens(\mathbf{T}, \mathbf{E});$
- $N_p(\mathbf{T} \mid \mathbf{E}) = ParSens(\mathbf{T}, \mathbf{E});$
- $N_e(\mathbf{T} \mid \mathbf{E}) = GivEvSens(\mathbf{T}, \mathbf{E}).$

4.2 An Example

To illustrate the use of the various relevance sets introduced in Sect. 3, we consider an example Bayesian network defining a joint probability distribution over eight nodes; the graph of the network is shown in Fig. 2(a). For the network, we consider output probability distributions $Pr(\mathbf{T} \mid \mathbf{E})$ for the target nodes $\mathbf{T} = \{T_1, T_2\}$ given observations for the evidence nodes $\mathbf{E} = \{E_1, E_2, E_3\}$. Using Bayes-ball, we find the following sensitivity sets, summarised in Fig. 2(b):

- $ParSens(\mathbf{T}, \mathbf{E}) = \{A, E_1, T_1, T_2\};$
- $PotEvSens(\mathbf{T}, \mathbf{E}) = \{A, C, T_1, T_2\};$
- $GivEvSens(\mathbf{T}, \mathbf{E}) = \{E_1, E_2\}.$

We recall that the parameter sensitivity set was designed to describe the nodes in a Bayesian network whose parameter inaccuracies may affect the output probabilities from the network. For the example network, we conclude that only changes in the parameter probabilities of the nodes A, E_1, T_1 and T_2 may influence the probabilities $Pr(\mathbf{T} \mid \mathbf{E})$. A parameter sensitivity analysis may thus be restricted to the parameters for these nodes and forego variation of the parameters of the nodes B, C, E_2 and E_3, that is, the parameters of only half of the nodes need be investigated upon the analysis.

The evidence sensitivity set captures the nodes for which a change of value or in observational status may affect the output probabilities established from

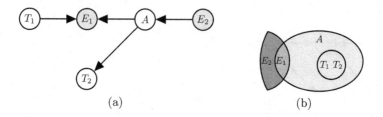

Fig. 3. (a) Graph of the example network after pruning all nodes outside $ParSens(\mathbf{T}, \mathbf{E}) \cup (\mathbf{E} \backslash IrrEv(\mathbf{T}, \mathbf{E}))$, and (b) a summary of the pruning result

the network. In the example network, only the evidence nodes E_1 and E_2 are contained in the given-evidence sensitivity set for $\mathbf{T}$ given $\mathbf{E}$. Changing their observed value, or removing their observations, may therefore change the output probabilities $\Pr(\mathbf{T} \mid \mathbf{E})$. Since node E_3 is not included in the given-evidence sensitivity set, we can change or remove its observation, without affecting the output probabilities. The network's output therefore is robust against an inaccurate observation for E_3. The potential-evidence sensitivity set for $\mathbf{T}$ given $\mathbf{E}$ provides information about the effects of additional evidence. The potential-evidence sensitivity set established from the example network shows that obtaining additional evidence for one of the nodes A, C, T_1 and T_2 may change the output. Since node B is not in the set, gathering an observation for this node cannot change the current distribution over $\mathbf{T}$. We note that such a finding may be exploited by a test-selection procedure. In fact, test selection can focus on collecting evidence for the nodes A and C, if appropriate.

The resulting computationally equivalent subgraph is shown in Fig. 3(a), along with a schematic summary of the roles of the remaining nodes (b). We would like to emphasize that as a result of the dynamics of the various sets upon changes in the observational status of nodes, a change in $\mathbf{E}$ may require a differently pruned graph. For example, if an observation would be entered for node C, the parameters of node E_3 would no longer be immaterial for the output distribution over the target nodes. We further note that the various sets of relevant nodes identified above can be instrumental in focusing the efforts of a large variety of inference tasks. We note for example that the above conclusions also pertain to MAP computations, that is, for establishing $\mathrm{MAP}(\mathbf{T}, \mathbf{e}) = \mathrm{argmax}_{\mathbf{t}} \Pr(\mathbf{t} \mid \mathbf{e})$ for a specific assignment $\mathbf{e}$ to $\mathbf{E}$: taking the output of the Bayes-ball algorithm in fact, we know that we can safely prune the nodes $\{B, C, E_3\}$ from the network without affecting the established MAP.

5 Conclusions and Future Research

Relevance of the nodes of a Bayesian network had so far been studied primarily in the context of probabilistic inference. In this paper we focused on a network's evidence nodes and addressed their relevance for such tasks as sensitivity-to-evidence analysis and diagnostic test selection. To this end, we defined two types of evidence sensitivity set and studied the relationships between these sets and with previously known sets of (ir)relevant nodes. We thereby presented a more complete picture of the relevance of various node sets for answering questions concerning inference and analysis in Bayesian network applications. By demonstrating that our evidence sensitivity sets can be determined from the well-known Bayes-ball algorithm, moreover, we provided an efficient way of establishing these sets from graphical considerations only.

The various relevance sets discussed in this paper are not static in a Bayesian network application, but will change dynamically as the set of observed nodes changes. More extensive sensitivity-to-evidence analyses and test-selection procedures therefore entail re-establishing the relevance sets after each change in observational status. In the near future we would like to study the dynamics involved and investigate whether we can predict, at least partly, how these sets will change without having to re-invoke the Bayes-ball algorithm. We would further like to extend our investigations and study the concept of relevance for yet other computational tasks in Bayesian network applications.

References

1. Baker, M., Boult, T.: Pruning Bayesian networks for efficient computation. In: Bonissone, P.P., Henrion, M., Kanal, L.N., Lemmer, J.F. (eds.) Uncertainty in Artificial Intelligence 6, pp. 225–232. Elsevier Science, Amsterdam (1991)
2. Coupé, V.M.H., van der Gaag, L.C.: Properties of sensitivity analysis of Bayesian belief networks. Ann. Math. Artif. Intell. **36**(4), 323–356 (2002)
3. Druzdzel, M., Suermondt, H.: Relevance in probabilistic models: "backyards" in a "small world". In: Working Notes of the AAAI 1994 Fall Symposium Series: Relevance, pp. 60–63 (1994)
4. Jensen, F.V., Aldenryd, S.H., Jensen, K.B.: Sensitivity analysis in Bayesian networks. In: Froidevaux, C., Kohlas, J. (eds.) ECSQARU 1995. LNCS, vol. 946, pp. 243–250. Springer, Heidelberg (1995)
5. Jensen, F.V., Nielsen, T.D.: Bayesian Networks and Decision Graphs. Springer, New York (2007)
6. Meekes, M.: Sensitivity to evidence in probabilistic networks. Master's thesis, Faculty of Science, Utrecht University (2013)
7. Park, J., Darwiche, A.: Complexity results and approximation strategies for MAP explanations. J. Artif. Intell. Res. **21**, 101–133 (2004)
8. Pearl, J.: Probabilistic Reasoning in Intelligent Systems: Networks of Plausible Inference. Morgan Kaufmann Publishers, San Mateo (1988)
9. Shachter, R.: Bayes-ball: The rational pastime (for determining irrelevance and requisite information in belief networks and influence diagrams). In: Cooper, G., Moral, S. (eds.) Proceedings of the Fourteenth Conference on Uncertainty in Artificial Intelligence, pp. 480–487. Morgan Kaufmann, San Francisco (1998)

Hybrid Time Bayesian Networks

Manxia Liu[1]([✉]), Arjen Hommersom[1,2], Maarten van der Heijden[1],
and Peter J.F. Lucas[1]

[1] ICIS, Radboud University, Nijmegen, The Netherlands
{m.liu,arjenh,m.vanderheijden,peterl}@cs.ru.nl
[2] Open University, Heerlen, The Netherlands

Abstract. Capturing heterogeneous dynamic systems in a probabilistic model is a challenging problem. A single time granularity, such as employed by dynamic Bayesian networks, provides insufficient flexibility to capture the dynamics of many real-world processes. The alternative is to assume that time is continuous, giving rise to continuous time Bayesian networks. Here the problem is that the level of temporal detail is too precise to match available probabilistic knowledge. In this paper, we present a novel class of models, called hybrid time Bayesian networks, which combine discrete-time and continuous-time Bayesian networks. The new formalism allows us to more naturally model dynamic systems with regular and irregularly changing variables. Its usefulness is illustrated by means of a real-world medical problem.

Keywords: Continuous time Bayesian networks · Dynamic Bayesian networks · Dynamic systems

1 Introduction

Many real-world systems exhibit complex and rich dynamic behavior. As a consequence, capturing these dynamics is an integral part of developing models of physical-world systems. Time granularity is an important parameter in characterizing dynamics as it determines the level of temporal detail in the model. In cases where one time granularity is coarser than another, dealing with multiple time granularities becomes significantly important, e.g., in the context of mining frequent patterns and temporal relationship in data stream and databases [1].

Dynamic Bayesian networks (DBNs) are a general framework for modeling dynamic probabilistic systems. DBNs are an extension of standard Bayesian networks (BNs) assuming a discretization of time [2], and where the distribution of variables at a particular time point is conditional on the state of the system at the previous time point. A problem occurs if temporal processes of a system are best described using different rates of change, e.g., one temporal part of the process changes much faster than another. In that case, the whole system

---

ML is supported by China Scholarship Council. AH and MVDH are supported by the ITEA2 MoSHCA project (ITEA2-ip11027).

© Springer International Publishing Switzerland 2015
S. Destercke and T. Denoeux (Eds.): ECSQARU 2015, LNAI 9161, pp. 376–386, 2015.
DOI: 10.1007/978-3-319-20807-7_34

has to be represented using the finest time granularity, which is undesirable from a modeling and learning perspective. In particular, if a variable is observed irregularly, much data on discrete-time points will be missing and conditional probabilities will be hard to estimate.

As an alternative to DBNs, temporal processes can be modeled as continuous time Bayesian networks (CTBNs), where time acts as a continuous parameter [3]. In these models, the time granularity is infinitely small by modeling transition rates rather than conditional probabilities, thus multiple time granularities, i.e., slow and fast transition rates, can easily be captured. A limitation from a modeling perspective is that all probabilistic knowledge, for example derived from expert knowledge, has to be mapped to transition rates which are hard to interpret. Moreover, the transition rates assume that the time until a transition is exponentially distributed, which may not always be appropriate.

In this paper, we propose a new formalism, which we call hybrid time Bayesian networks (HTBNs), inspired by discrete-time and continuous-time Bayesian networks. They facilitate modeling the dynamics of both irregularly-timed random variables and random variables which are naturally described in a discrete way. As a result, the new formalism increases the modeling and analysis capabilities for dynamic systems.

2   Motivating Example

To illustrate the usefulness of the proposed theory, we consider the medical problem of heart failure and, in particular, one possible cause of heart failure: heart attack (myocardial infarction). This usually occurs as the result of coronary artery disease giving rise to reduced blood supply to the heart muscle (myocardium). One consequence is that part of the heart muscle will die, which is revealed later in a blood sample analysis in the lab by an increased level of particular heart muscle proteins, in particular troponine. Loss of heart muscle will inevitably have an impact on the contractability of the myocardium, and thus heart function will be negatively affected. This is known as *heart failure*. In particular, the heart fails with respect to its function as a pump. This will enforce an increase in the amount of extracellular fluid (the patient is flooded with water), which can be measured quite simply by means of the body weight. With regard to treatment, digitalis is considered as one of the drugs to improve contractability. This causal knowledge is formalized as a directed graph in Fig. 1.

Heart attacks usually happen repeatedly in patients, although after some interval of time, and this may negatively affect heart function. After administration of digitalis it will take some time, in terms of days, before the drug has a diminishing effect on heart failure. Thus, the course of heart failure will likely depend on various factors, and how they interact. Of particular importance here is the dynamic over time of the probability distributions.

In modeling processes such as heart failure, it is essential to notice the existence of different time granularities. There are *discrete, regular* variables which are observed regularly such as a routine checkup for body weight and a regular

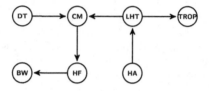

Fig. 1. Causal model for heart failure: CM = Contractility Myocardium, DT = Digitalis, LHT = Loss Heart Tissues, HA = Heart Attack, TROP = Troponine, HF = Heart Failure, BW = Body Weight.

intake of a drug. On the other hand, some variables are observed *irregularly*, such as the indicator troponine which is elevated after about half an hour after damage to the heart muscle is obtained; however its measurement is repeated with time intervals that increase after the patient's condition has been stabilized. Clearly, it is not possible to obtain a satisfactory representation of the clinical evolution of heart failure using only discrete time, regular or irregular, or continuous time. In the remainder of this paper we propose a method to deal with these heterogeneous time aspects.

3 Preliminaries

We start by introducing Bayesian networks, dynamic Bayesian networks and continuous time Bayesian networks. In the following, upper-case letters, e.g. X, Y, or upper-case strings, e.g. HA, denote random variables. We denote the values of a variable by lower-case letters, e.g. x. We will also make use of a successor function s, which is defined on a countable, linearly ordered set of numbers Z in which every element $z_i \in Z$ with index i is mapped to element $s(z_i) = z_{i+1} \in Z$.

Bayesian Networks. A Bayesian network is a probabilistic graphical model which represents a joint probability distribution of a set of random variables. A *Bayesian network* $\mathcal{B}$ is defined as a pair $\mathcal{B} = (G, P)$, where G is an acyclic directed graph with $G = (V(G), E(G))$, where $V(G)$ is a set of nodes, and $E(G) \subseteq V(G) \times V(G)$ a set of directed edges or arcs. A joint probability distribution P is defined by a set of conditional probabilities of each random variable X given its immediate parents $\pi(X)$ in G, formally: $P(V(G)) = \prod_{X \in V(G)} P(X \mid \pi(X))$.

Dynamic Bayesian Networks (DBNs). A DBN is defined as a pair $(\mathcal{B}_0, \mathcal{B}_\rightarrow)$ over discrete-time variables $\mathbf{D}$, where $\mathcal{B}_0$ is taken as the initial Bayesian network model and $\mathcal{B}_\rightarrow$ is defined as a conditional distribution for a 2-time-slice Bayesian network (2-TBN). Given a set of discrete time points of interest $A \subseteq \mathbb{N}_0$ that includes 0, the joint distribution for a DBN with $|A|$ slices is defined by a product of the CPDs in the initial model and in the 2-TBN:

$$P(\mathbf{D}_A) = \prod_{D \in \mathbf{D}} P_{\mathcal{B}_0}(D_0 \mid \pi(D_0)) \prod_{D \in \mathbf{D}} \prod_{\alpha \in A \setminus \{\max A\}} P_{\mathcal{B}_\rightarrow}(D_{s(\alpha)} \mid \pi(D_{s(\alpha)}))$$

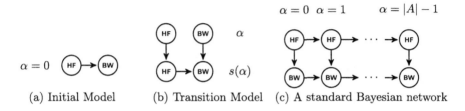

$$\alpha = 0 \quad \alpha = 1 \qquad \alpha = |A| - 1$$

(a) Initial Model   (b) Transition Model   (c) A standard Bayesian network

Fig. 2. A DBN and its corresponding Bayesian network.

where $D_{s(\alpha)}$ is the random variable D at time $s(\alpha)$. Parent set $\pi(D_{s(\alpha)})$ may be from the same or the previous time slice. We can obtain a standard Bayesian network by unrolling the DBN over the time points of interest. In the remainder it is assumed that the intra-slice arcs of this BN are the same for every α.

Example 1. Consider a dynamic Bayesian network that has two random variables, HF and BW (see Fig. 1), with an initial model and a transition model as shown in Figs. 2a and 2b, respectively. Then the joint distribution for the DBN over time points of interest A with the corresponding Bayesian network as shown in Fig. 2c is: $P(\mathrm{HF}_A, \mathrm{BW}_A) = P(\mathrm{HF}_0)P(\mathrm{BW}_0 \mid \mathrm{HF}_0) \prod_{\alpha=0}^{|A|-2} P(\mathrm{BW}_{s(\alpha)} \mid \mathrm{BW}_\alpha, \mathrm{HF}_{s(\alpha)})P(\mathrm{HF}_{s(\alpha)} \mid \mathrm{HF}_\alpha)$.

Continuous Time Bayesian Networks (CTBNs). CTBNs [3] represent dynamic systems with continuous-time variables as a factorized homogeneous Markov process parameterized by *intensity matrices*. An entry (i, j) with $i \neq j$ in an intensity matrix gives the intensity of transitioning from state i to state j. Furthermore, the main diagonal makes each row sum to zero.

Example 2. Suppose we want to model the random process of body weight as the variable BW, which describes a patient's weight. Variable BW has three possible states, i.e., BW = {low, normal, high}, with a transition matrix as follows:

$$Q_{\mathrm{BW}} = \begin{pmatrix} -0.13 & 0.09 & 0.04 \\ 0.13 & -0.23 & 0.1 \\ 0.07 & 0.16 & -0.23 \end{pmatrix}$$

For example, the entry $(3, 2)$ means that the process will transition from high at time β to normal at time $\beta + \epsilon$ with a probability of $0.16/0.23{=}0.696$ if a transition occurs at $\beta + \epsilon$.

The notion of a *conditional intensity matrix (CIM)* describes the dependence of a variable C on the current values of its parents $\pi(C)$. A *full amalgamation* product operator is defined over a set of CIMs to compute the joint intensity matrix, resulting in a single continuous-time Markov process for the entire system.

For a homogeneous Markov process over variables $\mathbf{C}$ with an intensity matrix $Q_{\mathbf{C}}$ and an initial distribution $P(\mathbf{C}_0)$, we can compute the distribution over the values of $\mathbf{C}$ at a particular time point or the joint distribution at different time points. The distribution at a point β is given by:

$$P(\mathbf{C}_\beta) = P(\mathbf{C}_0) \exp(Q_{\mathbf{C}}\beta)$$

The distribution over a finite set of time points of interest B is given by:

$$P(\mathbf{C}_B) = P(\mathbf{C}_0) \prod_{\beta \in B \setminus \{\max B\}} \exp(Q_{\mathbf{C}}(s(\beta) - \beta))$$

4   Hybrid Time Bayesian Networks

In this section, we define hybrid-time Bayesian networks, the semantics of these models in terms of its factorization, and finally, we show how such models can be interpreted as regular Bayesian networks. The latter is particularly important for practical purposes, as this implies that we may (dynamically) generate discrete-time versions of the model given time points for which we have observations, and in which we would like to compute marginals. After that, we can use existing methods for probabilistic inference in BNs.

4.1   Model Definition

The formal definition of hybrid time Bayesian networks is as follows.

Definition 1 (Hybrid Time Bayesian Networks (HTBNs)). *A hybrid time Bayesian network is a triple $\mathcal{H} = (G, \Phi, \Lambda)$, where $G = (V(G), E^t(G), E^a(G))$ is a directed graph with each vertex in $V(G)$ either a continuous-time variable, collectively denoted by $\mathbf{C}$, or a discrete-time variable, collectively denoted by $\mathbf{D}$, $E^t(G)$ and $E^a(G)$ are temporal and atemporal arcs, respectively, such that $(V(G), E^a(G))$ is acyclic, Φ is a set of conditional probability distributions for variables $\mathbf{D}$, and Λ is a set of conditional intensity matrices and initial distributions for variables $\mathbf{C}$.*

Furthermore, graph G has the following properties:

(i) Arcs connecting continuous-time and discrete-time variables are atemporal;
(ii) Arcs connecting continuous-time variables are temporal;
(iii) A continuous-time variable has a temporal arc to itself.

Property *(iii)* indicates that a discrete-time variable does not necessarily have temporal dependences on itself. It is worthwhile to notice that the temporal cyclic property is inherited from discrete-time and continuous-time Bayesian networks. A temporal cycle is possible in two cases, either between continuous-time variables or between discrete-time variables. However, an atemporal cycle is not allowed, that is, there is no cycle in the graph involving both continuous-time and discrete-time variables.

Example 3. In the example discussed in Sect. 2, regular variables, i.e., BW, DT, HF and hidden variable CM can be represented in a discrete-time manner. The irregular variables, i.e., LHT, TROP, HA are modeled as continuous-time variables. The example is then represented in a hybrid time Bayesian network $\mathcal{H}$ as shown in Fig. 3.

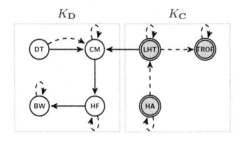

Fig. 3. An HTBN for the heart failure problem. Continuous-time variables are graphically represented by double-edged blue circles, atemporal arcs are solid, and temporal arcs are dashed.

4.2 Factorization

The joint probability distribution for hybrid time Bayesian networks is defined by multiplying the conditional joint probabilities for continuous-time and discrete-time Bayesian networks. To this end, we first need to introduce some new notions.

The *skeleton* $G^\sim$ of a directed graph G is obtained by changing the arcs in G by (undirected) edges. Every directed graph can be defined as the union of *connected components* by an equivalence relation $X - Y$, meaning that vertex Y can be reached by an undirected path from vertex X in its skeleton. Vertex X and Y are then members of the same equivalence class $[X]$ and the corresponding graph is a connected component. A graph $G' = (V(G'), E(G'))$ is said to be an *induced subgraph* of G if $E(G') = (V(G') \times V(G')) \cap E^t(G)$ and $V(G') = \mathbf{C}$, called a *continuous-time induced subgraph*, denoted as $G_{\mathbf{C}}$, or $E(G') = (V(G') \times V(G')) \cap (E^t(G) \cup E^a(G))$ and $V(G') = \mathbf{D}$, when it is called a *discrete-time induced subgraph*, denoted as $G_{\mathbf{D}}$.

Both $G_{\mathbf{C}}$ and $G_{\mathbf{D}}$ can be decomposed into connected components; each individual connected component is indicated by $K_{\mathbf{C}}$ and $K_{\mathbf{D}}$, respectively. Clearly connected components are disjoint as they represent equivalence classes and together the connected components form partitions of the continuous-time and discrete-time subgraphs, respectively. A subset $\mathbf{X} \subseteq V(G_{\mathbf{D}})$ is said to constitute the parents of $V(K_{\mathbf{C}})$, denoted as $\pi(V(K_{\mathbf{C}}))$, if and only if there exists an arc (D, C) in G, $C \in V(K_{\mathbf{C}})$, for every $D \in \mathbf{X}$. Parents $\pi(V(K_{\mathbf{D}}))$ are defined analogously. In the example shown in Fig. 3, there is only one continuous-time connected component with $V(K_{\mathbf{C}}) = \{\text{LHT}, \text{TROP}, \text{HA}\}$ and one discrete-time connected component with $V(K_{\mathbf{D}}) = \{\text{DT}, \text{CM}, \text{HF}, \text{BW}\}$.

We are now in the position to define a conditional distribution of connected components given their parents.

Definition 2 (Conditional Joint Distribution for Component $K_{\mathbf{D}}$). *Given a discrete-time component $K_{\mathbf{D}}$, the conditional joint distribution for $K_{\mathbf{D}}$ over time points of interest A is defined as:*

$$P(V(K_{\mathbf{D}})_A \mid \pi(V(K_{\mathbf{D}}))_A) = \prod_{D \in V(K_{\mathbf{D}})} (P(D_0 \mid \pi^a(D)_0) \prod_{\alpha \in A \setminus \{0\}} P(D_\alpha \mid \pi^a(D)_\alpha, \pi^t(D)_{\alpha-1}))$$

where $\pi^t(D)$ are the temporal and $\pi^a(D)$ are the atemporal parents of D.

Definition 3 (Conditional Joint Distribution for Component $K_{\mathbf{C}}$).
Given a continuous-time component $K_{\mathbf{C}}$ over variables $V(K_{\mathbf{C}})$ with an initial distribution $P(V(K_{\mathbf{C}})_0)$ and corresponding parents $\pi(V(K_{\mathbf{C}}))$ over time points of interest A. The conditional joint distribution for $K_{\mathbf{C}}$ over a finite set of time points of interest B, $\{0\} \subset A \subseteq B \subset \mathbb{R}^+$, is defined as:

$$P(V(K_{\mathbf{C}})_B \mid \pi(V(K_{\mathbf{C}}))_A)$$
$$= P(V(K_{\mathbf{C}})_0) \prod_{\beta \in B \setminus \{\max B\}} \exp(Q_{V(K_{\mathbf{C}}) \mid \pi(V(K_{\mathbf{C}}))_a}(s(\beta) - \beta))$$

$$a = \max\{\alpha \mid \alpha \leq \beta, \alpha \in A\}$$

where $Q_{V(K_{\mathbf{C}}) \mid \pi(V(K_{\mathbf{C}}))_a}$ is the conditional intensity matrix for variables $V(K_{\mathbf{C}})$ given the values of parents $\pi(V(K_{\mathbf{C}}))$ at time a.

Now we can define the full joint probability distribution of a hybrid-time BN given sets of time points of interest.

Definition 4 (Joint Probability Distribution). *Given a hybrid time Bayesian network $\mathcal{H}$ and sets of components $K_{\mathbf{D}}$, $K_{\mathbf{C}}$ with associated time points of interest A, B. The joint distribution for $\mathcal{H}$ over B is defined as:*

$$P(V(G)_B) = \prod_{K_{\mathbf{C}} \in K_{\mathbf{C}}} P(V(K_{\mathbf{C}})_B \mid \pi(V(K_{\mathbf{C}}))_A) \prod_{K_{\mathbf{D}} \in K_{\mathbf{D}}} P(V(K_{\mathbf{D}})_A \mid \pi(V(K_{\mathbf{D}}))_A)$$

The following propositions establish that HTBNs are proper generalizations of both DBNs and CTBNs.

Proposition 1. *A DBN $(\mathcal{B}_0, \mathcal{B}_\rightarrow)$ with random variables $\mathbf{D}$, and an HTBN $(G, \Phi, \varnothing)$ define the same joint probability distribution for any set of time points of interest A, if $V(G) = \mathbf{D}$; $E^a(G)$, $E^t(G)$ correspond to the temporal and atemporal arcs of $\mathcal{B}_\rightarrow$, and Φ are the parameters of the DBN.*

Proposition 2. *A CTBN with graph G and parameters Λ and an HTBN $(G, \varnothing, \Lambda)$ define the same probability distribution for any set of time points of interest B.*

4.3　Discrete-Time Characterization

A natural question is whether the joint distribution defined on a HTBN, given the fixed time points of interest, can also be graphically represented as a regular (discrete-time) Bayesian network. The benefit is that the parameters of the resulting Bayesian network are conditional probabilities, which are easier to understand for domain experts. Furthermore, this construction is convenient as it enables the use of standard software for inference in HTBNs.

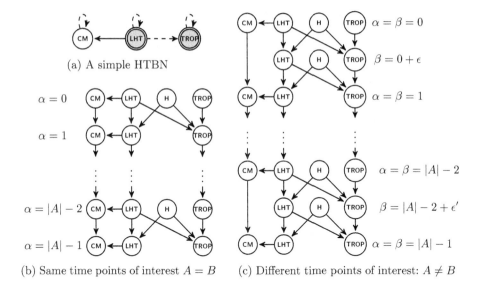

(a) A simple HTBN

(b) Same time points of interest $A = B$

(c) Different time points of interest: $A \neq B$

Fig. 4. Discretization of an HTBN.

Below we show that there is a construction to a regular Bayesian network possibly at the expense of introducing additional hidden variables that model the dependence structure of continuous-time variables. The reason for these hidden variables is as follows. Consider a simple structure $X \rightarrow Y \rightarrow Z$. In a regular Bayesian network, it holds that Z is independent of X given its parent Y. Interpreting this graph as a continuous-time component (where arcs are temporal), a continuous-time variable is conditionally independent of its non-descendants given the full trajectories of its parents. In the structure given, we thus can only conclude that Z at time β is independent of X given the full trajectory for Y from time 0 to time β, otherwise X and Z are dependent. In order to represent this, we introduce additional dependences between X and Z at each time point of interest using auxiliary hidden variables. We illustrate the process in Fig. 4.

Proposition 3 (Discretization). *Given a hybrid time Bayesian network $\mathcal{H}$ described by a graph G with associated probability distribution P and time points of interest, there exists a Bayesian network $\mathcal{B} = (G_{\mathcal{B}}, P_{\mathcal{B}})$, $P_{\mathcal{B}}(V(G)) = P(V(G))$, which represents all independences of $\mathcal{H}$.*

Proof (Sketch). We only show the construction of this Bayesian network $\mathcal{B}$.

Let $G_{\mathcal{B}} = (V(G_{\mathcal{B}}), E(G_{\mathcal{B}}))$. Set $V(G_{\mathcal{B}})$ are variables mapped from variables V. Set $V(G_{\mathcal{B}})$ is composed of three parts, i.e., $V(G_{\mathcal{B}}) = \Delta \cup \Omega \cup \Theta$, where: 1) Δ are variables $\mathbf{D}$ induced by time points A, 2) Ω are variables $\mathbf{C}$ induced by time points B, 3) Θ are hidden variables induced by temporal dependence between continuous-time variables and time points of interest B, $\Theta = \{H_{\beta}^{ij} \mid (C^i, C^j) \in E^t, \beta \in B\}$, where H_{β}^{ij} models the dependence between variable C^i and C^j.

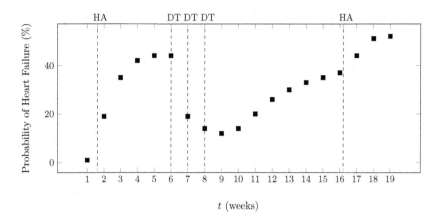

Fig. 5. Effects of heart attack and digitalis on heart failure. 'DT' indicates that digitalis was administered at that moment in time. 'HA' indicates that a heart attack was observed. Note that observations for HA are continuous-time, so observed at an arbitrary point in time; digitalis is observed once a week at most.

Set $E(G_{\mathcal{B}})$ are arcs mapped from E^a and E^t, $E(G_{\mathcal{B}}) \subseteq V(G_{\mathcal{B}}) \times V(G_{\mathcal{B}})$. Basically, the dependence mapping can be categorized by the type of dependences and variables, denoted as $E(G_{\mathcal{B}}) = \Xi \cup \Pi \cup \Upsilon \cup \Gamma$, where: (1) Ξ models the dependence for discrete-time child while its parents could be continuous-time or discrete-time, specified as $\Xi = \{(X_\alpha, D_\alpha) \mid X \in \mathbf{C} \cup \mathbf{D}, (X, D) \in E^a, \alpha \in A\}$, (2) The atemporal dependence for continuous-time variables conditioned on discrete-time parents is specified as $\Pi = \{(D_a, C_\beta) \mid (D, C) \in E^a, \beta \in B\}$, where $a = \max\{\alpha \mid \alpha < \beta, \alpha \in A\}$, (3) Temporal dependences for variables $\mathbf{C}$ and $\mathbf{D}$ are denoted as Υ: $\Upsilon = \{(C_\beta, C_{s(\beta)}) \mid \beta \in B \setminus \{\max B\}\} \cup \{(D_\alpha, D_{s(\alpha)}) \mid (D, D) \in E^t, \alpha \in A \setminus \{\max A\}\}$, 4) Γ are additional dependences for continuous-time variables, $\Gamma = \{(H_\beta^{ij}, C_{s(\beta)}^i), (H_\beta^{ij}, C_{s(\beta)}^j) \mid H_\beta^{ij} \in \Theta, \beta \in B \setminus \{\max B\}\} \cup \{(C_\beta^i, C_{s(\beta)}^j) \mid \beta \in B \setminus \{\max B\}\}$. Thus we have a graph $G_{\mathcal{B}} = (V(G_{\mathcal{B}}), E(G_{\mathcal{B}}))$.

It can be shown that G and $G_{\mathcal{B}}$ represent the same independences on $V(G)$ on the points of interest. Also, the parameters for $\mathcal{B}$ can be derived from $\mathcal{H}$. $\square$

5   Experiments

The power of HTBNs is illustrated in the domain of myocardial contractability in relationship to heart attack, heart failure and its medical treatment, introduced in Sect. 2 and summarized in Fig. 3. In particular, of interest is the question of how the dynamics of the occurrence of heart failure is affected by heart attacks and the administration of digitalis. As discussed in Sect. 2, a single DBN and CTBN can not provide a satisfactory representation of the evolution of variables with different rates: changes in the occurrence of heart failure happen often, in contrast to the more sparse and irregular occurrence of heart attacks.

We parameterized the model using medical expert knowledge given that discrete-time transitions occur weekly. Then, we computed the probability distribution of heart failure for a period of 19 weeks given the observed (regular or irregular) evidence. Results of this experiment are plotted in Fig. 5. The plot shows the negative effects of a heart attack (see the jumps at time $t = 2$, $t = 3$ and $t = 17$) and the positive effect of digitalis on heart failure (see the rapid fall at time $t = 7$). The model also implies that the condition of the heart stabilizes after administering the drug through an increase in the contractility. However, a damaged heart does not fully recover, not even with the help of digitalis.

6   Discussion

We have described hybrid time Bayesian networks for modeling dynamic systems with different types of time granularities: the proposed models provide a generalization of continuous-time and discrete-time Bayesian networks. As an inherited property from CTBNs, the joint distribution is propagated over time even when evidence is spaced irregularly. In addition, we established a mapping of hybrid-time networks into a standard BN given time points of interest.

The formalism is related to non-stationary dynamic Bayesian networks, where the structures and parameters are determined by time points of interest [4,5]. These are related in the sense that non-stationary Bayesian networks allow for different time granularities of the (complete) temporal process. The key difference here is that we consider the case where different random variables evolve at different kinds of rates.

A limitation of HTBN is that so far the granularities of discrete-time variables are assumed to be fixed, as the focus of this paper has been on the combination of continuous and discrete-time models. As future work, we will also combine different discrete-time granularities within the hybrid-time framework as proposed in irregular-time Bayesian networks (ITBNs) [6] and also discussed by van der Heijden and Lucas [7]. Furthermore, as a final piece of future work, we would like to extend the formalism to also allow random variables that are completely atemporal. For example, in classification, one might want to predict a single outcome indicator based on time-series. This would complete the full spectrum of temporal models of random variables.

References

1. Bettini, C., Jajodia, S., Wang, S.: Time Granularities in Databases, Data Mining, and Temporal Reasoning. Springer, Heidelberg (2000)
2. Murphy, K.P.: Dynamic Bayesian networks: representation, inference and learning. Ph.D. thesis, University of California, Berkeley (2002)
3. Nodelman, U., Shelton, C.R., Koller, D.: Continuous time Bayesian networks. In: Proceedings of the Eighteenth Conference on Uncertainty in Artificial Intelligence, pp. 378–387. Morgan Kaufmann Publishers Inc. (2002)
4. Grzegorczyk, M., Husmeier, D.: Non-stationary continuous dynamic Bayesian networks. In: Advances in Neural Information Processing Systems, pp. 682–690 (2009)

5. Robinson, J.W., Hartemink, A.J.: Non-stationary dynamic Bayesian networks. In: Advances in Neural Information Processing Systems, pp. 1369–1376 (2009)
6. Ramati, M., Shahar, Y.: Irregular-time Bayesian networks. In: UAI 2010: Proceedings of the 26th Conference on Uncertainty in Artificial Intelligence, pp. 484–491 (2010)
7. van der Heijden, M., Lucas, P.J.: Probabilistic reasoning with temporal indeterminacy. In: PGM 2012: Proceedings of the 6th European Workshop on Probabilistic Graphical Models (2012)

Learning Bounded Tree-Width Bayesian Networks via Sampling

Siqi Nie[1](✉), Cassio P. de Campos[2], and Qiang Ji[1]

[1] Department of Electrical, Computer and Systems Engineering,
Rensselaer Polytechnic Institute, Troy, USA
nies@rpi.edu
[2] School of Electronics, Electrical Engineering and Computer Science,
Queen's University Belfast, Belfast, Northern Ireland, UK

Abstract. Learning Bayesian networks with bounded tree-width has attracted much attention recently, because low tree-width allows exact inference to be performed efficiently. Some existing methods [12,14] tackle the problem by using k-trees to learn the optimal Bayesian network with tree-width up to k. In this paper, we propose a sampling method to efficiently find representative k-trees by introducing an Informative score function to characterize the quality of a k-tree. The proposed algorithm can efficiently learn a Bayesian network with tree-width at most k. Experiment results indicate that our approach is comparable with exact methods, but is much more computationally efficient.

Keywords: Bayesian network · Structure learning · Bounded tree-width

1 Introduction

Bayesian networks (BNs) are widely used probabilistic graphical models. Learning Bayesian networks from data has been widely studied in decades. In this paper we present our approach of score-based Bayesian network structure learning with some special constraint.

It is well known that the complexity of exact inference in a Bayesian network is related to the tree-width of the network [13]. To simplify the inference computation, one attempt that has received growing attention recently is to learn a Bayesian network with bounded tree-width. Moreover, some empirical results [10] demonstrate that bounding the tree-width of a Bayesian network achieves better generalization performance.

Several algorithms have been proposed to learn Bayesian networks with bounded tree-width. Korhonen and Parviainen [12] proposed a dynamic programming based algorithm for learning n-node Bayesian networks of tree-width at most k. Their algorithm guarantees to find the optimal structure maximizing a given score function subject to the tree-width constraint. Parviainen et al. [15] developed an integer programming approach to solve the problem. It iteratively creates a cutting plane on the current solution to avoid exponentially many constraints.

© Springer International Publishing Switzerland 2015
S. Destercke and T. Denoeux (Eds.): ECSQARU 2015, LNAI 9161, pp. 387–396, 2015.
DOI: 10.1007/978-3-319-20807-7_35

However, both algorithms work only with small tree-widths. Berg et al. [3] transferred the problem into a weighted maximum satisfiability problem and solved it by weighted MAX-SAT solvers. Nie et al. [14] introduced an integer programming and a sampling methods to address this problem.

In this work, we present a novel method of score-based Bayesian network structure learning with bounded tree-width via sampling. We design an approximate approach based on sampling k-trees, which are the maximal graphs of tree-width k. The sampling method is based on a fast bijection between k-trees and Dandelion codes [5]. We design a sampling scheme, called *Distance Preferable Sampling* (DPS), in order to effectively cover the space of k-trees using limited samples, in which we give a larger probability for a sample in the unexplored area of the space, based on the existing samples. Smart rules to explore the sample space are essential, because we can only compute a few best structures respecting sampled k-trees in a reasonable amount of time. To evaluate the sampled k-trees, we design an *Informative Score* (I-score) function as the criterion for accepting or rejecting k-trees based on independence tests and BDeu scores, which is used as a prior information for the k-trees. Different from the method proposed in [14], this work focuses on identifying high quality k-trees, instead of uniformly sampling. Given each sampled k-tree, we employ the algorithm of [12] to find the optimal Bayesian network as a subgraph of it, which we denote as K&P method from now on.

This paper is structured as follows. We first introduce some definitions and notations for Bayesian networks and tree-width in Sect. 2. Then we discuss the proposed sampling method for learning Bayesian networks with bounded tree-width in Sect. 3. Experimental results are given in Sect. 4. Finally we conclude the paper in Sect. 5.

2   Preliminaries

2.1   Learning Bayesian Networks

A Bayesian network uses a directed acyclic graph (DAG) to represent a set of random variables $X = \{X_i : i \in N\}, N = \{1, 2, ..., n\}$ and their conditional (in)dependencies. Arcs of the DAG encode parent-child relations. Denote X_{pa_i} as the parent set of variable X_i. Conditional probability tables $p(x_i|x_{pa_i})$ are given accordingly, where x_i and x_{pa_i} are instantiations of X_i and X_{pa_i}. We consider categorical variables in this work.

The structure learning task of Bayesian network is to identify the "best" DAG from data. In this paper we consider the score-based Bayesian network structure learning problem, in which a score $s(G)$ is assigned to each DAG G. The commonly used score functions (such as BIC [17], and BDeu [4,6,11]) are decomposable, i.e., the overall score can be written as the summation of local score functions, $s(G) = \sum_{i \in N} s_i(X_{pa_i})$. For each variable, its score is only related to its parent set. We assume that local scores have been computed in advance and can be retrieved in constant time.

2.2   Learning BN with Tree-Width Bound

The *width* of a tree decomposition of an undirected graph is the size of its largest clique minus one. The *tree-width* of an undirected graph is the minimum width among all possible tree decompositions of the graph. We define *tree-width* $tw(G)$ of a DAG G as the tree-width of its moral graph, which is obtained by connecting nodes with a common child, and making all edges undirected.

The objective of this work is to find a graph G^*,

$$G^* = \arg \max_{G} \sum_{i \in N} s_i(X_{pa_i}), \quad \text{s.t.} \quad tw(G) \leq k. \tag{1}$$

Directly computing the tree-width of a graph is intractable [1]. One way of imposing the tree-width constraint is to use the k-tree, the maximal graphs with tree-width k, and no more edges can be added to them without increasing the tree-width (see [16] for details). Therefore, every graph with tree-width at most k is a subgraph of a k-tree. Learning Bayesian network from a k-tree automatically satisfies the tree-width constraint if we ensure that the moral graph of the learned Bayesian network is a subgraph of the k-tree. A k-tree is denoted by $T_k \in \mathcal{T}_{n,k}$, where $\mathcal{T}_{n,k}$ is the set of all k-trees over n nodes.

3   Sampling k-trees Using Dandelion Codes

The basic idea is to efficiently search for k-trees with "high quality" and then use K&P algorithm to learn the optimal Bayesian network from the selected k-trees. This is accomplished in two steps. First, we propose a sampling method that can effectively cover the space of k-trees to obtain representative k-trees. Second, we establish an *informative score* (I-score) function to evaluate the quality of each k-tree.

3.1   Effective k-tree Sampling

Directly sampling a k-tree is not trivial. Caminiti et al. [5] proposed to establish a one-to-one correspondence between a k-tree and what is called *Dandelion* codes. The space of Dandelion codes is denoted by $\mathcal{A}_{n,k}$. A code $(Q, S) \in \mathcal{A}_{n,k}$ is a pair where $Q \subseteq N$ is a set of integers of size k and S is a $2 \times (n-k-2)$ matrix of integers drawn from $N \cup \{\epsilon\}$, where ϵ is an arbitrary number not in N (see [5] for details).

Dandelion codes can be sampled uniformly at random by a trivial linear-time algorithm that uniformly chooses k elements out of N to build Q, and then uniformly samples $n-k-2$ pairs of integers in $N \cup \{\epsilon\}$. Such property of Dandelion codes naturally makes a uniform prior for k-trees, which is a quite good prior in the absence of other prior knowledge [9]. However, uniform sampling generates each sample independently, and totally ignores previous samples, which makes it possible to generate the very same sample twice, or at least samples that are too close to each other. Considering the large size of the space of all Dandelion codes

$((\binom{n}{k})(k(n-k)+1)^{n-k-2})$ and the relatively small amount of samples that we can process, we would prefer the samples to be as evenly distributed as possible. This is accomplished by generating the next sample from some currently unexplored area of the sampling space. Driven by this idea, we define the *Distance Preferable Sampling* (DPS). Given the samples of Dandelion codes $A^{(1)}, A^{(2)}, \cdots, A^{(j-1)}$ obtained so far, we want to decide how to sample the next $A^{(j)}$. A kernel density function for a new sample can be defined as

$$q(A^{(j)}) = \frac{1}{j-1} \sum_{i=1}^{j-1} K(\|A^{(j)} - A^{(i)}\|), \qquad (2)$$

where $A^{(j)} \in \mathcal{A}_{n,k}$ is the jth Dandelion code sample. $q(A^{(j)})$ depends on all the previous samples, with its value decreasing as $A^{(j)}$ moves away from existing samples. $K(\cdot)$ is a kernel function, (e.g., a Gaussian). The distance between two Dandelion codes is defined as

$$\|A^{(j)} - A^{(i)}\| = \|Q^{(j)} - Q^{(i)}\|_2 + \|S^{(j)} - S^{(i)}\|_{2,1}, \qquad (3)$$

where $\|\cdot\|_2$ is the L_2 norm. $S^{(j)}$ is processed as a $2 \times (n-k-2)$ matrix, and $\|\cdot\|_{2,1}$ is the $L_{2,1}$ norm.

Since we intend to explore the regions which have not yet been sampled, we design a proposal distribution as follows:

$$p(A^{(j)}) = 1 - \frac{q(A^{(j)})}{K(0)}. \qquad (4)$$

$p(A^{(j)})$ increases as sample $A^{(j)}$ moves away from all the existing samples. Following the proposal distribution, we use the rejection sampling algorithm (Algorithm 1) to generate a sample of Dandelion codes, and then employ the implementation of [5] to decode it into a k-tree.

3.2   Informative Score for k-trees

Given a k-tree, the computational complexity of the method of [12] for constructing a Bayesian network subject to the k-tree is super-exponential in k $(O(k \cdot 3^k \cdot (k+1)! \cdot n))$. Hence, one cannot hope to use it with too many k-trees, given current computational resources. Instead of learning from every k-tree

---

Algorithm 1. Sampling a Dandelion code using Distance Preferable Sampling

Input Previous samples of Dandelion codes $A^{(1)}, \ldots, A^{(j-1)}$.
Output a new sample of Dandelion code $A^{(j)}$.
1 Uniformly sample a Dandelion code $A^{(j)}$ in the feasible region;
2 If $j = 1$, the sample is accepted. If not, the sample is accepted with probability $p(A^{(j)})$;
3 If $A^{(j)}$ is rejected, return to step 1 for another sample, until a sample is accepted.

---

without distinction, we define the I-score function to evaluate how well a k-tree "fits the data", hence can produce a Bayesian network with high quality. The I-score of a k-tree T_k is defined as

$$IS(T_k) = \frac{S_{mi}(T_k)}{|S_l(T_k)|}. \tag{5}$$

The numerator, $S_{mi}(T_k)$, measures how much information is lost by representing data using the k-tree. Let e_{ij} denote the edge connecting node i and j, and let I_{ij} denote the mutual information of node i and j. Then,

$$S_{mi}(T_k) = \sum_{i,j} I_{ij} - \sum_{e_{ij} \notin T_k} I_{ij}. \tag{6}$$

If an edge e_{ij} is not included in the k-tree, we subtract the mutual information corresponding to that edge from the optimal score. S_{mi} is a measurement of the consistency of the k-tree and the data, and can be interpreted either as the sum of the mutual information covered by the k-tree or as constant minus the sum of the mutual information lost by the k-tree. Larger S_{mi} indicates the k-tree fits the data well, from the independent test perspective.

On the other hand, the denominator $S_l(T_k)$ is defined as the score (e.g., BIC, BDeu scores) of the best pseudo subgraph of the k-tree by dropping the acyclic constraint.

$$S_l(T_k) = \max_{m(G) \subseteq T_k} \sum_{i \in N} s_i(x_{pa_i}), \tag{7}$$

where $m(G)$ is the moral graph of DAG G, and $s_i(x_{pa_i})$ is the local score function for x_i given parent set x_{pa_i}.

The best pseudo subgraph of a k-tree is constructed by choosing the best parent set for each node in terms of local scores, compatible with the k-tree, in a greedy way. Combining all the parent sets will result in a directed, possibly cyclic, graph. Therefore, given the pre-computed scores for each variable, score S_l can be computed in linear time. Since the value of S_l is negative, for practical reasons we use the term $1/|S_l(T_k)|$ in the I-score formulation.

The I-score for a k-tree combines the independence test approach and score-based approach for learning Bayesian networks. It can be very efficiently evaluated for any given k-tree, as computing S_{mi} requires only mutual information of pairs of nodes (which can all be pre-computed, so time complexity is at most $O(n^2)$ over all multiple runs of the algorithm).

With the I-score for a proposed k-tree, we then accept a k-tree with probability

$$\alpha = \min\left(1, \frac{IS(T_k)}{IS(T_k^*)}\right), \tag{8}$$

where T_k^* is the current k-tree with the largest I-score. Notice that we do not set a hard constraint for accepting or rejecting a k-tree, due to the fact that even for a k-tree with relatively small I-score, it is still possible for it to contain a good subgraph.

Algorithm 2. Learning a Bayesian network structure of bounded tree-width by sampling Dandelion codes.

Input score function s_i, $\forall i \in N$, mutual information I_{ij}, $\forall i,j \in N$
Output a DAG G^{best}.

1 Initialize Pa_i^{best} as an empty set for all $i \in N$;
2 (Rejection Procedure 1) Sample a Dandelion code $(Q, S) \in \mathcal{A}_{n,k}$ according to Algorithm 1;
3 (Rejection Procedure 2) Decode (Q, S) into $T_k \in \mathcal{T}_{n,k}$, accept it with probability α (Eq. 8);
4 Repeat Step 2 and 3 until m k-trees are accepted. Sort them in descending order based on their I-scores. From the top use the implementation of [12] to learn a Bayesian network. Keep the structure with the highest BDeu score.
5 If time limit is not reached after m k-trees, restart from step 2.

3.3   BN Learning from Sampled k-trees

Combining the ideas in Sects. 3.1 and 3.2, we present Algorithm 2 as an approximate algorithm for learning Bayesian networks of bounded tree-width. Due to the fact that k-trees with large I-scores are more likely to have better subgraphs, we give them high priority to learn the corresponding Bayesian network. This is reflected in Step 4 of Algorithm 2. A certain amount of k-trees are sampled, and then sorted based on their I-scores. The process starts with the k-trees of the largest I-score in the sorted list. If time allows, all k-trees are examined, and the procedure restarts. Given a k-tree as the super structure, the implementation of K&P is employed to learn the optimal Bayesian network. The goal of Algorithm 2 is to restrict the calls to K&P (which is a time consuming method in k, even if linear in n) only to k-trees that are promising.

Table 1. Dimensions of data sets.

Dataset	Nursery	Breast	Housing	Adult	Zoo	Letter	Mushroom	wdbc
Var.	9	10	14	15	17	17	22	31
Samples	12960	699	506	32561	101	20000	8124	569

4   Experiments

To empirically evaluate our method, we use a collection of data sets from the UCI repository [2] of varying dimensionality. Table 1 contains the details about the data sets used in the experiments. Firstly, we show the effectiveness of the I-score for accepting or rejecting a sampled k-tree. Secondly, we compare the BDeu scores of the learned Bayesian networks.

4.1   Informative Score

In this section, we evaluate the I-score as a measurement of how good a k-tree would be to "produce" a Bayesian network (moralized) structure as its subgraph.

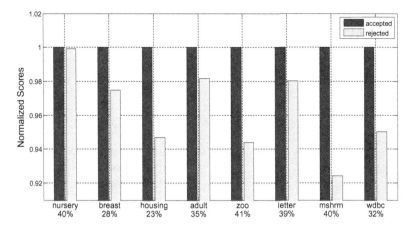

Fig. 1. Effect of the rejection process. The maximum BDeu scores of the Bayesian networks learned from the accepted k-trees, compared with those from the rejected k-trees. Best scores are normalized to 1. The rejection rates are presented at bottom.

Eight data sets are used (*nursery, breast, housing, adult, zoo, letter, mushroom,* and *wdbc*), whose dimensions are summarized in Tables 2 and 3. The numbers of samples vary from 100 to 20,000. Non-binary variables are binarized over the median value. In all experiments, we maximize the Bayesian Dirichlet equivalent uniform (BDeu) score with equivalent sample size equal to one [11]. To evaluate the effect of our rejection of k-trees, we sampled 500 k-trees, and counted the number of rejections during the k-tree selection (Step 3 in Algorithm 2). If a k-tree is rejected, we still compute the BDeu score of its optimal Bayesian network for comparison. Figure 1 shows the ratio of rejection (at bottom) and relation between best scores of Bayesian networks learned from both the accepted and the rejected k-trees. The scores are normalized so that best score is 1. In all data sets, BDeu scores of Bayesian network learned from rejected k-trees never exceeded the scores from accepted ones. Using the rejection process, we see that 20 % to 40 % of the k-trees were rejected. Such variation in the rejection rates is due to the randomness of the samples, because if a k-tree with high I-score is sampled in an early stage, later samples have a high probability to be rejected.

4.2   Bayesian Network Learning

In this section we compare the BDeu scores of structures learned by our method against scores from two exact methods as baseline methods, namely, the K&P algorithm[1] and the B&B method[2] [7,8]. The comparison with exact methods allows us to evaluate the proposed algorithm in terms of the difference in scores.

Due to the complexity of K&P method, it is only applicable to some relatively small data sets, hence our comparisons are restricted to those cases. The detailed

---

[1] http://www.cs.helsinki.fi/u/jazkorho/aistats-2013/.

[2] http://www.ecse.rpi.edu/~cvrl/structlearning.html.

Table 2. Computational time of the K&P method to find the optimal Bayesian network structure, and the proposed method to sample 100 k-trees, as well as the resulting BDeu scores of the networks found by both methods. Empty cells indicate that the method failed to solve the problem because of excessive memory consumption. s, m mean seconds and minutes, respectively.

Method	k	Time				Score			
		Nursery	Breast	Housing	Adult	Nursery	Breast	Housing	Adult
		$n = 9$	$n = 10$	$n = 14$	$n = 15$	$n = 9$	$n = 10$	$n = 14$	$n = 15$
K&P	2	7 s	26 s	128 m	137 m	−72160	−2688.4	−3295.4	−201532
	3	72 s	5 m	–	–	−72159	−2685.8	–	–
	4	12 m	103 m	–	–	−72159	−2685.3	–	–
	5	131 m	–	–	–	−72159	–	–	–
Proposed	2	5 s	8 s	16 s	18 s	−72218	−2690.5	−3409.6	−202852
	3	70 s	76 s	3 m	4 m	−72204	−2692.5	−3413.4	−204186
	4	9 m	10 m	36 m	50 m	−72159	−2691.9	−3285.0	−202432
	5	80 m	232 m	631 m	896 m	−72159	−2694.0	−3296.9	−202699

computational time that K&P uses is given in Table 2. The algorithm is run using a desktop computer with 64 GB of memory. Maximum number of parents is set to three. Due to the huge amount of memory cost, for *housing* and *adult* data sets with tree-width more than 2, as well as *breast* with tree-width bound 5, the algorithm failed to give a solution. Correspondingly, we sampled 100 k-trees and recorded the running time for the proposed algorithm to give a solution, given the same data set and the same choice of maximum tree-width. The BDeu scores of the best Bayesian networks found with both algorithms are also presented. By examining only a small portion of k-trees, the proposed algorithm finds solutions with an BDeu score difference less than 1 % for most cases. Only in the *housing* data set with tree-width equal to 2, our algorithm have a 3 % score difference to the exact solution, which is reasonable after only 16 seconds of computation. Generally speaking, the proposed algorithm achieves comparable results to those of the exact method in terms of BDeu score difference. Yet when considering the time and memory costs of the exact solution, the proposed algorithm is more efficient against the competing method by several orders of magnitude.

Besides efficiency, the proposed algorithm can be used on larger data sets with up to 31 nodes and larger values for the tree-width bound (*zoo, letter, mushroom*, and *wdbc*) (Table 3). Note that the B&B method does not have the tree-width constraint, so the learned structures are supposed to have larger BDeu scores. However, the score difference is not very significant, which indicates the bounding the tree-width can learn good structures in terms of scores.

To further study the benefit of the DPS and I-score based sampling, we also implemented the algorithm using the uniformly sampled Dandelion codes without sorting or rejection. The BDeu scores on the *letter* data set are compared, with different choices of tree-widths. According to Table 4, DPS outperforms uniform sampling, even if by a small margin. A great portion of the gain of performance is from rejecting k-trees based on I-scores. To summarize, we are

Table 3. BDeu scores for relatively larger data sets and lager tree-widths, compared with the B&B method without tree-width constraint. Running time is ten minutes. Averaged over ten repetitions.

Data set	Nodes	$k = 2$	$k = 3$	$k = 4$	$k = 5$	B&B
Zoo	17	−644.1	−623.8	−609.1	−649.1	−565.2
Letter	17	−195677	−192289	−192373	−194349	−184530
Mushroom	22	−73697	−74367	−68523	−73902	−68237
wdbc	31	−8435.1	−8320.8	−8352.1	−8316.9	−6933.8

Table 4. BDeu scores of BNs learned using different sampling methods with data set *letter*, normalized using the best score of each column. UNI means uniform sampling; DPS means Distance Preferable Sampling; α means that we employed the acceptance probability α. Larger numbers indicate worse performance.

Method	$k = 2$	$k = 3$	$k = 4$
UNI	1.019	1.046	1.039
DPS	1.018	1.045	1.038
DPS+α	1	1	1

able to focus on better k-trees by employing non-uniform sampling and sorting them according to some meaningful measure.

5   Conclusion

In this paper we present a sampling method for learning Bayesian networks with bounded tree-width. The sampling is based on a bijection between Dandelion codes and k-trees. We design a Distance Preferable Sampling scheme to effectively cover the space of k-trees, as well as an Informative score function to evaluate each k-tree. These ideas allow to quickly find representative k-trees of high quality. Experiments indicate that the proposed method reaches comparable accuracy to the exact algorithms in terms of BDeu scores, but is much more efficient in terms of learning speed, and can scale up to larger networks and larger tree-widths.

Acknowledgements. This work is supported in part by the grant N00014-12-1-0868 from the US Office of Navy Research.

References

1. Arnborg, S., Corneil, D.G., Proskurowski, A.: Complexity of finding embeddings in ak-tree. SIAM J. Algebraic Discrete Methods **8**(2), 277–284 (1987)
2. Bache, K., Lichman, M.: UCI machine learning repository (2013). http://archive.ics.uci.edu/ml

3. Berg, J., Järvisalo, M., Malone, B.: Learning optimal bounded treewidth bayesian networks via maximum satisfiability. In: Proceedings of the Seventeenth International Conference on Artificial Intelligence and Statistics, pp. 86–95 (2014)
4. Buntine, W.: Theory refinement on Bayesian networks. In: Proceedings of the 7th Conference on Uncertainty in AI, pp. 52–60 (1991)
5. Caminiti, S., Fusco, E.G., Petreschi, R.: Bijective linear time coding and decoding for k-trees. Theory Comp. Syst. **46**(2), 284–300 (2010)
6. Cooper, G.F., Herskovits, E.: A Bayesian method for the induction of probabilistic networks from data. Mach. Learn. **9**(4), 309–347 (1992)
7. de Campos, C.P., Ji, Q.: Efficient structure learning of Bayesian networks using constraints. J. Mach. Learn. Res. **12**, 663–689 (2011)
8. de Campos, C.P., Zeng, Z., Ji, Q.: Structure learning of Bayesian networks using constraints. In: Proceedings of the 26th Annual International Conference on Machine Learning, Montreal, Quebec, Canada, pp. 113–120 (2009)
9. Eaton, D., Murphy, K.: Bayesian structure learning using dynamic programming and MCMC. In: Proceedings of the 23rd Conference on Uncertainty in AI, pp. 101–108 (2007)
10. Elidan, G., Gould, S.: Learning bounded treewidth Bayesian networks. J. Mach. Learn. Res. **9**, 2699–2731 (2008)
11. Heckerman, D., Geiger, D., Chickering, D.M.: Learning Bayesian networks: the combination of knowledge and statistical data. Mach. Learn. **20**(3),, 197–243 (1995)
12. Korhonen, J.H., Parviainen, P.: Exact learning of bounded tree-width Bayesian networks. In: Proceedings of the 16th International Conference on AI and Statistics. JMLR W&CP, vol. 31, pp. 370–378 (2013)
13. Kwisthout, J.H.P., Bodlaender, H.L., van der Gaag, L.C.: The necessity of bounded treewidth for efficient inference in Bayesian networks. In: Proceedings of the 19th European Conference on AI, pp. 237–242 (2010)
14. Nie, S., Mauá, D.D., de Campos, C.P., Ji, Q.: Advances in learning Bayesian networks of bounded treewidth. In: Advances in Neural Information Processing Systems, pp. 2285–2293 (2014)
15. Parviainen, P., Farahani, H.S., Lagergren, J.: Learning bounded tree-width Bayesian networks using integer linear programming. In: Proceedings of the Seventeenth International Conference on Artificial Intelligence and Statistics, pp. 751–759 (2014)
16. Patil, H.P.: On the structure of k-trees. J. Comb. Inf. Syst. Sci. **11**(2–4), 57–64 (1986)
17. Schwarz, G.: Estimating the dimension of a model. Ann. Stat. **6**(2), 461–464 (1978)

Learning Conditional Distributions Using Mixtures of Truncated Basis Functions

Inmaculada Pérez-Bernabé[1]([⊠]), Antonio Salmerón[1], and Helge Langseth[2]

[1] University of Almería, 04120 Almería, Spain
{iperez,antonio.salmeron}@ual.es
[2] Norwegian University of Science and Technology, 7491 Trondheim, Norway
helgel@idi.ntnu.no

Abstract. Mixtures of Truncated Basis Functions (MoTBFs) have recently been proposed for modelling univariate and joint distributions in hybrid Bayesian networks. In this paper we analyse the problem of learning conditional MoTBF distributions from data. Our approach utilizes a new technique for learning joint MoTBF densities, then propose a method for using these to generate the conditional distributions. The main contribution of this work is conveyed through an empirical investigation into the properties of the new learning procedure, where we also compare the merits of our approach to those obtained by other proposals.

Keywords: Mixtures of truncated basis functions · Hybrid bayesian networks · Joint density · Conditional density

1 Introduction

Mixtures of truncated basis functions (MoTBFs) [2] have recently been proposed as a general framework for handling hybrid Bayesian networks, i.e., Bayesian networks where discrete and continuous variables coexist. Previous hybrid models as the so-called mixtures of truncated exponentials (MTEs) [7] and mixtures of polynomials (MoPs) [10] can be regarded as particular cases of MoTBFs.

Part of the success of MoTBFs is due to the fact that they can model hybrid Bayesian networks with no structural restrictions, unlike the conditional Gaussian (CG) model [6], where discrete variables are not allowed to have continuous parents. Furthermore, MoTBFs are closed under addition, multiplication, and integration, which facilitates the use of efficient inference methods like the Shenoy-Shafer architecture [9] or the *variable elimination* algorithm [12].

The problem of learning MoTBFs from data has been studied considerably already (see, e.g., [3,5]). However, even though a Bayesian network model populated with MoTBF distributions requires the specification of both marginal and conditional MoTBF distributions, only limited attention has been given to learning the *conditional* MoTBF distributions directly from data [1,11]. In this paper we first extend previous work on learning marginal MoTBF distributions [5] to also learn joint densities. These are in turn employed to generate the required conditional MoTBFs.

© Springer International Publishing Switzerland 2015
S. Destercke and T. Denoeux (Eds.): ECSQARU 2015, LNAI 9161, pp. 397–406, 2015.
DOI: 10.1007/978-3-319-20807-7_36

The remainder of the paper is organized as follows: The MoTBF model is introduced in Sect. 2. Next, techniques for learning marginal and joint MoTBF densities from data is described in Sect. 3, where we also detail how we define the conditional distributions. The main part of this work is given in Sect. 4, where our proposal is validated through a series of experiments. Finally, we give some conclusions in Sect. 5.

2   The MoTBF Model

The MoTBF framework is based on the abstract notion of real-valued *basis functions* $\psi(\cdot)$, which include both polynomial and exponential functions as special cases. Let X be a continuous variable with domain $\Omega_X \subset \mathbb{R}$ and let $\psi_i : \Omega_X \mapsto \mathbb{R}$, for $i = 0, \ldots, k$, define a collection of real basis functions. We say that a function $f : \Omega_X \mapsto \mathbb{R}_0^+$ is an MoTBF potential of level k wrt. $\Psi = \{\psi_0, \psi_1, \ldots, \psi_k\}$ if f can be written as

$$f(x) = \sum_{i=0}^{k} c_i \, \psi_i \, (x),$$

where c_i are real numbers [2]. The potential is a density if $\int_{\Omega_X} f(x) \, dx = 1$.

In this paper we will restrict our attention to the MoP framework, meaning that $\psi_i(x) = x^i$.

When there are more than one variable, we can use a joint MoP to capture the probability density function over the variables. Let $\mathbf{X}$ be a d-dimensional continuous variable, $\mathbf{X} = (X_1, \ldots, X_d)$ with domain $\Omega_\mathbf{X} \subset \mathbb{R}^d$. A function $f : \Omega_\mathbf{X} \mapsto \mathbb{R}^+$ is said to be an MoP potential of level k if it can be written as

$$f(\mathbf{x}) = \sum_{\ell_1=0}^{k} \cdots \sum_{\ell_d=0}^{k} c_{\ell_1, \ell_2, \ldots, \ell_d} \prod_{i=1}^{d} x_i^{\ell_i}, \tag{1}$$

or if there is a partition of $\Omega_\mathbf{X}$ into hypercubes where f can be written as in Eq. 1 for each part.

3   Learning MoPs from Data

We will now investigate how to learn MoP distributions for a given set of random variables. We start by looking at how to learn univariate MoP distributions from data, before we extend that approach to learning joint MoP distributions, and finally discuss how one can obtain conditional distribution functions.

3.1   Univariate MoPs

The learning of univariate MoTBFs from data was explored in [5], and we will briefly summarize that approach here in the special case of MoPs. The estimation procedure relies on the empirical cumulative distribution function (CDF) as a representation of the data $\mathcal{D} = \{x_1, \ldots, x_N\}$. The empirical CDF is defined as

$$G_N(x) = \frac{1}{N} \sum_{\ell=1}^{N} \mathbf{1}\{x_\ell \leq x\}, \quad x \in \Omega_X \subset \mathbb{R},$$

where $\mathbf{1}\{\cdot\}$ is the indicator function.

The algorithm in [5] approximates the empirical CDF by a function whose derivative is an MoTBF, using least squares. In our case, the role of the basis functions is taken by the polynomials, and since the integral of a polynomial is itself a polynomial, the target function is of the form $F(x) = \sum_{i=0}^{k} c_i x^i$, defined on an interval $\Omega_X = [a, b] \subset \mathbb{R}$. The optimization problem thus becomes

$$\textbf{minimize } \sum_{\ell=1}^{N} (G_N(x_\ell) - F(x_\ell))^2$$

$$\textbf{subject to } \frac{\mathrm{d}F(x)}{\mathrm{d}x} \geq 0 \quad \forall x \in \Omega_X, \tag{2}$$

$$F(a) = 0 \text{ and } F(b) = 1.$$

The probability density function (PDF) is found by simple differentiation of the estimated CDF. The constraints of the optimization program ensures that the result is a legal density; the first requirement ensures that the PDF is non-negative over the domain, the others ensure it integrates to one. Furthermore, [5] remarks that the solution obtained by solving program in Eq. 2 is a consistent estimator of the true CDF in terms of the mean squared error for all $x \in \Omega_X$.

Note that the optimization program is convex, and can be efficiently solved in theory. However, the infinite number of constraints introduced by requiring that $\frac{\mathrm{d}F(x)}{\mathrm{d}x} \geq 0$ for *all* $x \in \Omega_X$ complicates the implementation on a computer. In practice, we therefore only check that the constraint is fulfilled for a limited set of points spread across Ω_X.

In learning situations where we have lots of data (N is large), the solution of the program can be slow. In such cases we rather define a *grid* on Ω_X, where the grid is selected so that the number of observations is the same between each pair of consecutive grid-points. Then, the grid-points will play the role of the evaluation points in the objective function.

The level k of the estimated MoP can be decided using a multitude of different model selection techniques. For the results presented in this paper we have searched greedily for k, and chosen the value that maximized the BIC score [8]. This choice is motivated by [3], who showed that the estimators based on Eq. 2 are consistent in terms of the mean squared error for all $x \in \Omega_X$.

3.2   Joint MoPs

During the definition of the conditional distributions (described in Sect. 3.3), we will investigate the use of joint MoP densities to define conditional distributions. We therefore proceed by extending the program in Eq. 2 to arbitrarily dimensional random vectors. The procedure is very similar to the univariate case. The data now consists of d-dimensional observations, $\mathcal{D} = \{\mathbf{x}_1, \ldots, \mathbf{x}_N\}$, $\mathbf{x} \in \Omega_\mathbf{X} \subset \mathbb{R}^d$. We continue to use $\mathbf{1}\{\cdot\}$ to denote the indicator function, and the say that the event $\mathbf{x}_\ell \leq \mathbf{x}$ is true if and only if $\mathbf{x}_{\ell,i} \leq \mathbf{x}_i$ for each dimension $i = 1, \ldots, d$. For notational convenience we use $\Omega_\mathbf{X}^- \in \mathbb{R}^d$ to denote the minimal point of $\Omega_\mathbf{X}$ (obtained by choosing the minimum of $\Omega_\mathbf{X}$ in each dimension), and let $\Omega_\mathbf{X}^+ \in \mathbb{R}^d$ be the corresponding maximal point. Then, the empirical CDF is defined as

$$G_N(\mathbf{x}) = \frac{1}{N} \sum_{\ell=1}^{N} \mathbf{1}\{\mathbf{x}_\ell \leq \mathbf{x}\}, \quad \mathbf{x} \in \Omega_\mathbf{X} \subset \mathbb{R}^d.$$

Our goal is to find a representation of the empirical CDF of the form

$$F(\mathbf{x}) = \sum_{\ell_1=0}^{k} \cdots \sum_{\ell_d=0}^{k} c_{\ell_1, \ell_2, \ldots, \ell_d} \prod_{i=1}^{d} x_i^{\ell_i},$$

leading us to the optimization problem

$$\textbf{minimize} \quad \sum_{\ell=1}^{N} (G_N(\mathbf{x}_\ell) - F(\mathbf{x}_\ell))^2$$

$$\textbf{subject to} \quad \frac{\partial^d F(\mathbf{x})}{\partial x_1, \ldots, \partial x_d} \geq 0 \quad \forall \mathbf{x} \in \Omega_\mathbf{X}, \tag{3}$$

$$F\left(\Omega_\mathbf{X}^-\right) = 0 \text{ and } F\left(\Omega_\mathbf{X}^+\right) = 1.$$

The solution to this problem is the parameter-set that defines the joint CDF, and the density can be obtained simply by differentiation of the joint CDF. As in the univariate case, the problem is a quadratic optimization problem, that can be solved efficiently. When the amount of data and/or the dimensionality get large, we have used the same strategy wrt. grid-points for the joint density as we did when estimating the univariate PDFs.

The top of Fig. 1 shows the MoP density generated by solving the optimization program in Eq. 3. The model was learned from a database of 1000 observation generated from a bivariate standard normal distribution (i.e., with correlation-coefficient $\rho = 0$). In the bottom part of Fig. 1 we can see the model learned from same distributions but with correlation $\rho = 0.99$.

3.3   Conditional Distributions

The last piece of the puzzle is to learn the conditional density functions for a variable X with parents $\mathbf{Z}$, that will be used to populate the Bayesian network structure. Using the minimization program in Eq. 3, we can learn both $f(x, \mathbf{z})$ and $f(\mathbf{z})$, hence by the definition of a conditional probability density it seems natural to define $f(x|\mathbf{z})$ as

$$f(x|\mathbf{z}) \leftarrow \frac{f(x, \mathbf{z})}{f(\mathbf{z})}, \tag{4}$$

where both $f(\mathbf{z})$ and $f(x, \mathbf{z})$ are MoPs. Unfortunately, though, MoPs are not closed under division [2], thus $f(x|\mathbf{z})$ defined by Eq. 4 will not lead to a legal MoP-representation of a conditional density. An alternative was therefore pursued by [2], where the influence the parents $\mathbf{Z}$ have on X was encoded only through the partitioning of the domain of $\mathbf{Z}$ into hyper-cubes. Then, specific distributions for X that are valid as long as $\mathbf{Z}$ is inside a specific hypercube was learned from data.

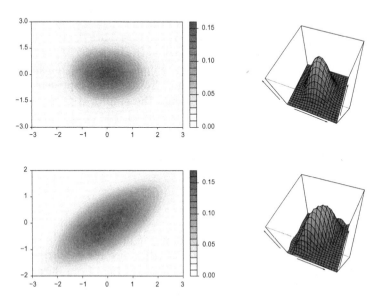

Fig. 1. The contour and the perspective plots of the result of learning a MoP from $N = 1000$ samples drawn from bivariate standard normal distributions with $\rho = 0$ (top) and $\rho = 0.99$ (bottom).

Here, however, we will follow an alternative strategy similar to the one pursued in [11]. The idea is to learn representations for $f(x, \mathbf{z})$ and $f(\mathbf{z})$, then utilize Eq. 4 to calculate $f(x|\mathbf{z})$. As already noted, this will not result in an MoP, and the next step is therefore to approximate this representation into an MoP by some means. Varando et al. [11] investigated two schemes: i) To use the representation in Eq. 4 to generate samples from the conditional distribution of x given $\mathbf{Z}$ and learn the MoP representation from the generated dataset; ii) to use numerical techniques to approximate the fraction directly (specifically, both Taylor series and Lagrange interpolation were considered). In our work we first learn an MoP representation for $f(x, \mathbf{z})$ using the program in Eq. 3, then *calculate* $f(\mathbf{z}) = \int_{\Omega_x} f(x, \mathbf{z}) \mathrm{d}x$ directly from the learned joint. Note that since $f(x, \mathbf{z})$ is a MoP the integral can easily be performed analytically. Next, the conditional distribution defined through Eq. 4 is our target, leading to the following optimization program:

$$\textbf{minimize} \quad \sum_{\ell=1}^{N} \left(\frac{f(x_\ell, \mathbf{z}_\ell)}{f(\mathbf{z}_\ell)} - f(x_\ell|\mathbf{z}_\ell) \right)^2 \tag{5}$$

$$\textbf{subject to} \quad f(x|\mathbf{z}) \geq 0 \quad \forall (x, \mathbf{z}) \in (\Omega_X \times \Omega_\mathbf{z}).$$

The solution to this problem is a parameter-set that defines an un-normalized conditional PDF (that is, we have no guarantee that $\int_{\Omega_x} f(x|\mathbf{z})dx = 1$ for all $\mathbf{z} \in \Omega_\mathbf{z}$). Hence, the procedure is finalized by partially normalizing the distribution [10]. The program is quadratic, and can therefore be solved efficiently.

We note that while the programmes in Eqs. 2 and 3 are defined to obtain the CDFs, the programme in Eq. 5 works directly with the PDF. The reason for the programmes in Eqs. 2 and 3 to work with the cumulative distribution functions is that the defined $G_N(\cdot)$ function is a more robust data-representation than, say, a histogram [5], and as $G_N(\cdot)$ represents the empirical CDF the result of these programs are also CDFs. On the other hand, the program in Eq. 5 does not work directly with representations of the data, but rather defines the target function through Eq. 4. Therefore, the objects under study by this program are PDFs.

4   Experimental Analysis

In this section, we compare the proposal given in Sect. 3 with the methods described in [5] (where the conditioning variables are discretized) and in [11] (where B-splines are used) for learning conditional MoPs from data.

We consider two different scenarios concerning two continuous variables, X and Y. In the first one, $Y \sim \mathcal{N}(\mu = 0, \sigma = 1)$ and $X|\{Y = y\} \sim \mathcal{N}(\mu = y, \sigma = 1)$. In the second scenario, $Y \sim \text{Gamma}(\text{rate} = 10, \text{shape} = 10)$ and $X|\{Y = y\} \sim \text{Exp}(\text{rate} = y)$. For each scenario, we generated 10 data-sets of samples $\{X_i, Y_i\}_{i=1}^{N}$, where the size is chosen as $N = 25, 500, 2500, 5000$. The effectiveness of the tested methods was measured by computing the mean square error for each set of samples. The results are showed in Tables 1 and 2.

The results in Table 1 indicate that the most accurate results for scenario 1 are achieved by the B-spline approach [11]. The worst results by far are obtained by the approach that discretizes the conditioning variables [5]. Both the proposed approach and the B-spline approach yield errors close to zero in most cases.

The results for scenario 2 are reported in Table 2. In this case, the most accurate results in terms of mean square error are provided by the MoTBF approach. Again, the method in [5] obtains the worst results overall.

The results are consistent with the plots in Fig. 2, where the MoTBF approach (bottom row in the figure) presented in this paper is able to resemble the shape of the exact conditional distribution (top row), specially in the non Gaussian scenario, while the method in [5] (middle row) is penalized by the fact that the estimated model is piecewise constant along the Y axis. The plots in Fig. 2 show the results obtained when learning from $N = 5000$ samples.

Table 1. Average MSE between the different methods to obtain MoP approximations and the true conditional densities for each set of 10 samples, where $Y \sim \mathcal{N}(0,1)$ and $X|Y \sim \mathcal{N}(y,1)$.

N	$f_{X|Y}(x|y)$	Split Method[5]	MoTBF Algorithm	B-Splines Method[11]
25	y=-0.6748	0.1276	0.0848	**0.0103**
	y=0.00	0.1254	0.0936	**0.0089**
	y=0.6748	0.1279	0.1416	**0.0105**
500	y=-0.6748	0.0256	0.0453	**0.0025**
	y=0.00	0.0317	0.0117	**0.0009**
	y=0.6748	0.0246	0.0411	**0.0020**
2500	y=-0.6748	0.0031	0.0019	**0.0006**
	y=0.00	0.0064	0.0010	**0.0002**
	y=0.6748	0.0058	0.0024	**0.0006**
5000	y=-0.6748	0.0019	0.0018	**0.0006**
	y=0.00	0.0074	0.0009	**0.0002**
	y=0.6748	0.0019	0.0020	**0.0006**

Table 2. Average MSE between the different methods to obtain MoP approximations and the true conditional densities for each set of 10 samples, where $Y \sim Gamma(rate = 10, shape = 10)$ and $X|Y \sim Exp(y)$.

N	$f_{X|Y}(x|y)$	Split Method[5]	MoTBF Algorithm	B-Splines Method[11]
25	y=0.7706	0.4054	**0.0083**	0.0131
	y=0.9684	0.4703	**0.0081**	0.0225
	y=1.1916	0.5473	**0.0229**	0.0374
500	y=0.7706	0.0158	0.0037	**0.0012**
	y=0.9684	0.0048	0.0034	**0.0022**
	y=1.1916	0.0118	**0.0039**	0.0057
2500	y=0.7706	0.0064	**0.0025**	**0.0025**
	y=0.9684	0.0080	**0.0024**	0.0043
	y=1.1916	0.0029	**0.0046**	0.0074
5000	y=0.7706	**0.0013**	0.0021	0.0015
	y=0.9684	0.0091	**0.0015**	0.0022
	y=1.1916	**0.0026**	0.0029	0.0032

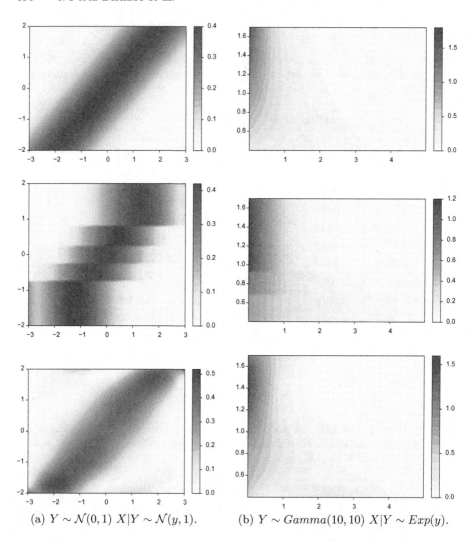

(a) $Y \sim \mathcal{N}(0,1)$ $X|Y \sim \mathcal{N}(y,1)$.   (b) $Y \sim Gamma(10,10)$ $X|Y \sim Exp(y)$.

Fig. 2. For the two scenarios (in columns), true conditional density (top row), the MoP produced by the method introduced in [5] (middle row) and the MoP obtained by the proposal in this paper (bottom row).

5   Concluding Remarks

In this paper we have extended the learning algorithm for univariate MoTBFs in [5] to multivariate and conditional densities. The advantage of the proposal described here with respect to the B-spline approach in [11] is that there is no need to split the domain of any variable. This is a fundamental issue in order to keep the complexity of inference in hybrid Bayesian networks under control. We note that while in theory high order polynomials may be required to model the distributions, the use of the BIC-score [8] leads to low-order polynomials being selected in practice [4,5].

The experimental analysis suggests that our proposal is competitive with the B-spine approach in a range of commonly used distributions. Even if the conditional distribution functions yielded by the method is this paper are not proper conditional densities, evidence so far indicates they are accurate approximations, which in practice allows the method to be used as a means of representing the parameters of a Bayesian network. This paves the way to envisioning structural learning algorithms for hybrid Bayesian networks parameterized by MoTBFs.

Finally, we note that even though the paper develops a learning method for MoPs, the techniques employed here can easily be extended to be applicable for MoTBFs in general.

Acknowledgments. This research has been partly funded by the Spanish Ministry of Economy and Competitiveness, through project TIN2013-46638-C3-1-P and by Junta de Andalucía through project P11-TIC-7821 and by ERDF funds. A part of this work was performed within the AMIDST project. AMIDST has received funding from the European Union's Seventh Framework Programme for research, technological development and demonstration under grant agreement no 619209.

References

1. Langseth, H., Nielsen, T.D., Rumí, R., Salmerón, A.: Maximum likelihood learning of conditional MTE distributions. In: Sossai, C., Chemello, G. (eds.) ECSQARU 2009. LNCS, vol. 5590, pp. 240–251. Springer, Heidelberg (2009)
2. Langseth, H., Nielsen, T.D., Rumí, R., Salmerón, A.: Mixtures of truncated basis functions. Int. J. Approximate Reasoning **53**, 212–227 (2012)
3. Langseth, H., Nielsen, T.D., Salmerón, A.: Learning mixtures of truncated basis functions from data. In: Proceedings of the Sixth European Workshop on Probabilistic Graphical Models (PGM 2012), pp. 163–170 (2012)
4. Langseth, H., Nielsen, T.D., Rumí, R., Salmerón, A.: Inference in hybrid Bayesian networks with mixtures of truncated basis functions. In: Proceedings of the Sixth European Workshop on Probabilistic Graphical Models (PGM 2012), pp. 171–178 (2012)
5. Langseth, H., Nielsen, T.D., Pérez-Bernabé, I., Salmerón, A.: Learning mixtures of truncated basis functions from data. Int. J. Approximate Reasoning **55**, 940–956 (2014)
6. Lauritzen, S.: Propagation of probabilities, means and variances in mixed graphical association models. J. Am. Stat. Assoc. **87**, 1098–1108 (1992)
7. Moral, S., Rumí, R., Salmerón, A.: Mixtures of truncated exponentials in hybrid Bayesian networks. In: Benferhat, S., Besnard, P. (eds.) ECSQARU 2001. LNCS (LNAI), vol. 2143, p. 156. Springer, Heidelberg (2001)
8. Schwarz, G.: Estimating the dimension of a model. Ann. Stat. **6**, 461–464 (1978)
9. Shenoy, P., Shafer, G.: Axioms for probability and belief function propagation. In: Shachter, R., Levitt, T., Lemmer, J., Kanal, L. (eds.) Uncertainty in Artificial Intelligence 4, pp. 169–198. North Holland, Amsterdam (1990)
10. Shenoy, P., West, J.: Inference in hybrid Bayesian networks using mixtures of polynomials. Int. J. Approximate Reasoning **52**, 641–657 (2011)

11. Varando, G., López-Cruz, P.L., Nielsen, T.D., Bielza, C., Larrañga, P.: Conditional density approximations with mixtures of polynomials. Int. J. Intell. Syst. **30**, 236–264 (2015)
12. Zhang, N., Poole, D.: Exploiting causal independence in Bayesian network inference. J. Artif. Intell. Res. **5**, 301–328 (1996)

MPE Inference in Conditional Linear Gaussian Networks

Antonio Salmerón[1], Rafael Rumí[1], Helge Langseth[2], Anders L. Madsen[3,4],
and Thomas D. Nielsen[4(✉)]

[1] University of Almería, 04120 Almería, Spain
{antonio.salmeron,rrumi}@ual.es
[2] Norwegian University of Science and Technology, 7491 Trondheim, Norway
helgel@idi.ntnu.no
[3] Hugin Expert A/S, 9000 Aalborg, Denmark
anders@hugin.com
[4] Aalborg University, 9220 Aalborg, Denmark
tdn@cs.aau.dk
http://www.amidst.eu

Abstract. Given evidence on a set of variables in a Bayesian network,
the most probable explanation (MPE) is the problem of finding a configuration of the remaining variables with maximum posterior probability.
This problem has previously been addressed for discrete Bayesian networks and can be solved using inference methods similar to those used
for finding posterior probabilities. However, when dealing with hybrid
Bayesian networks, such as conditional linear Gaussian (CLG) networks,
the MPE problem has only received little attention. In this paper, we provide insights into the general problem of finding an MPE configuration in
a CLG network. For solving this problem, we devise an algorithm based
on bucket elimination and with the same computational complexity as
that of calculating posterior marginals in a CLG network. We illustrate
the workings of the algorithm using a detailed numerical example, and
discuss possible extensions of the algorithm for handling the more general
problem of finding a maximum a posteriori hypothesis (MAP).

Keywords: MPE inference · Conditional linear gaussian networks ·
Hybrid Bayesian networks

1 Introduction

Probabilistic graphical models provide a well-founded and principled approach
for performing inference in complex domains endowed with uncertainty. A probabilistic graphical model is a framework consisting of two parts: a qualitative
component in the form of a graphical model encoding conditional independence
assertions about the domain being modeled as well as a quantitative component consisting of a collection of local probability distributions adhering to the
independence properties specified in the graphical model. Collectively, the two

© Springer International Publishing Switzerland 2015
S. Destercke and T. Denoeux (Eds.): ECSQARU 2015, LNAI 9161, pp. 407–416, 2015.
DOI: 10.1007/978-3-319-20807-7_37

components provide a compact representation of the joint probability distribution over the domain being modeled.

Given a Bayesian network where a subset of the variables is observed, we may, e.g., query the network for the posterior marginal distributions of the remaining variables or for a maximum a posteriori probability configuration for a subset of the variables. If this subset is a proper subset of the non-observed variables, then the problem is referred to as a maximum a posteriori (MAP) hypothesis problem [10]. On the other hand, if the variables of interest correspond to the complement of the observation set, then the problem is referred to as that of finding the most probable explanation (MPE) [2,6]; MPE can therefore be considered a specialization of MAP.

For Bayesian networks containing only discrete variables, there has been a substantial amount of work on devising both exact and approximate algorithms for performing MAP and MPE inference. However, for hybrid Bayesian networks, with both discrete and continuous variables, these types of inference problems have received only little attention [12]. In this paper we consider the problem of performing MPE inference in conditional linear Gaussian networks [7]. We propose an MPE algorithm based on bucket-elimination, which has the same computational complexity as that of standard inference for posterior marginals [8]. In contrast to the proposal in [12], we study the effect of entering evidence and also avoid the use of piece-wise defined functions by using an auxiliary tree structure keeping track of the functions used in previous calculations. The algorithm is illustrated using a detailed numerical example.

2   Preliminaries

Bayesian networks (BNs) [1,5,11] are a particular type of probabilistic graphical model that has enjoyed widespread attention in the last two decades. Attached to each node, there is a conditional probability distribution given its parents in the network, so that in general, for a BN with N variables $\mathbf{X} = \{X_1, \ldots, X_N\}$, the joint distribution factorizes as $p(\mathbf{X}) = \prod_{i=1}^{N} p(X_i | Pa(X_i))$, where $Pa(X_i)$ denotes the set of parents of X_i in the network. A BN is called *hybrid* if some of its variables are discrete while some others are continuous.

We will use lowercase letters to refer to values or configurations of values, so that x denotes a value of X and boldface $\mathbf{x}$ is a configuration of the variables in $\mathbf{X}$. Given a set of observed variables $\mathbf{X}_E \subset \mathbf{X}$ and a set of variables of interest $\mathbf{X}_I \subset \mathbf{X} \backslash \mathbf{X}_E$, *probabilistic inference* consists of computing the posterior distribution $p(x_i | \mathbf{x}_E)$ for each $i \in I$. If we denote by $\mathbf{X}_C$ and $\mathbf{X}_D$ the set of continuous and discrete variables not in $\{\mathbf{X}_i\} \cup \mathbf{X}_E$, and by $\mathbf{X}_{C_i}$ and $\mathbf{X}_{D_i}$ the set of continuous and discrete variables not in $\mathbf{X}_E$, the goal of inference can be formulated as computing

$$p(x_i | \mathbf{x}_E) = \left[\sum_{\mathbf{x}_D \in \Omega_{\mathbf{x}_D}} \int_{\mathbf{x}_C \in \Omega_{\mathbf{x}_C}} p(\mathbf{x}, \mathbf{x}_E) d\mathbf{x}_C \right] \Big/ \left[\sum_{\mathbf{x}_{D_i} \in \Omega_{\mathbf{x}_{D_i}}} \int_{\mathbf{x}_{C_i} \in \Omega_{\mathbf{x}_{C_i}}} p(\mathbf{x}, \mathbf{x}_E) d\mathbf{x}_{C_i} \right],$$

where $\Omega_{\mathbf{X}}$ is the set of possible values of a set of variables $\mathbf{X}$ and $p(\mathbf{x}, \mathbf{x}_E)$ is the joint distribution in the BN instantiated according to the observed values $\mathbf{x}_E$.

A particularly complex kind of inference in BNs is the so-called *maximum a posteriori (MAP)* problem. For a set of target variables $\mathbf{X}_I \subseteq \mathbf{X} \setminus \mathbf{X}_E$, the goal of MAP inference is to compute

$$\mathbf{x}_I^* = \arg \max_{\mathbf{x}_I \in \Omega_{\mathbf{X}_I}} p(\mathbf{x}_I | \mathbf{X}_E = \mathbf{x}_E), \tag{1}$$

where $p(\mathbf{x}_I | \mathbf{X}_E = \mathbf{x}_E)$ is obtained by first marginalizing out from the joint distribution $p(\mathbf{x})$ the variables not in $\mathbf{X}_I$ and not in $\mathbf{X}_E$. A related problem is *MPE* that stands for finding the *most probable explanation* to an observation $\mathbf{X}_E = \mathbf{x}_E$. It is a particular case of MAP, where $\mathbf{X}_I = \mathbf{X} \setminus \mathbf{X}_E$. Both MAP and MPE belong to the class of problems known as *abductive inference* [4].

2.1   Conditional Linear Gaussian Networks

A *Conditional Linear Gaussian Network* is a hybrid Bayesian network where the joint distribution is a conditional linear Gaussian (CLG) [7]. In the CLG model, the conditional distribution of each discrete variable $X_D \in \mathbf{X}$ given its parents is a multinomial, whilst the conditional distribution of each continuous variable $Z \in \mathbf{X}$ with discrete parents $\mathbf{X}_D \subseteq \mathbf{X}$ and continuous parents $\mathbf{X}_C \subseteq \mathbf{X}$, is given by

$$p(z | \mathbf{X}_D = \mathbf{x}_D, \mathbf{X}_C = \mathbf{x}_C) = \mathcal{N}(z; \alpha(\mathbf{x}_D) + \boldsymbol{\beta}(\mathbf{x}_D)^\mathsf{T} \mathbf{x}_C, \sigma(\mathbf{x}_D)), \tag{2}$$

for all $\mathbf{x}_D \in \Omega_{\mathbf{X}_D}$ and $\mathbf{x}_C \in \Omega_{\mathbf{X}_C}$, where α and $\boldsymbol{\beta}$ are the coefficients of a linear regression model of Z given its continuous parents; this model can differ for each configuration of the discrete variables $\mathbf{X}_D$.

After fixing any configuration of the discrete variables, the joint distribution of any subset $\mathbf{X}_C \subseteq \mathbf{X}$ of continuous variables is a multivariate Gaussian. Hence, the parameters of the multivariate Gaussian can be obtained from the ones in the CLG representation. For a set of n continuous variables $Z_1, \ldots, Z_n$ with a conditionally specified joint density $p(z_1, \ldots, z_n) = \prod_{i=1}^{n} f(z_i | z_{i+1}, \ldots, z_n)$, where the k-th factor, $1 \leq k \leq n$, is such that

$$p(z_k | z_{k+1}, \ldots, z_n) = \mathcal{N}(z_k; \mu_{z_k | z_{k+1}, \ldots, z_n}, \sigma_{z_k}),$$

it holds that the joint is $p(z_1, \ldots, z_n) = \mathcal{N}(z_1, \ldots, z_n; \boldsymbol{\mu}, \boldsymbol{\Sigma})$, where $\boldsymbol{\mu}$ is the n-dimensional vector of means and $\boldsymbol{\Sigma}$ is the covariance matrix of the multivariate distribution over random variables $Z_1, \ldots, Z_n$ and both $\boldsymbol{\mu}$ and $\boldsymbol{\Sigma}$ are derived from the parameters in Eq. (2) [9].

3   MPE Inference in CLG Networks

MPE inference can be carried out by adapting generic inference algorithms like *Bucket Elimination* [3]. The choice of bucket elimination as the underlying inference scheme for our proposal is motivated by its simplicity and flexibility, as well as the fact that it has been successfully employed in the MPE problem for discrete variables. The bucket elimination algorithm computes the MPE using local computations. A *bucket* containing probability functions is kept for each variable. Initially, an ordering of the variables in the network is established, and each conditional distribution in the network is assigned to the bucket corresponding to the variable in its domain holding the highest rank. Afterwards, the buckets are processed in a sequence opposite to the initial ordering of the variables. Each bucket is processed by combining all the functions it contains and by marginalizing the main variable in that bucket by maximization. The details of the algorithm are given in Algorithm 1.

Function Elim-MPE($\mathbf{X},P,\sigma,\mathbf{x}_E$)

Input: The set of variables in the network, $\mathbf{X} = \{X_1, \ldots, X_N\}$. The distributions in the network $P = \{p_1, \ldots, p_N\}$. An ordering, σ, of the variables in $\mathbf{X}$. Evidence $\mathbf{X}_E = \mathbf{x}_E$.

Output: $\mathbf{x}^{mpe}$, the configuration for which the posterior density reaches its maximum, and mpe, the density value at that point.

begin

    Initialization:

    Partition P into buckets $B_1, \ldots, B_N$, where B_i contains the conditional distributions in P whose highest index variable is X_i.

    Backward phase:

    for $p \leftarrow N$ **to** 2 **do**

        if $X_p \in \mathbf{X}_E$ **then**

            Replace X_p by $\mathbf{x}_{E_p}$ in each $h \in B_p$, and insert the resulting h in the bucket corresponding to its highest ranked variable according to ordering σ.

        end

        else

            $h^p \leftarrow \max_{x_p} \prod_{h \in B_p} h$

            Insert h_p in the bucket corresponding to its highest ranked variable.

        end

    end

    Forward phase:

    for $p \leftarrow 1$ **to** n **do**

        Let $h^{R(x_1, \ldots, x_p)}$ denote the restriction of each function $h \in B_p$ to the values $(x_1, \ldots, x_p)$.

        $x_p^{mpe} \leftarrow \arg\max_{x_p} \prod_{h \in B_p} h^{R(x_1, \ldots, x_p)}$.

    end

    return $\mathbf{x}^{mpe} = \{x_1^{mpe}, \ldots, x_N^{mpe}\}$ *and* $mpe = \max_{x_1} \prod_{h \in B_1} h$.

end

Algorithm 1. The Bucket elimination algorithm for computing the MPE as described in [3].

Example 1. Consider the network in Fig. 1 and the ordering $\langle Y, S, W, T, U \rangle$. According to such ordering, the initial setting of the buckets would be $B_Y = \{P(Y)\}$, $B_S = \{P(S)\}$, $B_W = \{f(w|Y)\}$, $B_T = \{f(t|w, S)\}$ and $B_U = \{f(u|w)\}$. The *backward* phase in Algorithm 1 conveys the processing of the buckets as follows. The first bucket to be processed is B_U. It is done by maximizing out u from $f(u|w)$. As $f(u|w) = \mathcal{N}(u; w, 1)$, the maximum is reached at the mean, which means that U is maximized out by replacing u in $f(u|w)$ by w, which results in a function $h^U(w) = \frac{1}{\sqrt{2\pi}}$. Hence, the obtained function is in fact a constant, that is shifted to bucket B_W. The next bucket to handle is B_T, where T is removed from $f(t|w,S)$ by replacing t by the mean of the conditional distribution, resulting again in a constant function $h^T(w,S) = \frac{1}{\sqrt{2\pi}}$. After this calculation, h^T is stored in B_W, which is itself processed by multiplying $f(w|Y), h^T(w,S)$ and $h^U(w)$ and maximizing out W from the result. Since h^T and h^U are constant, we just have to maximize $f(x|Y)$ and multiply by the constants afterwards. The result is $h^W(Y,S) = (\frac{1}{\sqrt{2\pi}})^3$, that is stored in B_S. Bucket B_S contains $P(S)$ and $h^W(Y,S)$, whose product is equal to $0.1(\frac{1}{\sqrt{2\pi}})^3$ when $S = 0$ and $0.9(\frac{1}{\sqrt{2\pi}})^3$ when $S = 1$. Hence, maximizing with respect to S yields $h^S(Y) = 0.9(\frac{1}{\sqrt{2\pi}})^3$, that is sent to bucket B_Y. The MPE configuration is actually obtained in the *forward* phase of the algorithm, where the bucket processing step is traced back.

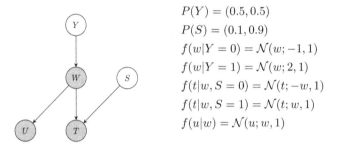

$$P(Y) = (0.5, 0.5)$$
$$P(S) = (0.1, 0.9)$$
$$f(w|Y = 0) = \mathcal{N}(w; -1, 1)$$
$$f(w|Y = 1) = \mathcal{N}(w; 2, 1)$$
$$f(t|w, S = 0) = \mathcal{N}(t; -w, 1)$$
$$f(t|w, S = 1) = \mathcal{N}(t; w, 1)$$
$$f(u|w) = \mathcal{N}(u; w, 1)$$

Fig. 1. A hybrid Bayesian network with two discrete and three continuous (shaded) variables.

The example above shows how maximizing out continuous variables is an easy task if the continuous variables are always removed first, as it just amounts to replacing the variable being removed by its mode (which in the Gaussian case is equal to its mean). The price to pay is that, in the worst case, a function containing all the discrete variables would be created, as is the case of $h^W(Y,S)$. It is an undesirable event, as the size of a probability function of discrete variables is exponential in the number of variables. This complexity blow-up can be avoided in many cases by allowing orderings for constructing the buckets where discrete and continuous variables can be arranged with no restrictions. But then a new problem arises, as the maximization operation becomes more complex. Assume, for instance, that we reach a point where Y is maximized out before W in Fig. 1. This amounts to computing

$$h^Y(w) = \max_y \{P(Y = y)f(w|Y = y)\} = \max\{0.5\mathcal{N}(w; -1, 1), 0.5\mathcal{N}(w; 2, 1)\}.$$

Therefore, h^Y is not a function with a single analytical expression, but it is piecewise defined instead. We show in the next section how it is possible to avoid piecewise representations of the result of maximizing out discrete variables. Instead, we will keep lists of the functions that take place in the max operation. In other words, the max operation is carried out in a lazy way. The counterpart is that the forward phase in Algorithm 1 requires us to keep track of the operations carried out over the potentials in the backward phase. We propose to use a tree structure to keep track of the functions involved in intermediate calculations as illustrated in Fig. 2 and which corresponds to Example 1.

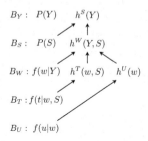

Fig. 2. Tree structure keeping track of the functions involved in the intermediate calculations performed during the backward phase of the bucket elimination algorithm.

3.1   Entering Evidence

If a variable is observed, no bucket is created for it. Instead, the variable is replaced by its observed value in every function where it appears. Assume a continuous variable X that is observed taking on value $X = x_0$. If the parents of X are $Y_1, \ldots, Y_n$, replacing variable X by value x_0 in its conditional density results in a function

$$\phi(y_1, \ldots, y_n) = \frac{1}{\sigma_x \sqrt{2\pi}} \exp\left\{ -\frac{(x_0 - (\beta_0 + \sum_{i=1}^{n} \beta_i y_i))^2}{2\sigma_x^2} \right\}. \tag{3}$$

Eventually, function ϕ will be passed to the bucket corresponding to one of its parents, where it will be multiplied by the parent's density prior to maximization. Let Y_j be such a parent of X. Its conditional density can be written as

$$f(y_j | Pa(Y_j)) = \frac{1}{\sigma_{y_j} \sqrt{2\pi}} \exp\left\{ -\frac{(y_j - \mu_{y_j | pa(y_j)})^2}{2\sigma_{y_j}^2} \right\}. \tag{4}$$

Maximizing the product of the functions in Eqs. (3) and (4) with respect to y_j is equivalent to maximizing the sum of their respective logarithms. It is obtained by solving the equation

$$\frac{\partial}{\partial y_j}\left(-\frac{(x_0 - (\beta_0 + \sum_{i=1}^{n} \beta_i y_i))^2}{2\sigma_x^2} - \frac{(y_j - \mu_{y_j | pa(y_j)})^2}{2\sigma_{y_j}^2} \right) = 0, \tag{5}$$

which simply amounts to maximizing a quadratic function.

4   A Numerical Example

In this section we illustrate our proposal through a detailed example. Consider the CLG network illustrated in Fig. 1, where the discrete variables Y and S are assumed to be binary with states 0 and 1. Assume now that the continuous variable U is instantiated to 1 and we seek an MPE configuration over the remaining variables.

For performing MPE inference in this network we proceed with bucket elimination using the order $\langle W, T, S, Y \rangle$. Thus, the buckets are initialized as $B_Y = \{P(Y), f(w|Y)\}$, $B_S = \{P(S), f(t|w, S)\}$, $B_T = \{1\}$, $B_W = \{f(u = 1|w)\}$, and $B_U = \{1\}$. The first bucket to be processed is B_Y, which involves maximizing Y from $P(Y)f(w|Y)$ and passing the result to bucket B_W.

$$h_1^Y(w) = \max_y P(y)f(w|y) = \max[P(Y = 0)f(w|Y = 0), P(Y = 1)f(w|Y = 1)],$$

where the super-script Y means that the potential contains two pieces indexed by Y; each of them corresponds to a scaled normal distribution (see Fig. 3). From an operational point of view, we use a list to store the components of $h_1^Y(w)$.

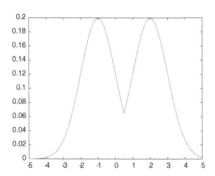

Fig. 3. The potential $h_1(w)$ obtained by maximizing Y out of $P(Y)f(w|Y)$.

The next bucket to process is B_S from which S should be eliminated. This operation produces the potential

$$h_2^S(t, w) = \max_s P(s)f(t|w, s) = \max[P(S = 0)f(t|w, S = 0),$$
$$P(S = 1)f(t|w, S = 1)],$$

which is passed to B_T; again, the super-script S indicates that $h_2^S(t, w)$ is a list with as many elements as states of S. When processing B_T, we maximize out T:

$$h_3(w) = \max_t h_2(w, t) = \max_t \max_s P(s)f(t|w, s) = \max_s P(s) \max_t f(t|w, s),$$

which produces a potential containing a contribution for each state of S. By following the arguments from Example 1, $f(t|w, S = i)$ is maximized at the conditional means $-w$ (for $S = 0$) and w (for $S = 1$), thus

$$h_3(w) = (\sqrt{2\pi})^{-1} \max[P(S = 0)\sigma_{T,S=0}^{-1}, P(S = 1)\sigma_{T,S=1}^{-1}],$$

which is a scalar value and constant wrt. W; since $h_3(w)$ contains only one element we omit the super-script index previously used. Based on the CLG specification above, we find that $h_3(w) = (\sqrt{2\pi})^{-1} \max[0.1 \cdot 1, 0.9 \cdot 1] = 0.9(\sqrt{2\pi})^{-1}$, which is passed to B_W.

Finally, we eliminate W based on the potentials $B_W = \{h_1(w), h_3(w), f(U = 1|w)\}$, but since $h_3(w)$ is constant wrt. w we can disregard it during maximization (algorithmically, we can also detect this from the network structure using d-separation analysis):

$$\begin{aligned}
h_4^Y &= \max_w [f(U = 1|w)h_1(w)] \\
&= \max_w [f(U = 1|w) \max[P(Y = 0)f(w|Y = 0), P(Y = 1)f(w|Y = 1)]] \\
&= \max[\max_w f(U = 1|w)P(Y = 0)f(w|Y = 0), \\
&\qquad \max_w f(U = 1|w)P(Y = 1)f(w|Y = 1)].
\end{aligned}$$

The two maximizations over w can easily be solved analytically (see the discussion in Sect. 3.1), since $\log(f(U = 1|w)P(Y = i)f(w|Y = i))$ is quadratic wrt. w, for $i = 0, 1$. That is, $\log(f(U = 1|w)P(Y = i)f(w|Y = i))$ is maximized when

$$\frac{\partial}{\partial w}\left(-\frac{1}{2}(1 - \beta_U w)^2 - \frac{1}{2}(w - \mu_{W,Y=i})^2\right) = 0,$$

which is achieved for $w_{Y=i}^{\mathrm{mpe}} = (\beta_U + \mu_{W,Y=i})/(\beta_U^2 + 1)$; here β_U is the regression coefficient for U wrt. w, $\mu_{W,Y=i}$ is the mean of W given $Y = i$ and the constant 1 in $(1 - \beta_U w)^2$ corresponds to the observed value of U. Using the numerical specification above, we get $w_{Y=0}^{\mathrm{mpe}} = 0$ and $w_{Y=1}^{\mathrm{mpe}} = 1.5$.

In order to find a full MPE configuration over all the variable (and thereby also a single MPE value for W), we need to retrace the maximizing arguments for the variables on which the current potential depends (a tree structure like the one displayed in Fig. 2 can be used). This set of variables can be identified from the functional arguments for the potential in question together with the variables that index the list structure of this potential (given above by the super-script indexes). Specifically, for h_4^Y we see that the potential depends on Y only, hence we look for the value y^{mpe} of Y maximizing $P(Y)f(w_Y^{\mathrm{mpe}}|Y)$ (corresponding to $h_1^Y(w_Y^{\mathrm{mpe}})$) and we get $y^{\mathrm{mpe}} = 1$ since $0.5 \cdot \mathcal{N}(1.5; 2, 1) > 0.5 \cdot \mathcal{N}(0; -1, 1)$. We thus also have $w^{\mathrm{mpe}} = 1.5$.

Next we proceed backwards in the elimination ordering and look for an MPE value for T. This is achieved by considering the maximizing arguments for h_3, which is the potential obtained when maximizing out T. From the discussion above we see that these maximizing arguments can immediately be identified as the conditional means of $f(t|w^{\mathrm{mpe}}, S = i))$ and we therefore find that $t_{S=0}^{\mathrm{mpe}} = -1.5$ and $t_{S=1}^{\mathrm{mpe}} = 1.5$. Lastly, we consider S and from the maximizing argument for $h_2^S(t, w)$ (obtained when maximizing out S) with t and w being fixed to

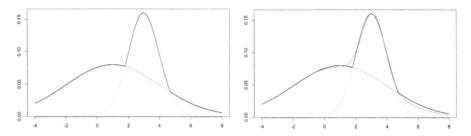

Fig. 4. Left part: Two Gaussian distributions (dashed lines) are shown together with their point-wise maximization (solid line). Right part: The max-potential is approximated by a mixture of Gaussians drawn using solid red line.

their MPE values ($t_S^{\text{mpe}} = 1.5$ and $w^{\text{mpe}} = 1.5$), we get that $s^{\text{mpe}} = 1$, since $0.1 \cdot \mathcal{N}(-1.5; 1.5, 1) < 0.5 \cdot \mathcal{N}(1.5; 1.5, 1)$, and thus $t^{\text{mpe}} = 1.5$.

As a final comment, we would like to reemphasize that the MPE inference scheme as proposed in this paper, and illustrated above, follows the same structure as standard algorithms for performing, say marginal, inference in CLG networks. Thus, the algorithms share the same computational complexity. In particular, in the example above we see that the elimination order is able to exploit the conditional independencies in the model structure, and we therefore avoid the computational blow-up of having to consider all combinations of the discrete variables, cf. the discussion in Sect. 3. Furthermore, when identifying MPE configurations for the continuous variables we see that these configurations can easily be identified as either corresponding to the conditional means of the densities involved or they can be found by maximizing a quadratic function.

5   Conclusion and Future Work

In this paper we have discussed the MPE problem in conditional linear Gaussian networks. The behavior of the proposed algorithm was illustrated with the help of a small example model, successfully calculating the most probable explanation over the variables in the domain. The run-time complexity of the proposed algorithm is identical to that of standard probabilistic inference in CLG networks, and all maximization operations can be done efficiently using analytic solutions. The key contributor to the complexity is maintaining the list of Gaussian components representing the densities of the unobserved continuous variables.

Our next step is to extend our results to the maximum a posteriori (MAP) problem. This is significantly more difficult than the MPE problem, as we will have to do both summation and maximization operations over the discrete variables. Consider again the model in Fig. 1, and assume we are interested in the MAP configuration over Y and T. Eliminating S (by summation) will result in a *mixture* of Gaussians potential, while eliminating T (by maximization) results in a *maximum* of Gaussians potential; the two potentials should later be combined. Maintaining these two separate types of potentials is inconvenient, as they are not closed under the required operations, something that is highly unsatisfactory from a computational point of view.

We are currently investigating a technique to approximate the max-potentials using sum-potentials, see Fig. 4, which will enable us to do the calculations using a single data structure. We are looking into the quality of the generated approximations, and we are also working towards an implementation of the approximate inference technique. We are also studying strategies for selecting optimal variable orders for computing the buckets.

Acknowledgments. This work was performed as part of the AMIDST project. AMIDST has received funding from the European Union's Seventh Framework Programme for research, technological development and demonstration under grant agreement no 619209.

References

1. Cowell, R.G., Lauritzen, S.L., Dawid, A.P., Spiegelhalter, D.J.: Probabilistic Networks and Expert Systems, 1st edn. In: Nair, V., Lawless, J., Jordan, M. (eds.) Springer-Verlag New York Inc., New York (1999)
2. Philip Dawid, A.: Applications of a general propagation algorithm for a probabilistic expert system. Stat. Comput. **2**, 25–36 (1992)
3. Dechter, R.: Bucket elimination: a unifiying framework for reasoning. Artif. Intell. **113**, 41–85 (1999)
4. Gámez, J.A.: Abductive inference in Bayesian networks: a review. In: Gámez, J.A., Moral, S., Salmerón, A. (eds.) Advances in Bayesian Networks. STUDFUZZ, vol. 146, pp. 101–117. Springer, Heidelberg (2004)
5. Koller, D., Friedman, N.: Probabilistic Graphical Models: Principles and Techniques. MIT Press, Cambridge (2009)
6. Kwisthout, J.: Most probable explanations in Bayesian networks: complexity and tractability. Int. J. Approximate Reasoning **52**, 1452–1469 (2011)
7. Lauritzen, S.L., Wermuth, N.: Graphical models for associations between variables, some of which are qualitative and some quantitative. Ann. Stat. **17**, 31–57 (1989)
8. Lerner, U., Parr, R.: Inference in hybrid networks: Theoretical limits and practical algorithms. In: UAI, pp. 310–318 (2001)
9. Nielsen, J.D., Gámez, J.A., Salmerón, A.: Modelling and inference with conditional Gaussian probabilistic decision graphs. Int. J. Approximate Reasoning **53**, 929–945 (2012)
10. Park, J.D.: Map complexity results and approximation methods. In: Darwiche, A., Friedman, N. (eds.) Proceedings of the Eighteenth Conference on Uncertainty in Artificial Intelligence (UAI 2002), pp. 388–396. Morgan Kaufmann Publishers Inc., San Francisco (2002)
11. Pearl, J.: Probabilistic Reasoning in Intelligent Systems: Networks of Plausible Inference. Morgan Kaufmann Publishers Inc., San Mateo (1988)
12. Sun, W., Chang, K.C.: Study of the most probable explanation in hybrid Bayesian networks. In: Signal Processing, Sensor Fusion, and Target Recognition XX, Proceedings of SPIE, vol. 8050 (2011)

Belief Functions

Dynamic Time Warping Distance for Message Propagation Classification in Twitter

Siwar Jendoubi[1,2,4(✉)], Arnaud Martin[2], Ludovic Liétard[2],
Boutheina Ben Yaghlane[3], and Hend Ben Hadji[4]

[1] LARODEC, ISG Tunis, Université de Tunis, Tunis, Tunisia
jendoubi.siwar@yahoo.fr
[2] IRISA, Université de Rennes I, Rennes, France
{Arnaud.Martin,ludovic.lietard}@univ-rennes1.fr
[3] LARODEC, IHEC Carthage, Université de Carthage, Tunis, Tunisia
boutheina.yaghlane@ihec.rnu.tn
[4] Centre d'Etude et de Recherche des Télécommunications, Tunis, Tunisia
hend.Benhji@cert.mincom.tn

Abstract. Social messages classification is a research domain that has attracted the attention of many researchers in these last years. Indeed, the social message is different from ordinary text because it has some special characteristics like its shortness. Then the development of new approaches for the processing of the social message is now essential to make its classification more efficient. In this paper, we are mainly interested in the classification of social messages based on their spreading on online social networks (OSN). We proposed a new distance metric based on the Dynamic Time Warping distance and we use it with the probabilistic and the evidential k Nearest Neighbors (k-NN) classifiers to classify propagation networks (PrNets) of messages. The propagation network is a directed acyclic graph (DAG) that is used to record propagation traces of the message, the traversed links and their types. We tested the proposed metric with the chosen k-NN classifiers on real world propagation traces that were collected from Twitter social network and we got good classification accuracies.

Keywords: Propagation Network (PrNet) · Classification · Dynamic Time Warping (DTW) · k Nearest Neighbor (k-NN)

1 Introduction

During the past decade, many classification methods have been appeared, like k Nearest Neighbors (k-NN), Naive Bayes, Support Vector Machines (SVM), etc. Those methods have been applied to several problems among them text classification and they proved their performance, [19]. However, when working with short text like online communications, chat messages, tweets, etc., we are face to a new challenge. In fact, in a short text there is no sufficient word occurrences or shared context for a good similarity measure. Let's take Twitter for example,

© Springer International Publishing Switzerland 2015
S. Destercke and T. Denoeux (Eds.): ECSQARU 2015, LNAI 9161, pp. 419–428, 2015.
DOI: 10.1007/978-3-319-20807-7_38

Twitter is a micro-blogging service that allows its users to share messages of 140 characters that are called *tweets*. As a consequence, using a traditional text classification technique to classify tweets, like the "Bag-Of-Words" method, fail to achieve good classification rates due to the message shortness. Existing works on classification of short text integrate meta-information from external sources like Wikipedia, World Knowledge and MEDLINE [3,11,17]. They tend to enrich the content of the message.

The purpose of this paper is to classify social messages without any access to their content. Our work is motivated by two facts; first, it is not always possible to have access to the content of the message but we may have access to its propagation traces, in such a case, our approaches are useful. Another motivation is that, text processing techniques, always, need a pre-processing step in which it is necessary to remove URLs, stop words, questions, special characters, etc. When working with tweets, for example, after the pre-processing step, it falls, very often, on empty messages. Those empty messages can not be classified by a text based classification technique. Hence comes the necessity of new classification approaches that consider the propagation of the message.

Our work is driven by the motivations above, and it achieves the following contributions: (1) we adapted the Dynamic Time Warping (DTW) distance [16] to be used to measure the distance between two propagation networks (PrNet for short)[1]. (2) we proposed to incorporate the proposed distance in the probabilistic k-NN and the evidential k-NN [8] to classify propagation networks of social messages. Then (3) we tested the classifiers on real world propagation traces collected from Twitter social network.

This paper is organized as follow: Sect. 2 discusses some related works. Section 3 provides relevant background. Section 4 introduces the proposed PrNet-DTW distance. And in Sect. 5 presents results from our experiments.

2   Related Works

2.1   Content Based Approaches

Methods that are used for text classification or clustering always have some limitation with short text, in fact, in short text there is no sufficient word occurrences. Then, traditional methods are not suitable for the classification of the social message that is characterized by its shortness. For example, the use of the traditional "Bag-Of-Words" method to classify tweets may fail to achieve good classification rates. This limitation has attracted the attention of many researchers who developed several approaches. The authors in [25] classified tweets to "News", "Events", "Opinions", "Deals" and "Private Messages" using a set of features among them author information and features extracted from the tweet. In [3] and [11], the authors propose approaches for short text clustering that use not only the content of the text but also an additional set of items that

---

[1] We call propagation network the network that conserves propagation traces of the message, *i.e.* traversed links and nodes.

is extracted from an external source of information like Wikipedia and World Knowledge. Also, [17] classify short and sparse text using a large scale external data collected from Wikipedia and MEDLINE.

Social messages are, also, classified for sentiment analysis and opinion mining purposes [13]. The task here, is to identify the dominant opinion about a product or a brand using text mining techniques. The author of [14] used 3516 tweets to identify costumer's sentiment about some well known brands. In [10], authors used text published on Twitter and Facebook to analyze the opinion about three chain of pizza. The reader can refer to [15] for a recent survey.

Our work is different from all of the above in that we propose to classify the social message without access to its content. In fact, we predict the class of the message by interpreting its propagation traces through the social network. We think that the proposed approaches will be useful in the case where there is no access to the content of the message or when text based methods are unable to classify the message due to its shortness.

2.2   Propagation Based Approaches

Now we move to present two methods that were used to classify propagation networks and that were published in [12]. The first method uses the probability theory and the second one incorporates the theory of belief functions. As we said above, existing classification approaches that are used for text classification and characterization, always, have some limitation with short text. To overcome this limitation, we propose to classify the propagation traces of the message instead of its content. For an illustrative example, when you receive a letter from your bank, it is likely to be about your bank account.

The PrNet classifiers work in two main steps, the first step, is used to learn the model parameters and the second step, uses the learned model to classify new coming messages (propagation network of the message). Both methods have the same principle in the two steps. In the parameter learning step, we need a set of propagation networks, PrNetSet that is used to estimate a probability distribution defined on types of links for each level[2]. In the belief PrNet classifier, we use the consonant transformation algorithm, also called inverse pignistic transformation, [1,2] that allows us to transform the probability distribution (output of the probabilistic parameter learning step) to a BBA distribution while preserving the least commitment principle [23]. Once model's parameters are learned, we can use it to classify a new message (propagation network of the message). The reader can refer to [12] for more details.

These classifiers need a transit step through a compact structure that assigns a probability distribution to each propagation level. This step leads to a loss of information that may be significant in the classification step. Another drawback is that these methods do not work with continuous types of links and a discretization step is always needed in such a case. We think that the proposed PrNet-DTW classifiers will avoid these problems.

---

[2] We call propagation level the number of links between the source of the message and the target node.

3   Background

3.1   Theory of Belief Functions

The *Upper and Lower probabilities* [7] is the first ancestor of the evidence theory, also called Dempster-Shafer theory or theory of belief functions. Then [20] introduced the *mathematical theory of evidence* and defined the basic mathematical framework of the evidence theory, often called *Shafer model*. The main goal of the Dempster-Shafer theory is to achieve more precise, reliable and coherent information.

Let $\Omega = \{s_1, s_2, ..., s_n\}$ be the frame of discernment. The basic belief assignment (BBA), m^Ω, represents the agent belief on Ω. $m^\Omega(A)$ is the mass value assigned to $A \subseteq \Omega$, it must respect: $\sum_{A \subseteq \Omega} m^\Omega(A) = 1$. In the case where we have $m^\Omega(A) > 0$, A is called focal set of m^Ω.

Combination rules are the main tools that can be used for information fusion. In fact, in real world applications, we do not have the same kind of information to be combined, that's why the same combination rule may performs well in some applications and may gives unsatisfiable results with other applications. Among these combination rules, we find the Dempster's rule [7], the conjunctive rule of combination (CRC) [21, 22] and the disjunctive rule of combination (DRC) [22].

3.2 k Nearest Neighbors

In this paper, we choose the k nearest neighbors classification technique because it is distance based. It will be used to classify propagation traces of social messages together with the proposed distance. In this section we present two k-NN based approaches which are the probabilistic k-NN and the evidential k-NN.

Probabilistic k Nearest Neighbors (k-NN) is a well known supervised method that is generally used for classification. It needs as input a set of training examples that we know their features values and their classes, and of course the object to be classified. Besides we have to specify a measure of distance that will be used to quantify the matching between the new object x and every object in the training set. First, the k-NN starts by computing the distance between x and every object in the training set, then, it selects the k nearest neighbors, *i.e.* that have the shortest distance with x. Finally, the object x is classified according to the majority vote principle, *i.e.* the algorithm chooses the class that has the maximum occurrence count in the k nearest neighbors set to be the class of x. The k-NN technique is surveyed in [5].

Evidential k Nearest Neighbors is an extension of the probabilistic k-NN to the theory of belief functions [8]. The probabilistic k-NN uses distances between the object x, to be classified, and objects in the training set to sort the training example, then it chooses the k nearest neighbors to x. However, according to [8], the distance value between x and its nearest neighbors may be significant. The evidential k-NN differs from the probabilistic one in the decision rule. Let $\Omega = \{s_1, s_2, ..., s_n\}$ the set of all possible classes, be our frame of discernment and d_j be the distance between x and the jth nearest neighbor.

The idea behind the evidential k-NN consists on representing each object of the k neighbors by a BBA distribution defined by:

$$m(\{s_i\}) = \alpha \tag{1}$$

$$m(\Omega) = 1 - \alpha \tag{2}$$

$$m(A) = 0 \,\forall A \in 2^C \setminus \{C_i\} \tag{3}$$

such that $0 < \alpha < 1$. If d_j is big, α have to be small. Then it will be calculated as follow:

$$\alpha = \alpha_0 \Phi_i(d_j) \tag{4}$$

$$\Phi_i(d_j) = e^{-\gamma_i d_j^\beta} \tag{5}$$

where $\gamma_i > 0$ and $\beta \in \{1, 2, \ldots\}$. After estimating a BBA distribution for each nearest neighbor, the decision about the class of x is made according to the following steps; first we combine all BBA distributions using a combination rule. Second, we apply the pignistic transformation, [24], in order to obtain a pignistic probability distribution. And finally, we choose the class that have the biggest pignistic probability. In the next section, we will introduce the dynamic time warping distance and its extension to compute similarity between propagation networks.

4 Proposed Dynamic Time Warping Distance for Propagation Networks Similarity

The propagation network is a graph based data structure that is used to store propagation traces of a message. The PrNet has two main characteristics that distinguish it from an ordinary DAG[3]; first, its arcs are weighted by the type of the relationship between users, and second, its paths are time dependent. In this paper, we choose to use distance based classifiers; the probabilistic and the evidential k-NN, then, we need to measure the distance between the PrNet to be classified and the training set. In [12], we presented two PrNet classifiers that are based on mathematical distances like the Euclidean distance and the Jaccard distance. This solution need to transform the PrNet to a set of probability or BBA distributions, then it computes the distance between those distributions instead of PrNets. This transformation may lead to a loss of the information. A second solution may be to use a graph distance metric to measure the similarity between PrNets. In the literature, we found several distances like *Graph edit distances* [9], and *Maximal common sub-graph based distances* [6]. However, all these distances do not consider the time dimension which is a character of the PrNet. Then comes the need of a new distance that is adapted to weighted time dependent DAGs like the PrNet. As a solution to this problem we propose the Dynamic Time Warping distance for propagation networks similarity (PrNet-DTW).

---

[3] Directed Acyclic Graph.

The Dynamic Time Warping similarity measure [18] was first proposed for speech recognition, it consider the fact that the speech is time dependent. Recently, [16] propose to use it to measure the similarity between two sequences, *i.e.* a sequence is an ordered list of elements. DTW distance is used to consider the order of appearance of each element in the sequences while computing the distance between them. Let $A = (a_1, a_2, \ldots, a_S)$ and $B = (b_1, b_2, \ldots, b_T)$ be two sequences. $DTW(A_i, B_j)$ is the DTW distance between A and B and it is defined as [16]:

$$DTW(A_i, B_j) = \delta(a_i, b_j) + \min \begin{cases} DTW(A_{i-1}, B_{j-1}) \\ DTW(A_i, B_{j-1}) \\ DTW(A_{i-1}, B_j) \end{cases} \tag{6}$$

Note that $\delta(a_i, b_j)$ is a the distance between the two elements $a_i \in A$ and $b_j \in B$. As mentioned in [16], the implementation of this recursive function leads to exponential temporal complexity. They propose the memoization technique as a solution to speed up the computation. Hence, we need a $\mid S \mid \times \mid T \mid$ matrix in which we record previous results in order to avoid their computation in next iterations. This computation technique maintain the time and space complexity of the DTW distance to $O(\mid S \mid \times \mid T \mid)$.

The PrNet-DTW distance is used to measure the distance between two propagation networks. In the first step, we transform each PrNet to a set of dipaths. We define a dipath as a finite sequence vertices connected with arcs that are directed to the same direction (line 1 and 2 in Algorithm 1). We note that all dipaths starts from the source of the message. In the second step, the PrNet-DTW algorithm loops on the DipathSet1, at each iteration, it fixes a Dipath and compute its DTW distance with all Dipaths in DipathSet2 and it takes the minimal value. Finally, it computes the mean of minimal distances between Dipaths in DipathSet1 and those in DipathSet2 to be the PrNet-DTW distance. Details are shown in Algorithm 1. We choose the k-NN algorithm and evidential k-NN algorithm to classify propagation networks because they are distance based classifiers and they can be used with the proposed PrNet-DTW distance.

5   Experiments and Results

We used the library Twitter4j[4] which is a java implementation of the Twitter API to collect Twitter data. We crawled the Twitter network for the period between 08/09/2014 and 03/11/2014. After a data cleaning step, we got our data set that contains tweets of three different classes: "Android", "Galaxy" and "Windows". To simplify the tweet classification step, we consider a tweet that contains the name of a class C, for example a tweet that contains the word "Android", of type that class C, i.e. the class "Android" in our example. Table 1 presents some statistics about the data set.

---

[4] Twitter4j is a java library for the Twitter API, it is an open-sourced software and free of charge and it was created by Yusuke Yamamoto. More details can be found in http://twitter4j.org/en/index.html.

Algorithm 1. PrNet-DTW algorithm

input : *PrNet1* and *PrNet2*: Two propagation networks
output: *Distance:* The distance between PrNet1 and PrNet2.
begin

1     $DipathSet1 \leftarrow PrNet1.TransformToDipathSet()$

2     $DipathSet2 \leftarrow PrNet2.TransformToDipathSet()$

3   **for** $i = 1$ **to** $DipathSet1.size()$ **do**

4        $D \leftarrow maxValue$

5   **for** $j = 1$ **to** $DipathSet2.size()$ **do**

6           $D \leftarrow \min(D, DTW(DipathSet1.get(i), DipathSet2.get(j)))$

7           $Distance \leftarrow Distance + D$

8        $Distance \leftarrow Distance/DipathSet1.Size();$

Table 1. Statistics of the data set

	#User	#Follow	#Tweet	#Retweet	#Mention	#Prop. links	#PrNet
Android	6435	9059	81840	3606	6092	7623	224
Galaxy	4343	4482	8067	2873	5965	6819	161
Windows	5775	12466	11163	2632	3441	11400	219

The remainder of this section is organized as follow: we present our experiments configuration, the method with which we extracted propagation and the computation process of link weights. Then, we compare the proposed classifiers with those of [12].

5.1 Experiments Configuration

In our experiments, we need to extract propagation traces of each type of message. Here, we consider that a tweet of type a was propagated from a user u to a user v if and only if u posts a tweet of type a before v and at least one of these relations between u and v exists: (1) v follows u, (2) u mentions v in a tweet of type a, (3) v retweets a tweet of type a written by u. After getting propagation traces we extract propagation networks such that each PrNet has to have one source.

We define types of links that are used to measure the similarity between propagation networks. In Twitter social network there are three possible relations the first one is explicit which is the follow relation, the second and the third relations are implicit which are the mention and the retweet. Another property of Twitter, is that between two users u and v we can have a follow, a mention and/or a retweet relation. We assign to each of those a weight [4] and we assign to each link a vector of weights that has the form (w_f, w_m, w_r). Let S_u be the set of successor of u, P_u the set of predecessor of u, T_u the set of tweets of u, $R_u(v)$ the set of tweets of u that were retweeted by v, $M_u(v)$ the set of tweets of u in which v was mentioned and M_u the set of tweets in which u mentions another user. We compute weights [4] as follow:

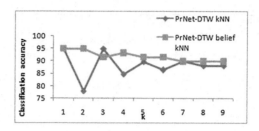

Fig. 1. k variation

- Follow relation: $w_f(u, v) = \frac{|S_u \cap (P_u \cap \{u\})|}{|S_u|}$
- Mention relation: $w_m(u, v) = \frac{|M_u(v)|}{|M_u|}$
- Retweet relation: $w_r(u, v) = \frac{|R_u(v)|}{|T_u|}$

Finally, we choose the euclidean distance to evaluate the $\delta(a_i, b_j)$ in the computation process of the PrNet-DTW.

5.2   Experiments Evaluation

In our experiments, we want to evaluate the performance of the PrNet-DTW distance, then, we integrate it in the k-NN and the evidential k-NN classifiers and we compare the proposed classifiers with those proposed in [12]. As PrNet classifiers works with a discrete types of links [12], a discretization step was needed, *i.e.* if the weight value (w_f, w_m or w_r) is greater than 0 we replace it by 1 in the discrete weight vector elsewere we replace it by 0. For example, if the link is weighted by the vector ($w_f = 0.5$, $w_m = 0$, $w_r = 0.25$), the output after the discretization step will be (1, 0, 1). In the remainder of our experiments, we divide, randomly, our data set into two subsets; the first one contains 90 % of PrNets and it is used for training and the second one (10 %) is used for testing.

The algorithm k-NN is known to be dependent to k value, and varying k may vary the classification accuracy. Then, to see the impact of the parameter k, we made this experiment; we run our k-NN based algorithms with multiple k values and we obtained results in Fig. 1. We note that odd values are more appropriate to k when we use PrNet-DTW Probabilistic k-NN. Moreover, the PrNet-DTW belief k-NN has not the same behavior as the PN-DTW Probabilistic k-NN. In fact, the curve of the evidential classifier is more stable than the curve of the probabilistic one and the variation of the value of k does not have a great effect on the classification accuracy.

A second experiment was done to evaluate and compare the proposed classification methods. We fixed the parameter k to 5 and we obtained results in Table 2. As shown in Table 2, the probabilistic and the belief classifiers do not give good classification accuracy, this behavior is a consequence of the discretization step that leads to the loss of the information given by weights values. In contrast, the PrNet-DTW based classifiers show their performance, indeed, we have got good accuracy rates: 88.69 % (± 3.39, for a 95 % confidence interval) and

Table 2. Comparison between PrNet classifiers

	Proba classifier	Belief classifier	PrNet-DTW k-NN	PrNet-DTW Belief k-NN
Accuracy	51.97% ±2.04	52.25% ±1.99	**88.69%** ±3.39	**89.92%** ±3.20

89.92 % (±3.20) respectively. We see also that the PrNet-DTW belief classifier gives slightly better results.

6 Conclusion

To sum up, we presented a new distance metric that we called PrNet-DTW. Our measure is used to quantify the distance between propagation networks. Also, we showed the performance of our measure in the process of classification of propagation networks, indeed, we defined two classification approaches that uses the PrNet-DTW measure which are the probabilistic k-NN and the evidential k-NN.

For future works, we will search to improve the PrNet-DTW based classifiers by taking into account the content of the message to be classified, in fact, we believe that a classification approach that uses information about the content of the message and information about its propagation will further improve the results.

Acknowledgement. These research works and innovation are carried out within the framework of the device *MOBIDOC* financed by the European Union under the *PASRI* program and administrated by the *ANPR*. Also, we thank the *"Centre d'Etude et de Recherche des Télécommunications"* (CERT) for their support.

References

1. Aregui, A., Denœux, T.: Fusion of one-class classifiers in the belief function framework. In: Proceedings of FUSION, Québec, Canada, Juillet 2007
2. Aregui, A., Denoeux, T.: Constructing consonant belief functions from sample data using confidence sets of pignistic probabilities. Int. J. Approximate Reasoning **49**(3), 575–594 (2008)
3. Banerjee, S., Ramanathan, K., Gupta, A.: Clustering short texts using wikipedia. In: Proceedings of ACM SIGIR Conference, pp. 787–788. ACM (2007)
4. Ben Jabeur, L.: Leveraging social relevance: Using social networks to enhance literature access and microblog search. Ph.D. thesis, Université Toulouse 3 Paul Sabatier (UT3 Paul Sabatier), October 2013
5. Bhatia, N.: Vandana: Survey of nearest neighbor techniques. IJCSIS **8**(2), 302–305 (2010)
6. Bunke, H., Foggia, P., Guidobaldi, C., Sansone, C., Vento, M.: A comparison of algorithms for maximum common subgraph on randomly connected graphs. In: Caelli, T., Amin, A., Duin, R.P.W., de Ridder, D., Kamel, M. (eds.) SSSPR 2002. LNCS, vol. 2396, pp. 123–132. Springer, Heidelberg (2002)

7. Dempster, A.P.: Upper and Lower probabilities induced by a multivalued mapping. Ann. Math. Stat. **38**, 325–339 (1967)
8. Denœux, T.: A k-nearest neighbor classification rule based on dempster-shafer theory. IEEE Trans. Syst., Man, Cybern.- Part A: Syst. Hum. **25**(5), 804–813 (1995)
9. Gao, X., Xiao, B., Tao, D., Li, X.: A survey of graph edit distance. Int. J. Future Comput. Commun. **13**(1), 113–129 (2010)
10. He, W., Zhab, S., Li, L.: Social media competitive analysis and text mining: A case study in the pizza industry. Int. J. Inf. Manage. **33**, 464–472 (2013)
11. Hu, X., Sun, N., Zhang, C., Chua, T.S.: Exploiting internal and external semantics for the clustering of short texts using world knowledge. In: Proceedings of CIKM, pp. 919–928. ACM (2009)
12. Jendoubi, S., Martin, A., Liétard, L., Ben Yaghlane, B.: Classification of message spreading in a heterogeneous social network. In: Laurent, A., Strauss, O., Bouchon-Meunier, B., Yager, R.R. (eds.) IPMU 2014, Part II. CCIS, vol. 443, pp. 66–75. Springer, Heidelberg (2014)
13. Lo, Y.W., Potdar, V.: A review of opinion mining and sentiment classification framework in social networks. In: Proceedings of DEST 2009, June 2009
14. Mostafa, M.M.: More than words: social networks text mining for consumer brand sentiments. Expert Syst. Appl. **40**, 4241–4251 (2013)
15. Othman, M., Hassan, H., Moawad, R., El-Korany, A.: Opinion mining and senti-mental analysis approaches: a survey. Life Sci. J. **11**(4), 321–326 (2014)
16. Petitjean, F., Inglada, J., Gancarski, P.: Satellite image time series analysis under time warping. IEEE Trans. Geosci. Remote Sens. **50**(8), 3081–3095 (2012)
17. Phan, X.H., Nguyen, L.M., Horiguchi, S.: Learning to classify short and sparse text and web with hidden topics from large-scale data collections. In: Proceedings of WWW 2009, pp. 91–100. ACM (2009)
18. Sakoe, H., Chiba, S.: A dynamic programming approach to continuous speech recognition. In: Proceedings of the Seventh International Congress on Acoustics, Budapest, vol. 3, pp. 65–69 (1971)
19. Sebastiani, F.: Machine learning in automated text categorization. ACM Comput. Surv. **34**(1), 1–47 (2002)
20. Shafer, G.: A mathematical theory of evidence. Princeton University Press, Princeton (1976)
21. Smets, P.: The Combination of evidence in the transferable belief model. IEEE Trans. Pattern Anal. Mach. Intell. **12**(5), 447–458 (1990)
22. Smets, P.: Belief functions: the disjunctive rule of combination and the generalized bayesian theorem. Int. J. Approximate Reasoning **9**, 1–35 (1993)
23. Smets, P.: Data fusion in the tranferable belief model. In: Proceedings of FUSION, Paris, France, vol. 1, pp. 21–33, (2000)
24. Smets, P.: Decision making in the TBM: the necessity of the pignistic transforma-tion. Int. J. Approximate Reasonning **38**, 133–147 (2005)
25. Sriram, B., Fuhry, D., Demir, E., Ferhatosmanoglu, H., Demirbas, M.: Short text classification in twitter to improve information filtering. In: Proceedings of ACM SIGIR, pp. 841–842. ACM (2010)

A Reliably Weighted Collaborative Filtering System

Van-Doan Nguyen[(✉)] and Van-Nam Huynh

Japan Advanced Institute of Science and Technology (JAIST), Nomi, Japan
nvdoan@jaist.ac.jp

Abstract. In this paper, we develop a reliably weighted collaborative filtering system that first tries to predict all unprovided rating data by employing context information, and then exploits both predicted and provided rating data for generating suitable recommendations. Since the predicted rating data are not a hundred percent accurate, they are weighted weaker than the provided rating data when integrating both these kinds of rating data into the recommendation process. In order to flexibly represent rating data, Dempster-Shafer (DS) theory is used for data modelling in the system. The experimental results indicate that assigning weights to rating data is capable of improving the performance of the system.

1 Introduction

Research on collaborative filtering systems (CFSs) has focused on the sparsity problem, which is that the total number of items and users is very large while each user only rates a small number of items. The challenge in this problem is how to generate good recommendations when a small number of provided rating data is available. Until now, various methods have been developed for overcoming the problem. In [14], the author introduced a method that employs additional information about the users, e.g. gender, age, education, interests, or other available information that can help to classify users. Recently, Matrix Factorization methods [8,10,15,18] have become well-known for combining good scalability with predictive accuracy; but they are not capable of tackling the data imperfection issue caused by some level of impreciseness and/or uncertainty in the measurements [9]. In [19], the authors proposed a new method that not only models rating data by using DS theory but also exploits context information of users for generating unprovided rating data. Further to the method developed in [19], the method in [12] employs community context information extracted from the social network for generating unprovided rating data. However, the methods in both [19] and [12] consider the role of the predicted rating data to be normally the same as that of the provided rating data, and they are not capable of predicting all unprovided rating data (see Example 1 in Sect. 4). In this paper, these two limitations will be overcome.

Additionally, over the years, management of data imperfection has become increasingly important; however, the existing recommendation techniques are

© Springer International Publishing Switzerland 2015
S. Destercke and T. Denoeux (Eds.): ECSQARU 2015, LNAI 9161, pp. 429–439, 2015.
DOI: 10.1007/978-3-319-20807-7_39

rarely capable of dealing with this challenge [19]. So far, a number of mathematical theories have been developed for representing data imperfection, such as probability theory [4], fuzzy set theory [20], possibility theory [21], rough set theory [13], DS theory [3,16]. Most of these approaches are capable of representing a specific aspect of data imperfection [9]. Importantly, among these, DS theory is considered to be the most general one in which different kinds of uncertainty can be represented [7,19].

For CFSs, DS theory provides a flexible method for modeling information without requiring a probability to be assigned to each element in a set [11]. It is worth to know that different users can have different evaluations on the same item in that users' preferences are subjective and qualitative. Additionally, the existing recommender systems usually provide rating domains representing as finite sets, denoted by $\Theta = \{\theta_1, \theta_2, ..., \theta_L\}$, where $\theta_i < \theta_j$ whenever $i < j$; these systems only allow users to evaluate an item as a hard rating value, known as a singleton, $\theta_i \in \Theta$. However, in some cases, users need to rate an item as a soft rating value, also referred to as a composite, representing by $A \subseteq \Theta$. For example, according to some aspects, a user intends to rate an item as θ_i, but regarding other aspects, the user would like to rate the item as θ_{i+1}; in this case, it is better to use a soft rating value as a set $A = \{\theta_i, \theta_{i+1}\}$. With DS theory, rating entries in the rating matrix can be represented as soft rating values. Besides, this theory supports not only modeling missing data by the vacuous mass structure but also generating both hard as well as soft decisions; here, hard and soft decisions can be known as the recommendations presented by singletons and composites, respectively. Specially, regarding DS theory, some pieces of evidence can be combined easily by using Dempster's rule of combination to form more valuable evidence. Under such an observation, DS theory is selected for modeling rating data in our system.

In short, the system in this paper is developed for not only dealing with the sparsity problem, but also overcoming the data imperfection issue. The main contributions of the paper include (1) a new method of computing user-user similarities which considers the significant role of the provided rating data to be higher than that of the predicted rating data, and (2) a solution for predicting all unprovided rating data using context information.

The remainder of the paper is organized as follows. In the next section, background information about DS theory is provided. Then, details of the methodology are described. After that, system implementation and discussions are represented. Finally, conclusions are illustrated in the last section.

2   Dempster-Shafer Theory

Let us consider that a problem domain is represented by a finite set, denoted as $\Theta = \{\theta_1, \theta_2, ..., \theta_L\}$, of mutually exclusive and exhaustive hypotheses, called frame of discernment [16]. A mass function, or basic probability assignment (BPA), $m : 2^\Theta \to [0, 1]$ is the one satisfying $m(\emptyset) = 0$ and $\sum_{A \subseteq \Theta} m(A) = 1$, where 2^Θ is the power set of Θ. The mass function m is called to be vacuous if $m(\Theta) = 1$

and $\forall A \subset \Theta$, $m(A) = 0$. A subset $A \subseteq \Theta$ with $m(A) > 0$ is called a focal element of m, and the set of all focal elements is called the focal set. If a source of information providing a mass function m has probability $\delta \in [0,1]$ of trust, the discounting operation is used for creating new mass function m^δ, which takes this reliable probability into account. Formally, for $A \subset \Theta$, $m^\delta(A) = \delta \times m(A)$; and $m^\delta(\Theta) = \delta \times m(\Theta) + (1 - \delta)$.

Two evidential functions, known as belief and plausibility functions, are derived from the mass function m. The belief function on Θ is defined as a mapping $Bl : 2^\Theta \rightarrow [0,1]$, where $A \subseteq \Theta$, $Bl(A) = \sum_{B \subseteq A} m(B)$; and the plausibility function on Θ is defined as mapping $Pl : 2^\Theta \rightarrow [0,1]$, where $Pl(A) = 1 - Bl(\bar{A})$. A probability distribution Pr satisfying $Bl(A) \leq Pr(A) \leq Pl(A), \forall A \subseteq \Theta$ is said to be compatible with the mass function m; and the pignistic probability distribution [17], denoted by Bp, is a typical one represented as $Bp(\theta_i) = \sum_{\{A \subseteq \Theta | \theta_i \in A\}} \frac{m(A)}{|A|}$. Additionally, a useful operation that plays an important role in the forming of two pieces of evidence into a single one is Dempster's rule of combination. Formally, this operation is used for aggregation of two mass function m_1 and m_2, denoted by $m = m_1 \oplus m_2$, in the following

$$m(A) = \frac{1}{1-K} \sum_{\{C,D \subseteq \Theta | C \cap D = A\}} m_1(C) \times m_2(D),$$

where $K = \sum_{\{C,D \subseteq \Theta | C \cap D = \emptyset\}} m_1(C) \times m_2(D) \neq 0$, and K represents the basic probability mass associated with conflict.

3   Methodology

3.1   Data Modeling

Let $\mathcal{U} = \{U_1, U_2, ..., U_M\}$ be the set of all users and let $\mathcal{I} = \{I_1, I_2, ..., I_N\}$ be the set of all items. Each user rating is defined as a preference mass function spanning over a finite, rank-order set of L preference labels $\Theta = \{\theta_1, \theta_2 ..., \theta_L\}$, where $\theta_i < \theta_j$ whenever $i < j$. The evaluations of all users are represented by a DS rating matrix created as $\mathcal{R} = \{r_{i,k}\}$, where $i = \overline{1,M}$, $k = \overline{1,N}$. For a provided rating entry regarding the evaluation of a user U_i on an item I_k, $r_{i,k} = m_{i,k}$, with $\sum_{A \subseteq \Theta} m_{i,k}(A) = 1$. Each unprovided rating entry is assigned the vacuous mass function; that means $r_{i,k} = m_{i,k}$, with $m_{i,k}(\Theta) = 1$ and $\forall A \subset \Theta$, $m_{i,k}(A) = 0$. All items rated by a user U_i, and all users rated an item I_k are denoted by $^I R_i = \{I_l \mid r_{i,l} \neq vacuous\}$, and $^U R_k = \{U_l \mid r_{l,k} \neq vacuous\}$, respectively.

3.2   Predicting Unprovided Rating Data

As mentioned earlier, each unprovided rating entry in the rating matrix is modeled by the vacuous mass function. It can be seen that this function has high

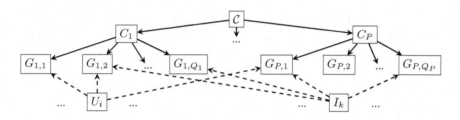

Fig. 1. The context information influencing on users and items

uncertainty. Thus, context information from different sources is used for the purpose of reducing the uncertainty introduced by the vacuous representation [19]. Here, context information, denoted by $\mathcal{C}$, is considered the concept for grouping users. Let us consider a movie recommender system. In this system, characteristics such as user gender, user occupation, movie genre can be considered concepts because they may have significantly influenced user ratings. Each concept can consist of a number of groups, e.g. the movie genre might contain some groups such as drama, comedy, action, mystery, horror, animation. We assume that, in our system, there are P characteristics considered as concepts, and each concept $C_p \in \mathcal{C}$, consists of Q_p groups [12,19], as shown in Fig. 1. Formally, the context information can be represented as follows

$$\mathcal{C} = \{C_1, C_2, ..., C_P\}; C_p = \{G_{p,1}, G_{p,2}, ..., G_{p,Q_p}\}, \text{ where } p = \overline{1, P}.$$

Simultaneously, a user U_i as well as an item I_k may belong to multiple groups from the same concept. For each $C_p \in \mathcal{C}$, the groups in which a user U_i is interested are identified by the mapping functions $f_p : \mathcal{U} \to 2^{C_p} : U_i \mapsto f_p(U_i) \subseteq C_p$; and the groups to which an item I_k belongs are determined by the mapping function $g_p : \mathcal{I} \to 2^{C_p} : I_k \mapsto g_p(I_k) \subseteq C_p$, where 2^{C_p} is the power set of C_p.

We also assume that the users belonging to a group can be expected to possess similar preferences. Based on this assumption, the unprovided rating entries are generated. For a concept $C_p \in \mathcal{C}$, let us consider an item I_k, the overall group preference of this item on each $G_{p,q} \in g_p(I_k)$, with $q = \overline{1, Q_p}$, is defined by the mass function $^G m_{p,q,k} : 2^\Theta \to [0,1]$. This mass function is calculated by combining all the provided rating data of the users who are interested in $G_{p,q}$ and have already rated I_k, as below

$$^G m_{p,q,k} = \bigoplus_{\{j|I_k \in ^I R_j, G_{p,q} \in f_p(U_j) \cap g_p(I_k)\}} m_{j,k}. \qquad (1)$$

If a user U_i has not rated an item I_k, the process for predicting the rating entry $r_{i,k}$ regarding the preference of user U_i on item I_k is performed as follows

– Firstly, the concept preferences corresponding to user U_i on item I_k, denoted by the mass functions $^C m_{p,i,k} : 2^\Theta \to [0,1]$, with $p = \overline{1, P}$, are computed by combining the related group preferences of item I_k as follows

$$^C m_{p,i,k} = \bigoplus_{\{q|G_{p,q} \in f_p(U_i) \cap g_p(I_k)\}} {}^G m_{p,q,k}. \qquad (2)$$

– Secondly, the overall context preference corresponding to a user U_i on item I_k, denoted by the mass function $^c m_{i,k} : 2^\Theta \to [0,1]$, is achieved by combining all related concept mass functions as below

$$^c m_{i,k} = \bigoplus_{p=\overline{1,P}} \, ^c m_{p,i,k}. \tag{3}$$

– Next, the unprovided rating entry $r_{i,k}$, which is vacuous, is replaced with its corresponding context mass function as follows

$$r_{i,k} = \, ^c m_{i,k}. \tag{4}$$

– Finally, in case the rating entry $r_{i,k}$ is still vacuous after replacing such as Example 1 in Sect. 4, we propose that this entry is assigned the evidence obtained by combining all preference mass functions of the users already rated item I_k as below

$$r_{i,k} = \bigoplus_{\{j | U_j \in ^U R_k\}} m_{j,k}. \tag{5}$$

Please note that, at this point, all unprovided rating data are completely predicted.

3.3 Computing User-User Similarities

In the DS rating matrix, every rating entry $r_{i,k} = m_{i,k}$ represents user U_i's preference toward a single item I_k. Let us consider that the focal set of $m_{i,k}$ is defined by $F_{i,k} = \{A \in 2^\Theta | m_{i,k}(A) > 0\}$. The user U_i's preference toward all items as a whole can be defined over the cross-product $\Theta = \Theta_1 \times \Theta_2 \times ... \times \Theta_N$, where $\Theta_i = \Theta, \forall i = \overline{1,N}$ [7,19]. The cylindrical extension of the focal element $A \in F_{i,k}$ to the cross-product Θ is $cyl_\Theta(A) = [\Theta_1 ... \Theta_{i-1} A \Theta_{i+1} ... \Theta_N]$. The mapping $M_{i,k} : 2^\Theta \to [0,1]$ generates a valid mass function defined on Θ by extending $r_{i,k}$; and if $B = cyl_\Theta(A)$, $M_{i,k}(B) = m_{i,k}(A)$, otherwise $M_{i,k}(B) = 0$ [7].

For a user U_i, let us consider the mass functions $M_{i,k}$ defined over the cross-product Θ, with $k = \overline{1,N}$. The mass function $M_i : 2^\Theta \to [0,1]$, where $M_i = \bigoplus_{k=1}^{N} M_{i,k}$, is referred to as the user-BPA of user U_i.

Consider user U_i's user-BPA M_i and the rating mass functions $m_{i,k}, k = \overline{1,N}$, each defined over Θ. The pignistic probability of the singleton $\theta_{i_1} \times ... \times \theta_{i_N} \in \Theta$, is

$$Bp_i(\theta_{i_1} \times ... \times \theta_{i_N}) = \prod_{k=1}^{N} Bp_{i,k}(\theta_{i_k}), \text{ where } \theta_{i_k} \in \Theta, \text{ and } Bp_i \text{ and } Bp_{i,k} \text{ are user}$$

U_i's pignistic probability distributions corresponding to its user-BPA and preference rating of user U_i on item I_k , respectively [19].

For computing the distance among users, we adopt the distance measure method introduced in [2]. According to this method, the distance between two user-BPAs M_i and M_j defined over the same cross-product Θ is $D(M_i, M_j) = CD(Bp_i, Bp_j)$, where CD refers to the Chan and Darwiche distance measure [2] represented as below

Table 1. The values of the reliable function

$x_{i,k}$	$x_{j,k}$	$\mu(x_{i,k}, x_{j,k})$
0	0	1
0	1	$1 - w_1$
1	0	$1 - w_1$
1	1	$1 - 2 \times w_1 - w_2$

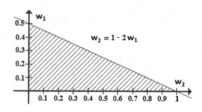

Fig. 2. The domains of w_1 and w_2

$$CD(Bp_i, Bp_j) = \ln \max_{\boldsymbol{\theta} \in \Theta} \frac{Bp_j(\boldsymbol{\theta})}{Bp_i(\boldsymbol{\theta})} - \ln \min_{\boldsymbol{\theta} \in \Theta} \frac{Bp_j(\boldsymbol{\theta})}{Bp_i(\boldsymbol{\theta})}.$$

In addition, $CD(Bp_i, Bp_j) = \sum_{k=1}^{N} CD(Bp_{i,k}, Bp_{j,k})$ [19]. Obviously, for each item I_k, it is easy to recognize as follows

- In case neither user U_i nor user U_j has rated item I_k, that means both $r_{i,k}$ and $r_{j,k}$ are predicted rating data. Since $Bp_{i,k}$ and $Bp_{j,k}$ are derived from entries $r_{i,k}$ and $r_{j,k}$, respectively, the value of the expression $CD(Bp_{i,k}, Bp_{j,k})$ is not fully reliable.
- The value of the expression $CD(Bp_{i,k}, Bp_{j,k})$ is also not fully reliable if either user U_i or user U_j has rated item I_k.
- The value of the expression $CD(Bp_{i,k}, Bp_{j,k})$ is only fully reliable if both user U_i and U_j have rated item I_k.

Under such an observation, in order to improve the accuracy of the distance measurement between two users, we propose a new method to compute the distance between two user-BPAs M_i and M_j, as shown below

$$\hat{D}(M_i, M_j) = \sum_{k=1}^{N} \mu(x_{i,k}, x_{j,k}) \times CD(Bp_{i,k}, Bp_{j,k}),$$

where $\mu(x_{i,k}, x_{j,k}) \in [0, 1]$ is a reliable function referring to the trust of the evaluation of both user U_i and user U_j on item I_k. $\forall (i, k), x_{i,k} \in \{0, 1\}$; $x_{i,k} = 1$ when $r_{i,k}$ is a provided rating entry, otherwise $r_{i,k}$ is a predicted rating one. Note that because of $\mu(x_{i,k}, x_{j,k}) \in [0, 1]$, the distinguishing of the provided and the predicted rating data does not destroy the elegance of the selected distance measure method [2]. When $\mu(x_{i,k}, x_{i,k}) < 1$ indicates that the distance between user U_i and user U_j is shorter than it actually is. That means user U_i has a high opportunity for being a member in user U_j's neighborhood set, and vice versa.

The reliable function $\mu(x_{i,k}, x_{j,k})$ can be selected according to specific applications. In the general case, we suggest that $\mu(x_{i,k}, x_{j,k}) = 1 - w_1 \times (x_{i,k} + x_{j,k}) - w_2 \times x_{i,k} \times x_{j,k}$, where $w_1 \geq 0$ and $w_2 \geq 0$ are the reliable coefficients representing the state when a user has actually rated an item and two users together have rated an item, respectively. Because of $\forall(i,k), x_{i,k} \in \{0,1\}$, the function $\mu(x_{i,k}, x_{j,k})$ has to belong to one of four cases as shown in Table 1. Under the condition $0 \leq \mu(x_{i,k}, x_{j,k}) \leq 1$, the domains of w_1 and w_2 must be in the parallel diagonal line shading area as illustrated in Fig. 2.

Consider a monotonically deceasing function $\psi: [0,\infty] \mapsto [0,1]$ satisfying $\psi(0) = 1$ and $\psi(\infty) = 0$. Then, with respect to ψ, $s_{i,j} = \psi(D(M_i, M_j))$ is referred to as the user-user similarity between users U_i and U_j. We use the function $\psi(x) = e^{-\gamma \times x}$, where $\gamma \in (0,\infty)$. Consequently, the user-user similarity matrix is then generated as $S = \{s_{i,j}\}, i = \overline{1,M}, j = \overline{1,M}$.

3.4   Selecting Neighborhoods

The method of neighborhood selection proposed in [5] is an effective one because it prevents the recommendation result from the errors generated from very dissimilar users. This method, selected to apply in our system. Formally, we need to select a neighborhood set $\mathcal{N}_{i,k}$ for a user U_i. First, the users already rated item I_k and whose similarities with user U_i are equal or greater than a threshold τ are extracted. Then, K users with the highest similarity with user U_i are selected from the extracted list. The neighborhood is the largest set that satisfies $\mathcal{N}_{i,k} = \{U_j \in \mathcal{U} \mid I_k \in {}^I R_j, s_{i,j} \geq \max_{\forall U_l \notin \mathcal{N}_{i,k}} \{\tau, s_{i,l}\}\}$. Note that for a new user, the condition $I_k \in {}^I R_j$ is removed.

The estimated rating data for an unrated item I_k of a user U_i is presented as $\hat{r}_{i,k} = \hat{m}_{i,k}$, where $\hat{m}_{i,k} = \bar{m}_{i,k} \oplus m_{i,k}$. Here, $\bar{m}_{i,k}$ is the mass function corresponding to the neighborhood prediction ratings, as shown below

$$\bar{m}_{i,k} = \bigoplus_{\{j|U_j \in \mathcal{N}_{i,k}\}} m_{j,k}^{s_{i,j}}, \text{ with } m_{j,k}^{s_{i,j}} = \begin{cases} s_{i,j} \times m_{j,k}(A), & \text{for } A \subset \Theta; \\ s_{i,j} \times m_{j,k}(\Theta) + (1 - s_{i,j}), & \text{for } A = \Theta. \end{cases}$$

3.5   Generating Recommendations

Our system supports both hard and soft decisions. For a hard decision, the pignistic probability is applied, and the singleton having the highest probability is selected as the preference label. If a soft decision is needed, the maximum belief with overlapping interval strategy (maxBL) [1] is applied, and the singleton whose belief is greater than the plausibility of any other singleton is selected; if such as class label does not exist, decision is made according to the favor of composite class label constituted of the singleton label that has the maximum belief and those singletons that have a higher plausibility.

4   Implementation and Discussions

Movielens data set[1], MovieLens 100 k, was used in the experiment. This data set consists of 100,000 hard ratings from 943 users on 1682 movies with the rating

---

[1] http://grouplens.org/datasets/movielens/.

value $\theta_l \in \Theta = \{1, 2, 3, 4, 5\}$, 5 is the highest value. Each user has rated at least 20 movies. Since our system requires a domain with soft ratings, each hard rating entry $\theta_l \in \Theta$ was transformed into the soft rating entry $r_{i,k}$ by the DS modeling function [19] as follows

$$
r_{i,k} = \begin{cases} \alpha_{i,k} \times (1 - \sigma_{i,k}), & \text{for } A = \theta_l; \\ \alpha_{i,k} \times \sigma_{i,k}, & \text{for } A = B; \\ 1 - \alpha_{i,k}, & \text{for } A = \Theta; \\ 0, & \text{otherwise}, \end{cases} \text{ with } B = \begin{cases} (\theta_1, \theta_2), & \text{if } l = 1; \\ (\theta_{L-1}, \theta_L), & \text{if } l = L; \\ (\theta_{l-1}, \theta_l, \theta_{l+1}), & \text{otherwise}. \end{cases}
$$

Here, $\alpha_{i,k} \in [0, 1]$ and $\sigma_{i,k}$ are a trust factor and a dispersion factor, respectively [19]. In the data set, context information is represented as below

$$
\mathcal{C} = \{C_1\} = \{Genre\}; C_1 = \{G_{1,1}, G_{1,2}, ..., G_{1,19}\} = \{Unknown, Action, Adventure, Animation,
$$
$$
Children's, Comedy, Crime, Documentary, Drama, Fantasy, Film\text{-}Noir,
$$
$$
Horror, Musical, Mystery, Romance, Sci\text{-}Fi, Thriller, War, Western\}.
$$

Because the genres to which a user belongs is not available, we assume the genres of a user U_i are assigned by the genres of the movies rated by user U_i. Each unprovided rating entry was replaced with its corresponding context mass function predicted according to Eqs. 1,2,3 and 5. Note that if the context mass functions are fused by using the methods in [12,19] (just applying Eqs. 1,2,3 and 4), some unprovided rating entries are still vacuous after replacing, as in Example 1.

Example 1. In the Movielens data set, let us consider a user U_c with $f_1(U_c) = \{G_{1,4}, G_{1,5}, G_{1,6}, G_{1,18}\} = \{Animation, Children's, Comedy, War\}$ and an item I_t with $g_1(I_t) = \{G_{1,17}\} = \{Thriller\}$. Assuming that user U_c has not rated item I_t and we need to predict the value for r_{ct}. The predicting process is as follows

- According to equation (1), $^Gm_{1,17,t} = \displaystyle\bigoplus_{\{j | I_t \in\ ^UR_j, G_{1,17} \in f_1(U_j)\}} m_{j,t};$

  $\forall G_{1,q} \in C_1$ and $q \neq 17$, $^Gm_{1,q,t} = vacuous.$
- Using equation (2), $^Cm_{1,c,t} = \displaystyle\bigoplus_{\{q | G_{1,q} \in f_1(U_c) \cap g_1(I_t)\}} {}^Gm_{1,q,t} = vacuous.$
- According to equation (3), $^Cm_{c,t} = {}^Cm_{1,c,t} = vacuous.$
- Applying equation (4), $r_{c,t} = {}^Cm_{c,t} = vacuous.$

Firstly, 10% of the users were randomly selected. Then, for each selected user, we accidentally withheld 5 ratings, the withheld ratings were used as testing data and the remaining ratings were considered as training data. Finally, recommendations were computed for the testing data. We repeated this process for 10 times, and the average results of 10 splits were represented in this section. Note that in all experiments, some parameters were selected as following: $\gamma = 10^{-4}$, $\beta = 1$, $\forall(i, k)\{\alpha_{i,k}, \sigma_{i,k}\} = \{0.9, 2/9\}$.

For recommender systems with hard decisions, the popular performance assessment methods are *MAE*, *Precision*, *Recall*, and F_β [6]. Recently, some new methods allowing to evaluate soft decisions are proposed, such as *DS-Precision* and

Table 2. Overall *MAE* versus w_1 and w_2

	w_1					
w_2	0.0	0.1	0.2	0.3	0.4	0.5
0.0	0.8361	0.8366	0.8363	0.8350	0.8342	0.8334
0.1	0.8363	0.8363	0.8363	0.8347	0.8342	
0.2	0.8366	0.8363	0.8363	0.8361	0.8342	
0.3	0.8366	0.8363	0.8361	0.8339		
0.4	0.8363	0.8363	0.8358	0.8339		
0.5	0.8363	0.8363	0.8355			
0.6	0.8363	0.8361	0.8355			
0.7	0.8363	0.8361				
0.8	0.8361	0.8361				
0.9	0.8358					
1.0	0.8358					

Table 3. Overall *DS-MAE* versus w_1 and w_2

	w_1					
w_2	0.0	0.1	0.2	0.3	0.4	0.5
0.0	0.8406	0.8406	0.8405	0.8402	0.8399	0.8397
0.1	0.8406	0.8406	0.8405	0.8401	0.8399	
0.2	0.8406	0.8406	0.8404	0.8401	0.8400	
0.3	0.8406	0.8405	0.8404	0.8400		
0.4	0.8406	0.8405	0.8405	0.8400		
0.5	0.8406	0.8406	0.8404			
0.6	0.8406	0.8405	0.8404			
0.7	0.8406	0.8405				
0.8	0.8406	0.8405				
0.9	0.8405					
1.0	0.8406					

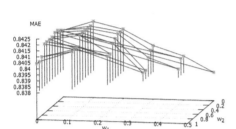

Fig. 3. Visualizing overall *MAE*

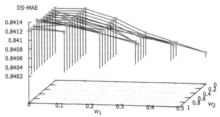

Fig. 4. Visualizing overall *DS-MAE*

DS-Recall [7]; *DS-MAE* and *DS-F_β* [19]. We adopted all these methods for evaluating the proposed system. Since the system is developed for aiming at extending CoFiDS [19], we also selected CoFiDS for performance comparison.

Tables 2 and 3 show the overall *MAE* and *DS-MAE* criterion results computed by mean of these evaluation criteria with $K = 15, \tau = 0$ according to two reliable coefficients w_1 and w_2, respectively. The statistics in these tables indicate that the performance of the proposed system is almost linearly dependent on the value of w_1; this finding is the same for the other evaluation criteria. The coefficient w_2 just slightly influences the performance in hard decisions, but seems not to affect the performance in soft decisions; the reason is that, in the data set, when considering two users, the number of movies rated by these users is very small while the total of movies is large. Figures 3 and 4 depict the same information as Tables 2 and 3 in a visualization way.

For comparing with CoFiDS, we conducted the experiments with $w_1 = 0.5$, $w_2 = 0, \tau = 0$, and several values of K. Figures 5 and 6 show the overall *MAE* and *DS-MAE* criterion results of both CoFiDS and the proposed system change with the neighborhood size K. According to these features, the performances of two systems are fluctuated when $K < 42$, and then appear to stabilize with $K \geq 42$. In particular, both features show that the proposed system is more effective in all cases.

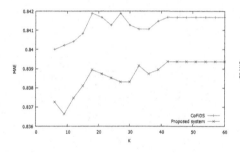

Fig. 5. Overall *MAE* versus *K*   **Fig. 6.** Overall *DS-MAE* versus *K*

Table 4. The comparison in hard decisions

Metric	True Rating					Overall
	1	2	3	4	5	
Proposed system:						
Precision	**0.3201**	**0.2210**	**0.3188**	**0.4002**	**0.4179**	**0.3630**
Recall	**0.0906**	**0.0892**	**0.3179**	0.6413	**0.1885**	**0.3709**
MAE	2.1368	1.4242	0.7790	0.4212	1.0175	0.8383
F₁	**0.1205**	**0.1245**	**0.3170**	0.4924	**0.2571**	**0.3384**
CoFiDS:						
Precision	0.3118	**0.2151**	0.3177	0.3996	0.4171	0.3609
Recall	0.0873	0.0872	0.3157	**0.6418**	0.1866	0.3697
MAE	2.1435	1.4325	0.7813	0.4224	1.0202	0.8413
F₁	0.1148	0.1216	0.3152	**0.4921**	0.2551	0.3366

Table 5. The comparison in soft decisions

DS -Metric	True Rating					Overall
	1	2	3	4	5	
Proposed system:						
Precision	**0.3001**	**0.2035**	**0.3150**	<u>0.3990</u>	0.4016	**0.3551**
Recall	**0.0663**	0.0926	**0.3164**	0.6391	**0.1847**	**0.3680**
MAE	2.1963	1.4313	0.7721	0.4122	1.0317	0.8405
F₁	**0.1036**	0.1248	**0.3147**	0.4909	**0.2507**	0.3349
CoFiDS:						
Precision	0.2926	0.2032	0.3148	<u>0.3990</u>	**0.4020**	0.3547
Recall	0.0658	**0.0934**	0.3155	**0.6398**	0.1837	0.3679
MAE	2.1973	1.4323	0.7724	**0.4118**	1.0359	0.8415
F₁	**0.1028**	**0.1255**	0.3141	**0.4911**	0.2500	0.3347

Tables 4 and 5 show the summarized results of the performance comparisons between the proposed system and CoFiDS in hard and soft decisions with $K = 30, w_1 = 0.5, w_2 = 0, \tau_2 = 0$, respectively. In each category in these tables, every rating has its own column; and the bold values indicate the better performance, and underlined values illustrate equal performance. Importantly, the statistics in both tables show that, except for soft decisions with true rating value $\theta_4 = 4$, the proposed system achieves better performance in all selected measurement criteria. However, the absolute values of the performance of the proposed system are just slightly higher than those of CoFiDS. The reason is that the MovieLens data set contains a small number of provided rating data. In case more provided rating data are available, the proposed system can be much better than CoFiDS.

5   Conclusions

In summary, in this paper, we have developed a CFS that uses the DS theory for representing rating data, and integrates context information for predicting all unprovided rating data. Specially, after predicting all unprovided data, suitable recommendations are generated by employing both predicted and provided rating data with the stipulation that the provided rating data are more important than the predicted rating data.

References

1. Bloch, I.: Some aspects of dempster-shafer evidence theory for classification of multi-modality medical images taking partial volume effect into account. Pattern Recogn. Lett. **17**(8), 905–919 (1996)
2. Chan, H., Darwiche, A.: A distance measure for bounding probabilistic belief change. Int. J. Approx. Reasoning **38**(2), 149–174 (2005)
3. Dempster, A.P.: Upper and lower probabilities induced by a multivalued mapping. Ann. Math. Stat. **38**, 325–339 (1967)
4. Feller, W.: An introduction to probability theory and its applications, vol. I. Wiley, New York (1968)
5. Herlocker, J.L., Konstan, J.A., Borchers, A.l., Riedl, J.: An algorithmic framework for performing collaborative filtering. In: SIGIR 1999, Proceedings of the 22nd Annual International ACM SIGIR Conference, pp. 230–237 (1999)
6. Herlocker, J.L., Konstan, J.A., Terveen, L.G., Riedl, J.: Evaluating collaborative filtering recommender systems. ACM Trans. Inf. Syst. **22**(1), 5–53 (2004)
7. Rohitha Hewawasam, K.K., Shyu, M.-L.: Rule mining and classification in a situation assessment application: A belief-theoretic approach for handling data imperfections. IEEE Trans. Syst. Man Cybern., Part B **37**(6), 1446–1459 (2007)
8. Jiang, M., Cui, P., Wang, F., Zhu, W., Yang, S.: Scalable recommendation with social contextual information. IEEE Trans. Knowl. Data Eng. **26**(11), 2789–2802 (2014)
9. Khaleghi, B., Khamis, A.M., Karray, F., Razavi, S.N.: Multisensor data fusion: A review of the state-of-the-art. Inf. Fusion **14**(1), 28–44 (2013)
10. Koren, Y., Bell, R.M., Volinsky, C.: Matrix factorization techniques for recommender systems. IEEE Comput. **42**(8), 30–37 (2009)
11. Maseleno, A., Hasan, M.M.: Dempster-shafer theory for move prediction in start kicking of the bicycle kick of sepak takraw game. CoRR, abs/1401.2483 (2014)
12. Nguyen, V.-D., Huynh, V.-N.: A community-based collaborative filtering system dealing with sparsity problem and data imperfections. In: Pham, D.-N., Park, S.-B. (eds.) PRICAI 2014. LNCS, vol. 8862, pp. 884–890. Springer, Heidelberg (2014)
13. Pawlak, Z.: Rough Sets: Theoretical Aspects of Reasoning About Data. Kluwer Academic Publishers, Norwell (1992)
14. Pazzani, M.J.: A framework for collaborative, content-based and demographic filtering. AI Rev. **13**, 393–408 (1999)
15. Pu, L., Faltings, B.: Understanding and improving relational matrix factorization in recommender systems. In: Seventh ACM Conference on Recommender Systems, pp. 41–48 (2013)
16. Shafer, G.: A Mathematical Theory of Evidence. Princeton University Press, Princeton (1976)
17. Smets, P.: Practical uses of belief functions. In: Proceedings of the Fifteenth Conference on Uncertainty in Artificial Intelligence, UAI 1999, pp. 612–621. Morgan Kaufmann Publishers Inc. (1999)
18. Sun, J.Z., Parthasarathy, D., Varshney, K.R.: Collaborative kalman filtering for dynamic matrix factorization. IEEE Trans. Sign. Proces. **62**(14), 3499–3509 (2014)
19. Wickramarathne, T.L., Premaratne, K., Kubat, M., Jayaweera, D.T.: Cofids: A belief-theoretic approach for automated collaborative filtering. IEEE Trans. Knowl. Data Eng. **23**(2), 175–189 (2011)
20. Zadeh, L.A.: Fuzzy sets. Inf. Control **8**(3), 338–353 (1965)
21. Zadeh, L.A.: Fuzzy sets as a basis for a theory of possibility. Fuzzy Sets Syst. **1**, 3–28 (1978)

A Comparison of Plausibility Conflict and of Degree of Conflict Based on Amount of Uncertainty of Belief Functions

Milan Daniel[(⊠)]

Institute of Computer Science, Academy of Sciences of the Czech Republic,
Pod Vodárenskou věží 2, CZ – 182 07 Prague 8, Czech Republic
milan.daniel@cs.cas.cz

Abstract. When combining belief functions by conjunctive rules of combination, conflicts often appear. Combination of conflicting belief functions and interpretation of conflicts is often questionable in real applications, thus a series of alternative combination rules was suggested and a series of papers on conflicting belief functions published in last years.

This theoretical contribution presents one of the perspective recent approaches — author's plausibility conflict — and Harmanec's approach which stands, unfortunately, aside the recent interest: conflict based on uncertainty measure and Dempster's rule. Both the approaches are analysed and compared here.

The compared approaches are based on completely different assumptions, thus some of their properties are very different almost counter-intuitive when first look at; on the other hand, they have some analogous properties, which distinguish them from other commonly used approaches to conflict between belief functions.

Keywords: Belief function · Dempster-Shafer theory · Internal conflict · Conflict between belief functions · Plausibility conflict · Amount uncertainty · Conflict based on amount of uncertainty

1 Introduction

The original Shafer's measure of conflict called *weight of conflict between belief functions*, unfortunately, does not fully correspond to reality see, e.g., [1,19]. Thus a series of alternative approaches was initiated, e.g., [12,18–22] and author's approaches [5,8,9,11].

Unfortunately all these approaches to conflict of belief functions ignore Harmanec's degree of conflict between BFs which is based on measure of uncertainty and Dempster's rule [14]. Amount of uncertainty comes from Harmanec & Klir research on theory of information [16,17]. For an overview of a long series of preceding definitions of uncertainty measures see SIPTA's Summary of uncertainty measures [15]. As Harmanec's approach is out of the scope of the above mentioned recent works on conflicts; and despite of its completely different foundation it has some features common with the plausibility conflict, we will analyze

© Springer International Publishing Switzerland 2015
S. Destercke and T. Denoeux (Eds.): ECSQARU 2015, LNAI 9161, pp. 440–450, 2015.
DOI: 10.1007/978-3-319-20807-7_40

and compare it with plausibility conflict here. Due to an extent limitation, for more detail, more explanations, and proofs see [10].

2   Preliminaries

We assume classic definitions of basic notions from theory of *belief functions* [23] on finite frames of discernment $\Omega_n = \{\omega_1, \omega_2, ..., \omega_n\}$, see also [3,4].

A *basic belief assignment (bba)* is a mapping $m : \mathcal{P}(\Omega) \longrightarrow [0,1]$ such that $\sum_{A \subseteq \Omega} m(A) = 1$; the values of the bba are called *basic belief masses (bbm)*. $m(\emptyset) = 0$ is usually assumed. A *belief function (BF)* is a mapping $Bel : \mathcal{P}(\Omega) \longrightarrow [0,1]$, $Bel(A) = \sum_{\emptyset \neq X \subseteq A} m(X)$. A *plausibility function* $Pl(A) = \sum_{\emptyset \neq A \cap X} m(X)$. There is a unique correspondence among m and corresponding Bel and Pl thus we often speak about m as of belief function.

A *focal element* is a subset X of the frame of discernment, such that $m(X) > 0$. If all the focal elements are *singletons* (i.e. one-element subsets of Ω), then we speak about a *Bayesian belief function* (BBF); in fact, it is a probability distribution on Ω. If there are only focal elements such that $|X| = 1$ or $|X| = n$ we speak about *quasi-Bayesian BF* (qBBF). In the case of $m(\Omega) = 1$ we speak about *vacuous BF* (VBF).

Dempster's (conjunctive) rule of combination $\oplus$ is given as $(m_1 \oplus m_2)(A) = \sum_{X \cap Y = A} K m_1(X) m_2(Y)$ for $A \neq \emptyset$, where $K = \frac{1}{1-\kappa}$, $\kappa = \sum_{X \cap Y = \emptyset} m_1(X) m_2(Y)$, and $(m_1 \oplus m_2)(\emptyset) = 0$, see [23]; if $\kappa > 0$ then we say that m_1 and m_2 are *combinable* (by Dempster's rule), see [14].

Normalized plausibility of singletons[1] of Bel is a probability distribution Pl_P such that $Pl\_P(\omega_i) = \frac{Pl(\{\omega_i\})}{\sum_{\omega \in \Omega} Pl(\{\omega\})}$ [4].

We may represent BFs by enumeration of their m-values, i.e., by $(2^n{-}1)$-tuples or by $(2^n{-}2)$-tuples as $m(\Omega_n) = 1 - \sum_{X \subsetneq \Omega_n} m(X)$; thus we have pairs $(a, b) = (m(\{\omega_1\}), m(\{\omega_2\}))$ for BFs on Ω_2.

Hájek-Valdés algebraic structure $\mathbf{D}_0$ of these pairs with Dempster's rule $\oplus$ is called *Dempster's semigroup*, see [13] and also (Fig. 1) it was further studied and generalised by the author, e.g., in [3,7]. In this study we need only a mapping $h(a, b) = (a, b) \oplus 0'$ which is a homomorphism of the structure to substructure of Bayesian BFs, i.e., $h((a, b) \oplus (c, d)) = h(a, b) \oplus h(c, d)$, where $h(a, b)$ is an abbreviation for $h((a, b))$; in general $h(Bel) = Bel \oplus U_n$, where $U_n = (\frac{1}{n}, \frac{1}{n}, ..., \frac{1}{n}, 0, 0, ..., 0)$,

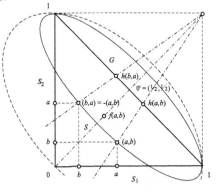

Fig. 1. Dempster's semigroup D_0. Homomorphism h is in this representation a projection of the triangle representing D_0 to its hypotenuse G along the straight lines running through the point $(1, 1)$.

---

[1] Plausibility of singletons is called *contour function* by Shafer in [23], thus $Pl\_P(Bel)$ is a normalization of contour function in fact.

$0' = (\frac{1}{2}, \frac{1}{2}) = U_2$. And mapping $-(a, b) = (b, a)$, which was generalized to Bayesian BFs (BBFs) in [6,7], such that $Bel \oplus -Bel = U_n$.

3 Plausibility Conflict of Belief Functions

Conflict between BFs is distinguished from internal conflict in [5,8], where internal conflict of a BF is included inside the individual BF. Total/global conflict of two BFs Bel_1, Bel_2, which is equal to sum of all multiples of conflicting belief masses: $m_{\ominus}(\emptyset) = \sum_{X \cap Y = \emptyset} m_1(X) m_2(Y)$, includes internal conflicts of both individual BFs Bel_1, Bel_2 and also a conflict between them.

Definition 1. *The internal plausibility conflict* $Pl\text{-}IntC$ *of BF Bel is defined as*

$$Pl\text{-}IntC(Bel) = 1 - max_{\omega \in \Omega_n} Pl(\{\omega\}),$$

where Pl is the plausibility corresponding to Bel (Fig. 2).

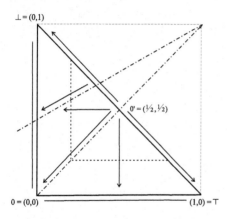

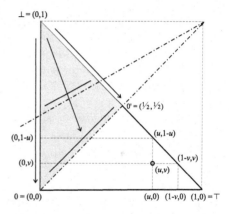

Fig. 2. Plausibility internal conflict; $Pl\text{-}IntC$ decreases in direction of arrows and it is constant along lines without arrows.

Fig. 3. Plausibility conflict between fixed BF (u, v) and general BF (a, b) on Ω_2; $Pl\text{-}C_0$ decreases in direction of arrows and it is constant along lines without arrows.

Definition 2. *Let Bel_1, Bel_2 be two belief functions on Ω_n given by bbms m_1 and m_2 which have normalised plausibility of singletons Pl_P_1 and Pl_P_2. The conflicting set $\Omega_{PlC}(Bel_1, Bel_2)$ is defined to be the set of elements $\omega \in \Omega_n$ with conflicting Pl_P masses, it is conditionally extended with union of sets max Pl_P_i value elements under condition that they are disjoint. Formally we have $\Omega_{PlC}(Bel_1, Bel_2) = \Omega_{PlC_0}(Bel_1, Bel_2) \cup \Omega_{smPlC}(Bel_1, Bel_2)$, where $\Omega_{PlC_0}(Bel_1, Bel_2) = \{\omega \in \Omega_n \mid (Pl\_P_1(\omega) - \frac{1}{n})(Pl\_P_2(\omega) - \frac{1}{n}) < 0\}$, $\Omega_{smPlC}(Bel_1, Bel_2) = \{\omega \in \Omega_n \mid \omega \in \{max_{\omega \in \Omega_n} Pl\_P_1(\omega)\} \cup \{max_{\omega \in \Omega_n} Pl\_P_2(\omega)\}$ & $\{max_{\omega \in \Omega_n} Pl\_P_1(\omega)\} \cap \{max_{\omega \in \Omega_n} Pl\_P_2(\omega)\} = \emptyset\}$.*

Plausibility conflict between BFs Bel_1 and Bel_2 is then defined by the formula

$$Pl\text{-}C(Bel_1, Bel_2) = min(Pl\text{-}C_0(Bel_1, Bel_2), (m_1 \ominus m_2)(\emptyset)),$$

where[2]

$$Pl\text{-}C_0(Bel_1, Bel_2) = \sum_{\omega \in \Omega_{PlC}(Bel_1, Bel_2)} \frac{1}{2} |Pl\_P_1(\omega) - Pl\_P_2(\omega)|$$

(Fig. 3).

4   Conflict Between Belief Functions Based on Amount of Uncertainty and the Dempster Rule

Definition 3. *Let Bel denote a belief function defined on a general frame of discernment Ω. A measure of the amount of uncertainty contained in Bel, denoted as $AU(Bel)$, is defined by*

$$AU(Bel) = max \left\{ -\sum_{\omega \in \Omega} p_\omega \, log_2 \, p_\omega \right\},$$

where the maximum is taken over all $\{p_\omega\}_{\omega \in \Omega}$ such that $p_\omega \in [0,1]$ for all $\omega \in \Omega$, $\sum_{\omega \in \Omega} p_\omega = 1$, and for all $A \subseteq \Omega$, $Bel(A) \le \sum_{\omega \in A} p_\omega$. See [16,17].

Theorem 1. *Let us suppose two combinable belief functions Bel_1 and Bel_2 on a two-element Ω_2 given by pairs (a_1, b_1), (a_2, b_2); assume further $a_1 \ge b_1$. Then*

$$AU(Bel_1 \oplus Bel_2) \le min(AU(Bel_1), AU(Bel_2))$$

if and only if at least one of the following holds

(i) $0 \le a_1, a_2, b_2 \le \frac{1}{2}$, (i.e. also $0 \le b_1 \le \frac{1}{2}$);   (see Fig. 4)
(ii) $a_2 \ge b_2$;   (see Fig. 5)
(iii) $a_2 < b_2$, $(1 - b_1)(1 - b_2) \ge (1 - a_1)(1 - a_2)$,
    $a_2(1 - b_1) \ge a_1 b_2$,
    $(1 - b_2)(1 - a_1 b_2 - b_1 a_2) \ge (1 - a_1)(1 - a_2)$; or
(iv) $a_2 < b_2$, $(1 - b_1)(1 - b_2) < (1 - a_1)(1 - a_2)$,
    $b_1(1 - a_2) \ge a_1 b_2$,
    $(1 - a_1)(1 - a_1 b_2 - b_1 a_2) \ge (1 - b_1)(1 - b_2)$.   For proof see [14].

Definition 4. *Let Bel_1 and Bel_2 denote combinable belief functions on Ω. We define the degree of conflict of Bel_1 and Bel_2 denoted $\mathbb{C}(Bel_1, Bel_2)$, by*

$$\mathbb{C}(Bel_1, Bel_2) = max \left(0, AU(Bel_1 \oplus Bel_2) - min_i AU(Bel_i) \right).$$

That is the degree of conflict is equal to the amount of uncertainty gained (or, equivalently, the amount of information lost[3]) by Dempster's combination. [14].

---

[2] $Pl\text{-}C_0$ is not a separate measure of conflict in general; it is just a component of $Pl\text{-}C$.
[3] The information gain $\mathcal{G}(Bel_1, Bel_2)$ is defined dually in [14].

5   A Comparison of the Approaches

5.1   Uncertainty and Internal Conflict

Unlike author's plausibility approach, there is no internal conflict specified in Harmanec's approach. On the other hand, there is uncertainty of individual beliefs Bel_1 and Bel_2, uncertainty of their combination $Bel_1 \oplus Bel_2$, and conflict between Bel_1 and Bel_2. Thus there is some kind of analogy of the approaches.

Let us present $AU(Bel)$ in two-element case on Fig. 4. For Bayesian BFs, AU is really analogous to $Pl\text{-}IntC(Bel)$, AU is maximal for $0' = U_2$ ($AU(U_2) = 1 = log_2\, n = log_2\, 2$) and it decreases to 0 towards both $(0,1)$ and $(1,0)$. On the other hand $AU(Bel)$ it is not decreasing towards VBF $0 = (0,0)$, but it is constant ($AU(Bel) = 1$) for all $Bel \in S$. VBF is completely without any internal conflict $Pl\text{-}IntC$, but it has maximal uncertainty $AU(VBF) = 1$. Non-analogous are also all simple (support) BFs $(a,0) \in S_1$ and $(0,b) \in S_2$, they are decreasing from 1 to 0, but $Pl\text{-}IntC(a,0) = Pl\text{-}IntC(0,b)$ are constantly equal to 0. Big difference is also maximal uncertainty $AU(a,b) = 1$ for all BFs such that $0 \leq a,b \leq \frac{1}{2}$ (the grey part of Fig. 4).

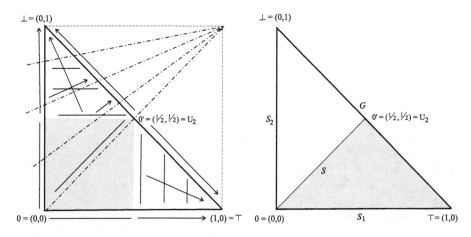

Fig. 4. Uncertainty $AU(Bel)$ of $Bel = (a,b)$ on Ω_2.; uncertainty decreases in direction of arrows; it is constant along the lines without arrows.

Fig. 5. Belief functions on Ω_2: $a \geq b$, $Bel(\{\omega_1\}) \geq Bel(\{\omega_2\})$.

In the case of Bayesian BFs on Ω_n, AU is maximal for U_n ($AU(U_n) = log_2\, n$) and it decreases towards categorical Bayesian BFs ($Bel_\omega : m(\{\omega\}) = 1$). For general BFs, AU is maximal for all symmetric BFs, for all qBBFs such that $m(\{\omega_i\}) \leq \frac{1}{n}$; and AU decreases towards categorical BFs. Note that $AU(Bel_C) = log_2\, |C|$, for any categorical BF on any frame, thus always $AU(Bel_\omega) = 0$.

5.2 Analysis of Conflict Between BFs on Ω_2

Let us start with mutual conflictness non-conflictness of two BFs. This is very easy in the case of plausibility conflict Pl-C. Two BFs $Bel_i = (a_i, b_i)$ on Ω_2 are mutually non-conflicting, i.e., there is no conflict between them if and only if, both of them support same ω_i and both of them oppose the other element of Ω_2 thus if and only if both of Bel_i are in grey part of the triangle on Fig. 5 or both of them are in the white part. Otherwise, the BFs are mutually conflicting.

In the case of Harmanec's conflict, Bel_i are mutually non-conflicting if and only if $AU(Bel_1 \oplus Bel_2) \leq AU(Bel_1), AU(Bel_2)$, i.e., if and only if the condition from Theorem 1 is satisfied (or its dual condition in the case that $a_1 \leq b_1$). Subcondition (i) says that both BFs are in a/the grey square on Fig. 4, subcondition (ii) says that both BFs are in the grey triangle on Fig. 5, while its dual subcondition is related to the white triangle (when $a_1 \leq b_1$); see detail in [10].

Theorem 2. *Let Bel_1, Bel_2 be two combinable BFs on two-element Ω_2, given by pairs (a_1, b_1) and (a_2, b_2). If Pl-$C(Bel_1, Bel_2) = 0$ then also $\mathbb{C}(Bel_1, Bel_2) = 0$.*

Conflict Between a Free *(a,b)* and a Fixed Bayesian *(u,1-u)*. Let us look at $\mathbb{C}((a, b), (u, v))$ analogously as at Pl-$C((a, b), (u, v))$ in Sect. 3. We will start with a simplified but important case of a Bayesian BF, thus $(u, v) = (u, 1-u)$. For a special case of Bayesian BF $0' = U_2 = (\frac{1}{2}, \frac{1}{2})$ we have the following lemma.

Lemma 1. *$U_2 = (\frac{1}{2}, \frac{1}{2})$ is non-conflicting with any belief function on two-element frame of discernment, i.e.. for any Bel on Ω_2 it holds that $\mathbb{C}(Bel, U_2) = 0$.*

Let us suppose $u > \frac{1}{2}$, $v = 1 - u$ now, see Fig. 6. If $a \geq b$ then $AU((a, b) \oplus (u, 1 - u) \leq AU(a, b), AU(u, 1-u)$ according to subcondition (i) from Theorem 1, hence $\mathbb{C}((a, b), (u, 1 - u)) = 0$. Maximal uncertainty $AU(\oplus) = 1$ (read: $AU((a, b) \oplus (u, 1 - u) = 1 = log_2|n|)$ appears for $(a, b) = (1 - u, u)$ and for all BFs lying on the same h-line as $(1 - u, u)$, i.e. such that $Pl\_P(a, b) = (1 - u, u)$.

$\mathbb{C}((a, 1 - a), (u, 1 - u))$:

Let assume $b = 1 - a$ for a moment: $AU(\oplus)$ increases for a decreasing from $\frac{1}{2}$ to $1 - u$, $AU(a, 1 - a) \geq AU(u, 1 - u)$ there (for $a \in [1 - u, \frac{1}{2}]$), thus conflict $\mathbb{C}((a, 1 - a), (u, 1 - u)) = AU(\oplus) - AU(u, 1 - u)$ increases with uncertainty from 0 for a decreasing from $\frac{1}{2}$ to $1 - u$. For $a \leq 1 - u$, $\mathbb{C}((a, 1 - a), (u, 1 - u)) = AU(\oplus) - AU(a, 1 - a)$, both $AU(\oplus)$ and $AU(a, 1 - a)$ decrease there, $AU(a, 1 - a)$ decreases more when closer to $(1 - u, u)$ thus the conflict still increases till its maximum for $(a_m, 1 - a_m)$, $0 < a_m < 1 - u$. Further it decreases till zero for $a = 0$. We can show that the conflict is positive for any $a > 0$, see [10]. This is represented by arrows from $(a_m, 1 - a_m)$ to $(0, 1)$ and to U_2 in Fig. 6.

Analogously we can analyse the other special cases: $\mathbb{C}((a, b), (u, 1 - u))$ for $a < b$, $b \leq u$, $\mathbb{C}((a, b), (u, 1 - u))$ for $a < b$, $b \geq u$, and $\mathbb{C}((0, b), (u, 1 - u))$, see [10], using homomorphic properties of h and h-lines on Fig. 6. From the analysis of the last case we obtain two subcases for $u \geq 0.618$ corresponding to Fig. 6, and for $\frac{1}{2} < u \leq \frac{1}{2}(\sqrt{5} - 1) \doteq 0.618034$ where non-conflicting area corresponding to subcondition (iv) from Theorem 1 appears, see a modification of the figure in [10].

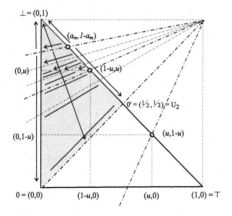

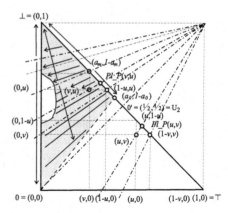

Fig. 6. Harmanec's conflict $\mathbb{C}((a,b),$ $(u, 1-u))$ for $u > 0.618$.

Fig. 7. Harmanec's $\mathbb{C}((a,b),(u,v))$. Modified figure with $u>v$ both relatively close to U_2; white area non-conflicting with (u,v).

Conflict Between a Free (a, b) and a Fixed General (u, v)

Lemma 2. *Any symmetric BF $Sym = (s, s)$ is non-conflicting with any other BF on Ω_2, i.e.. for any $Bel = (a, b)$ and any (s, s) it holds that $\mathbb{C}((a, b), (s, s)) = 0$.*

Let us assume that $u > v$, see Fig. 7, the situation is more complicated now. In Dempster's combination $Pl\_P(u, v)$ plays principal role (h-lines in Figures), whereas at $AU(u, v)$ directly u plays principal role (horizontal and vertical straight lines in Figures), hence there is more of important points in the Figure.

Special subcases are step by step analysed in [10]: $\mathbb{C}((a, 1-a), (u, v))$, $\mathbb{C}((a, b), (u, v))$, and $\mathbb{C}((0, b), (u, v))$; the results are displayed in Fig. 7: In this general case also area related to subcondition (iii) appears, a triangle $0 = (0, 0)$, U_2 and $(a_0, 1 - a_0)$. Fig. 7 is the modified version of the figure, which includes also non-conflicting area related to subcondition (iv): a white area aside of left leg of the triangle. For a (non-modified) figure without area related to (iv) see [10].

Theorem 3. *Let Bel_1, Bel_2 be two combinable BFs given by pairs (a_1, b_1) and (a_2, b_2) on Ω_2. It holds that $\mathbb{C}((a_1, b_1), (a_2, b_2)) \leq Pl\text{-}C((a_1, b_1), (a_2, b_2))$.*

5.3 Harmanec's Conflict and its Comparison to Plausibility Conflict of Quasi-Bayesian Belief Functions on Ω_n

We can represent any qBBF by enumeration of its singletons and their values or by n-tuples of all $m(\{\omega_i\})$ values. Analogously to the simplest case of Ω_2, where are only qBBFs, we can use h-lines defined by homomorphism h (straight lines through a qBBF in question and point $(1, 1, ..., 1)$ in this case. Similarly to Ω_2, AU decreases along h-lines in direction to BBFs as less and less iso-AU levels are crossed in this direction, analogously to Fig. 4. On the other side Harmanec's conflict $\mathbb{C}$ is again constant along h-lines or it increases towards Bayesian BFs. Thus we can relatively simply generalize the previous results.

Theorem 4. *Any symmetric quasi-Bayesian BF $Bel_S = (s, s...s)$ is non-conflicting with any other qBBF on general Ω_n, i.e.. for any qBBF Bel and any symmetric qBBF Bel_S both on Ω_n it holds $\mathbb{C}(Bel,Bel_S) = 0$; specially, $\mathbb{C}(Bel,U_n) = 0$.*

Theorem 5. *Let Bel_ω be a categorical singleton, i.e., BF such that $m_\omega(\{\omega\}) = 1$ for some $\omega \in \Omega_n$. For any qBBF Bel combinable with Bel_ω holds $\mathbb{C}(Bel,Bel_\omega) = 0$.*

Note that $\mathbb{C}(Bel, Bel_\omega)$ is not defined for Bel whose core does not include ω because $Bel_\omega \oplus Bel$ is not defined there. From the same reason $\mathbb{C}(Bel_1, Bel_2)$ is not defined either for any pair of BFs with disjunctive cores $(C)_1 \cap (C)_2 = \emptyset$. Hence full/total conflict is not defined by Harmanec degree of conflict $\mathbb{C}$.

Analysing situations analogous to those described for Ω_2, see Fig. 6, we obtain (for detail see [10]):

Theorem 6. *(max $\mathbb{C}$) Let Bel_u be a fixed quasi-Bayesian BF on Ω_n and Bel any qBBF on Ω_n combinable with Bel. Maximal $\mathbb{C}(Bel, Bel_u)$ appears for a BBF Bel_m, which lies between BBF $-h(Bel_u)$ and border of $n - 1$ dimensional simplex of BBFs in the direction opposite to the direction to BBF $h(Bel)$.*

Theorem 7. *If $Pl\text{-}C(Bel_1, Bel_2) = 0$ for any two combinable quasi-Bayesian BFs Bel_1, Bel_2 on a general frame of discernment Ω_n then also $\mathbb{C}(Bel_1, Bel_2) = 0$.*

Hypothesis 1. *Let us suppose two combinable quasi-Bayesian belief functions Bel_1 and Bel_2 on Ω_n. It holds that $\mathbb{C}(Bel_1, Bel_2) \leq Pl\text{-}C(Bel_1, Bel_2)$.*

5.4 A Comparison of the Approaches for General Belief Functions

Due to the proof of Theorem 5 holds for any BF Bel, we can simply formulate it also for general BFs. Nevertheless, situation is much more complicated for general belief functions, as there are not only one-dimensional h-lines, but multi-dimensional structures instead of them on Ω_n. For an introduction on algebra of belief functions on Ω_3 see [7].

Due to this, we can observe a difference in common properties of conflicts between belief functions which are not quasi Bayesian. Thus a symmetric BF Bel_S (even U_n) is not non-conflicting with any BF in general; and a simple generalization of Theorem 4 does not hold true in general. We have neither a simple generalization of Theorems 3 and 7, because, e.g., there is always $Pl\text{-}C(Bel, Bel_S) = 0$, but there are situations for which $\mathbb{C}(Bel, Bel_S) > 0$ thus $\mathbb{C}(Bel, Bel_S) \nleq Pl\text{-}C(Bel, Bel_S)$ in such situations. See the following example:

Example 1. Let $m_1(\{\omega_1\}) = \frac{1}{2}$, $m_1(\{\omega_2, \omega_3\}) = \frac{1}{2}$; $Bel_2 = (\frac{2}{10}, \frac{2}{10}, \frac{2}{10}, \frac{1}{10}, \frac{1}{10}, \frac{1}{10}; \frac{1}{10})$; $AU(Bel_1) = -\frac{1}{2}log_2\frac{1}{2} - 2\frac{1}{4}log_2\frac{1}{4} = 1.500$, $AU(Bel_2) = AU(U_3) = -3$

$\frac{1}{3}log_2\frac{1}{3} = 1.585.$ $Bel_1 \oplus Bel_2 = (\frac{4}{11}, \frac{3}{11}, \frac{3}{11}, 0, 0, \frac{1}{10}; 0)$, $AU(Bel_1 \oplus Bel_2) = -\frac{8}{22}$ $log_2\frac{8}{22} - 2\frac{7}{22}log_2\frac{7}{22} = 1.582$;

Thus $\mathbb{C}(Bel_1, U_3) = AU(Bel_1 \oplus U_3) - AU(Bel_1) = AU(U_3) - AU(Bel_1) = 0.085 > 0$ and also $\mathbb{C}(Bel_1, Bel_2) = AU(Bel_1 \oplus Bel_2) - AU(Bel_1) = 0.082 > 0.$

We have examples where U_3 and symmetric BFs are non-conflicting with other BFs and also counter-examples. Thus there arises an interesting open problem to specify conditions under which assertion of Theorem 7 holds for general BFs on a general frame. The related interesting open question is also generalization of Theorem 3 (including verification of Hypothesis 1) and Theorem 4.

6 Summary

We have seen that $\mathbb{C}(Bel_i, Bel_j)$ is a weaker measure of conflict than $Pl\text{-}C(Bel_i, Bel_j)$ on quasi-Bayesian BFs in the sense, that all non-conflicting couples of qBBFs with respect to $Pl\text{-}C$ are also non-conflicting with respect to $\mathbb{C}$. Moreover, we have Hypothesis $\mathbb{C}(Bel_i, Bel_j) \leq Pl\text{-}C(Bel_i, Bel_j)$, which has already been proved on a two-element frame of discernment. This is important as $Pl\text{-}C$ classifies as non-conflicting many cases which are considered to be positively conflicting by the other measures of conflict ($m(\emptyset)$, distances, Liu's cf, Martin's approach, Destercke-Burger's approach). A similar feature as we have observed at $Pl\text{-}C$ and $\mathbb{C}$ have also a new measure of conflict based on non-conflicting parts of BFs defined in [9] and measures defined by consonant conflict approach [11].

On the other hand, there are several properties of Harmanec's degree of conflict $\mathbb{C}$ which seem surprising or even strange and which are significantly different even from plausibility conflict $Pl\text{-}C$: e.g., decreasing of conflict in the direction to categorical singletons ($m_\omega(\{\omega\}) = 1$) and non-conflictness of categorical singletons with all combinable BFs, non-conflicting areas according to subconditions (iii) and (iv) from Theorem 1. This 'strange' behaviour is based on completely different assumptions. Harmanec's conflict does not measure either difference or opposition of beliefs, but increase/decrease of uncertainty when BFs are combined, thus this 'strange' property of $\mathbb{C}$-conflict is sound from its point of view. The 'strange' property of $\mathbb{C}$ comes from the nature of Dempster's rule. The plausibility conflict is quite different as it is based on accord/opposition of BFs.

All of these properties should be discussed (accepted or explicitly rejected) when a general axiomatic approach to conflicts between belief functions will be formulated based on Destercke & Burger [12], Martin's [20] and author's approaches [5,8,9] and his new consonant conflict approach [11].

When using Harmanec's conflict $\mathbb{C}$ we have to be careful about values (specially about values around 1) as rounding of the values may produce relatively different results, see Example in [10]. A disadvantage of $\mathbb{C}$ is its strong relation to Dempster's rule of combination[4], thus $\mathbb{C}$ is applicable only in the classic Dempster-Shafer approach with the Dempster's rule.

---

[4] We can, of course, generalise Harmanec's $\mathbb{C}$ by substitution of Dempster's rule by another rule of combination. But a nature of a such conflict may be substantially different from the nature of $\mathbb{C}$, thus a new analysis should be done. Analogously we can use instead of $\mathbb{C}$ Cattaneo's minimal joint conflict, see [2].

Let us close this Section by remark, that a reader can find a comparison of the plausibility conflict to $m_{\ominus}(\emptyset)$ and to Liu's degree of conflict in [8].

7   Conclusion

Two completely different approaches to conflict of belief functions were analysed and compared. The common features were observed and the significant difference in behaviour was explained. The warning for application of Harmanec's conflict was presented.

The theoretic analysis and comparison of the approaches coming from significantly different assumptions move us to better understanding of nature of conflicts of belief functions in general. This may consequently serve as a basis for better combination of conflicting belief functions in future, whenever conflicting belief functions appear.

Acknowledgements. The partial institutional support RVO: 67985807 is acknowledged.

References

1. Almond, R.G.: Graphical Belief Modeling. Chapman & Hall, London (1995)
2. Cattaneo, M.E.G.V.: Combining belief functions issued from dependent sources. In: Proceedings of the 3rd International Symposium, ISiPTA 2003, pp. 133–147. Carleton Scientific (2003)
3. Daniel, M.: Algebraic structures related to Dempster-Shafer theory. In: Bouchon-Meunier, B., Yager, R.R., Zadeh, L.A. (eds.) Advances in Intelligent Computing - IPMU 1994. LNCS, vol. 945, pp. 51–61. Springer-Verlag, Heidelberg (1995)
4. Daniel, M.: Probabilistic transformations of belief functions. In: Godo, L. (ed.) ECSQARU 2005. LNCS (LNAI), vol. 3571, pp. 539–551. Springer, Heidelberg (2005)
5. Daniel, M.: Conflicts within and between belief functions. In: Hüllermeier, E., Kruse, R., Hoffmann, F. (eds.) IPMU 2010. LNCS, vol. 6178, pp. 696–705. Springer, Heidelberg (2010)
6. Daniel, M.: Non-conflicting and conflicting parts of belief functions. In: Coolen, F., de Cooman G., Fetz T., Obergguggenberger M. (eds.) Proceedings of the 7th ISIPTA, ISIPTA 2011, pp. 149–158. SIPTA (2011)
7. Daniel, M.: Introduction to an algebra of belief functions on three-element frame of discernment — a Quasi Bayesian case. In: Greco, S., Bouchon-Meunier, B., Coletti, G., Fedrizzi, M., Matarazzo, B., Yager, R.R. (eds.) IPMU 2012, Part III. CCIS, vol. 299, pp. 532–542. Springer, Heidelberg (2012)
8. Daniel, M.: Properties of plausibility conflict of belief functions. In: Rutkowski, L., Korytkowski, M., Scherer, R., Tadeusiewicz, R., Zadeh, L.A., Zurada, J.M. (eds.) ICAISC 2013, Part I. LNCS, vol. 7894, pp. 235–246. Springer, Heidelberg (2013)
9. Daniel, M.: Conflict between belief functions: a new measure based on their non-conflicting parts. In: Cuzzolin, F. (ed.) BELIEF 2014. LNCS, vol. 8764, pp. 321–330. Springer, Heidelberg (2014)

10. Daniel, M.: A comparison of plausibility conflict of belief functions and of conflict based on amount of uncertainty of belief functions. Technical report. V-1221, ICS AS CR, Prague (2015)

11. Daniel, M.: An idea of consonant conflicts between belief functions. In: Augustin, T., Doria, S., Miranda, E., Quaeghebeur, E. (eds.) Proceedings of the 9th International Symposium on Imprecise Probability: Theories and Applications, ISIPTA'15, pp 336. SIPTA (2015)

12. Destercke, S., Burger, T.: Toward an axiomatic definition of conflict between belief functions. IEEE Trans. Cyber. **43**(2), 585–596 (2013)

13. Hájek, P., Valdés, J.J.: Generalized algebraic foundations of uncertainty processing in rule-based expert systems (dempsteroids). Comput. Artif. Intell. **10**(1), 29–42 (1991)

14. Harmanec, D.: A note on uncertainty, dempster rule of combination, and conflict. Int. J. Gen. Syst. **26**(1–2), 63–72 (1997)

15. Harmanec, D.: Measures of Uncertainty and Information. SIPTA (1999) (cited 1. 5. 2015) http://www.sipta.org/documentation/summary_measures/ippinfom.pdf

16. Harmanec, D., Klir, G.J.: Measuring total uncertainty in Dempster-Shafer theory: a novel approach. Int. J. Gen. Syst. **22**(4), 405–419 (1994)

17. Harmanec, D., Resconi, G., Klir, G.J., et al.: On the computation of the uncertainty measure for the Dempster-Shafer theory. Int. J. Gen. Syst. **25**(2), 153–163 (1996)

18. Lefèvre, É., Elouedi, Z., Mercier, D.: Towards an alarm for opposition conflict in a conjunctive combination of belief functions. In: Liu, W. (ed.) ECSQARU 2011. LNCS, vol. 6717, pp. 314–325. Springer, Heidelberg (2011)

19. Liu, W.: Analysing the degree of conflict among belief functions. Artif. Intell. **170**, 909–924 (2006)

20. Martin, A.: About conflict in the theory of belief functions. In: Denœux, T., Masson, M.-H. (eds.) Belief Functions: Theory and Applications. AISC, pp. 161–168. Springer, Heidelberg (2012)

21. Martin, A., Jousselme, A.-L., Osswald, C.: Conflict measure for the discounting operation on belief functions. In: Proceedings of the Fusion 2008. Cologne, Germany (2008)

22. Roquel, A., Le Hégarat-Mascle, S., Bloch, I., Vincke, B.: Decomposition of conflict as a distribution on hypotheses in the framework on belief functions. Int. J. Approximate Reasoning **55**, 1129–1146 (2014)

23. Shafer, G.: A Mathematical Theory of Evidence. Princeton University Press, Princeton (1976)

Weighted Maximum Likelihood for Parameters Learning Based on Noisy Labels in Discrete Hidden Markov Models

Pablo Juesas Cano and Emmanuel Ramasso$^{(\boxtimes)}$

Department of Applied Mechanics and Department of Automatic Control
and Micro-Mechatronic Systems, Technopôle TEMIS,
FEMTO-ST Institute, 25000 Besancon, France
`emmanuel.ramasso@femto-st.fr`

Abstract. In supervised time-series segmentation, each instance in the training set has to be assigned a label. However, elicitation of labels from experts or their estimation may be time consuming and prone to errors. The problem considered in this paper is focused on time-series segmentation based on noisy and uncertain labels by using discrete Hidden Markov Models (dHMM). Maximum likelihood parameter learning in dHMM with such labels is tackled by two methods: the Evidential Expectation-Maximization (E2M) algorithm where weights represent plausibility functions, and the Weighted Likelihood Principle (WLP) coupled with the usual Expectation-Maximization algorithm. The model is tested using the E2M solution on simulated datasets. The results allows to evaluating the sensitivity of the quantization phase, with report to the noise level and the level of uncertainty on labels, on the quality of the statistical modelling of continuous-valued time-series.

1 Introduction

Hidden Markov models (HMM) are powerful tools for sequence modeling and state sequence recognition that have been used in many different applications. Discrete HMM represents a particular of HMM where the observations are discrete symbols. One of the most extended use has been text character recognition from several scripts as Latin [9], Korean [11] or Farsi (Arabic) [6]. Other applications concerned signal processing [16], video event classification [3], medical applications [1] or transformer relaying protection [12].

A dHMM is composed of observed variables (outputs) $X_t, t = 1 \ldots T$ where t is a discrete time index and latent discrete random variables (hidden states) Y_t [14]. The sequence of states $Y_1, Y_2, \ldots Y_T$ is a first-order Markov chain and the distribution of the output X_t at time t depends only on Y_t.

One of the objective of a dHMM is to estimate the state sequence hidden within the observations. In order to improve the convergence (quicker and more precise) and to better estimate the parameters, it is proposed to use partial prior knowledge about the states. For that, we first apply the Evidential Expectation-Maximization (E2M) algorithm [8] by assuming that the prior is encoded by

© Springer International Publishing Switzerland 2015
S. Destercke and T. Denoeux (Eds.): ECSQARU 2015, LNAI 9161, pp. 451–460, 2015.
DOI: 10.1007/978-3-319-20807-7_41

a set of plausibility functions or basic belief assignments (Sect. 2). We then apply the Weighted Likelihood Principle (WLP) coupled with the Expectation-Maximization algorithm and we discuss the differences between both solutions. Experiments are focused on continuous-valued time-series segmentation with the solution provided by E2M. We illustrate the impact of the quantization phase with report to uncertain and noisy labels on the quality of the results (Sect. 3).

2   Developing the Model

2.1   Model and Notations

The following parameters are used to describe a HMM:

- Prior probabilities $\boldsymbol{\Pi} = \{\pi_1, ..., \pi_k, ..., \pi_K\}$, where $\pi_k = P(Y_1 = k)$ is the probability of being in state k at $t = 1$ being K the number of states;
- Transition probabilities $\mathbf{A} = [a_{kl}]$, where

$$a_{kl} = P(Y_t = l | Y_{t-1} = k), \quad (k, l) \in \{1, ..., K\}^2$$

is the probability for being in state l at time t given that it was in state k at $t - 1$ with $\sum_l a_{kl} = 1$;
- Observation symbol probabilities $\mathbf{B} = [b_{kv}]$ where

$$b_{kv} = P(x_t = v | Y_t = k), \quad k \in \{1, ..., K\} \ \& \ v \in \{1, ..., V\}$$

is the probability for being in state k at time t and observing symbol v with $\sum_v b_{kv} = 1$

The set of parameters is denoted as $\theta = (\mathbf{A}, \mathbf{B}, \boldsymbol{\Pi})$.

The complete data is defined as $\boldsymbol{z} = (\boldsymbol{x}, \boldsymbol{y})$ composed of the observed output sequence $\boldsymbol{x} = (x_1, ..., x_T)$ and the corresponding sequence of hidden states $\boldsymbol{y} = (y_1, ..., y_T)$. In the discrete case each observation takes a discrete value $v \in \{1, ..., V\}$ called symbol.

2.2   Learning Procedures Based on Soft Labels

E2M Algorithm. Let Y be a variable taking values in a finite domain $\Omega = \{1, 2 ... K\}$, called the *frame of discernment*. Uncertain information about Y (i.e. partial knowledge about hidden states, also called soft labels) is supposed to be represented by a mass function m on Ω, $\sum_{A \subseteq \Omega} m(A) = 1$ (assumed normalized).

Maximising the likelihood in presence of such uncertain information about hidden states can be performed by applying the E2M algorithm [8]. For that, it is first required to express the likelihood function over hidden and observed variables which, in the dHMM, is given by

$$L(\boldsymbol{\theta}; \boldsymbol{z}) = p(y_1; \Pi) \left(\prod_{t=2}^{T} p(y_t | y_{t-1}; \mathbf{A}) \right) \prod_{t=1}^{T} p(x_t | y_t; \mathbf{B})$$

$$= \left(\prod_{k=1}^{K} \pi_k^{y_{1k}} \right) \left(\prod_{t=2}^{T} \prod_{k,l} a_{kl}^{y_{(t-1,k)} y_{tl}} \right) \left(\prod_{t=1}^{T} \prod_{k=1}^{K} \prod_{v=1}^{V} b_{kv}^{y_{tk}} \right)$$

where y_{tk} is a binary variable such that $y_{tk} = 1$ if state k is true at time t. The second step is to take the conditional expectation of the log-likelihood given partial knowledge on states which can then be obtained at iteration q of E2M as [8]:

$$Q(\boldsymbol{\theta}, \boldsymbol{\theta}^{(q)}) = \mathbb{E}_{\boldsymbol{\theta}^{(q)}}[\log(L(\boldsymbol{\theta}; \boldsymbol{z}) | \boldsymbol{x}, pl] = \frac{\sum_{\boldsymbol{y} \in \Omega} \log(L(\boldsymbol{\theta}; \boldsymbol{z})) p(\boldsymbol{y} | \boldsymbol{x}, \boldsymbol{\theta}^{(q)}) pl(\boldsymbol{y})}{L(\boldsymbol{\theta}^{(q)}; \boldsymbol{x}, pl)}$$

where pl is the contour function (plausibility of singleton states) associated to m. $L(\boldsymbol{\theta}^{(q)}; \boldsymbol{x}, pl)$ is a generalized likelihood function [8] evaluated by using the forward-backward propagations [15]. By expanding the expectation, we get three terms:

- Two terms involving prior and transitions and similar to HMM with continuous observations [15];
- The third one is specific to the dHMM and concerns the emission probability model **B** from which the maximum likelihood estimate can be obtained as:

$$b_{kv}^{(q+1)} = \frac{\sum_{t=1}^{T} \gamma_{tk}^{(q)} \mathbb{1}\{x_t = v\}}{\sum_{t=1}^{T} \gamma_{tk}^{(q)}}$$

where $\gamma_{tk} = \mathbb{E}_{\boldsymbol{\theta}^{(q)}}[y_{t,k} | \boldsymbol{x}, pl]$ has the same expression as in [15].

Weighted Likelihood Principle (WLP). It is described in detail in [18,19] and aims at exploiting pieces of information obtained from independent samples generated by some distributions with unknown parameters that have justly to be estimated. In the WLP model, a sample is produced by a weighted likelihood function [13,18]. For the dHMM, it is given by

$$L(\boldsymbol{\theta}; \boldsymbol{z}, \mathbf{W}) = p(y_1; \Pi)^{w_{1k}} \left(\prod_{t=2}^{T} p(y_t | y_{t-1}; A)^{w_{(t-1,k)} w_{tl}} \right) \prod_{t=1}^{T} p(x_t | y_t; B)^{w_{tk}}$$

which can be rewritten by using multinomial variables as

$$L(\boldsymbol{\theta}; \boldsymbol{z}, \mathbf{W}) =$$
$$\left(\prod_{k=1}^{K} \pi_k^{w_{1k} y_{1k}} \right) \left(\prod_{t=2}^{T} \prod_{k,l} a_{kl}^{w_{(t-1,k)} y_{(t-1,k)} w_{tl} y_{tl}} \right) \left(\prod_{t=1}^{T} \prod_{k=1}^{K} \prod_{v=1}^{V} b_{kv}^{w_{tk} y_{tk}} \right) \quad (1)$$

where the weights $\mathbf{W} = \{w_{t,k}, t = 1 \ldots T, k = 1 \ldots K : w_{t,k} \geq 0\}$ can be obtained by optimization (given a target) [13,19] or provided by an end-user. By taking the logarithm of Eq. 1, we have:

$$\log L(\boldsymbol{\theta}; \boldsymbol{z}, \mathbf{W}) = \sum_{k=1}^{K} w_{1k} y_{1k} \log \pi_k + \sum_{t=2}^{T} \sum_{k,l} w_{(t-1,k)} y_{(t-1,k)} w_{tl} y_{tl} \log a_{kl}$$
$$+ \sum_{t=1}^{T} \sum_{k=1}^{K} \sum_{v=1}^{V} w_{tk} y_{tk} \log b_{kv} \tag{2}$$

We then apply the usual EM algorithm [7] to estimate the parameters $\boldsymbol{\theta}$ in an iterative way as in standard dHMM. Assuming independence between hidden variables and weights, the expression of the expectation of $\mathbb{E}[w_{tk} y_{tk} | \boldsymbol{x}, \boldsymbol{\theta}]$ can be obtained as:

$$\mathbb{E}[w_{tk} y_{tk}] = \frac{w_{tk} p(y_t = k | \boldsymbol{x}, \boldsymbol{\theta})}{\sum_{l=1}^{K} w_{tl} p(y_t = l | \boldsymbol{x}, \boldsymbol{\theta})}$$

This posterior distribution is then used to find the expectation of the complete-data log likelihood evaluated for some general parameter value [2]. The M-step then makes use of this posterior that relies on soft labels to estimate the parameters for the next iteration.

Differences Between the Two Models. The E2M and WLP models differ from two main points, independently on the statistical model considered (dHMM or another).

Firstly, in E2M, the prior on latent variables is expressed as a plausibility function (in $[0, 1]$), while the WLP allows more general weights provided positiveness. In practice, it permits more flexibility. Real applications are necessary to assess if this difference actually plays a role, either for weights elicitation or estimation, or concerning the performance.

Secondly, and more fundamentally, the plausibilities used in E2M play a role of weights on the emission model that generates the likelihood of the current data given the current state ($p(x_t | y_t)$). Therefore, the computation of the posterior probability on states (γ_t) at time t makes use of the plausibilities at t (in the forward propagation [2]) and on $t + 1$ (in the backward propagation [2]). In comparison, in the WLP model, the weights are combined conjunctively only once with the posterior probability on states ($p(y_t | \boldsymbol{x})$). Eventually, this difference leads to models with different likelihoods, and more interestingly, it shows that the WLP acts similarly as the approach proposed in [4,5].

3   Simulations

We consider a dHMM with 3 states and three symbols per state distributed with report to uniform distribution defined as:

$$\boldsymbol{\varPi} = (1/3, 1/3, 1/3)', \quad \mathbf{A} = \begin{pmatrix} 0.6 \ 0.3 \ 0.1 \\ 0.1 \ 0.6 \ 0.3 \\ 0.1 \ 0.3 \ 0.6 \end{pmatrix}$$

$$S_1 \sim \begin{cases} x \sim \mathcal{U}(0, 0.2) \\ y \sim \mathcal{U}(0.8, 1) \\ z \sim \mathcal{U}(0, 0.1) \end{cases} \quad S_2 \sim \begin{cases} x \sim \mathcal{U}(0.8, 1) \\ y \sim \mathcal{U}(0, 0.2) \\ z \sim \mathcal{U}(0, 0.1) \end{cases}$$

$$S_3 = \{S_{31}\} \cup \{S_{32}\} \quad S_{31} \sim \begin{cases} x \sim \mathcal{U}(0.4, 0.6) \\ y \sim \mathcal{U}(0, 1) \\ z \sim \mathcal{U}(0, 0.1) \end{cases} \quad S_{32} \sim \begin{cases} x \sim \mathcal{U}(0, 1) \\ y \sim \mathcal{U}(0.4, 0.6) \\ z \sim \mathcal{U}(0, 0.1) \end{cases}$$

Two sets of samples are represented in Fig. 1.

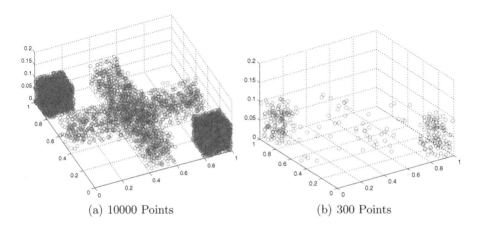

(a) 10000 Points   (b) 300 Points

Fig. 1. Distribution of signal points

The *Kmeans* algorithm was used for vector quantization [14] in order to transform those continuous-valued observations into discrete symbols. Different number of clusters were tested to estimate the impact of the quantization on the performance. Two different experiments were carried out with this model in order to study the influence of "label imprecision" and "labeling error" [5,8,15].

3.1   Influence of Label Imprecision

To study how the influence of imprecision of knowledge on hidden states affects the performing of the learning procedures described above, a learning sequence $(\boldsymbol{x}, \boldsymbol{y})$ of length T was generated using the model above. Uncertain labels were generated as follows:

$$pl_{tk} \begin{cases} 1 \text{ if } y_t = k, \\ \nu \text{ otherwise.} \end{cases}$$

ν represents the nonspecificity coefficient, which quantifies the imprecision of the contour function pl_t. To assess the quality of learning, a testing dataset of 1000 observations was generated following the same distribution. The most probable state at a given time was given by the maximum a posteriori probability [14], assuming no previous knowledge about hidden states in the test sequence. The precision of the predicted state sequences was assessed using the adjusted Rand index (ARI) [10] (equals 0 on average for a random partition, and 1 when comparing two identical partitions). The whole experiment (data generation, clustering and learning) was repeated 30 times, for different number of clusters and for $T = 100$ and $T = 300$.

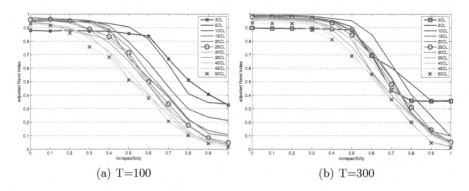

(a) T=100   (b) T=300

Fig. 2. Medians of the adjusted Rand index as a function of the nonspecificity coefficient over 30 repetitions for different number of clusters, from 3 to 50.

Results are shown in Figs. 2 and 3. We can observe that the results degrade from the fully supervised ($\nu = 0$) to the fully unsupervised ($\nu = 1$) case. In Fig. 2 we can see different curves representing the results for different number of clusters. For a small number of clusters, the results with precise knowledge about states ($\nu < 0.4$) are lower than for a larger number of clusters. However, from that point and till the fully unsupervised situation, curves representing larger number of clusters decrease faster and reach values near to 0. Those with fewer number of clusters keep a higher ARI till $\nu = 1$ and do not decrease so fast.

3.2   Influence of Labeling Error

To simulate a situation where information on states may be wrong, we proceed as proposed in [5,8,15]. At each time step t, an error probability q_t was drawn randomly from a beta distribution with mean ρ and standard deviation 0.2. With probability q_t, the state y_t was then replaced by a completely random value $\tilde{y}_t$ (with a uniform distribution over possible states). The plausibilities pl_{tk} were determined as

$$pl_{tk} = P(y_t = k|\tilde{y}_t) = \begin{cases} q_t/K + 1 - q_t & \text{if } \tilde{y}_t = k, \\ q_t/K & \text{otherwise.} \end{cases}$$

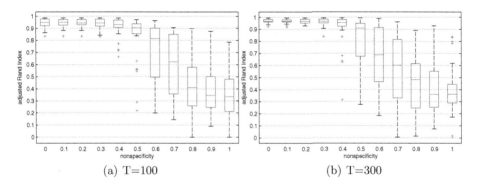

(a) T=100   (b) T=300

Fig. 3. Boxplots of the adjusted Rand index as a function of the nonspecificity coefficient over 30 repetitions for 5 clusters. Learning datasets of T=100 (left) and T=300
(right) observations.

Uncertain labels are more imprecise when the error probability is high. Training
and test data sets were generated as in previous section, and results were evaluated in the same way. For each randomly generated data set, the dHMM was
applied with uncertain labels pl_{tk}, noisy labels $\tilde{y}_{tk}$ and no information on states.

Figure 4 shows the ARI as a function of mean error ρ for uncertain (left) and
noisy (right) labels for different number of clusters and $T = 100$. As expected,
a degradation of the segmentation quality is observed when the mean error
probability ρ increases. The ARI tends to a value close to zero as ρ tends to 1
for a larger number of clusters. For fewer clusters, the results when ρ tends to
1 stay over 0. From the curves, we see that a smaller number of clusters give
generally better results. The number of clusters used for quantization produces
a side effect called distorsion [14] which remains difficult to assess in practice.

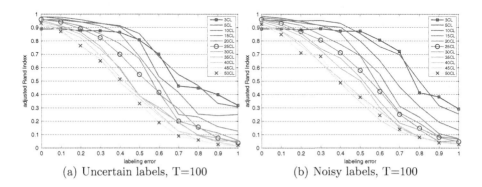

(a) Uncertain labels, T=100   (b) Noisy labels, T=100

Fig. 4. Medians of the adjusted Rand index as a function of the labeling error for
uncertain and noisy labels over 30 repetitions for different number of clusters, from 3
to 50. Learning datasets made of T=100 observations.

In Fig. 5 we show the same experiments as in Fig. 4 but with longer sequences ($T = 300$). Results are quite similar in both cases but we appreciate that with a larger number of observations, the curves scatter less and results are better for all values of ρ. This is an expected result since the dHMM is a statistical model where the parameters are learned by maximum likelihood and therefore the quantity of learning data may have an important impact on estimations.

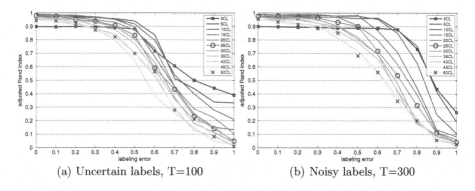

(a) Uncertain labels, T=100   (b) Noisy labels, T=300

Fig. 5. Medians of the adjusted Rand index as a function of the labeling error for uncertain and noisy labels over 30 repetitions for different number of clusters, from 3 to 50. Learning datasets made of T=300 observations.

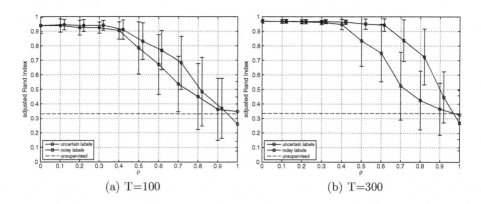

(a) T=100   (b) T=300

Fig. 6. Average values (plus and minus one standard deviation) of the adjusted Rand index over the 30 repetitions, as a function of the mean error probability for learning datasets of T=100 (left) and T=300 (right) observations

Figure 6 shows the evolution of both the noisy and uncertain labels for the experiment with 5 clusters. It is proved that the use of partial information on states in the form of uncertain or noisy labels allows to reach better results than the unsupervised case in every condition. Noisy labels reach better results than the uncertain labels till $\rho = 0.9$.

4   Conclusion

This paper studies the influence of labelling errors on the performance of of discrete Hidden Markov Models for continuous-valued time-series segmentation. Noisy and uncertain labels can be taken into account by the Evidential EM algorithm or by the weighted maximum likelihood principle, yielding two different results. The results shows that the degradation of the performance was accentuated when the quantization phase was inappropriately tuned. In contrast with the continuous HMM proposed in [15], the model can behave better when considering noisy labels than uncertain labels. The way to integrate imprecise knowledge on latent variables in HMM is under study. This would lead to imprecise transition matrices and observation models generating sets of possible sequences of states [17].

Acknowledgment. This work has been carried out in the framework of the Laboratory of Excellence ACTION through the program "Investments for the future" managed by the National Agency for Research (references ANR-11-LABX-01-01). The authors are grateful to the Région Franche-Comté and "Bpifrance financement" supporting the SMART COMPOSITES Project in the framework of FRI2.

References

1. Baldi, P., Chauvin, Y., Hunkapiller, T., McClure, M.A.: Hidden Markov models of biological primary sequence information. Proc. Nat. Acad. Sci. **91**(3), 1059–1063 (1994)
2. Bishop, C.: Pattern Recognition and Machine Learning. Springer, New York (2006)
3. Chen, H.S., Tsai, W.J.: A framework for video event classification by modeling temporal context of multimodal features using HMM. J. Vis. Commun. Image Represent. **25**(2), 285–295 (2014)
4. Cheung, Y.-M.: A rival penalized em algorithm towards maximizing weighted likelihood for density mixture clustering with automatic model selection. In: Proceedings of the 17th International Conference on Pattern Recognition, 2004. ICPR 2004, pp. 633–636, August 2004
5. Côme, E., Oukhellou, L., Denoeux, T., Aknin, P.: Learning from partially supervised data using mixture models and belief functions. Pattern Recogn. **42**(3), 334–348 (2009)
6. Dehghan, M., Faez, K., Ahmadi, M., Shridhar, M.: Handwritten Farsi (Arabic) word recognition: a holistic approach using discrete HMM. Pattern Recogn. **34**(5), 1057–1065 (2001)
7. Dempster, A.P., Laird, N.R.D.: Maximum likelihood from incomplete data via the EM algorithm. J. Roy. Stat. Soc. **39**(1), 1–38 (1977)
8. Denoeux, T.: Maximum likelihood estimation from uncertain data in the belief function framework. IEEE Trans. Knowl. Data Eng. **25**(1), 119–130 (2013)
9. Elms, A., Procter, S., Illingworth, J.: The advantage of using an HMM-based approach for faxed word recognition. Int. J. Doc. Anal. Recogn. **1**(1), 18–36 (1998)
10. Hubert, L., Arabie, P.: Comparing partitions. J. Classif. **2**(1), 193–218 (1985)
11. Kim, H.J., Kim, S.K., Kim, K.H., Lee, J.K.: An HMM-based character recognition network using level building. Pattern Recogn. **30**(3), 491–502 (1997)

12. Ma, X., Shi, J.: A new method for discrimination between fault and magnetizing inrush current using HMM. Electr. Power Syst. Res. **56**(1), 43–49 (2000)
13. Newton, M., Raftery, A.: Approximate bayesian inference with the weighted likelihood boostrap. J. Roy. Stat. Soc. **56**, 3–48 (1994)
14. Rabiner, L.: A tutorial on hidden Markov models and selected applications in speech recognition. Proc. IEEE **77**(2), 257–286 (1989)
15. Ramasso, E., Denoeux, T.: Making use of partial knowledge about hidden states in HMMs: an approach based on belief functions. IEEE Trans. Fuzzy Syst. **22**(2), 395–405 (2014)
16. Ranjan, R., Mitra, D.: HMM modeling for OFDM-BER performance. AEU-Int. J. Electron. Commun. **69**(1), 18–25 (2015)
17. Skulj, D.: Discrete time markov chains with interval probabilities. Int. J. Approximate Reasoning **50**(8), 1314–1329 (2009)
18. Wang, S.: Maximum Weighted Likelihood Estimation. Ph.D. thesis, British Columbia (2001)
19. Wang, X., Zidek, J.: Derivation of mixture distributions and weighted likelihood function as minimizers of KL-divergence subject to constraints. Ann. Inst. Stat. Math. **57**(4), 687–701 (2005)

Evidential Editing K-Nearest Neighbor Classifier

Lianmeng Jiao[1,2]([⊠]), Thierry Denœux[1], and Quan Pan[2]

[1] Sorbonne Universités, Université de Technologie de Compiègne,
CNRS, Heudiasyc UMR 7253, Compiègne, France
lianmeng.jiao@utc.fr
[2] School of Automation, Northwestern Polytechnical University,
Xi'an 710072, People's Republic of China

Abstract. One of the difficulties that arises when using the K-nearest neighbor rule is that each of the labeled training samples is given equal importance in deciding the class of the query pattern to be classified, regardless of their typicality. In this paper, the theory of belief functions is introduced into the K-nearest neighbor rule to develop an evidential editing version of this algorithm. An evidential editing procedure is proposed to reassign the original training samples with new labels represented by an evidential membership structure. With the introduction of the evidential editing procedure, the uncertainty of noisy patterns or samples in overlapping regions can be well characterized. After the evidential editing, a classification procedure is developed to handle the more general situation in which the edited training samples are assigned dependent evidential labels. Two experiments based on synthetic and real data sets were carried out to show the effectiveness of the proposed method.

Keywords: Data classification · K-nearest neighbor · Theory of belief functions · Evidential editing

1 Introduction

The K-nearest neighbor (KNN) rule, first proposed by Fix and Hodges [6], is one of the most popular and successful pattern classification techniques. Given a set of N labeled training samples $\mathcal{T} = \{(\mathbf{x}^{(1)}, \omega^{(1)}), \cdots, (\mathbf{x}^{(N)}, \omega^{(N)})\}$ with input vectors $\mathbf{x}^{(i)} \in \mathcal{R}^D$ and class labels $\omega^{(i)} \in \{\omega_1, \cdots, \omega_M\}$, the KNN rule classifies a query pattern $\mathbf{y} \in \mathcal{R}^D$ based on the class labels represented by its K nearest neighbors (according to, e.g., the Euclidean distance measure) in the training set $\mathcal{T}$. The basic rationale for the KNN rule is both simple and intuitive: samples close in feature space are likely to belong to the same class. The KNN rule is a suboptimal procedure. However, it has been shown that, in the infinite sample situation, the error rate for the 1-NN rule is bounded above by no more than twice the optimal Bayes error rate. Furthermore, as K increases, this error rate approaches the optimal rate asymptotically [7].

© Springer International Publishing Switzerland 2015
S. Destercke and T. Denoeux (Eds.): ECSQARU 2015, LNAI 9161, pp. 461–471, 2015.
DOI: 10.1007/978-3-319-20807-7_42

One of the problems encountered in using the KNN classifier is that each of the training samples is considered equally important in the assignment of the class label to the query pattern. This limitation frequently causes difficulty in regions where the data sets from different classes overlap. Atypical samples in overlapping regions are given as much weight as those that are truly representatives of the clusters. Furthermore, it may be argued that training samples containing noise should not be given equal weight. In order to overcome this difficulty, the editing procedure was proposed to preprocess the original training samples and the KNN rule was used to classify the query pattern based on the edited training samples [10,11,16]. According to the structure of the edited labels, the editing procedures can be divided into two categories: crisp and soft editing. In [16], Wilson proposed a simple editing procedure to preprocess the training set. This procedure classifies a training sample $\mathbf{x}^{(i)}$ using the KNN rule with the remainder of the training set, and deletes it from the original training set if its original label $\omega^{(i)}$ does not agree with the classification result. Later, concerned with the possibility of large amounts of samples being removed from the training set, Koplowitz and Brown [11] developed a modification of the simple editing technique. For a given value of K, another parameter K' is defined such that $(K+1)/2 \leq K' \leq K$. Instead of deleting all the conflicting samples, if a particular class (excluding the original class) has at least K' representatives among these K nearest neighbors, then $\mathbf{x}^{(i)}$ is labeled according to that majority class. Essentially, both the simple editing procedure and its modification belong to the category of crisp editing procedures, in which each edited sample is either removed or assigned to a single class. In order to overcome the difficulty of the crisp editing method in severely noisy conditions, a fuzzy editing procedure was proposed that reassigns fuzzy membership to each training sample $\mathbf{x}^{(i)}$ based on its K nearest neighbors [10]. This fuzzy editing procedure belongs to the soft editing category, in which each edited sample can be assigned to several classes. It provides more detailed information about the samples' membership than the crisp editing procedures.

Different kinds of uncertainty may coexist in real-world classification problems, e.g., fuzziness may coexist with imprecision or incompleteness. The fuzzy editing procedure, which is based on fuzzy set theory [17], cannot address imprecise or incomplete information effectively in the modeling and reasoning processes. In contrast, the theory of belief functions [1,14,15], also called Dempster-Shafer theory, can well model imprecise or incomplete information thanks to the belief functions defined on the power set of the frame of discernment. The theory of belief functions has already been used in the pattern classification field [2,4,8,9,12]. An evidential version of KNN, denoted by EKNN [2], has been proposed based on the theory of belief functions; it introduces the ignorance class to model the uncertainty. In [12], the EKNN was further extended to deal with uncertainty using a meta-class. Neither the EKNN method nor its extension consider any editing procedure and the original training set is used to make classification. More recently, an editing procedure for multi-label classification was developed in [9] based on an evidential multi-label KNN rule (EMLKNN) [5], but it essentially belongs to the crisp editing category as each edited sample is either removed or assigned to a new set of classes without considering the class membership degrees.

In this paper, an evidential editing K-nearest neighbor (EEKNN) is proposed based on the theory of belief functions. The proposed EEKNN classifier contains two stages: evidential editing and classification. First, an evidential editing procedure reassigns the original training samples with new labels represented by an evidential membership structure. Compared with the fuzzy membership used in fuzzy editing, the evidential labels provide more expressiveness to characterize the imprecision for those samples with great noise or in overlapping regions. For a training sample $\mathbf{x}^{(i)}$, if there is no imprecision among the frame of discernment, the evidential membership reduces to the fuzzy membership. After the evidential editing procedure, a classification procedure is developed to classify a query pattern based on the edited training samples.

The rest of this paper is organized as follows. In Sect. 2, the basics of belief function theory are recalled. The evidential editing K-nearest neighbor (EEKNN) classifier is developed in Sect. 3 and then two experiments are developed to evaluate the performance of the proposed EEKNN in Sect. 4. Finally, Sect. 5 concludes the paper.

2   Background on the Theory of Belief Functions

In the theory of belief functions [1,14], a problem domain is represented by a finite set $\Theta = \{\theta_1, \theta_2, \cdots, \theta_n\}$ of mutually exclusive and exhaustive hypotheses called the *frame of discernment*. A *basic belief assignment* (BBA) expressing the belief committed to the elements of 2^Θ by a given source of evidence is a mapping function m: $2^\Theta \rightarrow [0,1]$, such that

$$m(\emptyset) = 0 \text{ and } \sum_{A \in 2^\Theta} m(A) = 1. \tag{1}$$

Elements $A \in 2^\Theta$ having $m(A) > 0$ are called the *focal elements* of the BBA m. Each number $m(A)$ measures the degree of belief exactly assigned to a proposition A. The belief assigned to Θ, is referred to as the degree of *global ignorance*. A BBA is said to be *simple* if it has the following form

$$\begin{cases} m(A) = 1 - w \\ m(\Theta) = w, \end{cases} \tag{2}$$

for some $A \subset \Theta$ and $w \in [0,1]$. Let us denote such a mass function as A^w.

Shafer [14] also defines the *belief* and *plausibility functions* as follows

$$\text{Bel}(A) = \sum_{B \subseteq A} m(B) \text{ and } \text{Pl}(A) = \sum_{B \cap A \neq \emptyset} m(B), \text{ for all } A \in 2^\Theta. \tag{3}$$

$\text{Bel}(A)$ represents the exact support to A and its subsets, and $\text{Pl}(A)$ represents the total possible support to A and its subsets. The interval $[\text{Bel}(A), \text{Pl}(A)]$ can be seen as the lower and upper bounds of support to A.

For decision making, Smets [15] proposed the *pignistic probability* BetP to approximate the unknown probability in $[\text{Bel}(A), \text{Pl}(A)]$, given by

$$\text{BetP}(A) = \sum_{B \cap A \neq \emptyset} \frac{|A \cap B|}{|B|} m(B), \quad \text{for all } A \in 2^{\Theta}, \tag{4}$$

where $|X|$ is the cardinality of set X.

Two useful operations in the manipulation of belief functions are *Shafer's discounting operation* and *Dempster's rule of combination*. The discounting operation is used when a source of evidence provides a BBA m, but one knows that this source has a probability $\alpha \in [0, 1]$ of being reliable. Then, one may adopt $(1 - \alpha)$ as the discount rate, which results in a new BBA $^{\alpha}$m defined by

$$^{\alpha}\text{m}(A) = \begin{cases} \alpha m(A), & \text{for } A \neq \Theta \\ \alpha m(\Theta) + (1 - \alpha), & \text{for } A = \Theta. \end{cases} \tag{5}$$

Several distinct bodies of evidence characterized by different BBAs can be combined using Dempster's rule. Mathematically, the combination of two BBAs m_1 and m_2 defined on the same frame of discernment Θ yields the following BBA,

$$(\text{m}_1 \oplus \text{m}_2)(A) = \begin{cases} 0, & \text{for } A = \emptyset \\ \dfrac{\sum_{B \cap C = A} m_1(B) m_2(C)}{1 - \sum_{B \cap C = \emptyset} m_1(B) m_2(C)}, & \text{for } A \in 2^{\Theta} \text{ and } A \neq \emptyset. \end{cases} \tag{6}$$

To combine separable BBAs [14] induced by nondistinct bodies of evidence, a *cautious rule of combination* and, more generally, a family of parameterized *t-norm based combination rules* with behavior ranging between Dempster's rule and the cautious rule are proposed in [3]:

$$\text{m}_1 \circledast_s \text{m}_2 = \bigoplus_{\emptyset \neq A \subset \Omega} A^{w_1(A) \top_s w_2(A)}, \tag{7}$$

where m_1 and m_2 are *separable* BBAs, such that $m_1 = \bigoplus_{\emptyset \neq A \subset \Omega} A^{w_1(A)}$ and $m_2 = \bigoplus_{\emptyset \neq A \subset \Omega} A^{w_2(A)}$, and $\top_s$ is the Frank's parameterized family of t-norms:

$$a \top_s b = \begin{cases} a \wedge b, & \text{if } s = 0 \\ ab, & \text{if } s = 1 \\ \log_s \left(1 + \frac{(s^a - 1)(s^b - 1)}{s - 1} \right), & \text{otherwise,} \end{cases} \tag{8}$$

for all $a, b \in [0, 1]$, where s is a positive parameter. When $s = 0$, the t-norm based rule corresponds to cautious rule and when $s = 1$, it corresponds to Dempster's rule.

3   Evidential Editing K-Nearest Neighbor Classifier

Let us consider an M-class classification problem and let $\Omega = \{\omega_1, \cdots, \omega_M\}$ be the set of classes. Assuming that a set of N labeled training samples

$\mathcal{T} = \{(\mathbf{x}^{(1)}, \omega^{(1)}), \cdots, (\mathbf{x}^{(N)}, \omega^{(N)})\}$ with input vectors $\mathbf{x}^{(i)} \in \mathcal{R}^D$ and class labels $\omega^{(i)} \in \Omega$ are available, the problem is to classify a query pattern $\mathbf{y} \in \mathcal{R}^D$ based on the training set $\mathcal{T}$.

The proposed evidential editing K-nearest neighbor (EEKNN) procedure is composed of the following two stages:

1. *Preprocessing (evidential editing)*: The evidential editing algorithm assigns evidential labels to each labeled sample.
2. *Classification*: The class of the query pattern is decided based on the distance to the sample's K nearest neighbors and these K nearest neighbors' evidential membership information.

3.1   Evidential Editing

The goal of the evidential editing stage is to assign to each sample in the training set $\mathcal{T}$ a new soft label with an evidential structure as follows:

$$\mathcal{T}' = \{(\mathbf{x}^{(1)}, \mathrm{m}^{(1)}), (\mathbf{x}^{(2)}, \mathrm{m}^{(2)}), \cdots, (\mathbf{x}^{(N)}, \mathrm{m}^{(N)})\}, \tag{9}$$

where $\mathrm{m}^{(i)}$, $i = 1, 2, \cdots, N$, are BBAs defined on the frame of discernment Ω.

The problem is now to compute an evidential label for each training sample. In [2], an evidential K-nearest neighbor (EKNN) rule was proposed based on the theory of belief functions, where the classification result of the query pattern is a BBA. In the following part, we use the EKNN rule to carry out the evidential editing.

For each training sample $\mathbf{x}^{(i)}$, $i = 1, 2, \cdots, N$, we denote the leave-it-out training set as $\mathcal{T}^{(i)} = \mathcal{T} \setminus \{(\mathbf{x}^{(i)}, \omega^{(i)})\}$, $i = 1, 2, \cdots, N$. Now, we consider the evidential editing for one training sample $\mathbf{x}^{(i)}$ on the basis of the information contained in $\mathcal{T}^{(i)}$. For the training sample $\mathbf{x}^{(i)}$, each neighbor $\mathbf{x}^{(j)}$ ($j \neq i$) provides an item of evidence regarding the class membership of $\mathbf{x}^{(i)}$ as follows

$$\begin{cases} \mathrm{m}^{(i)}(\{\omega^q\} \mid \mathbf{x}^{(j)}) = \alpha \phi_q(d_{ij}) \\ \mathrm{m}^{(i)}(\Omega \mid \mathbf{x}^{(j)}) \quad = 1 - \alpha \phi_q(d_{ij}) \\ \mathrm{m}^{(i)}(A \mid \mathbf{x}^{(j)}) \quad = 0, \quad \forall A \in 2^\Omega \setminus \{\Omega, \{\omega_q\}\}, \end{cases} \tag{10}$$

where $d_{ij} = d(\mathbf{x}^{(i)}, \mathbf{x}^{(j)})$, ω_q is the class label of $\mathbf{x}^{(j)}$ (that is, $\omega^{(j)} = \omega_q$), and α is a parameter such that $0 < \alpha < 1$. As suggested in [2], $\alpha = 0.95$ can be used to obtain good results on average. When d is the Euclidean distance, a good choice for ϕ_q is

$$\phi_q(d) = \exp(-\gamma_q d^2), \tag{11}$$

with γ_q being a positive parameter associated to class ω_q and can be heuristically set to the inverse of the mean squared Euclidean distance between training samples belonging to class ω_q.

Based on the distance $d(\mathbf{x}^{(i)}, \mathbf{x}^{(j)})$, we select the K_{edit} nearest neighbors of $\mathbf{x}^{(i)}$ in training set $\mathcal{T}^{(i)}$ and calculate the corresponding K_{edit} BBAs in the above way. As the items of evidence from different neighbors are distinct (because the training samples are usually measured or collected independently), the $Kedit$ BBAs are combined using Dempster's rule displayed as Eq. (6) to form a resulting BBA $m^{(i)}$, synthesizing the final evidential membership regarding the label of $\mathbf{x}^{(i)}$ as

$$m^{(i)} = m^{(i)}(\cdot \mid \mathbf{x}^{(i_1)}) \oplus m^{(i)}(\cdot \mid \mathbf{x}^{(i_2)}) \oplus \cdots \oplus m^{(i)}(\cdot \mid \mathbf{x}^{(i_{Kedit})}), \qquad (12)$$

where $i_1, i_2, \cdots, i_{Kedit}$ are the indices of the $Kedit$ nearest neighbors of $\mathbf{x}^{(i)}$ in $\mathcal{T}^{(i)}$. Generally, the selection for parameter $Kedit$ depends on the specific classification problem. In practice, we can use cross-validation for the training set to search for the best value.

3.2   Classification

After the evidential editing procedure introduced in Sect. 3.1, the problem now turns into classifying a query pattern $\mathbf{y} \in \mathcal{R}^D$ based on the new edited training set $\mathcal{T}'$ as shown in Eq. (9). In this section, we extend the evidential K-nearest neighbor (EKNN) rule [2] to handle the more general situation in which the edited training samples are assigned dependent evidential labels. This classification procedure is composed of the following two steps: first, the BBAs from the query pattern's K nearest neighbors are computed; then, the K BBAs are combined to obtain the final result.

Determination of the BBAs. Considering the K nearest neighbors of the query pattern $\mathbf{y}$, if one training sample $\mathbf{x}^{(i)}$ is very close to $\mathbf{y}$, generally, it means that $\mathbf{x}^{(i)}$ is a very reliable piece of evidence for the classification of $\mathbf{y}$. In contrast, if $\mathbf{x}^{(i)}$ if far from $\mathbf{y}$, then it provides only little reliable evidence. In the theory of belief functions, Shafer's discounting operation can be used to discount the unreliable evidence before combination.

Denote $m^{(i)}$ as the class membership of the training sample $\mathbf{x}^{(i)}$, and β_i as the confidence degree of the class membership of $\mathbf{y}$ with respect to the training sample $\mathbf{x}^{(i)}$. The evidence provided by $\mathbf{x}^{(i)}$ for the class membership of $\mathbf{y}$ is represented with a discounted BBA $^{\beta_i}m^{(i)}$ by discounting $m^{(i)}$ with a discount rate $1 - \beta_i$. The confidence degree β_i is determined based on the distance d_i between $\mathbf{x}^{(i)}$ and $\mathbf{y}$, in such a way that a larger distance results in a smaller confidence degree. Thus, β_i should be a decreasing function of d_i. We use a similar decreasing function with Eq. (11) to define the confidence degree $\beta_i \in (0, 1]$ as

$$\beta_i = \exp(-\lambda_i d_i^2), \qquad (13)$$

where λ_i is a positive parameter associated to the training sample $\mathbf{x}^{(i)}$ and is defined as

$$\lambda_i = \left(\sum_{q=1}^{M} m^{(i)}(\{\omega_q\}) \overline{d}^q + m^{(i)}(\Omega) \overline{d} \right)^{-2}, \qquad (14)$$

with $\overline{d}$ being the mean distance between all training samples, and $\overline{d}^q$ being the mean distance between training samples belonging to each class ω_q, $q = 1, 2, \cdots, M$.

Combination of the BBAs. To make a decision about the class of the query pattern $\mathbf{y}$, the generated K BBAs should be combined to obtain the final fusion result. For combination, Dempster's rule lies in the assumption that the items of evidence combined be distinct or, in other words, that the information sources be independent. However, in the editing process, common training samples may be used for calculating the class membership of different edited samples. Therefore, the items of evidence from different edited samples to classify the query pattern $\mathbf{y}$ cannot be regarded as independent.

To account for this dependence, we use the parameterized t-norm based combination rule shown in Eq. (7) to obtain the final combination result for query pattern $\mathbf{y}$ as

$$\mathbf{m} = {}^{\beta_{i_1}}\mathbf{m}^{(i_1)} \circledast_s {}^{\beta_{i_2}}\mathbf{m}^{(i_2)} \circledast_s \cdots \circledast_s {}^{\beta_{i_K}}\mathbf{m}^{(i_K)}, \tag{15}$$

where $i_1, i_2, \cdots, i_K$ are the indices of the K nearest neighbors of $\mathbf{y}$ in T'. The selection of parameter s depends on the potential dependence degrees of the edited samples. In practice, we can use cross-validation to search for the optimal t-norms based combination rule.

For making decisions based on the above combined BBA m, the pignistic probability BetP shown in Eq. (4) is used and the query pattern $\mathbf{y}$ is assigned to the class with the maximum pignistic probability.

4   Experiments

The performance of the proposed evidential editing K-nearest neighbor (EEKNN) classifier was compared with other nearest-neighbor-based methods (the modified simple editing KNN (SEKNN) [11], the fuzzy editing KNN (FEKNN) [10] and the evidential KNN (EKNN) [2]) through two different types of experiments. In the first experiment, the behavior of the proposed method was studied using synthetic data sets. In the second experiment, six real benchmark data sets from the UCI repository [13] were used to compare the methods.

4.1   Synthetic Data Sets Test

This experiment was designed to evaluate the proposed EEKNN with other nearest-neighbor-based methods using synthetic data sets with different class overlapping ratios, defined as the number of training samples in the overlapping region divided by the total number of training samples. A training sample $\mathbf{x}^{(i)}$ is considered to be in the overlapping region if its corresponding maximum plausibility $\text{Pl}_{\max}^{(i)}$ after evidential editing is less than a set upper bound Pl^*, namely, $\text{Pl}^* = 0.9$. A two-dimensional three-class classification problem was considered. The following class-conditional normal distributions were assumed. For comparisons, we changed the variance of each distribution to control the class overlapping ratio.

Case 1 Class A: $\mu_A = (6, 6)^T, \Sigma_A = 3\mathbf{I}$; Class B: $\mu_B = (14, 6)^T, \Sigma_B = 3\mathbf{I}$;
Class C: $\mu_C = (14, 14)^T, \Sigma_C = 3\mathbf{I}$. Overlapping ratio $\rho = 6.67\%$

Case 2 Class A: $\mu_A = (6, 6)^T, \Sigma_A = 4\mathbf{I}$; Class B: $\mu_B = (14, 6)^T, \Sigma_B = 4\mathbf{I}$;
Class C: $\mu_C = (14, 14)^T, \Sigma_C = 4\mathbf{I}$. Overlapping ratio $\rho = 10.00\%$
Case 3 Class A: $\mu_A = (6, 6)^T, \Sigma_A = 5\mathbf{I}$; Class B: $\mu_B = (14, 6)^T, \Sigma_B = 5\mathbf{I}$;
Class C: $\mu_C = (14, 14)^T, \Sigma_C = 5\mathbf{I}$. Overlapping ratio $\rho = 21.33\%$

A training set of 150 samples and a test set of 3000 samples were generated from the above distributions using equal prior probabilities. For each case, 30 trials were performed with 30 independent training sets. Average test classification rates and the corresponding 95 % confidence intervals were calculated. For each trial, the best values for the parameters $Kedit$ and s in the proposed EEKNN method were determined in the sets $\{3, 6, 9, 12, 15, 18, 21, 24\}$ and $\{1, 10^{-1}, 10^{-2}, 10^{-3}, 10^{-4}, 10^{-5}, 0\}$, respectively, by cross-validation. For all the considered method, values of K ranging from 1 to 25 have been investigated. Figure 1 shows the classification results for synthetic data sets with different overlapping ratios. It can be seen that, for the three cases, the EEKNN method provides better classification performance than other nearest-neighbor-based methods. With the increase of the class overlapping ratio, the performance improvement becomes more important. Furthermore, the EEKNN method is less sensitive to the value of K and it performs well even with a small value of K.

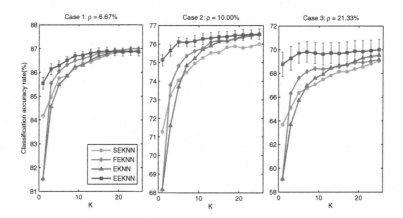

Fig. 1. Classification results for synthetic data sets with different overlapping ratios

4.2   Benchmark Data Sets Test

The main characteristics of the six real data sets used in this experiment are summarized in Table 1. To assess the results, we considered the resampled paired test. A series of 30 trials was conducted. In each trials, the available samples were randomly divided into a training set and a test set (with equal sizes). For each data set, we calculated the average classification rates of the 30 trials and the corresponding 95 % confidence intervals. For the proposed EEKNN method, the best values for the parameters $Kedit$ and s were determined with the same procedure used in the previous experiment. For all the considered method, values of K ranging from 1 to 25 have been investigated.

Table 1. Description of the benchmark data sets employed in the study

Data set	# Instances	# Features	# Classes	Overlapping ratio
Balance	625	4	3	19.23 %
Haberman	306	3	2	18.59 %
Liver	345	6	2	19.19 %
Pima	336	8	2	19.05 %
Vertebral	310	6	3	11.20 %
Waveform	5,000	21	3	19.60 %

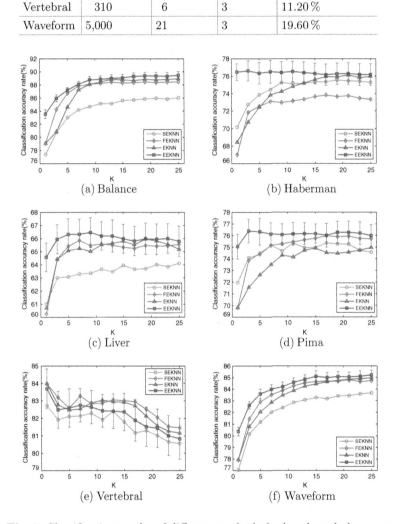

Fig. 2. Classification results of different methods for benchmark data sets

Figure 2 shows the classification results of different methods for benchmark data sets. It can be seen that, for data sets with high overlapping ratios, like *Balance, Haberman, Liver, Pima* and *Waveform*, the EEKNN method provides better classification performance than other nearest-neighbor-based methods, especially for small value of K. In contrast, for those data sets with relatively low overlapping ratios, like *Vertebral*, the classification performances of different methods were quite similar. The reason is that, for this data set, the best classification performance was obtained when K took a small value and, under this circumstance, the evidential editing cannot improve the classification performance.

5   Conclusions

An evidential editing K-nearest neighbor (EEKNN) classifier has been developed based on an evidential editing procedure that reassigns the original training samples with new labels represented by an evidential membership structure. Thanks to this procedure, patterns situated in overlapping regions have less influence on the decisions. Our results show that the proposed EEKNN classifier achieves better performance than other considered nearest-neighbor-based methods, especially for data sets with high overlapping ratios. In particular, the proposed EEKNN classifier is not too sensitive to the value of K and it can gain a quite good performance even with a small value of K. This is an advantage in time or space-critical applications, in which only a small value of K is permitted in the classification process.

Acknowledgments. This work was carried out in the framework of the Labex MS2T, which was funded by the French Government, through the program "Investments for the future" managed by the National Agency for Research (Reference ANR-11-IDEX-0004-02).

References

1. Dempster, A.: Upper and lower probabilities induced by multivalued mapping. Ann. Math. Stat. **38**, 325–339 (1967)
2. Denœux, T.: A k-nearest neighbor classification rule based on Dempster-Shafer theory. IEEE Trans. Syst. Man Cybern. **25**, 804–813 (1995)
3. Denœux, T.: Conjunctive and disjunctive combination of belief functions induced by nondistinct bodies of evidence. Artif. Intell. **172**, 234–264 (2008)
4. Denœux, T., Smets, P.: Classification using belief functions relationship between case-based and model-based approaches. IEEE Trans. Syst. Man Cybern. Part B Cybern. **36**, 1395–1406 (2006)
5. Denœux, T., Younes, Z., Abdallah, F.: Representing uncertainty on set-valued variables using belief functions. Artif. Intell. **174**, 479–499 (2010)
6. Fix, E., Hodges, J.: Discriminatory analysis, nonparametric discrimination: consistency properties. Technical report 4, USAF School of Aviation Medicine, Randolph Field, Texas (1951)
7. Fukunaga, K., Hostetler, L.D.: k-nearest neighbor Bayes risk estimation. IEEE Trans. Inf. Theory **21**, 285–293 (1975)

8. Jiao, L., Denœux, T., Pan, Q.: Fusion of pairwise nearest-neighbor classifiers based on pairwise-weighted distance metric and Dempster-Shafer theory. In: Proceeding of 17th International Conference on Information Fusion, pp. 1–7 (2014)

9. Kanj, S., Abdallah, F., Denœux, T., Tout, K.: Editing training data for multi-label classification with the k-nearest neighbor rule. Pattern Analysis and Applications, (2015). doi:10.1007/s10044-015-0452-8

10. Keller, J.M., Gray, M.R., Givens, J.A.: A fuzzy K-nearest neighbor algorithm. IEEE Trans. Syst. Man Cybern. **15**, 580–585 (1985)

11. Koplowitz, J., Brown, T.A.: On the relation of performance to editing in nearest neighbor rules. Pattern Recogn. **13**, 251–255 (1981)

12. Liu, Z., Pan, Q., Dezert, J.: A new belief-based k-nearest neighbor classification method. Pattern Recogn. **46**, 834–844 (2013)

13. Merz, C.J., Murphy, P.M., Aha, D.W.: UCI Repository of Machine Learning Databases. Department of Information and Computer Science, University of California, Irvine (1997). http://www.ics.uci.edu/mlearn/MLRepository.html

14. Shafer, G.: A Mathematical Theory of Evidence. Princeton University Press, Princeton, NJ (1976)

15. Smets, P.: Decision making in the TBM: the necessity of the pignistic transformation. Int. J. Approximate Reasoning **38**, 133–147 (2005)

16. Wilson, D.L.: Asymptotic properties of nearest neighbor rules using edited data sets. IEEE Trans. Syst. Man Cybern. **2**, 408–421 (1972)

17. Zadeh, L.A.: Fuzzy sets. Inf. Control **8**, 338–353 (1965)

Learning Contextual Discounting and Contextual Reinforcement from Labelled Data

David Mercier[1,2]([✉]), Frédéric Pichon[1,2], Éric Lefèvre[1,2],
and François Delmotte[1,2]

[1] University of Lille Nord de France, 59000 Lille, France
{david.mercier,frederic.pichon,eric.lefevre,
francois.delmotte}@univ-artois.fr
[2] UArtois, LGI2A, 62400 Béthune, France

Abstract. This paper addresses the problems of learning from labelled data contextual discounting and contextual reinforcement, two correction schemes recently introduced in belief function theory. It shows that given a particular error criterion based on the plausibility function, for each of these two contextual correction schemes, there exists an optimal set of contexts that ensures the minimization of the criterion and that finding this minimum amounts to solving a constrained least-squares problem with as many unknowns as the domain size of the variable of interest.

Keywords: Belief functions · Learning · Contextual discounting · Contextual reinforcement · Source biases · Expert tuning

1 Introduction

Classically, in belief function theory, the correction of the information provided by a source concerning a variable of interest $\mathbf{x}$ defined on a finite domain $\mathcal{X}$, is achieved using the discounting operation [8–10]. This operation admits one parameter, a real β belonging to $[0, 1]$, reflecting the degree of *reliability* of the source of information [9, Sect. 5.7] [5, Sect. 2.5].

Discounting operation has been extended by Mercier *et al.* in [5], where it is considered that one may have some knowledge about the reliability of a source, conditionally on different subsets (*contexts*) of $\mathcal{X}$, the set of contexts forming a partition of $\mathcal{X}$. This operation, called *contextual discounting based on a coarsening*, is controlled by a vector of parameters β_A, each β_A belonging to $[0, 1]$ and reflecting the degree of reliability of the source given context $A \subseteq \mathcal{X}$ (in other words, knowing that the true value of $\mathbf{x}$ lies in A). In this same article [5, Sect. 5], following preceding work from Elouedi *et al.* for the classical discounting [3], a computationally efficient method to automatically learn from labelled data the parameters β_A of a contextual discounting based on a coarsening, once a partition (a set of contexts) has been fixed, is also introduced; the idea is to find the

© Springer International Publishing Switzerland 2015
S. Destercke and T. Denoeux (Eds.): ECSQARU 2015, LNAI 9161, pp. 472–481, 2015.
DOI: 10.1007/978-3-319-20807-7_43

parameters values which minimize a measure of discrepancy between the ground truth and the outputs of the source corrected according to the parameters values. This method is potentially useful to improve a source performance in, *e.g.*, a classification application, as well as to discover its contextual reliability. However, the problem of finding the optimal partition of $\mathcal{X}$ for a given source was left open.

In [6], Mercier *et al.* have extended this contextual discounting based on a coarsening to be applicable to any set of contexts (*i.e.*, the set of contexts no longer needs to form a partition of $\mathcal{X}$). This mechanism is therefore simply called *contextual discounting (CD)*. The *contextual reinforcement (CR)* of a source is also introduced as the dual of CD. This new correction operation is also controlled by a vector of parameters β_A in $[0, 1]$ associated with a set of subsets (contexts) A of $\mathcal{X}$. However, the interpretation of CR was not clear (it was only known that CR amounts to the negation [2] of the CD of the negation of the information provided by the source) and the problem of learning CD and CR from labelled data was not tackled. Recently, in [7], Pichon *et al.* gave an interpretation to CR: it amounts to assuming, for each context A, that the source is truthful with mass β_A, and that with mass $(1 - \beta_A)$ it lies only when it tells that the true value of $\mathbf{x}$ is in $\overline{A}$; but the question of learning CD and CR from data remained open.

In this paper, we address the problems of learning from labelled data contextual discounting and contextual reinforcement, the former problem being only partially addressed so far – its solution is restricted to the case where a set of contexts has been fixed beforehand and where this set must also form a partition of $\mathcal{X}$ – and the latter problem not being addressed at all. Especially, we show that given the discrepancy measure used in [5], there exists an optimal set of contexts for the most general form of CD (the CD proposed in [6] and that does not require the set of contexts to form a partition of $\mathcal{X}$) that ensures the minimization of the measure, and that finding this minimum amounts to a computationally simple optimization problem (a constrained least-squares problem with K unknowns, K being the size of $\mathcal{X}$). Furthermore, we show that a similar result holds for CR. In addition, an illustrative example of the proposed learning of CD and CR is given. This example is also useful to make insightful additional remarks on CD and CR, and in particular the potential superiority of the recently introduced CR mechanism over CD, to improve a source performance.

This paper is organized as follows. Required basic concepts on belief functions and contextual correction mechanisms are exposed in Sect. 2. Learning of CD and of CR is formally studied in Sect. 3 and illustrated in Sect. 4, where a comparison of CD and CR correction capacities is also presented. Finally, Sect. 5 concludes the paper.

2 Belief Functions and Contextual Correction Mechanisms: Basic Concepts and Notations

2.1 Representation and Combination of Beliefs

The necessary background material on the representation and combination of beliefs is given here.

Representation of Beliefs. A *mass function (MF)* represents an agent's opinion regarding a variable of interest $\mathbf{x}$ taking values in a finite domain $\mathcal{X}$ [8,10]. It is defined as a mapping $m : 2^{\mathcal{X}} \to [0,1]$ verifying $\sum_{A \subseteq \mathcal{X}} m(A) = 1$. The negation $\overline{m}$ of a mass function m is defined as $\overline{m}(A) = m(\overline{A})$, $\forall A \subseteq \mathcal{X}$.

A MF m defined by $m(\mathcal{X}) = w$ and $m(A) = 1 - w$, with $w \in [0,1]$ and $A \subset \mathcal{X}$, can be conveniently noted A^w. Likewise a MF m such that $m(\emptyset) = v$ and $m(A) = 1 - v$, with $v \in [0,1]$, $A \subseteq \mathcal{X}$, $A \neq \emptyset$, can be conveniently noted A_v.

A MF m is in one-to-one correspondence with a plausibility function pl, a commonality function q and an implicability function b, which are respectively defined by: $pl(A) = \sum_{B \cap A \neq \emptyset} m(B)$, $q(A) = \sum_{A \subseteq B} m(B)$ and $b(A) = \sum_{B \subseteq A} m(B)$, for all $A \subseteq \mathcal{X}$.

Combination. Two MF m_1 and m_2 can be combined using the *conjunctive rule of combination* [10] denoted by $\bigcirc\!\!\!\cap$ and defined by:

$$(m_1 \bigcirc\!\!\!\cap m_2)(A) = \sum_{B \cap C = A} m_1(B) \cdot m_2(C), \quad \forall A \subseteq \mathcal{X}. \tag{1}$$

Numerous combination rules exist [11] to merge mass functions. The other combination of particular interest in this paper is the *disjunctive rule of combination* $\bigcirc\!\!\!\cup$ [2,9] defined by replacing the symbol $\cap$ in (1) by $\cup$.

Let us also recall that if $m = m_1 \bigcirc\!\!\!\cap m_2$, the corresponding commonality functions verify $q = q_1 \cdot q_2$, and if $m = m_1 \bigcirc\!\!\!\cup m_2$, the corresponding implicability functions verify $b = b_1 \cdot b_2$.

2.2 Contextual Discounting and Reinforcement of a Belief Function

Throughout this paper, m_S is a MF defined on $\mathcal{X}$, provided by a source S, and $\mathcal{A}$ is a set of subsets (contexts) of $\mathcal{X}$.

Contextual Discounting (CD). The contextual discounting [5–7] of m_S is the MF m defined, with $\beta_A \in [0,1]$, $\forall A \in \mathcal{A}$, by:

$$m = m_S \bigcirc\!\!\!\cup_{A \in \mathcal{A}} A_{\beta_A}. \tag{2}$$

The classical discounting [8,9] is retrieved when $\mathcal{A}$ is composed of just one element which is the whole domain $\mathcal{X}$:

$$m = m_S \bigcirc\!\!\!\cup \mathcal{X}_\beta = \beta \, m_S + (1 - \beta) m_{\mathcal{X}}, \tag{3}$$

with $m_{\mathcal{X}}$ defined by $m_{\mathcal{X}}(\mathcal{X}) = 1$.

In practice, β_A represents the proportion of $m_S(B)$ which remains on B, and $(1 - \beta_A)$ represents the part of $m_S(B)$ transferred to $B \cup A$, $\forall A \in \mathcal{A}$ and $\forall B \subseteq \mathcal{X}$.

Contextual Reinforcement (CR). The contextual reinforcement [6,7] of m_S is the MF m defined, with $\beta_A \in [0,1]$, $\forall A \in \mathcal{A}$, by:

$$m = m_S \bigcirc\!\!\!\cap_{A \in \mathcal{A}} A^{\beta_A}. \tag{4}$$

In practice, β_A represents the fraction of $m_S(B)$ remaining on B, and $(1 - \beta_A)$ the part of $m_S(B)$ transferred to $B \cap A$, $\forall A \in \mathcal{A}$ and $\forall B \subseteq \mathcal{X}$.

3   Learning CD and CR from Labelled Data

3.1   Description of the Learning Process

In this section, we study how to automatically learn CD and CR from:

1. A training set describing the outputs of a source (expressed in the form of a MF) regarding the classes in $\mathcal{X} = \{x_1, \ldots, x_K\}$ of n objects o_i, $i \in \{1, \ldots, n\}$ (A small illustrative example is given in Sect. 4 in Table 2);
2. And a measure of discrepancy to be minimized between the corrections of the mass functions provided by the source and the reality.

In this paper, the following measure of discrepancy between the corrected information and the ground truth has been chosen:

$$E_{pl}(\boldsymbol{\beta}) = \sum_{i=1}^{n} \sum_{k=1}^{K} (pl\{o_i\}(\{x_k\}) - \delta_{i,k})^2, \tag{5}$$

where $\forall i \in \{1, \ldots, n\}$, $pl\{o_i\}$ is the plausibility function obtained from a contextual correction of the output m_S of the source with a vector of coefficients $\beta \in [0,1]^{|\mathcal{A}|}$. The binary variable $\delta_{i,k}$ indicates the class of o_i as follows: $\forall i \in \{1, \ldots, n\}$, $\forall k \in \{1, \ldots, K\}$, $\delta_{i,k} = 1$ if object o_i belongs to the class x_k, and $\delta_{i,k} = 0$ otherwise.

Our choice to use measure E_{pl} (5) is mostly based on the fact that, as it will be seen in Propositions 2 and 4, its minimization has the advantage to yield constrained least-squares problems, which can be solved efficiently. Moreover, it was the one used in the approach proposed in [5], which we are clearly extending with this current work. At last, using the plausibility on singletons is in accordance with the Shafer [8] and Smets [10] *singular* [1] interpretation of belief functions, which is adopted in this paper. However, we may note that other measures of discrepancy could be used, *e.g.*, a measure based on the pignistic probability [10] or on a distance measure [4], but then it is not guaranteed that their minimization can be performed efficiently.

3.2   Learning CD

Plausibilities on the singletons after having applied CD on a MF m_S provided by a source are given by next proposition.

Proposition 1. *Let $m = m_S \bigcirc_{A \in \mathcal{A}} A_{\beta_A}$, $\beta_A \in [0,1]$, $\forall A \in \mathcal{A}$, be the CD of a MF m_S. The plausibility function associated with m is defined for all $x \in \mathcal{X}$ by:*

$$pl(\{x\}) = 1 - (1 - pl_S(\{x\})) \prod_{A \in \mathcal{A}, x \in A} \beta_A. \tag{6}$$

Proof. See Appendix A.1

Next proposition indicates that the minimization of E_{pl} when CD has been applied, is obtained using the vector β composed of the K parameters $\beta_{\{x_k\}}$, which means the parameters associated with the singletons of $\mathcal{X}$. Moreover the minimization of E_{pl} using this vector constitutes a constrained least-squares problem which can then be solved efficiently using standard algorithms.

Proposition 2. *The minimization of E_{pl} with CD is obtained using the vector $\beta = (\beta_{\{x_k\}}, k \in \{1, \ldots, K\})$ and constitutes a constrained least-squares problem as (5) can then be rewritten as:*

$$E_{pl}(\beta) = \|Q\beta - d\|^2 \; with \; Q = \begin{bmatrix} diag(\boldsymbol{pl}_1 - 1) \\ \vdots \\ diag(\boldsymbol{pl}_n - 1) \end{bmatrix} \; and \; d = \begin{bmatrix} \delta_1 - 1 \\ \vdots \\ \delta_n - 1 \end{bmatrix}, \quad (7)$$

with $diag(v)$ a square diagonal matrix with the elements of vector v on the main diagonal, and with $\boldsymbol{pl}_i = (pl_S\{o_i\}(\{x_1\}), \ldots, pl_S\{o_i\}(\{x_K\}))^T$, and $\delta_i = (\delta_{i,1}, \ldots, \delta_{i,K})^T$ the column vector of 0-1 class indicator variables for object o_i.

Proof. See Appendix A.2

This answers a prospect given in [5] concerning the study of the set of contexts which yields the best possible value for the measure of discrepancy E_{pl}. The answer given here is that there will be no smaller value reachable for E_{pl} than the one obtained with the set of the singletons of $\mathcal{X}$ with associated coefficients $\beta = (\beta_{\{x_k\}}, k \in \{1, \ldots, K\})$.

3.3   Learning CR

Plausibilities on the singletons after having applied CR are given in next proposition.

Proposition 3. *Let $m = m_S \bigcirc_{A \in \mathcal{A}} A^{\beta_A}$, $\beta_A \in [0, 1]$, $\forall A \in \mathcal{A}$, be the CR of a MF m_S. The plausibility function associated with m is defined for all $x \in \mathcal{X}$ by:*

$$pl(\{x\}) = pl_S(\{x\}) \prod_{A \in \mathcal{A}, x \notin A} \beta_A. \quad (8)$$

Proof. See Appendix A.3

Proposition 4. *The minimization of E_{pl} with CR is obtained using the vector $\beta = (\beta_{\overline{\{x_k\}}}, k \in \{1, \ldots, K\})$ and constitutes a constrained least-squares problem as (5) can then be written as:*

$$E_{pl}(\beta) = \|P\beta - \delta\|^2, \; with \; P = \begin{bmatrix} diag(\boldsymbol{pl}_1) \\ \vdots \\ diag(\boldsymbol{pl}_n) \end{bmatrix} \; and \; \delta = \begin{bmatrix} \delta_1 \\ \vdots \\ \delta_n \end{bmatrix}, \quad (9)$$

with the same notations as in Proposition 2.

Proof. See Appendix A.4

4   CD and CR Learnings: Comments and Illustration

4.1   CD and CR Respective Correction Capacities

The differences between CD and CR concerning their respective plausibilities ranges on singletons after having been applied are briefly discussed here.

With CD, as $pl(\{x_k\}) = 1 - (1 - pl_S(\{x_k\}))\beta_{\{x_k\}}$ for each $k \in \mathcal{X}$, $k \in \{1, \ldots, K\}$, with $\beta_{\{x_k\}}$ varying in $[0, 1]$, $pl(\{x_k\})$ can take any values in the interval $[pl_S(\{x\}), 1]$. It means that with CD the value on each singleton $pl_S(\{x\})$ can be shifted as close to 1 as required, in other words weakened as required.

In contrast, with CR, as $pl(\{x_k\}) = pl_S(\{x_k\})\beta_{\overline{\{x_k\}}}$ for each $x_k \in \mathcal{X}$, $k \in \{1, \ldots, K\}$, $pl(\{x_k\})$ can take any values in $[0, pl_S(\{x_k\})]$ with $\beta_{\overline{\{x_k\}}}$ varying from 0 to 1. With CR, the value of the plausibility on each singleton can then be carried as close to 0 as necessary. In other words, CR strengthens the information provided by the source by decreasing the plausibilities on certain singletons.

The following example illustrates these different capacities of adjustment to the reality on simple scenarios for CD and CR.

Example 1. Let us suppose that $\mathcal{X} = \{a, b, c\}$ and, without lack of generality, that the ground truth is a.

Let us suppose that a source n°1 outputs a mass $m_S(\{b, c\}) = 1$ which means that $pl_S(\{a\}) = 0$ and $pl_S(\{b\}) = pl_S(\{c\}) = 1$. To bring closer source n°1 output and the reality: CD can increase $pl_S(\{a\})$ to 1; CR can decrease $pl_S(\{b\})$ to 0 and $pl_S(\{c\})$ to 0.

This example is taken again in Table 1, and two more situations are considered: a source n°2 giving $m_S(\{c\}) = 1$, that is $pl_S(\{a\}) = pl_S(\{b\}) = 0$ and $pl_S(\{c\}) = 1$ and a source n°3 giving $m_S(\{a, b\}) = 1$, that means $pl_S(\{a\}) = pl_S(\{b\}) = 1$ and $pl_S(\{c\}) = 0$.

Table 1. Attainable plausibilities with CD and CR for three sources outputs.

	Ground truth	Source n°1	CD	CR	Source n°2	CD	CR	Source n°3	CD	CR
$pl(\{a\})$	1	0	1	0	0	1	0	1	1	1
$pl(\{b\})$	0	1	1	0	0	0	0	1	1	0
$pl(\{c\})$	0	1	1	0	1	1	0	0	0	0
		CD: $E_{pl} = 2$			CD: $E_{pl} = 1$			CD: $E_{pl} = 1$		
		CR: $E_{pl} = 1$			CR: $E_{pl} = 1$			CR: $E_{pl} = 0$		

As it can be observed in Table 1, CD can improve only one value of plausibility: the plausibility on the ground truth by increasing it as close as possible to 1, whereas CR can improve all the other plausibility values (all except the one associated with the ground truth) by decreasing them as near as possible to 0. CR has then more degrees of flexibility to improve the plausibility output of the source. Situations where CD can be of more help than CR, are in particular

Table 2. Ouputs of two sensors regarding the classes of 4 objects which can be airplanes (a), helicopters (h) or rockets (r). Data come from [3, Table 1].

		{a}	{h}	{r}	{a, h}	{a, r}	{h, r}	$\mathcal{X}$	Ground truth
Sensor 1	$m_{S_1}\{o_1\}$	0	0	0.5	0	0	0.3	0.2	a
	$m_{S_1}\{o_2\}$	0	0.5	0.2	0	0	0	0.3	h
	$m_{S_1}\{o_3\}$	0	0.4	0	0	0.6	0	0	a
	$m_{S_1}\{o_4\}$	0	0	0	0	0.6	0.4	0	r
Sensor 2	$m_{S_2}\{o_1\}$	0	0	0	0.7	0	0	0.3	a
	$m_{S_2}\{o_2\}$	0.3	0	0	0.4	0	0	0.3	h
	$m_{S_2}\{o_3\}$	0.2	0	0	0	0	0.6	0.2	a
	$m_{S_2}\{o_4\}$	0	0	0	0	0	1	0	r

Table 3. Results for the minimization of E_{pl} with the data in Table 2 for each contextual correction mechanism for both sensors 1 and 2.

Contextual correction	Sensor 1	Sensor 2
CD	$\beta = (0.76, 1.00, 1.00)$	$\beta = (0.74, 1.00, 1.00)$
	$E_{pl}(\beta) = 3.39$	$E_{pl}(\beta) = 4.81$
CR	$\beta = (0.94, 0.66, 0.38)$	$\beta = (0.65, 0.22, 0.55)$
	$E_{pl}(\beta) = 2.33$	$E_{pl}(\beta) = 2.39$

those where all the plausibilities on singletons which are not the ground truth are equal to zero, for example: $pl_S(\{b\}) = pl_S(\{c\}) = 0$ and $pl_S(\{a\}) = 0.5$, which means $m_S(\{a\}) = 0.5$ and $m_S(\emptyset) = 0.5$.

4.2   An Illustrative Example

Inspired from [3] and [5, Sect. 5], we consider the following small example of target recognition illustrated in Table 2.

Example 2. Two sensors are in charge of recognizing flying objects which can be airplanes (a), helicopters (h) or rockets (r). Data are composed of 4 known objects on which two sensors have expressed their outputs as MF on $\mathcal{X} = \{a, h, r\}$.

Results of the minimization of E_{pl} for CD and CR are summarized in Table 3 for both sensors 1 and 2. Let us recall that $\beta = (\beta_{\{a\}}, \beta_{\{h\}}, \beta_{\{r\}})$ for CD, and $\beta = (\beta_{\overline{\{a\}}}, \beta_{\overline{\{b\}}}, \beta_{\overline{\{c\}}})$ for CR with different meanings for each correction mechanism.

For CD it can be observed that $\beta_{\{h\}} = \beta_{\{r\}} = 1$ for both sensors, which means that both sensors are reliable to detect objects h and r. There is no need to transfer a portion of mass $m_S(B)$ to $B \cup \{h\}$ or $B \cup \{r\}$ with $B \subseteq \mathcal{X}$ ($1 - \beta_{\{h\}} = 1 - \beta_{\{r\}} = 0$). It is not the case for objects of type a which cause problems for both sensors, sensor 1 being slightly more reliable.

Minimizing E_{pl} with CR confirms that both sensors are more truthful to recognize objects h and r as $\beta_{\overline{\{a\}}} = 0.94 > \beta_{\overline{\{h\}}} > \beta_{\overline{\{r\}}}$ for sensor 1 and $\beta_{\overline{\{a\}}} = 0.65$ for sensor 2. In terms of mass transfers, there is less need to transfer a portion of mass $m_S(B)$ to $B \cap \overline{\{a\}} = B \cap \{h, r\}$ ($1 - 0.94 = 0.06$ for sensor 1, and $1 - 0.65 = 0.35$ for sensor 2) than to $B \cap \overline{\{h\}} = B \cap \{a, r\}$ (0.34 for sensor 1, and 0.78 for sensor 2) or $B \cap \overline{\{r\}} = B \cap \{a, h\}$ (0.62 for sensor 1, and 0.45 for sensor 2). With these data, CR also permits to obtain lower values for E_{pl} than those reached with CD, which confirms the advantages of CR over CD exposed in Sect. 4.1 and in Example 1 concerning the minimization of E_{pl}.

4.3   On the Absence of Link Between Learning CR and CD

Even if CR and CD are related (CR amounts to the negation of the CD of the negation of the information provided by the source [6]), CR and CD parameters minimizing E_{pl} (5) cannot be deduced analytically from each other.

Let us consider next example which is a slight modification of Example 2.

Example 3. By modifying in Table 2, MF $m_{S_1}\{o_1\}$ by $m_{S_1}\{o_1\}(\{r\}) = 0.5282$, $m_{S_1}\{o_1\}(\{h, r\}) = 0.3$ and $m_{S_1}\{o_1\}(\mathcal{X}) = 0.1718$ (information coming from Sensor 1 is slightly deteriorated, the truth being a), learning of CD parameters for sensors 1 and 2 yields the same vector $\beta = (0.74, 1.00, 1.00)$, while the learning of CR parameters yields $\beta = (0.92, 0.68, 0.38)$ for sensor 1 and $\beta = (0.65, 0.22, 0.55)$ for sensor 2.

Example 3 shows that knowing the vector β minimizing E_{pl} for CD does not imply knowing the vector β minimizing E_{pl} for CR.

5   Conclusion

In this paper, we have studied the learning of CD and of CR from labelled data, given a measure of discrepancy based on the plausibility function. We have shown that for each of these two contextual correction schemes, there exists an optimal set of contexts that ensures the minimization of the measure and that finding this minimum amounts to solving a constrained least-squares problem with K unknowns. These results can find applications in at least two domains: learning the biases of a source of information (what are the characteristics of a source?) and in source tuning (how to tune a source to obtain the best performances?). Future work will consist in exploiting these mechanisms in more complex applications and investigating the tuning of the combination of several sources.

A   Appendices

A.1   Proof of Proposition 1

As $m = m_S \textcircled{\cup}_{A \in \mathcal{A}} A_{\beta_A}$, CD is given in terms of implicability functions by: $b = b_S \prod_{A \in \mathcal{A}} b_{\beta_A}$ with $b_{\beta_A}(B) = 1$ if $A \subseteq B$, β_A otherwise, for all $B \subseteq \mathcal{X}$. Thus, for all $B \subseteq \mathcal{X}$: $b(B) = b_S(B) \prod_{A \in \mathcal{A}, A \not\subseteq B} \beta_A$, and consequently, for all $x \in \mathcal{X}$:

$$pl(\{x\}) = 1 - b(\overline{\{x\}}) = 1 - b_S(\overline{\{x\}}) \prod_{A \in \mathcal{A}, A \not\subseteq \overline{\{x\}}} \beta_A$$

$$= 1 - b_S(\overline{\{x\}}) \prod_{A \in \mathcal{A}, x \in A} \beta_A = 1 - (1 - pl_S(\{x\})) \prod_{A \in \mathcal{A}, x \in A} \beta_A.$$

A.2   Proof of Proposition 2

From Proposition 1, after having applied CD on m_S, the discrepancy measure E_{pl} (5) can be written: $E_{pl}(\boldsymbol{\beta}) = \sum_{k=1}^{K} E_{pl}(\boldsymbol{\beta}, x_k)$, with for all $k \in \{1, \ldots, K\}$:

$$E_{pl}(\boldsymbol{\beta}, x_k) := \sum_{i=1}^{n} \left(\left(1 - (1 - pl_S\{o_i\}(\{x_k\})) \prod_{A \in \mathcal{A}, x_k \in A} \beta_A \right) - \delta_{i,k} \right)^2. \quad (10)$$

As $E_{pl}(\boldsymbol{\beta}, x_k) \geq 0$ for all $k \in \{1, \ldots, K\}$, the minimum value of $E_{pl}(\boldsymbol{\beta})$ is obtained when each $E_{pl}(\boldsymbol{\beta}, x_k)$ reaches its minimum.

Besides, as all coefficients β_A belong to $[0, 1]$, for each x_k, $k \in \{1, \ldots; K\}$, the product $\prod_{A \in \mathcal{A}, x_k \in A} \beta_A$ of coefficients β_A in $E_{pl}(\boldsymbol{\beta}, x_k)$ (10) also belongs to $[0, 1]$ and can be denoted by a variable $\beta_k \in [0, 1]$. Hence, for each $k \in \{1, \ldots, K\}$, the minimum of $E_{pl}(\boldsymbol{\beta}, x_k)$ is reached for a particular value of β_k.

Now, we can remark that each coefficient $\beta_{\{x_k\}} \in [0, 1]$, $k \in \{1, \ldots, K\}$, only appears in the expression of $E_{pl}(\boldsymbol{\beta}, x_k)$ (10), $k \in \{1, \ldots, K\}$. Hence, choosing $\beta_k = \beta_{\{x_k\}}$ for all k (which means choosing $\mathcal{A}$ composed of the set of singletons of $\mathcal{X}$) constitutes then a solution, i.e., a set of contexts for which the minimum value of $E_{pl}(\boldsymbol{\beta})$ is reached.

Each value of E_{pl} is then reachable using the vector $\boldsymbol{\beta}$ of coefficients $\beta_k := \beta_{\{x_k\}}$, $k \in \{1, \ldots, K\}$, and as already mentioned in [5, Sect. 5.1], the computation of the coefficient $\boldsymbol{\beta}$ with CD based on the singletons is a constrained least-squares problem. Indeed, for all $k \in \{1, \ldots, K\}$, and for all $i \in \{1, \ldots, n\}$:

$$pl\{o_i\}(\{x_k\}) - \delta_{i,k} = 1 - (1 - pl_S\{o_i\}(\{x_k\}))\beta_k - \delta_{i,k} \quad (11)$$

$$= (pl_S\{o_i\}(\{x_k\}) - 1)\beta_k - (\delta_{i,k} - 1). \quad (12)$$

Then (5) can be rewritten as (7).

A.3   Proof of Proposition 3

As $m = m_S \bigcirc_{A \in \mathcal{A}} A^{\beta_A}$, the CR is determined in terms of commonality functions by $q = q_S \prod_{A \in \mathcal{A}} q^{\beta_A}$ with $q^{\beta_A}(B) = 1$ if $B \subseteq A$, β_A otherwise, for all $B \subseteq \mathcal{X}$. Then, for all $B \subseteq \mathcal{X}$: $q(B) = q_S(B) \prod_{A \in \mathcal{A}, B \not\subseteq A} \beta_A$, which means that after having applied CR, plausibilities on singletons are defined, for all $x \in \mathcal{X}$, by:

$$pl(\{x\}) = q(\{x\}) = q_S(\{x\}) \prod_{A \in \mathcal{A}, x \notin A} \beta_A = pl_S(\{x\}) \prod_{A \in \mathcal{A}, x \notin A} \beta_A$$

A.4 Proof of Proposition 4

From Proposition 3, for each $k \in \{1, \ldots, K\}$, coefficient $\beta_{\overline{\{x_k\}}}$ takes its values in $[0,1]$ and only appears in $pl(x_k)$ when a CR has been applied. Then, with the same reasoning as for the CD case, the minimum value of E_{pl} with CR can be reached using the set of contexts $\{\overline{x_k} = \mathcal{X} \setminus \{x_k\}, k \in \{1, \ldots, K\}\}$.

The minimization of E_{pl} with CR based on the vector $\boldsymbol{\beta} = (\beta_k := \beta_{\overline{\{x_k\}}}, k \in \{1, \ldots, K\})$ is also a constrained least-squares problem as (5) can be written as (9) (as $\forall k \in \{1, \ldots, K\}$ and $\forall i \in \{1, \ldots, n\}$, $pl\{o_i\}(\{x_k\}) - \delta_{i,k} = pl_S\{o_i\}(\{x_k\})\beta_k - \delta_{i,k}$).

References

1. Destercke, S., Burger, T.: Toward an axiomatic definition of conflict between belief functions. IEEE Trans. Cybern. **43**(2), 585–596 (2012)
2. Dubois, D., Prade, H.: A set-theoretic view of belief functions: logical operations and approximations by fuzzy sets. Int. J. Gen. Syst. **12**, 193–226 (1986)
3. Elouedi, Z., Mellouli, K., Smets, P.: Assessing sensor reliability for multisensor data fusion within the transferable belief model. IEEE Trans. Syst. Man Cybern. Part B. **34**(1), 782–787 (2004)
4. Jousselme, A.-L., Maupin, P.: Distances in evidence theory: comprehensive survey and generalizations. Int. J. Approx. Reason. **53**(2), 118–145 (2012)
5. Mercier, D., Quost, B., Denœux, T.: Refined modeling of sensor reliability in the belief function framework using contextual discounting. Inf. Fusion. **9**(2), 246–258 (2008)
6. Mercier, D., Lefèvre, É., Delmotte, F.: Belief functions contextual discounting and canonical decompositions. Int. J. Approx. Reason. **53**(2), 146–158 (2012)
7. Pichon, F., Mercier, D., Delmotte, F., Lefèvre, É.: Truthfulness in contextual information correction. In: Cuzzolin, F. (ed.) BELIEF 2014. LNCS, vol. 8764, pp. 11–20. Springer, Heidelberg (2014)
8. Shafer, G.: A mathematical Theory of Evidence. Princeton University Press, Princeton, N.J. (1976)
9. Smets, P.: Belief functions: The disjunctive rule of combination and the generalized Bayesian theorem. Int. J. Approx. Reason. **9**, 1–35 (1993)
10. Smets, P., Kennes, R.: The transferable belief model. Artif. Intell. **66**, 191–243 (1994)
11. Smets, P.: Analyzing the combination of conflicting belief functions. Inf. Fusion **8**, 387–412 (2007)

Logic

Symbolic Possibilistic Logic: Completeness and Inference Methods

Claudette Cayrol$^{(\boxtimes)}$, Didier Dubois, and Fayçal Touazi

IRIT, University of Toulouse, 118 rte de Narbonne, Toulouse, France
{ccayrol,dubois,faycal.touazi}@irit.fr

Abstract. This paper studies the extension of possibilistic logic to the case when weights attached to formulas are symbolic and stand for variables that lie in a totally ordered scale, and only partial knowledge is available on the relative strength of these weights. A proof of the soundness and the completeness of this logic according to the relative certainty semantics in the sense of necessity measures is provided. Based on this result, two syntactic inference methods are presented. The first one calculates the necessity degree of a possibilistic formula using the notion of minimal inconsistent sub-base. A second method is proposed that takes inspiration from the concept of ATMS. Notions introduced in that area, such as nogoods and labels, are used to calculate the necessity degree of a possibilistic formula. A comparison of the two methods is provided, as well as a comparison with the original version of symbolic possibilistic logic.

1 Introduction

Possibilistic logic [1] is an approach to reason under uncertainty using totally ordered propositional bases. In this logic, each formula is assigned a degree, often encoded by a weight belonging to $(0, 1]$, seen as a lower bound on the certainty level of the formula. Such degrees of certainty obey graded versions of the principles that found the notions of belief or knowledge in epistemic logic, namely the conjunction of two formulas is not believed less than the least believed of their conjuncts. This is the basic axiom of degrees of necessity in possibility theory [2]. See [3] for a recent survey of possibilistic logic. Deduction in possibilistic logic follows the rule of the weakest link: the strength of an inference chain is that of the least certain formula involved in this chain. The weight of a formula in the deductive closure is the weight of the strongest path leading from the base to the formula. Possibilistic logic has developed techniques for knowledge representation and reasoning in various areas, such as non-monotonic reasoning, belief revision and belief merging see references in [3].

About 10 years ago, a natural extension of possibilistic logic was proposed using partially ordered symbolic weights attached to formulas [4], we call here symbolic possibilistic logic, for short. Weights represent ill-known certainty values on a totally ordered scale. Only partial knowledge on the relative strength

© Springer International Publishing Switzerland 2015
S. Destercke and T. Denoeux (Eds.): ECSQARU 2015, LNAI 9161, pp. 485–495, 2015.
DOI: 10.1007/978-3-319-20807-7_44

of weights is supposed to be available, under the form of weak inequality constraints. In that paper, a possibilistic knowledge base along with the knowledge pertaining to weights is encoded in propositional logic, augmenting the atomic formulas with those pertaining to weights. They give a characterisation, and a deduction method for plausible inference in this logic using the idea of forgetting variables. This generalisation of possibilistic logic differs from other approaches that represent sets of formulas equipped with a partial order in the setting of conditional logics [5]. It also contrasts with another line of research consisting in viewing a partial order on weights as a family of total orders, thus viewing a symbolic possibilistic base as a set of usual possibilistic bases [6].

In this paper, we revisit symbolic possibilistic logic, first by assuming strict inequality constraints between weights and by focusing on the weighted completion of a possibilistic knowledge base. We provide an original completeness proof, absent from [4]. This proof is more general than the completeness proof of standard possibilistic logic as, contrary to the latter, we cannot rely on classical inference from sets of formulas having at least a given certainty degree. Specific inference methods to compute the symbolic weight attached to a conclusion are proposed, especially some inspired by the literature on abductive reasoning initiated by Reiter [7]. Our approach yields a partial order on the language, while the alternative partially ordered generalizations of possibilistic logic [4,6] only compute a set of plausible consequences.

2   Symbolic Possibilistic Logic Revisited

In this section, first we recall the construction of possibilistic logic. Then, we present symbolic possibilistic logic. In the paper, $\mathcal{L}$ denotes a propositional language. Formulas are denoted by $\phi_1 \cdots \phi_n$, and Ω is the set of interpretations. $[\phi]$ denotes the set of models of ϕ, a subset of Ω. As usual, $\vdash$ and $\models$ denote syntactic inference and semantic entailment, respectively.

2.1   Background on Standard Possibilistic Logic

Possibilistic logic is an extension of classical logic which handles weighted formulas of the form (ϕ_j, p_j) where ϕ_j is a propositional formula and $p_j \in \,]0, 1]$. (ϕ_j, p_j) is interpreted by $N(\phi_j) \geq p_j$, where N is a necessity measure, the conjugate of a possibility measure. A possibility measure [2] is defined on subsets of Ω from a possibility distribution π on Ω as $\Pi(A) = \max_{\omega \in A} \pi(\omega)$ expressing the plausibility of any proposition ϕ, with $[\phi] = A$, and the necessity measure expressing certainty levels is defined by $N(A) = 1 - \Pi(\overline{A})$ where $\overline{A}$ is the complement of A.

A possibilistic base is a finite set of weighted formulas $\Sigma = \{(\phi_j, p_j), j = 1 \cdots m\}$. It can be associated with a possibility distribution π_Σ on Ω in the following way:

$$\forall j, \pi_j(\omega) = \begin{cases} 1 & \text{if } \omega \in [\phi_j], \\ 1 - p_j & \text{if } \omega \notin [\phi_j] \end{cases} \qquad \pi_\Sigma(\omega) = \min_j \pi_j(\omega). \qquad (1)$$

Note that π_j is the least informative possibility distribution among those such that $N(\phi_j) \geq p_j$, where a possibility distribution π is less informative than ρ if and only if $\pi \geq \rho$. Likewise π_Σ is the least informative possibility distribution compatible with the base Σ, on behalf of *the principle of minimal specificity*. It can be checked that $N_\Sigma(\phi_j) = \min_{\omega \notin [\phi_j]}(1 - \pi_\Sigma(\omega)) \geq p_j$ is the least necessity degree in agreement with Σ. However, it may occur that $N_\Sigma(\phi_j) > p_j$. The (semantic) closure of Σ is then defined by $\{(\phi, N_\Sigma(\phi)) : \phi \in \mathcal{L} : N_\Sigma(\phi) > 0\}$, which simply corresponds to a ranking on the language. The semantics of possibilistic logic allows to replace weighted conjunctions $(\bigwedge_i \phi_i, p)$ by a set of formulas (ϕ_i, p) without altering the underlying possibility distribution, since $N(\phi \wedge \psi) = \min(N(\phi), N(\psi))$: from the minimal specificity principle, we can associate the same weight to each sub-formula in the conjunction. Therefore, we can turn any possibilistic base into a semantically equivalent weighted clausal base.

Syntactic Inference in Possibilistic Logic. A sound and complete syntactic inference $\vdash_\pi$ for possibilistic logic can be defined using axioms of classical logic turned into formulas weighted by 1 and inference rules [1]:

- Weakening rule: If $p_i > p_j$ then $(\phi, p_i) \vdash_\pi (\phi, p_j)$
- Modus Ponens : $\{(\phi \rightarrow \psi, p), (\phi, p)\} \vdash_\pi (\psi, p)$

This Modus Ponens rule embodies the law of accepted beliefs at any level, assumed they form a deductively closed set [8]. It is related to axiom K of modal logic. The soundness and completeness of possibilistic logic for the above proof theory can be translated by the following equality [1]: $N_\Sigma(\phi) = \max\{p : \Sigma \vdash_\pi (\phi, p)\}$.

Note that we can also express inference in possibilistic logic by classical inference on p-cuts $\Sigma_p^\geq = \{\phi_j : p_j \geq p\}$[1]: $N_\Sigma(\phi) = \max\{p : (\Sigma_p^\geq) \vdash \phi\}$.

Inconsistency degree $Inc(\Sigma)$ of a possibilistic base Σ is defined as follows: $Inc(\Sigma) = \max\{p | \Sigma \vdash_\pi (\bot, p)\}$. It can be proved that $N_\Sigma(\phi) = Inc(\Sigma \cup (\neg\phi, 1))$ [1,9].

2.2   Symbolic Possibilistic Logic (SPL)

In symbolic possibilistic logic (SPL), only partial knowledge is available on the relative strength of weights attached to formulas. So, weights are symbolic expressions taking values on a totally ordered necessity scale (such as $]0, 1]$), and there is a set of constraints over these weights, describing their relative strength. The name "symbolic possibilistic logic" indicates that we shall perform symbolic computations on the weights. The set $\mathcal{P}$ of symbolic weights p_j is recursively obtained using a finite set of variables (called elementary weights) $H = \{a_1, \ldots, a_k\}$ taking values on the scale $]0, 1]$ and max / min expressions built on H: $H \subseteq \mathcal{P}$, $1 \in \mathcal{P}$, and if $p_i, p_j \in \mathcal{P}$, then $\max(p_i, p_j), \min(p_i, p_j) \in \mathcal{P}$.

Let $\Sigma = \{(\phi_j, p_j), j = 1, \cdots, m\}$ be a symbolic possibilistic base where p_j is a max / min expression built on H. A formula (ϕ_j, p_j) is still interpreted as $N(\phi_j) \geq p_j$ [4]. The knowledge about weights is encoded by a finite set

$\mathcal{C} = \{p_i > p_j\}$ of constraints between max / min expressions, a partial ordering on symbolic expressions. We can prove $p > q$, denoted by $\mathcal{C} \models p > q$ if and only if every valuation of symbols appearing in p, q (on $]0, 1]$) which satisfies the constraints in $\mathcal{C}$ also satisfies $p > q$.

At the semantic level, $N_\Sigma(\phi)$ is now a symbolic max / min expression of the form

$$N_\Sigma(\phi) = \min_{\omega \not\models \phi} \max_{j : \omega \not\models \phi_j} p_j. \qquad (2)$$

We directly use the expression defined in standard possibilistic logic. The main difference with standard possibilistic logic is that we cannot simplify this expression down to a single weight. To perform inference at the syntax level, one must slightly reformulate the inference rules of possibilistic logic in order to account for the symbolic nature of weights:

- Fusion rule: $\{(\phi, p), (\phi, p')\} \vdash_\pi (\phi, \max(p, p'))$
- Weakening rule: $(\phi, p_i) \vdash_\pi (\phi, \min(p_j, p)), \forall p$
- Modus Ponens : $\{(\phi \rightarrow \psi, p), (\phi, p)\} \vdash_\pi (\psi, p)$

We call skeleton of a possibilistic base Σ the set of propositional formulas appearing in it, and denote it by Σ^*. If B is a subset of the skeleton Σ^* of Σ that implies ϕ, it is clear that $(\Sigma, \mathcal{C}) \vdash_\pi (\phi, \min_{\phi_j \in B} p_j)$. Using syntactic inference, we can compute the expression representing the strength of deduction of ϕ from Σ:

$$N_\Sigma^\vdash(\phi) = \max_{B \subseteq \Sigma^*, B \vdash \phi} \min_{j : \phi_j \in B} p_j. \qquad (3)$$

Note that in the above expression, it suffices to take max on all minimal subsets B for inclusion that imply ϕ. The aim of SPL is to compare the strength degrees of any two formulas in the language via their resulting weights.

Definition 1. $(\Sigma, \mathcal{C})$ *implies that ϕ is more certain than ψ $((\Sigma, \mathcal{C}) \models \phi > \psi)$ if and only if $\mathcal{C} \models N_\Sigma^\vdash(\phi) > N_\Sigma^\vdash(\psi)$.*

Example 1. *Let $\Sigma = \{(x, p), (\neg x \vee y, q), (\neg x, r), (\neg y, s)\}$, $\mathcal{C} = \{p > q, q > r, q > s\}$. Then, $N_\Sigma^\vdash(y) = \max(\min(p, q), \min(p, r)) = q$ and $N_\Sigma^\vdash(x) = p$. So, $x > y$.*

Note that in SPL, comparing the certainty degrees of formulas as per Definition 1 requires that the set of constraints $\mathcal{C}$ be not empty. Otherwise, no strict inequalities can be inferred between formula weights.

3   The Completeness of Symbolic Possibilistic Logic

The completeness of SPL comes down to proving that the two following expressions are equal : $N_\Sigma(\phi) = N_\Sigma^\vdash(\phi), \forall \phi \in \mathcal{L}$. This proof does not appear in [4], where the focus is on plausible inference.

Proposition 1. *SPL is sound and complete for the above inference system.*

The proof cannot rely on cuts, like for standard possibilistic logic, due to the fact that the weights are partially ordered. So we provide the sketch of a direct proof that the two expressions of $N_\Sigma(\phi)$ and $N_\Sigma^\vdash(\phi)$ coincide independently of constraints in $\mathcal{C}$. In this proof, we use the notion of hitting-set [7]:

Definition 2 (Hitting-Set). *Let $\mathcal{S}$ be a collection of sets. A hitting-set of $\mathcal{S}$ is a set $H \subseteq \cup_{S_i \in \mathcal{S}} S_i$ such that $H \cap S_i \neq \emptyset$ for each $S_i \in \mathcal{S}$. A hitting-set H of $\mathcal{S}$ is minimal if and only if no strict subset of H is a hitting-set of $\mathcal{S}$.*

Proof of Proposition 1: Due to the lack of space, we only give the list of steps and results needed. Let Σ_ω^- be the subset of formulas in Σ^* falsified by ω, and Σ_ω^+ be the subset of formulas in Σ^* satisfied by ω. We have to prove that $\min_{\omega \not\models \phi} \max_{j : \phi_j \in \Sigma_\omega^-} p_j = \max_{B \subseteq \Sigma^*, B \vdash \phi} \min_{\phi_j \in B} p_j$. We distinguish cases according to whether Σ^* is consistent or not.

1. Suppose that Σ^* is consistent. Then all B's implying ϕ are consistent. We note that:
   - For $N_\Sigma^\vdash(\phi)$, it is sufficient to consider the minimal (for set-inclusion) subsets of Σ^*, say $B_i, i = 1, n$, that imply ϕ: $N_\Sigma^\vdash(\phi) = \max_{i=1,\cdots,n} \min_{\phi_j \in B_i} p_j$.
   - For $N_\Sigma(\phi)$, it is sufficient to consider the interpretations ω such that $\omega \not\models \phi$ and Σ_ω^- is minimal (for set inclusion) : $N_\Sigma(\phi) = \min_{\omega \not\models \phi, \Sigma_\omega^- \text{ minimal}} \max_{j : \phi_j \in \Sigma_\omega^-} p_j$.

Lemma 1. *If Σ^* is a minimal (for set inclusion) base that implies ϕ, $N_\Sigma(\phi) = N_\Sigma^\vdash(\phi)$.*

We conclude that $N_\Sigma(\phi) \geq N_\Sigma^\vdash(\phi)$ since for each $B \subseteq \Sigma, N_\Sigma(\phi) \geq N_B(\phi) = N_B^\vdash(\phi)$. Using distributivity, we can rewrite the syntactic necessity degree in terms of the minimal hitting-sets of the set $\{B_1, \ldots, B_n\}$. By indexing all the minimal hitting-sets H_s of $\{B_1, \ldots, B_n\}$ by $s \in \mathcal{S}$ we obtain:

$$N_\Sigma^\vdash(\phi) = \max_{B \subseteq \Sigma^*, B \vdash \phi} \min_{\phi_j \in B} p_j = \min_{s \in \mathcal{S}} \max_{\phi_j \in H_s} p_j.$$

Lemma 2. $\forall \omega \not\models \phi, \Sigma_\omega^-$ *is a hitting-set of* $\{B_1, \ldots B_n\}$ *(that is $\forall i, B_i \cap \Sigma_\omega^- \neq \emptyset$).*

Note that the above result holds in particular when Σ_ω^- is minimal. The sub-bases Σ_ω^- such that $\omega \not\models \phi$ that are minimal are the complements of the maximal sub-bases $M_{\neg\phi}$ of Σ^* consistent with $\neg\phi$, the set of which we denote by $\mathcal{M}_{\neg\phi}$. Notice that:

Lemma 3. *The complement of each minimal hitting-set H_s of $\{B_1, \ldots B_n\}$ is a maximal sub-base of Σ^* consistent with $\neg\phi$.*

Then we can obtain the converse inequality $N_\Sigma(\phi) \leq N_\Sigma^\vdash(\phi)$ since: $N_\Sigma^\vdash(\phi) = \min_{s \in \mathcal{S}} \max_{\phi_j \in H_s} p_j = \min_{M_{\neg\phi} = \overline{H_s}, s \in \mathcal{S}} \max_{\phi_j \notin M_{\neg\phi}} p_j \geq \min_{M_{\neg\phi} \in \mathcal{M}_{\neg\phi}} \max_{\phi_j \notin M_{\neg\phi}} p_j = N_\Sigma(\phi)$.

2. Suppose that Σ^* is inconsistent with no constraint on the weights. Then, some of the minimal sub-bases that imply ϕ may be inconsistent. We have the following results:
   - Let $I_1, \ldots, I_p$ be the minimal inconsistent sub-bases of Σ^* (smallest inconsistent sub-bases in the sense of inclusion). The inconsistency degree of Σ is $Inc(\Sigma) = N_\Sigma^\vdash(\bot) = \max_{k=1}^p \min_{\phi_j \in I_k} p_j$, and $N_\Sigma^\vdash(\phi) = \max(Inc(\Sigma), \max_{i=1}^n \min_{\phi_j \in B_i} p_j)$, B_i being the minimal consistent sub-bases that imply ϕ (if any).
   - $N_\Sigma^\vdash(\phi) \geq Inc(\Sigma)$. However there is never strict inequality if $\mathcal{C} = \emptyset$.
   - The definition of $N_\Sigma(\phi)$ is the same as in the consistent case. However, $\forall \omega, \Sigma_\omega^+ \subset \Sigma$ (since Σ_ω^+ is consistent).

Now, we are able to prove completeness:

- Lemma 1 can be used. Now, Σ^* is a minimal inconsistent base implying ϕ, and none of its sub-bases implies ϕ. The inequality $N_\Sigma(\phi) \geq N_\Sigma^\vdash(\phi)$ still holds (note that minimality does not exclude inconsistency).
- For Lemma 2, Σ_ω^+ is always consistent. So in the case of an inconsistent set I_i, we cannot have $I_i \subset \Sigma_\omega^+$. The proof of Lemma 2 still holds, since the sets $\overline{H_s}$ are consistent, as the $M_{\neg \phi}$.

So completeness has been proved even if the base Σ^* is inconsistent. $\square$

Remark. However, it may happen that some minimal inconsistent subset I_i of Σ^* is not a minimal sub-base implying ϕ. For instance, if $\Sigma = \{(\phi, a), (\neg \phi, b)\}$ the unique minimal sub-base implying ϕ is $\{\phi\}$. In that case, $N_\Sigma^\vdash(\phi) = \max_{B \subseteq \Sigma^*, B \vdash \phi} \min_{\phi_j \in B} p_j = \max(\min(a, b), a) = a = N_\Sigma(\phi)$. Similarly, $N_\Sigma^\vdash(\neg \phi) = b$. So we have $N_\Sigma^\vdash(\bot) = \min(a, b) \leq N_\Sigma^\vdash(\phi)$ and $N_\Sigma^\vdash(\bot) \leq N_\Sigma^\vdash(\neg \phi)$. We have $\{a\} \subset \{a, b\}$ but it cannot be concluded that $N_\Sigma^\vdash(\bot) < N_\Sigma^\vdash(\neg \phi)$.

4   Toward Inference Methods in Symbolic Possibilistic Logic

In this section, we will present two syntactic inference methods that calculate the necessity degree $N_\Sigma^\vdash(\phi)$ of a possibilistic formula. The first method is based on the use of the notion of minimal inconsistent sub-base. The second one is inspired by abductive reasoning. We assume that the weights bearing on formulas of the original SPL base are elementary, with possibility of assigning the same weight to different formulas.

4.1   Syntactic Inference Based on Minimal Inconsistent Sub-bases

Given a formula ϕ, computing the expression in Eq. (3) requires the determination of all minimal sub-bases B_i such that $B_i \vdash \phi$. Some of the minimal sub-bases that imply ϕ may be inconsistent. In that case, they are minimal inconsistent in Σ^*.

Lemma 4. *Let $B \subseteq \Sigma^*$ inconsistent and minimal implying ϕ. Then B is minimal inconsistent in Σ^*.*

So, if $B \subseteq \Sigma^*$ is a minimal sub-base implying ϕ, either B is consistent or B is a minimal inconsistent sub-base of Σ^*. However, it may happen that some minimal inconsistent sub-base in Σ^* is not a minimal sub-base implying ϕ. It follows easily:

Proposition 2. *Let $B_1, \cdots, B_k$ be the minimal consistent sub-bases of Σ^* implying ϕ. Let $I_1, \cdots, I_l$ be the minimal inconsistent sub-bases in Σ^* which do not contain any B_j, $j = 1 \cdots k$, $N_\Sigma^\vdash(\phi) = \max(\max_{i=1}^k \min_{\phi_j \in B_i} p_j, \max_{i=1}^l \min_{\phi_j \in I_i} p_j)$.*

Besides, we know that $B \subseteq \Sigma^*$ is minimal implying ϕ if and only if B is minimal such that $B \cup \{\neg\phi\}$ is inconsistent. We can prove even more:

Proposition 3. *Let $(\Sigma, \mathcal{C})$ be an SPL base, and B a sub-base of Σ^*.*

- *If B is consistent and minimal implying ϕ then $B \cup \{\neg\phi\}$ is a minimal inconsistent sub-base of $\Sigma^* \cup \{\neg\phi\}$.*
- *If K is a minimal inconsistent sub-base of $\Sigma^* \cup \{\neg\phi\}$ containing $\neg\phi$, then $K \setminus \{\neg\phi\}$ is consistent, minimal implying ϕ.*

Due to Propositions 2 and 3, computing $N_\Sigma^\vdash(\phi)$ amounts to determining:

- the set of minimal inconsistent subsets K_i of $\Sigma^* \cup \{\neg\phi\}$ containing $\neg\phi$;
- the minimal inconsistent sub-bases of Σ^* which do not contain any of the $B_i = K_i \setminus \{\neg\phi\}$'s obtained in the previous step.

The above computation comes down to the well-known problem of determining the minimal inconsistent sub-bases, forming a set $MIS(S)$, of a given set of formulas S. Let $\mathcal{B}^\vdash(\phi) = \{B \subseteq \Sigma^* | B \cup \{\neg\phi\} \in MIS(\Sigma^* \cup \{\neg\phi\})\}$ and $\mathcal{B}_i(\phi) = \{B \in MIS(\Sigma^*) | B$ does not contain any base from $\mathcal{B}^\vdash(\phi)\}$. Then let $\mathcal{B}(\phi) = \mathcal{B}^\vdash(\phi) \bigcup \mathcal{B}_i(\phi)$. So, the necessity degree of a formula ϕ can be computed as follows:

$$N_\Sigma^\vdash(\phi) = \max_{B_i \in \mathcal{B}(\phi)} \min_{\phi_j \in B_i} p_j \tag{4}$$

The most efficient method for solving the MIS problem exploits the duality between minimal inconsistent subsets $MIS(S)$, and maximal consistent subsets $MCS(S)$, and the fact that checking the consistency of a base is less time-consuming than checking its inconsistency [10]. Given a propositional base S, $MIS(S)$ is obtained from $MCS(S)$ using hitting-sets [10,11].

Once we are able to compute the necessity degree of a formula, according to Definition 1, we can compare two SPL formulas by comparing their necessity degrees which are max / min expressions. So we have to check whether $\mathcal{C} \models N_\Sigma^\vdash(\phi) > N_\Sigma^\vdash(\psi)$ that is $\mathcal{C} \models \max_{B \in \mathcal{B}(\phi)} \min_{i:\phi_i \in B} a_i > \max_{C \in \mathcal{B}(\psi)} \min_{j:\phi_j \in C} b_j$. That amounts to finding an expression $\min(a_1, \cdots a_n)$ in $N_\Sigma^\vdash(\phi)$ which dominates all expressions $\min(b_1, \cdots, b_m)$ in $N_\Sigma^\vdash(\psi)$. Rather than applying this test in a brute force way, it is natural to use sets of elementary weights instead of formulas, and to simplify the expressions of $N_\Sigma^\vdash(\phi)$ and $N_\Sigma^\vdash(\psi)$ using $\mathcal{C}$ prior to comparing them. The inference technique proposed next is useful to that effect.

4.2   Syntactic Inference Based on ATMSs

In this section, we present another syntactic method for SPL inference, based on abductive reasoning. Namely, consider the weights involved in the computation of $N_\Sigma^\vdash(\phi)$ as assumptions that explain the certainty of ϕ. It suggests to use an Assumption-based Truth-Maintenance System (ATMS [12]), in which a distinction is made between two kinds of data, the data representing knowledge and the data representing assumptions. We first recall the basic definitions of ATMS, then we show how we encode an SPL base in order to use an ATMS for computing the necessity degree of a formula.

Definition 3. *Let $(\mathcal{J}, \mathcal{A})$ be an ATMS base where $\mathcal{J}$ is a consistent base of propositional formulas, and $\mathcal{A}$ is a set of propositional variables (the assumptions).*

- *Any subset E of $\mathcal{A}$ is called an environment*
- *An environment E is $\mathcal{J}$-incoherent if and only if $E \cup \mathcal{J}$ is inconsistent*
- *A nogood is a minimal $\mathcal{J}$-incoherent environment*
- *An environment E supports ϕ if and only if E is not $\mathcal{J}$-incoherent and $E \cup \mathcal{J} \vdash \phi$*

Given $(\mathcal{J}, \mathcal{A})$ and a formula ϕ, the ATMS is able to provide all the minimal environments that support ϕ, under the form of a set $Label(\phi)$.

Given an SPL base $(\Sigma, \mathcal{C})$, the possibilistic base Σ is encoded by a pair $(\mathcal{J}, \mathcal{A})$ as follows : each elementary weight a_i is associated with a propositional variable (for simplicity we keep a_i as propositional variable) and each SPL formula (ϕ_i, a_i) is encoded by the propositional formula $\neg a_i \vee \phi_i$.

Definition 4. *Let $(\Sigma, \mathcal{C})$ be an SPL base. The associated ATMS base $(\mathcal{J}_\Sigma, \mathcal{A})$ is defined by : $\mathcal{J}_\Sigma = \{\neg a_i \vee \phi_i | (\phi_i, a_i) \in \Sigma\}$ and $\mathcal{A} = \{a_i | (\phi_i, a_i) \in \Sigma\}$.*

As shown in Sect. 4.1, in order to compute $N_\Sigma^\vdash(\phi)$, we have to consider the sub-bases of Σ^* which are minimal implying ϕ and consistent, and then some of the minimal inconsistent sub-bases of Σ^*. Moreover, for computing $N_\Sigma^\vdash(\phi)$, we only need the weights associated with the formulas belonging to these sub-bases. With the encoding of Definition 4, it is easy to see that each consistent sub-base of Σ^* which is minimal implying ϕ exactly corresponds to an environment in $Label(\phi)$ with respect to the ATMS base $(\mathcal{J}_\Sigma, \mathcal{A})$. And each minimal inconsistent sub-base of Σ^* exactly corresponds to a nogood with respect to the ATMS base $(\mathcal{J}_\Sigma, \mathcal{A})$. So, it follows easily from Proposition 2 that:

Proposition 4. *Given an SPL base $(\Sigma, \mathcal{C})$ and the associated ATMS base $(\mathcal{J}_\Sigma, \mathcal{A})$, let $\mathcal{U}(\phi) = \{U_1, \cdots, U_k\}$ be the so-called useful nogoods for ϕ, i.e. the nogoods which do not contain any environment of $Label(\phi)$. Then we have:*

$$N_\Sigma^\vdash(\phi) = \max(\max_{E \in Label(\phi)} \min_{a \in E} a, \max_{i=1}^k \min_{a \in U_i} a).$$

See [13] for further details on calculating labels and nogoods.

Example 2. *Let* $\Sigma = \{(\neg x \vee y, a), (x, b), (\neg y, c), (\neg x, e)\}$. *This SPL base is encoded by the ATMS base:* $\mathcal{J}_\Sigma = \{\neg a \vee \neg x \vee y, \neg b \vee x, \neg c \vee \neg y, \neg e \vee \neg x\}$ *and* $\mathcal{A} = \{a, b, c, e\}$.

We obtain $Label(y) = \{\{a, b\}\}$. *The nogoods are* $\{a, b, c\}, \{b, e\}$, *hence only the second one is useful for* y. *So,* $N^\vdash_\Sigma(y) = \max(\min(a, b), \min(b, e))$.

4.3   Comparing Complex Symbolic Weights

One of the benefits of the last method lies in the fact that everything is computed only in terms of weights (in the label of the formula and the useful nogoods). Then constraints on weights can be used to simplify the max / min expressions, while in the previous method, we use all formulas in the symbolic possibilistic base. Moreover, in the ATMS method, one can think of exploiting constraints and simplify the sets of weights involved in the comparison of the necessity degrees at the moment we are producing them. So it is natural to simplify the expressions of $N^\vdash_\Sigma(\phi)$ and $N^\vdash_\Sigma(\psi)$ prior to comparing them,

- first by replacing each set of weights $B \in Label(\phi) \cup \mathcal{U}(\phi)$ by the reduced set of weights $W = \min_{\mathcal{C}}(B)$ consisting of the least elementary weights in B according to the partial order defined by the constraints in $\mathcal{C}$.
- Then by deleting the dominated sets W in the resulting family in the sense that $\mathcal{C} \models \min\{a \in W'\} > \min\{a \in W\}$ for some other set W', using Algorithm 1.

Of course we can apply these simplifications as soon as elements of the labels or useful nogoods are produced.

Example 2 (Continued). Consider again $\Sigma = \{(\neg x \vee y, a), (x, b), (\neg y, c), (\neg x, e)\}$ with $\mathcal{C} = \{a > b, a > c, b > e, c > e\}$. We want to check if $\mathcal{C} \models N^\vdash_\Sigma(y) > N^\vdash_\Sigma(\neg x)$. Note that $Label(y) = \{\{a, b\}\}$ and $\mathcal{U}(y) = \{\{b, e\}\}$. Likewise $Label(\neg x) = \{\{a, c\}, \{e\}\}$, and there is no useful nogood for $\neg x$.

Using $\mathcal{C}$ we can reduce $\{a, b\}$ to $\{b\}$ and $\{b, e\}$ to $\{e\}$ and the necessity degree of y to b, since $b > e \in \mathcal{C}$. Likewise we can reduce $\{a, c\}$ to $\{c\}$ and the necessity degree of $\neg x$ to c since $c > e \in \mathcal{C}$. Now, $b > c \notin \mathcal{C}$, so we cannot conclude $y > \neg x$ (nor the converse).

In general, the deletion of dominated sets of weights can be achieved by means of Algorithm 1 applied to all pairs of reduced sets in $Label(\phi) \cup \mathcal{U}(\phi)$. Finally we can compare the set of non-dominated reduced subsets from $Label(\phi) \cup \mathcal{U}(\phi)$ with the one for $Label(\psi) \cup \mathcal{U}(\psi)$, in order to decide if $\phi > \psi$, using Algorithm 2.

5   Related Works

The question of reasoning with a partially ordered knowledge base encoded in a symbolic possibilisitic logic has been addressed previously in [4]. These authors have proposed to encode symbolic possibilistic pairs in propositional logic like in Sect. 4.2. However there are several differences:

Algorithm 1. $Comp\_Min$

Data: F and G two sets of weights, C a set of constraints.

Result: $\min F > \min G$?

Dec:=false;
while *Dec=false and* $b_i \in G$ **do**
   Dec:=true;
   while *Dec=true and* $a_i \in F$ **do**
      Dec:=Dec $\land$ $a_i > b_i \in C$;
return *Dec;*

Algorithm 2. $Comp\_Max$

Data: $\mathcal{F}$ and $\mathcal{G}$ two families of sets of weights, C a set of constraints

Result:

$\max_{F \in \mathcal{F}} \min F > \max_{G \in \mathcal{G}} \min G$?

Dec:=false;
while *Dec=false and* $E_j \in \mathcal{F}$ **do**
   Dec:=true;
   while *Dec=true and* $E_i \in \mathcal{G}$ **do**
      Dec:=Dec
      $\land$ $Comp\_Min(E_i, E_j, C)$;
return *Dec;*

- A possibilistic formula (ϕ, a) in [4] is encoded as a formula $A \lor \phi$ where A is a variable supposed to mean "$\geq a$", i.e. $[a, 1]$ (while we use $\neg a \lor \phi \in \mathcal{J}_\Sigma$).
- Constraints between weights in [4] are reflexive (not strict), of the form $p \geq q$ with complex max-min weights. It allows them to be encoded also as propositional formulas (for elementary constraints, $\neg A \lor B$ encodes $a \geq b$). It is then possible to express all pieces of information (formulas and weights) about an SPL base in a single propositional base containing only clauses, which makes it natural to use the variable forgetting technique so as to deduce the necessity degree of a formula. We cannot encode strict constraints using a material implication, hence the use of the ATMS approach. We must encode the SPL base in two parts and we thus apply techniques such as MIS, and ATMS notions plus specific algorithms to compare complex weights.
- In [4], $C \vDash p > q$ means $C \vDash p \geq q$ and $C \nvDash q \geq p$ and is somewhat analogous to strict Pareto order between vectors. With this vision, from $\Sigma = \{(\phi, a), (\psi, b)\}$ and $C = \emptyset$ we could infer infer $N_\Sigma(\phi \lor \psi) > N_\Sigma(\phi)$. Indeed, one has $N_\Sigma(\phi) = a, N_\Sigma(\phi \lor \psi) = \max(a, b)$ $C \vDash \max(a, b) \geq a$ but not $C \vDash a \geq \max(a, b)$. This is problematic because it amounts to interpreting strict inequality as the impossibility of proving a weak one, which is non-monotonic. In our method, $p > q$ holds provided that it holds for all instantiations of p, q in accordance with the constraints. Only such strict constraints appear in C.

In the future it should be interesting to handle both strict and loose inequality constraints, since loose constraints between formula weights can be derived in our setting just by means of the weakening inference rule.

6 Conclusion

This paper is another step in the study of inference from a partially ordered propositional base. We present a version of possibilistic logic with partially ordered symbolic weights. It differs from conditional logic frameworks [5] by the use of the minimal specificity principle which is not at work in such logical frameworks. We provide a proof of the soundness and completeness of this logic.

Two syntactic inference methods are defined which allow us to infer new formulas with complex symbolic weights (necessity degrees of formulas): One that requires the enumeration of minimal inconsistent subsets to calculate necessity degrees. The other use results from the ATMS formalism. It enables constraints over weights to be taken into account so as to simplify the comparison of symbolic necessity degrees. This work has potential applications for the revision and the fusion of beliefs, as well as preference modeling [14].

References

1. Dubois, D., Lang, J., Prade, H.: Possibilistic logic. In: Gabbay, D., Hogger, C., Robinson, J., Nute, D. (eds.) Handbook of Logic in Artificial Intelligence and Logic Programming, vol. 3, pp. 439–513. Oxford University Press, Oxford (1994)
2. Dubois, D., Prade, H.: Possibility theory: qualitative and quantitative aspects. In: Smets, P. (ed.) Handbook on Defeasible Reasoning and Uncertainty Management Systems. Quantified Representation of Uncertainty and Imprecision, vol. 1, pp. 169–226. Kluwer Academic Publ., Dordrecht (1998)
3. Dubois, D., Prade, H.: Possibilistic logic - an overview. In: Gabbay, D., Siekmann, J., Woods, J., (eds.): Computational Logic. Handbook of the History of Logic. vol. 9, pp. 283–342. Elsevier (2014)
4. Benferhat, S., Prade, H.: Encoding formulas with partially constrained weights in a possibilistic-like many-sorted propositional logic. In: Kaelbling, L.P., Saffiotti, A., (eds.): IJCAI, pp. 1281–1286 Professional Book Center (2005)
5. Halpern, J.Y.: Defining relative likelihood in partially-ordered preferential structures. J. Artif. Intell. Res. **7**, 1–24 (1997)
6. Benferhat, S., Lagrue, S., Papini, O.: A possibilistic handling of partially ordered information. In: Proceedings 19th Conference on Uncertainty in Artificial Intelligence UAI 2003, pp. 29–36 (2003)
7. Reiter, R.: A theory of diagnosis from first principles. Artif. Intell. **32**, 57–95 (1987)
8. Dubois, D., Fargier, H., Prade, H.: Ordinal and probabilistic representations of acceptance. J. Artif. Intell. Res. (JAIR) **22**, 23–56 (2004)
9. Benferhat, S., Dubois, D., Prade, H.: Nonmonotonic reasoning, conditional objects and possibility theory. Artif. Intell. **92**, 259–276 (1997)
10. McAreavey, K., Liu, W., Miller, P.: Computational approaches to finding and measuring inconsistency in arbitrary knowledge bases. IJAR **55**, 1659–1693 (2014)
11. Liffiton, M.H., Sakallah, K.A.: On finding all minimally unsatisfiable subformulas. In: Bacchus, F., Walsh, T. (eds.) SAT 2005. LNCS, vol. 3569, pp. 173–186. Springer, Heidelberg (2005)
12. De Kleer, J.: An assumption-based tms. Artif. Intell. **28**, 127–162 (1986)
13. De Kleer, J.: A general labeling algorithm for assumption-based truth maintenance. AAAI **88**, 188–192 (1988)
14. Dubois, D., Prade, H., Touazi, F.: Conditional Preference Nets and Possibilistic Logic. In: van der Gaag, L.C. (ed.) ECSQARU 2013. LNCS, vol. 7958, pp. 181–193. Springer, Heidelberg (2013)

Probabilistic Common Knowledge Among Infinite Number of Agents

Siniša Tomović[1], Zoran Ognjanović[1], and Dragan Doder[2]([✉])

[1] Mathematical Institute of Serbian Academy of Sciences and Arts,
Kneza Mihaila 36, 11000 Belgrade, Serbia
{sinisatom,zorano}@turing.mi.sanu.ac.rs
[2] Computer Science and Communications Research Unit,
University of Luxembourg, Luxembourg, Luxembourg
dragan.doder@uni.lu

Abstract. We introduce an epistemic logic with probabilistic common knowledge and infinitely many agents, and provide its strong completeness for the class of measurable structures.

Keywords: Probabilistic epistemic logic · Strong completeness · Probabilistic common knowledge · Infinite number of agents

1 Introduction

Reasoning about knowledge, as well as reasoning about probability, are widely used in many applied fields such as computer science, artificial intelligence, economics, game theory etc. [4,6]. Notion of common knowledge has been shown as crucial for a variety of applications dealing with reaching agreements or coordinated action [4,9]. Infinite sets of agents can be convenient for modelling situations where the group of agents and its upper limit are not known apriori. Economies, when regarded as teams in a game, are often modeled as having infinite number of agents [7]. The main purpose of this paper is to prove strong completeness of the probabilistic common knowledge in a setting with possibly infinitely many agents.

We use the classical model for reasoning about knowledge based on the sematics of possible worlds, i.e. we say that an agent knows a fact φ, denoted by $K_i\varphi$, if that fact is true in all the worlds (or states) he considers possible. Group knowledge where all members of a group G know φ is denoted by $E_G\varphi$. Common knowledge $C_G\varphi$ informally means that everyone in group G knows φ, and everyone in G knows that everyone in G knows φ etc [8].

In many applied areas, it is often the case that reasoning about knowledge should be combined with reasoning about probabilities, which includes sentences like "according to agent i the probability of φ is at least 0.2", denoted by $P_{i,\geq 0.2}\varphi$ or "agent i knows that probability of φ is at least 0.5", $K_i(P_{i,\geq 0.5}\varphi)$. These situations occur for example in analysis of probabilistic programs and their behavior

© Springer International Publishing Switzerland 2015
S. Destercke and T. Denoeux (Eds.): ECSQARU 2015, LNAI 9161, pp. 496–505, 2015.
DOI: 10.1007/978-3-319-20807-7_45

in the context of distributed systems [3]. In game theory and economics, multi-agent framework typically incorporates assumptions about probability [8]. Since common knowledge in formal sense is not attainable in many practical systems, its close forms are being investigated, and probabilistic common knowledge $C_G^r \varphi$ is one of them [3,8,10].

Related work. Here we review some of the literature that is relevant for this paper, and compare the results with ours.

In the paper [5] Fagin et al. provide weakly complete axiomatization for a probability logic which includes linear inequalities involving probabilities e.g. expressions of the form: $a_1 p(\varphi_1) + \ldots + a_k p(\varphi_k) \geq b$, where $a_1, \ldots, a_k, b \in \mathbb{Q}$, $k \geq 1$. Our logic doesn't allow such linear expressions. Instead we use only unary operators for statements about probability as in [21], in order to gain simpler axiomatization for the purposes of this paper. With some straightforward changes, our language and results can be extended to include the more general polynomial weight formulas (see [23]).

In [3] Fagin and Halpern present a joint frame for reasoning about knowledge and probability, and prove weak completeness for a logic which combines expressions about knowledge with above mentioned linear probabilistic inequalities. In this setting, each agent in each state determines a probability space, and we use that approach in our paper. They also define probabilistic common knowledge and propose the corresponding axioms and rules. In this paper, we prove strong completeness for this notion of probabilistic common knowledge.

A strongly complete axiomatization of common knowledge which doesn't include reasoning about probabilities was proved in [16] by de Lavalette, Kooi and Verbrugge. The authors introduce an infinitary rule for obtaining common knowledge. The iterative property of this rule is convenient for proofs of the deduction theorem and strong necessitation.

We point out that the above mentioned epistemic logics do not support infinite group of agents. In [7], a weakly complete axiomatization for common knowledge with infinite number of agents (in non-probabilistic setting), is presented. In all the papers, knowledge $E_G \varphi$ of a finite group G is represented as a conjunction of knowledge of its members. In our axiomatization, the conjunction is replaced with an infinitary rule in the case of infinite number of agents.

From the technical point of view, we modify some of our earlier developed methods presented in [1,13–15,17,18,20–22].

2 Syntax and Sematics

In this paper, we consider a propositional modal logic with probabilistic common knowledge for a (possibly infinite) set of agents, denoted by PML_∞^{CP}.

Syntax. Let $[0,1]_\mathbb{Q}$ be the set of all rational numbers from the real interval $[0,1]$, $\mathbb{N}$ the set of positive integers, Ψ a denumerable set of primitive propositions, $\mathcal{A}$ an at most countable set of agents, and $\mathcal{G}$ a countable set of nonempty subsets of $\mathcal{A}$. We define our language $L_\mathcal{G}^{CP}$ as the least set L containing Ψ such that if

$\varphi, \psi \in L$ then $\neg\varphi$, $\varphi\wedge\psi$, $K_i\varphi$, $E_G\varphi$, $C_G\varphi$, $E_G^r\varphi$, $C_G^r\varphi$, $P_{i,\geq r}\varphi \in L$, where $i \in \mathcal{A}$, $G \in \mathcal{G}$, $r \in [0,1]_{\mathbb{Q}}$.

We use negation and conjunction ($\neg$ and $\wedge$) as the primitive connectives and we define other Boolean connectives ($\rightarrow$, $\vee$, $\equiv$) as abbreviations, in a usual way. Symbols $\bot$ and $\top$ abbreviate formulas $\varphi\wedge\neg\varphi$ and $\varphi\vee\neg\varphi$, respectively.

$K_i^r\varphi$ is an abbreviation for $K_i(P_{i,\geq r}\varphi)$. We define $(E_G)^1\varphi = E_G\varphi$, and $(E_G)^{k+1}\varphi = E_G((E_G)^k\varphi)$, $k \in \mathbb{N}$. Also $(F_G^r)^0\varphi = \top$, $(F_G^r)^{k+1}\varphi = E_G^r(\varphi \wedge (F_G^r)^k\varphi)$, $k \in \mathbb{N}$. We also introduce other probabilistic operators: $P_{i,<r}\varphi$ is $\neg P_{i,\geq r}\varphi$, $P_{i,\leq r}\varphi$ is $P_{i,\geq 1-r}\neg\varphi$, $P_{i,>r}\varphi$ is $\neg P_{i,\leq r}\varphi$ and $P_{i,=r}\varphi$ is $P_{i,\leq r}\varphi \wedge P_{i,\geq r}\varphi$.

For example, a formula $E_G(K_i^r\varphi \wedge \neg C_G\psi)$ says that everyone in a group G knows that agent i knows that the probability of φ is greater than or equal to r, and that ψ is not common knowledge in G.

We define $\Phi_{i,k}(\tau, (\theta_j)_{j<\omega})$ as a k-nested implication for the knowledge of an agent i and for formula τ based on the sequence of formulas $(\theta_j)_{j<\omega}$ in the following recursive way:

$$\Phi_{i,0}(\tau, (\theta_j)_{j<\omega}) = \theta_0 \rightarrow \tau, \ \Phi_{i,k+1}(\tau, (\theta_j)_{j<\omega}) = \theta_{k+1} \rightarrow K_i\Phi_{i,k}(\tau, (\theta_j)_{j<\omega}).$$

For example, $\Phi_{i,3}(\tau, (\theta_j)_{j<\omega}) = \theta_3 \rightarrow K_i(\theta_2 \rightarrow K_i(\theta_1 \rightarrow K_i(\theta_0 \rightarrow \tau)))$. This definition follows the form of probabilistic k-nested implication presented in [18]. The form is suitable for proving Deduction theorem and Strong necessitation theorem.

Semantics. The logic PML_∞^{CP} uses possible world semantics – it is based on Kripke structures and extended with probability spaces.

A *Kripke structure M for knowledge and probability* over a group $\mathcal{A}$ of agents and set Ψ is defined as a tuple $(S, \pi, \mathcal{K}, \mathcal{P})$, where:

- S is a nonempty set of *states* or *possible worlds*
- π associates with each state in S a truth assignment to the primitive propositions in Ψ, i.e. $\pi(s) : \Psi \rightarrow \{\mathbf{true}, \mathbf{false}\}$,
- $\mathcal{K} = \{\mathcal{K}_i \mid i \in \mathcal{A}\}$ is a set of binary relations on S, called *possibility relations*. We define $\mathcal{K}_i(s) = \{t \in s \mid (s,t) \in \mathcal{K}_i\}$.
- $\mathcal{P}$ is a probability assignment which assigns to each agent $i \in \mathcal{A}$ and state $s \in S$ a finitely-additive probability space $\mathcal{P}(i,s) = (S_{i,s}, \chi_{i,s}, \mu_{i,s})$, where $S_{i,s} \subseteq S$, $\chi_{i,s}$ is an algebra of subsets of $S_{i,s}$, and $\mu_{i,s}$ is a finitely-additive probability measure on $\chi_{i,s}$.

Now we introduce a binary satisfiability relation $\models_M$ for a Kripke structure M between a state s in M and formula φ, where $s \models_M \varphi$ is read as either "φ *is true at s*", "*s satisfies φ*" or "φ *holds at s*". When M is clear from the context, we will write $s \models \varphi$ instead of $s \models_M \varphi$.

1. $s \models p$, for $p \in \Psi$ iff $\pi(s)(p) = \mathbf{true}$
2. $s \models \varphi\wedge\phi$ iff $s \models \varphi$ and $s \models \phi$
3. $s \models \neg\varphi$ iff not $s \models \varphi$
4. $s \models K_i\varphi$ iff $t \models \varphi$ for all $t \in \mathcal{K}_i(s)$

5. $s \models E_G\varphi$ iff $s \models K_i\varphi$ for all $i \in G$
6. $s \models C_G\varphi$ iff $s \models (E_G)^k\varphi$ for every $k \in \mathbb{N}$
7. $s \models P_{i,\geq b}\varphi$ iff $\mu_{i,s}(\{s \in S_{i,s} \mid s \models \varphi\}) \geq b$
8. $s \models E_G^r\varphi$ iff $s \models K_i^r\varphi$ for all $i \in G$
9. $s \models C_G^r\varphi$ iff $s \models (F_G^r)^k\varphi$ for every $k \in \mathbb{N}$

Note that the possible problem with the definition of $\models$ is that $\{s \in S_{i,s} \mid s \models \varphi\}$ is not necessarily in $\chi_{i,s}$. If $\{s \in S_{i,s} \mid s \models \varphi\} \in \chi_{i,s}$ for all $i \in A$, $s \in S$ and $\varphi \in L_g(\Psi)^{CP}$, we say that M is a *measurable structure*. The class of all measurable Kripke structures is denoted by $\mathcal{M}_A^{MEAS}$.

Given a measurable structure $M = (S, \pi, \mathcal{K}, \mathcal{P})$, we say that φ is *valid in M*, noted as $M \models \varphi$, if $s \models \varphi$ for every state $s \in S$; we say that φ is *satisfiable in M* if $s \models \varphi$ for some state $s \in S$. A formula φ is *valid in a class* $\mathbb{M}$ *of structures* in notation $\mathbb{M} \models \varphi$ if φ is valid in all structures in $\mathbb{M}$. Similarly, φ is *satisfiable in a class of structures* $\mathbb{M}$ if φ is satisfiable in some structure in $\mathbb{M}$. A *set T of formulas is satisfiable* if there is a state s in some structure $M \in \mathcal{A}$ such that $s \models_M \varphi$ for every $\varphi \in T$.

Notice that the logic presented above is not compact, i.e. there exist infinite unsatisfiable sets of formulas such that all of their finite subsets are satisfiable. Examples of these sets are: $\{(E_G)^k\varphi \mid k \geq 1\} \cup \{\neg C_G\varphi\}$ or $\{P_{i,\geq 1-\frac{1}{k}}\varphi \wedge P_{i,\leq 1-\frac{1}{k}}\varphi \mid k \geq 1\} \cup \{\neg P_{i,\neq 1}\varphi\}$. As a consequence, there arises a problem of finding the corresponding axiomatization which is strongly complete (every consistent set of formulas has a model), since it cannot be finitary [12]. One of the approaches for solving this issue, which we follow here, is to introduce inference rules with countably many premises [16, 21], so the object language is countable, and formulas are finite, but proofs are allowed to be infinite.

3   The Axiomatization of PML_∞^{CP}

The axiomatic system Ax_∞^{MEAS} for PML_G^C contains the following axiom schemata and rules of inference:

I Axioms and rule for propositional reasoning
   Prop. All instances of tautologies of the propositional calculus
   MP. $\dfrac{\varphi, \varphi \to \psi}{\psi}$ (Modus Ponens)

II Axioms and rules for reasoning about knowledge
   AK. $(K_i\varphi \wedge K_i(\varphi \to \psi)) \to K_i\psi$, $i \in G$ (Distribution Axiom)
   RK. $\dfrac{\varphi}{K_i\varphi}$ (Knowledge Generalization)
   AE. $E_G\varphi \to K_i\varphi$, $i \in G$
   RE. $\dfrac{\{\Phi_{i,k}(K_i\varphi, (\theta_j)_{j<\omega}) \mid i \in G\}}{\Phi_{i,k}(E_G\varphi, (\theta_j)_{j<\omega})}$
   AC. $C_G\varphi \to E_G(\varphi \wedge C_G\varphi)$
   RC. $\dfrac{\{\Phi_{i,k}((E_G)^m\varphi, (\theta_j)_{j<\omega}) \mid \text{ for all } m \in \mathbb{N}\}}{\Phi_{i,k}(C_G\varphi, (\theta_j)_{j<\omega})}$

III Axioms and rule for reasoning about probabilities

P1. $P_{i,\geq 0}\varphi$

P2. $P_{i,\leq r}\varphi \rightarrow P_{i,<t}\varphi$, $t > r$

P3. $P_{i,<t}\varphi \rightarrow P_{i,\leq t}\varphi$

P4. $(P_{i,\geq r}\varphi \wedge P_{i,\geq t}\psi \wedge P_{i,\geq 1}\neg(\varphi \wedge \psi)) \rightarrow P_{i,\geq min(1,r+t)}(\varphi \vee \psi)$

P5. $(P_{i,\leq r}\varphi \wedge P_{i,<t}\varphi) \rightarrow P_{i,<r+t}(\varphi \vee \psi)$, $r + t \leq 1$

RP. $\dfrac{\varphi}{P_{i,\geq 1}\varphi}$ (Probabilistic Necessitation)

RA. $\dfrac{\{\Phi_{i,k}(P_{i,\geq s-\frac{1}{m}}\varphi, (\theta_j)_{j<\omega}) \mid \text{ for every } m \in \mathbb{N},\ m \geq \frac{1}{s} \text{ and } s > 0 \}}{\Phi_{i,k}(P_{i,\geq s}\varphi, (\theta_j)_{j<\omega}))}$

(Archimedean rule)

IV Axioms and rules for reasoning about probabilistic knowledge

APE. $E_G^r\varphi \rightarrow K_i^r\varphi$, $i \in G$

RPE. $\dfrac{\{\Phi_{i,k}(K_i^r\varphi, (\theta_j)_{j<\omega}) \mid i \in G\}}{\Phi_{i,k}(E_G^r\varphi, (\theta_j)_{j<\omega}))}$

APC. $C_G^r\varphi \rightarrow E_G^r(\varphi \wedge C_G^r\varphi)$

RPC. $\dfrac{\{\Phi_{i,k}((F_G^r)^m\varphi, (\theta_j)_{j<\omega}) \mid \text{ for all } m \geq 0\}}{\Phi_{i,k}(C_G^r\varphi, (\theta_j)_{j<\omega}))}$

Let us now discuss the given axioms and rules. They are divided in four sections according to the type of reasoning. The first part concerns the usual propositional reasoning. In the second part, axiom AK and rule RK are known from modal logics. Axiom AE and RE are used to obtain group knowledge, while AC and RC for common knowledge. Third part introduces probabilistic axioms and rules as in [21]. In the last part, axiom APC is as in [3], while other axiom and rules are by our definition.

$\varphi \in L_G^{CP}$ is a *theorem*, which we denote by $\vdash \varphi$ if there exists a countable sequence of formulas $\varphi_0, \varphi_1, \ldots, \varphi$ called the *proof*, such that every member of the sequence is an instance of some axiom schemata or is obtained from the previous formulas using an inference rule. Note that the length of a proof (the number of formulas in the corresponding sequence) is a countable successor ordinal. Thus, every proof has the last formula.

A formula φ is *derivable from* a set of formulas $(T \vdash \varphi)$ if there is an at most denumerable sequence of formulas $\varphi_0, \varphi_1, \ldots, \varphi$ called *the proof* such that each φ_i is an instance of some axiom schemata or a formula from the set T, or it is obtained from the preceding formulas by an inference rule, with the exception that the inference rules RK and RP can be applied to theorems only.

A set T of formulas is *inconsistent* if $T \vdash \varphi$ for every formula φ, otherwise it is *consistent*. Equivalently, T is inconsistent iff $T \vdash \bot$. A set of formula is maximal if for every formula φ either $\varphi \in T$ or $\neg\varphi \in T$.

Some parts of the following results can be proved in analogous way as in [11, 18, 21]. We point out main differences and results characteristic for our logic.

Theorem 1 (Soundness). *The axiomatic schemata* Ax_∞^{MEAS} *is sound with respect to the* $\mathcal{M}_\mathcal{A}^{MEAS}$ *class of measurable Kripke structures over* $\mathcal{A}$.

Proof. We show that rule RPC produces a valid formula from a set of valid premises by induction on k. The soundness for the rest of the infinitary rules is proved analogously. Suppose $s \models_M \Phi_{i,k}((F_G^r)^m\varphi, (\theta_j)_{j<\omega})$, for all $m \in \mathbb{N}$, $M \in \mathcal{M}_A^{MEAS}$. Then also $s \models_M \Phi_{i,k}(C_G^r\varphi, (\theta_j)_{j<\omega}$, for each state s in M:

Induction base. $k = 0$. Let $s \models \theta_0 \to (F_G^r)^m\varphi$, for all $m \in \mathbb{N}$. Assume that it is not $s \models \theta_0 \to C_G^r\varphi$, i.e. $s \models \theta_0 \wedge \neg C_G^r\varphi$. Then $s \models (F_G^r)^m\varphi$, for all $m \in \mathbb{N}$, and so $s \models C_G^r\varphi$, which is a contradiction.

Inductive step. Let $s \models \Phi_{i,k+1}((F_G^r)^m\varphi, (\theta_j)_{j<\omega})$, for all $m \in \mathbb{N}$, i.e. $s \models \theta_{k+1} \to K_i\Phi_{i,k}((F_G^r)^m\varphi, (\theta_j)_{j<\omega})$, for all $m \in \mathbb{N}$. Assume the opposite, that $s \not\models \Phi_{i,k+1}(C_G^r\varphi, (\theta_j)_{j<\omega})$, i.e. $s \models \theta_{k+1} \wedge \neg K_i\Phi_{i,k}(C_G^r\varphi, (\theta_j)_{j<\omega})$. Then also $s_V \models K_i\Phi_{i,k}((F_G^r)^m\varphi, (\theta_j)_{j<\omega})$, for all $m \in \mathbb{N}$, so for every state $t \in K_i(s)$ we have $t \models \Phi_{i,k}((F_G^r)^m\varphi, (\theta_j)_{j<\omega})$, and by the induction hypothesis $t \models \Phi_{i,k}(C_G^r\varphi, (\theta_j)_{j<\omega})$. Therefore $s \models K_i\Phi_{i,k}(C_G^r\varphi, (\theta_j)_{j<\omega})$, which is a contradiction. $\square$

Theorem 2 (Deduction Theorem). *Let T be a set of formulas in L_G^{CP}, and let φ be a formula. Then $T \cup \{\varphi\} \vdash \psi$ implies $T \vdash \varphi \to \psi$.*

Proof. We use the transfinite induction on the length of the proof of ψ from $T \cup \{\varphi\}$. We consider the case in induction step where ψ was obtained by the inference rule RPC. The proof for the rest of infinitary rules is analogous.

Assume that $T, \varphi \vdash \psi$ where $\psi = \Phi_{i,k}(C_G^r\eta, (\theta_j)_{j<\omega})$.

$T, \varphi \vdash \Phi_{i,k}((F_G^r)^m\eta, (\theta_j)_{j<\omega})$, for all $m \in \mathbb{N}$,
$T \vdash \varphi \to \Phi_{i,k}((F_G^r)^m\eta, (\theta_j)_{j<\omega})$, by the induction hypothesis,
$T \vdash \varphi \to (\theta_k \to K_i\Phi_{i,k-1}((F_G^r)^m\eta, (\theta_j)_{j<\omega}))$, by the definition of $\Phi_{i,k}$
$T \vdash (\varphi \wedge \theta_k) \to K_i\Phi_{i,k-1}((F_G^r)^m\eta, (\theta_j)_{j<\omega})$, by the propositional tautology
$(p \to (q \to r)) \longleftrightarrow ((p \wedge q) \to r)$.

If we denote by $(\overline{\theta}_j)_{j<\omega}$ the sequence which coincides everywhere with $(\theta_j)_{j<\omega}$ for $j \neq k$, with the exception that $\overline{\theta}_k \equiv \varphi \wedge \theta_k$, we get that:

$T \vdash \overline{\theta}_k \to K_i\Phi_{i,k-1}((F_G^r)^m\eta, (\overline{\theta}_j)_{j<\omega})$,
$T \vdash \Phi_{i,k}((F_G^r)^m\eta, (\overline{\theta}_j)_{j<\omega})$, for all $m \in \mathbb{N}$
$T \vdash \Phi_{i,k}(C_G^r\eta, (\overline{\theta}_j)_{j<\omega})$ by application of RPC
$T \vdash (\varphi \wedge \theta_k) \to K_i\Phi_{i,k-1}(C_G^r\eta, (\overline{\theta}_i)_{j<\omega})$
$T \vdash \varphi \to (\theta_k \to K_i\Phi_{i,k-1}(C_G^r\eta, (\theta_j)_{j<\omega}))$
$T \vdash \varphi \to \Phi_{i,k}(C_G^r\eta, (\theta_j)_{j<\omega})$
$T \vdash \varphi \to \psi$. $\square$

Lemma 1. *Let V be a maximal consistent set of formulas.*

1. *$E_G\varphi \in V$ iff ($K_i\varphi \in V$ for all $i \in G$)*
2. *$E_G^r\varphi \in V$ iff ($K_i^r\varphi \in V$ for all $i \in G$)*
3. *$C_G\varphi \in V$ iff ($(E_G)^k\varphi \in V$ for all $k \in \mathbb{N}$)*
4. *$C_G^r\varphi \in V$ iff ($(F_G^r)^k\varphi \in V$ for all $k \in \mathbb{N}$)*

502   S. Tomović et al.

Proof. 1–3. follow directly from the axioms AE, APE and AC, and the rules RE, RPE and RC where we choose $\Phi_{i,0}$ and $\theta_0 = \top$. Using $\vdash P_{i,\geq 1}(\alpha \to \beta) \to (P_{i,\geq r}\alpha \to P_{i,\geq r}\beta)$ (see [21] for the proof), one can show that if $\vdash \alpha \to \beta$ then $\vdash E_G^r\alpha \to E_G^r\beta$. We use that fact to we prove $\vdash C_G^r\varphi \to (F_G^r)^k\varphi$, for all $k \in \mathbb{N}$ (by induction on k). Now 4. follows immediately from the rule RPC and $\vdash C_G^r\varphi \to (F_G^r)^k\varphi$, $k \in \mathbb{N}$. □

4   Completeness

In order to achieve the completeness result, we extend the consistent set of formulas T to a maximal consistent T^*, and prove that T it is satisfiable in the corresponding state s_{T^*} of the canonical structure.

Theorem 3. *Every consistent set of formulas T can be extended to a maximal consistent set T^*.*

Proof. Let $\{\alpha_i \mid i \in \mathbb{N}\}$ be an enumeration of all formulas in $L_{\mathcal{G}}(\Psi)^{CP}$. We define a family $(T_i)_{i\in\mathbb{N}}$ of consistent sets of formulas, and a set T^* in the following way:

1. $T_0 = T$.
2. For every $i \in \mathbb{N}$:
    a. if $T_i \cup \{\alpha_i\}$ is consistent, then $T_{i+1} = T_i \cup \{\alpha_i\}$
    b. if $T_i \cup \{\alpha_i\}$ is inconsistent, and
        b1. $\alpha_i = \Phi_{l,k}(E_G\varphi, (\theta_j)_{j<\omega})$, then $T_{i+1} = T_i \cup \{\neg\alpha_i, \neg\Phi_{l,k}(K_j\varphi, (\theta_j)_{j<\omega})\}$, for some $j \in G$ such that T_{i+1} is consistent
        b2. $\alpha_i = \Phi_{l,k}(C_G\varphi, (\theta_j)_{j<\omega})$, then $T_{i+1} = T_i \cup \{\neg\alpha_i, \neg\Phi_{l,k}(E_G^m\varphi, (\theta_j)_{j<\omega})\}$, for some $m \in \mathbb{N}$ such that T_{i+1} is consistent
        b3. $\alpha_i = \Phi_{l,k}(E_G^r\varphi, (\theta_j)_{j<\omega})$, then $T_{i+1} = T_i \cup \{\neg\alpha_i, \neg\Phi_{l,k}(K_j^r\varphi, (\theta_j)_{j<\omega})\}$, for some $j \in G$ such that T_{i+1} is consistent
        b4. $\alpha_i = \Phi_{l,k}(C_G^r\varphi, (\theta_j)_{j<\omega})$, then $T_{i+1} = T_i \cup \{\neg\alpha_i, \neg\Phi_{l,k}((F_G^r)^m\varphi, (\theta_j)_{j<\omega})\}$, for some $m \in \mathbb{N}$ such that T_{i+1} is consistent
        b5. $\alpha_i = \Phi_{l,k}(P_{i,\geq r}\varphi, (\theta_j)_{j<\omega})$, then $T_{i+1} = T_i \cup \{\neg\alpha_i, \neg\Phi_{l,k}(P_{i,\geq r-\frac{1}{m}}\varphi, (\theta_j)_{j<\omega})\}$, for some $m \in \mathbb{N}$ such that T_{i+1} is consistent
        b6. Otherwise, $T_{i+1} = T_i \cup \{\neg\alpha_i\}$.
3. $T^* = \bigcup_{i=0}^{\infty} T_i$.

The existence of j and m in b1-b5. is a consequence of Deduction theorem and infinitary inference rules. T^* is maximal by its construction. It is straightforward to show that T^* is deductively closed, using the induction on the length of proof. The only problem could arise with infinitary rules. Here we prove that T^* is closed under RPC, and other cases can be considered in a similar way.

Suppose that $T^* \vdash \phi$ is obtained by application of the rule RPC, that is $T^* \vdash \{\Phi_{l,k}((F_G^r)^n\varphi, (\theta_j)_{j<\omega}) \mid n \in \mathbb{N}\}$ and $\phi = \Phi_{l,k}(C_G^r\varphi, (\theta_j)_{j<\omega})$. Then, by induction hypothesis, we have $\Phi_{l,k}((F_G^r)^n\varphi, (\theta_j)_{j<\omega}) \in T^*$ for all $n \in \mathbb{N}$ (1).

Assume that $\Phi_{l,k}(C_G^r\varphi(\theta_j)_{j<\omega}) \notin T^*$; if $\alpha_i = \Phi_{l,k}(C_G^r\varphi, (\theta_j)_{j<\omega})$, then $T_i \cup \{\alpha_i\}$ is inconsistent (otherwise $\Phi_{l,k}(C_G^r\varphi, (\theta_j)_{j<\omega}) = \alpha_i \in T_{i+1} \subset T^*$), so $T_{i+1} = T_i \cup \{\neg\Phi_{l,k}((F_G^r)^m\varphi, (\theta_j)_{j<\omega})\}$ for some m, and therefore $\neg\Phi_{l,k}((F_G^r)^m\varphi, (\theta_j)_{j<\omega}) \in T^*$, which contradicts (1) (because the formula and its negation are members of some consistent set T_j).

If $T^* \vdash \bot$, then $\bot \in T^*$ since T^* is deductively closed. This means that $\bot \in T_i$, for some i, which is impossible. Thus, T^* is consistent. $\square$

For a given set of formulas T, and $i \in \mathcal{A}$ we define the set $K_iT = \{K_i\varphi \mid \varphi \in T\}$.

Theorem 4 (Strong Necessitation). *If T is a set of formulas and $T \vdash \varphi$, then $K_iT \vdash K_i\varphi$ for all $i \in \mathcal{A}$.*

Proof. We use the transfinite induction on the length of proof of $T \vdash \varphi$. Suppose that $T \vdash \varphi$ where $\varphi = \Phi_{i,k}(C_G^r\psi, (\theta_j)_{j<\omega})$ is obtained by rule RPC. Then:

$T \vdash \Phi_{i,k}((F_G^r)^m\psi, (\theta_j)_{j<\omega})$, for all $m \in \mathbb{N}$
$K_iT \vdash K_i\Phi_{i,k}((F_G^r)^m\psi, (\theta_j)_{j<\omega})$, by induction hypothesis
$K_iT \vdash \top \to K_i\Phi_{i,k}((F_G^r)^m\psi, (\theta_j)_{j<\omega})$, for all $m \in \mathbb{N}$
$K_iT \vdash \Phi_{i,k+1}((F_G^r)^m\psi, \overline{(\theta_j)}_{j<\omega})$, where $\overline{(\theta_j)}_{j<\omega}$ is a nested k + 1-sequence such that $\overline{\theta_{k+1}} \equiv \top$, and which coincides everywhere with $(\theta_j)_{j<\omega}$ for $j \neq k+1$.
$K_iT \vdash \Phi_{i,k+1}(C_G^r\psi, \overline{(\theta_j)}_{j<\omega})$, by RPC
$K_iT \vdash \top \to K_i\Phi_{i,k}(C_G^r\psi, \overline{(\theta_j)}_{j<\omega})$
$K_iT \vdash \top \to K_i\varphi$
$K_iT \vdash K_i\varphi$. $\square$

Suppose $\mathcal{P}_{i,V}^\geq(\varphi) = \{r \mid P_{i,\geq r}\varphi \in V\}$. We define a special, so called *canonical* structure $M^* = (S, \pi, \mathcal{K}, \mathcal{P})$, where:

- $S = \{s_V \mid V \text{ is a maximal consistent set in } L_G^{CP}\}$,
- if $p \in \Psi$, then $\pi(s_V)(p) = \textbf{true} \iff p \in V$,
- $\mathcal{K} = \{\mathcal{K}_i \mid i \in G\}$, $\mathcal{K}_i = \{(s_V, s_U) \mid V/K_i \subseteq U\}$, where $V/K_i = \{\varphi \mid K_i\varphi \in V\}$.
- $\mathcal{P}(i,s) = (S_{i,s}, \chi_{i,s}, \mu_{i,s})$, where $S_{i,s} = S$,
- $\chi_{i,s} = \{[\alpha] \mid \alpha \in L_G^{CP}\}$, where $[\alpha] = \{s_V \in S \mid \alpha \in V\}$
- if $[\alpha] \in \chi_{i,s}$ then $\mu_{i,s_V}([\alpha]) = sup\,\mathcal{P}_{i,V}^\geq(\alpha)$.

Lemma 2. *M^* is a measurable Kripke structure for probability and knowledge.*

Theorem 5 (Strong Completeness). *Every consistent set of formulas is satisfiable.*

Proof. We prove that $\psi \in V$ iff $s_V \models_{M^*} \psi$ (*) by induction on complexity of ψ.

- $\psi = K_i\varphi$. Suppose $K_i\varphi \in V$, then $\varphi \in V/K_i$, so $\varphi \in U$ for each U - such that $s_V\mathcal{K}_is_U$ (by the definition of relation $\mathcal{K}_i$), therefore $s_U \models_{M^*} \varphi$ by induction hypothesis (φ is subformula of $K_i\varphi$), and then $s_V \models_{M^*} K_i\varphi$.

  Conversely, let $s_V \models_{M^*} K_i\varphi$ and assume the opposite i.e. that $K_i\varphi \notin V$. Then $V/K_i \cup \{\neg\varphi\}$ is consistent. Otherwise, by Theorem 2 we have $V/K_i \vdash \varphi$, and $V \supset K_i(V/K_i) \vdash K_i\varphi$ by Theorem 4, therefore $K_i\varphi \in V$, which is a contradiction. Thus, $V/K_i \cup \{\neg\varphi\}$ can be extended to a maximal consistent U, so we have $s_V \mathcal{K}_i s_U$. Since $\neg\varphi \in U$, then $s_U \models_{M^*} \neg\varphi$ by induction hypothesis, so $s_V \not\models_{M^*} K_i\varphi$, which is a contradiction.

– Case $\psi = P_{i,\geq r}\varphi$ can be proved as in [21]. The cases when ψ is one of the formulas $E_G\varphi, C_G\varphi, E_G^r\varphi, (F_G^r)^k\varphi, k \in \mathbb{N}, C_G^r\varphi$ are proved using Lemma 1.   □

5   Conclusion

The starting point for our research were the papers [3,7] where weakly complete axiomatizations for a logic combining knowledge and probability, and a non-probabilistic logic for knowledge with infinitely many agents (respectively), are presented. We combine those to approaches obtaining an expressive language, and we provide strongly complete xiomatization for our logic. Since the logic is not compact, we use infinitary rules of inference. We consider the most general semantics, with independent modalities for knowledge and probability. On the other hand, our axiomatization can be straightforwardly extended in different ways, to capture several interesting relationships between the modalities, considered in [3]. For example, if an agent knows a fact to be false, it seams natural to assume he doesn't place a positive probability on that fact, which is semantically represented by the condition: for all i, s, if $\mathcal{P}(i, s) = (S_{i,s}, \chi_{i,s}, \mu_{i,s})$, then $S_{i,s} \subseteq \mathcal{K}_i(s)$ [3]. The corresponding axiom is $K_i\varphi \to P_{i,=1}\varphi$.

A first-order logic extension of the logic PML_∞^{CP} is an idea to consider for further work on this topic. Since the language of such extension extends classical first order language, the set of all valid formulas is not recursively enumerable [2] and no (even weakly) complete finitary axiomatization is possible in this undecidable framework. On the other hand, our completion techniques are already applied to some first order probabilistic logics [17,19,21].

Acknowledgements. This work was supported by the National Research Fund (FNR) of Luxembourg through project PRIMAT, and by the Serbian Ministry of Education and Science through projects ON174026, OI174010 and III44006.

References

1. Doder, D., Ognjanović, Z., Marković, Z.: An axiomatization of a first-order branching time temporal logic. J. Univ. Comput. Sci. **16**(11), 1439–1451 (2010)
2. Jospeh, M.A., Halpern, Y.: Decidability and expressiveness for first-order logics of probability. Inf. Comput. **112**, 1–36 (1994)
3. Fagin, R., Halpern, J.Y.: Reasoning about knowledge and probability. J. ACM **41**(2), 340–367 (1994)
4. Fagin, R., Halpern, J.Y., Moses, Y., Vardi, M.Y.: Reasoning About Knowledge. The MIT Press, Cambridge (1995)
5. Fagin, R., Halpern, J.Y., Megiddo, N.: A logic for reasoning about probabilities. Inf. Comput. **87**(1–2), 78–128 (1990)

6. Geanakoplos, J.: Common knowledge. In: Aumann, R., Hart, S. (eds.) Handbook of Game Theory, vol. 2, pp. 1438–1495. Elsevier (1994)
7. Halpern, J.Y., Shoreb, R.A.: Reasoning about common knowledge with infinitely many agents. Inf. Comput. **191**(1), 1–40 (2004)
8. Halpern, J.Y.: Reasoning about knowledge: a survey. In: Gabbay, D., Hogger, C.J., Robinson, J.A. (eds.) Handbook of Logic in Artificial Intelligence and Logic Programming, pp. 1–34. Oxford University Press, Oxford (1995)
9. Halpern, J.Y., Moses, Y.: Knowledge and common knowledge in a distributed environment. J. ACM **37**(3), 549–587 (1990)
10. Halpern, J.Y., Tuttle, M.R.: Knowledge, probability, and adversaries. In: Proceedings of 8th ACM Symposium on Principles of Distributed Computing, pp. 103–118 (1989)
11. Halpern, J.Y., Moses, Y.: A guide to completeness and complexity for modal logics of knowledge and belief. Artif. Intell. **54**, 319–379 (1992)
12. van der Hoeck, W.: Some consideration on the logics $P_F D$. J. Appl. Non-Classical Log. **7**(3), 287–307 (1997)
13. Ikodinović, N., Ognjanović, Z., Rašković, M., Perović, A.: Hierarchies of probabilistic logics. Int. J. Approximate Reasoning **55**(9), 1830–1842 (2014)
14. Ilić-Stepić, A., Ognjanović, Z., Ikodinović, N.: Conditional p-adic probability logic. Int. J. Approximate Reasoning **55**(9), 1843–1865 (2014)
15. Stepić, A.I., Ognjanović, Z.: Complex valued probability logics. Publications de l'Institut Mathematique, N.s. tome **95**(109), 73–86 (2014)
16. de Lavalette, G.R., Kooi, B.P., Verbrugge, R.: Strong completeness for propositional dynamic logic. In: Balbiani, R., Suzuki, N.-Y., Wolter, F. (eds.) AiML2002 Advances in Modal Logic, pp. 377–393. Institut de Recherche en Informatique de Toulouse IRIT (2002)
17. Milošević, M., Ognjanović, Z.: A first-order conditional probability logic. Log. J. IGPL **20**(1), 235–253 (2012)
18. Milošević, M., Ognjanović, Z.: A first-order conditional probability logic with iterations. Publications de L'Institute Matematique, n.s. **93**(107), 19–27 (2013)
19. Ognjanović, Z., Perović, A., Doder, D.: A first-order dynamic probability logic. In: van der Gaag, L.C. (ed.) ECSQARU 2013. LNCS, vol. 7958, pp. 461–472. Springer, Heidelberg (2013)
20. Ognjanović, Z., Marković, Z., Rašković, M., Doder, D., Perović, A.: A probabilistic temporal logic that can model reasoning about evidence. Ann. Math. Artif. Intell. **65**(2–3), 217–243 (2012)
21. Ognjanović, Z., Rašković, M.: Some first order probability logics. Theoret. Comput. Sci. **247**, 191–212 (2000)
22. Ognjanović, Z., Rašković, M.: Some probability logics with new types of probability operators. J. Log. Comput. **9**(2), 181–195 (1999)
23. Perović, A., Ognjanović, Z., Rašković, M., Marković, Z.: A probabilistic logic with polynomial weight formulas. In: Hartmann, S., Kern-Isberner, G. (eds.) FoIKS 2008. LNCS, vol. 4932, pp. 239–252. Springer, Heidelberg (2008)

Towards Lifted Inference Under Maximum Entropy for Probabilistic Relational FO-PCL Knowledge Bases

Christoph Beierle[✉], Nico Potyka, Josef Baudisch, and Marc Finthammer

Department of Computer Science, University of Hagen,
58084 Hagen, Germany
beierle@fernuni-hagen.de

Abstract. A knowledge base in the logic FO-PCL is a set of relational probabilistic conditionals. The models of such a knowledge base are probability distributions over possible worlds, and the principle of Maximum Entropy (ME) selects the unique model having maximum entropy. While previous work on FO-PCL focused on ME model computation, in this paper we propose two possible approaches towards lifted inference based on independent rule sets.

1 Introduction

The logic FO-PCL [6] allows uncertain reasoning with probabilistic relational conditionals and is thus in the line of combining logic with probabilities (e.g. [4,8,13]). To select a best model among all probability distributions that satisfy an FO-PCL knowledge base $\mathcal{R}$, the principle of Maxmimum Entyropy (ME) [11,12,14] is employed.

Previous work on FO-PCL [2,5,6] focused on the computation of the ME model $p_{\mathcal{R}}^*$ of $\mathcal{R}$. FO-PCL inference under maximum entropy determines the probability of a query q under $p_{\mathcal{R}}^*$. While this can be done in a straightforward, but possibly quite inefficient way having the ME model $p_{\mathcal{R}}^*$ at hand, in this paper we will elaborate on approaches to lifted inference (cf. [15,16]) for FO-PCL. In particular, as new results, we will present a method that is based on maximal independent rule sets (Sect. 3) and an approach for answering queries that are independent of the size of the universe under consideration (Sect. 4). In Sect. 2, we briefly recall the basics of FO-PCL as required here, and in Sect. 5, we conclude and point out future work.

2 Background: FO-PCL and Parametric Uniformity

FO-PCL Syntax. FO-PCL uses function-free signatures of the form $\Sigma = (S, D, Pred)$ where S is a set of sorts, $D = \bigcup_{s \in S} D^{(s)}$ is a finite set of (disjoint) sets of sorted constant symbols, and $Pred$ is a set of sorted predicate symbols. Variables $\mathcal{V}$ also have a unique sort, and all formulas and variable substitutions

© Springer International Publishing Switzerland 2015
S. Destercke and T. Denoeux (Eds.): ECSQARU 2015, LNAI 9161, pp. 506–516, 2015.
DOI: 10.1007/978-3-319-20807-7_46

must obey the obvious sort restrictions. In the following, we will adopt the unique names assumption, i. e. different constants denote different elements.

An FO-PCL *conditional* $R = \langle (\phi_R | \psi_R)[\xi_R], C_R \rangle$ is composed of a *premise* ψ_R and a *conclusion* ϕ_R, which are quantifier and function free first-order formulas (over Σ and $\mathcal{V}$) without equality, a probability value $\xi_R \in [0, 1]$, and a *constraint formula* C_R which is a quantifier-free first-order formula using only the equality predicate. For $\neg(V = X)$ we also write $(V \neq X)$, and $\top$ resp. $\bot$ denote a tautology resp. a contradiction. An *FO-PCL knowledge base* is a pair $(\Sigma, \mathcal{R})$ where $\mathcal{R}$ is a set of conditionals over $\Sigma, \mathcal{V}$.

Example 1 (Misanthrope). The knowledge base $\mathcal{R}_{MI} = \{R_1, R_2\}$, adapted from [6], models friendship relations within a group of people, with one exceptional member, a misanthrope. In general, if a person V likes another person U, then it is very likely that U likes V, too. But there is one person, the misanthrope, who generally does not like other people: $R_1 : \langle (likes(U, V) | likes(V, U))[0.9], U \neq V \rangle$,
$$R_2 : \langle (likes(a, V))[0.05], V \neq a \rangle.$$

Please note that given the set of contants $D = \{a, b, c\}$, instantiating the conditionals in $\mathcal{R}$ without considering their constraint formulas would yield the contradictory conditional $\langle (likes(a, a) | likes(a, a))[0.9]$.

When the constraint formula of a ground instance of R evaluates to *true*, that instance is called *admissible*, and $gnd(R)$ denotes the set of all admissible instances of R (over Σ), in the following also just called instances.

FO-PCL Models. The Herbrand base $\mathcal{H}(\mathcal{R})$ is the set of all atoms in all $gnd(R_k)$ with $R_k \in \mathcal{R}$, and every subset $x \subseteq \mathcal{H}(\mathcal{R})$ is a Herbrand interpretation, also called *world*, defining a logical semantics for $\mathcal{R}$. The set $X(\mathcal{R}) = \{x \mid x \subseteq \mathcal{H}(\mathcal{R})\}$ denotes the set of all Herbrand interpretations. The probabilistic semantics of $\mathcal{R}$ is a possible world semantics [9]. An FO-PCL *interpretation* p of $\mathcal{R}$ is thus a probability distribution over $X(\mathcal{R})$. For performing lifted inference, it will be useful to regard $\mathcal{H}(\mathcal{R})$ as a tuple of binary random variables $\mathcal{X} = (X_1, \ldots, X_n)$ and p as a joint distribution $p(X_1, \ldots, X_n)$. A world $x \in X(\mathcal{R})$ will then be regarded as a variable assignment $(X_1 = x_1, \ldots, X_n = x_n)$, where, for $1 \leqslant i \leqslant n$, $x_i = 1$ if $X_i \in x$ and 0 otherwise. The notation $p(x)$ can then be regarded as a shorthand for $p(X_1 = x_1, \ldots, X_n = x_n)$. If $\mathcal{H}(\mathcal{R}) = \mathcal{Y}_1 \cup \mathcal{Y}_2$ and y_i is a variable assignment for $\mathcal{Y}_i$, we let $(\mathcal{Y}_1 = y_1, \mathcal{Y}_2 = y_2)$ denote the variable assignment for $\mathcal{H}(\mathcal{R})$ that assigns y_i to the variables in $\mathcal{Y}_i$. Correspondingly, the expressions $p(\mathcal{Y}_1, \mathcal{Y}_2)$ and $p(y_1, y_2)$ correspond to $p(\mathcal{X})$ and $p(\mathcal{Y}_1 = y_1, \mathcal{Y}_2 = y_2)$, respectively.

For $R_k \in \mathcal{R}$ and every $g_{R_k} \in gnd(R_k)$, let θ_{R_k} be an admissible ground substitution for the variables in R_k so that $g_{R_k} = \langle (\theta_{g_{R_k}}(\phi_{R_k}) \mid \theta_{g_{R_k}}(\psi_{R_k}))[\xi_{R_k}], \top \rangle$. Then $p_{X(\mathcal{R})}$ satisfies R_k iff for every instance $g_{R_k} \in gnd(R_k)$ we have:

$$p_{X(\mathcal{R})}(\theta_{R_k}(\phi_{R_k}) \wedge \theta_{R_k}(\psi_{R_k})) = \xi_{R_k} \cdot p_{X(\mathcal{R})}(\theta_{R_k}(\psi_{R_k})).$$

Note that for the case of $p_{X(\mathcal{R})}(\theta_{R_k}(\psi_{R_k})) > 0$, this equation is equivalent to $\frac{p_{X(\mathcal{R})}(\theta_{R_k}(\phi_{R_k}) \wedge \theta_{R_k}(\psi_{R_k}))}{p_{X(\mathcal{R})}(\theta_{R_k}(\psi_{R_k}))} = \xi_{R_k}$ and thus to $p_{X(\mathcal{R})}((\theta_{g_{R_k}}(\phi_{R_k}) \mid \theta_{g_{R_k}}(\psi_{R_k}))) =$

ξ_{R_k}, expressing conditional probability. A distribution $p_{X(\mathcal{R})}$ is a *model* of $\mathcal{R}$, denoted by $p_{X(\mathcal{R})} \models \mathcal{R}$, if it satisfies every $R_k \in \mathcal{R}$.

Maximum Entropy Model and Parametric Uniformity. A knowledge base $\mathcal{R} = \{R_1, \ldots, R_m\}$ may have many different models, and the principle of maximum entropy [11,12,14] provides a method to select a model that is optimal in the sense that it is the most unbiased one. The uniquely determined model of $\mathcal{R}$

$$p^*_{X(\mathcal{R})} = \arg \max_{p_{X(\mathcal{R})} \models \mathcal{R}} H(p_{X(\mathcal{R})}) \tag{1}$$

having maximum entropy $H(p^*_{X(\mathcal{R})})$ can be represented by a Gibbs distribution [7]:

$$p^*_{X(\mathcal{R})}(x) = \frac{1}{Z} \exp \left(\sum_{k=1}^{m} \sum_{g_{R_k} \in gnd(R_k)} \lambda_{g_{R_k}} f_{g_{R_k}}(x) \right) \tag{2}$$

where

$$f_{g_{R_k}}(x) = \begin{cases} 1, & \text{if } x \models \psi_{R_k}\phi_{R_k} \\ 0, & \text{if } x \models \psi_{R_k}\overline{\phi_{R_k}} \\ \xi_{R_k}, & \text{if } x \models \overline{\psi_{R_k}}. \end{cases} \tag{3}$$

is the feature function determined by g_{R_k}, $\lambda_{g_{R_k}}$ is a Lagrange multiplier [3] and Z is a normalization constant (see [6] for details). Note that according to Eq. (2), one optimization parameter $\lambda_{g_{R_k}}$ has to be determined for *each single ground instance* g_{R_k} of each conditional R_k. However, if $\mathcal{R}$ is parametrically uniform [6], it suffices to compute a single λ_{R_k} per conditional R_k :

$$p^*_{X(\mathcal{R})}(x) = \frac{1}{Z} \exp \left(\sum_{k=1}^{m} \lambda_{R_k} \sum_{g_{R_k} \in gnd(R_k)} f_{g_{R_k}}(x) \right) \tag{4}$$

By applying the set of transformations rules $\mathcal{PU}$ given in [2], each FO-PCL knowledge base $\mathcal{R}$ can be transformed into a parametrically uniform knowledge base that has the same ME model, see [2, Proposition 13].

Example 2 ($\mathcal{PU}(\mathcal{R}_{MI})$). When applying $\mathcal{PU}$ to $\mathcal{R}_{MI}$ (Example 1), in the first step, R_1 is replaced by the two conditionals $R_{1\cdot1}$: $\langle (likes(U, a)|likes(a, U)))[0.9], U \neq a \rangle$ and $R_{1\cdot2}$: $\langle (likes(U, V)|likes(V, U)))[0.9], U \neq V, V \neq a \rangle$. In the second step, $R_{1\cdot2}$ is replaced by the two conditionals $R_{1\cdot2\cdot1}$ and $R_{1\cdot2\cdot2}$, resulting in $\mathcal{PU}(\mathcal{R}_{MI})$ with:

$$R_{1\cdot1}: \langle (likes(U, a)|likes(a, U)))[0.9], U \neq a \rangle$$
$$R_{1\cdot2\cdot1}: \langle (likes(a, V)|likes(V, a)))[0.9], V \neq a \rangle$$
$$R_{1\cdot2\cdot2}: \langle (likes(U, V)|likes(V, U)))[0.9], U \neq V, V \neq a, U \neq a \rangle$$
$$R_2: \langle (likes(a, V)|\top)[0.05], V \neq a \rangle$$

3   FO-PCL Inference and Independent Rule Sets

Inference under maximum entropy inductively completes the knowledge given by a knowledge base $\mathcal{R}$ to the full probability distribution having maximum entropy, which will often be denoted by $p_{\mathcal{R}}^*$ in the following. Given a ground query q, ME inference returns the probability ξ such that $p_{\mathcal{R}}^*(q) = \xi$ holds.

Definition 1 (FO-PCL Entailment Relation). *Let $\mathcal{R}$ be a FO-PCL knowledge base, q a ground formula, and $\xi \in [0,1]$. $\mathcal{R}$ entails $q[\xi]$, denoted by $\mathcal{R} \sim^* q[\xi]$, iff $p_{\mathcal{R}}^*(q) = \xi$.*

For performing FO-PCL inference, one can thus distinguish two phases: (1) For given $\mathcal{R}$, determine $p_{\mathcal{R}}^*$, and (2), for a query q determine the probability ξ such that $p_{\mathcal{R}}^*(q) = \xi$ holds. Previous work on FO-PCL has focused on the computation of $p_{\mathcal{R}}^*$, and in [5] it is shown how parametric uniformity of $\mathcal{R}$ can be exploited to simplify the computation of $p_{\mathcal{R}}^*$. Using the following example, we will illustrate that for a given query q, we may not need to compute the full distribution $p_{\mathcal{R}}^*$ for determining $p_{\mathcal{R}}^*(q)$.

Example 3 ($\mathcal{R}_{dog}$). The knowledge base $\mathcal{R}_{dog} = \{R_{dog1}, R_{dog2}\}$ is a clone obtained from $\mathcal{R}_{MI}$ (Example 1) by replacing *person* by *dog*, $\{a, b, c\}$ by $\{e, f, g\}$ and *likes* by *dog_likes*: $R_{dog1} : \langle (dog\_likes(U,V) \mid dog\_likes(V,U))[0.9], U \neq V \rangle,$
$\qquad\qquad\qquad R_{dog2} : \langle (dog\_likes(a,V))[0.05], V \neq a \rangle.$
    Now $\mathcal{PU}(\mathcal{R}_{dog})$ is a corresponding clone of $\mathcal{PU}(\mathcal{R}_{MI})$. Moreover, when taking the union $\mathcal{R}_{MI}$ and $\mathcal{R}_{dog}$ (and the union of the corresponding signatures), we have $\mathcal{PU}(\mathcal{R}_{MI} \cup \mathcal{R}_{dog}) = \mathcal{PU}(\mathcal{R}_{MI}) \cup \mathcal{PU}(\mathcal{R}_{dog})$.

In Example 3, the sets $\mathcal{H}(\mathcal{R}_{MI})$ and $\mathcal{H}(\mathcal{R}_{dog})$ are disjoint. Statements referring to the probability of ground atoms of the person universe are not affected by the conditionals of $\mathcal{R}_{dog}$, and any statement about the probabilty of ground atoms from $\mathcal{H}(\mathcal{R}_{dog})$ is not influenced by rules outside the universe of dogs. In fact, the ME probability for any query q involving only persons is the same for both $\mathcal{R}_{MI}$ and $\mathcal{R}_{MI} \cup \mathcal{R}_{dog}$, i.e.

$$\mathcal{R}_{MI} \sim^* q[\xi] \quad \textit{iff} \quad \mathcal{R}_{MI} \cup \mathcal{R}_{dog} \sim^* q[\xi].$$

The following definitions generalize these observations.

Definition 2 (Independent Rule Sets). *Let $\mathcal{R} = \{R_1, ..., R_m\}$ be an FO-PCL knowledge base. R_i and R_j are directly connected, denoted by $R_i \sim R_j$, iff $\mathcal{H}(R_i) \cap \mathcal{H}(R_j) \neq \emptyset$. R_i and R_j are connected iff $R_i \sim^+ R_j$ holds where $\sim^+$ is the transitive closure of $\sim$. Two rule sets $\mathcal{R}_i, \mathcal{R}_j \subseteq \mathcal{R}$ are called independent rule sets iff for all $R_i \in \mathcal{R}_i$ and all $R_j \in \mathcal{R}_j$, R_i and R_j are not connected, i.e. $R_i \not\sim^+ R_j$.*

Definition 3 (Partition of Independent Rule Sets). *A partition $\mathcal{R}_1, ..., \mathcal{R}_k$ of an FO-PCL knowledge base $\mathcal{R}$ is called partition of independent rule sets iff for all different $i, j \in \{1, ..., k\}$, $\mathcal{R}_i$ and $\mathcal{R}_j$ are independet rule sets. In addition, the partition $\mathcal{R}_1, ..., \mathcal{R}_k$ is called maximal iff there is no other partition of independent rule sets of $\mathcal{R}$ consisting of more than k partition classes.*

If $\mathcal{R}_1, ..., \mathcal{R}_k$ is a maximal partition of independent rule sets for $\mathcal{R}$, then $\mathcal{H}(\mathcal{R}_i) \cap \mathcal{H}(\mathcal{R}_j) = \emptyset$ for any $i \neq j$. To see uniqueness of the maximal partition, consider the undirected graph $G_\mathcal{R}$ having the conditionals in $\mathcal{R}$ as nodes and an edge between nodes R and R' iff $\mathcal{H}(R) \cap \mathcal{H}(R') \neq \emptyset$. The subgraphs of $G_\mathcal{R}$ determined by $\mathcal{R}_1, \ldots, \mathcal{R}_k$ are exactly the connected components in $G_\mathcal{R}$. Since the connected components of a graph are uniquely determined, we get:

Proposition 1. *Every $\mathcal{R}$ has a unique maximal partition of independent rule sets.*

Since the $\mathcal{H}(\mathcal{R}_i)$ contain pairwise disjoint random variables, the knowledge bases $\mathcal{R}_i$ constrain independent languages, and general independence properties of ME distributions [17, page 33] yield:

Proposition 2. *Let $\mathcal{R}_1, ..., \mathcal{R}_k$ be the maximal partition of independent rule sets of $\mathcal{R}$, and let $i \in \{1, \ldots, k\}$. Then for any ground formula q containing only atoms from $\mathcal{H}(\mathcal{R}_i)$ we have $\mathcal{R}_i \vdash^* q[\xi]$ iff $\mathcal{R} \vdash^* q[\xi]$.*

Thus, in situations where the ME distribution that is relevant for a query can be computed with respect to a subset of the full knowledge base, exploiting this fact could significantly simplify ME inference.

Example 4 (Maximal partition of $\mathcal{R}_{MI}$). The maximal partition of $\mathcal{R}_{MI}$ (Example 1) is the trivial partion consisting of just $\mathcal{R}_{MI}$ itself. However, the maximal partition of $\mathcal{PU}(\mathcal{R}_{MI})$ is $\mathcal{R}_{MI(1)}$, $\mathcal{R}_{MI(2)}$ with $\mathcal{R}_{MI(1)} = \{R_{1\cdot1}, R_{1\cdot2\cdot1}, R_2\}$ and $\mathcal{R}_{MI(2)} = \{R_{1\cdot2\cdot2}\}$. Thus, applying $\mathcal{PU}$ to $\mathcal{R}_{MI}$ helps to split up the conditionals; thereby, the Herbrand base $\mathcal{H}(\mathcal{R}_{MI})$ is partitioned into the two subsets $\mathcal{H}(\mathcal{R}_{MI(1)})$ and $\mathcal{H}(\mathcal{R}_{MI(2)})$.

The observations above demonstrate that the $\mathcal{PU}$ transformation process, in addition to simplifying the ME model computation [5] may also enable a more efficient ME inference. This is the case for FO-PCL knowledge bases $\mathcal{R}$ where the maximal partition of independent rule sets of $\mathcal{PU}(\mathcal{R})$ results in a finer partition and where the corresponding Herbrand bases are smaller than those for the maximal partition of $\mathcal{R}$.

4   Answering Queries Independent from the Number of Constants

In the following, we will investigate how ME inference and entailment can be simplified when the number of available constants increases. To this end, we introduce the notion of an extended signature.

Definition 4 (Extended Signature). *Let $\Sigma = (S, D, Pred)$ be a signature. For $s \in S$ and $n \in \mathbb{N}$ let $\Sigma_s(n) = (S, D \cup \{c_1^s, \ldots, c_n^s\}, Pred)$ be the signature obtained from Σ by adding n new constants c_i^s of sort s, that is, $D \cap \{c_1^s, \ldots, c_n^s\} = \emptyset$. $\Sigma_s(n)$ is called the extended signature obtained from Σ by adding n new constants of sort s.*

Example 5 (Extended Signature for $\mathcal{R}_{MI}$). Let $\Sigma^{MI} = (S, D, Pred)$ be the signature with S and $Pred$ as for $\mathcal{R}_{MI}$ (Examples 1 and 3). For $n \in \mathbb{N}$, the signature $\Sigma^{MI}_{person}(n)$ has the set of constants $\{a, b, c, c_1, c_2, \ldots, c_n\}$. With $\mathcal{R}^n_{MI}$ we denote the corresponding knowledge base $\mathcal{R}_{MI}$ over the signature $\Sigma^{MI}_{person}(n)$ having $n + 3$ constants.

Remark 1. Since the transformation system $\mathcal{PU}$ is independent of any constants in D that are not explicitly mentioned in the conditionals of $\mathcal{R}$, we have $\mathcal{PU}(\mathcal{R}_{MI}) = \mathcal{PU}(\mathcal{R}^n_{MI})$ for any n (assuming that there are *enough constants* in the signature in order to avoid degenerated cases [2]). Hence, the maximal partition of $\mathcal{PU}(\mathcal{R}^n_{MI})$ is identical to the maximal partition of $\mathcal{PU}(\mathcal{R}_{MI})$ in Example 4.

One key insight that we are going to employ is that sometimes our ground query q depends only on a fixed number of ground conditionals that does not change if we add new constants to our language. To make this idea more precise, we need some additional definitions. The *dependency closure* of a set of ground atoms contains all ground conditionals on which the ground atoms depend.

Definition 5 (Dependency-Closure). *Let S be a set of ground atoms over a signature Σ and let $\mathcal{R}$ be a knowledge base over Σ. Define a sequence S_i of sets of ground atoms over Σ and a sequence $\mathcal{R}_i$ of sets of ground conditionals from $gnd(\mathcal{R})$ as follows:*

1. $S_1 = S$, $\mathcal{R}_1 = \{R \in gnd(\mathcal{R}) \mid \exists G \in S_1 : G \in \mathcal{H}(R)\}$,
2. $S_{i+1} = \mathcal{H}(\mathcal{R}_i)$, $\mathcal{R}_{i+1} = \{R \in gnd(\mathcal{R}) \mid \exists G \in S_{i+1} : G \in \mathcal{H}(R)\}$ *for $i \geqslant 1$.*

The dependency-closure *of S is defined as* $\mathrm{DepCl}(S) = \bigcup_i \mathcal{R}_i$.

Remark 2. How can we compute $\mathrm{DepCl}(S)$? Note that since there are at most $|\mathcal{H}(\mathcal{R})|$ ground atoms, $S_{i+1} = S_i$ for some $i < |\mathcal{H}(\mathcal{R})|$. If $S_{i+1} = S_i$, then $\mathcal{R}_i = \mathcal{R}_{i+1}$. But then $S_{i+2} = \mathcal{H}(\mathcal{R}_{i+1}) = \mathcal{H}(\mathcal{R}_i) = S_{i+1}$ and therefore $\mathcal{R}_{i+1} = \mathcal{R}_{i+2}$ and so on. Hence, there is an $n < |\mathcal{H}(\mathcal{R})|$ such that $\mathrm{DepCl}(S) = \bigcup_{i=1}^n \mathcal{R}_i = \mathcal{R}_n$. Equality holds because $\mathcal{R}_i \subseteq \mathcal{R}_{i+1}$ by definition. To generate $\mathrm{DepCl}(S)$ start with S_1 and for $i \geqslant 1$, generate $\mathcal{R}_i$ and S_{i+1} until $S_{i+1} = S_i$ or $\mathcal{R}_{i+1} = \mathcal{R}_i$. As explained before, the algorithm stops after at most $|\mathcal{H}(\mathcal{R})|$ iterations.

Example 6. Let $\mathcal{R}^n_{MI}$ be defined like in Example 5. Let us compute $\mathrm{DepCl}(\{likes(b, a)\})$ for $\mathcal{R}^n_{MI}$. For $n = 1$, we have the following steps:

$$S_1 = \{likes(b, a)\},$$
$$\mathcal{R}_1 = \{\langle(likes(a, b)|likes(b, a))[0.9], \top\rangle, \langle(likes(b, a)|likes(a, b))[0.9], \top\rangle\},$$
$$S_2 = \{likes(b, a), likes(a, b)\},$$
$$\mathcal{R}_2 = \mathcal{R}_1 \cup \{\langle(likes(a, b))[0.05], \top\rangle\},$$
$$S_3 = S_2,$$
$$\mathcal{R}_3 = \mathcal{R}_2.$$

Hence, we are done after three iterations. For the knowledge bases $\mathcal{R}^n_{MI}$ with $n > 1$, nothing changes since each ground instance of a conditional that contains a new constant c_i will contain only ground atoms $likes(c_i, const)$ or $likes(const, c_i)$ with $const$ being a constant in $\Sigma^{MI}_{person}(n)$, but neither $likes(b, a)$ nor $likes(a, b)$. Hence, the dependency closure $\text{DepCl}(\{likes(b, a)\}) = \{\langle(likes(a, b)|likes(b, a))[0.9], \top\rangle, \{\langle(likes(b, a)|likes(a, b))[0.9], \top\rangle, \langle(likes(a, b))[0.05], \top\rangle\}$ is independent of n.

Likewise, when computing $\text{DepCl}(\{likes(c_i, c_j)\})$ for $\mathcal{R}^n_{MI}$ with $i, j \leqslant n$, we get $\text{DepCl}(\{likes(c_i, c_j)\}) = \{\langle(likes(c_i, c_j)|likes(c_j, c_i))[0.9], \top\rangle, \langle(likes(c_j, c_i)|likes(c_i, c_j))[0.9], \top\rangle\}$ which does not change for $\mathcal{R}^{n'}_{MI}$ with $n' > n$.

In our running example, the ground atom $likes(b, a)$ depends only on three ground conditionals and $likes(c_i, c_j)$ depends only on two ground conditionals, independently of the number of additional constants in our language. In this sense, the queries $likes(b, a)$ and $likes(c_i, c_j)$ are *closed*. The following definition generalizes this observation. For an atom A, let $A^0 = \neg A$ and $A^1 = A$.

Definition 6 (Dependency-Closed Elementary Ground Query and Dependency Set). *Let $\mathcal{R}$ be a knowledge base over Σ and let $G_1, \ldots, G_k$ be ground atoms from $\mathcal{H}(\mathcal{R})$ over which we want to construct a conjunctive query. Let $\text{DepCl}(\{G_1, \ldots, G_k\})$ be the dependency closure of $\{G_1, \ldots, G_k\}$ with respect to Σ and $\mathcal{R}$. For all sorts $s \in S$ and all numbers $n \in \mathbb{N}$, let $\text{DepCl}^{s,n}\{G_1, \ldots, G_k\}$ denote the dependency closure of $\{G_1, \ldots, G_k\}$ with respect to $\Sigma_s(n)$ and $\mathcal{R}$.*

If for all sorts $s \in S$ and all numbers $n \in \mathbb{N}$, $\text{DepCl}(\{G_1, \ldots, G_k\}) = \text{DepCl}^{s,n}\{G_1, \ldots, G_k\}$ holds, then for all $e_1, \ldots, e_k \in \{0, 1\}$, the conjunction $\bigwedge_{i=1}^{k} G_i^{e_i}$ is called a dependency-closed elementary ground query with respect to Σ and $\mathcal{R}$. The set $\text{DepCl}(\{G_1, \ldots, G_k\})$ is called the dependency set of the query.

Remark 3. In general, $\text{DepCl}(\{G_1, \ldots, G_k\})$ can be large and in the worst-case it can be $gnd(\mathcal{R})$ itself. However, there are interesting special cases where $\text{DepCl}(\{G_1, \ldots, G_k\})$ is guaranteed to be small and easily computable. For instance, this is the case if all G_i are atoms whose corresponding predicate symbols appear only in conditionals that contain only a single variable. Another example of a small dependency closure was given in Example 6:

Example 7. As we saw in Example 6, $likes(b, a)$ is a dependency-closed elementary ground query and $\{\langle(likes(a, b)|likes(b, a))[0.9], \top\rangle, \langle(likes(b, a)|likes(a, b))[0.9], \top\rangle, \langle(likes(a, b))[0.05], \top\rangle\}$ is its dependency set.

To make full use of dependency-closed queries, it is desirable that our knowledge base is also closed in the sense that it is parametrically uniform and the Lagrange multipliers do not change if we increase n.

Definition 7 (Parameter-Closed Knowledge Base). *Let $\mathcal{R} = \{R_1, \ldots, R_m\}$ be a parametrically uniform knowledge base over Σ. For $1 \leqslant i \leqslant m$, let λ_i denote the Lagrange multiplier corresponding to R_i in the ME optimal Gibbs distribution with respect to $\mathcal{R}$ and Σ. Analogously, let for all $s \in S$ and $n \in \mathbb{N}$, $\lambda_i^{s,n}$ denote the corresponding Lagrange multiplier with respect to $\mathcal{R}$ and Σ. $\mathcal{R}$ is called parameter-closed with respect to Σ and $\mathcal{R}$ iff for all $s \in S$ and $n \in \mathbb{N}$, $\lambda_i = \lambda_i^{s,n}$.*

Example 8. $\mathcal{PU}(\mathcal{R}_{MI}^0)$ is indeed parameter-closed. That is, the Lagrange mutlipliers corresponding to ground instances of conditionals in $\mathcal{PU}(\mathcal{R}_{MI}^n)$ do not change as we increase n.

Definition 8 (Factor Corresponding to Ground Conditional). *Let* $\mathcal{R} = \{R_1, \ldots, R_m\}$ *be a knowledge base over* Σ *and let* $\mathcal{X} = \mathcal{H}(\mathcal{R})$. *For each ground conditional* $R \in gnd(\mathcal{R})$, *let*

$$\Phi_R(\mathcal{X}) = \exp(\lambda_R f_R(\mathcal{X})) \qquad (5)$$

where f_R *is the feature function corresponding to* R *and* λ_R *denotes the lagrange parameter corresponding to* R *in the ME-optimal Gibbs distribution with respect to* $\mathcal{R}$ *and* Σ. $\Phi_R(\mathcal{X})$ *is called the* factor corresponding to the ground conditional R *with respect to* $\mathcal{R}$ *and* Σ.

Remark 4. By definition of f_R, $\Phi_R(\mathcal{X})$ does not depend on the complete interpretation of $\mathcal{X}$ but only on the interpretation of $\mathcal{Y}_R = \mathcal{H}(R)$. Therefore, we will just write $\Phi_R(\mathcal{Y}_R)$ when exploting this property.

The following lemma says that all mentioned ME-optimal Gibbs distributions can be decomposed into two factors, where only the first factor depends on the ground atoms that Q depends on independently of s and n. In particular, the first factor itself is independent of s and n.

Lemma 1. *Let* $\mathcal{R}$ *be a parameter-closed knowledge base over* Σ, *let* $\mathcal{X} = \mathcal{H}(\mathcal{R})$, *and let* Q *be a dependency-closed elementary ground query with respect to* Σ *and* $\mathcal{R}$. *Let* $\mathcal{R}_Q$ *denote the dependency set of* Q *and let* $\mathcal{Y}_Q = \mathcal{H}(\mathcal{R}_Q)$. *Define*

$$\Phi_Q(\mathcal{Y}_Q) = \prod_{R \in \mathcal{R}_Q} \Phi_R(\mathcal{Y}_Q). \qquad (6)$$

Let $\mathcal{Y}_{\overline{Q}} = \mathcal{H}(\mathcal{R}) \setminus \mathcal{H}(\mathcal{R}_Q)$ *be the set of remaining ground atoms with respect* Σ *and* $\mathcal{R}$. *Then there is a factor* $\Phi_{\overline{Q}}(\mathcal{Y}_{\overline{Q}})$ *such that for the ME-optimal Gibbs distribution* p *with respect to* $\mathcal{R}$ *and* Σ,

$$p(\mathcal{X}) = \frac{1}{Z} \Phi_Q(\mathcal{Y}_Q) \Phi_{\overline{Q}}(\mathcal{Y}_{\overline{Q}}). \qquad (7)$$

For all $s \in S$ *and* $n \in \mathbb{N}$, *let* $\mathcal{Y}_{\overline{Q}}^{s,n} = \mathcal{H}^{s,n}(\mathcal{R}) \setminus \mathcal{H}(\mathcal{R}_Q)$ *be the set of remaining ground atoms with respect to* $\Sigma_s(n)$ *and* $\mathcal{R}$. *Then for all* $s \in S$ *and* $n \in \mathbb{N}$, *there is a factor* $\Phi_{\overline{Q}}^{s,n}(\mathcal{Y}_{\overline{Q}}^{s,n})$ *such that for the ME-optimal Gibbs distribution* $p^{s,n}$ *with respect to* $\mathcal{R}$ *and* $\Sigma_s(n)$

$$p^{s,n}(\mathcal{X}) = \frac{1}{Z^{s,n}} \Phi_Q(\mathcal{Y}_Q) \Phi_{\overline{Q}}^{s,n}(\mathcal{Y}_{\overline{Q}}^{s,n}). \qquad (8)$$

Proof. Note that $p^{s,0} = p$ for all $s \in S$, therefore it suffices to consider $p^{s,n}$. Each $p^{s,n}$ can be written in the form

$$p^{s,n}(\mathcal{X}) = \frac{1}{Z^{s,n}} \exp\left(\sum_{R \in gnd(\mathcal{R})} \lambda_R f_R(\mathcal{Y}_R)\right) = \frac{1}{Z^{s,n}} \prod_{R \in gnd(\mathcal{R})} \exp\left(\lambda_R f_R(\mathcal{Y}_R)\right)$$

$$= \frac{1}{Z^{s,n}} \prod_{R \in gnd(\mathcal{R})} \Phi_R(\mathcal{Y}_R),$$

where λ_R and f_R denote the lagrange multiplier and the feature function corresponding to the ground conditional R and $\mathcal{Y}_R$ is the set of ground atoms that f_R depends on. Since Q is a dependency-closed elementary ground query, only the feature functions of conditionals in $\mathcal{R}_Q$ depend on $\mathcal{Y}_Q$ independently of s and n. Therefore, each Gibbs distribution can be rewritten as

$$p^{s,n}(\mathcal{X}) = \frac{1}{Z^{s,n}} \prod_{R \in \mathcal{R}_Q} \Phi_R(\mathcal{Y}_Q) \prod_{R \in gnd(\mathcal{R}) \setminus \mathcal{R}_Q} \Phi_R(\mathcal{Y}_{\overline{Q}}^{s,n})$$

$$= \frac{1}{Z^{s,n}} \Phi_Q(\mathcal{Y}_Q) \Phi_{\overline{Q}}^{s,n}(\mathcal{Y}_{\overline{Q}}^{s,n}),$$

where $\Phi_{\overline{Q}}^{s,n}(\mathcal{Y}_{\overline{Q}}^{s,n}) = \prod_{R \in gnd(\mathcal{R}) \setminus \mathcal{R}_Q} \Phi_R(\mathcal{Y}_{\overline{Q}}^{s,n})$. Dependent on s and n, both $\mathcal{Y}_{\overline{Q}}^{s,n}$ and $\Phi_{\overline{Q}}^{s,n}(\mathcal{Y}_{\overline{Q}}^{s,n})$ can change, but only $\Phi_Q(\mathcal{Y}_Q)$ depends on $\mathcal{Y}_Q$. In particular, $\Phi_Q(\mathcal{Y}_Q)$ is independent of s and n because $\mathcal{R}$ is parameter-closed. $\square$

Theorem 1 (Domain-Size Independent Queries). *Let $\mathcal{R}$ be a parameter-closed knowledge base over Σ, let $\mathcal{X} = \mathcal{H}(\mathcal{R})$, and let Q be a dependency-closed elementary ground query with respect to Σ and $\mathcal{R}$. Let p be the ME-optimal Gibbs distribution with respect to $\mathcal{R}$ and Σ and, for $s \in S$ and $n \in \mathbb{N}$, let $p^{s,n}$ be the ME-optimal Gibbs distribution with respect to $\mathcal{R}$ and $\Sigma_s(n)$.*

Let $\mathcal{Y}_Q$ be defined like in Lemma 1. Let e_Q denote the variable assignment corresponding to Q, i.e., if $Q = \bigwedge_{i=1}^k G_i^{e_i}$, then $e_Q = (e_1, \ldots, e_k)$ and let $\mathcal{Z} = \mathcal{Y}_Q \setminus \{G_1, \ldots, G_k\}$ contain the ground atoms from $\mathcal{Y}_Q$ that do not appear in Q. Then

$$p^{s,n}(Q) = p(Q) = \frac{\sum_z \Phi_Q(e_Q, z)}{\sum_y \Phi_Q(y)} \tag{9}$$

for all $s \in S$ and $n \in \mathbb{N}$, where $\Phi_Q(\mathcal{Y}_Q)$ is defined like in Lemma 1 and y and z range over the possible truth assignments to the ground atoms in $\mathcal{Y}_Q$ and $\mathcal{Z}$, respectively.

Proof. We know from Lemma 1 that each of the mentioned Gibbs distributions (again $p = p^{s,0}$) can be rewritten as

$$p^{s,n}(\mathcal{X}) = \frac{1}{Z^{s,n}} \Phi_Q(\mathcal{Y}_Q) \Phi_{\overline{Q}}^{s,n}(\mathcal{Y}_{\overline{Q}}^{s,n}).$$

From normalization of $p^{s,n}$ it follows that $Z^{s,n} = \sum_{y_1} \sum_{y_2} \Phi_Q(y_1)\Phi_{\overline{Q}}^{s,n}(y_2)$, where y_1 ranges over $\mathcal{Y}_Q$ and y_2 over $\mathcal{Y}_{\overline{Q}}^{s,n}$. Then

$$p^{s,n}(Q) = \sum_z \sum_{y_2} p(e_Q, z, y_2) = \frac{\sum_z \Phi_Q(e_Q, z) \sum_{y_2} \Phi_{\overline{Q}}^{s,n}(y_2)}{\sum_{y_1} \Phi_Q(y_1) \sum_{y_2} \Phi_{\overline{Q}}^{s,n}(y_2)} = \frac{\sum_z \Phi_Q(e_Q, z)}{\sum_{y_1} \Phi_Q(y_1)}.$$

In particuar, the result is independent of s and n and therefore equal for all Gibbs distributions. □

Example 9. Consider the dependency-closed query $Q = likes(b, a)$ from Example 7. We have $\mathcal{R}_Q = \{\langle(likes(a, b)|likes(b, a))[0.9], \top\rangle, \langle(likes(b, a)|likes(a, b))[0.9], \top\rangle, \langle(likes(a, b))[0.05], \top\rangle\}$ and $\mathcal{Y}_Q = \{likes(a, b), likes(b, a)\}$. We denote the random variables corresponding to ground atoms in $\mathcal{Y}_Q$ by $X_{a,b}, X_{b,a}$ and the factors corresponding to the conditionals in $\mathcal{R}_Q$ by $\Phi_1(X_{a,b}, X_{b,a}), \Phi_2(X_{a,b}, X_{b,a}), \Phi_3(X_{a,b})$. Then

$$\Phi_Q(X_{a,b}, X_{b,a}) = \Phi_1(X_{a,b}, X_{b,a}) \cdot \Phi_2(X_{a,b}, X_{b,a}) \cdot \Phi_3(X_{a,b}).$$

If $p^{s,n}$ denotes the ME-optimal Gibbs distribution with respect to $\mathcal{R}_{MI}^n$ (cf. Example 5), then Theorem 1 says that

$$p^{s,n}(likes(b, a)) = p^{s,n}(X_{b,a}) = \frac{\Phi_Q(0, X_{b,a}) + \Phi_Q(1, X_{b,a})}{\Phi_Q(0, 0) + \Phi_Q(0, 1) + \Phi_Q(1, 0) + \Phi_Q(1, 1)}.$$

Note that when computing $p^{s,n}(likes(b, a))$ naively instead, the number of factors grows linearly with n and the number of sum terms grows exponentially with n (because we had to marginalize out all ground atoms but $likes(b, a)$).

In Theorem 1, we are in a situation, where our query depends only a subset of the knowledge base similar to Proposition 2. In particular, this subset is closed in the sense that it does not change if we add new constants. As in Proposition 2, we can apply general independence properties of ME distributions [17, page 33] to conclude that p_Q is the unique ME-optimal probability distribution over $\mathcal{Y}_Q$ that satisfies $\mathcal{R}_Q$.

Example 10. In Example 9, we computed p and then marginalized to obtain $p(X_{a,b}, X_{b,a})$. However, we can get $p(X_{a,b}, X_{b,a})$ immediately, by just computing the ME-optimal probability distribution over the random variables $X_{a,b}, X_{b,a}$ that satisfies $\{\langle(likes(a, b)|likes(b, a))[0.9], \top\rangle, \langle(likes(b, a)|likes(a, b))[0.9], \top\rangle, \langle(likes(a, b))[0.05], \top\rangle\}$.

5   Conclusions and Future Work

In this paper, we proposed two approaches towards lifted inference for FO-PCL knowledge bases under ME semantics. For answering queries independent of the size of the universe, we studied lifted inference for parameter closed knowledge bases and dependency closed queries. We are currently working on further elaborating these methods, aiming also at lifted ME model computation for parameter closed knowledge bases. Parts of the $\mathcal{PU}$ transformation process used in this paper are related to the shattering of parfactors [15,16], while the transformation rules removing intra-rule interactions [2] do not correspond to shattering. Our future work also includes investigating whether and to what extend aspects of lifted inference as in [1,10,15,16] can be transferred to the maximum entropy setting studied here.

References

1. Apsel, U., Kersting, K., Mladenov, M.: Lifting relational map-lps using cluster signatures. In: Proceedings AAAI-2014. pp. 2403–2409. AAAI Press (2014)
2. Beierle, C., Krämer, A.: Achieving parametric uniformity for knowledge bases in a relational probabilistic conditional logic with maximum entropy semantics. Ann. Math. Artif. Intell. **73**(1–2), 5–45 (2015)
3. Boyd, S., Vandenberghe, L.: Convex Optimization. Cambridge University Press, New York, NY, USA (2004)
4. Fagin, R., Halpern, J.Y.: Reasoning about knowledge and probability. J. ACM **41**(2), 340–367 (1994)
5. Finthammer, M., Beierle, C.: How to exploit parametric uniformity for maximum entropy reasoning in a relational probabilistic logic. In: del Cerro, L.F., Herzig, A., Mengin, J. (eds.) JELIA 2012. LNCS, vol. 7519, pp. 189–201. Springer, Heidelberg (2012)
6. Fisseler, J.: First-order probabilistic conditional logic and maximum entropy. Logic J. IGPL **20**(5), 796–830 (2012)
7. Geman, S., Geman, D.: Stochastic relaxation, gibbs distributions, and the Bayesian restoration of images. IEEE Trans. Pattern Anal. Mach. Intell. **6**, 721–741 (1984)
8. Getoor, L., Taskar, B. (eds.): Introduction to Statistical Relational Learning. MIT Press, Cambridge (2007)
9. Halpern, J.: Reasoning About Uncertainty. MIT Press, Cambridge (2005)
10. Kazemi, S.M., Buchman, D., Kersting, K., Natarajan, S., Poole, D.: Relational logistic regression. In: Proceedings KR-2014 (2014)
11. Kern-Isberner, G.: Conditionals in Nonmonotonic Reasoning and Belief Revision. LNCS (LNAI), vol. 2087. Springer, Heidelberg (2001)
12. Kern-Isberner, G., Lukasiewicz, T.: Combining probabilistic logic programming with the power of maximum entropy. Artif. Intell. **157**(1–2), 139–202 (2004)
13. Nilsson, N.: Probabilistic logic. Artif. Intell. **28**, 71–87 (1986)
14. Paris, J.: The uncertain reasoner's companion - A mathematical perspective. Cambridge University Press, Cambridge (1994)
15. Poole, D.: First-order probabilistic inference. In: Gottlob, G., Walsh, T. (eds.) Proceedings IJCAI-03, pp. 985–991. Morgan Kaufmann, Acapulco (2003)
16. de Salvo Braz, R., Amir, E., Roth, D.: Lifted first-order probabilistic inference. In: IJCAI 2005. pp. 1319–1325. Professional Book Center (2005)
17. Shore, J., Johnson, R.: Axiomatic derivation of the principle of maximum entropy and the principle of minimum cross-entropy. IEEE Transactions on Information Theory IT **26**, 26–37 (1980)

Probabilistic Graphical Models
for Scalable Data Analytics

Towards Gaussian Bayesian Network Fusion

Irene Córdoba-Sánchez[✉], Concha Bielza, and Pedro Larrañaga

Departamento de Inteligencia Artificial,
Universidad Politécnica de Madrid, Madrid, Spain
irene.cordoba.sanchez@alumnos.upm.es
{mcbielza,pedro.larranaga}@fi.upm.es

Abstract. Data sets are growing in complexity thanks to the increasing facilities we have nowadays to both generate and store data. This poses many challenges to machine learning that are leading to the proposal of new methods and paradigms, in order to be able to deal with what is nowadays referred to as Big Data. In this paper we propose a method for the aggregation of different Bayesian network structures that have been learned from separate data sets, as a first step towards mining data sets that need to be partitioned in an horizontal way, i.e. with respect to the instances, in order to be processed. Considerations that should be taken into account when dealing with this situation are discussed. Scalable learning of Bayesian networks is slowly emerging, and our method constitutes one of the first insights into Gaussian Bayesian network aggregation from different sources. Tested on synthetic data it obtains good results that surpass those from individual learning. Future research will be focused on expanding the method and testing more diverse data sets.

Keywords: Gaussian Bayesian network · Fusion · Scalability · Big data

1 Introduction

Nowadays, we are entering the *era of Big Data*, as a result of both the generalised trend of massive data collection and the increasing computer capabilities for processing and storage. These data sets are characterized mainly for their huge volume and complexity (they can be noisy, have a fast change rate, etc.). Machine learning methods are rapidly being revised and new paradigms are arising in order to be able to adapt to this kind of data.

One of the main approaches for dealing with high volume of data is to partition it across a cluster, perform some operations and then aggregate the results. This partition can be either horizontal (across the instances) or vertical (across the variables). Horizontal partitions can also naturally arise when we want to jointly analyse information contained at different sources, e.g. records of patients in different hospitals that store the same variables about each of them.

Bayesian networks (BNs) are well-known tools for modelling and dealing with uncertain knowledge and data. Their aggregation has been studied since the days of their conception as belief models from an expert. Martzkevich and

© Springer International Publishing Switzerland 2015
S. Destercke and T. Denoeux (Eds.): ECSQARU 2015, LNAI 9161, pp. 519–528, 2015.
DOI: 10.1007/978-3-319-20807-7_47

Abramson [7] consider the problem of fusing networks from different experts which shared some variables. They provide an algorithm which seeks to obtain a graph containing all the nodes and arcs from the individual networks, or their reversals. This however may not be the case of interest always when we are thinking about fusing networks that have been learned from data, since the individual networks in this case may contain spurious connections.

The work by del Sagrado and Moral [1] focuses on studying the fusion of DAGs by means of intersection and union of the independence statements represented by each of the involved networks. Richardson and Domingos [11] use knowledge from a group of experts to compute a prior distribution over the BN structures. They motivate their proposal by stating that knowledge elicitation can be facilitated if we allow experts to be noisy on their statements about the BNs, and make up for this flexibility by using multiple different experts. This argument is interesting because it can be compared with the case of huge, noisy data sets, where instead of sub-sampling and learning an individual network, an alternative approach could be to learn multiple networks on different partitions of data and aggregate them afterwards.

Another use case where horizontal partitioning arises naturally is the problem described by López-Cruz et al. [5]. In this case a set of experts were asked to classify different neurons, giving rise to one supervised training set from each expert. A cluster process was applied to the set of the individual BNs obtained and a representative BN for each cluster was constructed. These representative networks were then aggregated into a Bayesian multinet.

Regarding the aggregation of parameters, recently Etminani et al. [2] propose a method in which they cluster experts' parameters and aggregate only those that correspond to the cluster with the highest number of members, resembling democratic societies. Other popular strategies for parameter fusion in Bayesian networks are Linear Opinion Pools (LinOP) [6] and Logarithmic Opinion Pools (LogOP) [9].

We propose a method for the aggregation of Gaussian BNs (GBNs), which to the best of our knowledge is the first proposal of this kind. It covers both the structure of the network and the parameters of the Gaussian distribution encoded by it. The experiments carried out show promising results for the proposed method.

The paper is organised as follows. Section 2 introduces the necessary background knowledge for the rest of the paper. In Sect. 3 the details of the method are described, whose results from experimental evaluation are discussed in Sect. 4. Finally, the conclusions and future research lines are presented in Sect. 5.

2   Preliminaries

2.1   Bayesian Networks

A BN can be defined as a way of representing the factorization of a joint probability distribution over a random vector $X = (X_1, ..., X_p)$, where $Pa(X_i)$ are called the *parents* of X_i,

$$f(\boldsymbol{x}) = \prod_{i=1}^{p} f(x_i|\boldsymbol{pa}(x_i)). \tag{1}$$

A BN consists on a qualitative part, commonly called the structure, and a quantitative component, the parameters. More formally, it is defined [10] as a pair (G, Θ), where G is a DAG and Θ are the numerical parameters which define the factorization in Eq. (1). The nodes of G are the components of $\boldsymbol{X}$ and its arcs represent probabilistic dependencies between the variables, in such a way that the DAG satisfies the *Markov condition*: each variable is conditionally independent of its non-descendants given its parents. Two DAGs are *Markov equivalent* if they represent the same set of conditional independences between the variables. This defines a binary relation which gives rise to equivalence classes and partitions the DAG space.

In order to learn a BN from data it is necessary to learn both the structure (G) and the numerical parameters (Θ). There are two main approaches for BN structure learning: constraint based and score-and-search. Constraint based methods try to find the Bayesian network structure that represents most of the dependence relations present in data, detected by means of statistical tests. The PC algorithm [14], which has as output an equivalence class of DAGs, is a representative example of these types of methods.

On the other hand, score-and-search methods try to find the structure that best fits the data. They are characterized by a representation of the solution space, a search method and a score. The KES algorithm [8] is an example of such methods, which performs the search in the equivalence class space. Searching in this space has several advantages when compared to the DAG space, such as it being a more efficient and robust representation [16], although there is still some controversy regarding this choice. Many search heuristics and scores can be combined and give rise to the different methods appearing in the literature.

2.2 Gaussian Bayesian Networks

A GBN [4] encodes a joint Gaussian distribution over $\boldsymbol{X}$, i.e., with joint density function

$$f(\boldsymbol{x}) = \frac{1}{\sqrt{(2\pi)^p|\boldsymbol{\Sigma}|}} \exp\left\{-\frac{1}{2}(\boldsymbol{x} - \boldsymbol{\mu})^t \boldsymbol{\Sigma}^{-1}(\boldsymbol{x} - \boldsymbol{\mu})\right\},$$

where $\boldsymbol{\mu} = (\mu_1, ..., \mu_p)$ is the vector of unconditional means and $\boldsymbol{\Sigma}$ is the covariance matrix. Each factor in Eq. (1) corresponds in this case to a univariate normal distribution,

$$f(x_i|\boldsymbol{pa}(x_i)) \equiv \mathcal{N}\left(\mu_i + \sum_{x_j \in \boldsymbol{pa}(x_i)} \beta_{ji}(x_j - \mu_j), v_i\right), \tag{2}$$

where β_{ji} reflects the strength of the relationship between X_i and its j-th parent, and v_i is the conditional variance of X_i given its parents, i.e.,

$$v_i = \sigma_i - \boldsymbol{\Sigma}_{i\boldsymbol{Pa}(X_i)} \boldsymbol{\Sigma}_{\boldsymbol{Pa}(X_i)} \boldsymbol{\Sigma}_{i\boldsymbol{Pa}(X_i)}^t. \tag{3}$$

In Eq. 3 σ_i is the unconditional variance of X_i, $\boldsymbol{\Sigma}_{iPa(X_i)}$ is the matrix of covariances between X_i and $\boldsymbol{Pa}(X_i)$, and $\boldsymbol{\Sigma}_{\boldsymbol{Pa}(X_i)}$ is the covariance matrix of $\boldsymbol{Pa}(X_i)$.

Thus, the parameters of a GBN are the vector of means $\boldsymbol{\mu}$, the vector of conditional variances $\boldsymbol{v}$ and the coefficients β_{ji}. Assuming standardized data ($\mu_i = 0$ and $v_i = 1$), the parameter estimation is reduced to solving the linear regression model

$$x_i = \sum_{x_j \in \boldsymbol{pa}(x_i)} \beta_{ji} x_j + \epsilon_i,$$

with ϵ_i being the Gaussian noise term with zero expectation.

3   Method

Although the aggregation of different individual GBNs is a first step towards the analysis of massive data, where the data set would be split into slices distributed across a cluster, here we will assume that we already have different data sets over the same variables available (i.e., at this stage we are not concerned with the preprocessing and splitting processes).

The structure learning method we have used for learning the individual networks is the score-and-search hill climbing [15] with the Bayesian information criterion (BIC) [12] score on the DAG space. After each network has been learned, they are aggregated using majority vote below a threshold. This procedure is outlined in Algorithm 1.

Algorithm 1. Structure learning

Input: *datasets*. Data sets from where the individual Bayesian networks will be learned.
Input: *threshold*. Threshold for the majority arc voting.
Output: Aggregated Bayesian network structure learned with the specified thresholds.

1: $n\_bn \leftarrow$ size(*datasets*);
2: $bn\_list \leftarrow$ list();
3: **for** $i \in \{1, n\_bn\}$ **do**
4:     $bn\_list[i] \leftarrow$ learn_struc(*datasets*[i])
5: **end for**
6: $v\_matrix \leftarrow$ get_votes(bn_list);
7: $result \leftarrow$ bn_aggr(*threshold*, v_matrix);
8: **return** $result$;

The functions *get_votes* and *bn_aggr* in Algorithm 1 are further detailed in Algorithms 2 and 3 respectively. *get_votes* consists of the process of extracting how many networks contribute to the same arc, i.e., how common across the learned networks an arc is. Thus a matrix containing the sums of the appearances of each arc in the networks is obtained. The threshold for the majority vote is the

Algorithm 2. get_votes

Input: *bn_list*. List of BN structures already learned on each data set.
Output: Matrix containing the votes for each arc.
1: $n\_nodes \leftarrow$ nodes(bn);
2: $v\_matrix \leftarrow$ matrix(n_nodes, n_nodes);
3: **for** $bn \in bn\_list$ **do**
4:      $bn\_arcs \leftarrow$ arcs(bn);
5:      **for** $arc \in bn\_arcs$ **do**
6:          $from \leftarrow$ from(arc);
7:          $to \leftarrow$ to(arc);
8:          $v\_matrix[from][to] \leftarrow v\_matrix[from][to] + 1$;
9:      **end for**
10: **end for**
11: **return** v_matrix;

---

main parameter of this method and we will analyse it further on the experimental section.

In *bn_aggr* the threshold is compared with each of the entries in the matrix of arcs, and the corresponding arc is added to the final network if its value reaches the threshold. In the same algorithm we can notice that when an arc addition causes a cycle in the DAG it is discarded.

Algorithm 3. bn_aggr

Input: *threshold*. Threshold for the arc voting.
Input: Matrix containing the votes for each arc.
Output: *bn*. Aggregated Bayesian network.
1: $bn \leftarrow$ empty_dag();
2: **for** $i \in$ cols(v_matrix) **do**
3:      **for** $j \in$ rows(v_matrix) **do**
4:          **if** $v\_matrix[i][j] \geq threshold$ **then**
5:              **if not** arc_causes_cycle(bn, i, j) **then**
6:                  add_arc(bn, i, j);
7:              **end if**
8:          **end if**
9:      **end for**
10: **end for**
11: **return** bn;

After the aggregation of the structure has finished, the linear regression coefficients of each variable on its parents is learned by maximum likelihood estimation (MLE) from each data set, but this time using the aggregated structure. This is what del Sagrado and Moral [1] call *topological fusion*, that is, obtaining a consensus structure and then estimating the model parameters, as opposed to *graphical representation of consensus*, which consists of aggregating the probability distributions of each network and then obtaining the structure that represents it.

The aggregation of the parameters obtained from each data set is performed using the method explained hereafter. Consider a multiple linear regression model on $\{X_1, ..., X_n\}$ predictors. Assume that the data is distributed across k slices. Let $\hat{\boldsymbol{\beta}}_j = (\hat{\beta}_{1j}, ..., \hat{\beta}_{nj})$ be the vector of estimates obtained in slice j. For each predictor X_i, $i \in \{1, ..., n\}$, let

$$\tilde{\beta}_i = \sum_{j=1}^{k} w_{ij} \hat{\beta}_{ij}$$

be the aggregated estimate, where $w_{ij} = \sigma_{ij}^{-2} / \sum_{j=1}^{k} \sigma_{ij}^{-2}$, $\sigma_{ij} = var(\hat{\beta}_{ij})$. Because we are dealing with GBNs, MLE is equivalent to the least squares (LS) method, and thus $\tilde{\beta}_i$ is the estimator of minimum variance [3] among those with form

$$\sum_{j=1}^{k} w_{ij} \hat{\beta}_{ij}, \text{ where } \sum_{j=1}^{k} w_{ij} = 1,$$

Asymptotic normality is also established on Fan *et al.* [3].

The pseudo-code of the outlined procedure for learning the parameters of the linear regression for each variable on its parents can be found in Algorithm 4.

Algorithm 4. Parameter learning

Input: *datasets*. Data sets from where the individual parameters will be learned.
Output: Bayesian network parameters aggregated.
1: $n\_bn \leftarrow$ size($datasets$);
2: $param\_list \leftarrow$ list();
3: **for** $i \in \{1, n\_bn\}$ **do**
4:    $param\_list[i] \leftarrow$ learn_param($datasets[i]$);
5: **end for**
6: $n\_param \leftarrow$ size($param\_list$);
7: $n\_nodes \leftarrow$ nodes($param\_list$);
8: $param \leftarrow$ matrix(n_nodes, n_nodes);
9: **for** $i \in \{1, n\_param\}$ **do**
10:    **for** $node \in param\_list[i]$ **do**
11:       **for** $parent \in$ parents($node$) **do**
12:          $coef \leftarrow$ get_coeff($param\_list[i], node, parent$);
13:          $weight \leftarrow$ get_weight($param\_list[i], node, parent$);
14:          $param[node][parent] \leftarrow param[node][parent] + coef * weight$;
15:       **end for**
16:    **end for**
17: **end for**
18: **return** normalize($param$);

---

4   Experiments

We have used some utilities from the R package `bnlearn` [13] and tested the proposed method using synthetic data sets generated from a multivariate Gaussian distribution whose DAG structure is shown in Fig. 1.

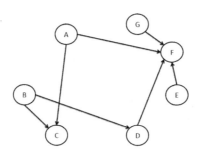

Fig. 1. Structure of the Bayesian network used for the experiments.

In a real use case of this method we could have been given a number of separate data sets over the same variables but differing in the number of instances each one contains. On the other hand, if we were to apply it to a huge data set, the different partitions would probably contain a similar amount of instances. In this synthetic experiment we have generated eight different data sets with a sample size of 50 instances each.

Figure 2 shows the different BN structures obtained from each data set. We can notice that a high portion of the original network is learned in most of the cases, being false positives the most common error. We have aggregated the results using all possible values for the threshold parameter, getting as result the networks that appear on Fig. 3.

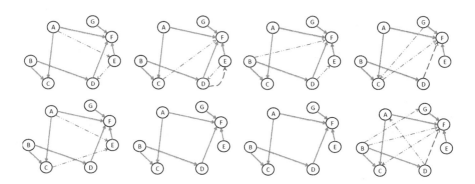

Fig. 2. Structure learned on each of the data sets. Green arcs are those correctly learned, red arcs are false positives and blue arcs are false negatives (Color figure online).

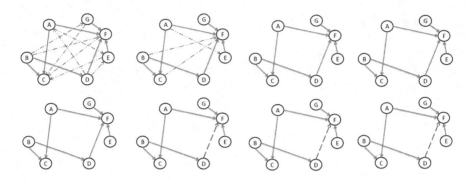

Fig. 3. Aggregated structures for the different thresholds (1 to 8), increasing from left to right and top to bottom. Green arcs are those correctly aggregated, red arcs are false positives and blue arcs are false negatives (Color figure online).

The metrics we are going to use to evaluate the results obtained with respect to the original structure are the false positive, false negative and true positive rate and the Structural Hamming Distance (SHD) [15]. The latter consists of the number of operations needed to match the Partial DAGs (PDAGs) representing the equivalence classes of each network. The operations considered are arc addition, deletion or reversal and edge addition or deletion. Therefore, the PDAG is extracted from the respective DAGs before calculating this metric. SHD provides a way to compare the two BNs in terms of the conditional independencies encoded by the BN, and thus avoids the penalization of differences in arcs that might be statistically undistinguishable.

In Table 1 we can see the value metrics for the individual structures (left) and the aggregated ones (right) when compared with the original network.

Table 1. Results of the GBN learned on each data set (left) and the aggregated GBN (right) compared with the original network. TP, FP and FN indicate the true positive, false positive and false negative rates (respectively). SHD denotes the Structural Hamming Distance. The networks are numbered according to their order of appearance in Fig. 2

Network	SHD	TP	FP	FN		Threshold	SHD	TP	FP	FN
1	3	7	2	0		1	8	7	8	0
2	3	6	2	1		2	3	7	3	0
3	2	7	2	0		3	0	7	0	0
4	3	6	2	1		4	0	7	0	0
5	2	7	2	0		5	0	7	0	0
6	0	7	0	0		6	1	6	0	1
7	0	7	0	0		7	1	6	0	1
8	5	6	4	1		8	1	6	0	1

Obviously when the threshold is 1 every arc that appears in the individual networks is added to the final one (unless a cycle is caused), so this produces worse results than any individual network when comparing it to the original structure. However, for thresholds above 1 the aggregated result is better than most of the isolated ones, because thanks to the majority threshold false dependences are eliminated. For too restrictive thresholds this can however result in the deletion of a valid arc, so it should be adjusted to an intermediate value for the best results. In a real use case this would depend on the data characteristics, the application domain and the availability of a training set.

Finally, parameter learning is influenced by noise if the structure is not correctly learned because false parents of variables arise, which means that false coefficients are estimated in the linear regression. However it is the case, as one would expect, that the coefficients corresponding to these false parents are very close to zero (e.g., 0.007 mean for the extreme case of threshold 1) and the variations on the value of the other parents are barely noticeable. This is not the case when we learn from a single network. For example, in the last network in Fig. 2, $\beta_{BF} = 1.5$, and B is a false parent of F.

5   Conclusions and Future Work

We have considered the problem of horizontal partitioning in the context of Big Data and proposed a method for aggregating several GBNs learned from different data sets as a first step towards scalable GBN learning. The method obtains good results both in the case of structure and parameter learning on synthetic data. The aggregated results surpass in most cases those derived from learning from a single data set by taking into account all the data available without the need of analysing it as a single block. This is specially useful for its potential applications when analysing partitions of massive data sets.

As a future line of research, when learning the aggregated structure the treatment of cycles will be refined and will involve more sophisticated techniques such as arc reversal, checking the strength of the connection in each of the individual networks (coefficients of the regression), establishing a suitable ordering of arc consideration, etc.

In the case of applying the proposed method on a distributed setting, where each data set is in a computer within a cluster, it would be interesting to define some communication protocol during the learning process. This would be useful for gathering stepwise information that could be used later on for example when aggregating the individual networks (e.g. cycles) but also for developing more sophisticated voting schemes which could depend on the adequateness of each data set for the learning process.

Finally, we will also focus on performing more testing with diverse (noise, missing values) and real data sets.

Acknowledgements. The authors thank the reviewers for comments and critics which significantly contributed to improve the paper; and also J.M. Peña, J. Nielsen,

J. Mengin and M. Serrurier for the valuable help. This work has been partially supported by the Spanish Ministry of Economy and Competitiveness through the Cajal Blue Brain (C080020-09; the Spanish partner of the Blue Brain initiative from EPFL) and TIN2013-41592-P projects, and by the Regional Government of Madrid through the S2013/ICE-2845-CASI-CAM-CM project.

References

1. del Sagrado, J., Moral, S.: Qualitative combination of Bayesian networks. Int. J. Intell. Syst. **18**(2), 237–249 (2003)
2. Etminani, K., Naghibzadeh, M., Peña, J.M.: DemocraticOP: A democratic way of aggregating Bayesian network parameters. Int. J. Approximate Reasoning **54**(5), 602–614 (2013)
3. Fan, T.H., Lin, D.K., Cheng, K.F.: Regression analysis for massive datasets. Data Knowl. Eng. **61**(3), 554–562 (2007)
4. Geiger, D., Heckerman, D.: Learning Gaussian networks. In: Proceedings of the Tenth International Conference on Uncertainty in Artificial Intelligence, pp. 235–243. Morgan Kaufmann Publishers Inc. (1994)
5. López-Cruz, P.L., Larrañaga, P., DeFelipe, J., Bielza, C.: Bayesian network modeling of the consensus between experts: an application to neuron classification. Int. J. Approximate Reasoning **55**(1), 3–22 (2014)
6. Maynard-Reid II, P., Chajewska, U.: Aggregating learned probabilistic beliefs. In: Proceedings of the Eighteenth International Conference on Uncertainty in Artificial Intelligence, pp. 354–361. Morgan Kaufmann Publishers Inc. (2001)
7. Matzkevich, I., Abramson, B.: The topological fusion of Bayes nets. In: Proceedings of the Eighth International Conference on Uncertainty in Artificial Intelligence, pp. 191–198. Morgan Kaufmann Publishers Inc. (1992)
8. Nielsen, J.D., Kočka, T., Peña, J.M.: On local optima in learning Bayesian networks. In: Proceedings of the Nineteenth International Conference on Uncertainty in Artificial Intelligence, pp. 435–442. Morgan Kaufmann Publishers Inc. (2002)
9. Pennock, D.M., Wellman, M.P.: Graphical representation of consensus belief. In: Proceedings of the Fifteenth International Conference on Uncertainty in Artificial Intelligence, pp. 531–540. Morgan Kaufmann Publishers Inc. (1999)
10. Pearl, J.: Probabilistic Reasoning in Intelligent Systems: Networks of Plausible Inference. Morgan Kaufmann Publishers Inc, California (1988)
11. Richardson, M., Domingos, P.: Learning with knowledge from multiple experts. In: Proceedings of the Twentieth International Conference on Machine Learning, pp. 624–631. AAAI Press (2003)
12. Schwarz, G.: Estimating the dimension of a model. Ann. Stat. **6**(2), 461–464 (1978)
13. Scutari, M.: Learning Bayesian networks with the bnlearn R package. J. Stat. Softw. **35**(3), 1–22 (2010)
14. Spirtes, P., Glymour, C.N., Scheines, R.: Causation, Prediction, and Search. MIT press, Cambridge (2000)
15. Tsamardinos, I., Brown, L.E., Aliferis, C.F.: The max-min hill-climbing Bayesian network structure learning algorithm. Mach. Learn. **65**(1), 31–78 (2006)
16. Vidaurre, D., Bielza, C., Larrañaga, P.: Learning an L1-regularized Gaussian Bayesian network in the equivalence class space. IEEE Trans. Syst. Man Cybern. Part B Cybern. **40**(5), 1231–1242 (2010)

Early Recognition of Maneuvers
in Highway Traffic

Galia Weidl[1(✉)], Anders L. Madsen[2,4], Viacheslav Tereshchenko[1,3],
Dietmar Kasper[1], and Gabi Breuel[1]

[1] Department of Driving Automation, Daimler AG, Group Research and AE,
71034 Böblingen, Germany
{galia.weidl,dietmar.kasper,gabi.breuel}@daimler.com
[2] HUGIN EXPERT A/S, Aalborg, Denmark
anders@hugin.com
[3] Institute of Automation and Software Technology, University of Stuttgart,
70550 Stuttgart, Germany
viacheslav.tereshchenko@gmail.com
[4] Department of Computer Science, Aalborg University, Aalborg, Denmark

Abstract. This paper presents an application of Bayesian networks where early
recognition of traffic maneuver intention is achieved using features of
lane change, representing the relative dynamics between vehicles on the same
lane and the free space to neighbor vehicles back and front on the target lane.
The classifiers have been deployed on the automotive target platform, which has
severe constraints on time and space performance of the system. The test driving
has been performed with encouraging results. Even earlier recognition is possible by considering the trend development of features, characterizing the
dynamic driving process. The preliminary test results confirm feasibility.

Keywords: Early recognition of maneuver intention · Dynamic bayesian networks · Situation analysis · Big data streams

1 Introduction

Highway traffic involves complex scenes with many vehicles, driving on several lanes at
high speed. To assess the situation and reduce any risks, a driver must interpret accurately the hazards. This requires correct assessment of driving behavior and intended
maneuvers of all neighboring vehicles. There are several approaches, which have been
be used for maneuver recognition, most of them originate from the research area of
"Detection and Pattern Recognition". All of them analyze continuously the traffic situation based on frequently sampled measurements (called features) of the dynamic

AMIDST (Analysis of Massive Data Streams) is a project, which has received funding from the
European Union's 7th Framework Programme for research, technological development and
demonstration under grant agreement no 619209.

© Springer International Publishing Switzerland 2015
S. Destercke and T. Denoeux (Eds.): ECSQARU 2015, LNAI 9161, 529–540, 2015.
DOI: 10.1007/978-3-319-20807-7_48

characteristics of a driving vehicle and its surrounding neighbor vehicles. One should distinguish between EGO-vehicle (own vehicle, performing the situation analysis) and OBJ-vehicles (surrounding vehicles, detected by the EGO-vehicle). Research in this area can be divided into three groups: 1) considers only the recognition of driving maneuvers for the EGO-vehicle; 2) considers only maneuvers of OBJ-vehicles and 3) investigates maneuvers of both. The works of [1] and [2] use physiological data, the driver's gaze direction (head position of driver) with other features to recognize EGO-maneuvers. Such data are not available for the driver of an OBJ-vehicle to predict a maneuver from EGO perspective. In [3] several approaches for maneuver recognition of the EGO-vehicle have been investigated. These include: neural networks and support vector machines (SVMs). SVMs are used in [4] together with Bayesian filtering for prediction of driving maneuvers of the EGO-vehicle. They show an average prediction time of the lane change maneuvers of about 1.3 s. In [5] the maneuver recognition is based on fuzzy logic and probabilistic finite-state machines (PFSM) with low computational complexity. Measurements (features) like velocity, acceleration, steering angle and the status of the turn indicator have been used. The approach of [6] extracts by feature selection the set, maximizing the predictive power of a classifier. The conditional probabilities of relevant features are obtained by Gaussian mixtures. It uses a Naive Bayesian classifier and is able to detect the maneuver up to 2.2 s earlier.

Our early work on maneuver recognition is based on the perception of EGO and its surrounding OBJ-dynamics, [7–10]. It represents our *application scenario 1:* approaching of lane marking, after a car (EGO or OBJ) was following another vehicle at a comparable speed. Here the situation features at each time step are analyzed independently during the transition from lane follow to lane change, involving lane marking crossing. In this work, we consider such lane change transition as a dynamic process, exploring the trend of features. The solution development is part of the RTD project AMIDST [12]. The recent automation challenges for maneuver recognition have given rise to the current objectives: 1) Meeting the requirements of the automotive target platform to ensure operation in real time. 2) Earlier maneuver recognition for future-situation awareness. The last requires analyzing the trend of features as well as the relative dynamics between vehicles (which defines *application scenario 2* described in Sect. 3) see Fig. 1, [11]. The combination of both scenarios allows continuous situation analysis of all surrounding vehicles, interpreting the development of a situation and assessment of possible collision risks, to ensure proactive safe driving. A detailed requirements analysis can be found in [13].

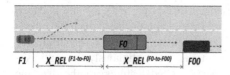

Fig. 1. Relative dynamics between EGO (= F1) and a slower moving vehicle (OBJ) in front F0 with its relation to a front vehicle F00.

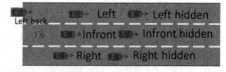

Fig. 2. EGO (own vehicle: red), OBJ-vehicles (blue) in-front (hidden ones - detected by radar) and one OBJ-vehicle left back (Color figure online).

The task we consider involves high speed analysis of massive amounts of streaming data. Consider a highway scenario involving a vehicle driving in a lane with three other vehicles driving in three different lanes in front of it. The data typically consists of 252 observations acquired with fixed sampling rate, a.k.a. cycle time ($\sim$ 42 or 60 ms, dependent on used cameras). If a test drive from only one hour is to be analyzed, this results in millions of database records/hour (total: 22.320.000). The raw data streams used for model development and testing are obtained from several sensors: 1) on-board sensors; 2) stereo camera & image processing; 3) radar sensors & data pre-processing. Their data are serving as an input to the Sensor Data Fusion (SDF) module, which generates the reconciled object data to extract the situation features and characterize each surrounding vehicle of the own or neighbor vehicles. Since the analyzed data are noisy and to resolve the combinatorial and interpretation issues of all possible maneuvers of surrounding vehicles, Bayesian networks (BN) (see [14, 15]) have been selected as the method for reasoning under uncertainty and to mimic the cognitive art of situation analysis.

2   Baseline Model: Bayesian Networks

All future developments for maneuver recognition are compared towards our earlier developed "Original OOBN" (Object-Oriented Bayesian Network), described in details in [7, 8, 10] and [12], which was also deployed in a prototype vehicle.

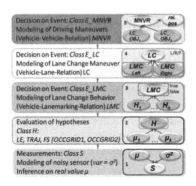

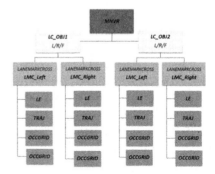

Fig. 3. Baseline model: OOBN structure   **Fig. 4.** Class hierarchy of the original OOBN, representing the original classifier ORIG

For easy reference, the overall structure of the original OOBN model is shown in Fig. 3, where OBJ_i can denote the own (EGO) or another vehicle. The *class S (Sensor)* is used to model uncertainties in features, extracted from measurements and thereof computed variables, which are used to characterize a traffic situation. The *class H (Hypothesis)* combines the features and is used to recognize situation changes. The set of used *hypotheses* H_i and their *features* S_i includes (see Figs. 3 and 4): a) H_1: *Lateral evidence (LE)* with $S_1 = \{lateral\ offset\ (O\_LAT)$ of the vehicle to the lane marking, *lateral velocity (V_LAT)*}; b) H_2: *Trajectory (TRAJ)* with $S_2 = \{steering\ angle\ (PSI)$ of the vehicle relative to road direction; *lateral acceleration (A_LAT); time to lane-marking crossing (T_LCR)*}; c) *H₃: Free space (FS)* on the target lane, represented by an *occupancy grid (OCCGRID)* with S_3 = {*times to enter (TTE)* and *disappear (TTD)* from surrounding occupancy cell and the corresponding *distances (S_{TTE}, S_{TTD})*}. The *class E (Event)* is used at three hierarchical levels of abstraction (Figs. 3 and 4). Event is modelling the relation of a vehicle: a) to the lane markings *(class LMC)*; b) to the lane of current motion *(class Lane Change (LC)* i.e. lane change towards left or right; or lane follow); c) to another neighbor vehicle *(class MNVR)*. The last event is recognized by the probability distribution of a random variable *"maneuver" (MNVR)*.

3   Static BN of "Relative Dynamics" for Earlier Recognition

The concept of relative dynamics explores the relation between vehicles driving on the same lane, providing a source for earlier recognition of possible driving intentions (or need) of lane change. It considers the relative states (distance, speed, acceleration) between the vehicles, see [6, 7]. This is realized in the following by extending the Original OOBN with these relative features. In the Original OOBN the BN-hypothesis *LE*, used for the evaluation of *LMC* (Figs. 3 and 4), can recognize a maneuver only when the car approaches the lane marking. Hence, the intention of a driver to make a lane change cannot be detected with it. Therefore, we explore for application scenario 2 the new hypothesis "Relative Dynamics" (*REL_DYN*), where we use the radar-measured features, extracted from vehicle-vehicle relations, providing additional advantage of a longer view-horizon (up to 200 m) than the camera (up to 60 m).

Since the hypotheses *REL_DYN* is contributing to maneuver recognition, it should be integrated into the forth layer LC of the Original OOBN (Fig. 3), since we use information on how fast the vehicles in front on the same lane are driving. At first, we apply a similar handling of uncertainties in measurements as in [7], see Fig. 3, layer 1. For simplicity, we will take two measured features (relative distance *X_REL_MEAS* and relative velocity *V_REL_MEAS* to the vehicle in front) and their variances σ^2 to improve the maneuver recognition time performance, i.e. earlier as in [7–9]. The structure of the static BN-Model on relative dynamics is shown in Fig. 5.

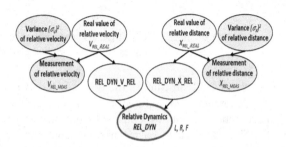

Fig. 5. Static BN-Model for hypothesis "Relative Dynamics". Evidence nodes are coded with blue color; chance nodes – with yellow; decision – with red border (Color figure online).

The new hypothesis should answer the question if the driver's intention is to change the lane to the left L, right R or follow F the lane. Therefore, the node Relative Dynamics *REL_DYN* models the recognized maneuver and has three states *LC = {Left L, Right R, Follow F)*. By domain knowledge, we model the node expressing the speed influence on the hypothesis *REL_DYN_V_REL* with 3 states: *faster, comparable* and *slower*. The distance influence on *REL_DYN_X_REL* is modeled with 3 states: *close, comfort distance* and *far away*. Their CPDs are defined through logistic functions, based on domain knowledge, expressing a general driving behavior in highway traffic. The CPD of *REL_DYN* expresses driving experiences, e.g. if a vehicle is approaching closer-and-closer with higher relative speed than the one in front, it will change the lane towards left. If it drives at nearly constant distance and comparable speed, then it follows the object on the lane. The CPTs for variance- and real-valued-nodes are defined with uniform distributions. The measurements-nodes are modeled with normal distributions. Hereby the measurement uncertainties are modeled with *class S* (see Fig. 3). Similarly to the free space hypothesis *OCCGRID* (in *class H* in Fig. 3, see also [9]), the "relative dynamics" is combined with a slightly modified (reflecting the dynamics shown in Fig. 2) safety concept (*Safe_RD*).

4   Deployment on Automotive Platform

After extending the Original OOBN with the relative dynamics, we have deployed the resulting models on the automotive platform. To study the effect of different parameters on recognition, we have defined three classifiers (called ORIG; STAT_TR; STAT) as shown in Table 1. **ORIG** classifier is the one using the Original OOBN (see Fig. 3 and [7, 8]). All three statical classifiers use hypotheses *LE* and *FS*, while only **ORIG** and **STAT_TR** use *TRAJ*. The concept of the three static classifiers (deployed in the same way) is based on the ORIG classifier. The automotive platform has severe constraints on time (0.1-0.15 ms) and space performance ($\sim 10^2$ kB in RAM and ROM) of the system. To meet the memory and time cost requirements of the target platform, we use the "Divide-and-Conquer" (D&C) method for the classifiers' implementation, see [10]. The idea of D&C implementation is to split the network into fragments (see Figs. 3 and 4) and to use the posterior distribution of its classification node (e.g. *LE*) as likelihood (soft evidence) over the corresponding (*LE*) node at the next level of an "upstream" network. To account for the extension with relative dynamics the *LMC* and *LC* models have been modified as shown in Figs. 6 and 7. The results from the statistical evaluation of the three implemented static classifiers (ORIG, STAT, STAT_TR) show earlier average recognition time (-0,84, -0.93, -0.96 s) and reduced false negatives for both classifiers, containing *REL_DYN*. The test drives on real highway confirm, that traffic scenarios with "relative dynamics" are recognized as intentions before a vehicle is initiating a maneuver due to the recognition of slower moving vehicle in front on the same lane, see Figs. 8 and 9. Thus, earlier recognition of the need for a lane is feasible, even when the OBJ (or EGO) vehicle is still driving on the same lane as the slower moving vehicle in front.

Table 1. Overview of the three deployed static classifiers (ORIG, STAT_TR, STAT). "X" shows which static BN fragment is included.

static BN (= hypothesis) Classifier	LE	TRAJ	Free Space (FS): OCCGR_OBJ1-OBJ2	REL_DYN	Free Space: Safe_RD
ORIG	X	X	X	–	–
STAT_TR	X	X	X	X	X
STAT	X	–	X	X	X

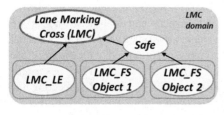

Fig. 6. Modified BN-fragment "Lane Marking Crossing" of the static classifiers: the *LMC* with *LMC_LE* contains only *LE*.

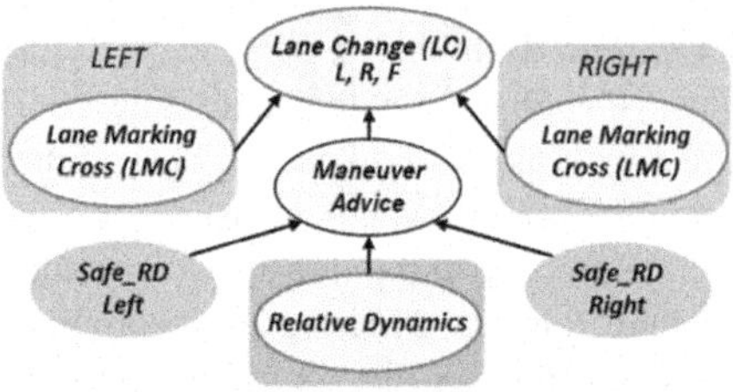

Fig. 7. Modified BN-fragment for recognition of Lane Change. It includes Maneuver Advice, based on *REL_DYN* and check for safety on the target lane.

Fig. 8. On-road demo with *REL_DYN* (scenario 2) shows early recognition of the need for a lane change, even when the OBJ vehicle is still on the same lane as the slower vehicle in front.

Fig. 9. Scenario 2 (at rainy weather conditions) with slower moving vehicle/truck (recognized by radar and symbolized by a blue vertical bar) in front of another vehicle/car (symbolized by a violet virtual box of data fusion) (Color figure online).

5   Dynamic Models for Earlier Recognition

Here, we focus on the use of two-time slice dynamic Bayesian networks DBNs (2T-DBNs) to achieve earlier recognition of traffic maneuvers, see [12]. They are characterized by an initial model representing the initial joint distribution of the process and a transition probability distribution (TPD) representing a standard BN repeated over time. They satisfy both the first-order Markov assumption and the stationary assumption. Figure 10 shows the graphical structure of a 2T-DBN model for the hypothesis LE, while Fig. 11 represents *REL_DYN*, which is a DBN extension of Fig. 5 with the hidden node $A_{REL\_REAL}(t)$, which was added for purposes as explained below. The TPD between the time slices t and t + 1 are assumed *conditional Gaussian $N(\mu, \sigma^2)$*. Here, since we do not have observations on the mean value μ, it is specified by physical models.

LE_DBN (Fig. 10) is combining the real values (inferred by Bayesian inference) of three lateral features (see Sect. 2): $O_{LAT\_REAL}(t)$, $V_{LAT\_REAL}(t)$ and $A_{LAT\_REAL}(t)$. When $O_{LAT\_REAL}(t)$ is steadily increasing and $V_{LAT\_REAL}(t)$ is high or increasing (requiring also $A_{LAT\_REAL(t)}$), their combination clearly indicates that the vehicle is leaving its lane. Note, that in [7, 8], A_{LAT_REAL} was included in hypothesis Trajectory (*TRAJ*) and not as part of *LE*. The TPDs for the *LE*-variables: $O_{LAT\_REAL}(t)$, $V_{LAT\_REAL}(t)$ and A_{LAT_REAL} are defined as given in (2)-(4):

$$O_{LAT\_REAL}(t) \sim N(O_{LAT\_REAL}(t-1) + V_{LAT\_REAL}(t-1) \cdot \Delta t, \quad \sigma_{O\_LAT(t)}{}^2) \quad (2)$$

$$V_{LAT\_REAL}(t) \sim N(V_{LAT\_REAL}(t-1) + A_{LAT\_REAL}(t-1) \cdot \Delta t, \quad \sigma_{V\_LAT(t)}{}^2) \quad (3)$$

$$A_{LAT\_REAL}(t) \sim N(A_{LAT\_REAL}(t-1), \quad \sigma_{A\_LAT(t)}{}^2) \quad (4)$$

The time step Δt is the cycle time, i.e., 42 ms or 60 ms depending on the camera used. The variances σ^2 are modeling the uncertainties of the variables. This dynamic extension incorporates the trend of real values, while their physics relations are represented as causal dependencies between time steps Δt. By analogy are defined the TPDs for the *REL_DYN* features: distance $X_{REL\_REAL}(t)$ and velocity $V_{REL\_REAL}(t)$ and the hidden variable relative acceleration $A_{REL\_REAL}(t)$.

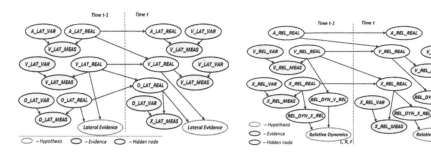

Fig. 10. *LE_DBN*: 2T-DBN structure for the hypothesis *LE* (Lateral Evidence) extended with the measured lateral acceleration *A_LAT*

Fig. 11. *REL_DYN_DBN*: The 2T-DBN structure for the hypothesis *REL_DYN* (Relative Dynamics) with *A_REL_REAL* as hidden node

5.1   The Method of Computing the Time Savings for Earlier Prediction

Due to the goal of early recognition of intended maneuvers, we have investigated two criteria (denoted below as A), B)) on how to interpret the inferred values of probability. For the classifier using static BNs, it is natural to base the decision on a statistical threshold value. For a DBN, following the development trend of features, it seems more natural, instead of using a threshold, to base the decision on the consistent growth of the trend of probability, thus reflecting its development over time.

A) Decision based on probability-threshold (p > 65 %): The choice of this probability-threshold value is based on statistical evaluation of the probability of "false positives" for the Original OOBN [7–9]. Thus, to avoid false recognized maneuvers, the system was allowed to classify a maneuver as recognized, only if its probability is bigger than the threshold. If no state has *p > 65 %,* no any maneuver is recognized.

B) Decision based on consistent trend growth of probability: If we base a decision not on a probability-threshold, but instead on the consistent growth of probability (over a certain number of time steps, e.g. 3-5 steps and above a certain value, e.g. 30 % or the highest probability value of modeled states of an event (i.e. maneuver), which is much lower than the threshold A), then the model may be able to achieve even earlier recognition, possibly at the cost of more false alarms, dependent on a situation and assuming that the initiated maneuver is not ceased due to new observations with possible safety impact. Both parameters are still to be defined by statistical analysis of all data in order to define the decision criteria for a consistent trend growth of probability.

5.2   Preparing the DBN Classifier for Automotive Integration

The deployment of a classifier, using the described DBNs is still work in progress. The main differences of a DBN-classifier compared to the statistical classifier (Table 1) are the DBN-fragments **LE** and **REL_DYN** (see Figs. 10 and 11), which follow the trend of features. The advantage in the implementation of the D&C-method is that the extended static classifiers, as well as the DBN classifier, employ at the higher abstraction levels (see Fig. 3) the same modified versions of logic BNs at level *LMC* (Fig. 6) and at *LC* (Fig. 7). D&C integrate the likelihoods of hypotheses from static BNs or DBNs.

The results for the DBN classifier for Scenario 1 (approaching of lane marking) are shown on a specific sequence in Fig. 12 and demonstrate the best recognition performance for a model, including $A_{LAT\_REAL}(t)$, which reflects driving experience with increased lateral acceleration shortly before the lane change. To be more explicit, in Figs. 12, 13 and 14 the x-axis represents the time steps of a maneuver sequence of streaming data, while the y-axis shows the probability of maneuver recognition for different variants of BN hypothesis and the red horizontal line marks the *probability-threshold p = 65 %.* Here, we compare recognition performance of different models at different abstraction levels (*H, LMC, LC,* except *MNVR,* see Fig. 3). Note that the performance at a certain level is not correlated 1-1 with the performance at other levels.

Figures 8 and 9 demonstrated early recognition of the need for a lane change maneuver with the static BN with relative dynamics. For the DBN classifier, the static BN is extended with *REL_DYN_DBN* (Fig. 11) combined with maneuver safety concept *Safe_RD* (Fig. 2). The possibility for earlier recognition in such situations is motivated by extensive driver experience and confirmed by the analysis results (by comparing the time gain on *LMC* and *LC* recognition, based on decision criteria with threshold and with trend growth of probability, shown in Figs. 13 and 14 respectively).

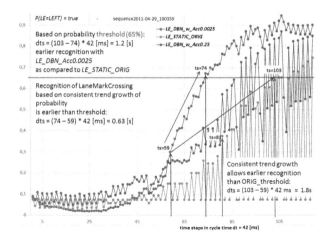

Fig. 12. BN-model performance for hypothesis LE_DBN as compared to LE_STATIC

A) *Based on the decision criteria with threshold:* The DBN model *REL_DYN_DBN* (Fig. 13) is recognizing a lane change maneuver towards left (*LC = LEFT*) earlier than both static models (the original *LE_STATIC_ORIG* and the extended *REL_DYN_STATIC*). Both (dynamic and static versions) of the extended with *REL_DYN* model are able to recognize the need for a lane change earlier than *LE_DBN* or *LE_STATIC*. The same holds for the test results (Fig. 14) on level *LC* (as of Fig. 3), integrating the results from the level *LMC* and hypotheses H_i. *REL_DYN_DBN* is recognizing the event at level *LMC* 0.76 s earlier (in Fig. 13) than *LE_STATIC_ORIG*, while in Fig. 14 the next level *LC* is recognized 0.46 s earlier.

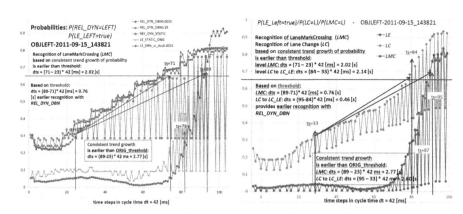

Fig. 13. Application scenario 2, level *LMC*: BN-model performance for the hypotheses *LE* and *REL_DYN*. Comparison on a selected sequence

Fig. 14. DBN-model performance on level *LC* (blue: using *LE_DBN* and *REL_DYN_DBN*) and same level *LC_LE* (orange: recognition using only *LE_DBN*). Comparison with results from Fig. 13 on level *LMC* and level *LC* (Color figure online).

B) Based on the decision criteria with consistent trend growth, Figs. 13 and 14 show that the same model can recognize the events *LMC* and *LC* earlier (2.02 s and 2.14 s correspondingly) than with the use of threshold. This is additionally improved by the use of a smaller variance parameter $\sigma^2 = 0.0025$ in the TPD. Moreover, if we consider the trend growth *P(LC)* for the extended model as compared to the threshold for the original *P(LE = true)* model, the recognition is even earlier (2.77 s at *LMC* and 2.6 s at *LC*). This confirms the initial assumption that the extension of the original model with the hypothesis "relative Dynamics" together with the trend development of its features in DBN, allows to reach the goal of earlier maneuver recognition. This is an argument in favor of the requirement on predicting the need for a lane change at least 2 s earlier than the actual lane marking crossing (*LMC*). Smoothing is still needed for the free space BN fragments in case of time cycles with missing data, e.g. by using its DBN extension.

6 Summary of Preliminary Results and Outlook

The static BNs have an inbuilt "mechanism" to check "collision avoidance" (for traffic safety) based on the free space hypotheses. Therefore, the probability drops when the evidence is not sufficient to confirm that LC is safe. And missing data leads to oscillating probability development (Figs. 12, 13 and 14), which is no problem for its implementation on the automotive platform, since in case of missing data, no propagation of evidence is performed. Extending the static BN to DBNs with smaller variance allows probability smoothing and achieving more robust performance, though at the price of growing size of memory requirements. For the DBNs, the contribution of adding $A_{LAT\_REAL}(t)$ and $A_{REL\_REAL}(t)$ with smaller variance $\sigma^2 = 0.0025$ is not only smoothing, but also earlier recognition. Thus, the analysis of the static and dynamic BN-fragments shows (see Figs. 12, 13 and 14) what is essential for deployment:

1. The moment of applied acceleration has an influence on the time step of maneuver recognition and contributes to recognition a few time steps (ts) earlier or later dependent on the traffic situation and driver behavior.
2. For the static BN (*REL_DYN_STATIC*): the oscillating development of probability is much stronger exhibited for the cases with missing data, thus the static BN can't compete with the DBN (on this driving sequence for application scenario 2).
3. Using DBNs extends the models and requires more memory. This has to be considered in relation to the space requirements of the target platform.
4. The decision criteria based on *consistent trend growth* allows earlier recognition than the criteria based on *threshold*.

For engineering purposes, "consistent trend-growth in probability" could be detected by observing a certain number of time steps in sequence (not counting a step with missing data), where the probability is growing consistently above a certain value (defined by statistical analysis). We have to develop this criterion formally to make sure it covers all cases/situations. Alternatively, a top level BN can monitor and recognize such trend of growth for earlier maneuver recognition. This will be a subject of further study. The preliminary results, described in Sects. 5 and 6, suggest that even earlier maneuver recognition by use of a DBN classifier is feasible. The implementation of an efficient inference algorithm for DBNs is work in progress. Finally, after DBN-deployment on the automotive platform, a comparison of static and DBN classifiers on the automotive platform and evaluation based on statistical analysis with all maneuver sequences will be a subject of further study.

References

1. Morris, B., Anup, D., Mohan, T.: Lane change intent prediction for driver assistance: on-road design and evaluation. In: IEEE Intelligent Vehicles Symposium, vol. IV, pp. 895-901 (2011)
2. Gerdes, A.: Automatic maneuver recognition in the automobile: the fusion of uncertain sensor values using bayesian models. In: 3rd International Workshop on Intelligent Transportation, Braunschweig (2006)
3. Dogan, Ü., Edelbrunner, J., Iossifidis, I.: Autonomous driving: a comparison of machine learning techniques by means of the prediction of lane change behavior. In: International Conference on Robotics and Biomimetics, Phuket, Thailand (2011)
4. Kumar, P., Perrollaz, M., Lef`evre, S., Laugier, C.: Learning-based approach for online lane change intention prediction. In: IEEE Intelligent Vehicles Symposium, Gold Coast, Australia (2013)
5. Hülnhagen, T., Dengler, I., Tamke, A., Dang, T., Breuel, G.: Maneuver recognition using probabilistic finite-state machines and fuzzy logic. In: 2010 IEEE Intelligent Vehicles Symposium, San Diego (2010)
6. Schlechtriemen, J., Wedel, A., Hillenbrand, J., Breuel, G., Kuhnert, K.-D.: A lane change detection approach using feature ranking with maximized predictive power. In: Proceedings on Intelligent Vehicles Symposium, 8-11 June 2014, pp. 108-114. IEEE (2014)
7. Kasper, D., Weidl, G., Dang, T., Breuel, G., Tamke, A., Rosenstiel, W.: Object-oriented Bayesian networks for detection of lane change maneuvers. In: Intelligent Vehicles Symposium. IEEE (2011)
8. Kasper, D., Weidl, G., Dang, T., Breuel, G., Tamke, A., Wedel, A., Rosenstiel, W.: Object-oriented Bayesian networks for detection of lane change maneuvers. IEEE Intell. Transp. Syst. Mag. **4**, 19–31 (2012)
9. Kasper, D.: Erkennung von Fahrmanöovern mit object-orientierten Bayes-Netzen in Autobahnszenarien, Ph.D. thesis. Tübingen University, Germany (2013). http://tobias-lib. uni-tuebingen.de/volltexte/2013/6800/pdf/thesis_kasper_20130426.pdf. Accessed 18 Feb 2015
10. Weidl, G., Madsen, A.L., Kasper, D., Breuel, G.:Optimizing Bayesian networks for recognition of driving maneuvers to meet the automotive requirements. In: Proceedings of the 2014 IEEE Multi-Conference on Systems and Control, October 8th to 10th, 2014, Nice/Antibes, France (2014)
11. Tereshchenko, V.: Relative object-object dynamics for earlier recognition of maneuvers in highway traffic. Master's thesis, University of Stuttgart, IAS, 30 October 2014
12. http://amidst.eu/use-cases/identification-and-interpretation-of-maneuvers-in-traffic. Accessed 18 Feb 2015, European Union FP7 project AMIDST grant no. 619209

13. http://amidst.eu/papersandpresentations/deliverables. Deliverable D1.2. Accessed 18 Feb 2015 European Union FP7 project AMIDST grant no. 619209
14. Friedman, N., Koller, D.: Probabilistic Graphical Models: Principles and Techniques. The MIT Press, Cambridge (2009)
15. Kjræulff, U.B., Madsen, A.L.: Bayesian Networks and Influence Diagrams - A Guide to Construction and Analysis. Springer, New York (2013)

Variable Elimination for Interval-Valued Influence Diagrams

Rafael Cabañas[1]([✉]), Alessandro Antonucci[2], Andrés Cano[1],
and Manuel Gómez-Olmedo[1]

[1] Department of Computer Science and Artificial Intelligence CITIC,
University of Granada, Granada, Spain
{rcabanas,acu,mgomez}@decsai.ugr.es
[2] Istituto Dalle Molle di Studi sull'Intelligenza Artificiale (IDSIA),
Galleria 2, Manno-Lugano, Switzerland
alessandro@idsia.ch

Abstract. Influence diagrams are probabilistic graphical models used to represent and solve decision problems under uncertainty. Sharp numerical values are required to quantify probabilities and utilities. Yet, real models are based on data streams provided by partially reliable sensors or experts. We propose an interval-valued quantification of these parameters to gain realism in the modelling and to analyse the sensitivity of the inferences with respect to perturbations of the sharp values. An extension of the classical influence diagrams formalism to support interval-valued potentials is provided. Moreover, a variable elimination algorithm especially designed for these models is developed and evaluated in terms of complexity and empirical performances.

Keywords: Influence diagrams · Bayesian networks · Credal networks · Sequential decision making · Imprecise probability

1 Introduction

Influence diagrams are probabilistic graphical models able to cope with decision problems with uncertainty. The parameters of an influence diagram are conditional probabilities for single variables given some other variables, or utilities depending on given sets of variables. The quantification of these parameters is based on a statistical processing of data or on the elicitation of expert knowledge.

Exactly as Bayesian networks, influence diagrams require sharp estimates of their parameters. Yet, when coping with expert knowledge, sharp values can be unfit to express judgements (e.g., which is the number modelling the probability for an option *more probable* than its negation?). This issue appears also when coping with scarce or missing data (e.g., probabilities conditional on rare events).

For reasons of this kind, in the last two decades, various extensions of Bayesian networks to support more general probabilistic statements have been proposed. These models have been developed in the field of possibility theory [2],

ⓒ Springer International Publishing Switzerland 2015
S. Destercke and T. Denoeux (Eds.): ECSQARU 2015, LNAI 9161, pp. 541–551, 2015.
DOI: 10.1007/978-3-319-20807-7_49

evidence theory [17], and imprecise probability [4]. The latter models, called *credal networks*, offer a direct sensitivity analysis interpretation: a credal network is a collection of Bayesian networks, all over the same variables and with the same graph, whose parameters are consistent with constraints (e.g., intervals) modelling a limited ability in the assessment of sharp estimates. Similarly, various extensions of decision trees have also been proposed [9,11]. The situation is different for influence diagrams. The early attempts of Fertig and Breese [7] first, and Zaffalon [6] after, to extend these models to non-sharp quantification are to the best of our knowledge the only works in this direction.[1] This is unfortunate as the above considerations about the difficulty of assessing sharp estimates for probabilities are even more compelling for utilities, which are supposed to model intrinsically qualitative objects such as preferences.

In this paper we extend to the interval-valued case the formalism of influence diagrams by keeping the same sensitivity-analysis interpretation of credal networks: a generalized influence diagram is a collection of classical influence diagrams consistent with the interval constraints. When coping with interval-valued utilities we might have overlaps between the different expectations. In these cases we adopt a conservative approach which rejects decisions leading to certainly dominated options and keeps all the other ones. A first example of *variable elimination* to compute inferences in these generalized models (arc reversal was considered in [7]) is also proposed together with some preliminary tests.

2 Basics

Let us first define the basic notation. We use upper-case letters for variables and lower-case for states. Given a variable X, x is an element of the domain of X, which we denote as Ω_X. Given a set of n variables $\boldsymbol{X} := (X_1, \ldots, X_n)$, and a multi-valued index $J \subseteq [1, n]$, X_J is the joint variable including any X_i such that $i \in J$. Thus, $\Omega_{X_J} = \times_{i \in J} \Omega_{X_i}$, where $\times$ is the Cartesian product. Given a second index I, notation $x_I \sim x_J$ is used to express *consistency*, i.e., to denote the fact that the two states have the same values on $X_{I \cap J}$. *Chance* variables are those whose actual value might be unknown, *decision* variables are those whose actual value can be set by the decision maker. A *potential* over X_J is a map $\psi : \Omega_{X_J} \to \mathbb{R}$. *Probability potentials* (PP, also called conditional probability tables) are special potentials. Given two disjoint set of variables X_I and X_J, $\phi(X_I, X_J)$ is a PP over X_I given X_J if and only if it is a nonnegative potential such that $\sum_{x_I \in \Omega_{X_I}} \phi(x_I, x_J) = 1$ for each $x_J \in \Omega_{X_J}$.

Influence Diagrams. Influence diagrams (IDs) [8] are a class of graphical models designed to formalize sequential decision problems with uncertainty. The uncertainty is represented by PPs, while the user preferences are represented by generic potentials called here *utility potentials* (UPs).

---

[1] Sensitivity analysis does not require the specification of more general class of models, being only focused on the results of the inferences. Thus, it should be regarded as a different topic, which, as a matter of fact, received more attention (e.g., [14]).

An ID over a set of variables $(\boldsymbol{X}, \boldsymbol{D})$ is made of a qualitative and a quantitative part. The qualitative part is a directed acyclic graph (DAG) $\mathcal{G}$ with three types of nodes. *Chance* nodes are depicted as circles and are in one-to-one correspondence with the chance variables, i.e., the variables in $\boldsymbol{X}$. Decision nodes are depicted as squares and associated to decision variables $\boldsymbol{D}$. Utility nodes are depicted as a diamonds and should be barren. For chance and decision variables we use the terms node and variable interchangeably. Utility nodes are not associated to variables. Still, these nodes are jointly denoted as $\boldsymbol{U}$. The immediate predecessors of a node Y according to the $\mathcal{G}$ are called *parents* and denoted as Π_Y. From the quantitative point of view, for each chance node, a PP over the corresponding variable and its parents is defined, while, for each utility node, a UP potential over the parents should be assessed. The formal definition of ID is the following.

Definition 1. *An influence diagram is a tuple* $\langle \mathcal{G}, \boldsymbol{X}, \boldsymbol{D}, \boldsymbol{U}, \Phi, \Psi \rangle$, *where* $\mathcal{G}$ *is a DAG over* $\boldsymbol{X} \cup \boldsymbol{D} \cup \boldsymbol{U}$, *while* $\Phi = \{\phi(X, \Pi_X)\}_{X \in \boldsymbol{X}}$ *and* $\Psi = \{\psi(\Pi_U)\}_{U \in \boldsymbol{U}}$ *are collections of, respectively, PPs and UPs.*

To model sequential decision problems with IDs, some additional information should be provided. A complete order of decision variables (e.g., $D_1 \prec \ldots \prec D_n$), and a partial order for $\boldsymbol{X} \cup \boldsymbol{D}$ consistent with the partial one for $\boldsymbol{D}$ should be formulated. Accordingly the partial order has form $\mathcal{I}_0 \prec D_1 \prec \mathcal{I}_1 \prec \cdots \prec D_n \prec \mathcal{I}_n$, with $\cup_{j=0}^{n} \mathcal{I}_j = \boldsymbol{X}$ and $\mathcal{I}_i \cap \mathcal{I}_j = \emptyset$ for each i, j. This reflects a temporal interpretation: the chance variables in $\mathcal{I}_i$ are observed before decision D_{i+1} is taken, and the ordering over $\boldsymbol{D}$ reflects the order in which the different decisions are taken. An ID of this kind is called *regular*. *Non-forgetting assumption* is usually required as well: previous decisions and observations are known at each decision. Here we only consider regular IDs with the non-forgetting assumption. A classical example is here below.

Example 1 (The oil wildcatter [15, 16]). An oil wildcatter must decide whether to drill or not. He is uncertain whether the amount of oil (O) in the place is empty (e), wet (w) or soaking (s). The wildcatter can make seismic tests (S) that will give a closed reflection pattern (c) indicating much oil, an open pattern (o) indicating for some oil, or a diffuse pattern (d) denoting almost no hope for oil. These two are chance variables, while the decision variables are T [to test (t) or not (nt)] and D [to drill (d) or not (nd)]. The utility nodes P and C describe the profit possibly obtained from the presence of oil and the cost of the tests. The DAG of an ID modelling this problem is in Fig. 1. Decision T precedes decision D, while the partial order is complete being $T \prec \{S\} \prec D \prec \{O\}$.

ID Evaluation. A *policy* for a decision variable D is a map $\delta_D : \Omega_{\Pi_D} \to \Omega_D$, i.e., a rule to assign D on the basis of the values of the parents. A *strategy* Δ is a collection of policies, one for each $D \in \boldsymbol{D}$. From a joint observation $\boldsymbol{x}$ of the chance variables and a strategy Δ, we deduce a joint specification of the decision variables, and hence of the values of the utilities, which are assumed additive. Accordingly, we can compute the expected utility of a strategy as follows:

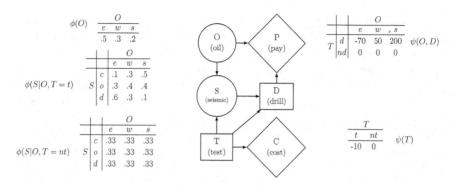

Fig. 1. The oil wildcatter's decision problem as an ID

$$\mathrm{EU}(\Delta) := \sum_{x} \prod_{X \in \boldsymbol{X}} \phi(x, \pi_X) \sum_{U \in \boldsymbol{U}} \psi(\pi_U), \tag{1}$$

with $x, \pi_X, \pi_U \sim x$, and the values of π_X and π_U also consistent with the values of $\boldsymbol{D}$ obtained from x and Δ. A typical task with IDs is to detect the strategy Δ^* maximizing the expected utility. This should respect the partial order, i.e.,

$$\mathrm{EU}(\Delta^*) = \sum_{\mathcal{I}_0} \max_{D_1} \cdots \max_{D_n} \sum_{\mathcal{I}_n} \prod_{X \in \boldsymbol{X}} \phi(X|\Pi_X) \sum_{U \in \boldsymbol{U}} \psi(\Pi_U) \tag{2}$$

The components of this optimal strategy, are called *optimal policies*, and they can be regarded as the intermediate steps of the above maximization. The optimal policy $\delta^*_{D_i}$ associated to D_i is therefore:

$$\delta^*_{D_i}(\Pi_{D_i}) = \arg\max_{D_i} \sum_{\mathcal{I}_i} \max_{D_{i+1}} \cdots \max_{D_n} \sum_{\mathcal{I}_n} \prod_{X \in \boldsymbol{X}} \phi(X|\Pi_X) \sum_{U \in \boldsymbol{U}} \psi(\Pi_U). \tag{3}$$

Example 2. In the oil wildcutter's problem (Ex. 1), when seismic tests have been done and returned a closed reflection pattern the right thing to do is to drill, i.e. $\delta^*_D(S = c, T = t) = d$ *as* $EU_D(S = c, T = t) = 77.5$.

Variable Elimination. *Variable elimination* (VE) is a typical approach to inference in graphical model. VE algorithms for IDs [10,18] are commonly used to solve Eq. (2). Unlike VE for Bayesian networks, in regular IDs the elimination order is not arbitrary: it should be the inverse of an order consistent with the partial order associated to the ID [12]. Furthermore, while chance variables are removed by sum, decision variables are instead eliminated by maximization. To describe VE, we first show how to remove a single variable Y in Algorithm 1. The whole algorithm consists in iterating the procedure over $\boldsymbol{X} \cup \boldsymbol{D}$. When the last variable is eliminated, the algorithm returns a potential with no arguments (i.e., a constant) with the value in Eq. (2).

The operator dom returns the variables in the argument of a potential. Sums in line 4 and maxima in line 6 of Algorithm 1 are two different forms (the first for

Algorithm 1. Removing a single (chance or decision) variable Y

1: $(\varPhi_Y, \varPsi_Y) \leftarrow (\{\phi \in \varPhi | Y \in \mathrm{dom}(\phi)\}, \{\psi \in \varPsi | Y \in \mathrm{dom}(\psi)\})$	▷ Select
2: $(\phi_Y, \psi_Y) \leftarrow (\otimes_{\phi \in \varPhi_Y} \phi, \otimes_{\psi \in \varPsi_Y} \psi)$	▷ Combine
3: **if** $Y \in X$ **then**	
4: $(\phi'_Y, \psi'_Y) \leftarrow (\sum_Y \phi_Y, \frac{\sum_Y \phi_Y \otimes \psi_Y}{\sum_Y \phi_Y})$	▷ Remove by sum (chance vars)
5: **else**	
6: $(\phi'_Y, \psi'_Y) \leftarrow (\phi_{Y=y}, \max_Y \psi_Y)$	▷ Remove by max (decision vars)
7: $\delta^*_Y \leftarrow \arg\max_Y \psi_Y$	▷ Optimal policy (as a byproduct)
8: **end if**	
9: $(\varPhi, \varPsi) \leftarrow (\varPhi \backslash \varPhi_Y \cup \{\phi'_Y\}, \varPsi \backslash \varPsi_Y \cup \{\psi'_Y\})$	▷ Update
10: **return** $(\varPhi, \varPsi)$	

decision, the second for chance variables) of *marginalization*, removing the variable from the argument of the potential. The division (line 4) is defined element-wise. For the PP in line 6, Y can be eliminated by instantiating an arbitrary value [12]. When eliminating a decision variable, the maximization of the UP also gives the corresponding optimal policy (line 7).

The operator $\otimes$ in Algorithm 1 combines pairs of potentials as explained here below. It is easy to check that these definitions are well-posed and that the operator is associative and commutative.

(i) given two UPs, say $\psi(X_I)$ and $\psi'(X_J)$, their combination $\psi \otimes \psi'$ is a UP over $X_{I \cup J}$ obtained by element-wise sums, i.e., $(\psi \otimes \psi')(x_{I \cup J}) := \psi(x_I) + \psi'(x_J)$ for each $x_{I \cup J} \in \Omega_{X_{I \cup J}}$, with $x_I, x_J \sim x_{I \cup J}$;

(ii) given a PP $\phi(X_I, X_J)$ and a UP $\psi(X_K)$, their combination $\phi \otimes \psi$ is a UP over $X_L := X_{I \cup J \cup K}$ defined by element-wise products, i.e., $(\phi \otimes \psi)(x_{I \cup J \cup K}) := \phi(x_I, x_J) \cdot \psi(x_K)$, for each $x_{I \cup J \cup K} \in \Omega_{X_{I \cup J \cup K}}$, with $x_I, x_J, x_K \sim x_{I \cup J \cup K}$;

(iii) finally, given two PPs, say $\phi(X_I, X_J)$ and $\phi'(X_K, X_L)$, their combination $\phi \otimes \phi'$ is a PP over $X_{I \cup K}$ given $X_{(J \cup L) \backslash (I \cup K)}$ defined by element-wise products, i.e., $(\phi \otimes \phi')(x_{I \cup K}, x_{(J \cup L) \backslash (I \cup K)}) := \phi(x_I, x_J) \cdot \phi(x_K, x_L)$ for each $x_{I \cup K} \in \Omega_{X_{I \cup K}}$ and $x_{(J \cup L) \backslash (I \cup K)} \in \Omega_{X_{(J \cup L) \backslash (I \cup K)}}$, with $x_I, x_J, x_K, x_L \sim x_{I \cup K}, x_{(J \cup L) \backslash (I \cup K)}$.

3   Interval-Valued Potentials

The main goal of this paper is to extend IDs to support interval-valued specifications. To do that, we first formalize the basic notion of interval-valued potential.

Definition 2. *An* interval-valued utility potential *(IUP) over X_I is a pair of UPs over X_I. We use the compact notation $\overline{\underline{\psi}}(X_I)$ for a IUP over X_I, $\underline{\psi}$ and $\overline{\psi}$ are the two UPs involved in the specification and are called, respectively, the* lower *and* upper *bounds of the IUP. The extension $\overline{\underline{\psi}}^*(X_I)$ of this IUP is the set of UPs consistent with the bounds, i.e.,*

$$\overline{\underline{\psi}}^*(X_I) := \left\{ \psi : \Omega_{X_I} \to \mathbb{R} \,\middle|\, \underline{\psi}(x_I) \leq \psi(x_I) \leq \overline{\psi}(x_I), \forall x_I \in \Omega_{X_I} \right\}. \quad (4)$$

The extension of a IUP $\overline{\underline{\psi}}$ is non-empty if and only if $\underline{\psi}(x_I) \leq \overline{\psi}(x_I) \ \forall x_I \in \Omega_{X_I}$. We similarly define an *interval-valued probability potential* (IPP) over X_I given X_J as a pair of (not necessarily normalized) PPs over X_I given X_J. We denote such a IPP as $\overline{\underline{\phi}}(X_I, X_J)$, where $\underline{\phi}(X_I, X_J)$ and $\overline{\phi}(X_I, X_J)$ are the two (unnormalized) bounds. The extension is also defined in terms of consistency.

$$\overline{\underline{\phi}}^{*}(X) := \left\{ \phi : \Omega_{X_I} \times \Omega_{X_J} \rightarrow \mathbb{R}_0^+ \ \middle| \begin{array}{l} \sum_{x_I} \phi(x_I, x_J) = 1, \\ \underline{\phi}(x_I, x_J) \leq \phi(x_I, x_J) \leq \overline{\phi}(x_I, x_J), \\ \forall (x_I, x_J) \in \Omega_{X_I} \times \Omega_{X_J} \end{array} \right\}. \quad (5)$$

Condition $\underline{\phi}(x_I, x_J) \leq \overline{\phi}(x_I, x_J)$ for each x_I, x_J, together with $\sum_{x_I} \underline{\phi}(x_I, x_J) \leq 1 \leq \sum_{x_I} \overline{\phi}(x_I, x_J)$, for each $x_J \in \Omega_{X_J}$ is necessary and sufficient for the extension of the IPP to be non-empty. The additional condition $\overline{\phi}(x_i') + \sum_{x_i \neq x_i'} \underline{\phi}(x_i) \leq 1$ and the analogous expression for the lower instead of the upper bounds is called *reachability* [5]. The meaning is that for each $p \in [\underline{\phi}(x_I, x_J), \overline{\phi}(x_I, x_J)]$, there is at least a PP $\phi \in \overline{\underline{\phi}}^{*}$ s.t. $\phi(x_I, x_J) = p$. Note also that an IPP with non-empty extension can be always reduced to a reachable one by shrinking its bounds. Both the extensions of a IUP and a IPP are therefore convex sets of, respectively, UPs and PPs. Vice versa, while any convex set of UPs can be regarded as the extension of a IUP, the same does not hold for IPPs.

Example 3. Figure 2 reports an interval-valued specification of the five potential associated to the ID in Fig. 1. It is a trivial exercise to check that: the IPPs have non-empty extensions and are reachable, and the UPs and PPs of the original model are included in the extensions of their interval-valued counterparts.

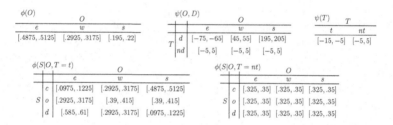

Fig. 2. A set of IUPs and IPPs for the oil wildcatter's decision problem

Combining Interval-Valued Potentials. The combination operation over potentials in Algorithm 1 can be extended to interval-valued potentials as follows:

(i) given two IUPs, say $\overline{\underline{\psi}}(X_I)$ and $\overline{\underline{\psi}}'(X_J)$, their combination $\overline{\underline{\psi}} \otimes \overline{\underline{\psi}}'$ is a IUP over $X_{I \cup J}$ s.t. $(\underline{\psi} \otimes \underline{\psi}')(x_{I \cup J}) := \underline{\psi}(x_I) + \underline{\psi}'(x_J)$ for each $x_{I \cup J} \in \Omega_{X_{I \cup J}}$ with $x_I, x_J \sim x_{I \cup J}$; and similarly for the upper bounds;

(ii) given a IPP $\overline{\underline{\phi}}(X_I, X_J)$ and a IUP $\overline{\underline{\psi}}(X_K)$, their combination $\overline{\underline{\phi}} \otimes \overline{\underline{\psi}}$ is a IUP over $X_{I \cup J \cup K}$ s.t. $(\underline{\psi} \otimes \underline{\psi})(x_{I \cup J \cup K}) := \underline{\phi}(x_I, x_J) \cdot \underline{\psi}(x_K)$ for each $x_{I \cup J \cup K} \in \Omega_{X_{I \cup J \cup K}}$, with $x_I, x_J, x_K \sim x_{I \cup J \cup K}$; if $\underline{\psi}(x_K) < 0$ the lower bound of the combination is obtained by multiplying the lower bound of the IUP for the upper bound of the IPP (and vice versa for the upper bound);

(iii) given two IPPs, say $\overline{\underline{\psi}}(X_I, X_J)$ and $\overline{\underline{\psi}}'(X_K, X_L)$, their combination $\overline{\underline{\psi}} \otimes \overline{\underline{\psi}}'$ is a IPP over $X_{I \cup K}$ given $X_{(J \cup L) \setminus (I \cup K)}$ s.t. $(\underline{\psi} \otimes \underline{\psi}')(x_{I \cup K}, x_{(J \cup L) \setminus (I \cup K)}) :=$ $\underline{\psi}(x_I, x_J) \cdot \underline{\psi}(x_K, x_L)$, for each $x_{I \cup K} \in \overline{\Omega}_{X_{I \cup K}}$ and $x_{(J \cup L) \setminus (I \cup K)} \in \Omega_{X_{(J \cup L) \setminus (I \cup K)}}$, with $x_I, x_J, x_K, x_L \sim x_{I \cup K}, x_{(J \cup L) \setminus (I \cup K)}$. If $\overline{\underline{\psi}} \otimes \overline{\underline{\psi}}'$ is not reachable, the transformation to make it reachable is performed.

The following result, whose proof is left to the reader provides a sensitivity-analysis justification for the proposed generalization of the combination operator.

Proposition 1. *Given potentials (no matter whether IUPs or IPPs)* $\overline{\underline{\psi}}$ *and* $\overline{\underline{\phi}}$ *the extension of their combination is s.t.* $(\overline{\underline{\psi}} \otimes \overline{\underline{\phi}})^* = \left\{ \psi \otimes \phi \middle| \psi \in \overline{\underline{\psi}}^*, \phi \in \overline{\underline{\phi}}^* \right\}.$

4   Interval Influence Diagrams

IDs can be extended to the interval framework by simply replacing the PPs and UPs in Definition 1 with an equal number of IPPs and IUPs defined on the same domains. We call a model of this kind an *interval-valued influence diagram* (IID). As an example, the ID in Example 1 with the interval-valued quantification in Fig. 2 is an IID over the graph in Fig. 1. Before applying to IIDs the VE scheme in Algoritm 1, the different operations over the potentials involved in the algorithm should be extended to intervals. In the previous section we discussed how to do that with the combination. Here we generalize the operations in lines 4 and 6.

Eliminating Chance Variables. We start from line 4. To sum out a variable from a IPP, we sum out the variable from the two bounds and, if needed, we make the result reachable. Concerning the sum and division in the second term, given an IPP $\overline{\underline{\phi}}(X_I \cup Y, X_J)$ and a IUP $\overline{\underline{\psi}}(X_K \cup Y)$, we set the result as a IUP $\overline{\underline{\hat{\psi}}}$ over $X_{I \cup J \cup K}$ s.t.

$$\overline{\underline{\hat{\psi}}}^*(X_{I \cup J \cup K}) := \left\{ \hat{\psi}(X_{I \cup J \cup K}) \middle| \begin{array}{l} \hat{\psi}(x_{I \cup J \cup K}) = \frac{\sum_y \phi(x_I, y, x_J) \cdot \psi(y, x_K)}{\sum_y \phi(x_I, y, x_J)} \\ \forall x_{I \cup J \cup K}, \forall \phi \in \overline{\underline{\phi}}^*, \forall \psi \in \overline{\underline{\psi}}^* \end{array} \right\}. \quad (6)$$

This allows to obtain a result as in Proposition 1. Note that the argument of the sum in the numerator can be regarded as an element of $(\overline{\underline{\phi}} \otimes \overline{\underline{\psi}})^*$. By computing the bound of the extension in Eq. (6), we eventually obtain the required IUP. Because of Eqs. (4) and (5), the extensions $\overline{\underline{\psi}}^*$ and $\overline{\underline{\phi}}^*$ are convex regions defined by linear constraints. Furthermore, the objective function to optimize is linear-fractional. So the task reduces to a linear program by the Charnes-Cooper transformation. Equivalently, the task can be regarded as a combinatorial optimization by considering only the extreme points of the feasible region.[2] Faster, but approximate, approaches can be also considered. To obtain the lower bound, we can take the lower bound of the numerator and the upper bound of the denominator in Eq. (6) (and vice versa for the upper bound). This induces an outer

---

[2] The solution of a linear program is an extreme point of the feasible region.

approximation. A heuristic alternative consists in consider as PP specifications a lower bound for a value of Y and the upper bounds for the other values (or vice versa).

Eliminating Decision Variables. Here we discuss the operations in lines 6 and 7. The arg max operation is intrinsically related to the fact that a UP has sharp values. The problem of deciding the "maximal" options in the interval case might be arguable. The most conservative approach is the following.

Definition 3. Let $\overline{\underline{\psi}}$ be a IUP over $Y \cup \boldsymbol{X}_I$. An element $y \in \Omega_Y$ is interval-maximal given $x_I \in \Omega_{\boldsymbol{X}_I}$ if there is no $y' \in \Omega_Y$ s.t. $\underline{\psi}(y', x_I) > \overline{\psi}(y, x_I)$.

Let D be a decision to be eliminated from $\overline{\underline{\psi}}(D, \boldsymbol{X}_I)$. To detect the optimal policy $\delta_D^*(\boldsymbol{X}_I)$ we compute the interval-maximal states of D given each $x_I \in \Omega_{\boldsymbol{X}_I}$. This corresponds to a so-called *credal* policy allowing for indecision between two or more possible options. Finally the maximization of the IUP is done as usual by acting separately on the two bounds.

Example 4. In the oil wildcutter's problem (Example 1), if the combinatorial approach is used, $\delta_D^*(S = c, T = t) = \{d\}$ as $EU_D(S = c, T = t) \in [46.24, 115.78]$.

Complexity Analysis. VE in IDs takes time exponential in the maximum clique size (i.e., the arity of the biggest potential generated during the evaluation). The same holds for IIDs, apart from a possible bottleneck during the elimination of the chance variables as in Eq. (6). This is the case when the combinatorial optimization is adopted: the number of extreme points to be evaluated is exponential in the number of states. This is not the case with the outer approximation and the heuristic, as well as the linear programming which is polynomial in the number of constraints, and hence in the number of states.

5   Empirical Validation

For a preliminary validation of the VE algorithm we consider six IDs [1,3,13,15]. Table 1 details the number of nodes of each type for these models. These IDs are transformed in IIDs by a perturbation of the original parameters. The approaches in Sect. 4) are compared. Figure 3 shows the computation times. As expected, the outer approximation and the heuristic method roughly take the double of the time required by the precise evaluation. The exact approach with the extreme

Table 1. Number of chance, decision and utility nodes for the benchmark IIDs

	NHL	Jaundice	Appendicitis	Comp. Assym	Oil	Thinkbox
$|\boldsymbol{X}|$	17	21	4	3	2	5
$|\boldsymbol{D}|$	3	2	1	5	2	2
$|\boldsymbol{U}|$	1	1	1	2	1	4

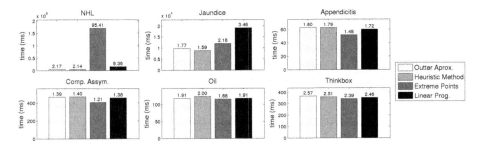

Fig. 3. Evaluation times for the IIDs in Table 1 and relative duration w.r.t. the evaluation of the corresponding IDs

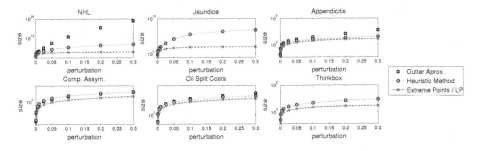

Fig. 4. Size of $EU(\Delta^*)$ for different sizes of the IPPs

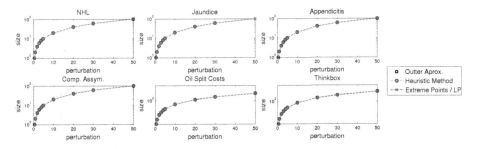

Fig. 5. Size of $EU(\Delta^*)$ for different sizes for the IUPs

points might be very slow if there are chance variables with many states, this being the case of NHL, which has a chance variable with 12 states. The exact approach based on linear programming is slightly slower than the heuristic and the outer approximation.

A sensitivity analysis has also been done to evaluate the effect of the size of the intervals of the initial potentials affects the informativeness of the solutions. Figure 4 shows the size of the (interval-valued) expected utility of the optimal policy $EU(\Delta^*)$ as a function of the sizes of the intervals of the potentials. The results based on the linear programming and on the enumeration of the extreme points are exact and therefore coincide. As expected the heuristic is more precise than the outer approximation, which in some cases returns infinite values because of a division by zero. If sharp values are assumed for the IPPs and the intervals are only in the IUPs, the results are those in Fig. 5. The four methods, which differs only in the treatment of the IPPs, produce the same results. Comparing the scales of Figs. 4 and 5, it can be observed that the imprecision in the IPPs has a stronger effect that in the IUPs.

6   Conclusions and Future Work

We have generalized the formalism of influence diagrams to the interval framework by allowing both probabilities and utilities to take interval values. A variable elimination algorithm has been also proposed and preliminary tested. In the experimental part, four different methods for eliminating chance variables have been compared, showing that the best results are obtained if the linear programming approach is considered. As a future work intend to develop approximate evaluation algorithms for these models.

Acknowledgments. This research was supported by the Spanish Ministry of Economy and Competitiveness under project TIN2013-46638-C3-2-P, the European Regional Development Fund (FEDER), the FPI scholarship program (BES-2011-050604) and the short stay in foreign institutions scholarship EEBB-I-14-08102. The authors have also been partially supported by "Junta de Andalucía" under projects TIC-06016 and P08-TIC-03717.

References

1. Hugin Expert network repository. http://www.hugin.com/technology/samples
2. Benferhat, S., Smaoui, S.: Hybrid possibilistic networks. Int. J. Approximate Reasoning **44**(3), 224–243 (2007)
3. Bielza, C., Gómez, M., Insua, S.R., del Pozo, J.A.F., Barreno, P.G., Caballero, S., Luna, M.S.: IctNEO system for jaundice management. Revista de la Real Academia de Ciencias Exactas, Físicas y Naturales **92**(4), 307–315 (1998)
4. Cozman, F.G.: Credal networks. Artif. Intell. **120**, 199–233 (2000)
5. de Campos, L.M., Huete, J.F., Moral, S.: Probability intervals: a tool for uncertain reasoning. Int. J. Uncertainty Fuzziness Knowl. Based Syst. **2**(02), 167–196 (1994)
6. Fagiuoli, E., Zaffalon, M.: Decisions under uncertainty with credal influence diagrams. Technical report, pp. 51–98, IDSIA (1998). (unpublished)
7. Fertig, K.W., Breese, J.S.: Probability intervals over influence diagrams. IEEE Trans. Pattern Anal. Mach. Intell. **15**(3), 280–286 (1993)
8. Howard, R.A., Matheson, J.E.: Influence diagram retrospective. Decision Anal. **2**(3), 144–147 (2005)
9. Huntley, N., Troffaes, M.C.M.: Normal form backward induction for decision trees with coherent lower previsions. Ann. Oper. Res. **195**(1), 111–134 (2012)
10. Jensen, F.V., Nielsen, T.D.: Bayesian Networks and Decision Graphs. Springer Verlag, New York (2007)
11. Kikuti, D., Cozman, F.G., de Campos, C.P.: Partially ordered preferences in decision trees: computing strategies with imprecision in probabilities. In: IJCAI Workshop on Advances in Preference Handling, pp. 118–123 (2005)

12. Kjaerulff, U.: Triangulation of graphs - algorithms giving small total state space. Research report R-90-09, Department of Mathematics and Computer Science, Aalborg University, Denmark (1990)
13. Lucas, P.J.F., Taal, B.: Computer-based decision support in the management of primary gastric non-hodgkin lymphoma. In: UU-CS, vol. 33 (1998)
14. Nielsen, T.D., Jensen, F.V.: Sensitivity analysis in influence diagrams. IEEE Trans. Syst. Man Cybern. Part A Syst. Hum. **33**(2), 223–234 (2003)
15. Raiffa, H.: Decision Analysis: Introductory Lectures on Choices Under Uncertainty. Addison-Wesley, Boston (1968)
16. Shenoy, P.P.: Valuation-based systems for Bayesian decision analysis. Oper. Res. **40**(3), 463–484 (1992)
17. Xu, H., Smets, P.: Reasoning in evidential networks with conditional belief functions. Int. J. Approximate Reasoning **14**(2–3), 155–185 (1996)
18. Zhang, N.L., Poole, D.: Exploiting causal independence in Bayesian network inference. J. Artif. Intell. Res. **5**, 301–328 (1996)

Author Index

Printed in the United States
By Bookmasters